Mac OS X Snow Leopard for Power Users

Scott Granneman

Apress®

Mac OS X Snow Leopard for Power Users

ISBN-13 (pbk): 978-1-4302-3030-4

ISBN-13 (electronic): 978-1-4302-3031-1

Printed and bound in the United States of America 9 8 7 6 5 4 3 2 1

President and Publisher: Paul Manning
Lead Editor: Clay Andres
Development Editor: Douglas Pundick
Technical Reviewer: Kunal Mittal
Editorial Board: Clay Andres, Steve Anglin, Mark Beckner, Ewan Buckingham, Gary Cornell, Jonathan Gennick, Jonathan Hassell, Michelle Lowman, Matthew Moodie, Duncan Parkes, Jeffrey Pepper, Frank Pohlmann, Douglas Pundick, Ben Renow-Clarke, Dominic Shakeshaft, Matt Wade, Tom Welsh
Coordinating Editor: Kelly Moritz
Copy Editor: Ralph Moore
Compositor: MacPS, LLC
Indexer: BIM Indexing & Proofreading Services
Artist: April Milne
Cover Designer: Anna Ishchenko

Distributed to the book trade worldwide by Springer Science+Business Media, LLC., 233 Spring Street, 6th Floor, New York, NY 10013. Phone 1-800-SPRINGER, fax (201) 348-4505, e-mail orders-ny@springer-sbm.com, or visit www.springeronline.com.

For information on translations, please e-mail rights@apress.com, or visit www.apress.com.

Apress and friends of ED books may be purchased in bulk for academic, corporate, or promotional use. eBook versions and licenses are also available for most titles. For more information, reference our Special Bulk Sales–eBook Licensing web page at www.apress.com/info/bulksales.

To my toddler son Finn, who's started on iOS already but will graduate to Mac OS X soon.

Contents at a Glance

Contents

About the Author

 **Scott Granneman** is an author, Adjunct Professor, and partner in a technology firm. Scott has written five books—*Don't Click on the Blue E!: Switching to Firefox* (O'Reilly Media, 2005), *Hacking Knoppix* (Wiley, 2006), *Linux Phrasebook* (Sams, 2006), *Podcasting with Audacity: Audio Editing for Everyone* (Prentice Hall, 2007), and *Google Apps Deciphered: Compute in the Cloud to Streamline Your Desktop* (Prentice Hall, 2008)—and contributed to several more. In addition, he was a columnist for SecurityFocus, The Open Source Weblog, and *Linux Magazine*.

As an educator, Scott has taught thousands of people of all ages—from pre-teens to senior citizens—on a wide range of topics covering everything from technology to literary representations of Hell. He is currently an Adjunct Professor at Washington University in St. Louis, where he teaches courses on Technology & the Law, Using Everyday Technology, Web Development, From Blogs to Wikis, Technology for Managers, and Technology in Our Changing Society.

As a Principal of WebSanity, he works with businesses and non-profits to plan, develop, and host web sites using a robust open source Content Management System. In particular, he manages the firm's UNIX-based server environment, writes all the documentation, and works closely with other partners on the company's software and systems.

Scott started using Macs in 1985, and has been using them almost continuously ever since. As with his high school mullet, he prefers to forget his brief flirtation with Windows when he was younger and sometimes lacked good taste.

About the Technical Reviewer

 **Kunal Mittal** serves as an Executive Director of Technology at Sony Pictures Entertainment where he is responsible for the SOA and Identity Management programs. He provides a centralized engineering service to different lines of business and consults on the open-source technologies, content management, collaboration, and mobile strategies.

Kunal is an entrepreneur who helps startups define their technology strategy, product roadmap, and development plans. Having strong relations with several development partners worldwide, he is able to help startups and large companies build appropriate development partnerships. He generally works in an advisor or consulting CTO capacity, and serves actively in the Project Management and Technical Architect functions.

He has authored and edited several books and articles on J2EE, cloud computing, and mobile technologies. He holds a Master's degree in Software Engineering and is an instrument-rated private pilot.

Acknowledgments

I wrote this book in many locations over the span of many months, including WebSanity's office, Denise Lieberman's house and car, Missouri Scholars Academy (www.moscholars.org), my Mom's house in Marshall, a car between St. Louis and Marshall, CWE-LUG meetings (www.cwelug.org), several coffee shops, Washington University in St. Louis, and last, but certainly not least, the cozy home Robin Woltman and I share.

A lot of people at Apress helped make this book possible, including Clay Andres (Acquisitions Editor), Douglas Pundick (Development Editor), Ralph Moore (Copyeditor), Kunal Mittal (Technical Reviewer), and Kelly Moritz (Coordinating Editor). They were always supportive, and I thank them for their aid—and their willingness to lay on the pressure to get this thing done! I truly appreciate it.

I've known Jans Carton since 5th grade, and he's shown his loyalty to me and to the Mac countless times. Jans let me bounce ideas off of him several times. Thanks, buddy!

Denise Lieberman read over several chapters and suggested some very clever edits. Her editing reflected her background in journalism, and I thank her for them. I also appreciate that she let me use her and her MacBook as guinea pigs for a few ideas of mine! Thanks, D.D.!

I often had to write while my toddler son Finn Scott Granneman Jaeger tried his hardest to distract me. More often than not, he succeeded, which is easy when you're the cutest little boy in the world. I look forward to the day when you finally read this book, Finny. By then, though, Apple may have used all the big cats as names for Mac OS X. Maybe it will decide to use "Bear" in honor of your favorite stuffed animal!

Speaking of cute, my lil' shih tzu Libby was a constant companion for much of the writing of this book. She's getting on in years, but she's still a fun distraction. When faced with a choice between wrting another few paragraphs or giving a sweet dog a few scratches behind the ears, I always find that it's no choice at all.

Finally, Robin Woltman read nearly every line of this book and gave me fabulous feedback. When my writing wasn't clear, she asked me to clarify it, and when it was clear, she tested it. And always she tried to keep me on task so I could finish this book. Thank you thank you thank you! I honestly couldn't get nything done without you!

Scott Granneman

Chapter **1**

Introduction: Advanced Secrets of Mac OS X

I've been using a Mac as my desktop since 1985, with a short detour into Windows (don't hate me!) in the late 1990s and a much longer detour into Linux in the early and mid 2000s (I still love Linux, but now my usage of it is pretty much limited to servers, where it is excellent). When Mac OS X came out, I thought it was a brilliant move on Apple's part: take a rock solid, dependable UNIX core and put a beautiful, supremely usable GUI on top of it. As a confirmed UNIX lover (and author!), moving back to the Mac was easy and exciting for me, and my appreciation has only grown as Apple has further developed Mac OS X with Snow Leopard. When I was asked to write this book, I jumped at the chance.

The title of this book is *Mac OS X Snow Leopard for Power Users*. So what's a Power User? Why should power users be interested in Mac OS X, an operating system famed for its ease-of-use? And what will power users learn in this book?

Power Users and Mac OS X

A power user is defined by Wikipedia as "a user of a personal computer who has the ability to use advanced features of programs which are beyond the abilities of 'normal' users, but is not necessarily capable of programming and system administration" (http://en.wikipedia.org/wiki/Power_user). That's pretty accurate, except that I would contend that any reasonably competent computer user has to be a system administrator these days, as computers (and yes, even Macs) have gotten more complex. Fortunately, Macs are still much easier for individual users to administer than Windows machines, so they have that advantage.

So if power users are interested in "advanced features," why should they be interested in Mac OS X? Isn't the Mac focused on usability and ease-of-use? What's there for power users?

My answer is, a lot! First of all, remember that Mac OS X is UNIX under the hood, which means that a whole universe of programs, techniques, and tools is available to those who are curious (this was one of the big reasons that I happily switched back to Mac OS X as my full-time operating system). In fact, the combination of UNIX automation tools plus Apple's own work in that area (AppleScript and Automator, which I cover quite a bit in this book, are pre-eminent here) means that power users can get more done, much faster.

Unfortunately, a few misinformed folks still hold the erroneous belief that Apple so tightly controls Mac OS X that users face limited choices in almost every area: settings, programs, and usage. This is just not true, and power users in particular will find that Mac OS X has both power and a kind of elegantly hidden complexity, in which it is possible to get under the hood and tweak and change things at will, while at the same time preserving the Mac's famed ease of use, consistency, and refinement.

Here's one example of that elegantly hidden complexity: when quote-unquote normal users look at the Mac's System Preferences, they see a (perhaps) overwhelming number of choices. When power users look at System Preferences, they see options, but they also notice things that are not there. It turns out that System Preferences only displays a subset of the total number of preferences that are possible on Mac OS X. Apple effectively hides the rest by not presenting them in the GUI (Graphical User Interface); instead, you enable and disable those preferences on the command line using Terminal.

Want to automatically play movies when you open them in QuickTime Player? Enter this on the command line:

```
defaults write com.apple.QuickTimePlayerX MGPlayMovieOnOpen 1
```

Likewise for QuickTime Player, if you'd like to automatically show subtitles on movies that support them, try this on the command line:

```
defaults write com.apple.QuickTimePlayerX MGEnableCCAndSubtitlesOnOpen 1
```

Don't like the stripes that show in Finder's List View? Use this on the command line and then restart the Finder:

```
defaults write com.apple.finder FXListViewStripes -bool FALSE
```

Hate the way that iTunes 10 runs the Close, Minimize, and Zoom buttons vertically, like a stoplight? Want to go back to the old horizontal view? Type this on the command line:

```
defaults write com.apple.iTunes full-window -1
```

That's the kind of stuff that power users love. But here's what's nifty about Mac OS X—if you want to use the command line to make those changes, great. You can, and it's no problem.

But if you don't want to have to remember those, or you get sick of looking them up, or you just don't want to have to whip out Terminal all the time ("What's wrong with you?!" he asked in mock horror), you can instead use a third-party Preference Pane called Secrets, available for free from http://secrets.blacktree.com. Install Secrets, go to ⬧ > SYSTEM PREFERENCES > SECRETS, and you'll see the hundreds of possibilities shown in Figure 1–1.

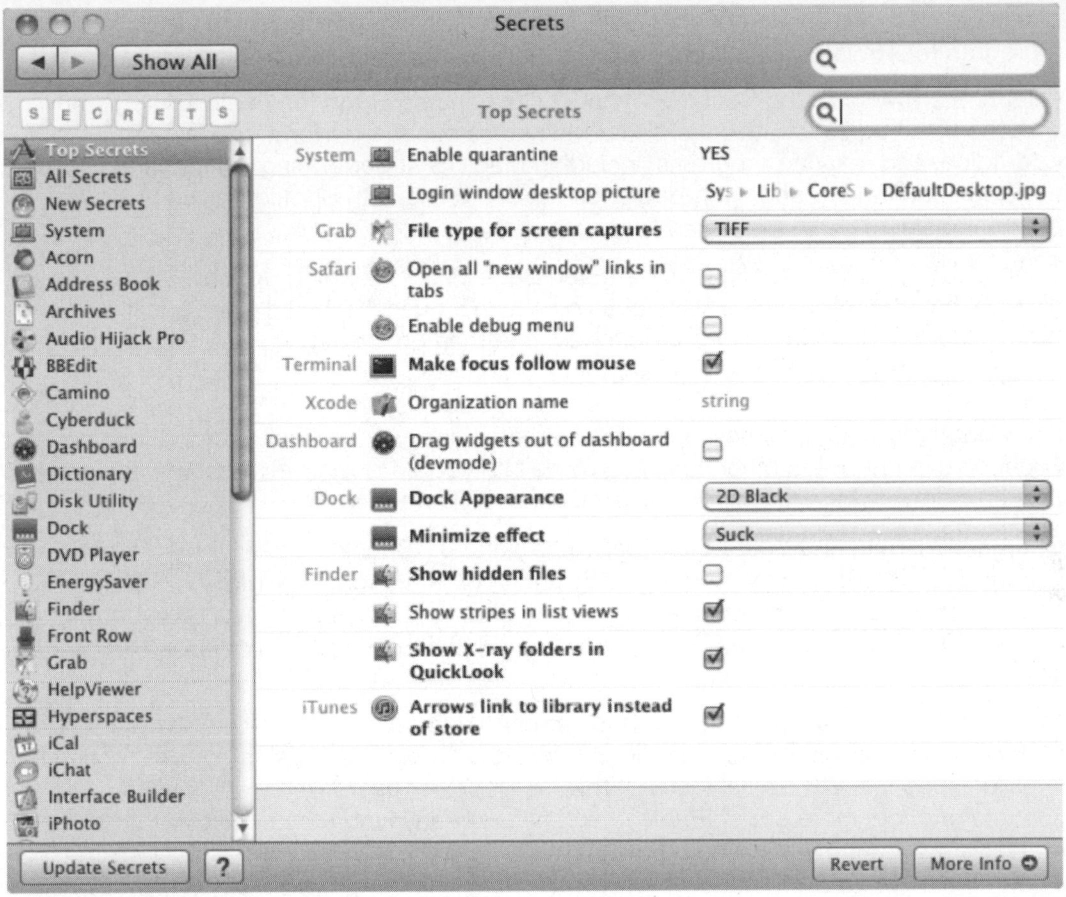

Figure 1-1. *Hidden settings galore!*

Secrets doesn't just stick to Apple's hidden prefs—it also brings in lots of third-party software as well. Spend some time with Secrets, and you'll find out literally hundreds of things that you didn't know your Mac could do. Now that's perfect for power users!

> **TIP:** Secrets is free and focuses on hidden preferences. If you're willing to spend $20, MacPilot (available at www.koingosw.com/products/macpilot.php) does everything Secrets does and a *lot* more. Check it out!

What You'll Learn

The definition of power users I quoted earlier nicely covers what I'm going to focus on in this book: advanced features of the operating system and other programs, as well as cool and useful programs that help perform advanced tasks. I'll show you some sysadmin tasks and tools, and I'll give you some code that you can enter in various places, even if you don't know the first thing about programming (which is cool—I'm not a programmer myself, even if I can write simple shell scripts and the like).

Chapters 2 ("Maintaining Your Mac") and 3 ("Expanding Upon the Basic Tools") start with the basic administrative tasks that Mac users need to perform: managing, upgrading, and deleting programs, including Mac OS X; performing maintenance; fixing the Dock and Finder; and an in-depth look at searching with Spotlight... on the command line!

Chapters 4 ("Making a Great Browser Even Better"), 5 ("Stepping Beyond Safari"), and 6 ("Using the Internet to its Fullest") focus on—take a guess!—the Internet. You'll find out how to extend Safari in every possible way, and then go far beyond Safari by meeting pretty much every other web browser that runs on Mac OS X, including the very cool group of tools called SSBs. That stands for *Site Specific Browsers*, and you'll find out just what that means and how you can use them. Finally, you'll find out how to integrate Facebook, Twitter, and other social software into your Mac, as well as how to download files efficiently, with a revealing look at the best BitTorrent apps.

Chapters 7 ("Securing Your Mac & Networks") and 8 ("Backing Up Your Mac") focus on security. Need to protect your passwords and your other sensitive info? Use SSH heavily to run commands on other computers (Mac and non-Mac)? Worried about backing up all your data, both locally and remotely? Then these two chapters are for you.

Chapters 9 ("Manipulating and Sharing Pictures") and 10 ("Having More Fun with Audio and Video") are all about the fun stuff: multimedia. These chapters aren't for Photoshop whizzes and Final Cut ninjas; instead, they're for power users who want to take screenshots, get more out of iPhoto, watch virtually any kind of video file out today, and convert and change images and movies quickly, and in as automated a fashion as possible. I'm pretty particular about my music files, so I'm going to spend some time showing you how to keep the metadata in your MP3s accurate and orderly.

Chapters 11 ("Key Utility Tools for Text and Archives") and 12 ("Digging Deep as an Admin") circle around to administrative kinds of tasks again, but these are a bit more advanced than those at the beginning of the book. Automation is key here, whether it's about entering text accurately, unarchiving gigabytes of files, monitoring what's happening on your Mac and your network connection, running jobs at pre-determined times and events. Automator is key, and even though I'll discuss it throughout the book where appropriate, I really dig in here. Finally, I wrap up with a few admin odds and ends, such as changing DNS and fixing a few little nagging hardware issues.

A short appendix ("Learning as Much as You Can") rounds things off with a list of resources, both off- and online, that serious Mac users can't be without.

So that's the book, in a nutshell. Whew!

What You Need to Already Know

In addition to letting you know what you're going to find in this book, I also want you to know my expectations of you, my reader. This book is for power users, so I'm dispensing with a lot of basic Mac info that you can find in any introductory book or on countless websites. That means that I expect you to already know:

How to install software. DMG, PKG, MPKG, ZIP, or something else: I'm not going to cover how to get software you've downloaded, installed, and are running on your Mac. It's pretty simple, actually—so much so that I often tell Mac newbies that installing software on a Mac is so easy that it's not obvious, especially to Windows converts. Drag and drop? That's it? Yep. For a refresher, check out "Installing Applications in Mac OS X" (http://guides.macrumors.com/Installing_Applications_in_Mac_OS_X).

How to find apps. Many times I'm going to tell you to open a program that's on your Mac already. You should know how to find an app using the Finder, or Spotlight if necessary, or the Terminal if it uses the command line. That way I don't have to waste time saying things like "Open the Finder, now go to Applications, now look for Foobar, now click on Foobar."

How to use the Terminal. You don't have to be a command-line whiz or a Bash shell junkie like I am, but you also can't freak out if I ask you to open the Terminal and type a few commands. If you've configured your own .bashrc file, welcome! If you have no idea what that means, don't panic. As long as you're willing to monkey around on the Terminal and learn a few new things, you'll be fine.

> **NOTE:** Here's a bit of shameless self-promotion that you are free to ignore. I wrote a very good book all about the Linux command line called *Linux Phrasebook* (Sams, 2006). The cool part is that almost everything I wrote in that book is also applicable to the command line in Mac OS X as well. If you don't know much about the command line and want to learn more, or even if you already know a lot and just want a handy reference, check out *Linux Phrasebook*. I use it all the time, and I wrote the book!

How to navigate around Mac OS X. You don't need to know every file deep in the bowels of Mac OS X—Quick! Explain what every file in /System/Library/CoreServices does! You have three minutes!—but you should be comfortable poking around the filesystem. I'm going to be taking you into some areas of your Mac that you may not normally visit. It's safe to touch things (if I say it's OK), but things may be a bit dusty due to a lack of recent visitors!

Basic folder structure of Mac OS X. Again, you don't need to have everything memorized, but you should be comfortable leaving your Home directory. If I mention something in /System/Library, you should have a rough idea of what that part of your Mac does.

What ~/ means. If you don't know already, it's shorthand on the command line for your Home directory. So if I talk about ~/bin, that refers to the bin folder in your Home directory.

How to create and use ~/bin. I'm going to give you a few cool command-line tips throughout the book, and I almost always put all of mine in ~/bin. That is, I create a bin directory in my Home to store command-line scripts, Automator actions, and things I've created that are personalized for me. But convention, UNIX systems—and remember, Mac OS X is a variant of UNIX!—want you to put things like that in ~/bin (putting them in ~/bin also makes them easy to back up). After you create ~/bin, don't forget to update your .profile file by adding this line so your system knows to look there:

```
export PATH=$PATH:~/bin
```

> **NOTE:** If you didn't know already, bin is short for *binary*.

How to turn filename extensions on. I'll be referring to files and programs with their extensions, so it would help if you have extensions turned on. This is also a good idea because extensions are important, and your ability to see them can help you keep things straight so you know which kind of files you're seeing, which tells you which kinds of programs can open them. To see extensions, go to Finder ➤ Preferences ➤ Advanced and check the box next to Show All Filename Extensions.

How to select items in the Finder with Command or Shift. This is just good, basic Mac OS X knowledge to have. To select contiguous items (things that are next to each other), click on the first item, then press Shift and click on the last item. All of the files and folders, from the first to the last, should be selected. To select non-contiguous items (things that are not next to each other), click on the first item, and then press Command as you click on the others, until you're finished.

What a good text editor is and where yours is. You're going to occasionally be writing some code, and to do that, you need a good text editor. Sure, you could use an actual IDE (Integrated Development Environment; for more, see http://en.wikipedia.org/wiki/Integrated_development_environment), but that's overkill. Besides, a good text editor is like a web browser: it's something every computer user should have and know how to use.

For most people, TextWrangler is perfect. It's free and powerful, yet easy to use, and you can get it at www.barebones.com/products/textwrangler/. If you're feeling uber-nerdy, however, you can go the route I've chosen and download MacVim, free from http://code.google.com/p/macvim/. However, be forewarned! MacVim is based on vim, and vim isn't at all like your normal text editor, so you absolutely need to do some reading about vim first. Start with Wikipedia's article at http://en.wikipedia.org/wiki/Vim_(text_editor), and then check out some tutorials at http://blog.interlinked.org/tutorials/vim_tutorial.html and www.linuxconfig.org/Vim_Tutorial. The documentation is at http://vimdoc.sourceforge.net/htmldoc/version7.html. Finally, before starting out down the vim path, you may want to read the answers given to this question: "Is learning VIM worth the effort?"

(http://stackoverflow.com/questions/597077/is-learning-vim-worth-the-effort). My answer is "Yes," but I'm a nerd and I absolutely adore and depend upon vim (and now, MacVim).

Why I'm not covering iOS. Finally, keep in mind that this book is about Mac OS X Snow Leopard, not iOS. My iPhone is definitely an extension of my hand, and I certainly tie many things on it to my Mac, but fundamentally they're two separate devices. This book will mention the iPhone (and iPod Touch, and maybe even the iPad) every once in a while, but nothing here will depend upon any device running iOS.

Now that you know what you need to know, and also what you'll be learning, let's dive right in and start finding out about Mac OS X Snow Leopard for Power Users!

## Chapter 2

Maintaining Your Mac

Computer makers—yes, even Apple!—tell people that computers are easy to use. Granted, Macs are easier to use than computers running any other operating system, but they're still computers, and computers are not devices that you simply turn on and use (the exception here is the iPad, but that's a different animal, since I would argue that it's actually a consumer electronic appliance rather than a traditional computer). You have to administer a computer, and you have to take constant care of it, which means maintainance. In this chapter, I'm going to cover the important maintainance tasks Mac users need to perform.

Managing & Upgrading Your Apps

It was a big deal when Microsoft introduced Windows Update along with Windows 98 (perhaps the best thing about that misbegotten OS, which also saw the inextricable welding together of Windows and Internet Explorer at the system level, the most egregious security error Microsoft ever made), as it certainly made keeping Windows up-to-date with the latest bug fixes and changes much easier. Likewise, when Mac OS 9 unveiled Software Update, it was a similarly big deal, and Mac OS X has continued, and improved, this great feature.

Windows Update and Software Update are nice, sure. However, neither one holds a candle to the way Linux users keep their systems fresh. In the Linux world, the operating system comes with *package managers*, software that serves to upgrade not just system software, but also virtually every piece of software on the system. Sometimes called APT (the *Advanced Packaging Tool*), and sometimes called YUM (the *Yellowdog Updater, Modified*), depending upon the variant of Linux, package managers make it a breeze to update virtually everything on the computer.

> **TIP:** For more on the actual commands that Linux uses to update software, see my *Linux Phrasebook* (Sams, 2006), available at better bookstores everywhere.

Think about it: Windows Update updates, what, exactly? Windows—and a few hardware drivers, sure, although those don't always work as well as one would hope. And Apple's Software Update updates… yep! Mac OS X only. And Apple's own software, such as Final Cut Express and Aperture. But that's it.

If I'm using Ubuntu (the most popular desktop version of Linux), on the other hand, when I run APT, it updates the Linux kernel. And any hardware drivers I have installed. And KDE, one of the main Linux GUIs. And Firefox. And Google Chrome. And my text editor. And on and on. This makes it an absolute breeze to keep my Linux box safe, secure, and running well.

Of course, things are easier in the Linux world when it comes to updating software. Virtually all Linux software (with a few exceptions) is open source and free to acquire and use. This isn't the case in Windowsworld and the Macverse. No way, no how. So it's not a big deal for Linux distributions like Ubuntu to create gigantic repositories of code covering every possible program and then allow users to run an app like APT that connects to those repositories to download the latest and greatest release of all those programs. If Apple or Microsoft tried that, it would be a great day for lawyers.

Sure, there have been efforts to help ameliorate the situation for Mac users. Andy Matuschak came up with *Sparkle*, a free framework that any developer can insert into her program to automatically check for the latest software update and then ask the user if he'd like to download and install it. Two problems, however: first, not every developer uses Sparkle, so it's only a partial solution; and second, you have to actually open and run the software for Sparkle to kick in, so there's no automatic way to upgrade all of your software without remembering which ones use Sparkle and then opening them all up!

In this chapter, we're going to look at more comprehensive solutions that try to emulate APT or YUM from Linux. All of them are worth checking out, and you can definitely install more than one on your Mac, which is actually a recommended idea. None of them is perfect (though several are very good) and, while there is considerable overlap in the software packages they cover (they all keep an eye on Firefox, for instance), they all have a few holes in their coverage.

VersionTracker Pro

NOTE: Just as this book was about to be printed, it was announced that VersionTracker has been absorbed by CNET, and the paid VersionTracker Pro service will be discontinued. Treat all information in this VersionTracker section with not a grain of salt, but an entire salt lick.

The VersionTracker website has been around quite a while, and it's one of the best of its kind for Mac users. Want to know if a particular app has been updated and when? Check out www.versiontracker.com. In addition to its website, VersionTracker offers software you can download from www.versiontracker.com/subscribe/ that will help keep your Mac running the latest releases of your programs. It's a nice service with one big gulp: the price. At $80 a year for three machines, it's a sizable investment. Keep reading to see how it works.

When you open VersionTracker Pro on your Mac, it begins scanning your software and looking for updates. After it's done, you'll see a screen like that in Figure 2–1.

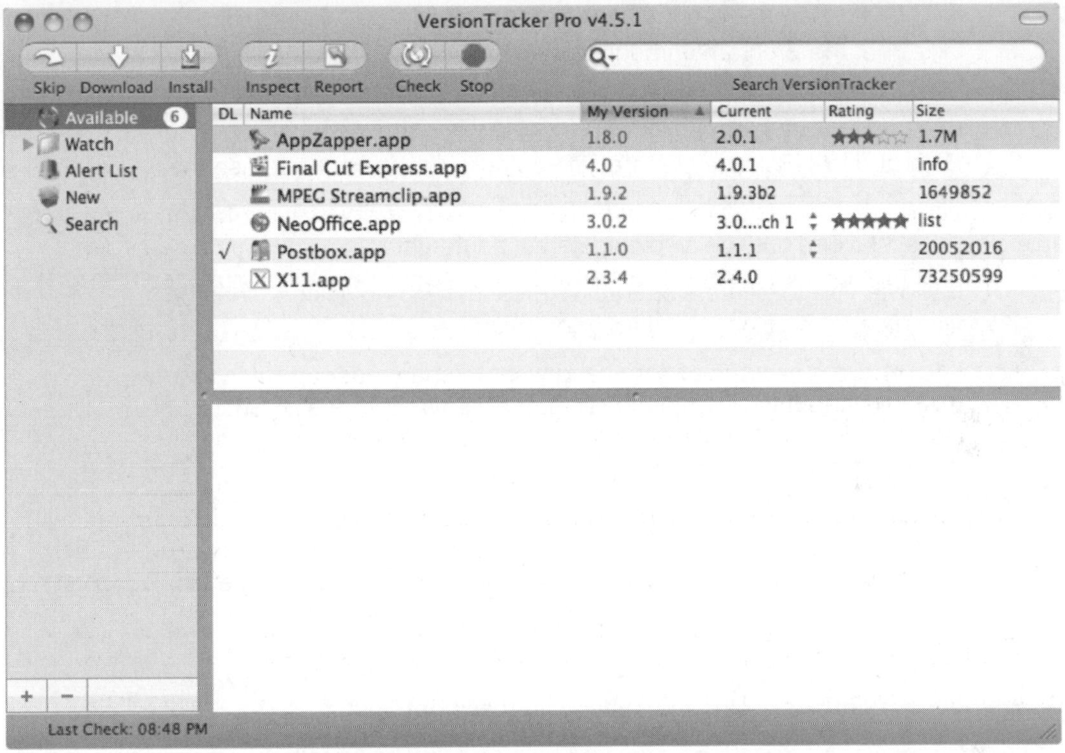

Figure 2–1. *VersionTracker Pro identifies outdated software.*

To make VersionTracker Pro easier to use, go to **View ➤ Columns** and make sure that the following items are checked: Current Version, Download Status, Name, My Version, Rating (only if you want; it's kind of useless), and Size. The three most important are Name (gotta have that one!), My Version (the one you have installed), and Current Version (the newest one to which you can upgrade). You can rearrange the columns by dragging; I like to put My Version in front of, and next to, Current to make it easy to see the difference.

Once VersionTracker Pro has listed any programs that have new versions, choose the ones you want to update and click the Download button. If you want VersionTracker Pro to download and install the app, click the Install button instead; even after its done, VersionTracker Pro keeps the installer for you so you can archive it if you'd like.

To change how VersionTracker Pro functions, go to **VersionTracker Pro ➤ Preferences**. I'm not going to go over every panel here in order to focus instead on the important details.

On the Updates screen, pay attention to the following:

- You can set Check For Updates, which determines how often the program looks for new software for you. Weirdly, I've had mine set to Every Four Hours for a long time, but this doesn't seem to affect anything.

- I like that the program immediately begins working if you select Check For Updates On Launch.

- If you want to walk the safe path, check the box next to Don't Show Beta and Pre-Release Updates; if you're like me and like to use the newest of the new, leave it unchecked.

The Download screen has the following items of interest:

- It allows you to tell VersionTracker Pro where to download files; the Downloads directory is a darn good place.

- If you have a network of Macs and want to share your updates, check the boxes next to Download From Local Network Peers or Share My Downloads With Local Network Peers, depending on which machines you want to act as servers and which you want to be clients.

- For automatic downloading, check the box next to Download New Updates Every Day At and then set a time (I don't do this, for reasons you'll discover in "Which One Should You Use?" later in this section).

- Finally, if you want to have to avoid double-clicking on ZIP files and DMGs, go ahead and check Unpack Archives Automatically.

Scanning makes things easier and faster with these options:

- I recommend selecting Software I Use next to The Installed Software Watchlist Scans, as it's faster and not full of the endless minutiae of the other choice, All Of My Software. If you're a control freak (and you know if you are), you can instead choose Only Items I Add.

- For On, think about where your software is located. Most likely, it's on your Mac's internal hard drive, not on an external drive and not on your Boot Camp partition, if you have one. The best thing to do is choose Selected Volumes and then check only your internal hard drive, to speed up VersionTracker Pro's scanning process.

- Filtering For lets you exclude apps written for Mac OS 9 and below; to do that, uncheck Classic. By and large, any app written for any version of Mac OS X should work with your version of OS X, so I leave all the OS X items checked. If you're trying to free your system of PowerPC apps, however, make sure you uncheck everything except the Intel options.

VersionTracker Pro is easy to use and will definitely keep your system up-to-date, but how well does it do when compared to the competition? You'll find out in the upcoming "Which One Should You Use?" section.

AppFresh

AppFresh is free and available for you to download at http://metaquark.de/appfresh/. Keep in mind that the website explains that it's "still work in progress and released as a Development Preview." As such, it's free now while in beta; however, the developers have emphasized on their blog that even after it reaches a 1.0 release, they still plan to keep it free for personal use. It's been in development for at least two years, though, and progress toward that 1.0 release at times seems painfully slow, so I wouldn't worry about having to pay for the program any time soon.

AppFresh claims that it integrates into one interface a wide variety of programs that serve to check for updates on a Mac, including:

- Apple's Software Update

- Sparkle

- Microsoft's AutoUpdate

- Adobe's Updater

- osx.iusethis.com (a website where people can indicate the software they use)

Of course, AppFresh updates your apps, but it also checks your Dashboard widgets, Preference Panes, and plug-ins for a variety of programs, including Web browsers, Address Book, iPhoto, and Mail.

One you open AppFresh, it starts scanning your system for programs. It then uses the various update checkers listed previously to see if any of your programs have new releases. If they do, they're listed, as you can see in Figure 2–2.

Once AppFresh has listed programs with new versions, you choose the ones you want to bring up-to-date and click the Update button. At that point, depending on the settings you've made to AppFresh (which I'll cover in just a moment), those new versions are either downloaded and installed for you, or just downloaded so you can install them manually.

If you go to **AppFresh ➤ Preferences**, you'll be able to set how AppFresh behaves. On the General screen, I recommend you uncheck Check For Available Apple Updates, since you probably have Apple's Software Update set to take care of that already, and because it causes AppFresh to take an inordinate amount of time to perform its initial scan for new software.

Also on the General screen, you can set how often the program checks for new software and what it updates. For Schedule, you can set it to automatically check Daily, Weekly, or Monthly; Weekly makes the most sense to me. For AppFresh Updates, you can choose either Stable Releases or Nightly Builds. I prefer to live on the edge with the latest and greatest, so I went with Nightly Builds, but more careful folks ought to select Stable Releases.

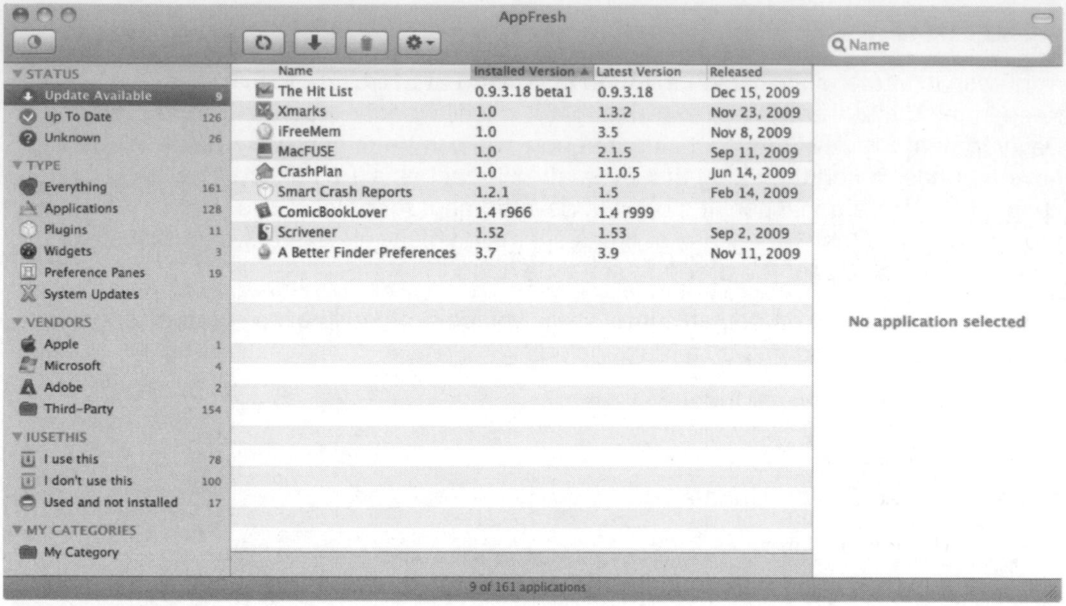

Figure 2–2. *AppFresh found some programs that need to be updated.*

The Update screen contains some very important choices. If you check Unpack Downloaded Files, AppFresh will do just that: either unzip updates that are zipped, or mount DMGs. Related to that is Install Updates If Considered Safe; if that is selected, in addition to unpacking downloads, AppFresh will go ahead and install them for you, if that's possible. You will still have to install apps that use a wizard-like interface, where you click Next, then Next, then Finish, manually. If an app is automatically installed for you, AppFresh moves the old version to the Trash, so you can recover it if something doesn't work with the new one (so wait to empty your Trash!).

Personally, I like to keep my installers and do everything manually to know exactly what's going on, so I keep both Unpack Downloaded Files and Install Updates If Considered Safe unchecked. But on a spare machine I do everything automatically, and things have been fine. It's really up to you and your level of control.

Those are the main things I would pay attention to in AppFresh's preferences. There are other screens with other settings, but most of them are pretty self-explanatory.

So should you use AppFresh or not? For the answer, check out "Which One Should You Use?," later in this section.

MacUpdate Desktop

The MacUpdate website has been around since the mid-1990s and now tracks around 30,000 Mac apps. Want to find out about a particular program, including if there's an update? Head over to www.macupdate.com and check it out.

In October 2009, MacUpdate released a brand new version of MacUpdate Desktop, software that compares the software on your Mac with those 30,000 apps and makes it easy for you to upgrade to the newest release. You can try it for free for ten days; after that, it'll cost you $20 each year.

To get it, head to www.macupdate.com/desktop/ and begin your free trial. If you don't already have a MacUpdate account, you can create one the first time you launch the program. After the account info is set up, MacUpdate Desktop will go to work analyzing your software. After a short period of time, MacUpdate Desktop will display all of your software, with the outdated stuff in red. To see just the programs that need your attention, click on Outdated, which will show you something like the screenshot you see in Figure 2–3.

Figure 2–3. *MacUpdate Desktop has found quite a bit of outmoded software.*

At this point, you can download and install software using one of the following methods:

- Double-click on it in the software list.

- Select the package in the software list and click on the Download+Install button in the Version Info (the bottom) pane.

- Select the package in the software list, click on the sprocket at the bottom of the window, and choose Download+Install.

- Select the package in the software list and go to **Updates ➤ Download+Install Update.**

- Select the package in the software list and press ⌘-D.
- Right-click on the package in the software list and select Download+Install.

Good gravy! I think they have it covered!

If you want to download and install all the software packages listed (not a good idea, actually, as I'll make clear shortly in the coming section, "Which One Should You Use?"), go to **Updates ➤ Download+Install All Updates**, or press ^-⌘-D.

If you just want to download the package and install it manually, select it and go to **Updates ➤ Download Update**, or press ⇧-⌘-D.

By default, the updates get delivered into `~/Downloads/MacUpdate Desktop/MacUpdate Desktop 2010-02-20` (the date changes to today's whenever you download anything). All the updates you do on a particular day will have their installers in that folder. The software that was replaced will be in the Trash, so you can revert back to an older version if necessary.

You'll notice in Figure 2–3 that MacUpdate also categorizes updates not just into Applications, but also into Widgets, Screen Savers, and Preference Panes. Click on those buttons and follow the same procedures to download and install the new software.

MacUpdate Desktop doesn't have a lot of preference screens, but what's there is important to the program. Go to **MacUpdate Desktop ➤ Preferences**, and you'll see two screens; for each one, I'll walk you through the notable settings.

Settings

- *Show Version Info*: Leave this checked, as it shows the bottom pane when you select an item in the software list.

- *Show Beta Versions In Outdated Listings*: Check it if you want to be able to update to betas of your software; uncheck it if you don't. You'll need to restart MacUpdate Desktop if you change this setting.

- *Only Scan Recently Used Applications*: If this is checked, only apps you used in the last 30 days are scanned. I would not check this, as MacUpdate Desktop is pretty fast already.

- *Show Community Applications*: If checked, then the MacUpdate Community section appears in the left pane of the program, with MacUpdate Promo under it; if unchecked, it disappears. I don't see how it harms anything, so I leave it checked.

- *Show Hot Picks and Popular Listings*: If this is checked, these additional sections appear under MacUpdate Community. They can be useful, but they do add a little bit of time when MacUpdate Desktop first runs and checks software.

- *Show Latest Updates Added To MacUpdate*: Yet another section under MacUpdate Community, yet more time added when MacUpdate Desktop checks for updates... thankfully, not a lot, but still.

Updates

- Keep Downloads Sorted By Date Folders: Don't like how MacUpdate Desktop automatically downloads updates into a folder that has the date appended to its name? Uncheck this box.

- Automatically Install Updates: Want to download updates but leave it to you to actually install them? Uncheck this box.

- Archive Old Version Before Updating: Checking this means that after an app is updated, the old version is zipped and stored in the Applications folder; in other words, update Transmission, and next to the new Transmission.app will appear Transmission (old).zip as well. Yuck! I do not want my Applications folder cluttered like that, so thank goodness for the next option, which is...

- Move Archive To Downloads Location: If you choose to keep an archive of the old version of software that you're replacing, you can have the resulting ZIP file placed in the same location as the downloaded installer by checking this box.

- Downloads Folder: Want the updates to end up somewhere besides ~/Downloads/MacUpdate Desktop? Change it here.

My one complaint with how MacUpdate Desktop operates is that updating is a one-or-all proposition. You can either update each app individually by using one of the methods I listed previously, or you can update all of them at once. You can't, though, select multiple apps with your ⌘ or Shift key and then update those, which is quite annoying, especially given my findings in the upcoming "Which One Should You Use?" section. Overall, though, MacUpdate Desktop is a great program for updating your software, but is it the best? To find out, keep reading.

Bodega

Bodega really wants to be the equivalent of the iPhone's App Store, but for Mac OS X. But is it everything it hopes to be?

To find out, you can download it from www.appbodega.com for free. The program is free because it makes money from ads, and not by taking a cut of app purchases à la Apple. When you open Bodega, the Featured screen opens up, as you can see in Figure 2–4.

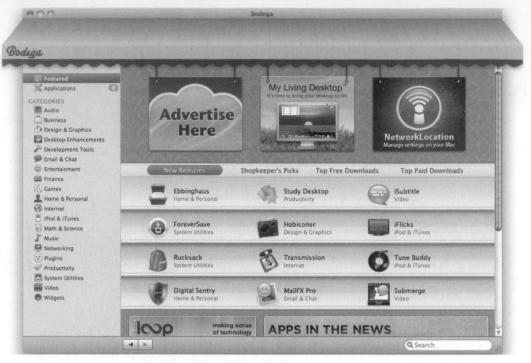

Figure 2–4. *Bodega features certain programs when you open it.*

The Featured screen has ads along the top and four buttons: New Releases (the default), Shopkeeper's Picks, Top Free Downloads, and Top Paid Downloads. Click on those to see the software Bodega has available categorized in different ways, or use the list of Categories (Audio, Email & Chat, Internet, and Video, to name but a few) on the left side of the program's window. This is a nice way to find out about new software that you may or may not have (and in fact, it will show you software you already have installed, which is a bit of a bummer). If you see something you like, you're taken to the developer's website, where you can purchase and download it.

Nice as Bodega's efforts to show you new stuff are, I'm really more interested in how well Bodega keeps my apps up-to-date. Unfortunately, it's here that problems begin to appear. To see your installed programs in Bodega, go to the Applications screen, shown in Figure 2–5.

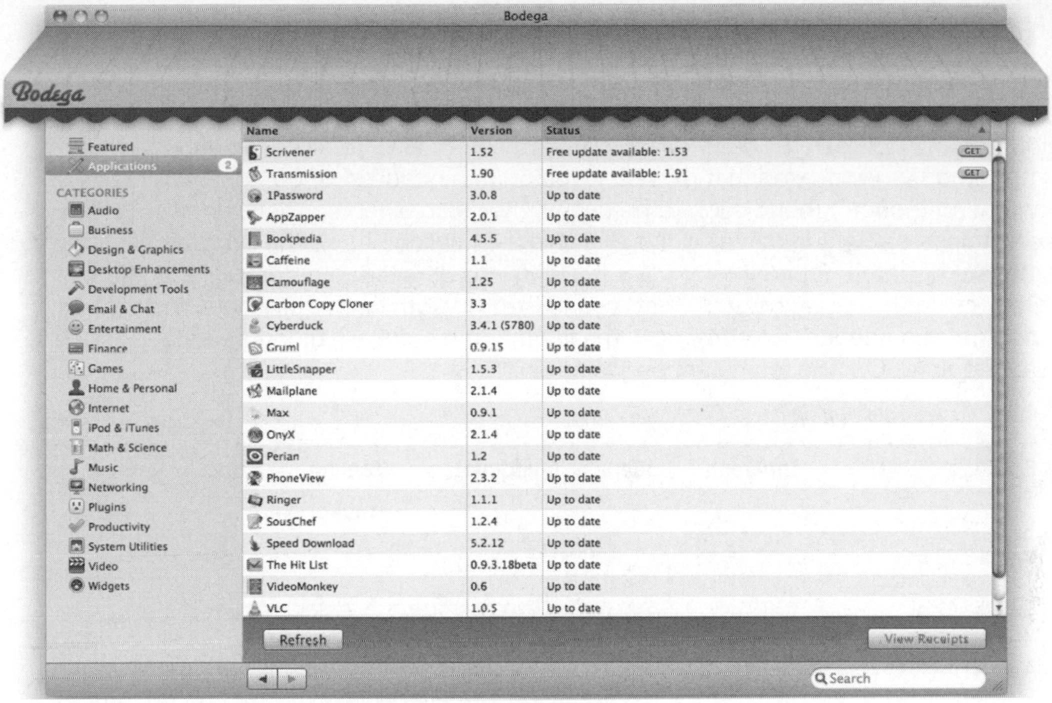

Figure 2–5. *Bodega lists your installed apps… well, some of them.*

Bodega found only 23 of my apps, with just two needing an update. I know this is way off, and further examination yields another interesting tidbit: nothing by Apple, Adobe, Microsoft, or any other large company shows up. In fact, at the time of this writing, Bodega's website shows that it is tracking 866 apps in total. What gives?

It turns out that developers have to request inclusion in Bodega, and enough have done so to bring the total number of apps to 866. But none of the big guns have added themselves, and obviously not that many developers have done so. The missing word, of course, is *yet*. Bodega has only been in general release since August 2009, so maybe it will eventually prove to be incredibly popular and considered *de rigueur* by developers, even the powerhouses, to add themselves to its database. I hate to sound defeatist, but I'm not so sure that's likely to happen.

Still, it's a nice little program if you want to discover new apps, and its updating features aren't terrible—just very incomplete.

NOTE: Bodega has some visual flourishes, like a large graphical awning at the top of the window, that some people like and others dislike. I actually kind of dig the idea of the awning—it fits with the program's name—although it has a tendency to separate from the main window if you grab it and move the window quickly, which looks janky. But this is a personal decision, so I'll leave the weighing of the program's aesthetics up to you.

Which One Should You Use?

I've covered the four major choices out there when it comes to updating your Mac automatically, but which one should you choose? I've been using all four software updaters—AppFresh, Bodega, MacUpdate Desktop, and VersionTracker Pro—for a while, and I've wondered that myself. I would often notice strange behaviors by all of them, and though I found each to be useful, they also exhibited deficiencies. To help keep things straight in my mind, I built Table 2–1, which shows the programs that all four software updaters found on my Mac. It's long and detailed, but complete. If you see "Correct" in the Notes column, that means that the software rightly detected that an upgrade was needed. An empty cell means that the software didn't see that an update was required. Other circumstances are noted.

Table 2–1. *The Four App Updaters, Compared.*

Software	AppFresh	Bodega	MacUpdate	Version Tracker	Notes
Applications					
1Password			✓	✓	Correct
Acorn	✓		✓		Correct
AppZapper				✓	Already up-to-date, so I don't need an upgrade
Combine PDFs	✓		✓		Correct
ComicBookLover	✓				Correct
CrashPlan	✓		✓		Versions are very confused[1]
Final Cut Express			✓	✓	Correct
Houdini			✓		Correct
iFreeMem	✓		✓		Wrong version detected[2]

[1] Both AppFresh and MacUpdate report that I have version 1.0 installed. AppFresh, however, reports that the current version is 11.0.5, while MacUpdate reports that the currect version is 11.05.2009 (so is AppFresh confused by dates as version numbers?). In any case, CrashPlan reports on its website that the current version is 11.5.2009; if I open CrashPlan on my Mac, it reports, if I go to the Settings screen and then Account, that my current installed version is in fact 11.5.2009, which differs from both AppFresh and MacUpdate!

[2] I have version 3.5 installed, but both AppFresh and MacUpdate think I have version 1.0 instead.

Software	AppFresh	Bodega	MacUpdate	Version Tracker	Notes
Little Snitch			✓		Correct
MPEG Streamclip			✓	✓	Correct
NeoOffice				✓	Already up-to-date
OmniGraffle			✓		Correct
Postbox				✓	Already up-to-date
QuickTime Player 7			✓		Comes with Snow Leopard, but Apple doesn't allow updates
Scrivener	✓	✓	✓		Wrong, but appears to be the app's fault; see Finding the Wrong Software later
Smart Crash Reports	✓				Argh! This shouldn't even be on my Mac![3]
Snood			✓		Snood misreports itself as v. 1, when it is in fact v. 4
Synchronize! X Plus			✓		Correct

---

[3] Smart Crash Reports is a hack to send crash reports to developers when their programs fail (you can read more about it at www.red-sweater.com/blog/860/crash-reporter-roundup). However, it relies on Input Managers, which don't even work in Snow Leopard (the last time Smart Crash Reports was updated was mid-year 2008), and that inject themselves into every running program on your system, which is bad bad bad. Unfortunately, even if you delete Smart Crash Reports, other programs can sneakily reinstall it the next time you open them, without any warning! To get rid of Smart Crash Reports, look for its folder in /Users/[yourname]/Library/InputManagers (where I found it), /Library/InputManagers, and /System/Library/InputManagers and delete it. To prevent it from ever coming back again, empty the contents of the InputManagers folder and then run this command in Terminal (/Applications/Utilities/Terminal): ln -s /dev/null /Users/[yourname]/Library/InputManagers. Now anything that tries to write to the InputManager directory will be sending data into a black hole (for more on /dev/null, see http://en.wikipedia.org/wiki//dev/null—note the two forward slashes before dev!). Repeat as necessary for any other InputManagers folders.

Software	AppFresh	Bodega	MacUpdate	Version Tracker	Notes
The Hit List	✓				Already up to date
Toodledo			✓		An app I created with Fluid, so doesn't apply
Transmission	✓	✓	✓	✓	Correct
VideoMonkey			✓		Confused with another piece of software that has nothing to do with VideoMonkey
X11				✓	Points to a non-Apple source that doesn't work on Snow Leopard
xchm			✓		Confused between UNIX source code and Mac GUI versions[4]
XMLEditor			✓		Correct
Screen Savers					
FieldLines			✓		Correct
iSight Screensavers SL			✓		Correct
Preference Panes					
A Better Finder Preferences	✓		✓		Correct, but with complications[5]

---

[4] The current version of xhcm is 1.17, which is what MacUpdate reports, but that is UNIX source code that would have to be compiled to run as a Mac program. The last pre-compiled version for Mac OS X is 1.13, the current version I have installed.

[5] This is the preferences pane for A Better Finder Rename, which is easily updateable, but there is no apparent way to update just the preferences pane! And frankly, it's very annoying that the app even requires a pref pane in the first place, since it does virtually nothing. Finally, MacUpdate thinks that this is the pref pane for A Better Finder Attributes, when I don't even have that program installed.

Software	AppFresh	Bodega	MacUpdate	Version Tracker	Notes
MacFUSE	✓				Wrong version detected[6]
Secrets			✓		Wrong software[7]
TeX Distribution			✓		Wrong software[8]
TypeIt4Me			✓		Correct, mostly[9]
Xmarks	✓				Wrong version detected[10]

Now that we have data, let's analyze it according to the following aspects:

- Missed software: what apps did the updaters fail to see?

- Finding the wrong software: what apps did the updaters want to erroneously upgrade?

- Finding outdated software: what apps did the updaters correctly identify as needing to be upgraded?

- Cost: how much do these updaters cost, and are they worth it?

With those in mind, let's proceed.

---

[6] Version 2.0.3 is installed, but AppFresh reports it as 1.0, perhaps because it is a 32-bit preferences pane instead of the 64-bits that Snow Leopard likes?

[7] MacUpdate thinks that I have Secrets (a password manager by Severn Software) installed, instead of what I really have: a pref pane by Blacktree that gives me GUI access to hidden settings on Mac OS X (and which is discussed in Chapter 1, "Introduction"). What's interesting is that MacUpdate recognizes that Secrets is a pref pane, but then points to the program by Severn that certainly is *not* a pref pane.

[8] I have BasicTeX, a separate software package from the complete TeX distribution (known as TeXShop), but MacUpdate thinks I have the complete TeX, so it points to the TeXShop release. The purpose of the TeX Distribution pref pane is to allow users to pick which TeX they want to use, even if they only have one installed, as I have. MacUpdate, however, just sees TeX in the title and points to the complete TeX release.

[9] MacUpdate says the latest version I can update to is 4.2, but the developer's website has 4.2.1.

[10] Version 1.3.2, the current one, is installed, but AppFresh reports that I have 1.0 installed. Again, Xmarks (like MacFuse) is 32-bit; could this be the cause?

Missed Software

MacUpdate Desktop missed the following software entirely and didn't recognize them at all, so they apparently are not in its database (you can find these by clicking on All and looking for the grayed-out items in the list):

- Amazon MP3 Downloader
- Bodega (That's funny!)
- CrossOver
- Photo Booth (Really?)
- Seesmic Desktop
- Shrink O'Matic
- Times Reader
- TweetDeck
- Zenmap

Among those listed, Seesmic Desktop, Shrink O'Matic, Times Reader, and TweetDeck are all Adobe AIR apps, which might help to explain MacUpdate Desktop's blindness toward them. Even so, Seesmic Desktop and TweetDeck are two of the most common Twitter apps for the Mac, and Times Reader is pushed by *The New York Times*, so they're surprising omissions.

> **TIP:** At least MacUpdate Desktop makes it easy to let the company know about a program it has missed: just select the app and select **Updates ➤ Submit to MacUpdate**.

AppFresh missed these programs (you can tell by going to the Up To Date section and seeing what AppFresh considers up-to-date, even when it's not):

- Chromium (That's not good)
- ForkLift
- MyMahjGL
- Shrink O'Matic
- Snood

Chromium is Google's open source version of its web browser, Chrome, while ForkLift is a pretty well-known Mac program (discussed in the next chapter). Those two absences are surprising. Shrink O'Matic is a little-used Adobe AIR app, and MyMahjGL and Snood, while fun, are really old games ported to run on Macs, so it's no surprise that they're not on AppFresh's radar.

Bodega missed so many programs that it was, frankly, not very useful when it comes to updating your Mac (but that goes back to the fact that the only programs that show up were added by the program's developers). Put it this way: MacUpdate Desktop reported that I had 157 apps installed, while Bodega only showed 23 *total*.

Finding the Wrong Software

One annoying, potentially problematic, thing that these programs do is find false positives: apps they claim need to be updated when in fact they need no such thing.

For instance, AppFresh, Bodega, and MacUpdate Desktop all claim that Scrivener needs to be updated and have for months. You can update every day if you like, and they will still claim that Scrivener has a new version available. This, I think, is Scrivener's fault—I think that it is reporting the wrong version number to these programs. The same thing is true for Snood, which fools MacUpdate Desktop, and for CrashPlan, which tricks AppFresh and MacUpdate Desktop with a confusing version-numbering scheme.

Weirdly, though, a lot of times these updating programs just don't seem to get the message that I've updated the apps they found, using their updating programs to do so! It doesn't seem to be the updated apps' fault, as they appear to report their version numbers correctly; rather, it's like the updating program has myopia when it comes to a few apps on my Mac.

For example, VersionTracker Pro consistently tells me to update AppZapper, even though I did almost two months ago, and it often seems confused by all the various versions and patches for NeoOffice. AppFresh urges me to update The Hit List and MacFUSE every time I run it, even though I did so two and four months ago, respectively.

You'd also expect some better intelligence from the updater apps, which display shocking ignorance at times. MacUpdate Desktop wants me to update QuickTime Player 7, but I'm running Snow Leopard. Apple provides QuickTime Player 7 as a sop to the fact that QuickTime Player X, Snow Leopard's default media player, is under-featured when compared to its predecessor. However, Apple also doesn't allow (yet) QuickTime Player 7 to be updated; you can only update version 7 if you're using Leopard. Why can't MacUpdate Desktop tell that I'm using Snow Leopard and then hide QuickTime Player 7, since I can't update it?

MacUpdate Desktop also thinks that Toodledo, an SSB I created using Fluid (more on that and other SSBs in Chapter 5 "Using the Web to Its Fullest"), actually has something to do with Toodledo, the website that the SSB points to, which makes no sense, since you can't update an app with a website. And it also urges me to update xchm from 1.13 to 1.17, but there's a problem it's ignoring: 1.13 was the last GUI release for Macs, and 1.17 is just source code that I'd have to compile, so the two are not equivalent.

Finally, the updater programs sometimes seem to get completely befuddled by a particular piece of software on my Mac, and actually point to a program that has nothing to do with the software I'm running!

To illustrate, MacUpdate Desktop wants me to update VideoMonkey (video conversion software discussed in Chapter 10, "Having More Fun With Audio & Video") with FontSee (a Dashboard widget for previewing fonts), and Secrets (a control panel for accessing command-line-only preferences discussed in Chapter 1, "Introduction") with Secrets (a password safe that shares a name and nothing else)!

> **NOTE:** You'll notice that Bodega didn't mis-identify items, at least during my testing. This could be because it's much better than the other apps, but I'm pretty certain it's because it doesn't identify that many programs to begin with (only 866 so far, remember?)!

These are disconcerting, to say the least. Fortunately, most all of the programs have a way to tell them to stop bugging you about a problematic program. AppFresh lets you click on software, then use the **Application** menu to choose **Exclude**, **Skip Update**, or **Report As Broken**. MacUpdate Desktop gives you the option to select the **Updates** menu and from there pick **Don't Check For Updates**, **Set Version To Current**, or **Report Bad Match**. And VersionTracker Pro allows you to go to **File** and then use **Remove** or **Skip Version** (with no apparent way to report mistakes, which is badly needed). Those are all nice, but accurate matching would be far better.

Finding Outdated Software

Of course, the main thing you expect from updater programs is that they'll find apps that are out of date so you can update them. So how did they do?

At the low end, Bodega found only two apps to update (both, though, were correct). Contrast that with MacUpdate Desktop, which found 24. Eleven of those were problematic, as Table 2–1 shows, but I blame two of those on the apps themselves mis-reporting their version numbers, so 9 of 24 had issues, which means that 15 were correctly diagnosed as needing to be updated.

VersionTracker Pro found just eight apps that needed upgrading, but four of those were incorrect, as shown in Table 2–1. It found 4 that correctly needed to be updated, but MacUpdate Desktop found all of those too, as well as an additional *11* that correctly needed to be updated that were missed by VersionTracker Pro.

Clearly, when it comes to finding apps on your Mac that need to be updated, the best program by a mile is MacUpdate Desktop (of course, MacUpdate Desktop also found the most false positives as well, as I discussed in the previous section).

Cost

However, MacUpdate Desktop costs $20 each year, which still seems to me a pittance when it comes to keeping your software up-to-date. If you just can't swing $20, then the next best is AppFresh, which is free, but won't find nearly as many updates as MacUpdate Desktop.

VersionTracker Pro's price—$50 for up to three Macs—just doesn't seem worth it considering that MacUpdate Desktop found far more updates. The fact that

VersionTracker Pro allows you to use it on three Macs is nice, but it's obviously not worth it if you only have one or two to administer. And even if you have three, you'd only pay $10 more for MacUpdate Desktop but get far more accurate software, as I've shown throughout this section.

Who's It For?

Keep in mind, though, that *all* of the software I've covered in this section—AppFresh, Bodega, MacUpdate Desktop, and VersionTracker Pro—are best used by power users. Don't install these on your non-power-user friends' and family members' Macs and expect them to use any updating program to keep their Macs up-to-date without constant confusion on their parts and phone calls to you. They're just not going to understand why a program they updated keeps insisting that it hasn't yet been updated, or why an update to a program installs a completely different program. Sure, they can indicate that a particular package should be ignored, but that's what power users do, not what quote-unquote normal computer users do.

I hope this complex situation changes in the future, but I doubt it will without a concerted, centralized effort to track and manage all Mac software… which ain't gonna happen. In the Linux world, such centralization is possible, thanks to the open source licenses that virtually all software is under, but in the Mac world, diversity reigns, for better, or, as in this case, for worse.

Further Resources

For more on Sparkle, which I mentioned at the very beginning of this section, see `http://sparkle.andymatuschak.org`.

If you're really into Dashboard widgets, then you might like App Update (`http://gkaindl.com/software/app-update`), which updates your Mac's software, or Widget Update (`http://gkaindl.com/software/widget-update`), which updates Dashboard widgets. Yes, a widget that updates widgets!

Deleting Apps

I will say one positive thing about Windows: most of the time, it's pretty darn easy to install software. You double-click on the installer, click Next about six or seven times, click Finish, and your software is installed. The real problem, however, comes later, when you want to uninstall the software. Anyone who's ever used Windows for any length of time knows that you must use the Add or Remove Programs Control Panel, or you're in for a world of hurt.

Why? Because when you install software on Windows, that software typically spews itself all over the system, in every conceivable nook and cranny and folder. If you don't use the Add or Remove Programs Control Panel, and you simply try to drag an app to the Windows Recycle Bin (don't *ever* do that!), you'll end up leaving little bits of that program all over Windows, cluttering up your system and potentially leading to big problems (not to mention the horror known as the Windows Registry, where data about programs can reside, squirreled away in dark corners, forever).

In the Mac world, we're told that things are simpler. We're told that when we're done with an app, we can simply drag it to the Trash, and that's it. That's not 100% true, however. You can do that, and the vast majority of the time things will be just fine. However, many apps do store data files in your ~/Library folder. Occasionally, some programs may store files in a few other places, such the OS's Library folder, found at /System/Library. If you're a neat freak like I am, you'll want to make sure that all of those little files leave your Mac when the program does.

You could go hunt them down manually, but we're talking about a computer here. Computers are designed to do the tedious grunt work that we humans don't like doing. So let's use some programs to delete other programs that we no longer want on our Mac (yes, it's all very self-referential, which is part of the fun).

AppZapper

The first app on my list is AppZapper (www.appzapper.com), and it's perfect for most people, with one small caveat. It does exactly what you want in a program like this—it deletes apps and their related files quickly, easily, and efficiently. The caveat? It costs money, while the other programs in this section are free. However, AppZapper does such a good job that it's worth paying for. And besides—the program's icon, shown in Figure 2–6, is one of the coolest third-party icons in the Macverse, and icon development like this should be rewarded!

Figure 2–6. *AppZapper's awesomely cool ray gun icon.*

Let's say that I want to uninstall the Opera web browser. I simply drag Opera from the Applications folder onto the very cool AppZapper ray gun icon, also in Applications (if the icon is on your Dock, it's an even shorter process). A few seconds later, the window shown in Figure 2–7 appears.

Figure 2–7. *AppZapper detects the program and its related files.*

AppZapper figures out all of the other files that Opera installed or created on my Mac and displays them for me as well. If I'm happy with what I see, I can go ahead and press the Zap! button. Instantly, I hear a nifty ray gun noise and see a flash of light on my screen, all in tune with AppZapper's icon. The files are moved to my Trash and can now be deleted.

AppZapper provides another way for me to choose the program I want to delete. If you look in the top right of Figure 2–7, you'll notice a slider. If I click on it after I've opened AppZapper and before I've dragged an app onto it, I instead see what AppZapper calls the Hit List—a list of programs, Dashboard widgets, Preference Panes, and web browser plug-ins that I can select and delete.

Figure 2–8 shows AppZapper in Hit List mode, after I've selected Opera for deletion (nothing against Opera—it's a fine browser).

Again you'll notice the AppZapper detects any files related to Opera and offers to delete them as well. If I don't want a particular file deleted for some reason, I can uncheck it in the upper left; if I'm not sure where a file is located on my hard drive, I can click the little magnifying glass icon in the upper right and the Finder will open at the folder containing that file.

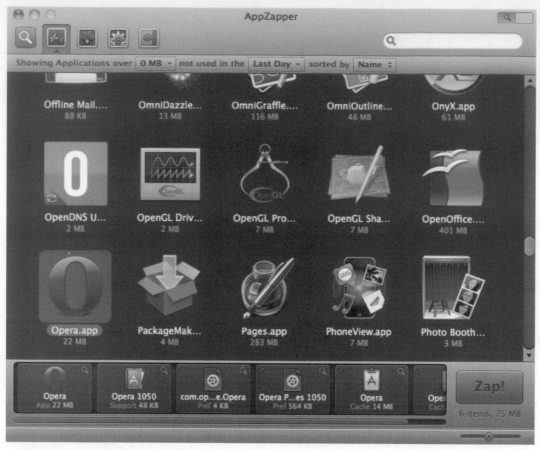

Figure 2–8. *AppZapper in Hit List mode*

In the upper left of the Hit List window shown in Figure 2–8, you notice five icons that allow you to narrow down your search for the items you want to delete. In order, they are:

- Everything

- Applications

- Widgets (for Dashboard)

- Preference Panes

- Plug-ins (for your web browsers)

I can search for items using the familiar Spotlight-like search bar in the upper right, or I can filter the items I'm looking for by size and date of last use, and then sort the results by Name or Date.

TIP: AppZapper has another feature called My Apps that allows you to catalog your programs, which you can access by going to **Window ➤ My Apps**. It's nice to have, but 1Password is much better for this purpose than AppZapper, so I recommend you skip this extra in AppZapper.

Here's a tip that may save you some head scratching: if you're like me, you may want to uninstall one of Apple's apps that you just don't use in order to save space. In my case, I don't use GarageBand and would rather free up the space it takes on my hard drive. If I try to delete it with AppZapper, however, the program refuses to remove it, explaining that it's a protected system app. The solution? Go into AppZapper's preferences and uncheck Keep Apple Applications Safe. Be careful, though—this now means that you could accidentally delete Mail or iTunes, and getting those back could be a lot of work.

AppZapper costs a measly $12.95, payable solely via PayPal, or you can buy the three-user Family Pack for only $18, which is quite a steal. If you bought version 1, the upgrade to version 2 was free, which is always much appreciated and is hopefully a policy that will continue in the future version 3.

AppTrap

AppTrap (http://onnati.net/apptrap/) is a much simpler program compared to AppZapper, with a low-key aesthetic that goes along with its price: free. It's not a pretty program, but it's clever in just how out-of-the-way it is, appearing only when you need it. I know that might be confusing, so let me explain.

It turns out that AppTrap doesn't go into your Applications folder at all—it's a Preference Pane that you can see in Figure 2–9.

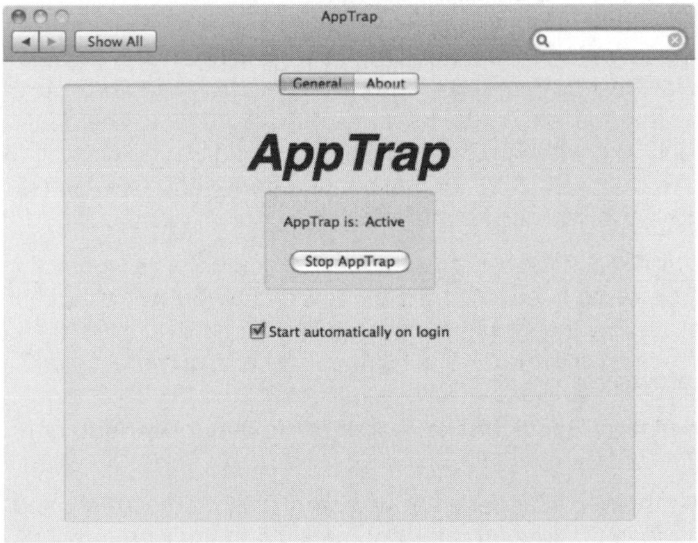

Figure 2–9. *AppTrap is a pref pane, and a simple one at that.*

It doesn't get much easier than that! A button to manually start or stop the program, and a check box to start AppTrap automatically when you log in to your Mac—that's it. My recommendation: check the box so that AppTrap is running all the time (it takes about 11 MB of RAM and 0% of CPU while it idles, which is pretty good) and start the program if it's not already running. That's it!

> **TIP:** The About tab on the AppTrap pref pane might seem unnecessary, but it actually tells you how to uninstall the AppTrap pref pane (as the authors say there, "ah, the irony!"). As with most pref panes, you can right-click on AppTrap while you're viewing System Preferences and select Remove AppTrap Preference Pane, but that doesn't get rid of everything, hence the extra instructions on the About tab.

Once AppTrap is running, just drag the program you want to uninstall to the Trash. After a few seconds, a window like that in Figure 2–10 appears.

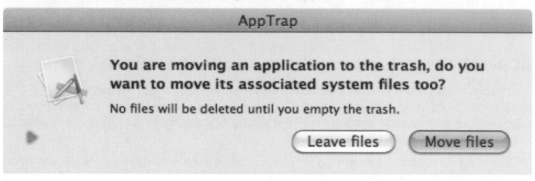

Figure 2–10. *After dragging a program to the Trash, AppTrap springs into action.*

At this point, click Move Files and anything associated with your no-longer-desired app is moved to the Trash for you. However, I tend to want more information first, and you probably do as well, so click the little triangle on the left side of the window to see a full list of files that will be trashed. Just like with AppZapper, uncheck the files you want to keep, click Move Files, and you're done. No cool ray gun sound effect, though, which is too bad—every app should have a cool ray gun sound effect!

So if it's free, why not just use AppTrap instead of AppZapper? A couple of reasons. First, even on a fast Mac, AppTrap takes a few seconds to realize that you've thrown out a program and then display the window that asks you if you'd like to remove all files associated with the app. If you're fast on the draw like I sometimes am, and press ⌘-⌫ to put something in the Trash and then ⌘-Space-⌫ to delete what's in the Trash, you could potentially delete a program before AppTrap even opened, which could be confusing.

Second, even though it's simpler than AppZapper—throw a program into the Trash, and then get asked if you'd like to remove the files for that program—I find the wording ("associated system files," anyone?) to be a bit jargony.

If AppTrap's free status means that it wins out for you over AppZapper, however, just hold on until you see AppCleaner, discussed next.

AppCleaner

AppCleaner is a neat little hybrid of AppZapper and AppTrap, as you'll see. It's got the best features from both, and it's free to boot, making it an excellent choice for most folks.

AppZapper allows you to delete a program by either dragging it onto the AppZapper icon or window, or by selecting the program from within AppZapper using the Hit List feature. AppTrap deletes a program only if you first move it to the Trash. AppCleaner combines all three methods into one program!

When you open AppCleaner, you see a window telling you to Drag Apps Here. Drag a program into that window (or onto the AppCleaner icon) and you see that program and a list of related files in the window that you can then delete.

Want to see a list of your installed programs instead, much like AppZapper's Hit List? Click the Applications button and you'll see a list of programs much like that shown in Figure 11.

Figure 2–11. *A list of programs you can select and delete.*

Check the boxes next to any programs you want to remove, click Search, and AppCleaner will show you a list of files it has found related to the selected programs, ready to be deleted.

Next to Applications is a button for removing Dashboard widgets, and following that is a button labeled Others that does double duty, finding both browser plug-ins and pref panes.

But that's not all. If you open AppCleaner's preferences, you'll find some interesting goodies. Let's start with the General screen, shown in Figure 2–12.

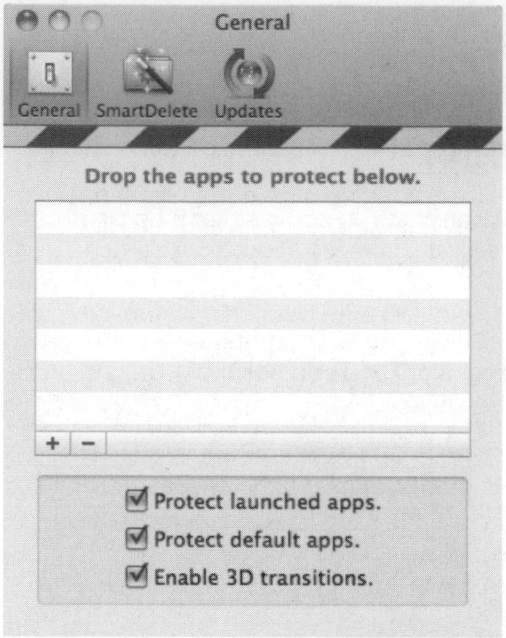

Figure 2–12. *Protect apps from being deleted accidentally.*

The first two check boxes on this screen are similar to AppZapper, in that they stop you from deleting Apple's apps that come with your Mac, as well as anything running. However, it goes beyond AppZapper in that you can also define other key apps that shouldn't be tossed out either, which is a very nice touch.

The next screen, SmartDelete, is similar to AppTrap's main function: throw a program into the Trash, and AppCleaner detects it and its related files so you can nuke 'em all at the same time. Click the button labeled Enable SmartDelete, and you're covered.

AppCleaner is a very cool little app, and the fact that it's free is icing on the cake. My only issue is the lack of help files it provides. Granted, it's a pretty obvious program, but I'm a power user with experience with other, related programs, so I can figure everything out. The website isn't much better, with basically a single short page to cover AppCleaner and its functions.

Further Resources

The apps I've covered in this section aren't the only ones out there that do this job. For instance, there's AppDelete (www.reggieashworth.com), Uninstaller (macmagna.com/uninstaller/), CleanApp (www.synium.de/products/cleanapp/), and Amnesia (www.koingosw.com/products/amnesia.php). Feel free to check those out, but the three I covered here are definitely worth your attention, for the reasons I've outlined.

No matter what you choose, an uninstaller is a great tool to have in your arsenal. Macs make it easy to remove the big chunk of a program you don't want any longer by simply dragging the app to the Trash, but sometimes bits of those programs are left behind. For those of us who obsessively like to keep our systems clean and organized, uninstallers come in handy.

Keeping Your Mac Running Well

Mac OS X is famously stable, but that doesn't mean that you can just set it up and ignore it. You still need to update it, for instance, and you really should run certain maintenance tasks regularly if you want to keep things in tip-top shape. And even if you don't want to tinker around obsessively in the guts of OS X to keep it finely tuned, you'll still need to get under the hood every once in a while to fix a nagging problem. In this section, I'm going to show you a few tools that help you keep Mac OS X running well.

OnyX

One of my favorite third-party system utilities is OnyX, a Swiss army knife of a program that does at least 100 different, useful things. You can get it for free at www.titanium.free.fr—just be sure to get the release that matches your version of OS X.

Every time you start up OnyX (unless you go into the program's Preferences and change this), it will offer to Check S.M.A.R.T. Status, which means it will verify that your hard drive is functioning correctly. You can refuse, but if you choose to allow it, the check usually takes just a moment.

After that, OnyX next offers to Verify Startup Volume. This process actually checks your system files to make sure everything is in its right place, and while it's a good thing to do, you'd better pay attention to the warning that OnyX provides:

> As some processes can affect the results, OnyX will quit all applications (please remember to save your work!). During the verification, you may see the Spinning Wheel, the Finder might slow down and your computer might seem to be unresponsive (freeze). This is normal. Please wait!

This can take a few minutes or more, and any open programs will be closed, so consider yourself forewarned. It's a good thing to do, but if you want to skip this check, just click Cancel. You'll be prompted to enter your password, and you can finally use OnyX freely. To begin with, you'll see the screen shown in Figure 2–13.

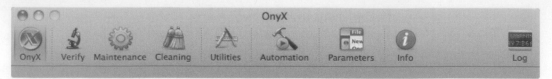

Figure 2–13. *OnyX's first screen once it's available for your use.*

I'm not going to go over every single option and task you can perform with OnyX—that would be an entire chapter to itself!—but I'll instead call out the highlights that I use regularly.

> **WARNING:** After you run many of these options, OnyX will inform you that you need to reboot. If you're finished with OnyX, definitely go ahead and reboot. If, however, you want to continue using OnyX, do so—and *then* reboot at the end of the process. Either way, reboot at the end of your OnyX session, *if* OnyX has told you that you need to reboot.

Verify

- *Preferences*: Checks syntax of all User and System Preference files. Before you run this one, check the box next to Show Only Corrupt Preference Files so you don't clutter the interface with useless information.

Maintenance

- *Permissions*: Verifies and repairs file permissions for the entire system, which can take a while. On my 2.5 GHz Intel Core 2 Duo MacBook Pro with 4 GB of RAM and a 250 GB hard drive, it took over 7 minutes.

- *Rebuild*: Rebuilds various collections of data maintained by Mac OS X. Normally, you don't need to mess around here unless you're having a problem with a program that uses one of those collections. For instance, if Mail is having issues, you may want to check the box next to Mail Envelope Index; if the Sidebar in the Finder is acting weird, check the box next to Sidebar Of Finder Windows. If you right-click on a file and select Open With, and something seems wrong—duplicate listings of programs are the most common issue I've experienced— check the box next to LaunchServices.

Cleaning

- *System*: To keep your system clean, check all the boxes on this screen and get rid of those System cache files.

- *User*: To keep your system clean of cache files associated with your user account, check the boxes on this screen.

- *Internet*: If you're super-paranoid, check all the boxes on this screen; if you just want to clear up space on your hard drive, but want to keep data that makes using the Web more convenient, check everything except Form Values and Cookies.

- *Fonts*: Fonts have caches too, and they can sometimes get corrupted, so checking the boxes on this page can fix some font problems. Pay attention to the note that warns that restarting some programs after clearing the font cache may "take an unusually long time," so you don't have any unpleasant surprises.

- *Logs*: Logs can be extremely helpful if you know how to use them, but they take up a lot of room. If you need to free up room on your drive, checking all the boxes here can sometimes make a big difference. At the least, checking System Archived Logs will get rid of old stuff while keeping current logs that may be helpful for diagnostic reasons.

- *Misc*: Feel free to check items on this screen as you see necessary, with one warning: if you have more than one iTunes library, be careful checking Previous iTunes Libraries, as you may lose a library you want.

Automation

This screen combines features from the Maintenance and Cleaning screens (so I'm not quite clear about why it exists, to be honest). If you want a quick way to run a few of those commands, try checking boxes here.

Parameters

This section duplicates a small subset of the features in a Preference Pane called Secrets that I discussed in Chapter 1, "Introduction." That doesn't mean it's not useful, so feel free to make changes here if they seem useful. I'm not going to go through them here, as most are self-explanatory (and if one is not, click on the little question mark icon in the bottom left of a screen, and OnyX's help will open, detailing the features found there), with one exception that could save your bacon.

On the Login screen, check the box next to Show Message in the Login Window, and then enter something like the following, using your real cell phone number and e-mail address (although if you do use mine, I'm happy to take your Mac off your hands):

This Mac belongs to Scott Granneman: scott@granneman.com or 314-555-1234. Reward if found.

Press Apply, and now you may—*may*—get your Mac back if it's ever lost or stolen.

Info

This is the same data you can get from going to > About This Mac, and then selecting More Info. The one exception is the Misc tab, which actually displays some pretty cool files that are well hidden on your system. Check 'em out!

As you can see from this review of OnyX's feature set, it's a powerful piece of software with a huge range of tools. You probably won't use it a lot, but when you do need one of its capabilities, it's fantastic that you have it in your Applications folder. Check it out and play with it!

Repair Permissions Weekly With Automator

Mac OS X is a UNIX system, and as such, permissions on files and folders that determine who owns them and what owners can do (read, write, or execute) play a key role in keeping things running smoothly. If either you or a program changes permissions on system files without being careful, then things could grind to a halt, or at the least, start getting very funky.

In light of this, one of the best ways to keep things running smoothly under the hood of your Mac is to repair permissions on your file system. The manual way to do this task involves the following steps:

1. Open Disk Utility (/Applications/Utilities/Disk Utility).

2. Select the partition on your hard drive that contains your Mac OS X system. This is easy if you do not dual boot with Boot Camp, as there will only be one partition on your hard drive. If you dual-boot with Boot Camp, just make sure you don't choose the Windows partition. Figure 2–14 shows how I've selected my Mac OS X partition on my internal hard drive, ignoring my Windows partition and my external hard drive.

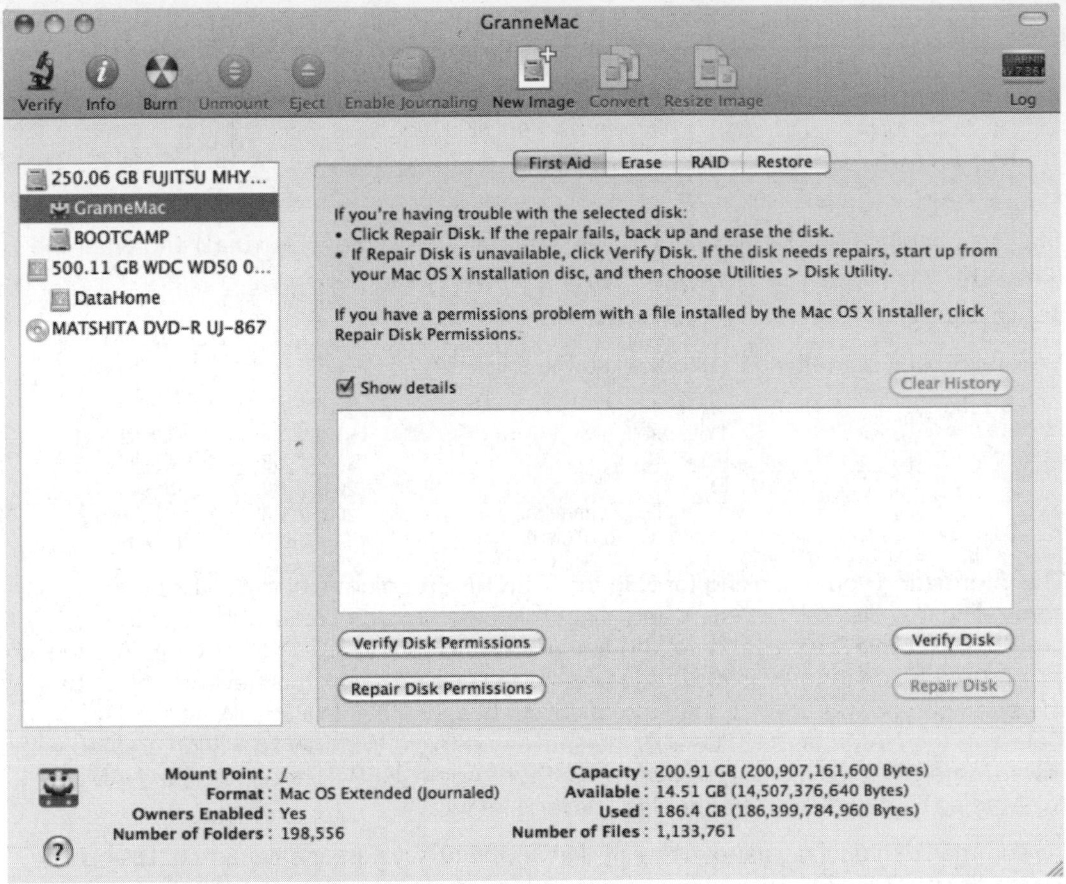

Figure 2-14. *Select the Mac OS X partition in Disk Utility*

3. Click the Repair Disk Permissions button and wait. My 2.5GHz MacBook Pro took almost 13 minutes to check my 200GB partition.

> **TIP:** You could click Verify Disk Permissions and then select Repair Disk Permissions if Disk Utility found an issue, but if you skip ahead to Repair, it will first Verify automatically and then take the appropriate action if it finds problems.

This isn't a difficult process, but it's manual. Why do something manually when it's super-easy to automate it and have your Mac do this task on a regularly timed basis? This is a job for Automator!

> **TIP:** Although I'm demonstrating a great use for Automator in this section, you could also create a cron job using /etc/crontab (see man cron for more details, or find an old UNIX hand who can help you) or regularly run a repair permissions script with Lingon, discussed later in this book in Chapter 12, "Digging Deep as an Admin."

Start by opening your Terminal app (/Applications/Utilities/Terminal) and enter the following:

```
diskutil list
```

You'll get back something that looks like the following:

```
/dev/disk0
   #:                       TYPE NAME              SIZE          IDENTIFIER
   0:      GUID_partition_scheme                  *250.1 GB      disk0
   1:                       EFI                    209.7 MB      disk0s1
   2:                Apple_HFS GranneMac           200.9 GB      disk0s2
   3:       Microsoft Basic Data BOOTCAMP          48.8 GB       disk0s3
```

The information you're looking for is in the IDENTIFIER column, and it will look something like diskXsY, where X and Y are numbers. You can ignore disk0 in the previous example, because that's the actual disk itself, not a partition (it's missing the sY part). You can ignore disk0s1, because its TYPE is EFI, which is never going to be the partition you want. You can ignore disk0s3, because the TYPE is Microsoft Basic Data and the NAME is BOOTCAMP, indicative that this a Windows partition created with Boot Camp. That leaves disk0s2, with a TYPE of Apple_HFS (Bingo!) and the NAME of my Mac's OS X partition, GranneMac (clever, I know).

To summarize, you'll now know how diskutil, the command-line version of Disk Utility, identifies your Mac OS X partition: as disk0s2 (or whatever yours is). Write that down.

> **NOTE:** EFI, according to the man page for diskutil, is "specialized data ... required for the system software" having to do with booting your Mac.

Now open Automator (/Applications/Automator). When it opens and asks you to "Choose a template for your workflow," select iCal Alarm and press Choose. On the left side of the Automator window, select Library, then Utilities, then Run Shell Script, as shown in Figure 2–15.

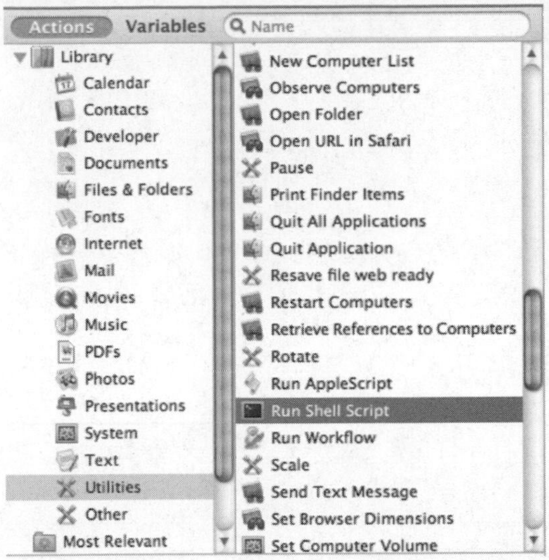

Figure 2–15. *Run Shell Script is a fantastically useful action in Automator.*

TIP: If you don't see the Library, go to the **View** menu and choose **Show Library**. If you still don't see it after that, make sure that Actions is selected instead of Variables.

Drag Run Shell Script to the right side of the Automator window. When the action appears, delete `cat` and replace it with the following line, using the Identifier you wrote down after previously running the `diskutil` command (in my case, disk0s2):

```
diskutil repairPermissions disk0s2
```

To test your little script, click the Run button in the upper right of Automator and then wait (again, this will probably take at least ten minutes to run). If you want to watch the script's progress, click on Results under your script (next to the spinner). When everything finishes, the Log section at the bottom of the Automator window will show that the script has finished running, with a green check mark indicating success.

TIP: Don't see the Log section? Go to View ➤ Log and it will appear.

Now that you know your one-line script works, it's time to save it. Go to **File ➤ Save**, and when you're asked what to Save iCal Alarm As, enter something meaningful, like Repair Permissions. Click Save, and a moment later, iCal will open, with a new entry displayed on the Automator calendar (which will be enabled if you've never seen it before), as in Figure 2–16.

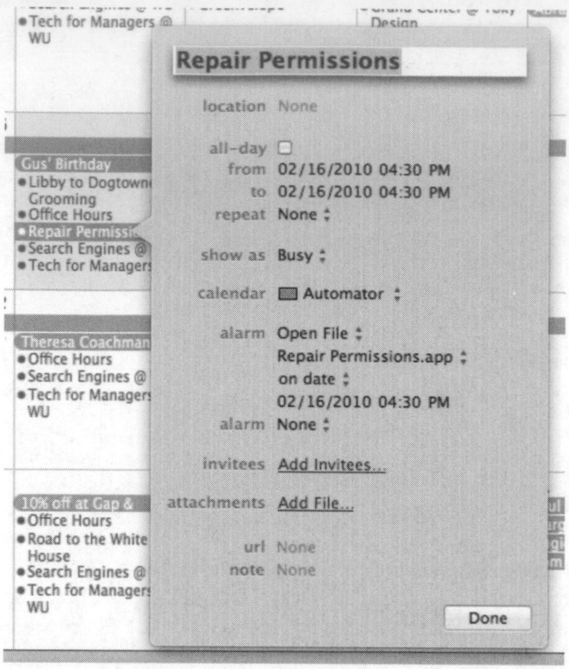

Figure 2–16. *iCal has a new entry for my now-automated task!*

Let's run down this calendar entry, as there are a few items on it you'll want to change.

- Name: You can change the name if you'd like.

- Location: None because that doesn't matter.

- All-day: Don't check this, as the next fields are where you want to focus.

- From And To: This is the date and time your newly created event will run. In my case, I don't want to repair permissions on Tuesdays at 4:30 PM, so I'd change it to something like Wednesdays at 3:30 AM.

- Repeat: Here's where the automation comes in. Click on the drop-down that currently says None and change it to Every Week, with an End date of Never. Now my computer will repair permissions every Wednesday at 3:30 AM, automatically.

- Show As: This really doesn't matter, unless you share your Automator calendar with someone else, in which case you could change it to Free (since you're not going to be Busy during that time), but really, you're not going to share this calendar, so why bother?

- *Alarm*: This is where the magic occurs, and where iCal really shows its power. Essentially, iCal allows you to set alarms to run at certain times; we've already set the time, and here's the alarm: our script to repair permissions, which Automator saved as an app. Yes, iCal has several types of alarms, including pop-up messages, sounds, e-mails, and opening files. In our case, Automator has helpfully told iCal to open (and thereby run) our Repair Permissions app as an alarm.

- *Invitees*: Unnecessary. Who are you gonna invite?

- *Attachments*: Again, unnecessary.

- *URL*: Same thing as Invitees and Attachments.

NOTE: If you really want to leave a Note for yourself to explain what you're doing, go ahead.

Click Done, and that's it—once a week, iCal will invoke the Repair Permissions app you created with Automator, which will scan your Mac fixing any errant permissions on key system files. You'll know it's running because while it is, you'll see a new addition to your menu bar, as shown in Figure 2–17: a rotating sprocket.

Figure 2–17. *It's easy to tell that your Automator app is running.*

Click on that sprocket, and you'll be able to stop running the script, as you can see in the figure. I've found that the script takes very few system resources, so you should be able to run it without a problem while you use your Mac, even if you have some hefty programs open.

TIP: If you ever want to delete the Repair Permissions app that you created with Automator, or if you just want to admire your handiwork, you can find it in `~/Library/Workflows/Applications/iCal`.

Of course, this is just another demonstration of how you can combine Automator and iCal. Use your imagination, and I'm sure you can come up with other tasks that you need to perform on a regular basis that would make great iCal alarms!

Further Reading

Another program similar to OnyX that some Mac users like is MainMenu, which you can get at `http://creativebe.com/mainmenu/`. It costs $20 and hangs out in your Menu Bar (which might be enough to annoy some folks). To run one of its functions, click on the icon in the Menu Bar and select a task. While OnyX is more full-featured than MainMenu, if you find yourself running maintenance tasks constantly, then the easy access to MainMenu may make it more invaluable to you.

Another recommended program—but again, one that costs and does pretty much what the free OnyX and Secrets together do—is Cocktail. You can download a free trial from www.maintain.se/cocktail/. It's very Mac-like in appearance and behavior, more so, in fact, than OnyX, but OnyX appears to me to do much more, and in a clearer fashion. However, your mileage may vary, so give Cocktail a whirl. If you decide to keep it, it's only $15.

Finally, TinkerTool was for a while the main show in town when it came to multi-purpose system maintenance tools, but then OnyX and others eclipsed it. It's still around, and some still prefer it. You can find out for yourself at www.bresink.com/osx/ TinkerTool.html; it's free.

Upgrading Mac OS X Point Releases

Upgrading your Mac from Leopard to Snow Leopard is an obviously big deal, but it's not always so obvious when you perform a point update within Snow Leopard, from 10.6.8 to 10.6.9, for instance (at the time of this writing, the current version is 10.6.2, so we're a long way off from 10.6.9!). And keep in mind, Apple can release a lot of point updates: Leopard went to 10.5.8, while Tiger went all the way up to 10.4.11!

In this section, I'm going to cover upgrading those point releases, from 10.6.8 to 10.6.9, going over what to do before, during, and after the upgrade. However, much of what I'm saying here is also applicable to major upgrades as well, from Leopard to Snow Leopard, say, or from Snow Leopard to whatever comes next. With that understood, let's get to work!

What to Do Before Your Upgrade

Before a big upgrade, there are a few tasks you should perform to increase the likelihood that everything will be as smooth as Al Green's voice (and the likelihood is already high to begin with, as the vast majority of Mac users never experience any issues upgrading point releases).

Search

If you can wait a few days or even weeks, do so. Let other, braver folks try out the new release of OS X and report (or decry!) their experiences on blogs, Twitter, and Apple support forums. Let's say the new release of Mac OS X is out, and it's 10.6.9. Search Google for the new release using search terms such as this:

- Snow Leopard upgrade
- Mac OS X 10.6.9
- Mac update
- 10.6.9 sucks
- Problems Mac OS 10.6.9

Here's the trick, at least at Google (I wrote a book on Google—*Google Apps Deciphered* (Prentice Hall, 2008)—so my biases are definitely in that direction): on the top of the search results list, you'll see a link that says Show Options, as shown in Figure 2–18.

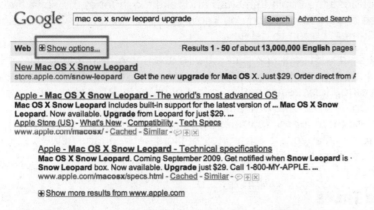

Figure 2–18. *You can specify certain options for Google's Web search.*

Click that link, and along the left side of the page, you'll see a variety of different options, grouped together. Among those groups is time, as you can see in Figure 2–19.

Figure 2–19. *Google lets you specify the time from which results come.*

By default, Google shows you results from Any Time, but you can change this with a click. If the new release for Mac OS X came out in the past week, change Any time to Past week. If it's been in the past three weeks, select Specific date range and adjust accordingly. By adjusting the date, you know the results you're seeing are targeted at the specific release of Mac OS X in which you're interested, so you'll know your information is current!

In addition to Google, you can use the other search engine, Bing (I'm leaving out Yahoo! because its results now come from Bing, sadly), but don't forget social networks such as Facebook and Twitter. A quick search on Twitter can be very helpful, as it's a great source of instantaneous commentary on any new event, such as an OS upgrade.

Check Login Items

Go to > System Preferences > Accounts and select your account on the left side of the window. On the right side, choose the Login Items tab and take a gander at the software listed there. If something has a generic icon and you know you uninstalled it a while ago, select the software and click the – button to delete it.

Look at the other items that start with your computer. If you see something you know you don't need, remove it! If it's old, get the most current version of the software using AppFresh or MacUpdate Desktop (discussed earlier in this chapter in "Managing and Upgrading Your Apps"); if AppFresh or VersionTracker Pro can't find it, go to the developer's website and check there for an upgrade. If you're really feeling paranoid, search Google and Twitter to see if anyone's reporting conflicts between the new version of OS X you're about to install and particular startup items.

Perform Maintenance Tasks

Open OnyX, discussed previously in this chapter in "Keeping Your Mac Running Well," and go to Maintenance, then Scripts. Check the boxes next to Daily, Weekly, and Monthly, and click Execute. Reboot and re-open Onyx. Go to Cleaning and methodically go through each tab (System, User, Internet, Fonts, Logs, and Misc), selecting the items to clean up and clicking Execute. Don't be excessive here—refer to my earlier look in this chapter at Onyx for advice about cleaning your system with the software. When you're finished, reboot your Mac and continue to the next section.

Verify Permissions and Your Hard Drive

Open Disk Utility (/Applications/Utilities/Disk Utility) and choose your hard drive's Mac OS partition on the left side of the window. On the right side, click Verify Disk Permissions; if Disk Utility detects a problem, click Repair Disk Permissions.

> **NOTE:** If you created an iCal Alarm, as detailed earlier in this chapter in the "Repair Permissions Weekly With Automator" section, you probably don't need to Verify or Repair Disk Permissions here, since your regularly scheduled alarm took care of it for you. But hey, if you want to be positively certain, go right ahead—it doesn't hurt anything.

After taking care of permissions, click Verify Disk and then Repair Disk if Disk Utility found an issue.

Now you know that your hard drive and the permissions on your system files are good, let's back everything up for safekeeping!

Create a Clone

Before doing an upgrade, back up your computer! If things go kablooey, you can restore from your backup and do more research, a far better prospect than having to reinstall everything from scratch.

Later in this book, in Chapter 8, "Backing Up Your Mac," I'll cover software you can use to clone your hard drive to an external drive. Jump ahead to that chapter if you need to learn more, but for now, the words to remember are "Carbon Copy Cloner." Use it!

What to Do During Your Upgrade

You can actually download the update in one of two ways: manually, or using Apple's Software Update tool. Each has its advantages; it just depends on which method makes the most sense to you and your particular needs.

Downloading Manually

Open Software Update (yes, I know we're here to talk about upgrading manually, but you need it in order to know what software to update in the first place, assuming you don't just go by what you read on the Web!), select the software package you want to upgrade, and go to **Update ➤ Go To Apple Downloads Page** (or just point your web browser to `http://support.apple.com/downloads`). From there, you'll need to either search to find the download you need, or browse the list of downloads until you find it.

However, if you want to make it easy to find the right package to download, search for the word "combo." Why? Because what you really want is the combo update. Apple releases two kinds of updates for point releases to Mac OS X: a regular update—"Mac OS X v10.6.9 Update," for instance—and a combo update—"Mac OS X v10.6.2 Update (Combo)". So what's the difference?

The most obvious is size. Regular ol' updates (called a "standard" or "delta" update) are smaller than combo updates, most of the time quite a bit so. For instance, the 10.5.5 standard update was 316MB, while the combo update was 601MB, almost double. But it's not always such a huge difference: the standard update for 10.6.2 was 473MB, while the combo update for the same release was 479MB.

Besides size, you can only apply delta updates to an Mac OS X system that is one version back; in other words, if the delta update will bring your Mac up to 10.6.9, you can only apply it to 10.6.8, and that's it. Combo updates, however, can update from *any* version of the main release (the first two numbers separated by a dot), so if the combo is for 10.6.9, then you can update anywhere from 10.6.0 to 10.6.8, but you cannot update from any version of 10.5, because it's a different main release.

Why is the delta smaller and only good for one version back? Because the deltas mostly just patch existing files with updated code, while combo updates actually replace existing files with totally new versions. Instead of a few KB or even MB of patches, the combo updater contains complete copies of the files to update, which causes the increase in size.

> **NOTE:** *Delta* is actually a common term in computer programming, which is the source from which Apple derives its term: "Delta encoding is a way of storing or transmitting data in the form of differences between sequential data rather than complete files.... The differences are recorded in discrete files called 'deltas' or 'diffs'." You can read the rest at http://en.wikipedia.org/wiki/Delta_encoding.

Downloading with Software Update

Software Update is pretty easy to run—open the program, select the software you want to upgrade, click the Install button, and soon enough you're finished. But there are a few tricks to Software Update that are useful to know.

> **NOTE:** Keep in mind that Software Update will only download the delta update, never the combo update.

In the Leopard edition of Software Update, you could go to the **Update** menu and select either **Download Only** or **Install and Keep Package**. Either way, you would have an installer that you could use on other Macs or back up for future installs, or both. Snow Leopard completely removes those options. So if you want to use Software Update to download the update, how can you do it?

In good UNIX fashion, Software Update isn't just a GUI program—it also has a command-line equivalent, called, cleverly enough, softwareupdate. Open your Terminal (/Applications/Utilities/Terminal) and enter this:

```
softwareupdate --list
```

If you have any updates, you'll see something like this:

```
Software Update found the following new or updated software:
   * FCE401-4.0.1
       Final Cut Express Update (4.0.1), 125240K [recommended]
```

The item next to the * is Apple's code for the update, while the third line is the longer description, the version number, the size, and whether it is recommended or not. In addition, you may also see [restart], which let's you know that a restart is required.

If you want to install a specific update, you would now type the following:

```
sudo softwareupdate -ia
```

You have to use sudo, because only root can install software. The options mean the following:

> i: Install the software after downloading it.

> a: Get all appropriate updates.

If you want to install only required updates, you would use -r instead of -a, so the command would be:

```
sudo softwareupdate -ir
```

The command will now do what you ordered, and inform you when it has finished.

If you want to download the updates without actually installing them, you would instead use this command:

```
softwareupdate -da
```

You don't need to be root to download software, so sudo isn't needed. Once again, use -a for all and -r for required updates. The big difference is -d instead of -i, where the -d means, obviously, "download."

If you want to install (or download) specific packages instead of all or required packages, just specify them using Apple's codes. So if I have several updates listed, but I only want to install the latest version of Final Cut Express, I would use this command:

```
sudo softwareupdate -i FCE401-4.0.1
```

By using Software Update's command-line tool, you end up with a lot more power and control, which can be exactly what you need. As the author of a book that delves extensively into the Linux command line, this is exactly what I'd expect, and it makes me—and hopefully you—very happy.

Which Option to Choose?

So you have a choice: manually go to Apple's website, find the updates you need, and then download and install them, or automate the process using Software Update's command-line tool. Which one should you pick?

The answer is, it depends.

If you want to run the combo update, then it's an easy choice: you have to use the manual method, since Software Update (even on the command line) only provides the delta version.

If, on the other hand, you're in a hurry, or you don't feel like you need the combo package since you're upgrading from the immediately previous release to the newest one (from 10.6.8 to 10.6.9, in other words), then Software Update makes sense. And it's certainly easier—you don't have to poke around Apple's website trying to find the packages you need. Even so, I'm a very big proponent of downloading installers, so they're available to run later in case you ever re-install or want to give them to a friend.

The final thing to think about: downloading manually via Apple's website lets you choose where you want the installers to go; if you use Software Update instead, they will always end up in /Library/Updates. Not that it's a huge pain to get there in your Finder, but it might be an easy thing to forget (so I guess you'd better keep this book around!).

What to Do After Your Upgrade

Before you installed an upgrade, you used Disk Utility to Verify Permissions. Now that the upgrade is done, it's time to do it again. Yes, this seems excessive, I know, but funky permissions can cause a funky Mac OS X experience, and it doesn't take that long, so just do it.

And with that, your upgrade is good to go! Enjoy it!

Summary

In this chapter, I've looked at four important areas you need to consider when it comes to maintaining your Mac and keeping it healthy and productive:

- Managing and Upgrading Your Apps
- Deleting Apps
- Keeping Your Mac Running Well
- Upgrading Mac OS X Point Releases

All of these are tasks that have to be done, some more often than others. Fortunately, there are great tools that make them easy to do, with MacUpdate Desktop, AppCleaner, and OnyX the standouts. No matter which you choose, though, take care of your Mac, so it can take care of you.

## Chapter 3

Expanding Upon the Basic Tools

The Dock. The Finder. Spotlight. These are basic parts of Mac OS X that a new user has to learn soon in his process of becoming a Mac user. And once he does learn about these vital components, he will probably soon forget about them. Oh, he doesn't forget they exist. It's just that they're used so constantly that they essentially fade into the background, unthought of in the same way that the wallpaper and art in your office quickly fades away so that you just don't see them.

Even if you've been using Mac OS X since it came out a decade ago, even if you've been using the Finder since the original Mac came out almost three decades ago (and it's truly incredible how similar the Finder's behaviors are today to that oh-so-crude yet oh-so-amazing Finder of 1984), there are still new things to learn, improvements that you can make, and techniques that can make you even more productive with these essential tools. After reading this chapter, I guarantee you're going to know a lot that was unknown before, and I think you'll be able to immediately start using what you find out. Let's dive in!

Improving the Dock

The Dock is integral to Mac OS X. That doesn't mean, however, that everything about it is obvious, or that you cannot improve it. In fact, there are features of the Dock that are wonderfully useful, but are not self-evident, and you can definitely improve with some useful tweaks and additions. In this section, I'll show you how to use—and improve—the Dock to make it even better. A lot of these will be quick, simple things that you can immediately use, so let's jump in.

Navigating the Dock

I vastly prefer using my keyboard to my mouse, so I'm always looking for keyboard shortcuts for everything. Here are a few for the Dock that are handy to know:

- ^-F3: Send keyboard focus to the Dock so you can use your keys to navigate and use the Dock.

- Arrow keys: Navigate between items on the Dock.

- Tab: Navigate forward to items on the Dock.

- ⇧-Tab: Navigate backward to items on the Dock.

- Letters: Jump to an item on the Dock by pressing the first few letters of the item's name.

- Return: Open selected item on the Dock.

- ⌘-Q: Quit selected item on the Dock.

- ↺: Remove keyboard focus from the Dock.

Try it—after you do it a few times, those key commands will be burned into your muscle memory so you can use them whenever you need them.

A 2D Dock

I never have liked the 3D shelf look for the Dock in Snow Leopard, so one of the first things I do on a new Mac is change its appearance. To do this, I use Onyx (see Chapter 2 for more). Open Onyx and head to **Parameters ➤ Dock**. Next to Appearance, select 2D With Transparency Effect. Press Continue to relaunch the Dock, and it will now look something like what you see in Figure 3–1.

Figure 3–1. *It's a different look, and I actually prefer it greatly to the default.*

You can also do this same trick with Secrets (discussed in chapter 1). Open ➤ System Preferences ➤ Dock, and next to Dock Appearance, select 2D Black. Click Quit This to relaunch the Dock. Done!

To reverse the way the Dock looks and go back to 3D, just revisit the locations in either Onyx or Secrets and select the other style.

Faster Force Quit

It's a fact of life on all operating systems: sometimes apps lock up. You try to Quit an app, but nothing happens. At that point, savvy Mac users will open ➤ Force Quit and kill the misbehaving program. However, there's a quicker way: ⌥ - right click on the running app on the Dock. Instead of Quit on the bottom of the menu, you'll instead see Force Quit. Choose it, and the app is killed immediately. Quick! Easy!

Adding Spacers to Your Dock

By default, Apple groups everything on the Dock right next to each other. Some folks, though, would like the ability to put spacers in between Dock items. How do you do that?

It's no problem, if you have Onyx. Open Onyx and go to **Parameters ➤ Dock**. At the very bottom of the window, press the Applications button to insert a spacer on the left side of the Dock. Press the Others button to insert a spacer on the right side of the Dock. Press either one again to insert more. Press Continue to relaunch the Dock. When you do, the results appear as in Figure 3–2.

Figure 3–2. *Spacers help you group things on the Dock, but they're a bit big.*

That definitely worked, but the spacers are a bit on the large side. I wish there was a way to size them, but there's not. If you decide you don't like one, just grab it and drag it off the Dock, and it will disappear in a puff of smoke.

If you don't like or use Onyx, you can also use Secrets. Go to **➤ System Preferences ➤ Secrets ➤ Dock**, and you'll see buttons next to Add Separator To Left Side and Add Separator To Right Side. Once you click them, be sure to click Quit This at the bottom of the window to restart the Dock.

If you don't want spaces, you can use something else to separate your Dock items. For instance, try the free Dock Dividers at www.artofadambetts.com/weblog/?p=35. Unzip the small file and you'll find six apps that go into /Applications (or wherever you want them to live) that you can drag onto the Dock: Black Bar, Black Dots, Blank, Panel Divider, White Bar, and White Dots. They're not really apps; instead, they're basically fake apps (so they can go on the Dock) that have graphics for icons, and the icons serve as dividers, as you can see in Figure 3–3, where I've used two of them.

Figure 3–3. *White Dots and White Bar look better with the 2D Black Dock style.*

This is a cool idea and it works well, as they're much smaller in width than the standard spacer. The only problem is that you can have only one of them on the Dock at a time (which makes sense—you can have only one Firefox on the Dock at a time too, and the Dock Dividers *are* apps, after all). There's an easy workaround, though: just duplicate the Dock Dividers you want to use, so you have White Dots.app, White Dots 2.app, White Dots 3.app, and so on. Then you can drag those to the Dock and have as many White Dots dividers as you'd like. Crude, but it works.

Lock the Dock

Back when my father-in-law used Linux (yeah, that was my idea), I'd get a call every few months that the "bar" at the bottom of his screen had "gotten really big." It turns out that when he went to click on an icon or minimized window on the Linux taskbar (a lot like the one in Windows), he kept the mouse button down while he dragged upward, causing the taskbar to become three to six times its normal height (the same thing would sometimes happen when he used Windows, a long time ago).

This was frustrating, because back then, there was no way I could tell the Linux taskbar not to change its height. When I switched him to a Mac, I was mindful that the variable-height-by-dragging problem would no longer exist with the Dock, but I was instead worried about another biggie: dragging icons off the Dock accidentally, only for them to vanish into a literal puff of smoke. Then he'd call me for tech support because he couldn't open Firefox or Mail or his Bridge game.

Thinking ahead, I installed Onyx—as I do on every Mac I set up—and went to **Parameters ➤ Dock**. There you'll see a check box next to Lock The Icons, which explains underneath it that checking it will prevent moving and removing Dock icons. Perfect! Check that box, click Continue when you're asked to restart the Dock, and you have yourself a locked-down Dock.

> **TIP:** This might seem obvious, but make sure the Dock is set up exactly the way you want it before you check that box, or be prepared to uncheck and check it until things are the way you want them. And don't forget that you checked that box in the first place! I had a heck of a time figuring out why I couldn't add something to my father-in-law's Dock until I remembered that I had locked it via Onyx. Duh!

By the way, just so it's clear: this setting affects only Dock items that you try to drag or move. It has nothing to do with icons that appear when apps are launched. Those still appear and disappear just like normal.

Secrets allows you to lock the Dock too, with other options as well. Open ➤ **System Preferences ➤ Secrets ➤ Dock** and go to the Restrictions section. There you can check boxes next to several items, including these:

- Prevent Changes To Dock Contents
- Prevent Changes To Autohide Preference
- Prevent Changes To Dock Size
- Prevent Changes To Magnification Preference
- Prevent Changes To Position

If you have issues with people doing weird things to the Dock that are giving you grief, try some of these tools. They'll reduce your tech support calls, I promise.

Hiding Instead of Minimizing Apps on Your Dock

Almost all Mac users know that if they press the yellow button in the upper left of every window, the window is minimized. Easy.

A problem appears if a user then tries to switch back to the program using ⌘-Tab. Sure, the program then becomes active, but the window stays minimized, something that Windows (and Linux) switchers in particular find weird. In Windows, if you minimize something and then switch to it via Alt-Tab, the app and its windows open back up. On the Mac, the app becomes active again—you can see it in the Menu Bar—but the window doesn't reappear. Why not?

The reason is that Mac OS is doing what you told it to do: you instructed it to minimize the window, but keep the app still running. When you switch back to the app with ⌘-Tab, Mac OS does just that—it switches back to the app. The window is still minimized, however, because you haven't told Mac OS to restore it.

This is something central to Mac OS, but it's sometimes easy to forget: there is a total separation (most of the time) between programs and windows. Not so in Windows and Linux—in those operating systems, when you close the window, you close the program. In the Mac, as you know, you can close all the windows, and the program keeps on chugging along.

I love using ⌘-Tab to switch between apps, but I still wanted the ability to do what minimizing does—get windows out of the way temporarily—and then use ⌘-Tab to get those windows back. Like so many things, Apple already has a solution, but it might not be obvious.

Instead of minimizing windows, hide them. Press ⌘-H (or use **(Name of App) ➤ Hide App**) and the app and its windows all disappear. Use ⌘-Tab to switch to the app—or click on it on the Dock—and it's front and center again: app, windows, everything. Plus, you never have to take your fingers off the keyboard—⌘-H to hide, ⌘-Tab to switch to a different program, ⌘-H to hide that one, and then ⌘-Tab back to the original one, which reappears. It's efficient and fast, and it's the only way I work.

Calling Out Hidden Dock Items

If you follow my practice in the previous section and you hide things instead of minimizing them, you might like to also make it very clear on your Dock which items are hidden and which are not. This is easy with Onyx—go to **Parameters ➤ Dock** and check the box next to Use Transparent Icons For Hidden Applications. Restart the Dock when prompted, and voila!

You can also use Secrets, if you'd like. Open ➤ System Preferences ➤ Secrets ➤ Dock and check the box next to Dim Hidden Apps. Click Quit This on the status bar to restart the Dock, and now your hidden programs will be quite obvious when you look at your Dock.

Making an App Dockless

Hiding windows and apps is sure useful, and making hidden apps have transparent Dock icons is icing on that cake. But what if you don't want to see an app's icon on the Dock at all? What if you want to go … Dockless?

There are apps that help you hide other apps on the Dock. The best of them is Dock Dodger, which is available for free (donations requested) at `http://foggynoggin.com/dockdodger`.

> **NOTE:** I just have to say this: if we still have Macs in 350 years, then we may need Dock Dodgers in the 24 1/2 Century! Looney Tunes fans, rejoice in my bad pun; others, go here: `http://en.wikipedia.org/wiki/Duck_Dodgers_in_the_24½th_Century`.

Dock Dodger is pretty easy to use. Run the program, and a window appears with three words: Drag Application Here. Do that, and the program's icon no longer appears on the Dock. Drag it back, and the program's icon now appears on the Dock again.

If you're really feeling ambitious, you can manually make apps dockless. Right-click on the program in /Applications and choose Show Package Contents. Find the program's info.plist file and edit it with a text editor. Look for the LSUIElement key. If you see it, change the value from 0 to 1. If you don't see the LSUIElement key, add the following *in alphabetical order* to the plist file:

```
<key>LSUIElement</key>
<string>1</string>
```

Save the plist file, close the Finder window, and start the app. You shouldn't see an icon on the Dock. Your dream has been achieved!

> **WARNING:** There's a big caveat with removing icons from the Dock: not all programs like having their Dock icon disappear. In fact, many react quite badly to this, so be prepared to give up with that app or deal with the problems that will crop up. And if something doesn't work, remember that you can always switch back.

Hovering and Highlighting Stacks

This is a small effect, but I really like it. Open ➤ System Preferences ➤ Secrets ➤ Dock and check the box next to Highlight Stack Items On Hover (10.6). Restart the Dock by clicking Quit This at the bottom of the Secrets window. Now as you move your mouse over the various choices in your Grid-based Stacks (or move around them with your keyboard), the currently selected item has a nice highlighted box behind it, as in Figure 3–4.

Figure 3–4. *See the highlight in the third row down? Nice, ain't it?*

You can also set this with Onyx. On **Parameters ➤ Dock**, check the box next to Enable Mouse-Over On Stacks Displayed In Grid-Mode, and you'll get that nice effect. Like I said, it's a small thing, but I find it helps me navigate.

A Nicer List View for Stacks

List view for Stacks normally looks like what you see in Figure 3–5.

Figure 3–5. *The normal look for List view*

However, if you know what to do, you can get a nicer List view, as in Figure 3–6.

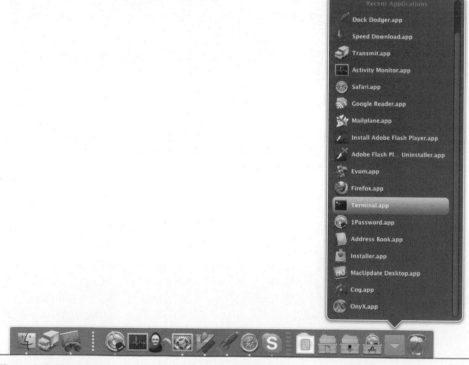

Figure 3–6. *You have to admit, it's snappier and easier to read.*

If you do this, though, all Stacks with List view will change. You can't just make the change for one Stack and leave others with the old view. As long as you understand that, here's how to do it:

- Secrets: On Dock, check the box next to Enable New List View In Stacks and click Quit This to restart the Dock.

- Onyx: On **Parameters ➤ Dock**, check the box next to Non Hierarchical List Menu and then restart the Dock when prompted.

The new list view is bigger—and therefore easier to read with older eyes like mine—but it may be too big for some, especially those with small screens. If you don't like it, reverse it!

Creating New & Useful Stacks

There are two extra stacks I like to create on my Dock: Recent Applications and Templates. The first is pretty easy to make, while the second takes a bit more work, but they're both very useful.

Recent Applications

To prepare for this Stack, first go to ➤ **System Preferences ➤ Appearance** and find the Number Of Recent Items section. For Applications, change 10 to 20. Also, I would definitely turn on highlighting, as I showed you earlier in the section called "Hovering and Highlighting Stacks."

That's the preliminary part. To actually create the new Recent Applications Stack, you can use either Onyx or Secrets.

- Onyx: On **Parameters ➤ Dock**, click the Add button next to Recent/Favorite Items Stack.

- Secrets: On Dock, click the Add button next to Add Recents/Favorite Stack To Right Side. Restart the Dock by clicking Quit This at the bottom of the window.

A new Stack should appear next to your Trash Can on the Dock. When you click it, you should see the last 20 apps you used, making this a super-quick way to launch programs. I prefer the Grid view, so if you don't see it, right-click on the Stack and choose Grid.

Note also while you're right-clicking that you can choose from Recent Applications, Recent Documents, and Recent Servers, as well as Favorite Volumes and Favorite Items. In fact, if you want a Recent Documents Stack in addition to one for Recent Applications, go back to Onyx or Secrets and simply click Add again, then right-click and change what the Stack displays.

If you want to see what my Recent Applications stack looks like, take a look at Figure 3–4, which shows it in all its glory.

Templates

The idea for a Templates Stack came from an article by Lukas Mathis called "Creating New Documents," available at `http://ignorethecode.net/blog/2009/05/31/creating-new-documents/`. It's a fascinating look at how and why Mac OS X creates documents as it does, and how other operating systems—including earlier incarnations of the Mac!—have tried to deal with the issue themselves. I've modified what he says a bit, but I did want to give him credit for a good idea.

The concept is simple: create a series of templates for the various documents you use and make them available in a convenient way so that you can easily choose a template and begin working. Once you try it, I think you'll find it as indispensible as I have.

To begin, create a Template folder somewhere it can live forever. In my case, I put it in my Home directory, at `~/Templates`. Insert template files you create into the Templates directory; again, in my case, these are the ones I made:

- Bash shell script.sh
- HTML 4.01 Strict.htm
- HTML 4.01 Transitional.htm
- HTML 5.htm
- Keynote.key
- Text file.txt
- XHTML 1.0 Strict.htm
- XHTML 1.0 Transitional.htm

Each one contains the appropriate contents for a template that I need; in your case, of course, you will more than likely have completely different templates and contents.

The Templates folder is going to end up on the Dock in just a moment, which is why I like to take this next step, although it's completely optional. I went on the Net and found a nice icon that I named " Template.gif" (note the space at the beginning) and also placed in the Templates folder. Because its name began with a space, it's at the top of the list, and since it's at the top of the list, it becomes the default icon for the Stack, which is what I wanted.

> **TIP:** If you want to find your own Template icon, try searching Google for open `source icons`. Also, go to Smashing Magazine's website, at `www.smashingmagazine.com`, and search for `icon set`. You'll find tons of great graphics that you can use, for free!

Now that the contents of the Templates folder are ready, let's get the show on the road!

Right-click on each file and choose Get Info. In the Get Info window, check the box next to Locked, which you can find in the General section, and close Get Info.

Now right-click on the Templates folder and do the same thing: Get Info and check the box next to Locked.

For the final step, drag the Templates folder to the Dock. I like to right-click on the Templates icon on the Dock and set the View to List. Since I also changed the default List view according to my advice earlier in "A Nicer List View for Stacks," the end result is what you see in Figure 3–7.

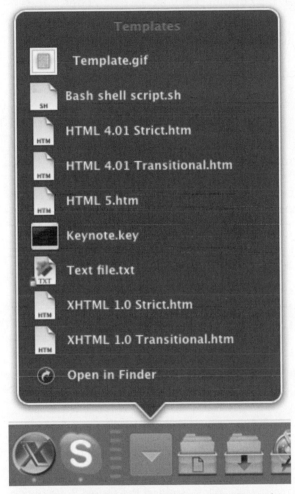

Figure 3–7. *My templates on the Dock, ready to be used.*

I can use the templates in one of two ways:

- Open the Stack and drag the template I need to the Finder. Since the Templates folder is locked, a copy of the template is made in the Finder. Before I can use it, though, I need to Get Info on the new file and uncheck Locked. After I do that, I can edit the file to my heart's content.

■ Open the Stack and click on the template I need. I then immediately do a Save As so I have a copy of the template that I can work with and edit. This new copy of the file isn't locked since I did a Save As, so I don't need to Get Info to unlock it.

If I ever want to add a new one to the batch, I create the template, Get Info on the ~/Templates folder and uncheck Locked, drag the template into the folder, and check Locked for both the file and and the folder. It's not that big of a deal since I don't add templates that often.

It's great to have a set of customized templates available to me that I can use any time. These are files that I find myself creating all the time, and now they're available with just a click on my Dock. Now that is convenient!

Further Resources

Want to be radical? Then give your Dock a whole new theme! You can find collections of themes at Leopard Docks (http://leoparddocks.com) or Dockulicious (http://dockulicious.com). Keep in mind, though, that changing the Dock theme without a third-party app like Dockulicious or Candybar (www.panic.com/candybar/) is complicated, so I'd use one of those apps if you want to go down that road.

Docker (http://download.cnet.com/Docker/3000-18487_4-175638.html) offers a number of customizations for the Dock, to make it look exactly how you want it to look. Read more about it at http://reviews.cnet.com/8301-13727_7-10388290-263.html.

Fixing the Finder by Improving Open and Save

When you're busy using your favorite apps, you're probably looking at Open/Save dialog boxes far more than you realize. They're kind of like the artwork in a room—after a short while, you don't even notice them because they're just *there*. Even though Open and Save are incredibly common, that doesn't mean you can't customize them in some ways to make them more useful.

For instance, when you're in an Open/Save dialog and you want to quickly move to a folder you know but are far away from, or to one that Mac OS X makes it hard to get to by default, such as /etc, just press ~ (the *tilde*, at the top left of your keyboard). When you do so, a drawer will appear that says Go To The Folder and gives you a nice long text box in which to type. Type in the path you want, click Go, and the Open/Save dialog box whisks you there.

That's nice, but here's something that some of you will love. I'm a UNIX guy at heart, so I often want to edit hidden files or mess around in hidden folders. Since Mac OS X is a UNIX-based OS, all files and folders whose name begins with a period are hidden by default. If I'm using Terminal, I can see them by typing ls -a (the -a means to show all files and folders, even the hidden ones).

But if I'm in the Finder, there's no easy way to view hidden stuff. I wish that Apple would come up with a nice key command that would toggle back and forth between hiding and showing dot files, but it hasn't yet. So what to do?

I can use Onyx or Secrets to toggle between showing and hiding dot files in the Finder, but I find that kind of clumsy—I have to open those apps, navigate to where the setting is, click it, go back to the Finder, navigate to the now-visible location, do what I need to do, then go back to Onyx or Secrets, reverse the setting, and close the program. Like I said, clumsy.

> **NOTE:** You might be wondering why I just don't use Onyx or Secrets to show all hidden files and then just leave it at that. I don't do that for the same reason the `ls` command doesn't show hidden files by default: I don't want to see all the clutter.

Fortunately, there's a faster way: Houdini, a free app you can download from `www.macupdate.com/info.php/id/26729/houdini`. When you open Houdini, you see the window shown in Figure 3–8.

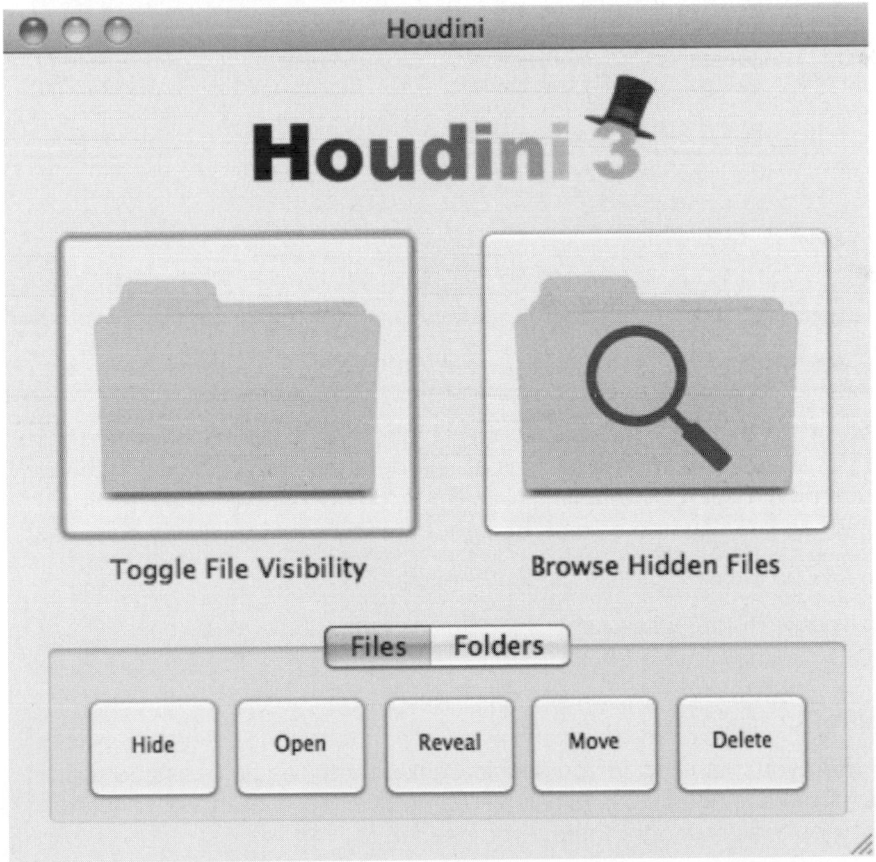

Figure 3–8. *Houdini makes it very easy to see and work with invisible files and folders.*

As you can see in Figure 3–8, Houdini is a simple app, and that's a good thing. Click the Toggle File Visibility button, and hidden files and folders appear; click it again, and they disappear. There are other buttons on Houdini's screen, but they're just add-ons to the main feature, that big Toggle File Visibility button.

If you find yourself working with hidden files often, then, I'd advise putting Houdini on your Dock. Open Houdini, click Toggle File Visibility, do what you need to do, click Toggle File Visibility, and quit Houdini. Much faster, and much less clunky.

If you really want to do this pioneer style, open the AppleScript Editor on your Mac and paste the following in (you can also copy it from http://files.granneman.com/maxosxpowerusers/Toggle_Hidden_Files.txt):

```
tell application "Finder"
        activate
        set showAllFilesState to "NO"
        set showAllFilesState to do shell script "defaults read com.apple.finder
AppleShowAllFiles"

        if showAllFilesState is "ON" then
                do shell script "defaults write com.apple.finder AppleShowAllFiles OFF"
                quit
        end if
        if showAllFilesState is "OFF" then
                do shell script "defaults write com.apple.finder AppleShowAllFiles ON"
                quit
        end if
end tell

delay 3
tell application "Finder" to launch
```

> **NOTE:** Ideas and code for this script came from the always-excellent Mac OS X Hints website, specifically from www.macosxhints.com/article.php?story=20030409015020645.

What does this script do? Simple—it toggles between showing all files and hiding those that begin with a dot. Select the app, and if files are hidden, they now appear; if they were visible, they're now hidden. After telling Mac OS X to show or hide the files, the Finder is relaunched so you can immediately see your results.

To finalize your work, go to **File ➤ Save**; I suggest the following settings:

- Save As: Toggle Hidden Files.app
- Where: ~/bin
- File Format: Application

Click Save. Now drag your new app to your Dock. Click on it to toggle back and forth between hiding and viewing dot files. You can also drag the app to the toolbar in the Finder, so that the app is always right there if you need it.

TIP: To really make the Toggle Hidden Files.app look nice, you should find an icon for it, or otherwise it will be just a generic AppleScript icon. Right-click and Get Info on both Toggle Hidden Files.app and the graphic whose icon you want to use. Click on the icon at the top of the Get Info window for the graphic and use **Edit ➤ Copy**, then click on the icon at the top of the Get Info window for Toggle Hidden Files.app and use **Edit ➤ Paste**, thus transferring the icon.

Replacing the Finder

In the previous section, I showed you a few things that fix the Finder, but what if you just want to replace the darned thing altogether? You have options, some of them nicer than others. Let's look at three of them so you have an idea about the pros and cons of leaving the Finder behind for something else.

NOTE: Of course, you can't ever completely leave the Finder behind. It's an integral part of Mac OS X, and you can't remove it. It's always there, always running. You can, though, use the other programs discussed here to act as replacements for functions performed by the Finder, such as file management.

ForkLift

One of the premier Finder replacements is ForkLift, available at www.binarynights.com/forklift. It's a commercial app that'll run you $30, but it's worth it, since it does about a million different things, some of them that the Finder does, many of them that it does not. Let's start with what ForkLift looks like, so take a look at Figure 3–9.

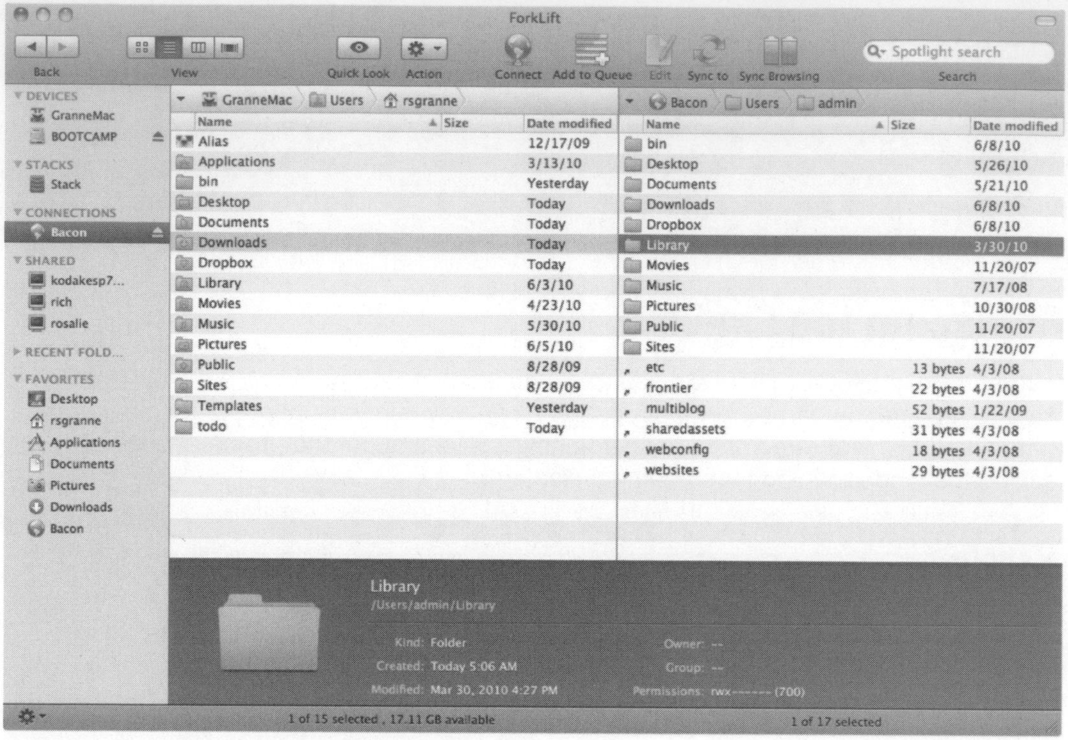

Figure 3–9. *ForkLift is one heck of a Finder replacement!*

ForkLift's Cool Features

There's a lot going on in Figure 3–9, but the best way to understand some of what you're seeing is to leap in. Following are some of the major features that ForkLift has that the Finder does not.

> **NOTE:** As I'm writing this chapter, the current stable release of ForkLift is 1.7.8, but beta 2 of version 2 is due soon, and that's the version I'm basing my discussion on here. In fact, when you buy the current version of ForkLift, it includes a free upgrade to version 2 when it comes out. That said, some things may change between the time I finish this chapter and the final release of ForkLift 2, but I don't think (or hope!) those changes will be a big deal.

Dual-pane UI: As you can see in Figure 3–9, one of the biggest UI differences that ForkLift has from the Finder is that ForkLift has a dual-pane interface. Instead of having to create two Finder windows to drag and drop files back and forth, a maneuver I've had to do too many times, you can do everything in one ForkLift window. In fact, if you explore ForkLift's View menu, you'll see several commands that let you maximize your use of panes:

- Select Left Pane (⌘-left arrow): Move focus to the pane on the left.

- Select Right Pane (⌘-right arrow): Move focus to pane on the right.

- Zoom Pane In (⌘-⇧-P): This switches ForkLift from a dual-pane UI to a single-pane UI like the Finder, with the currently focused pane assuming control over the window. To restore the dual-pane interface, use **View ➤ Zoom Pane Out** or press ⌘-⇧-P again.

- Clone Pane (⌘-⇧-C): The current pane is cloned in the other pane, so you now see the same files and folders in both.

- Flip Panes: Switch the right and left panes.

- Sync Browsing: Let's say you have two directories that you want to compare. They could both be local, or one could be local and one remote. Get them both loaded, one in each pane, and then turn on Sync Browsing. As you go up or down the folder structure in one pane, the exact movement occurs in the other pane as well, allowing you to easily compare the two directories and their sub-directories.

Tabs: In addition to a dual-pane UI, ForkLift also features tabs. Each pane can have one or more tabs; in fact, when you create a new tab (**File ➤ New Tab**, or ⌘-T), the tab is created in the pane with focus. This is counter to several other dual-pane apps (such as Transmit, for instance)—in those, when you create a new tab, it creates two new panes inside the tab. In other words, with ForkLift, tabs live inside panes; with other apps, panes live inside tabs.

The View menu allows you to Select Next Tab (⌘-⇧-right arrow) and Select Previous Tab (⌘-⇧-left arrow), as needed.

Open In Terminal: If you're a big Terminal user, you'll find the fact that you can use **File ➤ Open In Terminal** to open a command line window to be quite nice. The fact the Terminal opens to where you were in ForkLift is an even bigger help. And if you go to **View ➤ Customize Toolbar**, you can add a button for Open In Terminal to ForkLift's toolbar, so the command is just a click away.

Batch rename files: ForkLift will rename hundreds of files at once, which can be the difference between a quick task that takes a few seconds and a tedious one that stretches out forever. To use this feature, select several files and then go to **File ➤ Multi Rename**. When you do, a new window opens that you can see in Figure 3–10.

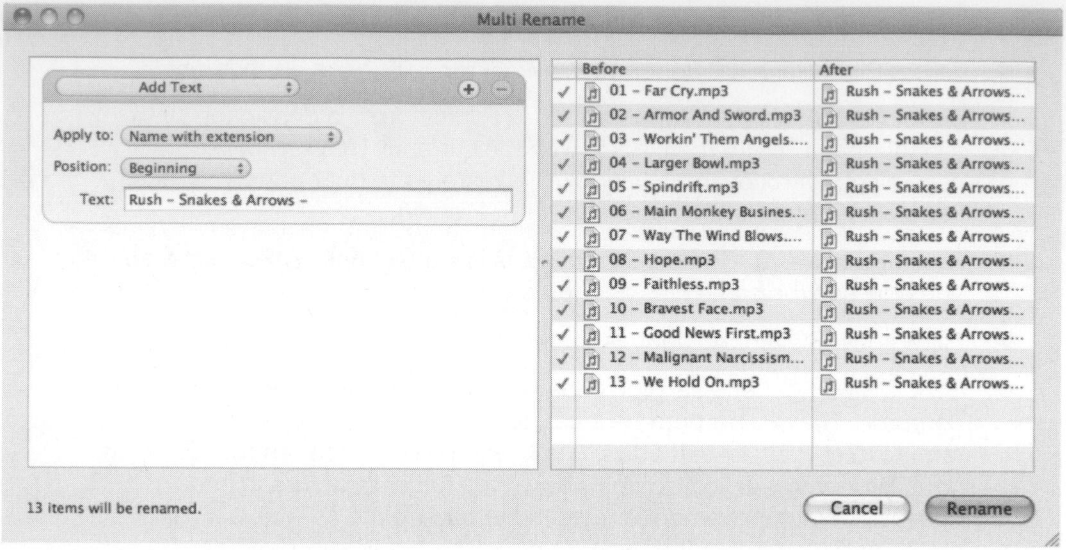

Figure 3–10. *You can do many things to files; in this case, I'm adding text to the beginning.*

ForkLift allows you to do the following to files and folders:

- Replace Text

- Replace RegExp (replace text using regular expressions)

- Add Text

- Change Case

- Add Sequence

- Add Modification Date

- Add Creation Date

For each of those, you can select which part of the file name you want to affect (Name With Extension, Name, Extension, Extension With Dot) and be specific as to the exact changes you want to make.

In addition to all that, if you click the + in the corner of the procedure, you can add others, chaining a detailed process together out of several different steps. To delete a step, click the –.

NOTE: There are other, more sophisticated programs that will batch rename files, but ForkLift will do the job in many cases. If you need something more powerful, check out A Better Finder Rename ($20 from www.publicspace.net/ABetterFinderRename/), which is the most feature-complete of all these apps on the Mac, and Name Mangler ($10 from www.manytricks.com), which is simpler and quite fast.

Create new text file: Sure, both the Finder and ForkLift can create new folders with ease. But only ForkLift let's you use File ➤ New File (or press ⌘-⌥-N) to create a new text file.

Group files from different folders into a Stack: This is a pretty neato ability to have. Basically, a Stack is a virtual folder that contains files you've added from various folders (and has nothing to do with the Stacks you find on the Dock). If you've ever created a playlist in iTunes, you have the idea: you can drag songs into the playlist, but you're not actually moving the songs—you're just grouping them together in a way that's useful to you.

- To create a Stack, click on the Action menu in the bottom left of ForkLift and go to New ➤ Stack. To rename the Stack, right-click on it and select Rename.

- To add files—and folders!—just drag them onto the Stack.

- To remove items from the Stack, right-click and choose Remove From Stack. Do not select the item and press ⌘-⌫, or you will move it to the Trash!

- To remove the Stack, right-click on it and choose Delete Stack.

Built-in app deletion: In Chapter 2, I looked at several uninstallers for the Mac, but ForkLift has one built in. Select a program and then go to Tools ➤ Delete App to move an app and its associated files to the Trash. You're asked before anything is deleted, and you can select which files get trashed, which is the correct behavior.

Empty Trash toolbar button: You have to add it yourself, but if you select View ➤ Customize Toolbar, there it is—an Empty Trash button you can add to ForkLift's toolbar.

Connect to remote servers: ForkLift is more than just a file manager for local files. It's also a full-fledged network-based file transfer app, connecting to remote machines using a variety of protocols:

- FTP

- FTP (TLS/SSL)

- SFTP

- WebDAV

- WebDAV (HTTPS)

- iDisk

- Amazon S3

To start a new connection, use Go ➤ Connect, which brings up a window like that in Figure 3–11.

Figure 3–11. *SFTP is one of the most common protocols for file transfer on the Net.*

In Figure 3–11, I'm showing you the settings for SFTP, but the UI changes depending upon the protocol you select. When it comes to SFTP, a protocol I rely on every day, ForkLift supports what I need: public key authentication instead of passwords and configurable port numbers. Enter your settings, click Connect, and a moment later ForkLift displays the contents of your remote server in one of its panes.

If you want to save the connection for use again later, head to **Go ➤ Add To Favorites**. By default, your saved connection goes under Favorites on the sidebar, along with your home, Applications, Documents, and the rest of the standard directories the Finder displays. If you want to put your servers in a different group, go to the action menu at the bottom of ForkLift and select **New > Group**. Right-click on the group to rename it and then drag your favorites into the new group. It's a great way to organize your connections the way *you* want them to be organized.

I still prefer Transmit for transferring files (discussed in Chapter 6, it's faster and has a gorgeous UI), but ForkLift is a fine program for throwing bits around networks.

Mount servers as local devices: If you connect to a remote machine via a network protocol such as SFTP, then you can mount it like it's a local disk under Devices, a process ForkLift calls Disklets. To create a Disklet, right-click on a bookmark and choose Mount As Disk, or click the Mount button when you're creating a new connection through **Go > Connect** (⌘-K). Once a Disklet has been created and mounted, any app on your Mac can access and use the files on that machine as though they were connected directly to your Mac. This is very similar to what the file transfer app Transmit can do (see Chapter 6).

Sync directories: Need to sync directories, local to local, local to remote, or even remote to remote? How about within archives (remember, you can open archives inside ForkLift)? You can with ForkLift. Get the two directories open in ForkLift's panes, with the Source on the left and the Target on the right, and head to **File > Sync To**. A window will open like the one in Figure 3–12.

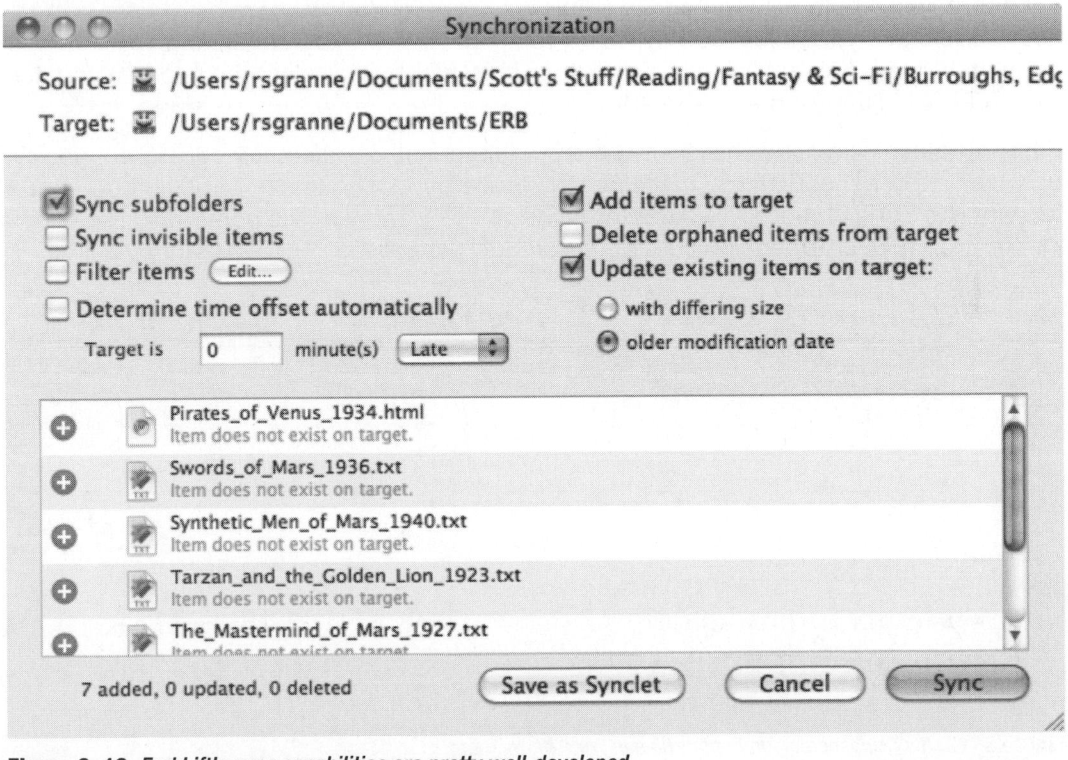

Figure 3–12. *ForkLift's sync capabilities are pretty well-developed.*

As you can see in Figure 3–12, ForkLift has quite a few capabilities wrapped up in its Synchronization window. You can sync subfolders and invisible items, or filter the items you want to sync. Of course, you can copy items over, but you can also delete items on the Target that have been deleted from the Source. Once you have your settings in place, click Sync and watch the files fly.

Synclets: When the Synchronization window is open, you might notice a button at the bottom that says Save As Synclet. Similar to Droplets in other programs (such as Photoshop, for instance), Synclets save specific sync configurations. When you click on the Synclet—which can be found in /Applications, the Dock, the Finder's toolbar, and so on—the sync runs. Two ideas for Synclets: use them with Automator, or use them with folder actions to auto-sync as soon as a file changes or appears in a specific folder.

Create aliases and symbolic (soft) links: Sure, ForkLift can create aliases (File ➤ Make Alias, or ⌘-L), but so can the Finder. But only ForkLift can create UNIX soft links (File ➤ Make Symlink, or ⌘-⇧-L). If you don't know what I'm talking about, you probably don't need this, but if you want to learn more, open Terminal and type man ln. As you read, keep in mind that ForkLift creates soft (or symbolic), not hard, links.

View folder sizes: If you want to see the sizes of folders alongside those of files, open View ➤ Show View Options and then check the box next to Calculate All Sizes. Keep in mind that this will slow down ForkLift a little bit, since it has to add up the contents of all your folders every time you view them, so you might not want to enable this permanently. If you want to see it on a folder-by-folder basis, select the folder(s) and use File ➤ Calculate Sizes (or press ⌘-⇧-S).

Filtering files: What if you have a directory with a bunch of different files in it, but you only want to see the ZIP files? In the Finder, you're supposed to use Spotlight, but that's too slow. In ForkLift, use Edit ➤ Filter (or press ⌘-⌥-F) and you see something like Figure 3–13 (I've cropped out most of the window except the important stuff).

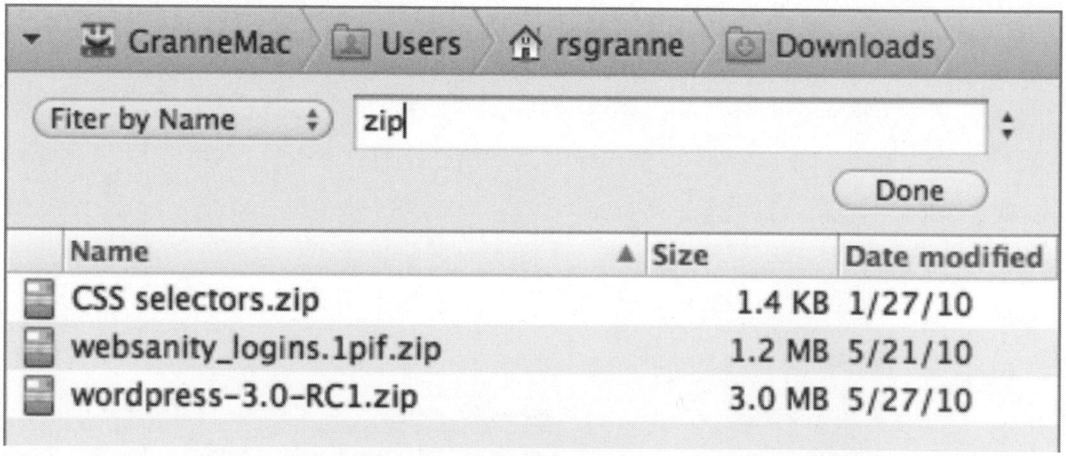

Figure 3–13. *It's fantastically fun to filter files in ForkLift, forsooth!*

You can filter by name, kind of file, or extension. It's amazingly convenient to have such easy filtering right at your fingertips!

Configurable search: Filtering only shows files in the current directory, and is not recursive, so if there are ZIP files in subdirectories, they won't show up. Searching, however, *is* recursive, and ForkLift supports it, and exactly where you'd think to look for it: in the upper right corner of the app.

By default, ForkLift does a Spotlight search of your current folder, but you can switch to a Mac-wide search if you click the drop-down in the search box. Even better, you can use ForkLift's search capabilities and look for files by name, kind, and extension, exactly like Filtering, except that searches are always recursive.

Archiving and compression: The Unarchiver (discussed in Chapter 11) is built in to ForkLift. That means ForkLift can now work with almost every common (and even many uncommon) archiving and compression format, not just ZIP, TAR, and GZ. Just double-click on an archived file, or use **File ➤ Extract** (or ⌘-X—a key command that is not kosher, by the way).

Better Get Info (in some ways): ForkLift has its own Get Info window, which you can see in Figure 3–14, that provides several functions missing in Mac OS X's Get Info window.

Much of the Get Info window seen in Figure 3–14 is just like Mac OS X's, which is fine, but look at the Permissions section. ForkLift's method for setting permissions on files and folders is much easier to understand and set, and whoa mama! you can actually indicate that a file is executable in Get Info. What a nutty idea! (Yes, I'm being sarcastic—the fact that you still can't do this in Mac OS X's default Get Info window is annoying as heck.)

Also, if you click on the Action menu at the bottom of the Permissions section (the sprocket), you can apply your permissions to Enclosed Files, Enclosed Folders, or All Enclosed Items, a very nice feature.

To be fair, Mac OS X's built-in Get Info has check boxes for Stationery Pad (not that useful, IMHO) and Locked (very useful), and the +/– at the bottom of the Sharing & Permissions section allows you to set up ACLs (Access Control Lists) for specific users. However, since ForkLift doesn't remove the Finder, you can still use the Finder (or, heck, the Terminal) to do those tasks if you need them.

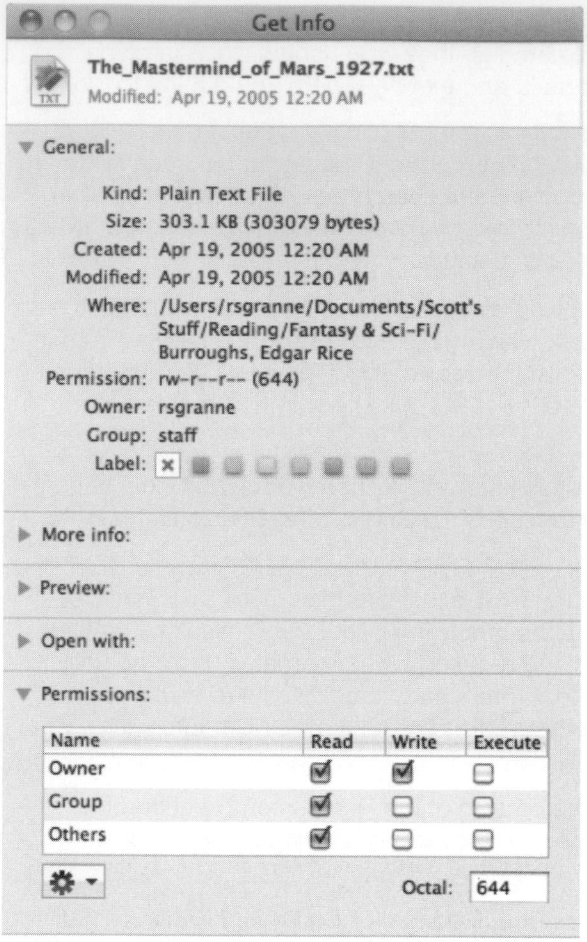

Figure 3–14. *See the new stuff?*

ForkLift's Annoyances

As great as ForkLift is, it's not perfect. There are a few annoyances, and here are a few:

Some (very) poor choices for key commands: For example, QuickLook is ⌘-Y instead of Space. I hate having to re-learn system-wide key commands. Even worse is when an app decides to ignore over 20 years of standardization, as ForkLift has done by making ⌘-X the key command for Extract instead of Cut. What the …? Not cool, guys. Not cool at all. Especially in a program that otherwise tries to closely copy the key commands of the Finder, the app it's trying to replace.

Difficulty copying between panes: If all the rows in a pane are full and you try to copy anything into that pane, there's no safe place to drag and drop files. In Transmit, for instance, there are safe areas on rows—usually in the Size and Date columns—where you can drop things you want to copy. In other words, in Transmit—and many other apps—if you drag files onto a folder listed in a pane, the files are copied into the folder, but if you drag files onto the safe areas of a row, the files are copied into the containing folder listed in the pane.

With ForkLift, all parts of a row are hot, so you end up containing files into sub-folders, which is annoying. There is a solution—drag the files onto the last folder listed in the path found at the top of the pane, but below the tabs, and the files will copy into the containing folder listed in the pane. The problem is that such a move isn't obvious. Oh, and I don't want to use File ➤ Copy To every time, either. I just want to quickly and easily drag the files!

Get Info doesn't always give you info you need: When you're connected via SFTP to a server and you Get Info on a file or folder, ForkLift doesn't tell you who the owner or group is for the item. That's important info to have!

Ineffectual progress bar: By default, ForkLift's progress bar lives in the bottom left of the program's window, at the very bottom of the sidebar. That means it's pretty narrow, which effectively cuts off a lot of important info I'd like to see during a copy, as you can see in Figure 3–15.

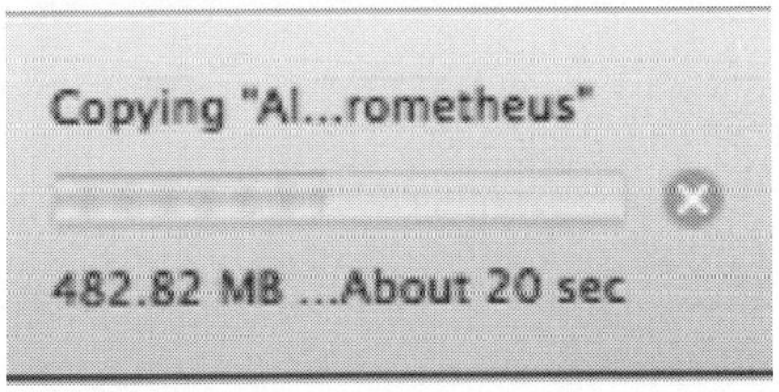

Figure 3–15. *Not the most communicative, is it?*

It gets worse when you start another copy while the first copy is still doing its thing. Take a look at Figure 3–16—that's even worse!

Figure 3–16. *Uhhhh ... thanks? I think?*

Now, granted, you can resize the sidebar to see more info, but why should I have to do that? The larger problem is that the bottom of the sidebar is a bad place to put the progress bar. How about the very bottom of the ForkLift window?

There's also a bad inconsistency in the UI design of the progress bar. If you're copying only one thing and you click on the small X next to the progress bar, it stops the copy. If, however, you're copying several things (you start one copy, and while that's working, you start another) and you press the X, a window opens showing you the progress of all your copy jobs. This is unclear and inconsistent, to say the least.

Let's all hope this is fixed soon. Maybe it will be fixed by the time you're reading this. If so, good! If not, fix it!

> **NOTE:** A later beta that came out as this book neared print fixes the problems with the progress bar. Yay!

Those are my criticisms of ForkLift, and as you can tell, none of them are devastating. Overall, ForkLift is darn good, and a worthy Finder replacement—and then some. If you're a power user, download it, use it during the free trial period, and see what you think. It may be just the thing you're looking for.

Path Finder

The other big competitor in the "let's replace the Finder" sweepstakes is Path Finder, which you can see in Figure 3–17.

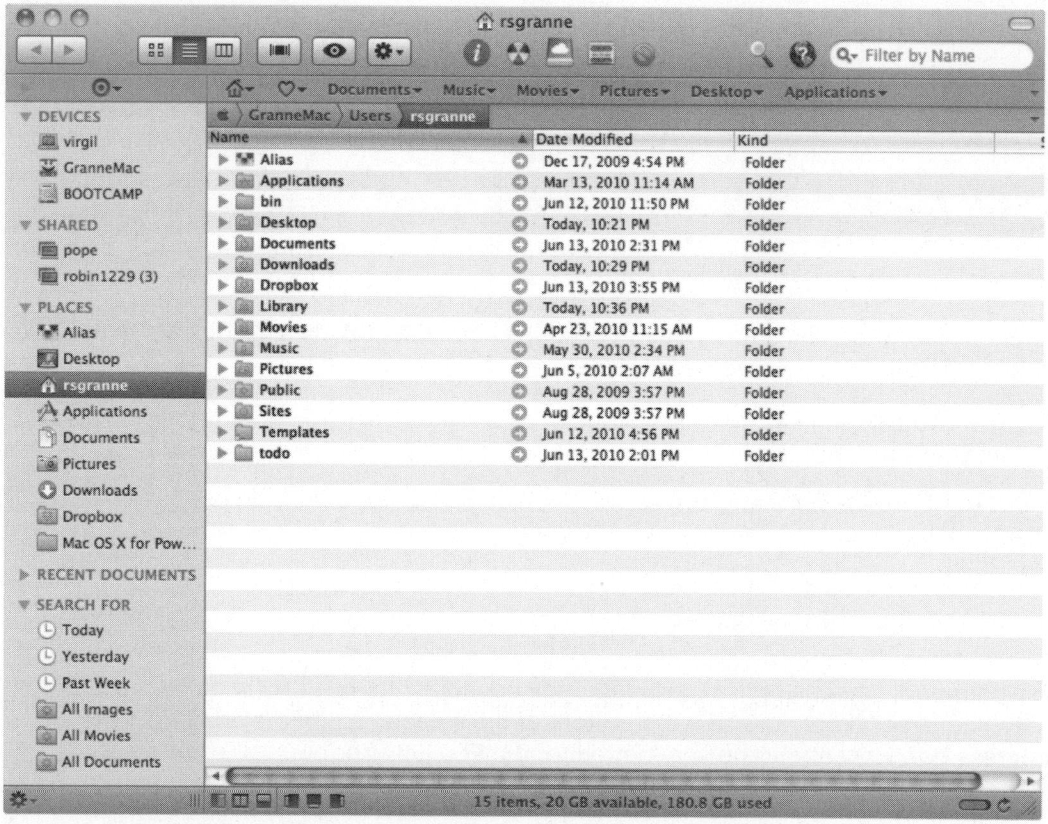

Figure 3–17. *It starts out simply, but it can easily be transformed into much more.*

You can download it from www.cocoatech.com. When you do, you'll get a ten-day free trial; after that, it costs $40.

I'm not going to go over every single feature that Path Finder has in its arsenal. There are a lot, and many of them are the same as those I've already covered with ForkLift. That's not to say that Path Finder copied its ideas from ForkLift; in fact, Path Finder came first, appearing in 2001 while ForkLift wasn't released until 2007. But it's obvious to me that the developers of both apps are watching each other and getting inspiration from their competitor, which is just fine.

Comparison and Contrast of ForkLift and Path Finder

So here are some similarities—and differences:

Dual-pane UI: Both support a dual-pane interface, although ForkLift starts out with that UI and Path Finder starts with a single-pane look. To get two panes, click on the little bitty Dual Browser button in Path Finder's status bar, or use **View** ➤ **Dual Browser**. Unfortunately, I don't see any key commands to select or switch different panes like you get with ForkLift, so you're stuck with the mouse.

Tabs: Both support tabs, and both create tabs inside of panes, instead of panes inside of tabs (see my earlier discussion of ForkLift for more on this difference). Like ForkLift, Path Finder enables you to flip between tabs with key commands: ⌘-} for the next tab and ⌘-{ for the previous tab (or you can use **Window** ➤ **Select Next Tab** and **Window** ➤ **Select Previous Tab**).

Open In Terminal: Both allow you to open a Terminal window that immediately loads the current directory you were viewing in the app. Where ForkLift hands the job off to Apple's Terminal, however, Path Finder uses its own app, or at least wraps its own window dressing around Apple's Terminal, which is kind of annoying.

In fact, this is a big difference between ForkLift and Path Finder: ForkLift sometimes comes up with its own tools (Get Info, for instance), but it tends to hand jobs off to Apple's built-in apps, while Path Finder is much more likely to develop its own stuff to replace Apple's. Which direction you prefer depends upon how satisfied you are with Apple's programs and how good of a job you think Path Finder does replacing them.

Batch rename files: Path Finder doesn't have this feature, which surprises me; that said, it has several features that ForkLift doesn't have either, as I'll shortly demonstrate.

Create new text file: ForkLift will create a new text file in the current folder and leave it up to you to decide what to do with it, but Path Finder goes further in terms of choices and actions. Under **File** ➤ **New File** you'll find the following:

- New File: creates a new file with the default extension of TXT; once the title is entered, you start editing it in Path Finder's text editor.

- New Text File: actually creates a new RTF file that opens in Path Finder's RTF editor; you can save the file you create as RTF, text (stripping out the formatting), and Microsoft Word (DOC only, not DOCX).

- New HTML File: creates a new HTML file that opens in Path Finder's text editor, a pretty bare-bones affair that requires that you know HTML thoroughly.

Do I like this? Not really. I like my text editors of choice—MacVim and BBEdit—and I certainly don't want to use Path Finder's. When I create a file, just create the file and then let me decide what program to use to open it. Don't force me to use a substandard tool that I immediately have to close.

Group files from different folders into a Stack: Yup, both ForkLift and Path Finder do this. ForkLift calls these Stacks, while Path Finder calls them Drop Stacks, but in practice they're the exact same thing. To access Path Finder's implementation, select a file or folder, click on the icon that looks like a target at the top of the sidebar, and choose Add To Drop Stack (or go to **File ➤ Add To Drop Stack**).

Built-in app deletion: Unique to ForkLift (which also surprises me).

Empty Trash toolbar button: Ditto.

Connect to remote servers: Path Finder supports the protocols built in to the Finder: AFP, FTP, SMB/CIFS, NFS, and WebDAV. No SFTP, though.

Mount servers as local devices: Sure, Path Finder can do it … if you're connecting to the server via FTP or one of the other protocols the Finder supports. That pretty much makes it useless for anyone who uses SFTP because they care about security.

Sync directories and Synclets: Not found in Path Finder.

Create aliases and symbolic (soft) links: Like ForkLift, Path Finder does this. Go to **File ➤ Make Alias**, and you have three choices:

- Make Alias (⌘-L)
- Make Symbolic Link (⌘-⇧-L)
- Make Path Finder Alias (⌘-^-⇧-L)

That last one bothers me. The first two are great—aliases are Mac-specific, and symbolic links are UNIX-specific—but the third is application-specific. I'd recommend sticking to the first two, as they'll work with pretty much every app on your Mac, and avoiding something that ties you to one vendor.

View folder sizes: ForkLift has a menu command and a key command to see folder sizes, or you can open View Options to toggle a check box to make a long-term setting. Path Finder requires you to go to **View ➤ Show View Options**, and then check a box next to Calculate All Sizes, which isn't nearly as handy.

Filtering files: Path Finder combines filtering, searching, and Spotlight in one place: in the upper right search bar. If you click on the little drop-down arrow in the menu, you'll see your choices, shown in Figure 3–18.

```
No Recents

Filter
✓ by Name
   by Extension
   by Kind
Spotlight
   Computer
   Home
   Selection
   Servers
Search
   Computer
   Home
   Selection
   Servers

Spotlight Panel
```

Figure 3–18. *Path Finder cleverly combines several modes of searching in one place.*

Filtering looks in only the current directory, without progressing recursively down into sub-folders. Spotlight is, well, Spotlight. And Search proceeds recursively through sub-folders to find what you're looking for. My only beef is that the search is limited to the four starting points you see in Figure 3–18. The third choice, Selection, allows customizability, which is great, but it seems weird to me that it's third on the list, and it searches the selected folder on down, and does not start in the current folder shown in Path Finder.

Archiving and compression: When it comes to compressing, Path Finder provides lots of nice options. Under the Commands menu are several choices, including Compress and Email (very nice), Compress (which uses ZIP by default), and Compress With Format, which itself offers support for over ten different archival formats. At the bottom of the Compress With Format menu is Decompress, which detects the format of the archived file and acts accordingly. Or you can just double-click the compressed file and it will open, just like in the Finder.

Better Get Info: Like ForkLift, Path Finder also has a more detailed Get Info window than the Finder, as you can tell from Figure 3–19 (the window is so long that I wrapped it in two columns).

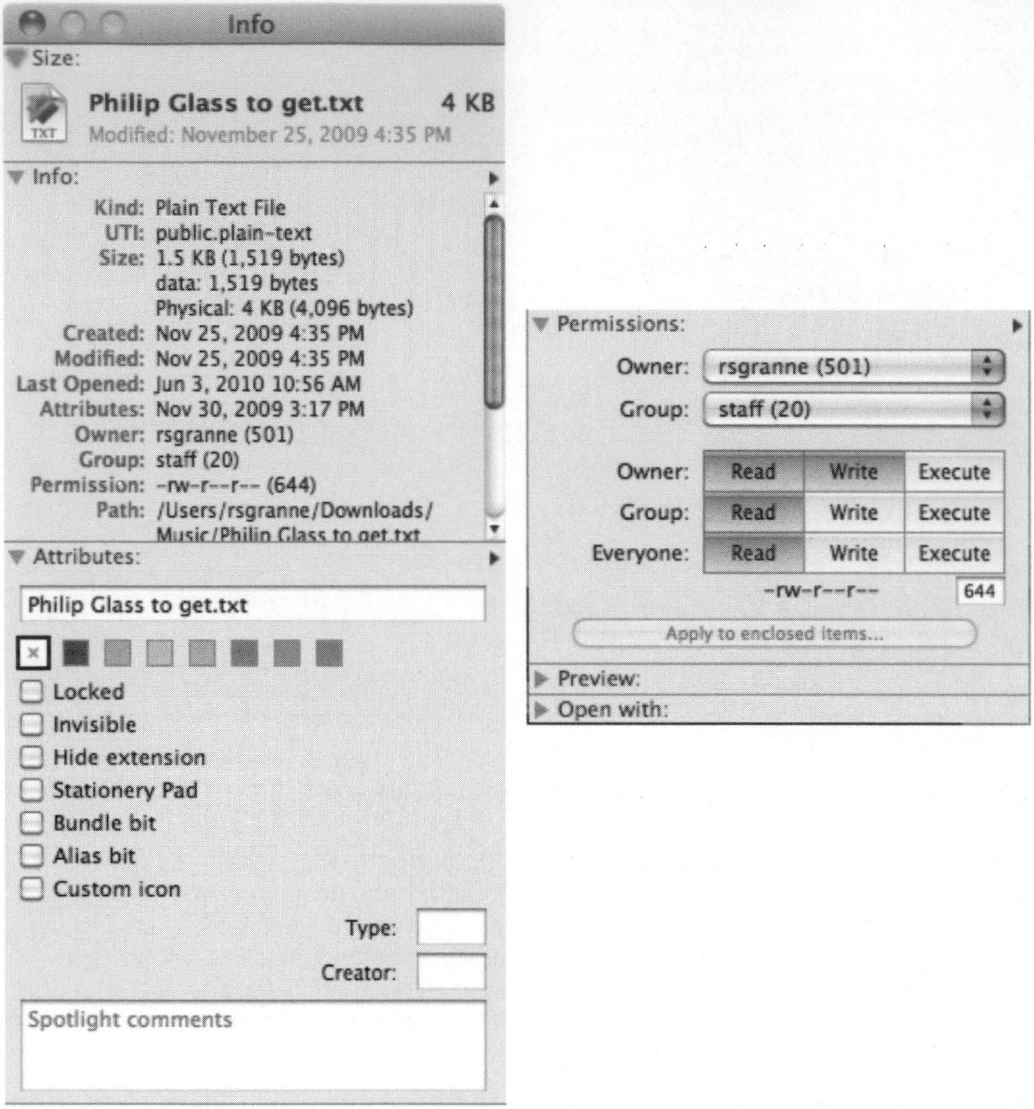

Figure 3–19. *Path Finder's Get Info window has a lot of information in it, but is it presented well?*

Path Finder's Get Info has a ton of great detail in it, but it's not presented in the most attractive or beneficial manner. The big Info block is so long, in fact, that it needs a scroll bar, and the layout of the check boxes in the Attributes section leaves an enormous amount of whitespace that is then weirdly offset by the Type and Creator boxes. So while there's good stuff here, the window isn't Mac-like and attractive, which always bums me out. I like my apps to be both incredibly functional and beautiful too, and this is an example of a larger problem with Path Finder: it has the features, but too often, it's just too plain and cluttered for me.

That's my major beef with Path Finder vis-à-vis ForkLift: it's just not as attractive as the other program. There's too much going on, and it's not displayed as nicely as it could be to the user (for an example of an app that manages to posses both a great number of capabilities and a beautiful UI, see Transmit, covered in Chapter 6, "Using the Internet to Its Fullest").

Path Finder's Cool Features

Now, that said, lots of people think Path Finder is the bee's knees, and I'm certainly not here to slag it—just critique it. I don't want to leave an entirely negative impression of the program, as it actually has lots of very cool features, including these:

Change attributes easily: Select a file or folder and go to File ➤ Attributes and you can make several key changes to a file's state quickly, such as Locked and Invisible, as well as Owner and Group.

Copy paths: I like this one a lot. Select something in Path Finder and use Edit ➤ Copy Path to, well, copy the path of the selected item. What's neat is that Path Finder will format the path in a variety of ways, including UNIX, Windows, Terminal, and URL. Very cool.

Drawers: Some folks love love love this, but I find it more clutter. On Path Finder's status bar are several icons; three of them open, respectively, Left Drawer, Bottom Drawer, and Right Drawer (you can also find these in the View menu). The left and right drawers contain different useful tools that you can make visible on demand, such as Recent Applications, Selection Path (a hierarchical, clickable path for the current file or folder), Terminal, Trash, Recent Documents, Recent Folders, and more. The bottom drawer is a Terminal that opens to the current folder.

Copy and move anywhere: When I used Ubuntu Linux as my main OS for a while, one of my favorite touches was that I could right-click on a file or folder, select either Copy To or Move To, and then indicate the location to which I'd like the file or folder to go. It was a great time-saver, and I missed it when I returned to Mac OS X. However, Path Finder has it. Under Commands, you'll find both Copy To and Move To. Nice!

***Really* delete files:** Feeling paranoid about a particular file or folder that you need to delete? You could go to Finder ➤ Preferences ➤ Advanced and check Empty Trash Securely, which then overwrites the hard drives sectors several times with random data when you empty your Trash. The problem is that this setting greatly slows down emptying the Trash, especially if you don't care about 99% of the stuff you delete. And if you have a lot of files to plow through, it can take forever.

To get around that annoyance, you could leave that checkbox unchecked, but then go to Commands ➤ Secure Delete in Path Finder instead. That way, the vast majority of the time, stuff you aren't concerned about is quickly deleted from the Trash but still recoverable by the NSA if they grab your hard drive (like you're worried about pix of your kid's birthday party or your e-mail), but if you need to really wipe something off your hard drive, it's easy to do.

There are other features, but those should start to give you an idea of Path Finder's comprehensiveness.

Should you try Path Finder? Absolutely. It's got a ten-day free trial, so take advantage of that. Should you adopt Path Finder? That's up to you. I prefer ForkLift, but I can see why others might prefer Path Finder. What's nice is that you can try out both, see which one suits you more, and then adopt that one for day-to-day use.

Xfile

And then we get to Xfile. This one is a nerd's dream come true—well, a rich nerd's dream come true. The nerd part: it's not just 1 tool, it's actually over 90, and most of those tools are designed in a way that would appeal to, well, nerds. The rich part: it's $60.

I'm slightly torn when it comes to Xfile: it does tell you lots of useful information that could be helpful in some situations. But the way that information is presented leaves a lot to be desired. Let me show you the main Xfile app in Figure 3–20.

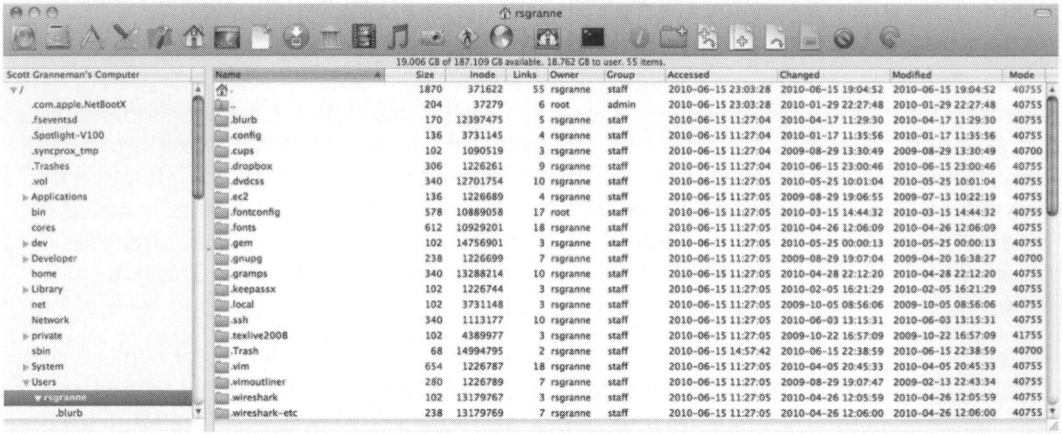

Figure 3–20. *Xfile in all of its tell-you-everything-and-then-some glory.*

See the huge row of icons in the toolbar? See the list of files and folders, and how those that are hidden (that have dots in front of them) are shown by default? See the columns of information that are shown by default? And forget right-clicking. If you want something, you need to use the menus or the buttons. If all that floats your boat, then Xfile may be for you.

But there's more! Figure 3–21 shows Xfile's Get Info window (yes, like the other apps, it has its own).

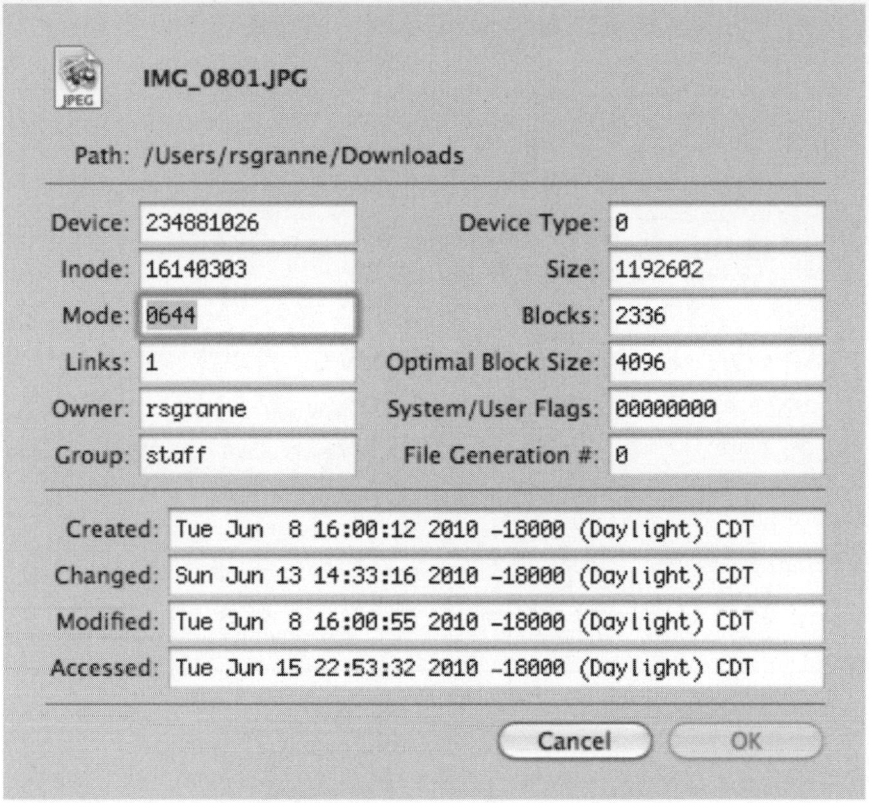

Figure 3-21. *Lots of great info—perhaps too much—and so, so ugly.*

There's a ton of data in this window that you can find in the normal Get Info window—Owner, Group, Size, Path—and even more that you can't: Links. File Generation #. System/User Flags? Inode number? I mean, I know what an inode number is (see http://en.wikipedia.org/wiki/Inode), but how often do I need it? Enough that it's part of the Get Info window? Nah. And not to mention, it's just an ugly window with ugly fonts.

A final example: Xattrib, one of the 90+ programs that come with Xfile. Take a look at Figure 3-22, and compare it to Figure 3-21, the Get Info window.

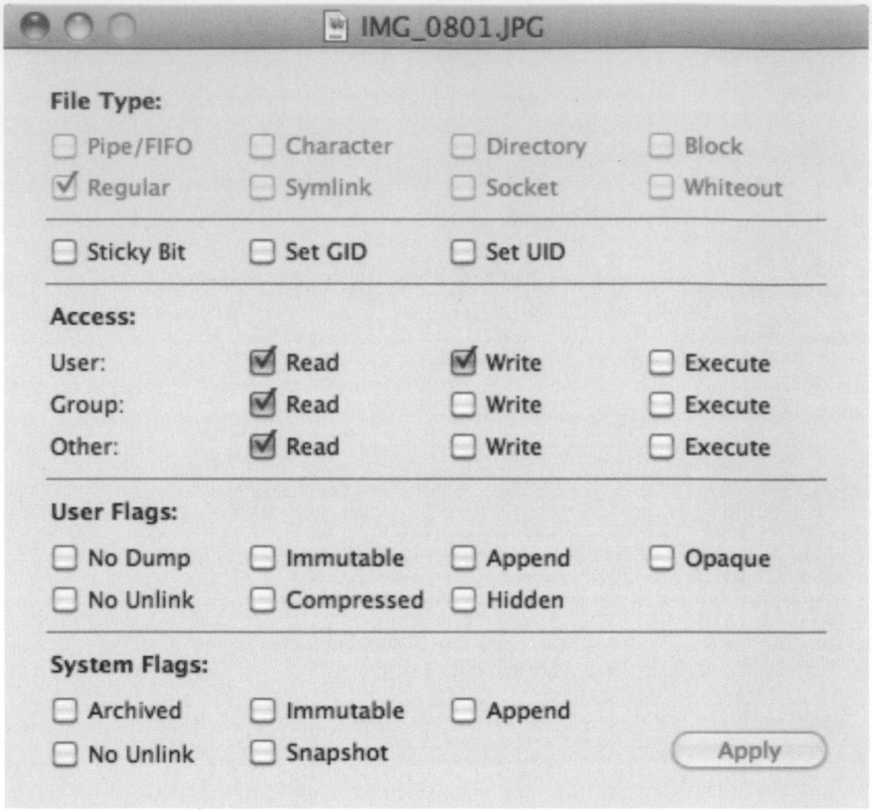

File Type:

☐ Pipe/FIFO   ☐ Character   ☐ Directory   ☐ Block
☑ Regular   ☐ Symlink   ☐ Socket   ☐ Whiteout

☐ Sticky Bit   ☐ Set GID   ☐ Set UID

Access:

User: ☑ Read   ☑ Write   ☐ Execute
Group: ☑ Read   ☐ Write   ☐ Execute
Other: ☑ Read   ☐ Write   ☐ Execute

User Flags:

☐ No Dump   ☐ Immutable   ☐ Append   ☐ Opaque
☐ No Unlink   ☐ Compressed   ☐ Hidden

System Flags:

☐ Archived   ☐ Immutable   ☐ Append
☐ No Unlink   ☐ Snapshot   (Apply)

Figure 3–22. *So, some info is new, and some is repeated from Get Info?*

Notice that Xattrib shows you permissions with a grid and check boxes, as does the Get Info window, except that it does it with numbers. And notice all the other stuff that Xatttrib shows you, such as File Type. And all the stuff it let's you set: the Sticky Bit, and various flags, including Hidden, Compressed, and Snapshot. Again, all nerdy and good, but is it really something you need? Perhaps you do.

If you do—if you're looking at these screenshots and thinking, "Man, I gotta get me some of that!"—then by all means, proceed! Download and buy Xfile.

The final thing you should know, though, concerns Xfile's free trial policy. Hey, I understand that it's certainly within a developer's right to do as he pleases. It's his software, his business model, and his choice. But that doesn't mean I can't point out that during its trial period, Xfile is as annoying as a buzzing mosquito in your ear. Figure 3–23 shows you a window that you will become intimately familiar with if you try out Xfile.

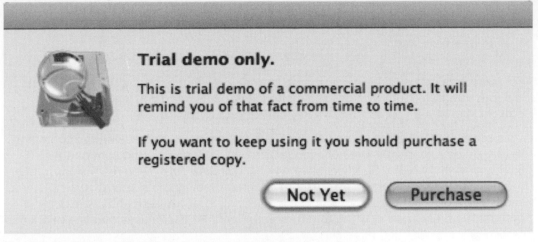

Figure 3–23. *I hope you like that window, because you're going to see it a lot.*

You will see that window when:

- You open an app

- You close an app

- Every couple of minutes (not every ten minutes, which wouldn't be horrible, just annoying, but every couple of minutes, which is horribly annoying)

- You try to use certain functions of an app (and often it will inform you that it can't use the function you wanted to because you don't have the full version)

I find this sort of behavior on the part of a developer offputting. Again, I'm not saying he shouldn't, since it's his choice how he wants to present his software. But when I'm constantly aggravated to the point of exasperation while I'm just trying to test software that I might actually, y'know, *buy*, I don't want to use or recommend it to my friends. Or, to be sure, buy it.

So, to recap: Xfile is very nerdy and will tell you everything about the files on your Mac. And a whole lot more besides. But it's nothing you can't get from the command line or from other programs, it will cost you a good chunk o' change, and it will probably drive you batty while you're trying it out. If that intrigues you, go for it!

Spotlight

All UNIX boxes—and that includes Mac OS X—come with a fantastic command-line tool for searching the file system: find. The find command is tremendously useful and powerful, and actually does far more than simply locate files. For instance, you can tell find to run a program on every file that it locates, which allows you to do some amazing things. Compared to Mac OS X's Spotlight, it has far more options and can do more.

> **TIP:** For more on `find`, see my *Linux Phrasebook*, which contains a chapter on the command, along with lots of examples.

That said, Spotlight is great. It can search for metadata that `find` can't see, and since it's tightly integrated into Mac OS X, it's often faster. The more you learn about Spotlight, the better you can utilize a key part of your Mac.

In this section, we're going to look at Spotlight, but I'm going to focus on the command line (heck, some readers might not even realize that you can use Spotlight on the command line!). I use the Spotlight search box all the time, but if you really want to dig down and locate things, and if you want to integrate Spotlight into your own scripts, you need to learn how to utilize Spotlight in the Terminal. After we learn about wielding Spotlight like a ninja, we're going to move on to Spotlight alternatives that you might find interesting.

Spotlight via the Command Line

The Terminal-based Spotlight is actually four different programs:

- `mdfind`: Search Spotlight's indices to find files matching your query. For Apple's documentation, see http://developer.apple.com/mac/library/documentation/Darwin/Reference/ManPages/man1/mdfind.1.html.

- `mdimport`: Add files to Spotlight's indices. For Apple's docs, see http://developer.apple.com/mac/library/documentation/Darwin/Reference/ManPages/man1/mdimport.1.html.

- `mdls`: List the metadata for a particular file. For more from Apple, see http://developer.apple.com/mac/library/documentation/Darwin/Reference/ManPages/man1/mdls.1.html.

- `mdutil`: Manage Spotlight's indices. This command allows you to turn off indexing for a volume, delete an index, and view the indexing status. For details from Apple, see http://developer.apple.com/mac/library/documentation/Darwin/Reference/ManPages/man1/mdutil.1.html.

> **NOTE:** Some of you, like me, are probably thinking, "What's with the md in front of everything?" Turns out that it's short for "metadata." Of course!

Since I'm focusing on searching using Spotlight, we're going to use `mdfind` almost exclusively, although `mdls` will make an appearance.

Search for Files

The easiest way to search for files is to simply use `mdfind`, followed by a word for which you're searching:

```
$ mdfind Groucho
```

By default, `mdfind` searches the names of files, the contents of files, and the metadata associated with files. That explains the results I got on my Mac for that search (which have been greatly truncated):

> **NOTE:** For future reference, assume results are always truncated to present only the most important info.

```
/Users/rsgranne/Dropbox/Mac OS X for Power Users/Chapters/03 Expanding Upon the Basic
Tools/7 Spotlight.txt
/Users/rsgranne/Library/Caches/Metadata/Safari/History/http:%2F%2Fen.wikipedia.org%2Fwik
i%2FThe_Coo-Coo_Nut_Grove.webhistory
/Users/rsgranne/Documents/Scott's Stuff/Music/Lists/Elvis Costello's Top 500 Albums.txt
/Users/rsgranne/bin/email/quotes.xml
/Users/rsgranne/Library/Mail/IMAP-
scott@granneman.com@imap.gmail.com/PER/Entertainment.imapmbox/Messages/905837.emlx
/Users/rsgranne/Pictures/Covers/Albums/Comedy/Groucho/An Evening With Groucho.jpg
/Users/rsgranne/Pictures/People/Entertainers/Comedians/Groucho Marx/Groucho Marx 06.jpg
```

What if I want to search for a string of text, with spaces between the words? No problem—just wrap the search string in quotation marks:

```
$ mdfind "Groucho Marx"
/Users/rsgranne/Dropbox/Mac OS X for Power Users/Chapters/03 Expanding Upon the Basic
Tools/7 Spotlight.txt
/Users/rsgranne/Library/Caches/Metadata/Safari/History/http:%2F%2Fen.wikipedia.org%2Fwik
i%2FThe_Coo-Coo_Nut_Grove.webhistory
/Users/rsgranne/Documents/Scott's Stuff/Music/Lists/Elvis Costello's Top 500 Albums.txt
/Users/rsgranne/bin/email/quotes.xml
/Users/rsgranne/Pictures/People/Entertainers/Comedians/Groucho Marx
/Users/rsgranne/Pictures/People/Entertainers/Comedians/Groucho Marx/Groucho Marx 06.jpg
```

Note that the first search brought up a result that the second did not: /Users/rsgranne/Pictures/Covers/Albums/Comedy/Groucho/An Evening With Groucho.jpg. Why? Because while "Groucho" was in the result, "Groucho Marx" was not.

Search for Files by Name

By default, `mdfind` searches file names, file contents, and file metadata. This is powerful and often very useful, but sometimes I don't need all that. I just want to search files by name. In those cases, I would use the –name parameter.

```
$ mdfind -name Mars
/Users/rsgranne/Documents/Reading/Burroughs, Edgar Rice/Mars/03 - Warlord of Mars.txt
/Users/rsgranne/Documents/Reading/Burroughs, Edgar Rice/Mars/02 - Gods of Mars.txt
```

```
/Users/rsgranne/Documents/Reading/Burroughs, Edgar Rice/Mars/01 - Princess of Mars,
A.txt
/Users/rsgranne/Documents/Reading/Burroughs, Edgar Rice/Mars
/Users/rsgranne/Documents/Reading/Arnold, Edwin/Gulliver of Mars.txt
/Users/rsgranne/Documents/Reading/Simak, Clifford D/Madness From Mars.txt
/Users/rsgranne/Documents/Reading/Campbell, John W/The Brain Stealers of Mars.txt
/Users/rsgranne/Pictures/iPhoto Library/Originals/2007/Marshall & Arrow Rock
/Users/rsgranne/Pictures/Nature/Space/mars/marsglobe1.jpg
/Users/rsgranne/Pictures/RSG/20030704_marshall_fireworks
```

Keep in mind that I'm searching only the file names, not the directory path, which is why the Edgar Rice Burroughs items came up: because they had "Mars" in the file names, not because they were in the directory "Mars." To prove it, this result did *not* appear:

```
/Users/rsgranne/Documents/Reading/Burroughs, Edgar Rice/Mars/10 - Llana of Gathol.txt
```

Why? Because the name of the file is "10 - Llana of Gathol.txt," and there's nary a "Mars" in it.

However, notice that /Users/rsgranne/Documents/Reading/Burroughs, Edgar Rice/Mars does appear. Why? Because Mars is the final object at the end of the path, so it matches. It's not the path—so Llana of Gathol doesn't appear, even though it's in Mars—that's unimportant; instead, what's important is the actual file (or folder, but remember, on a UNIX system like Mac OS X, folders are just special files) itself at the end of the path.

Search for Files in Specific Folders

By default, mdfind searches all attached volumes, but often that's overkill. What if you just want to look in a particular folder and its sub-folders? No problem: just use the –onlyin parameter. So, for example, if I just want to search for "Louis Armstrong" in my Music directory, I'd use this command:

```
$ mdfind –onlyin ~/Music "Louis Armstrong"
/Users/rsgranne/Music/Music/Compilations/Louis Armstrong Plays W.C. Handy/02 Yellow Dog
Blues.mp3
/Users/rsgranne/Music/Music/Compilations/Louis Armstrong Plays W.C. Handy/01 St. Louis
Blues.mp3
/Users/rsgranne/Music/Music/Compilations/Louis Armstrong Plays W.C. Handy
/Users/rsgranne/Music/Music/Ella Fitzgerald & Louis Armstrong
/Users/rsgranne/Music/Music/Ella Fitzgerald & Louis Armstrong/Ella And Louis/11 April In
Paris.mp3
/Users/rsgranne/Music/Music/Ella Fitzgerald & Louis Armstrong/Ella And Louis/02 Isn't
This A Lovely Day.mp3
```

You're going to see me using –onlyin contantly throughout the rest of this chapter, in order to keep my results smaller, and because that's how I almost always search.

Search for Files in the Current Folder

What if you're already at the folder you want to search? You could do this, of course:

```
$ cd "~/Documents/Reading/Burroughs, Edgar Rice/Mars"
$ mdfind -onlyin ~/Documents/Reading/Burroughs\,\ Edgar\ Rice/Mars -name Mars
/Users/rsgranne/Documents/Reading/Burroughs, Edgar Rice/Mars/05 - Chess Men of Mars.txt
/Users/rsgranne/Documents/Reading/Burroughs, Edgar Rice/Mars/04 - Thuvia Maid of
Mars.txt
/Users/rsgranne/Documents/Reading/Burroughs, Edgar Rice/Mars/03 - Warlord of Mars.txt
/Users/rsgranne/Documents/Reading/Burroughs, Edgar Rice/Mars/02 - Gods of Mars.txt
/Users/rsgranne/Documents/Reading/Burroughs, Edgar Rice/Mars/01 - Princess of Mars,
A.txt
/Users/rsgranne/Documents/Reading/Burroughs, Edgar Rice/Mars
```

That's great, but I sure don't want to have to type out the full path if I don't have to. Instead, use this:

```
$ cd "~/Documents/Reading/Burroughs, Edgar Rice/Mars"
$ mdfind -onlyin "$(pwd)" -name Mars
/Users/rsgranne/Documents/Reading/Burroughs, Edgar Rice/Mars/05 - Chess Men of Mars.txt
/Users/rsgranne/Documents/Reading/Burroughs, Edgar Rice/Mars/04 - Thuvia Maid of
Mars.txt
/Users/rsgranne/Documents/Reading/Burroughs, Edgar Rice/Mars/03 - Warlord of Mars.txt
/Users/rsgranne/Documents/Reading/Burroughs, Edgar Rice/Mars/02 - Gods of Mars.txt
/Users/rsgranne/Documents/Reading/Burroughs, Edgar Rice/Mars/01 - Princess of Mars,
A.txt
/Users/rsgranne/Documents/Reading/Burroughs, Edgar Rice/Mars
```

You have to admit, `"$(pwd)"` is a lot easier to type. But what's going on here?

Let's start with `pwd`, which is a command name short for "print working directory." This command instructs your shell to echo back the complete path to the current directory you're in. In other words, based on where I am in the previous example, if I was to type `pwd` and hit Enter, I'd see this:

```
/Users/rsgranne/Documents/Reading/Burroughs, Edgar Rice/Mars
```

When you enclose a command inside $(and), that is called Command Substitution, and it means that your shell runs that command first and then uses its output inside another command. So I'm telling my shell to get the full path to the working directory— /Users/rsgranne/Documents/Reading/Burroughs, Edgar Rice/Mars—and then use it in my `mdfind` command.

So why surround $(pwd) with the quotation marks? Because if I don't, the spaces in the path really screw things up, and I get no results at all. You can see why if you use `ls`:

```
$ ls $(pwd)
ls: /Users/rsgranne/Documents/Reading/Burroughs,: No such file or directory
ls: Edgar: No such file or directory
ls: Rice/Mars: No such file or directory
```

Every place there's a space, the command gets confused and thinks it's another directory. The `mdfind` command thinks I'm looking in the

`/Users/rsgranne/Documents/Reading/Burroughs`, directory, which doesn't exist, and then gets baffled.

Moral of the story? Just to be safe, enclose $(pwd) in quotation marks. It can't hurt, and it can definitely prevent errors.

There's one other way to use the pwd trick, and some might consider it easier to type (I'm so used to command substitution that it's quicker for me, but it might not be so for you). Instead of actually running the pwd command and inserting it via command substitution, just refer to the environment variable $PWD that your shell keeps constant track of.

```
$ cd "~/Documents/Reading"
$ echo $PWD
/Users/rsgranne/Documents/Reading
$ cd "~/Documents/Reading/Burroughs, Edgar Rice/Mars"
$ echo $PWD
/Users/rsgranne/Documents/Reading/Burroughs, Edgar Rice/Mars
$ mdfind -onlyin "$PWD" -name Mars
/Users/rsgranne/Documents/Reading/Burroughs, Edgar Rice/Mars/05 - Chess Men of Mars.txt
/Users/rsgranne/Documents/Reading/Burroughs, Edgar Rice/Mars/04 - Thuvia Maid of
Mars.txt
/Users/rsgranne/Documents/Reading/Burroughs, Edgar Rice/Mars/03 - Warlord of Mars.txt
/Users/rsgranne/Documents/Reading/Burroughs, Edgar Rice/Mars/02 - Gods of Mars.txt
/Users/rsgranne/Documents/Reading/Burroughs, Edgar Rice/Mars/01 - Princess of Mars,
A.txt
/Users/rsgranne/Documents/Reading/Burroughs, Edgar Rice/Mars
```

I put the echo $PWD in there to show you that the environment variable constantly changes as you move about the file system. And when using mdfind, note also that you have to enclose $PWD inside quotation marks just as you did with $(pwd), for the same reason—to make sure spaces don't cause any problems.

Search for Files by the Kind of File

So let's say I want to find that copy of the 1918 Tarzan movie starring Elmo Lincoln that I know is somewhere in my home directory. I could just do this:

```
$ mdfind -onlyin ~ Tarzan
```

The problem is that I get 312 results! Everything having Tarzan in the file name or contents is listed. So I get smart and decide to use the -name parameter:

```
$ mdfind -onlyin ~ -name Tarzan
```

I still get 54 results. Not so bad, but I'm feeling very lazy. So let's try this:

```
$ mdfind -onlyin ~ -name Tarzan kind:movie
/Users/rsgranne/Downloads/ERB/Tarzan of the Apes (1918).mp4
```

Perfect! Keep in mind that kind is not searching the extensions of files, so don't try using those.

Table 3–1 is a list of `kind:` keywords that Apple makes available to use. This isn't comprehensive, so the best way to discover new ones is to try them out. That's how I found out about `text` and `excel`.

Table 3–1. *Major Keywords for the kind: Attribute*

Type	kind: Attribute
Aliases	alias
Applications	application, applications, app
Audio	audio
Bookmarks	bookmark, bookmarks
Browser history	history
Contacts	contact, contacts
Email	email, emails, mail message, mail messages
Excel	excel
Folders	fol, folder, folders
Fonts	font, fonts
iCal events	event, events
iCal to dos	todo, todos, to do, to dos
Images	image, images
JPEGs	jpeg
Keynote	keynote
Movies	movie, movies
MP3	mp3
Music	music
Numbers	numbers
Pages	pages
PDF	pdf, pdfs
PowerPoint	powerpoint
Preferences	system preferences, preferences
Presentations	presentations, presentation
QuickTime	quicktime
Text	text
TIFF	tiff
Word	word

Try those and you can start to get very precise in your Spotlight searches.

NOTE: Yes, I could have used `grep`.

```
$ mdfind -onlyin ~ -name Tarzan | grep mp4
```

That would work perfectly fine if you didn't want to just stick with the built-in parameters that `mdfind` has.

Search for Files by Date

Often you'll want to find files based on a particular date. For instance, what if I had two Tarzan movies on my hard drive, but one of them had been downloaded a year ago, and I wanted the one that was downloaded yesterday? Sure, I could just look for all the Tarzan movies on my Mac (there are only two), but I'm trying to be precise here!

```
$ mdfind -onlyin ~ -name Tarzan kind:movie date:yesterday
/Users/rsgranne/Downloads/Movies/Tarzan of the Apes (1918).mp4
```

There are three words you can use with `date`: `yesterday`, `today`, and `tomorrow` (tomorrow is for calendar appointments, since obviously you can't save a file in the future!). You're not limited to those dates, however, but to use others requires more work and a new syntax.

You've probably noticed by now that the syntax you use when you're searching Spotlight using the Finder is different from that used when you're searching via the Terminal. However, you can still use the Finder syntax on the command line, if you include the `-interpret` parameter, which tells `mdfind` to convert on-the-fly the Finder syntax into something it can use. Everything that is to be interpreted goes inside quotation marks, and there are a couple of different ways you can structure your command, as you can see in the following:

```
$ mdfind -onlyin ~ -name Tarzan kind:movie -interpret "date:6/13/2010-6/20/2010"
/Users/rsgranne/Downloads/Movies/Tarzan of the Apes (1918).mp4
$ mdfind -onlyin ~ -name Tarzan -interpret "kind:movie date:6/13/2010-6/20/2010"
/Users/rsgranne/Downloads/Movies/Tarzan of the Apes (1918).mp4
$ mdfind -onlyin ~ -interpret "Tarzan kind:movie date:6/13/2010-6/20/2010"
/Users/rsgranne/Downloads/Movies/Tarzan of the Apes (1918).mp4
```

In the `date:` parameter, I was searching the past week, but you can use any of these (dates must be entered using the short numeric date format that is shown on ➤ System Preferences ➤ Language & Text ➤ Formats):

- date:6/10/2010
  A specific day.

- date:>6/10/2010
  On or after a specific day.

- date:<6/10/2010
  On or before a specific day.

- date:1/1/2009-6/10/2010
  During that range of days.

By default, date: is actually looking at the date the file was modified. In fact, if you want to be specific, you can use modified: instead of date:, as you can see here:

```
$ mdfind -onlyin ~ -name Tarzan -interpret "kind:movie modified:>6/19/2010"
/Users/rsgranne/Downloads/Movies/Tarzan of the Apes (1918).mp4
```

You can also use created: to look for files authored on a date or during a date range.

Learn About the Metadata Spotlight Knows About Files

Granted, the searches I've been showing you all use metadata of one sort or another, but in this section, I'm talking about something a bit more complicated: metadata attribute keys that Spotlight indexes and that you can view using mdls, which I mentioned earlier in this section. To see what I'm talking about, let's look at the complete metadata for various files.

First, let's look at a text file:

```
$ mdls "02 - Gods of Mars.txt"
kMDItemContentCreationDate     = 2005-04-19 00:20:59 -0500
kMDItemContentModificationDate = 2005-04-19 00:20:59 -0500
kMDItemContentType             = "public.plain-text"
kMDItemContentTypeTree         = (
    "public.plain-text",
    "public.text",
    "public.data",
    "public.item",
    "public.content"
)
kMDItemDisplayName             = "02 - Gods of Mars.txt"
kMDItemFSContentChangeDate     = 2005-04-19 00:20:59 -0500
kMDItemFSCreationDate          = 2005-04-19 00:20:59 -0500
kMDItemFSCreatorCode           = ""
kMDItemFSFinderFlags           = 10
kMDItemFSHasCustomIcon         = 0
kMDItemFSInvisible             = 0
kMDItemFSIsExtensionHidden     = 0
kMDItemFSIsStationery          = 0
kMDItemFSLabel                 = 5
kMDItemFSName                  = "02 - Gods of Mars.txt"
kMDItemFSNodeCount             = 0
kMDItemFSOwnerGroupID          = 20
kMDItemFSOwnerUserID           = 501
kMDItemFSSize                  = 454144
kMDItemFSTypeCode              = ""
kMDItemKind                    = "Plain Text File"
kMDItemLastUsedDate            = 2005-04-19 00:20:59 -0500
kMDItemUsedDates               = (
    "2005-04-19 00:00:00 -0500"
```

```
)
```

Second, an MP3:

```
$ mdls "02 - Chapter 01.mp3"
kMDItemAlbum                      = "A Princess Of Mars"
kMDItemAudioBitRate               = 64000
kMDItemAudioChannelCount          = 1
kMDItemAudioSampleRate            = 22050
kMDItemAudioTrackNumber           = 2
kMDItemAuthors                    = (
    "Edgar Rice Burroughs"
)
kMDItemComment                    = "Processed 20060812"
kMDItemContentCreationDate        = 2006-08-12 12:05:47 -0500
kMDItemContentModificationDate    = 2008-11-30 13:46:24 -0600
kMDItemContentType                = "public.mp3"
kMDItemContentTypeTree            = (
    "public.mp3",
    "public.audio",
    "public.audiovisual-content",
    "public.data",
    "public.item",
    "public.content"
)
kMDItemDisplayName                = "02 - Chapter 01.mp3"
kMDItemDurationSeconds            = 1005.58975
kMDItemFSContentChangeDate        = 2008-11-30 13:46:24 -0600
kMDItemFSCreationDate             = 2006-08-12 12:05:47 -0500
kMDItemFSCreatorCode              = ""
kMDItemFSFinderFlags              = 0
kMDItemFSHasCustomIcon            = 0
kMDItemFSInvisible                = 0
kMDItemFSIsExtensionHidden        = 0
kMDItemFSIsStationery             = 0
kMDItemFSLabel                    = 0
kMDItemFSName                     = "02 - Chapter 01.mp3"
kMDItemFSNodeCount                = 0
kMDItemFSOwnerGroupID             = 20
kMDItemFSOwnerUserID              = 501
kMDItemFSSize                     = 8120762
kMDItemFSTypeCode                 = ""
kMDItemKind                       = "MP3 Audio File"
kMDItemLastUsedDate               = 2008-11-30 13:46:24 -0600
kMDItemMediaTypes                 = (
    Sound
)
kMDItemMusicalGenre               = "Spoken Word - Audiobook"
kMDItemTitle                      = "Chapter 01"
kMDItemTotalBitRate               = 64000
kMDItemUsedDates                  = (
    "2008-11-30 00:00:00 -0600"
)
```

Third, a PNG image that is a digital copy of an illustration:

```
$ mdls "Frazetta - John Carter of Mars.png"
kMDItemBitsPerSample              = 32
```

```
kMDItemColorSpace            = "RGB"
kMDItemContentCreationDate   = 2010-06-20 11:41:26 -0500
kMDItemContentModificationDate = 2010-06-20 11:41:26 -0500
kMDItemContentType           = "public.png"
kMDItemContentTypeTree       = (
    "public.png",
    "public.image",
    "public.data",
    "public.item",
    "public.content"
)
kMDItemDisplayName           = "Frazetta - John Carter of Mars.png"
kMDItemFSContentChangeDate   = 2010-06-20 11:41:26 -0500
kMDItemFSCreationDate        = 2010-06-20 11:41:26 -0500
kMDItemFSCreatorCode         = ""
kMDItemFSFinderFlags         = 0
kMDItemFSHasCustomIcon       = 0
kMDItemFSInvisible           = 0
kMDItemFSIsExtensionHidden   = 0
kMDItemFSIsStationery        = 0
kMDItemFSLabel               = 0
kMDItemFSName                = "Frazetta - John Carter of Mars.png"
kMDItemFSNodeCount           = 0
kMDItemFSOwnerGroupID        = 20
kMDItemFSOwnerUserID         = 501
kMDItemFSSize                = 2079427
kMDItemFSTypeCode            = ""
kMDItemHasAlphaChannel       = 0
kMDItemKind                  = "Portable Network Graphics image"
kMDItemLastUsedDate          = 2010-06-20 11:41:27 -0500
kMDItemOrientation           = 1
kMDItemPixelCount            = 1094400
kMDItemPixelHeight           = 1200
kMDItemPixelWidth            = 912
kMDItemResolutionHeightDPI   = 96
kMDItemResolutionWidthDPI    = 96
kMDItemUsedDates             = (
    "2010-06-20 00:00:00 -0500"
)
```

Finally, a photo of my cute lil' son Finny:

```
$ mdls "2010 0611 Mr. Sincere.jpg"
kMDItemAcquisitionMake       = "KONICA MINOLTA "
kMDItemAcquisitionModel      = "DiMAGE Z3"
kMDItemBitsPerSample         = 32
kMDItemColorSpace            = "RGB"
kMDItemContentCreationDate   = 2010-06-14 17:10:33 -0500
kMDItemContentModificationDate = 2010-06-14 17:10:33 -0500
kMDItemContentType           = "public.jpeg"
kMDItemContentTypeTree       = (
    "public.jpeg",
    "public.image",
    "public.data",
    "public.item",
    "public.content"
)
kMDItemCreator               = "QuickTime 7.6.6"
```

```
kMDItemDisplayName           = "2010 0611 Mr. Sincere.jpg"
kMDItemEXIFVersion           = "2.2"
kMDItemExposureMode          = 0
kMDItemExposureTimeSeconds   = 0.025
kMDItemFlashOnOff            = 1
kMDItemFNumber               = 2.799999952316284
kMDItemFocalLength           = 5.859375
kMDItemFSContentChangeDate   = 2010-06-14 17:10:33 -0500
kMDItemFSCreationDate        = 2010-06-14 17:10:33 -0500
kMDItemFSCreatorCode         = ""
kMDItemFSFinderFlags         = 0
kMDItemFSHasCustomIcon       = 0
kMDItemFSInvisible           = 0
kMDItemFSIsExtensionHidden   = 0
kMDItemFSIsStationery        = 0
kMDItemFSLabel               = 0
kMDItemFSName                = "2010 0611 Mr. Sincere.jpg"
kMDItemFSNodeCount           = 0
kMDItemFSOwnerGroupID        = 20
kMDItemFSOwnerUserID         = 501
kMDItemFSSize                = 1436095
kMDItemFSTypeCode            = ""
kMDItemHasAlphaChannel       = 0
kMDItemHeadline              = "Finn 2010-06-11"
kMDItemISOSpeed              = 200
kMDItemKeywords              = (
    2010,
    truck,
    sweet,
    toddler,
    cute,
    finn
)
kMDItemKind                  = "JPEG image"
kMDItemLastUsedDate          = 2010-06-15 22:45:36 -0500
kMDItemOrientation           = 0
kMDItemPixelCount            = 3871488
kMDItemPixelHeight           = 1704
kMDItemPixelWidth            = 2272
kMDItemProfileName           = "sRGB IEC61966-2.1"
kMDItemRedEyeOnOff           = 0
kMDItemResolutionHeightDPI   = 72
kMDItemResolutionWidthDPI    = 72
kMDItemUsedDates             = (
    "2010-06-14 00:00:00 -0500",
    "2010-06-15 00:00:00 -0500"
)
kMDItemWhereFroms            = (
    "http://farm5.static.flickr.com/4036/4691905627_c1a38272ce_o.jpg"
)
kMDItemWhiteBalance          = 0
```

Take a few minutes and look over the four examples I've provided. Notice that some of those attribute keys are repeated for all of the files, no matter what kinds of files they are:

- kMDItemContentModificationDate
- kMDItemContentType
- kMDItemContentTypeTree
- kMDItemDisplayName
- kMDItemFSLabel
- kMDItemFSOwnerUserID
- kMDItemFSSize
- kMDItemLastUsedDate

And notice also that some attributes are only for music files, such as the MP3:

- kMDItemAlbum
- kMDItemAudioBitRate
- kMDItemAudioTrackNumber
- kMDItemAuthors
- kMDItemDurationSeconds
- kMDItemMusicalGenre

Images have many special attributes too, but the format of the image is important too. Here's a PNG:

- kMDItemBitsPerSample
- kMDItemColorSpace
- kMDItemOrientation
- kMDItemPixelHeight
- kMDItemPixelWidth

And here's a JPEG—note how many of them are based on the camera that took the picture:

- kMDItemAcquisitionMake
- kMDItemAcquisitionModel
- kMDItemCreator
- kMDItemExposureTimeSeconds
- kMDItemFocalLength
- kMDItemKeywords
- kMDItemWhereFroms

This all comes from the mdls tool, and if you want to get more advanced in your usage of mdfind, you're going to have to get familiar with mdls.

NOTE: Apple has a list of Common Metadata Attribute Keys at
`http://developer.apple.com/mac/library/documentation/Carbon/Reference/Me`
`tadataAttributesRef/Reference/CommonAttrs.html`. This web page is very helpful,
especially as it also explains what each of the attributes means, but you're still going to have to
use `mdls` to get the full picture.

Learn About Search Operators

So now that we know the metadata associated with some files, how can we use it? You
construct `mdfind` searches that use the metadata attribute keys, and you get the keys
and the values you want to look for from `mdls`.

There are several operators you can use to format your query, some of which you'll see
in detail in the following pages. But you should know all the possibilities now for
reference, so here they are, in Table 3–2.

Table 3–2. *Operators that Can Be Used to Create a Spotlight Query on the Command Line*

Operators	Meaning
()	Nesting
==	Comparison: Equal
!=	Comparison: Not equal
<	Comparison: Less than
>	Comparison: More than
<=	Comparison: Less than or equal
>=	Comparison: More than or equal
||	Logical Or
&&	Logical And
InRange (attributeName,minValue,maxValue)	Numeric values within a range
*	Wildcard
\	Escape character

> **NOTE:** For more on the operators and how you can use them, see Apple's "Query Expression Syntax" at
> `http://developer.apple.com/mac/library/documentation/Carbon/Conceptual/S`
> `potlightQuery/Concepts/QueryFormat.html`.

With that out of the way, let's look at some examples.

Search for Files by Type (Kind)

You can use the attribute keys instead of the parameters I earlier showed you. For instance, instead of kind:, you can instead use kMDItemContentType:

```
$ mdfind -onlyin "$PWD" "kMDItemContentType == 'public.jpeg'"
/Users/rsgranne/Documents/Reading/Burroughs, Edgar Rice/Art/Frazetta - John Carter & the
Savage Apes of Mars.jpg
/Users/rsgranne/Documents/Reading/Burroughs, Edgar Rice/Art/Frazetta - A Princess of
Mars.jpg
/Users/rsgranne/Documents/Reading/Burroughs, Edgar Rice/Art/Frazetta - A Fighting Man of
Mars.jpg
/Users/rsgranne/Documents/Reading/Burroughs, Edgar Rice/Art/John Carter of Mars - action
figures.jpg
```

You can actually use any item in the kMDItemContentTypeTree key as a replacement for kind:, but remember that the key word in that attribute is Tree. Take a look at that attribute key for any JPEG:

```
kMDItemContentTypeTree = (
    "public.jpeg",
    "public.image",
    "public.data",
    "public.item",
    "public.content"
)
```

The list starts with the most specific type of content—public.jpeg—and proceeds down until it gets to the most general type of content: public.content, which matches almost every file on your Mac. So if you want to find all images—not just JPEGs, but all images—you could use this:

```
$ mdfind -onlyin "$PWD" "kMDItemContentTypeTree == 'public.image'"
/Users/rsgranne/Documents/Reading/Burroughs, Edgar Rice/Art/Frazetta - John Carter & the
Savage Apes of Mars.jpg
/Users/rsgranne/Documents/Reading/Burroughs, Edgar Rice/Art/Frazetta - A Princess of
Mars.jpg
/Users/rsgranne/Documents/Reading/Burroughs, Edgar Rice/Art/Frazetta - A Fighting Man of
Mars.jpg
/Users/rsgranne/Documents/Reading/Burroughs, Edgar Rice/Art/John Carter of Mars - action
figures.jpg
/Users/rsgranne/Documents/Reading/Burroughs, Edgar Rice/Art/Frazetta - John Carter of
Mars.png
/Users/rsgranne/Documents/Reading/Burroughs, Edgar Rice/Mars/02 - Gods of Mars.gif
```

> **NOTE:** Of course, if I removed `-inonly "$PWD"` from my search, I'd be looking over all volumes, which could come in handy if I had no idea where the files might be located.

With a little practice, you can get very precise when it comes to looking for files of a certain type. Just use `mdls` first on a sample file and you'll have the info you need.

For instance, here are a few values for `kMDItemContentType` that you might find handy to know (again, you can find these and more by running `mdls` against a sample file). I'm not going to tell you what they are, since you should be able to tell!

- `com.microsoft.word.doc`
- `com.adobe.pdf`
- `public.zip-archive`
- `com.apple.disk-image-udif`
- `com.apple.iwork.keynote.sffkey`

Search for Images Taken with a Particular Camera

You might have noticed that JPEGs (sometimes) have two attribute keys that pertain to the camera that took the picture: kMDItemAcquisitionMake and kMDItemAcquisitionModel. Here are two files with just those keys listed:

```
$ mdls "2010 0611 Mr. Sincere.jpg"
kMDItemAcquisitionMake        = "KONICA MINOLTA "
kMDItemAcquisitionModel       = "DiMAGE Z3"
$ mdls "2010 0613 Eating a bagle.jpg"
kMDItemAcquisitionMake        = "Apple"
kMDItemAcquisitionModel       = "iPhone 3GS"
```

You can use either of those in your searches. Say you want to find all the images on your hard drive that you took with your iPhone 3GS:

```
$ mdfind "kMDItemAcquisitionModel == 'iPhone 3GS'" -onlyin ~/Pictures/iPhoto\ Library
[Thousands of lines snipped]
```

OK, but what if I want to find pix snapped with my iPhone 3GS and original iPhone, but not with the iPhone 3G? Time to combine my search terms! But first I need to know the kMDItemAcquisitionModel for the original iPhone. I find a picture that I know was taken with the original iPhone and run `mdls` against it, discovering this:

```
$ mdls IMG_0371.JPG
kMDItemAcquisitionMake        = "Apple"
kMDItemAcquisitionModel       = "iPhone"
```

So now I have my answer. Time to build a search:

```
$ mdfind "kMDItemAcquisitionModel == 'iPhone 3GS' || kMDItemAcquisitionModel ==
'iPhone'" -onlyin ~/Pictures/iPhoto\ Library
[Thousands of lines snipped]
```

Notice how that query was constructed. Quotation marks surround the query itself, with the values inside quotation marks. Between the two key/value pairs is the | |, the OR logical operator.

Search for Images of a Particular Size

Two of the common attributes for all images are kMDItemPixelHeight and kMDItemPixelWidth. You can use them together to find images that are an exact size, and to do so, you'll need to use the AND logical operator. Here's an example:

```
$ mdfind "kMDItemPixelWidth == 1024 && kMDItemPixelHeight == 768" -onlyin
~/Pictures/iPhoto\ Library
/Users/rsgranne/Pictures/iPhoto Library/Originals/2010/Apr 15, 2010/IMG_0736.JPG
/Users/rsgranne/Pictures/iPhoto Library/Originals/2009/Nov 7, 2009/IMG_0321.JPG
```

NOTE: Notice that I didn't need to put apostrophes around the numbers. You need to do that only for text strings.

What if I wanted to find images of a particular size that are not JPEGs? Time for some nesting *and* comparision.

```
$ mdfind "(kMDItemPixelWidth == 1024 && kMDItemPixelHeight == 768) && kMDItemContentType
!= 'public.jpeg'" -onlyin ~/Pictures/iPhoto\ Library
/Users/rsgranne/Pictures/iPhoto Library/Originals/2006/Mar 26, 2006/1998 Portland
flower.bmp
```

There it is—that really cool picture from years ago! But how did my query work?

First, I needed to search for the dimensions, so I put it in parentheses for nesting purposes. Then I indicated that I was also looking for files that were not—hence the ! =— JPEGs. Put it all together inside the quotation marks, and you get the query shown.

Search for MP3s of a Particular Length and Bitrate

Spotlight's metadata for audio files contains several useful attribute keys that can help you zero in on the exact files you need. For instance, let's say you want MP3s and M4As (MPEG 4 Audio files) that are longer than five minutes and have been encoded at high bitrates.

So let's start with an easy piece: all MP3s that are over five minutes long. The key/value pair I need is kMDItemDurationSeconds >= 300, which looks for audio files that are longer than five minutes (which is 300 seconds):

```
$ mdfind -onlyin ~/Music "kMDItemContentType == 'public.mp3' && kMDItemDurationSeconds
>= 300"
/Users/rsgranne/Music/Music/Lucinda Williams/Little Honey/08 Jailhouse Tears.mp3
/Users/rsgranne/Music/Music/Lucinda Williams/Little Honey/07 If Wishes Were Horses.mp3
/Users/rsgranne/Music/Music/Levon Helm/Electric Dirt/01 Tennessee Jed.mp3
/Users/rsgranne/Music/Music/Big Star/Radio City/01 O My Soul.mp3
/Users/rsgranne/Music/Music/Crystal Method/Vegas/01 Trip Like I Do.mp3
```

OK, that worked. Now how about all MP3s and M4As that are over five minutes long? To find out how to refer to M4As, I used `mdls` on an M4A file and discovered that it's `public.mpeg-4-audio`, giving me this:

```
$ mdfind -onlyin ~/Music "(kMDItemContentType == 'public.mp3' || kMDItemContentType ==
'public.mpeg-4-audio') && kMDItemDurationSeconds >= 300"
/Users/rsgranne/Music/Louis Armstrong/Greatest Hits/03 Hello Dolly.m4a
/Users/rsgranne/Music/Louis Armstrong/Greatest Hits/01 April in Paris.m4a
/Users/rsgranne/Music/Music/Levon Helm/Electric Dirt/01 Tennessee Jed.mp3
/Users/rsgranne/Music/Music/Big Star/Radio City/01 O My Soul.mp3
/Users/rsgranne/Music/Music/Crystal Method/Vegas/01 Trip Like I Do.mp3
```

Now I'm starting to nest, since I want all audio files that are either `public.mp3` or `public.mpeg-4-audio`—which needs to be nested together—and are at least five minutes long. The `kMDItemDurationSeconds` goes at the end of the query because it is an attribute key that can be found for both MP3s and M4As.

I want audio files that have bit rates between 192 and 256, and when I use `mdls` to look at an MP3 file, I find that the attribute is `kMDItemAudioBitRate` and the value is `192000`. Ah—so the bitrates for the MP3s I want will be expressed as between 192000 and 256000. There are actually two ways I can express that range. I could do it with the AND operator, giving me this:

```
(kMDItemAudioBitRate >= 192000 && kMDItemAudioBitRate <= 256000)
```

Or, I could use the InRange operator that I discussed earlier in Table 3–1, which would be expressed this way:

```
InRange (kMDItemAudioBitRate,192000,256000)
```

Either one is fine, but I'm gonna go old skool and use the AND operator, giving me this query, in which I look for files that are either MP3 or M4A, and have bitrates betwen 192100 and 256000, and are longer than five minutes:

```
$ mdfind -onlyin ~/Music "(kMDItemContentType == 'public.mp3' || kMDItemContentType ==
'public.mpeg-4-audio') && (kMDItemAudioBitRate >= 192000 && kMDItemAudioBitRate <=
256000) && kMDItemDurationSeconds >= 300"
```

… and that didn't work. Hmmm. I figured that would do the job, but it didn't—M4As that I knew would match weren't showing up. Time to use `mdls` on an M4A file (I'll show you only the relevant part):

```
$ mdls 03\ Hello\ Dolly.m4a
kMDItemAudioBitRate = 320
```

Ohhh. MP3s have values in the thousands when it comes to `kMDItemAudioBitRate`, but M4As just measure the value in the tens or hundreds. That means that I'm going to have to associate the separate way in which each audio format reports `kMDItemAudioBitRate` with each individual audio format. More nesting!

First, though, let's test it and see if I can find M4As by bitrate. In the interests of mixing it up, I'm going to use the InRange operator with this one instead of the old skool && that I used with MP3s:

```
$ mdfind -onlyin ~/Music "kMDItemContentType == 'public.mpeg-4-audio' && InRange
(kMDItemAudioBitRate,192,256) && kMDItemDurationSeconds >= 300"
```

```
/Users/rsgranne/Music/Louis Armstrong/Greatest Hits/03 Hello Dolly.m4a
/Users/rsgranne/Music/Music/D'Angelo/Voodoo/09 Spanish Joint.m4a
```

That worked! OK, now to combine the whole furshlugginer mess into one big query:

```
$ mdfind -onlyin ~/Music "((kMDItemContentType == 'public.mp3' && (kMDItemAudioBitRate
>= 192000 && kMDItemAudioBitRate <= 256000)) || (kMDItemContentType == 'public.mpeg-4-
audio' && InRange (kMDItemAudioBitRate,192,256))) && kMDItemDurationSeconds >= 300"
/Users/rsgranne/Music/Louis Armstrong/Greatest Hits/03 Hello Dolly.m4a
/Users/rsgranne/Music/Music/D'Angelo/Voodoo/09 Spanish Joint.m4a
/Users/rsgranne/Music/Music/Lucinda Williams/Little Honey/08 Jailhouse Tears.mp3
/Users/rsgranne/Music/Music/Lucinda Williams/Little Honey/07 If Wishes Were Horses.mp3
/Users/rsgranne/Music/Music/Levon Helm/Electric Dirt/01 Tennessee Jed.mp3
```

Bee-yoo-teeful! That worked, but whew! That one is a citizen in the City of
Nestingopolis! I know there are a lot of parentheses there, but if you count them and
work your way from the inside out, you'll see that they all match and are all necessary.

This example should show you that you can construct some very precise queries using
Spotlight on the command line. You'll have to spend some time with `mdls`, but with
some patience and thought you can use `mdfind` to do some powerful things.

Construct Complex Queries Using Smart Folders

It's fun to come up with complex queries just using your brain, but we're using a
computer, so why not leverage the computer to construct those queries for us? Here's a
neat trick that isn't obvious, but once you know it, you'll find it to be a great time-saver.

Go to **File ➤ Find** (or press ⌘-F) while you're in the Finder, and the Spotlight query
window will open, shown in Figure 3–24.

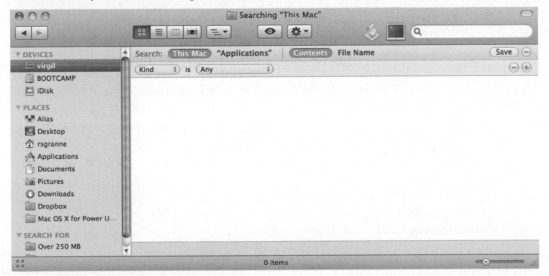

Figure 3–24. *What do you want to find today?*

Now use the UI to construct a complex query. Let's say I want to find MP3s by Louis Armstrong that have the word "Blues" in the title. I start by making sure my Finder window is in Music when I go to File ➤ Find so that the window opens ready to search in Music. I also change the search's area of interest from Contents to File Name.

Next, I choose Kind from the first select menu, and Music from the next select menu. When I do that, a third menu appears with a tiny few choices in it (too few, in my opinion), one of which is MP3, which I also choose. A lot of files appear, way more than I'm interested in, all of them MP3s. Louis is in there somewhere.

> **TIP:** If you want to learn more about Louis Armstrong and his music, you should check out *Pops: A Life of Louis Armstrong*, by Terry Teachout (Houghton Mifflin Harcourt, 2009), a fascinating and enjoyable biography. And then download *The Best of Louis Armstrong: The Hot Five and Hot Seven Recordings* (Sbme Special Mkts., 2009) and enjoy some of the greatest music ever made.

I have more details to add, so I click the + at the end of the row to add another attribute to my query. Now I need to add Louis Armstrong. Since there's nothing in the first select menu that applies, I choose Other at the bottom, which opens a sheet that allows me to select from a large number of additional attributes. The one I want is Authors, which seems a little strange, but it's correct (if you doubt me, use `mdls` on an MP3 and note where the artist's name is found). I can simply select it and click OK, or, if I know I'm going to be using it constantly, I can check the box under In Menu to make it a permanent part of the first select menu.

> **TIP:** My sheet of additional attributes has one that seems useful—`Artist`, described as "CDpedia artist attribute"—which has never once worked, much less been useful.

After I choose Authors, I'm back in the Search window, with Authors in the first select list. For the second I choose Contains, and in the text box that appears, I enter `Louis Armstrong`. Now I see far fewer audio files, just MP3s by Louis Armstrong. We're getting there!

Finally, it's time to find just those songs with "Blues" in the name. I click + to add another attribute, and from the first select list, I choose Name. In the second select list, I choose Contains, and in the text box, I enter `Blues`. And there are my results, which you can see in Figure 3–25.

Figure 3–25. *Blues played by Louis Armstrong—what could be better?*

NOTE: Yes, I know that you can't construct a query in the GUI that's as complex as the one I created in the last section. However, you can make the GUI a lot more useful. I'm going to get to that in the next section!

Now that's nice, but here's where it really gets cool. I've constructed a nice query that works like I want it to, so now I click the Save button in the Finder Search window to preserve my query as a Smart Folder. I give it a name—something clever like `Blues by Louis`—and save it in the default location, Saved Searches (which actually lives at `~/Library/Saved Searches`), making sure that Add To Sidebar is checked.

The new Smart Folder appears in the Finder sidebar, under Search For. If you click it, the search is performed and the results appear in the Finder. However, if you right-click on the saved search and choose Get Info, you'll find something very interesting in the resulting window, which I've zoomed in on in Figure 3–26.

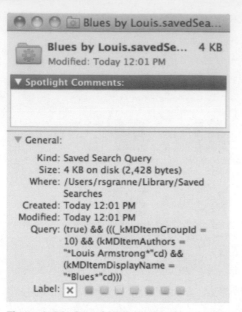

Figure 3–26. *Query? Well, that's new... and very useful!*

See the Query field? See what's after it? Recognize that sort of thing from what we did in the previous section? You should! Here's the whole thing:

```
(true) && (((_kMDItemGroupId = 10) && (kMDItemAuthors = "*Louis Armstrong*"cd) &&
(kMDItemDisplayName = "*Blues*"cd)))
```

> **NOTE:** If you're wondering about the cd that appears after Louis Armstrong and Blues, wait one moment—I'll explain it later in this section.

I'll remove the stuff at the very beginning, which I don't need, so I now have this:

```
(((_kMDItemGroupId = 10) && (kMDItemAuthors = "*Louis Armstrong*"cd) &&
(kMDItemDisplayName = "*Blues*"cd)))
```

If you look carefully, you'll figure out that we don't need all those parentheses at all, since there's no nesting in the query. So I can remove them, giving me this:

```
_kMDItemGroupId = 10 && kMDItemAuthors = "*Louis Armstrong*"cd && kMDItemDisplayName =
"*Blues*"cd
```

> **NOTE:** So why are the parentheses there? Because a computer is generating this stuff, and computers overdo things to try to cover any problems that stupid humans might introduce. The parentheses aren't a mistake or bad; they're just unnecessary.

If I cut and paste that into a typical mdfind query, and put the quotation marks around the query like I'm supposed to do, I'd get this:

```
$ mdfind -onlyin ~/Music "_kMDItemGroupId = 10 && kMDItemAuthors = "*Louis Armstrong*"cd
&& kMDItemDisplayName = "*Blues*"cd"
```

Trust me, that's not going to work. The quotation marks around Louis Armstrong and Blues will cause problems, so I need to format the query with apostrophes around text strings, like I've been doing in this chapter. Once I do that, I get this query:

```
$ mdfind -onlyin ~/Music "_kMDItemGroupId = 10 && kMDItemAuthors = '*Louis Armstrong*'cd
&& kMDItemDisplayName = '*Blues*'cd"
/Users/rsgranne/Music/Music/Compilations/Louis Armstrong Plays W.C. Handy/10 Hesitating
Blues.mp3
/Users/rsgranne/Music/Music/Compilations/Louis Armstrong Plays W.C. Handy/08 Ole Miss
Blues.mp3
/Users/rsgranne/Music/Music/Compilations/Louis Armstrong Plays W.C. Handy/07 Beale
Street Blues.mp3
```

That worked! So now you see how to use the Finder to create a Smart Folder, and then take the Query from the Get Info box to construct a query you can use with mdfind. You'll have to manipulate the query you copy from Get Info a little bit, but it can save you time—and you'll learn some new attribute keys. For instance, I certainly didn't know that another way to refer to MP3s is _kMDItemGroupId = 10. That could be useful.

Before we leave this section, though, what about the cd we saw, as in '*Louis Armstrong*'cd? Those are modifiers that you can apply to individual text strings within a query. You have three you can use, and you can combine them:

- c: Case insensitive
- d: Diacritical insensitive
- w: Word-based, and detects transitions from lower- to uppercase

So how would you use these? Here are a few examples:

- 'louis'c matches "Louis" and "louis" but not "Louis Armstrong"
- 'Louis'd matches "Louis" and "Louís"
- 'louis'w matches "Louis" and "louis" and also "Louis Armstrong" and "louis_armstrong.jpg"
- 'louis'cd matches "Louis", "louis", "Louís", and "louís", but not "Louis Armstrong", "Louís Armstrong", or "louis_armstrong.jpg"
- 'louis'cdw matches "Louis", "louis", "Louís", "louís", "Louis Armstrong", "Louís Armstrong", and "louis_armstrong.jpg"

These can be very helpful if case or diacritical marks matter for your query.

Use Complex Queries in Smart Folders

You undoubtedly noticed that the query that I created by building a Smart Folder was limited in several ways. Two big absences should leap out: no logical OR (the ||), and no nesting. There's a way around that, however. In the previous section, we built an mdfind query using what we generated from a Smart Folder; in this section, we're going to build a Smart Folder using an mdfind query. To quote Alfred Hitchcock's *Strangers on a Train* (Warner Bros., 1951), criss-cross! Criss-cross!

It's actually very easy. Here's the query that I created earlier (in "Search for MP3s of a Particular Length and Bitrate") that was used along with mdfind:

```
$ mdfind -onlyin ~/Music "((kMDItemContentType == 'public.mp3' && InRange
(kMDItemAudioBitRate,192000,256000)) || (kMDItemContentType == 'public.mpeg-4-audio' &&
(kMDItemAudioBitRate >= 192 && kMDItemAudioBitRate <= 256))) && kMDItemDurationSeconds
>= 300"
```

Copying just the query—the stuff inside the quotation marks—gives me this, which I copy to the clipboard:

```
((kMDItemContentType == 'public.mp3' && InRange (kMDItemAudioBitRate,192000,256000)) ||
(kMDItemContentType == 'public.mpeg-4-audio' && (kMDItemAudioBitRate >= 192 &&
kMDItemAudioBitRate <= 256))) && kMDItemDurationSeconds >= 300
```

Now I go to the Finder, navigate to ~/Music, and choose **File ➤ Find**, which opens the Finder's Search window, giving me something like back in Figure 3–24. Using the first select list, I choose Other, and then, in the sheet that lists all the additional attributes, I scroll down to Raw Query and choose that. Back in the Search window, I paste the contents of the clipboard into the text box next to Raw Query, and boom! The results show up immediately in the window, as you can see in Figure 3–27.

Figure 3–27. *Man, that Raw Query works like a charm!*

Is that not cool or what? If you need to create something complex, go ahead and do it, test it on the command line, and then paste it in to a Finder search as a Raw Query. Click Save to preserve it as a Saved Search, and you have the best of both worlds. That is just fantastic!

Further Resources

Spotlight is an awesome tool, whether in the GUI or on the command line, but there are alternatives. One of the best is the Google Quick Search Box (QSB), which actually integrates Spotlight's results (if you tell it to). However, the QSB can go way beyond Spotlight, even incorporating results from Google, Google Docs, Picasa, Wikipedia, and much more. If you use GlimmerBlocker, read an article at MacOSXHints.com that will help you integrate GlimmerBlocker keywords into your QSB results (www.macosxhints.com/article.php?story=2009091410132731). Heck, you can use it to post to Twitter!

The software and basic documentation is available at www.google.com/quicksearchbox, but Google open sourced the project, and the latest and greatest code and help is now at http://code.google.com/p/qsb-mac/. Be sure to read all the documentation you can find, as the QSB has a lot of features that are not obvious at first glance, but once you learn them, they'll become an integral part of your Mac use.

> **NOTE:** Those of you who use Quicksilver (www.blacktree.com) should recognize the Google QSB as very similar in many ways to Quicksilver. That's no surprise, since the initial developer of Quicksilver got hired by Google and went on to develop the QSB!

Summary

This has been a long chapter, which is strange considering that it was all about taking some of the most common, basic things in Mac OS X—the Dock, the Finder, and Spotlight—and making them better. That's not because those three things are terrible, because they're not. Millions of Mac users happily launch programs, manage files, and search for content on their computers every day. But you can definitely improve those three key software tools, and power users love to improve things they use, especially those things they use every day. This chapter has given you lots of improvements to try, and now it's up to you to test them and adopt the ones that make you productive and happy. Have fun!

Using Safari to Its Fullest

Apple has put a lot of spit and polish into Safari, and it shows. It's fast, attractive, and powerful, all typical for Apple software and products. At the same time, it's intentionally limited in the name of simplicity and control by Apple—there's still no official extension architecture, for instance! In this section, I'll show you how to soup up Safari to be even better—and I'll show you how to get around Apple's limitations on extensions.

NOTE: Right before this book was going to press, Apple released Safari 5, which contains many new features:

- The JavaScript engine is 30% faster.

- The Bing search engine is an additional option.

- Safari Reader (**View ➤ Enter Reader**) removes all the unnecessary junk off a web page so you can read it without distractions.

- Extensions!

Yes, Safari now supports extensions, and there are many excellent ones for you to install and use. You can visit the official list maintained and vetted by Apple (**Safari ➤ Safari Extensions Gallery**, or go to http://extensions.apple.com), or you can check out the massive, unofficial yet still very useful list at http://safariextensions.tumblr.com. Here are a few of my favorites:

- Sessions
  Save and reload groups of tabs when you restart Safari. Way better than going to **History ➤ Reopen All Windows From Last Session**.

- Better Facebook
  Makes Facebook a lot better to use. Warning: there are a lot of options here!

- Google Reader Background Tabs and Better Google Reader
  Makes using Google Reader bearable on Safari.

■ Coda Notes
  Annotate Web pages and then mail off a screenshot.

■ JavaScript Blacklist
  Die, Tynt, IntelliTXT, and Snap, die!

As you read this chapter, you may notice references to Safari lacking extensions. Now you know the truth!

Speeding Up Safari

Safari is wicked fast (although Google Chrome can feel faster at times), but in my experience with it, I've found two built-in features that can cause slowdowns, during which the browser feels like it's stuck in molasses.

WebpageIcons.db

The first of these involves the favicon database that Safari uses. *Favicons* (yes, that's the spelling) are the little icons that websites use, icons that usually appear to the left of a website's URL in a browser's Address Bar and in your list of bookmarks. They're not required for websites; instead, they help brand a website while making it easier for you to find it in your bookmarks and history.

> **NOTE:** For more on favicons, see Wikipedia's article, at
> `http://en.wikipedia.org/wiki/Favicon`.

Safari stores the favicons of all the websites you visit in a database file, located at `~/Library/Safari/WebpageIcons.db`. The problem is that the more websites you visit, the fatter that database grows, and the slower Safari becomes. If you close Safari, delete WebpageIcons.db, and then start Safari back up, it will be speedy again—at the cost of lost favicons, which to me is no big deal. Sure, they're cute, but if they slow down your web browser, to heck with 'em (this is a Safari problem, by the way—other Web browsers don't have this issue).

You have several choices about how to deal with WebpageIcons.db:

■ Manually delete it

■ Automatically delete it

■ Permanently delete it

Let's quickly look at each of those options.

Manually delete the file whenever you notice Safari is starting to get slow. You could do this, but why wait until there's a problem? And why not automate things so you don't even have to worry about it? Still, this is a good method if your Safari never seems to slow down due to a bloated WebpageIcons.db file.

Automatically delete the file on a timed basis. Open Automator and create an iCal Alarm. Your workflow will consist of six parts. In order, they are:

1. **Utilities ➤ Run AppleScript**. Replace the default code with the following:

```
activate application "Safari"
tell application "System Events"
        try
                tell process "Safari"
                        keystroke "q" using command down
                        try
                                click button "Quit" of window 1
                        end try
                end tell
        end try
end tell
```

> **WARNING:** The code in step 1 will not work if you previously went into **Safari ➤ Preferences ➤ Tabs** and unchecked **Confirm Before Closing Multiple Tabs Or Windows**. If you did that, either check the box again, or use this code instead:
>
> ```
> on run {input, parameters}
>         tell application "System Events"
>                 if exists (some process whose name contains "Safari") then
>                         tell application "Safari" to quit
>                 end if
>         end tell
> end run
> ```

2. **Utilities ➤ Run Shell Script**. Replace the default code with this:

```
if [-e $HOME/Library/Safari/WebpageIcons.db]
then
 rm $HOME/Library/Safari/WebpageIcons.db
fi
```

3. **Utilities ➤ Pause**. Set it to ten seconds. This gives the script time to finish. If, when you test it, it's not enough, feel free to increase it, but remember that it will be longer the first time if you've never deleted WebpageIcons.db file before.

4. **Utilities ➤ Launch Application**. Select Safari.

5. **Utilities ➤ Pause**. Set it to ten seconds.

6.   Utilities ➤ Run AppleScript. Replace the default code with the following:

```
tell application "System Events"
        tell process "Safari"
                click menu item "Reopen All Windows from Last Session" of menu 1 of menu
bar item "History" of menu bar 1
        end tell
end tell
```

> **NOTE:** In order for this to work at all, you must have first gone to **Apple ➤ System Preferences ➤ Universal Access ➤ Seeing** and checked the box next to Enable Access For Assistive Devices.

Test the Automator workflow by clicking the Run button. Usually you'll see failure at step 6, which means you need to increase the length of time in step 5. Do so in increments of ten seconds at a time until you hit the magic number for your Mac.

Once everything works to your satisfaction, go to **File ➤ Save**. Remember that iCal will open, allowing you to set up your alarm according to when you want to run the workflow. Once a week should be sufficient, but feel free to alter as you desire.

Permanently delete the file so you never have to worry about it. This is the hardcore solution, for those who don't care about favicons. If you want to go this route, the easiest thing to do is open the Secrets Preference Pane, select Safari in the left pane, and then uncheck the box next to Enable Favicon Database (which is equivalent to entering defaults write com.apple.Safari WebIconDatabaseEnabled -bool NO in Terminal).

The choice is up to you. Keep in mind that you can always reverse whatever you choose by deleting the iCal Alarm or by re-checking the box next Enable Favicon Database in Secrets, so pick the solution that best meets your needs.

Top Sites

The second thing that can really slow down Safari is a new features introduced in Safari 4 called Top Sites. As you can see in Figure 4–1, it displays thumbnails of the websites you've visited so you can easily choose to go to a site again. You can easily make Top Sites very prevalent within Safari (by going to Safari's Preferences, then choosing Top Sites for both New Windows Open With and New Tabs Open With, and by setting the Home Page to topsites:—yes, with the colon).

Figure 4–1. *Top Sites shows screen shots of your most-visited websites.*

Although it's much better now, at one point, Top Sites was causing Safari to open painfully slooooooow. If this happens to you, there are several ways to fix the problem.

Start with deleting existing web-site screenshots by going to Safari ➤ Reset Safari. Uncheck everything except Remove All Webpage Preview Images and click OK (to do this manually, empty out ~/Library/Caches/com.apple.Safari/Webpage Previews).

After that, hide Top Sites from view by reversing the choices made a few paragraphs back, so it doesn't show up when you open new windows or tabs (I like to set these to just use empty pages, as it's quicker), and change your Home Page to something else.

To completely disable Top Sites, close Safari, open the Secrets Preference Pane, choose Safari on the left pane of the window, and then uncheck Enable Top Sites (the same thing as opening Terminal and running defaults write com.apple.Safari DebugSnapshotsUpdatePolicy -int 2; to reverse it and re-enable Top Sites, run defaults delete com.apple.Safari DebugSnapshotsUpdatePolicy).

If you've disabled Top Sites, there's no reason to still have a Top Sites button on your Safari toolbar, so you should remove that. Do so by going to **Safari ➤ Preferences ➤ Bookmarks** and unchecking Include Top Sites.

> **WARNING:** If you disable Top Sites, you also remove the website screenshots that show up when you view Safari's History in Cover Flow mode. That might be enough to stop many people from disabling Top Sites altogether, and instead emptying it out periodically using Reset Safari, as shown previously.

Be sure you understand me when it comes to Top Sites: I am not advocating messing with the Top Sites features unless Safari is starting or running slowly. In that case, it may be necessary to go through the previous steps, trying the first one and then testing to see if that fixes the problem. If it does, great; if it doesn't, try the next, more drastic step, and give that a whirl. Top Sites is a cool addition to Safari, and it would be a shame to disable it if it's not necessary.

Enabling the Develop Menu

If you're a Web developer and you use Safari (which is a silly statement, since any good Mac-using Web developer would at least use Safari to test her sites!), you're undoubtedly familiar with the Develop menu. Hidden by default, it's easy to turn this menu on: go to **Safari ➤ Preferences ➤ Advanced** and check the box next to Show Develop Menu In Menu Bar.

> **NOTE:** If you're still using an older version of Safari, you can enable the menu by opening the Secrets pref pane, selecting Safari in the left pane, and then checking the box next to Enable Web Inspector (which is the same thing as entering `defaults write com.apple.Safari WebKitDeveloperExtras -bool true` into Terminal, with `defaults write com.apple.Safari WebKitDeveloperExtras -bool false` hiding the menu once again).

Once you do so, a bevy of treats for Web devs appears, which you can see in Figure 4–2. I'm not going to go into most of them, since this isn't a book for people who make web pages, but I do want to call out a few items of general interest.

Open Page With	▶
User Agent	▶
Show Web Inspector	⌥⌘I
Show Error Console	⌥⌘C
Show Snippet Editor	
Start Debugging JavaScript	
Start Profiling JavaScript	⌥⇧⌘P
Disable Caches	
Disable Images	
Disable Styles	
Disable JavaScript	
Disable Runaway JavaScript Timer	
Disable Site-specific Hacks	

Figure 4–2. *Safari's Develop menu has some very useful items in it.*

Open Page With can be wonderfully useful if you want to view a particular web page in another browser. Safari automagically detects all the other Web browsers on your Mac and lists them in alphabetical order in this menu, so if you hit a web page that doesn't look right in Safari, it's a simple matter to switch to Firefox, Google Chrome, or something else (assuming those browsers are installed, of course).

User Agent allows you to fool websites by hiding your real identity—Safari on a Mac—to instead present yourself as Safari on Windows, or Mobile Safari on an iPhone, or Firefox on Windows, or even Internet Explorer on you know what. Run into a website that (stupidly) won't let you use it because you're running Safari on a Mac? Try switching your User Agent to something more to that website's taste and see if things work. If they still don't, try Open Page With instead. Later, fire an e-mail to that website's owner asking him why he doesn't want to support Web standards.

Even if you're not a Web developer, the Develop menu can be a handy thing to have in Safari's arsenal, so I don't see a reason why you shouldn't enable it. It could really come in handy.

Picking the Best Add-ons

If you use Firefox or Chrome, you have thousands of extensions available to you that you can download and add to your Web browser. Apple, however, has never officially supported extensions for Safari that modify how the browser acts (it does, however, support plug-ins such as Flash, QuickTime, and the like). Prior to Snow Leopard, developers were able to utilize Input Managers, software built into Mac OS X by Apple, to create pseudo-extensions for Safari. That really wasn't a good thing, however, and Apple altered the way Safari works with Input Managers in Snow Leopard.

To understand why Apple did this, and why it's ultimately a good thing that the company did so, let's first look at why Apple included Input Managers in Mac OS X at all. Brad Choate explains the reasons in his post "Input Managers and Leopard" (http://bradchoate.com/weblog/2008/03/01/input-managers-and-leopard), taken from his blog:

> *The original intent of Input Managers was to provide a means for customizing the operation of the keyboard and/or mouse to support things like locale-specific input behavior (treating keyboard input differently for different languages or regions) and software that aids handicapped individuals. The name "Input Manager" is thus appropriate for these intended uses. ...*

> *However, it wasn't long before Mac developers found this to be a useful way to graft additional functionality into other applications. There are several OS X software products out there that are input managers which have little to do with input management ... These products are typically unstable in nature, since they often times rely on undocumented aspects of the "host" application. But when they work, they can add real useful functionality to other programs.*

> *The downside to Input Managers is that it is a tempting means for rogue software to exploit.*

John Gruber, in his post "Smart Crash Reports" (http://daringfireball.net/2006/01/smart_crash_reports) on his widely read Mac blog Daring Fireball, explains another big problem with Input Managers:

> *Input managers are loaded by most Mac OS X applications—including all Cocoa apps, but also many modern Carbon apps as well—soon after they launch.*

> *The supported purpose for input managers is to allow developers to define new ways for users to enter text. However, the code in an input manager can pretty much do what it wants to inside an application's address space, and so thus, input managers have turned into an unofficial channel for hacking system and application behavior. E.g., most of the hacks euphemistically described as "plug-ins" on Jon Hicks's Pimp My Safari website—such as Saft and PithHelmet—are input manager hacks. "Plug-ins" implies the use of a legitimate API intended for extending or modifying an application; Safari, unfortunately, has no plug-in API,*

so any developer wishing to extend or modify Safari must resort to unsupported mechanisms such as input managers.

As stated before, every installed input manager loads into (nearly) every application. Input managers that are targeting one specific application, such as the way Saft and PithHelmet patch Safari ..., typically perform some identifier checking so as only to deliver their actual payload inside the application they're targeting. But, no bones about it, the nature of input managers is such that they're loaded into every app on your system. The basic gist is that when they're loaded, they check to see whether this app is the app they're looking to patch, and if it isn't, do nothing more.

Prior to Leopard, Input Managers could reside anywhere. Starting with Leopard, they were still allowed, but Input Managers had to reside in /Library/InputManagers. Snow Leopard changed this entirely. Along with the move to 64-bit apps system-wide in Snow Leopard came a new restriction: 64-bit apps can't use Input Managers.

NOTE: You can get around this restriction easily, if you'd like—right-click on Safari in /Applications, choose Get Info, and check the box next to Open In 32-Bit Mode. Since Safari will then run in 32-bit mode, the restrictions on Input Managers will vanish. This is a bad idea, however. The 64-bit apps in Snow Leopard bring better performance, especially when it comes to JavaScript, so you would be hobbling Safari in important ways in order to bring yourself minor benefits. In addition, the 64-bit Safari sandboxes plug-ins such as Flash and Java into processes separate from Safari, so that when those plug-ins crash, Safari continues to run unaffected. 32-bit Safari bundles everything together, so when Flash crashes, Safari crashes.

Since Safari can't use Input Managers any longer, several so-called extensions no longer function. That doesn't mean that there aren't add-ons for Safari—there are still very clever, legitimate ways for apps to work like extensions in Safari—but it does mean that several no longer work. In addition to those "extensions" that no longer work are those that have proven to be problematic and should be dropped, and those that are no longer actively developed. Gentle readers, I present you with ... the Safari Add-On Dead Pool!

NOTE: Want to find out a clever way that some of these add-ons are able to work under the new 64-bit Safari? Read Kevin Ballard's "1Password extension loading in Snow Leopard," available at http://kevin.sb.org/2009/09/02/1password-extension-loading-in-snow-leopard/.

The Safari Add-On Dead Pool

Inquisitor: This add-on made the Search Bar in Safari much handier by giving you more suggestions matching your query while also making it easy to move your search to a different search engine. Although it's still available for download at `www.inquisitorx.com/safari/index_en.php`, it doesn't work at all with Snow Leopard. Now you know why!

Google Gears: Gears (`http://gears.google.com`) allowed browsers to store and access data offline, but Google never updated it for Snow Leopard. In an official blog post dated February 19, 2010 and titled "Hello HTML5" (`http://gearsblog.blogspot.com/2010/02/hello-html5.html`), Google announced it was ending support for Gears and moving to HTML5 for offline storage.

PithHelmet: An ad-, annoyance-, and cookie-blocker, PithHelmet (`www.culater.net/software/PithHelmet/`) doesn't work in Snow Leopard, the sure sign of an Input Manager.

Saft: One of the most feature-filled Input Manager–based extensions for Safari, Saft (`http://haoli.dnsalias.com/Saft/`) no longer works with Snow Leopard unless you run Safari in 32-bit mode. That's just as well—the registration and payment system the developer uses is cumbersome and annoying, so good riddance.

There are others in the Safari dead pool, but those are some of the biggies. The point is, if a quote-unquote extension doesn't work in Snow Leopard's Safari, it's probably something you should avoid anyway.

Glims

Glims is a powerful, free add-on for Safari that adds a lot of very nice features. A lot of people love it, but I removed it from my Mac a while ago because it was causing Safari to move like a tree sloth high on opiates. That said, it might work beautifully for you, so at least give it a try (and when I later tried it again for this book, things seemed better).

You can download it at `www.machangout.com`. Once installed, Glims shows up as another screen in Safari's Preferences, as shown in Figure 4–3.

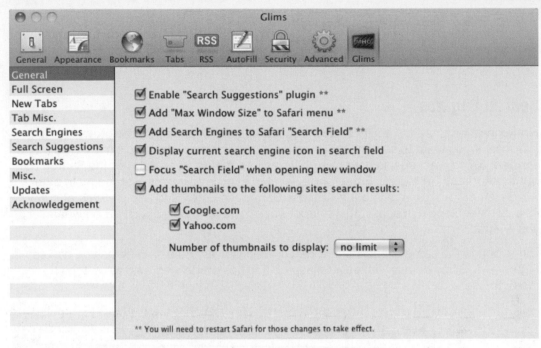

Figure 4–3. *Glims and its many features appears in Safari's Preferences.*

The ten sub-screens run down the left side and offer a wide number of settings and changes to Safari, many of them quite beneficial. I can't go over all of them, but let me point a few out, by screen.

General

Enable Search Suggestions Plugin: Start typing in the Search Bar, and suggestions appear for various websites, along with snippets and icons from the sites. The number of results and the information that shows up depend upon what you select on the Search Suggestions screen.

Add Thumbnails To The Following Sites [sic] Search Results: Check the boxes next to Google and Yahoo, and when you search those sites, thumbnails for each site in the list appear next to each result.

Tab Misc.

Re-Open Last Session When Safari Starts: If Safari crashes or you quit it, when you start the program back up, Safari—alone of all major Web browsers on the Mac—doesn't automatically restore your tabs and windows (your "session," in other words). Sure, you can go to **History ➤ Reopen All Windows From Last Session**, but if you check this box, it'll happen without any work required by you.

Undo Close Tab: Ever accidentally closed a tab in Safari? To restore it, you need to open a new tab, then go to the History menu and find it there. Check this box, and you just press ⌘-Z, which is much easier and accurate, and conforms to the Mac conventions for Undo. Why doesn't Apple just do this?

Search Engines

Firefox has long had the ability to add website-specific searches to the browser. For instance, if you want to search Google Images for "shih tzu," you can simply type a shortcut to the website and your search terms into the Address Bar (not the Search Bar, but the Address Bar), press Enter, and see the results load in your web page. In other words, enter gi shih tzu into the Address Bar, press Enter, and see pictures of cute little dogs at Google Images. The shortcut doesn't have to be gi; it could be whatever you wanted.

Glims brings the same capabilities to Safari, which is very cool. In fact, as you can see in Figure 4–4, Glims comes with several search engines predefined for you so they're ready to use.

Figure 4–4. *Glims makes searching from the Safari Address Bar easy.*

If you don't like one of the search engines—let's say you never search at Yahoo, for instance—you can easily delete it by selecting it and clicking Remove. If you want to edit the keyword for a search engine—say you want to invoke Bing by typing b instead of bi—then select it, click Edit, and make your change.

And if you want to add a new search engine, go to its website in Safari and perform a simple search. So if I wanted a new search shortcut for Apple's Support site, I'd head there (www.apple.com/support/) in Safari and search for something like iPhone. Copy the complete URL from Safari's Address Bar, which will look something like this:

```
http://support.apple.com/kb/index?page=search&src=support_site.home&locale=en_US&q=iPhone
```

Replace iPhone (or whatever term you used) with #query# so that it now looks like this:

```
http://support.apple.com/kb/index?page=search&src=support_site.home&locale=en_US&q=#query#
```

Copy that, open Glims in Safari's Preferences, choose Search Engines, and click Add. Fill in the fields as follows:

Name: Apple Support (you can use whatever you'd like, but be descriptive)

Type: Search Engine

Query URL: Paste the URL with #query# here

Keyword: appsup (or whatever you'd like to use and can remember)

Click Add and close Safari's Preferences. Now when you'd like to search Apple's Support site, just enter "appsup" followed by your search terms into Safari's Address Bar and press Enter. It's that easy!

Bookmarks

Safari has a nice manager for bookmarks, but Glims finds a couple of ways to make it more efficient.

Replace Bookmark Titled "-" With Menu Separator: Like to group bookmarks with a horizontal rule between groups? Create a bookmark with a hyphen for a title and Glims turns it into a horizontal rule. Neatniks rejoice!

Enable Action "Add Folder Here" In Bookmark Bar Menu: To create a folder for a group of bookmarks, you would normally go to Bookmarks ➤ Show All Bookmarks, select the folder into which you want to insert a new folder, and then go to Bookmarks ➤ Add Bookmark Folder (or press ⇧-⌘-N). With this feature enabled in Glims, you click on Bookmarks, navigate to the place in which you'd like the folder, and select Add Folder Here from the list of options at the bottom of the menu. Boom! Instant bookmark folder.

Enable Action "Add Bookmark Here" In Bookmark Bar Menu: The same concept as the previous feature, but for bookmarks themselves instead of folders.

Glims Annoyances

All of these nice features—and they are quite nice—don't hide the fact that Glims has some glaring annoyances, beyond the whole slowness issue that I've experienced. In order to uninstall Glims, you have to download a separate uninstaller from the program's website, at www.machangout.com/faq, which always causes me to grate my teeth.

Another thing that rubs me the wrong way is the cutesy tone that the developers use when talking about themselves and their software. Both in the installer and on the website, the developers say that "We are a group of kids having fun so please don't take us too seriously." That's nice, but we're talking about software that can screw up a major component of an operating system, so I need to take their work seriously, indeed. On top of that, nowhere do they identify themselves, so we have no idea who's creating Glims, which doesn't exactly inspire confidence.

Others might object to the way that Glims rewrites links to Amazon and eBay so that a referral fee is paid to the developers when you buy things on those websites. The "kids" are upfront about this, stating in the installer and on the Acknowledgements screen of Glims that:

> *When you use our plugin and click on an Amazon or eBay result that we formatted, you support our project. Amazon and eBay gives us a small percentage in referral fees on all qualifying revenue made through their links. Please note that this only happens on our formatted links. Other websites or links are not reformatted.*

I personally wouldn't mind this if I knew who these "kids" were, but since they refuse to tell me who they are.... Not to mention, if I was a person or organization who had my own affiliate links to Amazon and eBay set up, this would enrage me—how dare these people rewrite my links without a way to disable this on certain sites! The developers should make this voluntary, not mandatory; most people won't have a problem with it, but those that do should be able to disable it to serve their own needs.

Finally, if you are using Saft (which I mentioned previously and do not recommend), you really shouldn't use Glims too. The developers behind Glims warn that you could experience "unexpected results" if you try to run both at the same time, which makes sense, since there's so much overlap between the two programs.

Xmarks

One browser extension I immediately install on any of my browsers running on any of my computers, Mac or otherwise, is Xmarks. It's a no-brainer, as it's free, performs a vital service, and works bee-yoo-tifully. What's it do? It synchronizes my bookmarks among all my browsers (Mozilla Firefox, Internet Explorer, Google Chrome, and Apple Safari—no Opera), so they're the same everywhere. Add a new bookmark in Firefox? It'll show up soon in Safari. Rename a bookmark folder in Safari? See it change in Chrome. Delete a bookmark while holding my nose and running Internet Explorer on Windows? Firefox will soon enough remove the same bookmark. Like I said, absolutely vital!

NOTE: Xmarks began life as an extension for Firefox called Foxmarks, but in 2009 it changed its name to Xmarks as it began to work on browsers besides Firefox.

Another neat thing about Xmarks: in addition to syncing your bookmarks between your Web browsers, you can also access them by logging in to `https://my.xmarks.com` (it's a secure site—note the "s" in "https"). Once there, you can view, add, change, or delete bookmarks, and even perform various other tasks, which I'll cover in subsequent pages.

Xmarks is available from its website, at `www.xmarks.com`, or you can go directly to the download page for all the various browsers it supports at `http://download.xmarks.com/download/all/`. Understand that the Xmarks you download for Safari works only for Safari; if you want Xmarks for Firefox or Chrome, you need to download those separately.

This difference becomes very obvious when you install Xmarks. Firefox and Chrome install Xmarks as browser extensions that you access inside those browsers. Since Safari doesn't have a built-in extensions architecture, Xmarks for that browser ends up installed as a Preference Pane in System Preferences, under Other, as you can see in Figure 4–5.

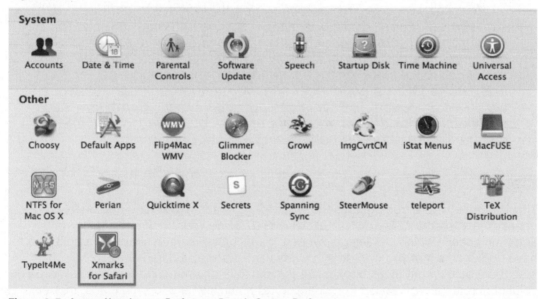

Figure 4–5. *Access Xmarks as a Preference Pane in System Preferences.*

Open that pref pane and you can start configuring and using Xmarks. I'm going to walk you through each screen of Xmarks, pointing out important stuff that you should notice and set.

General

Current Status: Shows you if Xmarks is running or not. To stop it for some reason, click the Stop Xmarks button; click that button again to restart the service. Below the current status indicator is a box that shows you the last date and time Xmarks synced your bookmarks, along with a button labeled Synchronize Now that lets you sync immediately.

Enable Automatic Synchronization: Check this box so syncing happens in the background, all the time. If you want total control, uncheck this box, which means you'll have to manually click Synchronize Now when you want Xmarks to do its thing.

Launch At Login: Check this so that Xmarks loads when you log in to your Mac. Again, this is for convenience, so it's always running for you. On my MacBook Pro, an idling Xmarks takes up 0% of my CPU and around 50MB of RAM, which isn't bad at all.

Detect Local Bookmark Changes: I'll let Eric, an Xmarks employee, explain what this means and why you might want to disable it (http://getsatisfaction.com/foxmarks/ topics/help_with_feature_description):

> *The option in Xmarks for Safari is available because the OS X sync code we use for detecting local bookmark changes can sometimes report false positives, causing Xmarks for Safari to synchronize more frequently than it really needs to. With that option disabled ..., Xmarks simply synchronizes on a regular basis and finds bookmark changes during synchronization rather than listening to OS X's announcements regarding bookmark changes, which can often be misleading from our narrower sync perspective. Kind of a roundabout way of saying: Feel free to disable it if Xmarks is synchronizing too frequently.*

Profiles

This is a neat feature from Xmarks that will be vital to some folks and completely unnecessary to others. Basically, it allows you to divide your bookmarks into profiles, and then specify which profiles get synced to which browsers. A simple example: you have bookmarks that you want to sync between Firefox and Safari on your personal Mac, but you do want those bookmarks to sync to IE on your Windows box at work. The solution: create a profile titled Personal and tell Xmarks where to sync it and, more importantly, where not to sync it.

Xmarks has a page at http://wiki.foxmarks.com/wiki/Product_Features: _Sync_Profiles that explains how to set Profiles up. Rather than regurgitate their concise explanation, I'll just point you there.

If you do use Profiles for your bookmarks, this screen in the Xmarks pref pane is where you determine which profiles you want to sync to Safari.

Advanced

Encryption: I can see absolutely no reason why you shouldn't select Encrypt All. If encryption is offered, take it!

Overwrite Server Bookmarks With Local Bookmarks: If you decide to do some big-time spring cleaning on your bookmarks in Safari and want to overwrite everything Xmarks has stored on its servers with your shiny new collection from Safari, click this button. If you stepped in it and blew away bookmarks you shouldn't have, don't panic. Log in to http://my.xmarks.com, go to Tools ➤ Explore & Restore Old Bookmarks, and revert to an earlier set of bookmarks.

Overwrite Local Bookmarks With Server Bookmarks: This is the reverse of the previous feature. If you know the server set of bookmarks is absolutely correct and you want to blow away the set that Safari is using, click this button. I've found this to be very helpful—just be sure to log in to www.myxmarks.com and verify that everything is copacetic *before* you use it!

Display Xmarks Status In The Menu Bar: I uncheck this, as I don't need yet another icon in my Mac's menu bar, especially since I check the box next to the next feature, listed after this one.

Use Growl For Sync Notifications: Instead of an icon on my Mac's menu bar, I prefer a Growl notification. It appears for a few seconds and then vanishes, letting me know that my bookmarks have synced. Perfect.

Network: You probably don't need to enter a proxy at all, but if you do, enter it here.

About

Automatically Check For Updates: Check this. Why not?

By now, I hope you see how useful Xmarks is. One final word on privacy: while individual users of Xmarks cannot see other people's bookmarks, it is true that Xmarks' employees could see your bookmarks. Obviously, this would completely destroy their business once word of such a grave privacy violation got out, so I don't worry too much about that happening. If you're still paranoid, however, don't use Xmarks with Safari and instead only use it with Firefox. With that particular browser, you can store your bookmarks on your own WebDAV or FTP server, completely bypassing Xmarks' servers altogether (that's not all the Firefox version of Xmarks does, as you'll see later in this chapter).

GlimmerBlocker

There are legitimate reasons to block ads on websites; likewise, there are legitimate reasons *not* to block ads on websites. I'm not going to get into the debate here, other than to point out a very powerful tool for blocking ads and web annoyances. If you don't think it's ethical to use an ad blocker, then by all means, don't; if you do, read on. But do be aware that this particular software lets you get as fine-grained as you'd like, allowing you to view ads on the websites you want to support while blocking them on websites that run abusive, obnoxious ads.

The name of this software is GlimmerBlocker, and it's a doozy. It's not an Input Manager or hack; instead, it's a free, open source proxy server that installs as a Preference Pane in System Preferences and intercepts Safari's requests for ads and stops them. Because it's not a Safari hack, but instead something that Safari's network connections interact with, you can upgrade Safari at any time without having to worry about its compatibility with GlimmerBlocker.

In fact, it's not just for Safari. Since it's a system-wide proxy server, any app that relies on the Network pref pane's proxy settings will use GlimmerBlocker, so ads are blocked in virtually every Internet-accessing program on your Mac.

> **TIP:** Firefox users have an extension that does much of what GlimmerBlocker does: AdBlock Plus, available at https://addons.mozilla.org/en-US/firefox/addon/1865. It's fantastic at blocking ads, but, unlike GlimmerBlocker, that's all it does, and it works only for Firefox. That said, you can set Firefox to use GlimmerBlocker if you want and skip AdBlock Plus; if you're interested, check out http://glimmerblocker.org/wiki/Firefox.

Let's first make sure it's working, and then I'll walk you through each of GlimmerBlocker's screens to hit the high points.

Download GlimmerBlocker at http://glimmerblocker.org and install it. To verify that it's running, you need to look at two Preference Panes in System Preferences: GlimmerBlocker and Network.

After installing it, go to **Apple ➤ System Preferences ➤ GlimmerBlocker**. On the Setup screen, Activate GlimmerBlocker should be checked. If it's not, check it. Now go to the Network screen and notice the Proxy Port Number that GlimmerBlocker uses: 8228. That's it for GlimmerBlocker.

Now head to **System Preferences ➤ Network** and select your connection from the left side (AirPort, in my case), then click Advanced. On the resulting screen, pick the Proxies tab. Web Proxy (HTTP) should be checked; if you select it by clicking on the line (don't uncheck it!), you should see that the Web Proxy Server has been set to 127.0.0.1, with the port number at 8228, the port that GlimmerBlocker is using. At the bottom, Bypass Proxy Settings For These Hosts & Domains should have this in it: `*.local, 169.254/16`. Finally, Use Passive FTP Mode (PASV) should be checked. If this is all correct—and it should be out of the box—click OK to close the network interface settings so you're back at the Network pref pane. Time to go back to GlimmerBlocker and check out its settings!

Setup

Activate GlimmerBlocker: I already mentioned this setting, which needs to be checked or the program ain't gonna work!

Automatically Check For Updates To GlimmerBlocker: I see no reason not to check this. You want to keep the program up-to-date, don't you?

Filters

This is a key screen, as the stuff that gets blocked is determined here. Five categories of filters are provided with GlimmerBlocker, but only three are checked:

- **Ad-networks:** This is the hardest-working filter on the screen, the one that blocks ads from atdmt.com, doubleclick.com, and other websites whose sole purpose is delivering ads. It's truly amazing how many ads get blocked thanks solely to this filter.

- **Site-specific Ad Removal:** This one blocks annoying (read: animated, loud, or obnoxious) ads run on specific websites.

- **Safari Keyword Expansions:** Earlier I discussed how Glims lets you define keywords that you can use to search websites from the Address Bar, so that if you type g H.P. Lovecraft a search at Google is done for H.P. Lovecraft. GlimmerBlocker offers the same sort of feature, and you can see the pre-defined filters here.

There are two others that are not enabled by default. If you want them, you need to check them.

- **Intrusive/Fragile Ad Filtering:** This blocks words in URLs that may or may not be indicative of ads (such as "banners" and, yes, "ads"— you'd be surprised how many websites use these words for non-ads!) and things on web pages that could change at any time, hence the "Fragile." Only enable it if you're willing to fiddle with it as necessary.

- **Site Enhancements:** Feel like adding things to sites, such as download links at YouTube and larger images in RSS feeds than are usually provided by default? Then enable this. To be honest, almost all of the enhancements are for websites in Denmark, but they're still helpful as examples if you want to learn how to make your own.

That last statement is true—there's a lot of powerful ways you can adjust GlimmerBlocker, and the best way to learn about those methods is to look at the myriad examples that GlimmerBlocker provides.

There are some things you should know about these filters. First, see those blue dots to the right of each filter? Click on one of those to view key information and settings about a filter, including its URL, how often it updates, and how much you're willing to trust the filter.

Second, to the far left of each rule is a check box. That check box can have three states: checked, minus, or blank. Blank is easy—that means GlimmerBlocker won't use that particular rule (the fact that the word in the Action column turns red is another indication). However, I can find no difference between a minus and a check in terms of whether or not the rule is applied by GlimmerBlocker—in both cases, the rule is used.

Third, due to the way Safari works, you can't block ads served via HTTPS using GlimmerBlocker. The developer of the software explains why at `http://glimmerblocker.org/wiki/FAQ`: "When Safari fetches an HTTPS page using a proxy, it doesn't really use the HTTP protocol, but makes a tunneled TCP connection." Because of this, GlimmerBlocker can't really see the traffic, so it can't affect it. Fortunately, hardly any ads and annoyances are served via HTTPS, so this restriction isn't really that painful.

Fourth, you need to know that you can't change the rules found in each filter. You can view a rule by double-clicking on it, but you can't change anything about that rule. You can't even see all of the information in a text box if the text box isn't long enough, which is annoying if you want to learn how that rule works.

> **NOTE:** The filters are located in `/Library/GlimmerBlocker/Filter subscriptions`; if you look at the permissions on the files, you'll see that they are set to be read-only by everyone except the files' owner, _glimmerblocker.

Creating and Modifying Filters

So if the filters are read-only, what do you do then? For example, what if you want to add your own filters and rules? Or what if you want to modify ones that already exist? The answer to that last question is based on the second.

Let's start with creating your own filter. To do so, click the + under the list of Filters—not the list of Rules, the list of Filters—and give your new Filter a name. I like to name mine with my initials at the beginning and then something descriptive, like RSG Ads. Now you can start adding rules for that filter by clicking on the + under Rules.

For instance, I hate hate hate those ads that show up as double green underlines under certain words on websites; mouse over those words with their special links, and a tiny popup appears with ads in them. Usually, web pages with those ads have oodles of those links on them, which means that moving your mouse anywhere on the page turns into an exercise in frustration. Let's block 'em!

Click on the + to add a new rule and you'll see a screen like that in Figure 4–6.

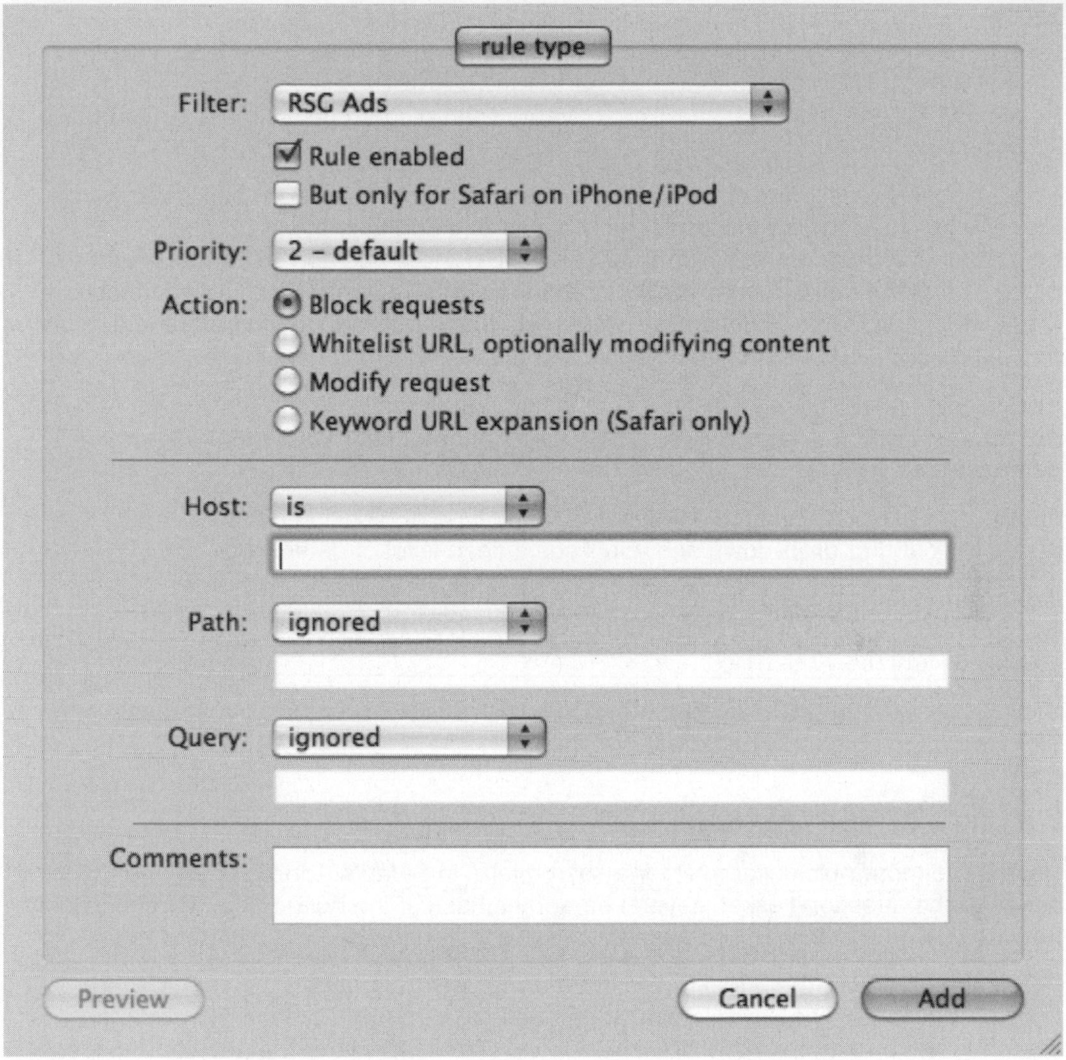

Figure 4–6. *GlimmerBlocker gives you a lot of options when you create a new rule.*

Here's what I'd do in each field:

Filter: Leave it set to RSG Ads, the name of my personal filter; if it's not already set, do so.

Rule Enabled: Check it, or the rule isn't used by GlimmerBlocker.

But Only For Safari On iPhone/iPod: Leave this unchecked, since it doesn't apply to this situation (but more on what this means soon).

Priority: 2 - default is fine, but I can set it lower or higher if need be.

Action: Here's where you really see how complete GlimmerBlocker is. In this case, I want to choose Block Requests, but if I wanted to always allow something, I could select Whitelist URL. Modify Request lets me rewrite URLs and content on-the-fly, while Keyword URL Expansion enables me to create search shortcuts I can use in Safari's Address Bar.

Host: In this case, I know that I want to block anything coming from intellitxt.com, no matter what subdomains are used (in other words, I don't just want to block techradar.uk.intellitxt.com, which is just one site using those annoying ads; I want to block *everything* coming from intellitxt.com). Because I want to block an entire domain, I set Host to Is In Domain and enter `intellitxt.com`, which will take care of the domain and all subdomains.

Path: I don't need to set this, since I'm blocking by domain. But if I needed to, I could be incredibly precise, as one look at the options in the drop-down next to Path demonstrates.

Query: Again, I don't need to set this due to the type of blocking I'm performing, but take a look at that drop-down and you'll see a deep level of detail.

Comments: It's always a good idea to enter comments explaining the purpose of a rule, but you don't have to. In this case, I might put in something like `Block those annoying double-underline green text ads`.

Click Save and you just created a new rule—and helped lower your blood pressure as well.

Working with Read-Only Filters

Here's one more quick example, for a search term in Safari's Address Bar, and this also ties in to the question I asked several paragrahs back: if the built-in filters are read-only, how do you modify them? The answer is: you don't; instead, you go around them.

For example, one of the built-in rules in Safari Keyword Expansions is for Google Images: to search Google Images from the Safari Search Bar, type in `gim` and then your search term (for example, `gim Cthulhu`). I don't like the keyword the developer chose, though: `gim`. Why not `gi`, which is what I use in Firefox, Chrome, and anywhere else I can use such shortcuts? I can't change it, since it's a default, but I can disable it, so I do that. And now to add it back to GlimmerBlocker, but using my preferred keyword.

I like to create another set of filters for my Safari Keyword Expansions, called, cleverly enough, `RSG Safari Keyword Expansions`. Using the filter, I add a new rule, and I use the same settings as I did previously to block intellitxt.com, but with these changes:

Filter: Obviously, this is different. It doesn't have to be, but I like segregating my rules into the appropriate filters.

Action: Select Keyword URL Expansion. Notice when you do that the fields below this change to accommodate this choice.

Keyword: Why you'd want anything besides Is isn't obvious to me. In the textbox, I enter my new keyword, gi.

Use Simple Macro Expansion: I have a choice between this and Use JavaScript Expansion, which is quite a bit more sophisticated and requires some programming knowledge (for more on this option, see `http://glimmerblocker.org/wiki/KeywordExpansion`). Since I'm going the easier route, I do a search at Google Images, copy the URL, and replace my search term in the URL with %s, which is what GlimmerBlocker uses as a substitute, leaving me with `http://images.google.com/images?q=%s` in the textbox.

Click OK, and you can now test your new search by typing gi `Pellucidar` in Safari's Address Bar.

Keyword Expansion Caveats

There are two caveats you need to know about GlimmerBlocker's Safari Keyword Expansions, however. First, if you're using Glims, you may have conflicts, so it's best to compare Glims' Search Engines with GlimmerBlocker's Safari Keyword Expansions to weed out duplicates.

Second, some Keyword Expansions don't work—at least, not the way you might expect them to. I like to search AllMusic.com for information on bands, albums, and more, so I created three Keyword Expansions in GlimmerBlocker to help me search the website. Here are the keywords, Simple Macro Expansions, and Comments for each one:

```
allm
        http://www.allmusic.com/cg/amg.dll?P=amg&opt1=1&sql=%s
        AllMusic Artists
allma
        http://www.allmusic.com/cg/amg.dll?P=amg&opt1=2&sql=%s
        AllMusic Albums
allms
        http://www.allmusic.com/cg/amg.dll?P=amg&opt1=3&sql=%s
        AllMusic Songs
```

I started testing what I'd just created by typing in the following:

```
allm Rolling Stones
allma Koyaanisqatsi
allms Afternoon Delight
```

So far, so good. Then I threw a spanner in the works. I searched for `allma Bags'` `Groove`, and got an error. Safari thought I was trying to go to `http://allma%20Bags'%20Groove/`, which of course doesn't exist, so Safari complained. The same thing occurred if I tried `allma 'round About Midnight` or `allma Steamin'`. But when I tried `allma Bags Groove` or `allma Round About Midnight` or `allma Steamin`, things worked. What was going on?

The answer is on the GlimmerBlocker wiki, at `http://glimmerblocker.org/wiki/FAQ`. It turns out that apostrophes and quotation marks cause Safari to sidestep GlimmerBlocker and treat whatever is typed in the Address Bar as an address, which is why `allma Bags' Groove` gets transmogrified into `http://allma%20Bags'%20Groove/`. You have two solutions: remember to always leave out quotation marks and apostrophes, or use the Search Engines feature of Glims, which doesn't have this annoyance.

There are many more things you can do on the Filters tab of GlimmerBlocker—enough, easily, for an entire chapter—but I'll leave discovering them to you and the GlimmerBlocker web site.

History

Enable History: Check the box to see recent URLs that were blocked or modified by GlimmerBlocker. It's kind of amazing—and sad, and also infuriating—when you see just how many get blocked. To see why a particular URL was blocked, select it, and GlimmerBlocker shows you why in the box at the bottom of the screen.

Suspects

This is a very handy screen, but to make it work, you have to check the box next to Find Candidates For New Rules. I would also check the boxes next to Show Details—so you can see what website serves up the offending ad—and next to Show JavaScripts, if you really want to block the potentially bad stuff. Check this screen periodically and scan it for offenders that you may want to block. When you see one, select it and click Create Filter Rule. The create-a-rule screen will appear, and you can customize as you wish. Handy!

Network

There are some interesting, clever items on this screen.

Proxy Port Number: Leave this set to 8228 unless you have a really good reason to change. Remember that if you do change it, you're going to need to change the port on the Proxies screen in the Network pref pane as well.

Allow iPhone, iPods, And Other Computers To Use GlimmerBlocker On This Mac: If you own an iPhone, iPod Touch, or iPad, you may have noticed that it's impossible to block ads when using Mobile Safari. Not any longer! Check this box, and then go into the Settings app on your iPhone/iPod Touch/iPad and configure your Wi-Fi connection to use your Mac as a proxy. Bam! No more ads in Mobile Safari (at least while you're in proximity to your iDevice). You can find full instructions, with screenshots, at `http://glimmerblocker.org/wiki/iPhoneiPodProxy`.

Ask For Confirmation Of Changes To HTTP Proxy In Network Setup: Check this for an added level of safety—if changes are made to the Proxies setting in the Network pref pane in System Preferences, you'll be prompted first, in order to make sure that GlimmerBlocker continues to work. And if you ever add another network interface and want to insert the correct proxy settings so that it will work with GlimmerBlocker, click the Update Now button located here.

Site-Wide Proxy: Most people can leave this alone, set to None. But if you have an additional proxy to which you need to connect—like at work, for instance—you can enter it here, with Always Use This Proxy. If you want something that changes automatically depending upon your location—with one proxy at work, another at home, and another at a coffee shop—choose Dynamic Configuration Using JavaScript and then head over to `http://glimmerblocker.org/wiki/Proxies` for the complete skinny.

> **TIP:** If you need to connect to another proxy that requires a password, check out the developer's advice on `http://glimmerblocker.org/wiki/FAQ`, in answer to the question, "My company proxy needs a password."

Developer

The only reason to enable any of the boxes on this page is if you are a programmer and want to dig deep into GlimmerBlocker, with one exception.

Use Checkerboard Pattern For Blocked Images: Want to see exactly what you're missing when GlimmerBlocker hides ads? Check this and Safari will display a checkboard box in place of blocked images. I don't bother, as I don't care and I find checkerboard patterns ugly, but you may find it amusing or useful.

And that, finally, is GlimmerBlocker. Out of the box, with very little fiddling by a user, it will do a lot to make the Web a saner place, but if you want to tinker and customize, you can do so to your heart's content. GlimmerBlocker is an amazing piece of software, and I hope you find it useful.

> **TIP:** If you implement GlimmerBlocker and also use Little Snitch, which I'll cover in Chapter 11, "Digging Deep as an Admin," you really need to understand how the two work together, or you're going to have problems. In my case, I simply told Little Snitch to allow any connection from GlimmerBlocker, and that will serve for most people. If you're very paranoid or really want to get your hands dirty, check out more advanced solutions at `www.macosxhints.com/article.php?story=20091228114759199` (be sure to read the comments too!) and `http://glimmerblocker.org/wiki/LittleSnitch`.

1Password

1Password is one of the best programs I ever put on my Mac, as I'm going to show you in Chapter 7, "Securing Your Mac and Networks." Because I'm going to talk so much about it there, I'll just say here that if you install 1Password, you absolutely *must* install the 1Password plug-in for Safari. It will make interacting with password-protected websites so much easier, safer, and enjoyable that you'd be a fool not to.

ClickToFlash

Flash isn't all bad, but it sure is annoying a lot of the time. Couple that with the fact that Flash has never run all that well on Mac OS X, and add on top of that all of the stupid, grating, animated Flash-based ads that clutter the Web, and its obvious why a good Flash-blocker is a necessity. Firefox has had good ol' FlashBlock for ages, but Safari users had to suffer... until ClickToFlash made its appearance. The person who programmed it remains a mystery, but the code isn't, since it's all open source. Thank you, mysterious unnamed developer who made this beautiful open source software!

To get ClickToFlash, head over to http://github.com/rentzsch/clicktoflash/. After installing it, when you go to a web page that uses Flash, instead of the animation, you'll see a gray box with the words "Flash" (or sometimes "QuickTime," on such sites as YouTube that substitute MP4 videos for Flash) in the middle. You can see the effect in Figure 4–7.

Figure 4–7. *No annoying animation in sight!*

Click in that gray box, and the Flash loads and plays; don't click, and Flash remains blocked. It's that simple.

In the upper left corner of any Flash that ClickToFlash blocks, you'll see a sprocket, as shown in Figure 4–7. If you click on that sprocket, you'll see a menu, shown in Figure 4–8, that gives you several features.

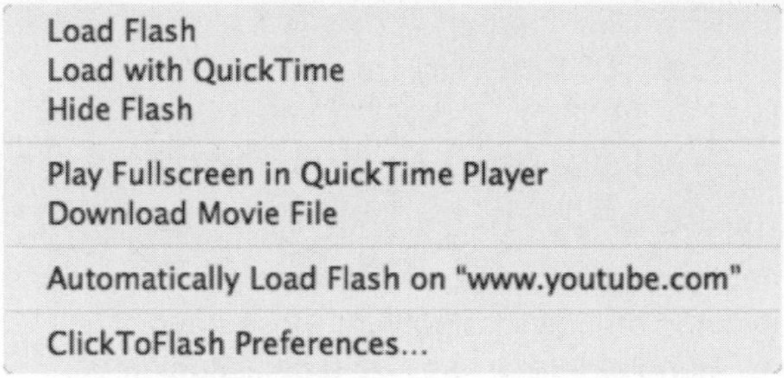

Load Flash
Load with QuickTime
Hide Flash

Play Fullscreen in QuickTime Player
Download Movie File

Automatically Load Flash on "www.youtube.com"

ClickToFlash Preferences...

Figure 4–8. *ClickToFlash allows you to work with Flash movies in several ways.*

Most of these options are self-explanatory, but I want to delve into a few.

Load With QuickTime: If the website supports substituting MP4 movies instead of Flash, this will load them.

> **NOTE:** To read more about ClickToFlash's support for QuickTime and MP4 videos, see
> http://rentzsch.github.com/clicktoflash/killers.html.

Automatically Load Flash: If you know that you always want Flash to load on the current website, click on this option. YouTube is often a good choice for this.

ClickToFlash Preferences: Yes, ClickToFlash has preferences. This isn't the only way to access those prefs, though. In Safari and some other apps, you'll find a new ClickToFlash menu under the application's menu; in other words, at **Safari ➤ ClickToFlash ➤ Preferences**. The main thing ClickToFlash's Preferences allow you to do is remove sites that you told ClickToFlash to automatically load using the previously mentioned option.

Before you start getting serious with ClickToFlash, you need to fix one issue that could potentially drive you nuts. ClickToFlash doesn't just block Flash in Safari; it blocks it in any app that uses software found in ~/Library/Internet Plug-Ins. Included in that group is Apple Mail. Except that Apple Mail doesn't play well with ClickToFlash, and tends to crash when viewing certain rich-text emails (at least in my experience; YMMV).

Fortunately, ClickToFlash recognizes that some programs don't work well with it, and allows you to whitelist certain apps so that ClickToFlash loads all Flash in them. Unfortunately, you have to do this on the command line, and it's a rather arcane process.

You first have to find out the Bundle ID of the app you want to whitelist. What's a Bundle ID? Remember that Mac apps are really bundles, which are directories with a special flag set that makes the Finder display those directories as files (Terminal, however, ignores that flag, which is why you can run commands such as cd and ls on programs in the /Applications directory and see them behave like directories—because to Terminal, they *are* directories!). Apple requires application bundles to contain certain files, among them Contents/Info.plist. Info.plist is a key file, as it's supposed to contain the name of the app, the version, the kinds of files the app can handle, and a string of text that uniquely identifies the app: the Bundle ID.

NOTE: To learn more about bundles, read Apple's "Mac OS X Reference Library — Bundle Structures"
(`http://developer.apple.com/mac/library/documentation/corefoundation/conceptual/CFBundles/Introduction/Introduction.html`).

Data in an Info.plist file is organized by keys and strings that go with those keys. If you're looking for the Bundle ID, find the CFBundleIdentifier key, and its associated string is the Bundle ID. For example, here are a few keys and strings identifying the Bundle IDs of various programs on my Mac:

```
Safari
  <key>CFBundleIdentifier</key>
  <string>com.apple.Safari</string>
1Password
  <key>CFBundleIdentifier</key>
  <string>ws.agile.1Password</string>
MacVim
  <key>CFBundleIdentifier</key>
  <string>org.vim.MacVim</string>
```

To find out a program's Bundle ID, you can do one of the following:

In the Finder, right-click on the app & select Show Package Contents. In the resulting Finder window that will open, navigate into Contents and open Info.plist in a text editor or, if you don't have a text editor, view the file with QuickLook by pressing Spacebar. Look around in the file (or search) until you find the CFBundleIdentifier key. Right under that is the Bundle ID.

In Terminal, cd into the app (remember, to Terminal, the bundle will still look like a folder) and then into the Contents folder. Use less or some other pager to view the contents of the file until you find the CFBundleIdentifier key and its Bundle ID.

I prefer using Terminal, but I'm also very lazy, so I'd just use this command:

```
grep CFBundleIdentifier -A 1 /Applications/Mail.app/Contents/Info.plist
```

After running this command, you should see this:

```
<key>CFBundleIdentifier</key>
<string>com.apple.mail</string>
```

NOTE: The grep command searches files, in this case for CFBundleIdentifier. Normally the command prints matching lines to the Terminal, but in this case I used -A 1, which tells grep to append one following line to the output. For more on grep, see my book *Linux Phrasebook*.

Now that we know Mail's Bundle ID, we can tell ClickToFlash to whitelist Mail using this command in Terminal:

```
defaults write com.github.rentzsch.clicktoflash applicationWhitelist -array-add
com.apple.mail
```

Restart Mail, and the big bad crashes will have gone away, at least from ClickToFlash.

> **TIP:** This may have been improved, but I found myself re-entering that line every time ClickToFlash updated, which meant I had to re-find the command and figure out Mail's Bundle ID, which quickly grew tedious. To get around that, I created an alias in `.bash_aliases` like this:
>
> ```
> alias clicktoflashnomail='defaults write
> com.github.rentzsch.clicktoflash applicationWhitelist -array-add
> com.apple.mail'
> ```
>
> Now I just type `clicktoflashnomail` in Terminal and Mail is whitelisted. Much easier.
>
> Oh, and if you don't know what `.bash_aliases` is or how to use it, take a look at `www.linux.com/learn/tutorials/278507-bash-201-intermediate-guide-to-bash`—it's for Linux, but it applies to Mac OS X just as much.

Working with the Bookmarks Bar

While a lot of people know how to use bookmarks, I'm always surprised that more folks don't know how to use the Bookmarks Bar to its fullest. The Bookmarks Bar, for those who don't know what it's called, sits at the top of Safari's window, above the Tab Bar and below the Address Bar. It's designed to hold bookmarks that you need to quickly access, or that you use constantly. You can see mine in Figure 4–9.

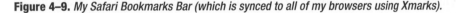

Figure 4–9. *My Safari Bookmarks Bar (which is synced to all of my browsers using Xmarks).*

So here's my advice on the Bookmarks Bar.

Use folders. It's easy to add bookmarks to the Bar—just go to **Bookmarks ➤ Add Bookmark** and save the bookmark on the Bookmarks Bar using the dropdown menu, or drag the address from the Address Bar to the Bookmarks Bar—but you should create folders for your bookmarks, with very few exceptions. Folders organize your bookmarks better and are a more efficient use of the limited space afforded you by the Bookmarks Bar. You can see those folders in Figure 4–9: Bonjour (that's actually added by Apple), RSG, WS, Soc, lets, G-RSG, News, and Save. And don't forget you can put sub-folders in those folders as well.

Use short names for folders and bookmarks. Notice my folders' names. RSG are my initials, and that folder is for personal websites. WS are the initials of my company, WebSanity. Soc stands for "Social" and that's where Facebook, Twitter, and other social software sites live. I'm going to discuss Bookmarklets in the next section, and that's what "lets" is short for. G-RSG is for all the Google-based accounts and websites that I use. News is easy, while Save is for sites that make it easy to save content I find on the Web, either by printing efficiently, or emailing, or republishing.

I even keep actual bookmarks short. If I select a word or phrase on a webpage and then press G, a Google search is done using my selection. Mail uses Gmail to email the URL of the webpage I'm currently viewing to whomever I'd like.

Understand how multi-tab bookmarks work. If you close Safari or it crashes, you can restore the tabs you were working on by going to **History ➤ Reopen All Windows From Last Session**. However, if you'd like, you can also bookmarks groups of tabs by selecting **Bookmarks ➤ Add Bookmark For These X Tabs**, where X is the number of current tabs open in Safari. You can save that bookmark anywhere, but the Bookmarks Bar is often a good place to put it, especially if you're heavy into research and need to temporarily sideline a group of tabs while you move on to something else.

Just be aware of one possible gotcha: when you click on that multi-tab bookmark, it will *replace* any tabs that are currently open, which can be very disconcerting. My advice is to therefore open a new Safari window before you click on that bookmark, so as to minimize disruption. However, if you do click that multi-tab bookmark and it appears to obliterate your current tabs, just immediately click the Back button, and your original set of tabs will be restored.

Adding the Best Bookmarklets

Bookmarklets have been around since the late 1990s, and they're a cool implementation of a smart idea. Basically, a bookmarklet is a short program—almost always written in JavaScript—that is stored as the URL of a bookmark. Click on the bookmark(let), and you run the program. Being JavaScript, the bookmarklet can query or alter a web page in almost limitless ways. In this section, I'd like to present a few of my favorites, most of which I keep in a folder on my Bookmarks Bar labeled "lets," as I discussed in the previous section.

> **NOTE:** I'm only covering a few bookmarklets in this book, but there are several websites that contain collections of bookmarklets that you can search and try out. Try Bookmarklets at www.bookmarklets.com, the granddaddy of such websites, and the Bookmarklet Directory at www.marklets.com/bookmarklets/. The blog Digital Inspiration has a very nice "Guide to Most Useful Bookmarklets for Chrome, Firefox, Safari, etc." at www.labnol.org/internet/guide-to-useful-bookmarklets/7931/.

ToRead

I do a lot of research, for my teaching at Washington University in St. Louis, for my Web development company, and certainly for books like this. Different people have different ways of keeping track of their research materials, but in my case, I like to use e-mail to store the articles I find on the Web; specifically, in Gmail, using several different labels. That way, I can use Gmail's awesome search capabilities to find the info I saved.

There are various ways to grab those articles, but my favorite method is with a service called ToRead. With ToRead, when I find a web page that I want to save, I simply click the ToRead bookmarklet, and a moment later, the contents of the web page is in my Gmail inbox. It's about as easy as could be.

To start using ToRead, go to `http://toread.cc` and sign up by entering your e-mail address (yes, that's all you need!) and then click the Start Now button. You'll receive an e-mail that contains the links that you'll turn into bookmarklets: [toread] and [toread+]. At that point, you can use the service.

Yes, there are two. Let's say I went to the BBC's page about RSS (`http://news.bbc.co.uk/2/hi/help/rss/3223484.stm`) and wanted a copy of it for my files. Here's what happens when you use each bookmarklet:

When I click [toread], the page fades out for a second (if I look at the Status Bar, Safari tells me that it's "Contacting toread.cc") and then the page is restored. If I then check my e-mail, there's an e-mail with this Subject:

`[toread] BBC NEWS | Help | RSS | News feeds from the BBC`
`(http://news.bbc.co.uk/2/hi/help/rss/3223484.stm)`

The [toread] bookmarklet inserts [toread] at the beginning of the Subject, followed by the web page's title and its URL in parentheses. The body of the message is the web page, but at the top, ToRead places additional information:

> *This is a cached page retrieved by "toread" on 03/11/2010 04:30:23 GMT. Original: BBC NEWS | Help | RSS | News feeds from the BBC (http://news.bbc.co.uk/2/hi/help/rss/3223484.stm) [del.icio.us] [Furl] [Reddit] [Scouter] * This page may contains images/external files which are no longer available. * Page may not include frames, iframes and/or scripts. * "toread" is neither affiliated with the authors of this page nor responsible for its content.*

Much of it is repeated from the Subject, but it's still nice to have, and the links to bookmarking services such as del.icio.us and Furl, and news sites such as Reddit, can be very helpful.

The [toread+] bookmarklet does everything that [toread] does, but adds one excellent feature (hence the +). When I click the bookmarklet, Safari opens a prompt that asks you for a comment. In the case of the BBC's RSS page, I went there for my class on social software, so I'd enter `social software` in the prompt (I wouldn't need to enter "RSS," since that word is already in the title of the web page, and therefore ToRead will include it in the e-mail's Subject). I can include several words in the prompt, but there appears to be a limit of about 50 characters or so.

When I click OK, the prompt closes, the page fades out for a second, and is then restored. My e-mail now shows a new message, with this as the Subject:

[toread][social software] BBC NEWS | Help | RSS | News feeds from the BBC (http://news.bbc.co.uk/2/hi/help/rss/3223484.stm)

The subject is exactly the same as if I'd used the first bookmarklet, except that my additional words are included in square brackets immediately after [toread] at the beginning. Now my searching in Gmail can be even more precise, and therefore more useful.

As cool as ToRead is, it has a few limitations. This might be obvious, but the content in the e-mail is that on the web page at the time you clicked on the bookmarklet—it does not auto-update. Also, any images in the e-mail are on the original Web server, so if the images get taken down, or move, or the URL changes, the images won't appear in your e-mail. And finally, as the note at the top of every e-mail processed by ToRead makes clear, ToRead really can't handle Web pages with frames, inline frames (iframes), or JavaScripts on them.

Even with those limitations, though, ToRead is still an invaluable service that has helped me do many research-related tasks, such as write this book. Give it a try—it's free, and it's fantastic.

Readability/Readable

Too many web pages look like New York's Times Square at night: loud, bright, garish, and with everything competing for your attention in an orgy of distraction. That's not to put down Times Square—it's an awesome landmark and it can be great fun. But when you want to concentrate and focus, Times Square isn't the place to be. Likewise, it's amazing how many web pages contain content that needs to be read with solid attention, but then subvert themselves by making it difficult to give that attention to the content. Ads ads ads, sidebars, photos, multiple groups of navigation, and everything else take away from the reason you came to the web page in the first place: to read what the web page has to say!

In early 2009, a solution to this problem appeared: Readability. Basically a bookmarklet that loads a series of style sheets and scripts, Readability strips out all of the crud on a web page and reformats it in a simpler format that enhances the web page's, well, readability. To install and use Readability, go to http://lab.arc90.com/experiments/readability/. There you make three settings regarding how you want Readability to format web pages: Style, Size, and Margin.

Style basically consists of five pre-determined looks for text: Newspaper, Novel, eBook, Inverse, and Athelas. Newspaper, for instance, creates pages with a white background and serif fonts, while eBook uses a very light gray background and sans-serif fonts. Size lets you adjust how big the fonts are, from Extra Small through Extra Large. Margin determines how wide the text is on the page, from Extra Narrow through Extra Wide. What's really cool is that Readability shows you a preview below your settings that changes as you make your choices, so you can see exactly what you're getting.

When you're done, click on the Readability badge and drag it to Safari's Bookmarks Bar (make sure you click and drag; don't just click). Next time you're on a web page that needs some simplification, click on the Readability bookmarklet, and poof! the page will change to display your settings. Easy peasy!

However, as nice as Readability is, it wasn't long before a developer named Gabriel Coarna decided he could do better, so he created Readable (`http://readable-app.appspot.com`). Interestingly, according to Coarna on `http://readable-app.appspot.com/more.html`, he had already created Readable when Readability appeared. What's really amazing is that as nice as Readability is, Readable is much better in several ways.

Non-destructive: Readability completely changes the web page on which it's used; Readable keeps the page intact but overlays the newly cleaned-up design over the original page, which is grayed out.

Selectivity: Readability automatically affects an entire web page, and there's not getting around that. Readable can do that, or you can select some text and Readable will only fix up that particular part of the page.

Flexibility: When you go to Readable's setup page, at `http://readable-app.appspot.com/setup.html`, you're presented with far more choices than offered by Readability, as you can tell in Figure 4–10.

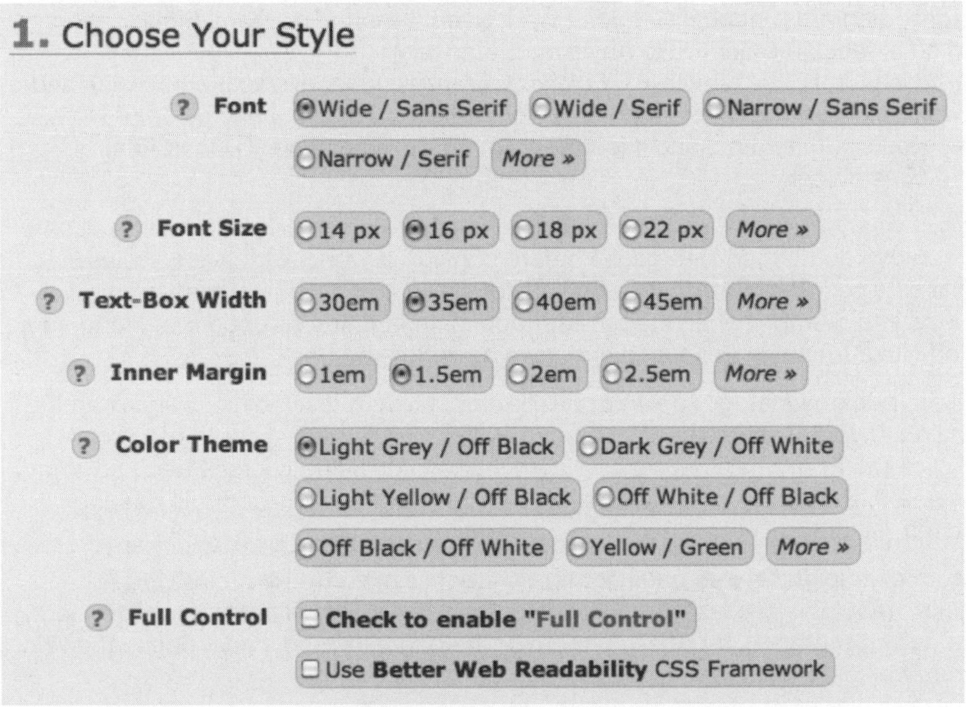

Figure 4–10. *Readable makes it easy to highly customize how the final product looks.*

That might seem like a lot of options, but that's nothing. First, notice the More next to each choice, which allows you to extend things further. Second, see the box next to Check To Enable Full Control? Check that, and the types of options explode. Now you have Line Height, Text Align, Outer Margin, Transparency, Video Options, and several more. That doesn't mean you should use Full Control, but it's nice to know it's there if you want it.

There are other bookmarklets designed to clean up web pages to make them easier to read—one of them is Clippable, which you can find at http://brettterpstra.com/share/readability2.html—but Readable is really the best that I've seen. If you do a lot of reading on the Web—and who doesn't nowadays?—then you really need to give Readable a spin.

NOTE: You can use Safari 5's Reader feature to strip the garbage away from web pages too, but you get a lot more customization from Readability and Readable.

PrintWhatYouLike

I hate wasting ink or toner when I print, so I always use the print-friendly version of a web page. The problem is that a lot of so-called print-friendly pages are anything but. Ads, images, diagrams, sidebars—I don't want to print them! For years, Firefox users have had an extension called Nuke Anything Enhanced (https://addons.mozilla.org/en-US/firefox/addon/951) that allows them to pick and choose which items to remove temporarily from a web page. It's a fine piece of work, but it only works with Firefox, and it loads into memory every time you load Firefox, which can cause bloat.

That's why I was thrilled to discover PrintWhatYouLike, a web service that allows users to easily remove content on web pages before printing. It works with every browser, since it's a service instead of locally installed software, and it's a bookmarklet, so it doesn't load into memory when the browser opens. In fact, it's so good that I long ago uninstalled Nuke Anything Enhanced and have never looked back.

To install the bookmarklet, go to www.printwhatyoulike.com/bookmarklet and drag the specified link to your Bookmarks Bar. When you get to a page that could use some pruning, click the PrintWhatYouLike bookmarklet and you'll find yourself whisked away to its namesake's website, with the web page on the right and the controls running down the left.

Let's use an example: the web page at http://www.businessinsider.com/google-picnik-photo-editing-tool-2010-3, which you can see in Figure 4–11. If you go there, you'll see a Print button, but it doesn't reformat the page; instead, it just opens the Print dialog box. Well gee, thanks!

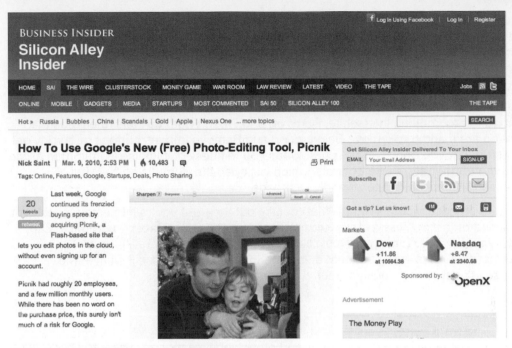

Figure 4–11. *Eeek! This page needs to be reformatted to print!*

That page needs a bunch of junk removed, so it's time to use PrintWhatYouLike. Click on the bookmarklet, and the web page reloads with the PrintWhatYouLike controls on the left, as in Figure 4–12.

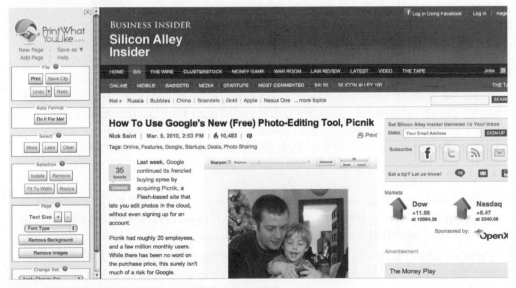

Figure 4–12. *PrintWhatYouLike's controls load on the left*

As you mouse over the web page on the right, red boxes will appear over objects, including images, paragraphs, groups of paragraphs, columns, and even the page itself. When the red box surrounds an object you want to affect, click on it to select it, which will highlight it in yellow, and then use the controls on the left to change it.

Figure 4–12 is undoubtedly too small for you to see all the details, but that's okay, because the best way to figure out PrintWhatYouLike is to actually use it for yourself. In particular, I recommend the Isolate, Remove, and Fit To Width buttons to change the selection area, and the Remove Background and Remove Images buttons to quickly get rid of stuff that you don't want to print. When you're finished, click the Print button at the top of the PrintWhatYouLike controls, which will open the Print dialog box, but containing your clean, printer-friendly web page.

There are other services like PrintWhatYouLike out there—if you're interested, check out Printliminator (`http://css-tricks.com/examples/ThePrintliminator/`) and Click2Zap (`http://mrclay.org/index.php/2006/02/18/click2zap-bookmarklet/`)—but PrintWhatYouLike is easily the best of its type that I've found. I use it all the time because I find it tremendously useful, & I hope you do as well.

Bit.ly

As the popularity of Twitter, Facebook, and other websites that ask users to share links, updates, and news has exploded, so has the growth of URL shortening sites. The first successful site was TinyURL (`http://tinyurl.com`), but now there are oodles of such sites—for proof, check out the list at `http://code.google.com/p/shortenurl/wiki/URLShorteningServices`, which has 179 listed!

The king of the URL shorteners is Bit.ly, however, and for good reason. It was the first service of its type to provide users with statistical tools so they could track the popularity of the links they created with Bit.ly. Then, in May 2009, Twitter made Bit.ly its default link-shortening tool. At that point, Bit.ly's use skyrocketed, and it's currently the number one URL shortening service by a mile.

To really use Bit.ly effectively, you need to set up an account with the service, so head over to `http://bit.ly`, click on Sign Up, and do so. To add the bookmarklet, go to `http://bit.ly/pages/tools`, scroll down to the Standard Bit.ly Bookmarklet section, and drag the Shorten With Bit.ly link to your Bookmarks Bar (I find that name to be too long, so I'd go to **Bookmarks ➤ Show All Bookmarks** and change the name to something shorter, like Bit.ly).

When I find myself on a page with a URL that I want to shorten using Bit.ly, I select the bookmarklet, and a moment later I'm at Bit.ly, with my new short link sitting there ready to copy and share. Now that's simple!

Under the short link is a list of other links I've created using Bit.ly, along with statistics and other interesting information. For instance, it tells me that an article about my brother that I shared using the URL `http://bit.ly/6wF9I0` has been clicked on 60 times, 48 of which were thanks to me. If that's a bit confusing, remember that when you create a short link using Bit.ly, it associates that short link with the longer URL permanently, so if anyone tries to use Bit.ly for the same longer URL, the same short link is created. In fact, Bit.ly will show you just who else created that link, and what services—Twitter, Facebook, and so on—they used. It's all pretty fascinating when you start delving into that data, and also amazing how fast links spread around the world.

Add to Amazon Wish List

Amazon is the 800-pound gorilla of online commerce, and one of its most-used features is the Wish List. I use my Amazon Wish List constantly as a place to store a list of books, movies, and music that I'd like to get someday. I have two big issues with my Amazon Wish List, however: I can't search it, which drives me batty, and I can only add things from Amazon to it.

I can't do much about the first problem until Amazon decides to fix it (and for Cthulhu's sake, it really should!), but I can do something about the second. After all, Amazon is my main wish list online, and most other websites don't offer anything like it, so if I find something I want to remember on a different site, I either have to bookmark it, which would clutter my bookmarks, or e-mail it, but neither is optimal. I already have a wish list—it's just stored at Amazon!—so why can't I just add items from other websites to that wish list?

Amazingly, Amazon realized this need and added a new feature in 2008: the Universal Wish List, which allows you to add items from any website to your Amazon Wish List. To use this feature, go to www.amazon.com/wishlist/get-button and drag the Add To Wish List button to your Bookmarks Bar.

When I get to a site that has something interesting on it that I want to add to my Amazon Wish List—like the fabulously gross Spinning Eyeball Fountain found at www.buycostumes.com/Spinning-Eyeball-Fountain/58451/ProductDetail.aspx—I click on the Add To Wish List bookmarklet. A small window appears, which you can see in Figure 4–13.

As you can see in Figure 4–13, the name field is pre-filled in for me using the title of the web page, but that could be wrong, so I can change it to whatever is meaningful. The price field is blank, so I need to fill that in. Quantity is pre-filled to 1, which is fine. I can enter up to 500 characters in the Comments field; what I usually do is copy the description from the web page and then paste that in so I have something there to help me.

Amazon usually does a very good job picking the correct image of the item I'm adding to the Wish List, but if it's wrong, I can click on the tiny right and left arrows under the image to move between all visible images on the page. Finally, I can choose which Wish List to add this Spinning Eyeball Fountain to, if I have more than one. Once everything's entered, I click Add To List; if I change my mind and decide I don't want that awesome toy, I can Cancel instead (never!).

Figure 4–13. *It's so easy to add the Spinning Eyeball Fountain to my Amazon Wish List!*

And that's it. The Spinning Eyeball Fountain is now on my Amazon Wish List. As I cruise about the Web, if I see something interesting that I might want to buy some day, I can add it to the one Wish List I keep: my personal list at Amazon. It's utterly convenient.

Further Resources

Apple provides a couple of good overviews of Safari that are worth reviewing, even if you think you know everything about that web browser: "Mac 101: Safari 4" (http://support.apple.com/kb/HT3643) and "Safari - 150 Features" (www.apple.com/safari/features.html). Sometimes you stumble across the neatest stuff on Apple's help sites—for instance, did you know that if you load file:///Applications/Safari.app/Contents/Resources/Shortcuts.html in Safari, you get a nice page that lists all of its keyboard shortcuts?

For more on Top Sites, read Ars Technica's "Safari 4 how-to: Top Sites Browser in a nutshell," at http://arstechnica.com/apple/guides/2009/02/safari-4-focus-top-sites-browser-in-a-nutshell.ars.

Input Managers have been a contentious issue for years, and many people still confuse them with real, supported browser plug-ins. MacJournals does a great job explaining the difference in "Input Managers are not 'plug-ins'" (www.macjournals.com/news/inputmanagerhacks.html).

Xmarks isn't the only way to synchronize your bookmarks, but it's free, cross-platform, and cross-browser, which is far more than virtually all the other solutions. If you're curious, check out Wikipedia's "Comparison of browser synchronizers" at http://en.wikipedia.org/wiki/Comparison_of_browser_synchronizers.

There are other ways to block ads besides GlimmerBlocker. Privoxy is a free, open source proxy software that's been around for a while, but it really doesn't work on Macs very well, as you can see in the comments to "10.6: Run Privoxy 3.0.16 on Snow Leopard" (www.macosxhints.com/article.php?story=20100227045756617). FloppyMoose details its very limited Cascading Style Sheet-based solution in "Better Ad Blocking for Firefox, Mozilla, Camino, and Safari" (www.floppymoose.com).

If you want to learn more about bookmarklets, read Wikipedia's article at http://en.wikipedia.org/wiki/Bookmarklet.

Summary

Safari is great, but like everything on the third rock from the sun, it's not perfect (although the new version 5 brings it closer!). Nonetheless, you can definitely improve it, and I've given you several directions for improvement in this chapter. First, speed up Safari—after all, who doesn't like more speed?—and then install add-ons and extensions and bookmarklets that customize the browser to fit your needs exactly. Apple started out with an iron grip on Safari (as Apple is wont to do), but, like my aunt after her late afternoon nip of gin, it's loosened up greatly. Take advantage of Apple's growing willingness to allow greater customization of Safari and try new things!

## Chapter 5

Stepping Beyond Safari

Safari is a really great web browser—and so is Firefox, and so is Google Chrome. And in addition to those, there are others that are also great, which you'll learn about in this chapter. Still, while I use Safari quite a bit, I don't use it exclusively. I like to bounce around between several different browsers, using each as my main web tool for a couple of weeks, and then switching to a different one. During this time, I still continue to use others for minor tasks, so I'm constantly seeing what works and what doesn't with the range of web browsers for Mac OS X.

In this chapter, I'm going to go way beyond Safari and cover a range of other web browsers for the Mac, some well-known—such as Firefox and Chrome—and others not very well-known, such as Stainless and Arora. Finally, I'll finish up with Site-Specific Browsers (SSBs), which allow you to turn websites and web apps into programs that run on your Mac. Well, kinda. You'll see.

Exploring Web Browser Alternatives

Safari is a great—no, an *excellent*—web browser for the Mac, but it's not the only contender. Mac OS X has a number of browsers available for it, some excellent, some good, and some not so good. In this section, I'm going to give an overview of other significant web browsers you can run on your Mac:

- WebKit
- Firefox
- Camino
- Chrome/Chromium
- Opera
- Stainless

For each browser, I'll summarize the ideas behind it, tell you what's unique, good, and bad, let you know who should use it, and give you some pointers for further reading and exploration. I'll also cover a few lesser-known browsers as well and give you the quick skinny on each.

Finally, to close out this section, I'll look at a few tools that make it very easy to work several different web browsers on your Mac, at the same time.

WebKit

Every web browser has a layout engine built inside of it that turns HTML and CSS and other building blocks into finished web pages. Firefox has Gecko, Internet Explorer has Trident, Opera has Presto, and Safari and Chrome have WebKit. WebKit is an open source project overseen by Apple at http://webkit.org; as part of that project, every night a build of the current WebKit source code is compiled together and made available for download. This is bleeding edge stuff—on the positive side, you get to try out new features and capabilities long before they appear in Safari, but on the negative side, you may experience bugs and crashes galore (although they're usually not that bad).

To try out WebKit, go to http://webkit.org and click on the Download Nightly Builds button. On the page that loads, click the big yellow arrow next to Mac OS X, download the DMG, and install it. Run it and you'll see something like Figure 5–1.

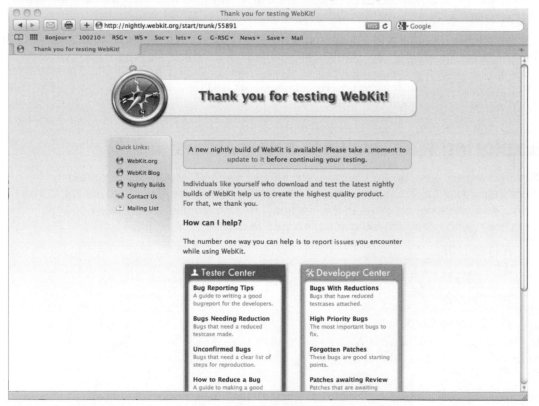

Figure 5–1. *WebKit looks like Safari, which is entirely intentional.*

TIP: You can install and run WebKit without affecting Safari, so don't be afraid to give it a whirl. The one area of overlap is in bookmarks, so don't go crazy and delete bookmarks in WebKit, unless you also want them deleted in Safari as well.

When you load WebKit, you'll see that it looks exactly like Safari. In fact, your Mac's Menu Bar says Safari next to the , which is confusing, but it's actually the latest, greatest version of WebKit, which will one day grow up to become Safari.

What's Unique?

If you want to see the future of Safari, check out WebKit. Other than that, it *is* Safari.

What's Good?

It can be faster than Safari, and new features and capabilities are introduced first in WebKit.

What's Bad?

You're using a nightly build, so this browser changes every day. You could get a fast, stable version with really neat-o features one day, and the next day get a slow, crashy version with messed-up features that don't work correctly. The latter rarely happens, but it can. At the least, expect WebKit to be less stable than Safari—in fact, it crashed while I was writing this paragraph!

Who Should Use WebKit?

Web developers and testers. Brave souls who enjoy living on the bleeding edge. The incorrigibly curious.

Further Resources

Wikipedia has a nice article about WebKit that tells the history of the layout engine at http://en.wikipedia.org/wiki/Webkit. If you're a Web developer and want to keep up-to-date with WebKit's progress, follow The WebKit Blog (http://webkit.org/blog/). Like everyone else in the world, the developers even have a Twitter feed you can follow: http://twitter.com/webkit. Finally, a surprising number of web browsers have decided to use WebKit as their layout engine; you can find a list of them on Wikipedia, at http://en.wikipedia.org/wiki/List_of_web_browsers#WebKit-based_browsers.

Firefox

The late 1990s were the era of the so-called "browser wars," when Microsoft and Netscape were duking it out to see who would dominate the web browser market. Thanks to illegal abuse of its operating system monopoly, Microsoft began to crush Netscape, and Netscape could see it coming.

> **NOTE:** When I say "illegal abuse," I'm not being hyperbolic; I'm stating a legal finding of fact. For more on the case and Microsoft's misdeeds, see `http://cyber.law.harvard.edu/ msdoj/conclusions-l.html` for the judge's actual Conclusions of Law and Final Order, or take a look at Wikipedia's article on the case at `http://en.wikipedia.org/wiki/ United_States_v._Microsoft`.

In January 1998, Netscape decided to throw a Hail Mary pass, and it open sourced the code to the Netscape web browser under the name of the Mozilla Project. Even though Netscape eventually went off to die in the bowels of AOL, the Mozilla Project continued work, and finally version 1.0 of the Mozilla web browser was released in June 2002.

While there was much to like about the new Mozilla, there was a glaring problem as well. Mozilla wasn't just a web browser; it was in reality of suite of programs, including an e-mail and news reader, an address book, a web-page creator, an Internet Relay Chat (IRC) client, and it even had tools for synchronizing data with Palm Pilot PDAs. All this extra stuff meant that it was bloated, complicated, and slow.

As a result, a group of developers basically took the web browser component out of Mozilla and began to simplify and refine it. This eventually, after a few name changes, became Firefox, which debuted in November 2004. Eventually, Firefox proved so successful that the Mozilla Foundation elected to focus future development resources on Firefox instead of Mozilla (although Mozilla is still developed by the community, but now under the name of SeaMonkey, which you can read about at `www.seamonkey-project.org`).

Today, Firefox is an excellent browser that millions of people around the world use every day. In fact, it's the second most popular web browser in the world, which is a pretty impressive achievement for an open source project that was originally a side project for a group of programmers!

What's Unique?

Why, almost infinite customizability with extensions and themes, of course! Chrome has extensions too, but nowhere near as many as Firefox does. It's really amazing just how much Firefox's community has contributed to the browser's development.

What's Good?

Firefox has a lot to recommend it:

- All the standard features you'd expect in a modern web browser—tabs, spell checking, incremental find, bookmarks, a download manager, private mode, geolocation, and integrated search engines—are present; in fact, Firefox popularized many of those features.

- Excellent support for web standards, such as HTML, CSS, XML, SVG, JavaScript, and many more.

- A fast JavaScript engine that's getting faster all the time, thanks to competition from Chrome's JavaScript engine.

- Thousands of extensions and themes at `http://addons.mozilla.org` that enable you to customize Firefox exactly to your liking.

- The ability to create different profiles containing different bookmarks, settings, and extensions allows users to create unique, customized versions of Firefox to perform wildly divergent tasks (for more on profiles, start with `http://kb.mozillazine.org/Profile_folder_-_Firefox`).

- Constant innovation in features and underlying technologies, many of which are later adopted by other browsers.

- An open source development process helps both developers and users.

- An open bug tracker makes it easy for users to find out if issues they're encountering are known and are being fixed, something that can be very frustrating with more closed environments, like those at Microsoft, Apple, and Opera.

- A good security record, and when vulnerabilities are found, they tend to be patched more quickly than with other browser makers (especially when compared to that security abomination, Internet Explorer on Windows).

- If you create websites, Firefox is easily the best browser in terms of tools, with Firebug alone keeping many developers I know using Firefox as their primary browser.

What's Bad?

Firefox is great, but that doesn't mean it's perfect. Here are a few imperfections:

- Because it's built first and foremost as a cross-platform web browser (in fact, Firefox runs on Windows, Mac OS X, Linux, BSD UNIX, Solaris, and others), Firefox isn't the most Mac-like web browser out there. It still doesn't support several Apple technologies, libraries, and conventions (such as Apple Keychain, Services, AppleScript, key commands, and keyboard navigation—for a good list, see `https://wiki.mozilla.org/Firefox/Feature_Brainstorming:Platform _Integration`), although it's slowly getting better all the time.

- Firefox can be slow to launch, especially if you install lots of extensions, but that could very well be the fault of the extensions.

- Anecdotally, Firefox doesn't feel as fast as Safari and Chrome, but I'm well aware that the exact opposite is true for some folks!

Who Should Use Firefox?

Every Mac user should have Firefox on his computer, at least as an alternative to Safari. Because you can create highly customized versions of Firefox, with unique profiles, extensions, themes, and bookmarks, it can be both a general-purpose browser and a tool specifically designed to perform a specific function. If you haven't ever used Firefox, give it a whirl today; if you already use Firefox, learn more about it, as I guarantee there are lots of cool things you don't know that will knock your socks off once you learn about them.

NOTE: My point about customization can't be over-emphasized. In my case, for instance, I have four Firefox profiles, which helps keep me from trying to load 50 extensions at one time. By segregating extensions into different profiles, I help keep the bloat down. My four profiles are:

- Default, for general web surfing
- Web Dev, for web development
- Multimedia, for working with music and movies online
- Virgin, for screenshots of Firefox in its untouched state

Profiles are a feature that most Firefox users just don't know much about, which is too bad, considering how useful they really are. If you don't know how to create or access Firefox profiles, the best place to start is MozillaZine's excellent introduction at `http://kb.mozillazine.org/Profile_Manager`. If you're ready to go beyond that, one article that should make power users happy is Asa Dotzler's "Shortcut to launch a specific Firefox profile on Mac" (`http://weblogs.mozillazine.org/asa/archives/2008/ 08/shortcut_to_lau.html`).

Further Resources

My first book (*Don't Click on the Blue E!: Switching to Firefox* (O'Reilly Media, 2005)) was about Firefox 1.0, and even though much of it is completely out-of-date, there's still a lot of good information in it. In particular, the first chapter, a history of web browsers, is one of my favorite things I've written.

Wiki has several great articles on Firefox, but one that I'd recommend particularly is "Features of Mozilla Firefox" (http://en.wikipedia.org/wiki/Features_of_Mozilla_Firefox). The best website I know of for all things Mozilla is http://kb.mozillazine.org, with the Firefox articles on http://kb.mozillazine.org/Category:Firefox. Two that I suggest you bookmark are "Frequently encountered issues" with Firefox (http://kb.mozillazine.org/Category:Issues_%28Firefox%29) and "Problematic extensions" (http://kb.mozillazine.org/Problematic_extensions), both of which contain lists of problems and how to deal with them.

Camino

Firefox is a great browser—one of the best in the world—but as you saw in the previous section, it's not very Mac-like (that's not to say that it's not Mac-friendly, as it definitely is, but there's a big difference between Mac-like and Mac-friendly—Mac-like means it conforms to Mac OS X's user interface guidelines, while Mac-friendly means that, well, it works pretty darn well on the Mac). In response, several developers decided to take the heart of Firefox—the Gecko layout engine that turns HTML and CSS and other web code into a finished web page that you see in your Web browser—and build a Mac-centric environment around it, creating a free and open source browser they named Camino, which you can see in Figure 5–2.

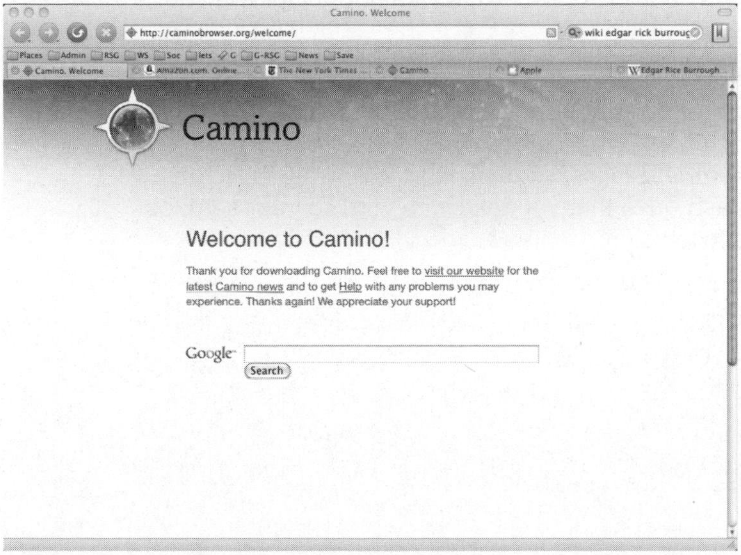

Figure 5–2. *Camino is Firefox at the core but all Mac on the outside.*

In November 2009, Camino 2.0 was released, and work continues on the browser today. It's not used by a lot of folks, but it's worth taking a look at for the benefits it brings.

What's Unique?

Camino is basically Firefox, Mac-ified. It combines the standards-compliant, fast, widely compatible Gecko layout engine that Firefox uses with Mac-native software libraries, so that is a Mac app through and through. It looks like a Mac app, and it behaves like a Mac app. It's part of the family!

What's Good?

Camino has a lot going for it, including:

- Because it's built first and foremost as a Mac OS X web browser, Camino is a very Mac-friendly and Mac-like web browser. It supports several Apple technologies, libraries, and conventions (such as Apple Keychain, Services, AppleScript, Spotlight, Bonjour, key commands, and keyboard navigation).

- Gecko, the layout engine used by Firefox and Camino, is one of the best on the planet, so you can expect accuracy, speed, and wide compatibility.

- Even though Firefox extensions and themes don't work in Camino (see "What's Bad," next), you can still find several for Camino at Pimp My Camino (www.pimpmycamino.com).

- The Mozilla Foundation considers Camino to be an officially supported project (see www.mozilla.org/projects/), so it's not going away any time soon.

- Because Camino is open source, folks can do some interesting things with it that are harder to do with closed source software. One big example of this principle is Portable Camino (www.freesmug.org/portableapps/camino), which allows you to run Camino on a USB flash drive that you take with you, so your settings and everything else follows you.

What's Bad?

I'd love to be able to tell you that all is swell in the land of Camino, but that's not quite true, for these reasons:

- Even though Camino is based on Firefox's layout engine, none of Firefox's extensions or themes work in Camino, due to the fact that Camino is built using Apple's libraries and tools. There are extensions and themes available for Camino (see "What's Good," previously), but there aren't a lot, and many of them are hit-and-miss or poorly maintained, or both.

- Development on Camino is slow. It's also steady, and it's very much a live project, but don't expect constant updates. If history is any guide, you can expect a new, small release of Camino once a year, with a bigger release coming every three years.

Those aren't horrible, but they do explain why Camino isn't the default browser for most people.

Who Should Use Camino?

If you like Firefox but are really bothered that it's not Mac-like enough, fire up Camino and see what you think. To be honest, I've used Camino for weeks at a time, but I personally don't find anything super-compelling about it, as opposed to other web browsers. But hey, it's free and you might love it, so download it and see what you think.

Further Resources

The Camino Wiki, at `http://wiki.caminobrowser.org`, is an essential stop for users. Another good source of the latest info is The Camino Blog, at `http://caminobrowser.org/blog/`.

MozillaZine has an active support forum for Camino users at `http://forums.mozillazine.org/viewforum.php?f=12`, so head there if you have questions or need help.

Chrome/Chromium

Ever since Google announced Chrome in September 2008, it's been the topic of thousands of articles, blog posts, and discussions. With Chrome, Google aimed to bring the web browser into the modern age by integrating the best features from other browsers with new technologies and ideas, all with a stated focus on security, speed, and stability. In less than two years, Chrome is already the number three web browser in the world in terms of users, an impressive accomplishment. Of course, the fact that Chrome has the Google powerhouse behind it has played a major role in that popularity, but even so, there are very good reasons to use Chrome, shown in Figure 5–3.

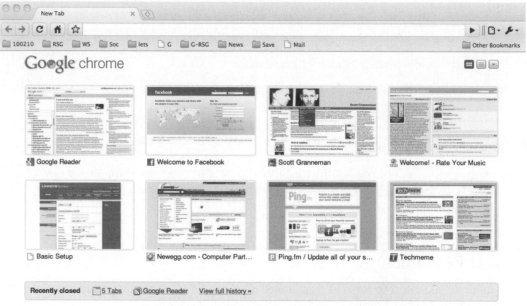

Figure 5–3. *Chrome's default New Tab page shows you your most-visited websites.*

Chrome is a great web browser already, and it shows enormous promise. Like Safari, it uses WebKit as its layout engine, but unlike Safari, it's a lot more flexible, with an official extension architecture that's produced thousands of extensions in just a few months. If you want to jump on board the Chrome train, head to www.google.com/ chrome?platform=mac and download it. I think you'll be very glad you did.

At the same time Google announced Chrome, it also let the world know about Chromium, the open source project behind Chrome. Chromium is available for anyone to contribute to and use, and periodically Google takes the code, adds Google branding and other pieces of code, and releases the result as Chrome. Features (and bugs!) get introduced in Chromium before they ever get to Chrome, so it can be a sometimes frustrating glimpse of the future.

What's Unique?

Chrome is Google's web browser, and it is the most modern, most secure web browser out there today. One feature in particular embodies the new thinking behind Chrome: process separation. Basically, Chrome spawns a new process for every tab you open as you use the browser. Google's decision to build Chrome this way brings three huge benefits:

- **Better Security:** WebKit's only access to the network is through the parent's browser process, and its access to the file system is restricted by Mac OS's built-in permissions. Even if a criminal compromises one tab, the others are unaffected, which is obviously a safer model for users. In fact, Chrome was the only browser not compromised during the Pwn2Own contest, during which experts attempted to exploit security holes in web browsers, a feat attributed to Chrome's separation of processes. The winner of Pwn2Own, who was able to easily manipulate the other browsers, said exploiting Chrome would be "a formidable challenge," which is impressive (http://arstechnica.com/security/news/2009/03/chrome-is-the-only-browser-left-standing-in-pwn2own-contest.ars).

- **Better Stability:** Think about how other Web browsers work: if a plug-in or tab hangs, the entire browser hangs, forcing you to have to restart the browser. Why? Because everything the browser is doing is running as a single process. Chrome, however, splits everything into multiple, independent processes. If one tab goes haywire, you'll see the Sad Tab of Death (see http://commons.wikimedia.org/wiki/File:SadTab.png), but Chrome will keep running happily, so you can easily reload or close the bad tab.

- **Better Information:** In line with the fact that Chrome is a multi-process browser, it makes sense that it provides users with a Task Manager to manage those processes. You can get to it at **View ➤ Developer ➤ Task Manager**, and it allows you to view every tab, plug-in, and extension's usage of memory, CPU, and the network. If one is misbehaving, click the End Process button to kill it.

Google's decision to develop Chrome with multiple processes has benefited the company and the browser's users tremendously. But that's not all that's great about Chrome, as you're about to see.

> **NOTE:** Independently of Chrome, Microsoft's Internet Explorer 8 also introduced what it calls Loosely Coupled Internet Explorer (LCIE) architecture, which basically runs things in separate processes (see `http://blogs.msdn.com/ie/archive/2008/03/11/ie8-and-loosely-coupled-ie-lcie.aspx` for a technical explanation). Stainless, which I'll introduce you to shortly, is a Chrome-like browser that runs tabs in separate processes, but then goes Chrome (and every other browser I know) one better, as I'll show you. Finally, Firefox is also proceeding with a rewrite of the browser that will result in separated processes, a project that has the cool code name "Electrolysis." You can read more about it at `https://wiki.mozilla.org/Electrolysis`.

What's Good?

Fast: Chrome feels really, really fast. The browser opens quickly, pages load quickly, and web-based apps run quickly. When I convince people to try Chrome and then talk to them a week later, the thing they all say to me is "Wow! It's fast!" I'll admit, Chrome and Safari often feel equally sprightly, but they both feel much more sleek than Firefox.

> **NOTE:** There are several technical reasons for the speediness, detailed in Google's blog post "Technically speaking, what makes Google Chrome fast?" (`http://blog.chromium.org/2009/12/technically-speaking-what-makes-google.html`).

Security: Besides the factors I already discussed previously in What's Unique?, Chrome features anti-malware and anti-phishing protection to warn users about bad stuff on the Web. The anti-malware part isn't as vital to Mac users (but boy is it helpful for Windows users!), but the anti-phishing aspect is quite useful.

> **NOTE:** If you don't know what phishing is, see Wikipedia's article at http://en.wikipedia.org/wiki/Phishing.

Omnibox: Chrome folds the Search Box (found in Firefox and Chrome) into the Address Bar so that you now use the Address Bar for both URLs and web searches. Type a URL in, and Chrome takes you there; enter a word or phrase, and Chrome searches for it. What could be easier or more logical?

Extensions: Starting in January 2010, Chrome began to support extensions, and currently there are thousands of them. Unlike Firefox, you don't have to restart your browser when you install a theme in Chrome, which is great; also unlike Firefox, Chrome themes are very limited and cannot change the browser in fundamental ways, which isn't so great. You can find extensions at `https://chrome.google.com/extensions`; be sure to Google for "best Chrome extensions" to find scads of lists on blogs and websites all over the Net.

Themes: Chrome supports themes, which allow you to turn the browser from a boring gray to a hideous, unreadable mess of colors and images. Yes, I'm overstating things, but not by much. You can download themes from two official places: Google Chrome's Themes Gallery (`https://tools.google.com/chrome/intl/en/themes/`), which features themes by artists and by Google, and from Google Chrome Extensions (`https://chrome.google.com/extensions/search?q=theme`), which provides themes from developers.

Automatic updates: IE 8 was released in March 2009, one year ago at the time of this writing, yet only 37% of IE users are using it—23% still use IE 7, and a whopping 34% still use the putrid IE 6. The story's not quite as bad with Firefox: 3.6 was released in January 2010, 2 months ago, and 21% of Firefox users have it, while 60% still run 3.5, 15% run Firefox 3, and only about 3.5% run Firefox 2 or earlier. In contrast, 97% of Chrome users are using the current version. Why? Because Chrome updates itself silently, every five hours, without any user involvement. That's great, since most people just don't pay attention to updating when it's manual.

> **NOTE:** The IE numbers came from `http://en.wikipedia.org/wiki/Template:Msieshare1`, and the Firefox numbers were on `http://en.wikipedia.org/wiki/Template:Firefox_usage_share`. Chrome's numbers were reported at `www.informationweek.com/news/internet/security/showArticle.jhtml?articleID=217300466`.

Cookies Manager: Like virtually all contemporary web browsers, Chrome includes the ability to manage cookies (though it's a bit hidden, at **Chrome ➤ Preferences ➤ Under The Hood ➤ Privacy ➤ Content Settings ➤ Cookies**). However, Chrome is the first browser I've seen that provides a link to Adobe Flash Player Storage Settings, which lets you manage Flash cookies. I'm not that concerned about normal web cookies, as browsers come with tools built in that let me manage those, but Flash cookies are another thing entirely. They're far worse than regular browser cookies (see why at `http://en.wikipedia.org/wiki/Flash_cookies`), and no browser has built-in management tools for them—even Chrome simply provides a link to the page that Adobe provides for overseeing them. What Chrome's doing is nice, but all browsers need to do more.

NOTE: For information about Flash cookies and why they're really a bad thing, see Wikipedia's "Local Shared Object" (`http://en.wikipedia.org/wiki/Flash_cookies`) and the Electronic Privacy Information Center's "Local Shared Objects - Flash Cookies" (`http://epic.org/privacy/cookies/flash.html`).

New Tab page: When you open a new tab in Chrome, it displays thumbnails of your eight most-visited websites (which you can delete, rearrange, or pin so they stick), a list of recently closed web pages, and tips for using Chrome. This is wonderfully useful, as you'll quickly see when you start using it.

Incognito Mode: Like many other browsers, Chrome supports a private browsing mode that doesn't store cookies, history, or other personal data. To use this feature, select **File** ➤ **New Incognito Window**.

AutoFill: Like many other browsers, Chrome allows you to fill in fields for such personal data as Name, Address, E-mail, Company Name, even Credit Cards; then, when you get to a form that requests that information, Chrome makes it easy to enter it, saving you time and work. To enter your data, go to **Chrome** ➤ **Preferences** ➤ **Personal Stuff** ➤ **Form Autofill**.

Translate Infobars: When you hit a web page that contains a language on it that's different from your preferred language (**Chrome** ➤ **Preferences** ➤ **Under The Hood** ➤ **Web Content**), Chrome displays an Infobar that drops down over the top of the web page and offers to translate the content for you using Google Translate.

Greasemonkey support: I'm a huge fan of the Greasemonkey extension for Firefox, and starting in early 2010, Chrome started supporting (most) Greasemonkey scripts natively. In other words, you don't need to install a Greasemonkey extension first; instead, just click on any Greasemonkey script and Chrome converts it into a Chrome extension on-the-fly and installs it. At this time, about 80% of the scripts at `http://userscripts.org`, the main repository for Greasemonkey scripts, work in Chrome, with more expected. Some recommendations: Google Reader - Colorful List View (`http://userscripts.org/scripts/show/8782`), Linkification (`http://userscripts.org/scripts/show/67744`), Wikipedia Auto-Login (`http://userscripts.org/scripts/show/4971`), and YouTube Enhancer (`http://userscripts.org/scripts/show/33042`).

NOTE: Don't know what Greasemonkey does or what it's good for? Oh, you're in for a treat! Go read Wikipedia's article on the subject at `http://en.wikipedia.org/wiki/Greasemonkey`, and then hie thee to `http://userscripts.org` and start downloading some Greasemonkey scripts! They work in Firefox, Prism (some of the time), and Chrome and Fluid (most of the time). By the way—you'll find out about Prism and Fluid later in this chapter, so hold your horses.

What's Bad?

As great as Chrome is, it's still missing features that other web browsers have, such as:

- **64-bit support:** Nope, Chrome is still just 32-bits. Safari is 64-bits. Get with it, Google!

- **Toolbar customization:** Beyond adding the Home button and the Page and Tools menus, you can't customize Chrome's toolbar at all. This grows especially problematic as you start adding extensions, many of which stick their buttons in... you guessed it! The toolbar.

- **Advanced print controls:** Sure, you get the basics, but you have absolutely no choices about the headers and footers you print (something that's always chapped me about Safari as well, although Firefox gives you complete control).

- **RSS support:** Chrome doesn't recognize RSS feeds or, shockingly, offer to add them to Google Reader. There are extensions that take care of it, but why isn't it built-in?

- **Simple image properties:** Sure, you can right-click and use Inspect Element, but that's way more complicated than what you do in Firefox, in which you can right-click and select View Image Info.

In addition to the features Chrome lacks that you can find in other browsers, there are also missing features that the Windows version of Chrome *does* have, such as:

- **App Mode:** In Chrome on Windows, users can go to **Page ➤ Create Application Shortcuts** to turn the current website into a desktop/web app hybrid, with Chrome as the SSB (more on those coming up, when we'll talk about Prism and Fluid). That menu is grayed out in the Mac version of Chrome, so it's coming soon. Hurry!

- **Tab pinning:** In Windows, you can pin important tabs that you use all the time. They'll never close, and they'll shrink down to the size of their icon on the tab. No such luck on the Mac side.

NOTE: Just as this book was going to press, I checked the latest Chrome, and Mac users now have Tab Pinning. To use this feature, right-click on a tab you want to pin and select Pin Tab. Woohoo!

Who Should Use Chrome/Chromium?

In my opinion, all Mac users should have at least three web browsers on their machines in order to meet different needs: Safari (no getting around that one!), Firefox, and Chrome. In fact, as I've introduced people to Chrome, I've found that many of them—both Windows and Mac users—switch once they try it. They like its speed, its simplicity, and its extensions. Granted, it's not as Mac-like as Safari or even Camino, but Chrome is moving very fast, so it's likely that it will get more integrated with Mac OS X over time—heck, Chrome is still in beta as I'm writing this! Based on Google's achievements so far with Chrome, and the positive reaction users have to it, I foresee a strong future for that web browser.

Chromium, on the other hand, is for a very limited audience: developers who want to test new features, users curious about the future of Chrome, and those who don't mind testing new, potentially buggy software. I run Chromium as well as Chrome, and Chromium is sometimes weird and buggy, but Chrome is not.

TIP: If after all that you still want to run Chromium, the best way to keep up-to-date with it is to go to `http://techcrunch.com/2009/08/16/our-mac-chromium-updater-stay-up-to-date-on-the-best-versions-of-chrome-for-mac/` and download the Mac Chromium Updater introduced in the post. If you want to create your own script, or use the command line, check out Mac OS X Hints' "Update to latest Chromium build via shell script" at `http://www.macosxhints.com/article.php?story=20090604081030791`.

Further Resources

Google announced Chrome by publishing a 48-page comic book, *Google Chrome: Behind the Open Source Browser Project*. The comic is brilliant in how well it presents the ideas and technologies behind Chrome (no surprise, since it was drawn by Scott McCloud, an expert in visual communications through comics), and I really can't recommend it enough. You can read it at Google Books (www.google.com/googlebooks/ chrome/), or download a PDF at `www.docstoc.com/docs/1084148/Google-Chrome-Comic-Book/`.

Google's hub for Chrome support is at www.google.com/support/chrome/; in particular, the Google Chrome Help Forum, at www.google.com/support/forum/p/Chrome, can be tremendously helpful. The official Google Chrome Blog, at `http://chrome.blogspot.com`, is usually a great source of news and info. Finally, to keep up with what's happening in the fast-moving world of Chrome, check out Google Chrome Releases Announcements and Release Notes, at http://googlechromereleases.blogspot.com/.

If you want to geek out and learn a lot more about Chrome's method of process separation, read Marc Chung's "Chrome's Process Model Explained" (http://blog.marcchung.com/2008/09/05/chromes-process-model-explained.html), Charlie Reis' "Using Processes to Improve the Reliability of Browser-based Applications" (www.cs.washington.edu/homes/creis/publications/UW-CSE-07-12-01.pdf), which inspired Chrome's developers, and the Chromium "Design Documents" (www.chromium.org/developers/design-documents).

For more on Chrome's security and why it works, take a look at "Browser Security: Lessons From Google Chrome" (http://queue.acm.org/detail.cfm?id=1556050), by Charles Reis, Adam Barth, and Carlos Pizano. Another interesting read is Roger Grimes' "How Secure Is Google Chrome?" (www.pcworld.com/businesscenter/article/158400/how_secure_is_google_chrome.html) , but keep in mind that many of his complaints in the "Questionable controls" and "Bugaboos" sections have pretty much been fixed.

Opera

Opera has long been the leader in browser innovation, even if most people have never heard of it. For instance, Opera was the first browser to introduce tabs (2000), sessions that save your windows and tabs and then restore them when you restart (2000), pop-up blocking (2000), mouse gestures that let you control the browser by moving your mouse in pre-defined ways (2001), and Speed Dial, which Apple copied and rebranded as Top Sites (2007). So if Opera is so ahead of the curve, why isn't it more widely used?

That actually depends on what you're talking about. True, Opera only has about a 2% market share in English-speaking countries, but it's far more popular in many part of Europe, where its use approaches 25% in some nations. When you move beyond computers, things get even more interesting. Opera is the only commercial web browser you can get for your Nintendo Wii, and when it comes to mobile phones, Opera is widely popular. It's estimated that over 100 million cell phones have shipped with Opera pre-installed—as long as those phones were using Symbian or Windows Mobile operating systems, or could run Java ME apps.

So Opera is widely used, just not on computers in the US. I think a lot of that comes down to the fact that Opera used to cost $40, which turned a lot of people off, since they could use Netscape or IE for free. Opera tried to change this by switching to an ad-supported model in 2000 and then finally becoming completely free in 2005, but by then the damage was done. This is really too bad, as Opera, shown in Figure 5–4, really is a great browser in many ways.

Figure 5-4. *Opera keeps adding cool new features and getting better all time.*

Opera has a history of innovation, and it's continuing that tradition in the newest versions. In addition, competition from Chrome and Firefox are pushing it to become faster, which is great for consumers.

What's Unique?

Opera has many features that distinguish it from competitors, including:

- **Mouse gestures:** Opera has had this feature built-in since 2001, as I mentioned previously. In addition to clicking on buttons, selecting menus, and pressing key commands, a user can also control Opera by moving her mouse in pre-defined ways. For instance, to go back a page, right-click and hold while moving the mouse left, then release. To create a new tab and give it focus, right-click and hold while moving the mouse down, then release. Some people *love* mouse gestures; for them, Opera is a dream.

- **E-mail client and contact manager:** Opera is the only web browser that comes with its own built-in e-mail client and contact manager. Some Opera users think this is a huge plus for the browser, but I've never been that impressed when I tried to use it. To try it out, go to Tools ➤ Mail And Chat Accounts.

- **IRC client:** Opera is the only web browser that comes with built-in support for IRC, which enables users to chat with people all over the globe in rooms dedicated to every topic under the sun. To use it, go to Tools ➤ Mail And Chat Accounts.

- **BitTorrent:** Opera is the only web browser that comes with a BitTorrent client built-in (are you seeing a theme here?), which allows users to download and share files using the awesome BitTorrent protocol. I prefer other BitTorrent clients, which I'll cover in the next chapter, so it's nice that you can disable Opera's BitTorrent client by following the instructions at www.opera.com/support/kb/view/840/. That said, you may very well like it, so give it a chance.

- **Private browsing:** Plenty of other browsers support some sort of private browsing mode, during which your history, cookies, and other data aren't saved. Opera, however, lets you browse privately on a per-tab basis, which is unique, to my knowledge. You can select either File ➤ New Private Tab or File ➤ New Private Window. Very smart! I wish more browsers did it this way.

- **Opera Unite:** Opera doesn't just allow users to view web pages; it also makes it easy for users to publish them using Opera Unite. Set it up, and you can serve a website, photos, files, chat rooms, and streaming media from your Mac, as long as Opera is running. The speed depends on your Internet connection, of course, and you wouldn't want to serve your company's website using this feature, but it's good for quick-and-dirty stuff. To get started, click on Tools ➤ Opera Unite Server.

- **Opera Link:** Chrome makes it easy to back up and synchronize your bookmarks, Safari uses MobileMe to sync bookmarks and some other data, and Firefox has an official plug-in called Weave that syncs bookmarks, saved passwords, browsing history, and open tabs. Opera Link is built in, and backs up and syncs bookmarks (including the Bookmarks Bar, called the Personal Bar by Opera), notes, and Speed Dial.

- **Paste And Go:** I do this constantly in other Web browsers: copy a link, paste it into the browser's Address Bar, press Return to load the URL. Not in Opera, where I copy a link and then right-click in the Address Bar and select Paste And Go, which sticks the URL in and immediately takes me there (I can also use ⌘-⇧-V on the keyboard). Every browser should do this (Chrome does)!

What's Good?

In addition to those features unique to Opera, there are lots of great aspects to the browser.

- **Fast:** Safari, Chrome, Firefox, and Opera are locked in a back-and-forth battle for speediest browser. Opera has always been fast, and the competition has only helped spur it on, which is great for all web users.

- **Security:** Opera has an excellent security record in terms of number of vulnerabilities found and the speed with which those vulnerabilities get fixed. In addition to that admirable record, Opera has built-in anti-phishing and anti-malware protection.

- **Cross-platform:** As Mac users, we obviously focus on that operating system, but Opera also runs on Windows, Linux, FreeBSD, and Solaris, so if you want to use Opera on one of your other computers, you're probably covered.

- **Speed Dial:** Like Top Sites, Opera automatically shows you a list of your most-visited websites when you open a new tab (and remember, Opera did it first). Opera will show up to 25 sites, but you can add more if you edit a config file, speeddial.ini.

- **Ad Blocking:** Opera calls this a Content Blocker in an effort to prevent the displeasure of advertisers. But it is what it is. It's also hidden well: right-click on a blank area of a web page and select Block Content to access it (to manage your settings, go to **Tools ➤ Preferences ➤ Advanced ➤ Content ➤ Blocked Content**). It's not as powerful as the solutions in other browsers—nor is it automated with ad lists you can subscribe to—but it does work.

- **Standards:** Opera has always been at the forefront when it comes to supporting Web standards; in fact, an Opera employee helped develop CSS. In addition to CSS, Opera supports a wide litany of standards, including HTML, XHTML, WML, XSLT, XPath, JavaScript, DOM, XMLHttpRequest, Unicode, SVG, and PNG (including alpha transparency). Opera also passes the Acid2 test, which tests how well browsers support Web standards, and scored 100/100 on the Acid3 test, which primarily focuses on JavaScript.

- **Customization:** Of all the Web browsers, Opera is easily the most customizable. You can change how it looks, how it acts, key commands, and much more. **Opera ➤ Preferences** opens up a world of settings that you can tweak to your heart's content. And if what you want to change isn't in the GUI, you can more than likely manually edit a config file to make your change (for more on this, read "Finding and Editing the Opera INI Files" at http://operawiki.info/EditingINIFiles).

- **Accessibility:** If you're physically disabled, using a mouse can be arduous; Opera, however, makes it easy to control virtually everything about it using the keyboard. For those with visual disabilities, Page Zoom (**View ➤ Zoom**) enlarges everything on a web page—text, images, Flash, even Java applets—up to 1000%. Even for those of us who just suffer from aging eyes, this can be tremendously useful!

- **Web Development:** Developers who use Firefox have the excellent Firebug extension available to them, but Opera comes with Dragonfly, a Firebug-like tool, as part of the browser. To invoke it, go to **Tools ➤ Advanced ➤ Developer Tools**. Once it's open, you can do an amazing number of things with it, so spend some time learning it.

What's Bad?

Opera doesn't have a lot of negatives, as you can see:

- **No extensions:** Opera tightly limits what plug-ins can do and lacks a full-fledged API for extensions, which is why such software as 1Password can't work with it, which makes me sad.

- **Mail:** Opera's built-in e-mail client doesn't do it for me at all. I know that some people like it, but I find Opera's strengths to be in the area of web browsers, not e-mail clients.

- **Key commands:** Some standard Mac OS X key commands are ignored by, or conflict with, Opera. One huge annoyance for me: I like to Hide instead of Minimize windows, but when I press ⌘-H while using Opera, the History panel opens. Opera's key command to show History is ⌘-⇧-H, but that conflicts with ⌘-H, which is very frustrating, since this is the *only* program on my Mac that has this problem.

- **Incompatibilities:** There are still sites that don't really work well in Opera, causing things to look or act weird; worse, some sites—and this is very bad—don't support Opera, forcing you to switch to Firefox, Chrome, Safari, or (blech!) Internet Explorer. As more websites switch to supporting common Web standards, however, this should be less of an issue all the time.

Who Should Use Opera?

Opera is a great browser, but it's always been a lesser contender on the desktop in terms of market share. The company's decision to charge for its product at a time when all of the other competing products were free has perhaps doomed it to a permanently small market share. It's certainly attractive to power users, with its customization and built-in features, but it's often been seen as over-complicated for quote-unquote normal web users. This may change as Opera strives to push its way into more markets and onto more desktops. In my case, while I like and respect Opera, after using it for a few weeks I always return back to Safari, Firefox, and Chrome. Give it a try, however, as you never know: you may be one of those people who love Opera passionately.

Further Resources

There's one central place you should go if you want to find out pretty much anything about Opera: the Opera Wiki, at `http://operawiki.info/Opera`. That site is a fabulous repository of knowledge, tips, and tricks about all things Opera. If you're even thinking about using Opera, you must must must visit that site.

Stainless

When Google announced Chrome, the company made it clear that Mac users were going to have to wait a while before the browser would be out on our favorite operating system. So we waited. And waited. And waited some more. The waiting got to be too much for the developers at Mesa Dynamics, a small software company (now MD Software), so they went ahead and created Stainless, a Web browser inspired by Chrome, which you can see in Figure 5–5.

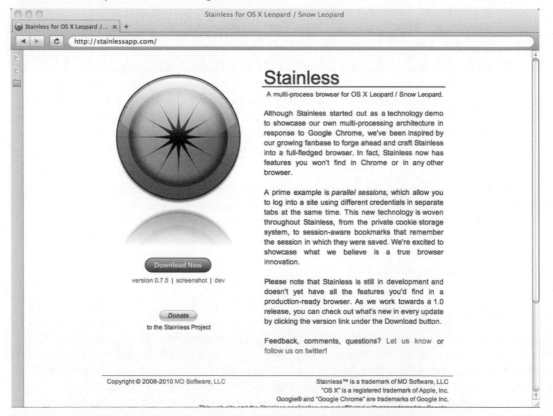

Figure 5–5. *Stainless is a WebKit-based browser with some clever tricks up its sleeve.*

Like Chrome, Stainless uses WebKit to render web pages, and also like Chrome, Stainless runs each tab as a separate process, bringing with it stability and control. Originally, Stainless was more of a lark for MD Software, but now, according to the company's website, "we've been inspired by our growing fanbase to forge ahead and craft Stainless into a full-fledged browser." As you're about to see, this is very good news.

What's Unique?

I probably should have put Stainless in the Others section that's coming up soon, in which I give quick looks at the browsers with teeny-tiny market shares (many undeservedly, it should be said). After all, Stainless has a teeny-tiny market share. However, I wanted to call it out because it does something that no other browser does, on any platform (that I know of) and that makes Stainless truly unique.

Here's the scenario that so many other browsers fail: you have two Twitter accounts, or two Gmail accounts, or two accounts at any website. On one tab, you log in with one account, and then you log in on another tab with the second account. Now go back to the first tab—you're no longer logged in with the first account; instead, you're logged in with the second account. Both tabs are now using the second account. Why? Because every browser except Stainless allows you to have only one cookie from a site for the entire browser. The first account writes info to the site's cookie, but when you log in with the second account, that account overwrites the site's cookie with that information. When the first tab looks at the cookie, it sees the second account, so that's the account you're now using.

Stainless has this one solved, with a feature it calls Parallel Sessions. Unlike the other browsers, Parallel Sessions allows you log in to the same site with different accounts, each on a different tab in the browser, by going to **File ➤ New Single Session Tab**. How? Stainless uses a private cookie storage system that segregates cookies in memory while the tabs are loaded. In addition, you can bookmark the different tabs, and when you click on a bookmark, it will load with the appropriate account. Sweet!

This one feature is reason enough to keep Stainless on your Mac, just to log in to sites on which you have more than one account. Yes, I know you could open multiple browsers to do the same thing, but that always seemed wildly inefficient to me, as well as confusing: "Wait... do I have my work account in Firefox or Safari?" Use well-labeled bookmarks in Stainless, and you can do it all in one browser. Much easier, much cleaner, much more efficient.

What's Good?

Stainless has many nice features, even for a relatively newly minted browser:

- **Separate processes:** As I just pointed out, in emulation of Chrome, every browser tab runs as a separate process, bringing greater stability and security.

- **Process Manager:** Since every tab runs as a different process, it makes sense that—also like Chrome—Stainless has a Process Manager that allows you to monitor those processes. To use it, go to Window ➤ Process Manager.

- **Private browsing:** Like most other browsers nowadays, Stainless has a private browsing mode (File ➤ New Private Browsing Window) that doesn't save history, cache, cookies, or other info.

- **Omnibox:** Also like Chrome, Stainless combines the Address Bar and the Search Bar into one unified field, which I much prefer.

- **Cookies:** This is another option I haven't seen before. Open Stainless ➤ Preferences ➤ Security, and you'll notice the check box next to Shutdown Actions: Delete All Unbookmarked Session Cookies. That's an interesting way to dispose of tracking cookies from websites you don't care about. If you bookmark it, Stainless assumes you want the cookie; otherwise, toss it. Smart.

- **Source code:** If you're a web developer, you'll like this one: if you select View ➤ Page Source, the HTML you see is color-coded and numbered. That's always helpful.

- **Bookmark strip:** Here's one that some may like & others may hate: there's no bookmarks menu. Instead, bookmarks are saved in a vertical strip that runs down the left side of the browser. Further, you see only a website's icon, not text, until you hover your mouse over the icon, which does display information about the bookmark. Personally, I find it difficult to use.

What's Bad?

Stainless is a young program, which explains why a lot of standard browser features are M.I.A., such as:

- **Extensions:** There are no extensions for Stainless, because Stainless doesn't provide an architecture for extensions.

- **Themes:** Likewise, there are no themes.

- **Bookmarks:** Bookmarking is pretty anemic. Other than the vertical strip, which I just covered in "What's Good?," you're out of luck. No bookmarks manager, and no import or export. That's no good.

- **Overwriting tabs:** This is a pet peeve of mine with Firefox as well, and with Safari: if you add bookmarks to a folder, and then right-click on that folder and choose Open In New Tabs, any currently opened tabs will be overwritten, which is highly annoying. New Tabs should be appended to current tabs, not nuke them!

Who Should Use Stainless?

If the Parallel Sessions feature gets your heart a-racin', then you know you need to try out Stainless. That's really the big reason to use Stainless. It's a nice browser overall, and I hope the developers at MD Software keep working on it, but now that Chrome is out with full extension and theme support, it's going to be hard for Stainless to compete unless they really advertise and explain Parallel Sessions and how it can be helpful.

Further Resources

You can read the Release Notes for Stainless at www.stainlessapp.com/doc/releasenotes.htm, which is a good idea if you want to keep up with new features and improvements. If you're feeling brave, download Stainless Development Builds from www.stainlessapp.com/doc/dev.htm. Finally, you can follow the Stainless team on Twitter, at http://twitter.com/mesadynamics.

Others

I could probably write an entire book about all of the browsers available on Mac OS X. There are many more than those I just covered, but I want to quickly focus on a few of the top also-rans. Many of these are quite good and are definitely worth investigating, at least to verify that innovation is found in many places besides Apple, Google, and Mozilla. I've listed them in alphabetical order, not in any sort of preferential order.

Arora: Arora is a bit different from most of the other web browsers in this chapter. It uses WebKit to display web pages, but it uses the cross-platform Qt framework for everything else, which means that Arora runs on Linux, UNIX, Windows, and Mac OS X. Unfortunately, this also means that Arora is very un-Mac-like. To give just one example: **Arora ➤ Preferences** is all about search and not really about the browser's settings, while **Tools ➤ Options** opens another window, also named Preferences, that does contain all of the browser's settings. On top of that, it's buggy and crashed constantly, on almost every page, on my MacBook Pro. Arora is a mess for Mac users, but if you're a masochist, go check it out at http://code.google.com/p/arora/. Figure 5–6 shows what Arora looks like when it's not busy crashing.

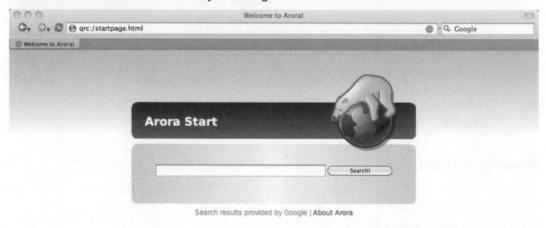

Figure 5–6. *Normally I don't say this, but here it's appropriate: avoid!*

Cruz: You'll learn about Todd Ditchendorf and his wonderful SSB, Fluid, later in this chapter. In addition to Fluid, Ditchendorf also codes Cruz, a web browser built using the same framework that Fluid uses, and with the WebKit layout engine underneath. It's still early days for Cruz, but it already boasts interesting features, such as tight Twitter integration and split views, which allows you to browse several web pages simultaneously in the same window. You can read more about Cruz and download it at http://cruzapp.com; view it in Figure 5–7.

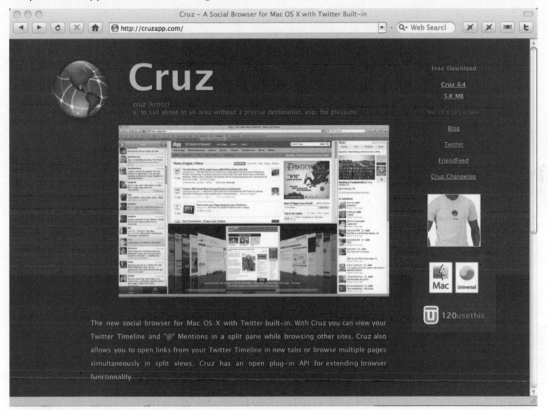

Figure 5–7. *Cruz has a long way to go before it reaches maturity.*

Flock: If you're a social networking or social media addict, then Flock is for you. Basically a highly customized Firefox (actually, the developers just announced that it's now going to be based on Google Chrome!), Flock integrates Facebook, Flickr, Twitter, Delicious, and many other services. It's free, open source, cross-platform, and updated regularly, but it's never really attracted that many users. You can check it out at http://flock.com and Figure 5–8.

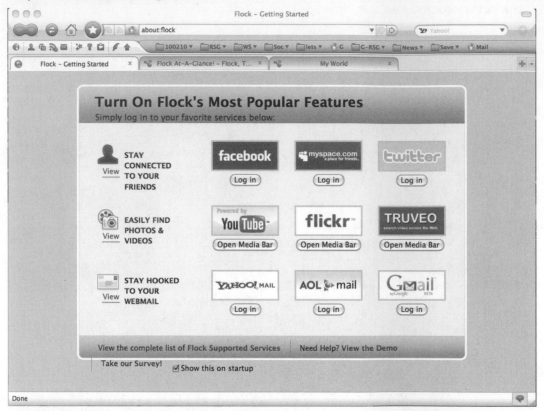

Figure 5–8. *If you're a social media addict, then Flock is for you.*

iCab: This is the best decade-old, highly customizable, fully featured, innovative, powerful web browser that almost no one uses. Why? Originally, iCab used its own proprietary layout engine that didn't really work that well, and by the time it switched to WebKit, Safari had conquered the Mac world. Add on to that the fact that iCab's free version constantly nags you to pay $15, in a world where all the major web browsers are completely free, and you can see why it has minuscule market share. Too bad—it's definitely worth taking for a spin. Get it at `www.icab.de`, and take a look at it in Figure 5–9.

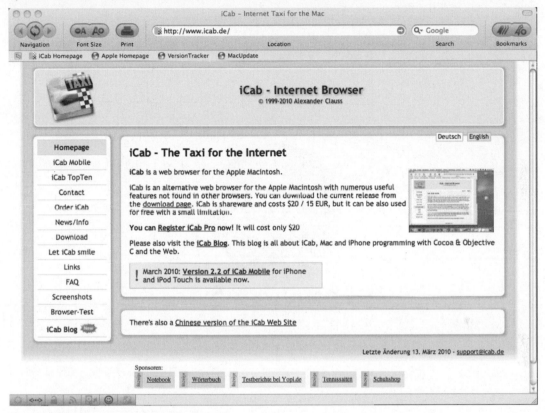

Figure 5–9. *iCab showing the iCab home page.*

OmniWeb: The Omni Group produces some of the best software available on the Mac, and it charges a pretty penny for it. For several years, they sold a web browser named OmniWeb that coupled its own proprietary layout engine with several interesting, formidable features. Two big changes—switching to WebKit and giving OmniWeb away for free—unfortunately occurred too late. Not very many people use it today, which is too bad, since it really does offer a lot; not to mention, it's pretty, as you can see in Figure 5–10. You can download it at www.omnigroup.com/products/omniweb; do so and give it a try, as it's a fine piece of work.

Figure 5–10. *OmniWeb has lots of great features, and it's now free.*

Shiira: Shiira is a Japanese web browser (don't worry, the UI is in English) that's based on WebKit. It's released under an open source license, but that hasn't helped it much, since the last update was in 2007. To all appearances this is a dead project, but for some reason, websites listing Mac browsers always list Shiira. Don't bother—it's so bad that I can't even show you a picture because it wouldn't open on my Mac running Snow Leopard.

Sunrise: Like Shiira, Sunrise is a Japanese web browser based on WebKit, which you can see in Figure 5–11. It has a few interesting features, like thumbnailed bookmarks, web-page screenshots, and more, but it's just not that compelling. You can find out more at www.sunrisebrowser.com.

Figure 5–11. *Sunrise is rather anemic when it comes to features.*

Choosing Between Browsers

As I said at the beginning of this chapter, I keep several web browsers on my Mac at all times, and I like to switch back and forth between them. In fact, sometimes I'll click on a link and want to open it in Safari, because I want to print the page and I find Safari does that better than any other browser, but a few minutes later I'll click on a link and want to open it in Firefox, because I have that browser set up to handle downloading music and movies. In Mac OS X, as in Windows and Linux, I can specify a default browser for my system, but that browser is used for everything. Wouldn't it be nice if I could choose between browsers on the fly, as needed?

Now I can, with Choosy. Choosy is a Preference Pane that runs as your Mac's default web browser. You configure Choosy by telling it which web browsers are installed on your Mac that you want to use, and which rules need to apply to start which web browsers. This can be as simple as telling Choosy to always display a list of web browsers when you click on a link in e-mail (which you can see in Figure 5–12), to ordering Choosy to open Chrome when you click on a link in Firefox that's been shortened using bit.ly.

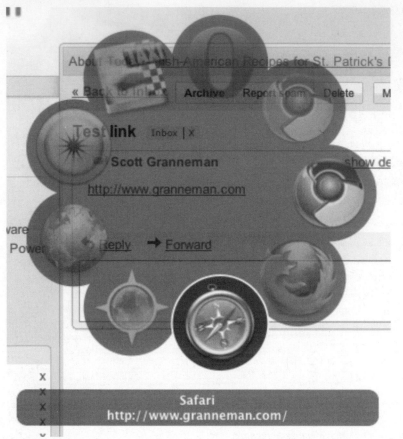

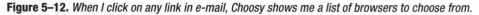

Figure 5–12. *When I click on any link in e-mail, Choosy shows me a list of browsers to choose from.*

After you download Choosy from www.choosyosx.com and install it, go to ➤ **System Preferences** and select Choosy. There are six tabs in Choosy; I'm going to cover the important stuff that you need to know.

General

Enable Choosy For Links: Check this for links in e-mail and other programs that display URLs. Yes, this includes web browsers, but by default Choosy will not interrupt you if you click on a link in a web browser; instead, it will let Chrome, Firefox, Safari, and the others all handle their own links, just like normal. You can change this, if you want, on the Advanced tab.

Enable Choosy For HTML Files: Check this if you want Choosy to appear if you click on HTML files in the Finder. If you create web pages, this will be handy; most people, though, probably don't need to worry about this.

Start Choosy Helper At Login: Check this if you want Choosy to run when you log in to your Mac. I would advise doing so, or you won't get the full benefits of the program.

Display Choose Icon In The Menu Bar: Uncheck this—you don't need more stuff cluttering up your Menu Bar.

Browsers

Add your browsers to this list by clicking the + on the bottom left and selecting browsers from your /Applications folder; remove browsers by selecting them in the list and then clicking -. Your favorite should be in the 1 position, because it will be selected by default when you invoke Choosy. Try to order your browsers from most to least favorite, as that will help when you move your mouse to select a browser when Choosy appears after you click on a link.

Behaviour

Now you get to make several choices about when Choosy should appear, which you can see in Figure 5–13.

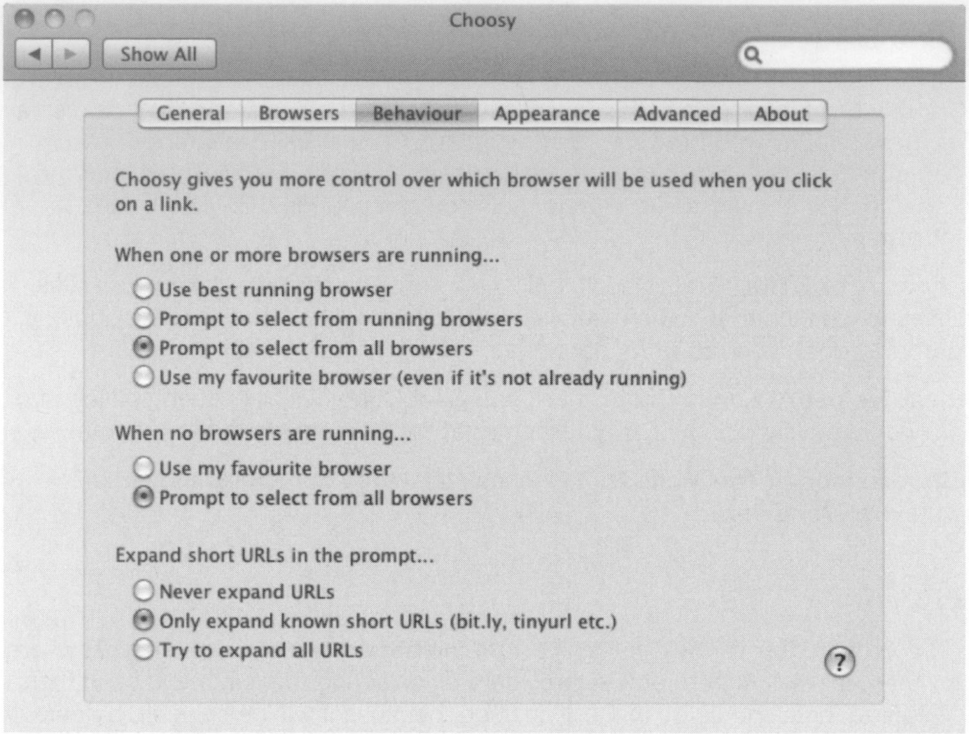

Figure 5–13. *Which browser appears when you click on a link? You decide.*

As you can see in Figure 5–13, you can be very specific here.

When One Or More Browsers Are Running and **When No Browsers Are Running:** I prefer to always select from all browsers, but it's really up to you. You might have noticed that you can tell Choosy to pick the "best running browser," where "best" is determined by the order you put your browsers in on the Browsers tab.

Expand Short URLs In The Prompt: I think it's a really good idea to expand short URLs—after all, you have no idea what lies behind them! I chose Only Expand Known Short URLs because I tend to only click on those from services I've heard of, and the list that Choosy understands (which you can view in the program's Help) contains all of the big ones. Besides, the Help also shows you to add new services yourself by creating and editing a file named short_urls.plist.

Appearance

Browser Prompt Style: I prefer to have the browser icons appear in a circle, as in Figure 5–12, instead of a row, due to the fact that I have so many of them (and, to be honest, because I think it looks cooler). If you only have one or two browsers, a row would probably be fine.

Display The URL In The Prompt: Absolutely! I want to see where I'm going.

Display Browser Names In The Prompt: When you have nine or so browsers on your Mac, sometimes it's easy to forget which icon goes with which browser, so I enable this.

Advanced

By default, Choosy simply displays itself based on your choices on the General tab. But as I mentioned in the introduction to this section, you can be very precise as to how Choosy works and when it shows itself. This is the tab to set that up. To add new rules, click on the + in the bottom left corner; to delete a rule, use the - in the same place. I simply don't have the space to go into this in detail, but it's also not something your usual power user can't figure out for herself by experimenting and reading the Help. The key takeaway here is that you can completely control Choosy, which is very impressive.

Rules have three parts:

Title: Use something meaningful to you.

Choosy Should Use This Rule When: First, determine if your specifications have to be met when All, Any, or None are true. Then, you can specify details about such things as Web Address, Source Application, Modifier Keys, URL Shortening Service, and more. Create as many specifics as you need.

When This Rule Is Used Choosy Should: So when your specifics are met, what should Choosy do? Choices include such things as Use The Default Behaviour, Use My Favorite Browser, Prompt To Select From All Browsers, Always Use This Browser, and more. You can even select Use All Of These Browsers if you want the link to open in more than one browser at the same time, which is very cool for Web developers.

I actually don't have that many rules, because the default behaviors satisfy most of my needs, but it's great that I have so many options that I can tailor to my needs. George Brocklehurst, the guy who created Choosy, has really done an excellent job making it as flexible and powerful as possible, while keeping it simple for those who prefer to keep it that way.

Choosy costs $12, which is cheap for the benefits it can bring you, but the developer generously gives you 45 days to try it out to see if it works for you. As a web developer, a lover of web browsers, and a writer of technical books, Choosy has been invaluable to me, and I really can't recommend it enough. Go to `www.choosyosx.com` and give it a spin today.

Further Resources

There are a few other programs that kinda sorta do the same things Choosy does—Choose Wisely, at `http://blog.tigion.de/2010/02/16/software-choose-wisely/` (in German, so use Google Chrome with auto-translate if necessary) is one of the closest—but none of them come anywhere near the functionality that Choosy offers. Sure, the others are free, and Choosy costs money, but it's a measly $12, and it's head and shoulders above the others, so don't waste your time.

SSBs: Site Specific Browsers

The web browser is probably the most important software tool developed in the last two decades. Over that time, web browsers have added new features that many now consider essential: tabs, auto-fill, and extensions, to name just a few. But sometimes the added features and complexity can actually get in the way of productivity, which is why there's been a movement in the last couple of years to create SSBs—Site Specific Browsers (although I prefer defining them as Single Site Browsers myself).

An SSB is still a web browser at its core, but it's a vastly simplified browser with the menus and toolbars removed, and instead of using it to visit any old website you wish, you use it for a specific, single site (hence the name!). In other words, instead of having Facebook open in one tab and Gmail open in another and TUAW open in still another, you'd create a Facebook SSB, and a Gmail SSB, and open those separately, like they are actual apps on your Mac. You would use the Facebook SSB only to access Facebook, and you would use the Gmail SSB only to access Gmail. You typically create SSBs for web apps—such as Facebook and Gmail—and not for websites, such as TUAW, or *The New York Times*, or Techmeme.

I know many of you reading this are thinking to yourself, "Why the heck would I use an SSB? Why don't I just open Facebook or Gmail as a tab in my web browser of choice and use that?" There are actually very good reasons to consider using an SSB instead of a tab in your usual web browser:

- **Minimize distractions:** Other tabs can distract you from your research and work. By segregating the web apps that tempt you and eat your time, you can get more done in your web browser. Think of this also as a separation of purpose—treat web apps like they're apps that deserve their own program, and your web browser as a general-purpose device.

- **Web apps that act like desktop apps:** Your SSB apps go in /Applications, just like every other app on your Mac (by and large). You can drag the SSB for Facebook to your Dock and launch it, or you can use Spotlight to search for the Gamil SSB. Basically, you launch your SSB like any other app, because to your Mac, your SSBs *are* just other apps.

- **Stability:** If the SSB crashes or locks up, your regular web browsers keep on going, and vice versa.

- **Autostart favorite websites:** If, after you log in to your Mac, you always open your web browser so you can see Gmail or another web app, then you can instead set your Gmail SSB to launch on log in ( ➤ System Preferences ➤ Accounts ➤ Login Options).

- **Different accounts in different SSB apps:** If you have to keep separate sets of credentials for work & personal accounts for web services, no need to log in and out repeatedly—just set up a Prism SSB for one of the accounts, and the passwords & cookies will stay as they need to be.

As you can see, there are substantial benefits to using SSBs. At the least, try one for yourself and see if it meets your needs. To give you some ideas, here are a few sites that work well as SSBs (besides Gmail and Facebook, since I already mentioned them):

- Amazon deals (see `http://probargainhunter.com/2006/11/28/amazon-shopping-tips-and-hacks/` to help you build the URLs)

- Basecamp (`http://YOURCOMPANY.basecamphq.com`)

- Google Buzz (`https://mail.google.com/mail/?shva=1#buzz` if you don't use Google Apps; if you use Google Apps, at this time you can't use Buzz, but that will change eventually)

- Google Reader (`https://www.google.com/reader/view`)

- Google Tasks (use `https://mail.google.com/tasks/ig` if you don't use Google Apps, or `https://mail.google.com/tasks/a/YOURDOMAIN.COM/canvas` if you do)

- Google Voice (`https://www.google.com/voice`)

- Google Wave (`https://wave.google.com`)

- Picnik (online photo editor; use `www.picnik.com`)

- Quake Live (free online Quake—woot!; use `www.quakelive.com` for the website and download `www.cocoia.com/QuakeLiveIcon.zip` for the SSB icon)

- Toodledo (the best to-do web app out there; use `www.toodledo.com`)

Basically, any website that's really a Web app makes a good candidate for an SSB. Think about the sites you visit every day and try them out using one of the SSB software tools that I'll cover next.

Prism

SSBs had been around for a few years when Mozilla announced in 2007 that it had created a technology that allowed users to create Mozilla-based SSBs. Now known as Prism, these SSBs are essentially very stripped-down versions of Firefox, so they have all the stability and compatibility of that excellent web browser.

There are actually two ways to create a Prism-based SSB:

The Prism extension for Firefox: Go to `https://addons.mozilla.org/en-US/firefox/addon/6665` and install the extension. Restart Firefox, browse to a site you want to access via the Prism SSB, and select Tools ➤ Convert Website to Application. Fill in the appropriate info, click OK, and you're finished.

A standalone application, also named Prism: Go to `http://prism.mozillalabs.com/started/` and click on Download Prism. Install the app and then run it when you find a website you want to turn into an SSB app. Fill in the appropriate info, click OK, and you're finished.

The extension is nice, but personally, I don't like to clutter Firefox with yet another extension if I can help it. Also, I don't create SSB-based sites all the time, so I don't need it constantly sitting in Firefox. For those reasons, I prefer the stand-alone app Prism, so that's what I'm going to focus on. Fortunately, virtually everything I'm going to say about it applies to the Firefox extension, so you're still covered if you go that route.

I'll start with the initial screen you see when you create an SSB app, shown in Figure 5–14.

Figure 5–14. *Creating an SSB app with Prism is just a matter of filling in the right fields.*

Be careful with what when you enter, because—incredibly—you can't change it once you're done, which seems crazy to me (and is one of the reasons I prefer Fluid, coming up next). My advice for the fields in that window is as follows:

URL: The address of the website that you want to run in Prism. If there's an https option, use that for added security.

Name: Enter the name of the website, or something else that's meaningful to you. This will become the name of the SSB app that you see on your Mac.

Show Navigation Bar: If you need to see the four main navigation buttons—Back, Forward, Home, and Reload—then check here. For a true web app, however, you shouldn't need those buttons. Think about it—you don't use the browser's buttons to go back in Gmail; you use links in Gmail's interface. Unfortunately, sometimes things go kooky in your browser and you need to reload the page. It appears that the only way to do this is either to restart the SSB app or click on the Reload button, *if* it's enabled. So best to enable it (again, Fluid does this better).

Show Status Messages And Progress: Check it, as the only way to get to Prism's meager Preferences is through an icon on the Status Bar. Prism developers, is this really a good idea?!

Enable Navigation Keys: Check this If the website you're converting allows you to press keys to enter commands (like Gmail does, for example), or those key commands won't work.

Create Shortcuts: I just don't understand why Applications Folder (AKA, /Applications) is even an option. Of course you'll want an app—it's what you're creating—in /Applications. Checking Desktop is up to you. What really gets me is that you can fail to check both, which means that your app isn't reachable—why is that even possible?

Icon: By default, Prism grabs the favicon (the little 16x16 icon next to the URLs of most websites) of the website you entered into the URL field and uses that for your SSB app's icon. Since favicons are 16x16 pixels, and Mac OS X icons can go all the way up to 512x512 pixels, with the default for the Desktop at 48x48, this results in absolutely horrible-looking icons. Pixelated junk, basically. Better instead to click on **Settings ▸ Choose Image** and use an image that looks good at large sizes. But where to find such images? See "SSB Icons" later in this section for the answer.

Click OK and you can start using your SSB app.

You might be thinking, "What about Firefox extensions?" Even though Prism and Firefox have the same Mozilla layout engine at their cores, they are not the same thing, and *very* few Firefox extensions work with Prism. One of the most important Firefox extensions, however, does work, and that's great news: Greasemonkey, which I discussed earlier in the section on Chrome. However, you can't just install the Greasemonkey extension for Firefox; instead, you need to download the source code for a version of Greasemonkey that was specially written by a programmer named "teramako" to run in Prism.

Get the code from `http://github.com/teramako/greasemonkey-for-prism` by clicking the Download Source button; when prompted, choose Zip. Unzip the file, open your

Terminal, and cd into the folder that was created when you unzipped the file. Run this command to create the Greasemonkey extension for Prism:

```
sh ./build.sh
```

When that command finishes, you'll have a new file named something like greasemonkey-for-prism-0.8.20100301.0.xpi in the folder. To install that extension into Prism, open the app you create using Prism, click on the sprocket in the bottom right of the window, go to **Tools ➤ Add-ons**, click Install on the bottom left of the Add-ons window, select greasemonkey-for-prism-0.8.20100301.0.xpi (or whatever your XPI is named), and click Open. Whew! When you're finished, if you click on the sprocket, you'll see a new Greasemonkey menu from which you can install and manage your Greasemonkey scripts. Remember, a great place to go to find those scripts is at www.userscripts.org.

Fluid

The other popular SSB for Macs is Fluid, which is actually the one I prefer, for lots of reasons. For one, it doesn't have the user interface issues that Prism does. Another big difference: it uses WebKit to render web pages like Safari and Chrome do, instead of Gecko, which is what Firefox (and therefore Prism) uses.

However, Fluid and Prism differ in one other big way as well, and this may be a real pain for some people. Prism does not share its cookies and cache with Firefox, which means that you can have one Gmail account in Prism and another, separate account in Firefox. Fluid, however, shares its cookies and cache with Safari, which is both an advantage and a disadvantage, depending upon your needs. The advantage is that if you've already set up a login in Safari, that same login will be ready to go in Fluid; the disadvantage, though, is that you can't be logged into one Gmail account in Safari and another Gmail account in an SSB app created with Fluid. The last one you log in to becomes the account that the other one uses, too.

Fluid has some other advantages over Prism. It has built-in support for Greasemonkey userscripts (yay!), which change how a web page behaves, and userstyles, which are scripts that change how a web page looks (you can find those at http://userstyles.org). To install either, after you create a Fluid-based SSB app, go to the **AppleScript icon ➤ Browse Userscripts.org**, which opens a new Fluid window at http://userscripts.org. Find the script you want, click Install, close the window open at userscripts.org, then reload your main SSB app window, and you should see your new userscript in action.

> **TIP:** To install userstyles, you can download the one you want and put it in ~/Library/Application Support/Fluid/SSB/[Your SSB]/Userstyles/. Or, in your SSB app's Preferences, go to the Userstyles screen and add the userstyle there. Restart your SSB app, and your userstyle should now work.

To create a new SSB app with Fluid, open Fluid and take care of four fields:

URL: The address of the website that you want to turn into an SSB app. If there's an https option, use that for added security.

Name: Enter the name of the website, or something else that's meaningful to you. This will become the name of the SSB app that you see on your Mac.

Location: By default, Fluid wants to put the SSB app in /Applications, which makes sense to me. But if you have another need, select Other and indicate a new location.

Icon: By default, Fluid grabs the favicon (the little 16x16 icon next to the URLs of most websites) of the website you entered into the URL field and uses that for your SSB app's icon. Since favicons are 16x16 pixels, and Mac OS X icons are usually much bigger, this results in absolutely awful icons. Instead, click on Icon ➤ Other and use an image that looks good at large sizes. But where to find such images? See "SSB Icons" later in this section for the answer.

When you've decided everything, click Create. Open the SSB app, and you can start using it immediately, but it's probably a good idea to make a few changes, so open the app's Preferences. A Fluid-based SSB app has 14 screens in Preferences, and I obviously can't go through all of them, so I'll just cover the important stuff.

General

Restore Last Browsing Session On Startup: Check this if you want your SSB app to re-open the page it was on when you closed it.

Appearance

Standard Font: Times New Roman is an awful font for reading web pages. Change it to Verdana, or Georgia if you want a serif font.

Fixed-Width Font: Courier isn't awful, but it's not super-great either. Mac OS X comes with two good monospaced fonts: Menlo and Monaco. Pick one.

Advanced

By default, the radio button next to Allow Browsing To Any URL is checked. However, this will cause problems because many sites actually utilize more than one URL, such as a login page and the main page. For that reason, I highly recommend clicking the second radio button, next to Browsing To URLs Matching These Pattens, and selecting Allow from the drop-down. Then you need to add URLs by clicking the + and entering them in. This can sometimes be difficult to figure out, so it's often easiest just to insert wildcards around the domain name, like *facebook.com* or *toodledo.com*, for instance. Or, in the name of security, you can be more precise, as I was with Google Reader:

```
*reader*google.com*
*google.com*/accounts/ServiceLogin*
*google.com*reader*
```

```
*fusion.google.com*
feed://*
```

To be honest, this is the first pref screen I go to, because without it, a lot of SSB apps won't work.

Fluid has all the standard SSB features that Prism does, but it has a better user interface and much more detailed preferences. But that's not all! It has some other features that really put it over the top when it comes to Mac SSBs.

Menu Bar SSB: By default, Fluid-based SSB apps run in big windows like a web browser does. But they don't have to. You can also access the SSB app from an icon on your Mac's Menu Bar, which is perfect for such narrow sites as Twitter or the iPhone-formatted version of Google Reader (at https://www.google.com/reader/i/ — try it!). Go to the **name of your SSB app ➤ Convert To MenuExtra SSB**. When you do, an icon appears on your Menu Bar; when you click on it, a small window appears for your SSB app, which you can resize. If you want to change back to a non-Menu Bar SSB app, right-click on the icon and select Convert To Normal Application.

Embedded SSB: Want your SSB app to run as your desktop background, but still featuring clickable links? (My answer would be "No," since doing this covers up your Desktop icons, but some people might like this.) On your Mac's Menu Bar, go to the **name of your SSB app ➤ Convert To Embedded SSB**. To convert back to the regular style of SSB app, left-click on the icon in the Menu Bar and select Convert To Normal Application.

Check if the website is down: This is a very cool feature for an SSB, and it is found only in Fluid. If the website isn't loading in the SSB app, go to **File ➤ Down For Everyone Or Just Me**. This loads a new window at, yes, http://downforeveryoneorjustme.com that tells you if the site is down for everyone or just you!

Show toolbars at any time: Want to see the Address Bar temporarily? Choose **View ➤ Show Toolbar**. When you're finished, choose **View ➤ Hide Toolbar**. Prism doesn't let you have this choice—you're stuck with what you selected when you set up the SSB app, which is very annoying.

Fluid is a great SSB for Mac users, and it's the one I recommend. It's full-featured, powerful, and it does the job beautifully. Best of all, like Prism, it's open source and free, so there's no reason not to try it out today.

SSB Icons

I mentioned much earlier in this section on SSBs that by default, both Prism and Fluid use websites' favicons as the icons for SSB apps, which means that the icons tend to look terrible. When you blow a 16x16 icon up to 48x48 (the Finder's default), or even bigger, bad things happen. So where can you get nice-looking icons for your SSB apps?

You can search for them using Google or your favorite search engine—something like "Google Reader Fluid icon" would probably work (substituting "Google Reader" with the name of the website you used, of course)—but there's another place I'd check first.

Go to www.flickr.com/groups/fluid_icons/, which is a Flickr group dedicated to Fluid icons, which of course you can also use with Prism (or any SSB, actually). Here you'll find nice, large (512x512 pixels for many of them, the maximum size on Snow Leopard), attractive icons that you can save to your Desktop and then use with your SSB app. At the time I'm writing this, they have 536 images, which means there's a pretty good chance someone has created an icon you can use. Granted, many of them are duplicates—there are a bunch for Gmail, for instance—but that also means you can pick the one you like.

I've found this particular Flickr pool very helpful, and I know you will too.

Further Resources

To find out more about Prism, check out the official Mozilla website, at http://prism.mozillalabs.com. The Prism project has also posted two official videos on YouTube to help new users: Prism Firefox Extension How-To (www.youtube.com/watch?v=_q6SMRaCEsQ) and Prism Standalone App How-To (www.youtube.com/watch?v=UeRukM1VteI).

The Productive Geek blog has a great post covering how to make Prism SSB apps portable, so you can distribute them to other users; see "Make Mozilla Prism Portable" (http://productivegeek.com/forums/topic/make-mozilla-prism-portable). It's written for Windows, but you should be able to modify it to get it to work on Macs as well.

There's been quite a bit written about efforts to get Prism to support more Firefox extensions. Articles on the subject include the Mozilla Development Center's "Extensions" (https://developer.mozilla.org/en/Prism/Extensions), Matthew Gertner's "Prism and Extensions" (http://browsing.justdiscourse.com/2009/10/22/prism-and-extensions/), and Lucky Disasters' "Here's How To Make An Extension Compatible With Prism" (www.luckydisasters.com/2008/06/10/heres-how-to-make-an-extension-compatible-with-prism-two-ish/). In particular, you can find all of Lucky Disasters' blog posts on Prism at www.luckydisasters.com/category/xulapps/prism/; they're definitely worth reading.

If you're really into Fluid, then should read what Todd Ditchendorf, the creator of the program, has to say about his "plans for future of Fluid, Cruz, and Fluidium" in "Fluid Goes Open Source" (http://fluidapp.com/blog/2010/03/18/fluid-goes-open-source/).

Summary

Web browsers are the central tools on our Macs nowadays, and with more software and services moving to the web at breakneck speeds, they're only to become more important. It's fantastic that Mac OS X has such a powerful built-in browser in Safari, but it's even better that we have so many other choices. Competition is a great thing, and the big winner—as Apple, Google, Mozilla, Opera, and the other companies and developers strive to make their web browsers faster, better, and more useful—is the happy Mac user, who has so many wonderful choices!

## Chapter 6

Using the Internet to Its Fullest

The Internet is one of the most amazing inventions of the last century, probably of all time, and it has inexorably changed our lives in countless ways. The Mac was an early sojourner on the Net when it began its climb to ubiquity in the 1990s, and in many ways Mac OS has always led the way when it comes to usable, beautiful, powerful software that lets people work and play in cyberspace. In this chapter, I'm going to look at software that works with four things people do on the Internet: e-mail, participate in social networking and sharing, transfer files, and share files with BitTorrent. There are some truly amazing apps in this chapter, and I think you'll find out about some things you'll be using for years to come.

Building a Better Mail and Address Book

Mail is a powerful app, but it's also been covered widely in many places, and Apple's Help for the program is pretty darn good, so I'm not going to rehash the obvious in this section. However, before proceeding, I should at least mention that there are several other e-mail programs that are better than Mail, at least in some ways. You may have heard of these and dismissed them, but they're free, or at least have free trials, so you should give them a try.

> **TIP:** Testing e-mail programs is much easier if you're using IMAP instead of POP3, and it's super-easy if you're using Gmail, since it supports IMAP quite well. If you don't know what I'm talking about, then you need to read Wikipedia's article about POP3 first (`http://en.wikipedia.org/wiki/Post_Office_Protocol`), and then its article about IMAP (`http://en.wikipedia.org/wiki/Internet_Message_Access_Protocol`), paying close attention to the section in IMAP about its advantages over POP.

The competitors to Mail that I would check out are:

- **Thunderbird:** Open source, free, powerful, and cross-platform. It used to be very noticeably *not* a Mac app, but version 3 fixed that in many big ways, chief among them that it now uses the Apple Address Book. Just like its cousin Firefox, there are add-ons and themes a-plenty that will let you do things that Mail only dreams of doing. Highly recommended. Download it from the Mozilla Foundation at `www.mozillamessaging.com` and read all about it at `http://kb.mozillazine.org/Category:Thunderbird`.

- **Postbox:** Thunderbird is an open source project, so if someone gets a better idea about how Tbird should function, they can modify the code and test it out with the world. The guys at Postbox think they have a better Thunderbird, and I have to agree—in many ways, it is a definite, strong improvement. More Mac OS X integration, better ways to search and sort and filter your mail, powerful sidebars that display key information from messages in a thread, and lots more. The level of thought and detail that has gone into this app is incredible. That said, it costs $40, which may cause some people to hesitate, so try the free trial and see what you think. Get it at `www.postbox-inc.com`.

- **Mailplane:** I love this program, and it's the e-mail program I use almost every day. Then again, I'm in a unique situation, as all of my e-mail is routed through several different accounts at Google's Gmail. Mailplane is basically a desktop app that shows you Gmail's web interface. I understand that might sound a bit strange, but the screenshots and screencasts at `http://mailplaneapp.com` will make it more understandable. The program costs $25, but it's totally worth it, as the developer updates it constantly, keeping up with Google's rapid changes. If you live in Gmail like I do and want to get the most out of your mail, this is the app for you.

Sure, there are others, but those are the best alternatives.

Going back to Apple's Mail, there are always cool tips and tricks to learn about it, such as these:

- How do you open another window, so you can see two messages at the same time? **File ➤ New Viewer Window**.

- Annoyed that when you click on a link in Mail, it opens in a web browser but also takes the focus away from Mail and puts it on the browser? To open a link in the background, right-click on the link and choose Open Link Behind Mail, or ⌘-click on the link.

- Like Gmail's conversation view, which shows all the messages in a thread, including those that you sent? Select **View ➤ Organize By Thread**, and then ⌘-click on the folders whose contents you want to view. Mail will group the messages from those folders together and display them by thread, in a close approximation of Gmail's conversation view. It's not perfect, and it's kind of clunky, but it works.

Those are helpful, but now let's look at some larger ways to make Mail even better that don't just require learning more about built-in features, but actually require some outside assistance. A big part of this concerns your Address Book, a key part of Mail's infrastructure.

Making Mail Faster

If you're a heavy user of Mail, you may find that over time the program takes longer and longer to open, and operates more and more sluggishly. There's a trick to making things faster, one that never fails to work. Open Terminal and run the following:

```
sqlite3 ~/Library/Mail/Envelope\ Index vacuum
```

This command basically cleans old and discarded crud out of the database that Mail uses to keep track of messages. When old messages are deleted, Mail unfortunately keeps some information about them around, and that's what you're nuking from orbit. Here's an example on my machine that shows the before and after (I've removed everything but the relevant information to keep it short):

```
$ cd ~/Library/Mail
$ ls -l
-rw-r--r-- 1 rsgranne  staff 43M Apr 15 23:14 Envelope Index
$ sqlite3 ~/Library/Mail/Envelope\ Index vacuum
$ ls -l
-rw-r--r-- 1 rsgranne  staff 35M Apr 16 18:35 Envelope Index
```

If you want to run it often on the Terminal, I'd make an alias for it, either in .bashrc or .bash_aliases (if you've created such a file, which I have and swear by):

```
alias vacuummail='sqlite3 ~/Library/Mail/Envelope\ Index vacuum'
```

If you're really feeling ambitious, you could create an Automator action that would shut down Mail, run the command, and start Mail back up. Make it an iCal Alarm and set it to run once a week, and you will guarantee that Mail runs lean and mean. Or, if you don't like Automator, use Lingon to run the command for you at a set time. For more on Automator and Lingon, check out Chapter 12.

Finally, if you use Onyx (discussed in Chapter 2), you could go to **Maintenance ➤ Rebuild**, then check Mail Envelope Index and click Execute. That will do the same thing as the command, but Onyx will quit all running apps, which is a drag, and is another reason I prefer to use the command line.

Syncing Your Address Book with Facebook

Apple's Address Book is a nice program that I use constantly, especially because so many other programs use its data. Many of the people in my Address Book are also friends on Facebook, but a lot of the info that's on Facebook isn't in my Address Book. Wouldn't it be nice if I could somehow suck the data from Facebook into my Address Book?

There are two ways to get Facebook stuff on your Mac. The first way is to go to http://danauclair.com/addressbooksync/ and download the free AddressBookSync program. AddressBookSync allows you to synchronize—or add—a subset of the data Facebook has about your friends to your Apple Address Book: profile pictures, birthdays, profile URL, and current location. What about phone numbers and addresses? No dice—that's against Facebook's terms of service.

Still, profile pix are nice, especially if you have an iPhone—when those people call you, you'll see their smiling faces. And birthdays are good to have too, especially if you add the Birthdays calendar to iCal so you'll never forget another one (in iCal, go to **Preferences ➤ General** and check Show Birthdays Calendar). Profile URL and current location? Sure, whatever.

When you open AddressBookSync, you're prompted to authorize it with Facebook. After doing so, the program will connect to Facebook and begin downloading information about all of your Facebook friends. A few moments later, depending upon how many friends are in Facebook and how big your Address Book is, AddressBookSync will display a window like that in Figure 6–1.

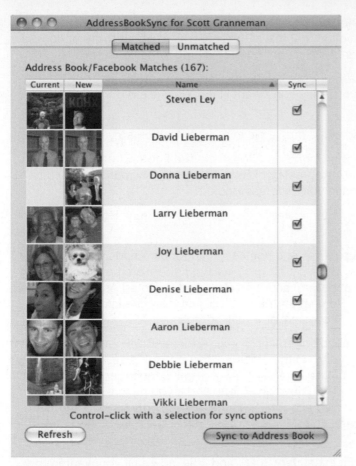

Figure 6–1. *There are 167 people in both my Facebook account and my Address Book.*

AddressBookSync groups people into two tabs: Matched and Unmatched. Matched contains people that are in both your Address Book and Facebook friends, while Unmatched contains people that are Facebook friends but are not in your Address Book.

On the Matched tab you'll see four columns:

- **Current:** The current photo you have for this person in your Address Book.

- **New:** The profile photo the person is using on Facebook, which will be imported into your Address Book, replacing the current photo.

- **Name:** The name of the person.

- **Sync:** If the box is checked, then the person's photo, birthday, and current location (if specified on Facebook) will be imported into Address Book. If unchecked, the person will be skipped over.

If you right-click anywhere on the row for a person, a menu pops up with a few interesting choices (and keep in mind that this is the only way to reach these options, as they don't exist on the Menu Bar, which is not good Mac app behavior):

- **Sync Options:** This lets you turn off sync for data items on a person-by-person basis. So if you really don't want Uncle Gussie's birthday, here's where you'd go.

- **Crop/Zoom:** See the person's profile pic in a larger fashion so you can change what is saved into Address Book.

- **Unmatch Selection:** Tells AddressBookSync it erroneously matched people on Facebook and in your Address Book.

When you have everything you want checked, press Sync To Address Book, and you're finished.

The Unmatched tab shows you pictures and names of Facebook friends. Select people you want to add to your Address Book by ⌘- or ⇧-clicking (there are no check boxes here, which is inconsistent and annoying) and then click Add Selected As New to make your Address Book a bit bigger. Remember that you will just have the info Facebook allows, with no phone numbers, or physical or e-mail addresses.

There's another way to add Facebook contacts to your Address Book, but this one uses your iPhone. I've tried to avoid relying on the iPhone in this book (it's called *Mac OS X Snow Leopard for Power Users*, after all, not *Mac OS X Snow Leopard and the iPhone*); still, this is super-easy and quick if you have an iPhone and if you have the Facebook app on your iPhone. And if you sync Facebook with the data on your iPhone, then the next time you sync the iPhone with your Mac's Address Book, the Facebook data should show up there.

The new Facebook app came out in January 2010, and it asked you if you wanted to "Add Facebook profile pictures and links to your contacts" when you first ran it after installing or updating it. If you already had it installed and ignored that request and now want to change your mind and do it, open the Facebook app and select Friends (if you've never installed the Facebook app on your iPhone, do so and answer Yes when asked). Once there, press the Sync button in the upper right, and you'll see the screen in Figure 6–2.

Figure 6-2. *Facebook's Sync is even more bare-bones than AddressBookSync!*

Basically, you can turn syncing on and off. You can also choose whether or not to replace Address Book photos with Facebook profile pix. And that's it as far as customization. If a person in your Address Book doesn't have a home page URL, then their Facebook URL is used instead, and you can't prevent it. Facebook URL's look like `fb://profile/667422834`, and if you click on one on your iPhone, it will open in the Facebook app.

I find that I get more data into my Mac's Address Book by using AddressBookSync, but I also sync my iPhone Contacts to Google Contacts, and sync my Address Book to Google Contacts as well, so some things could be getting lost between all three (for instance, none of the `fb://` links show up on my Mac's Address Book, and I'm pretty sure it's because Google refuses them, since they're not the standard `http://`). Still, it's nice to have both options available, especially as Facebook continues its inexorable movement toward ubiquity. Want to find people? Increasingly, Facebook is the Web's contact repository, so it's nice to add some of that to your personal Address Book as well.

Keeping Up with Twitter, Facebook, and Other Social Services

Like it or not, Twitter and other social networking services have become juggernauts in the last few years, with millions of people posting, sharing, linking, and discussing the things that they find interesting, annoying, funny, or just plain weird. You can use the web pages for those services, but that's not always convenient (although the SSBs I discussed in Chapter 5 sure help) and sometimes you get far better usability by avoiding the websites.

In cases like that, turn to a Mac app to access, read, and comment at Twitter. There are a lot for the Mac (and I do mean a lot), but I've narrowed the list down to the top choices. Even better, some of these programs incorporate several services into one app, so that you can check Twitter, Facebook, and even more services with one tool. If you use Twitter or Facebook, you're going to find something to try out in this section.

TweetDeck and Seesmic Desktop

I'll come right out and say it: sure, TweetDeck (www.tweetdeck.com) and Seesmic Desktop (http://seesmic.com/seesmic_desktop/air/) will show you your Twitter feeds, and Facebook news, and let you post to multiple Twitter accounts at the same time, and search and filter Twitter posts, buuuuut...

- They're not native Mac apps. They're written in Adobe AIR, which is cross-platform, and it shows. They're simply not Mac-like in any way, frustratingly so.

- They're complicated, busy apps. I've used them both extensively, and I still have to figure things out and scratch my head to remember how to do certain things. They're just not easy to use.

- They're ugly. This is subjective, of course, but a large part of it is because they're not native Mac apps, and another large part is that they're complicated and busy. No matter the reason, they're just not pretty apps to look at.

- They can be memory hogs. This is undoubtedly more the fault of Adobe AIR, but both apps have caught flack in the past about memory leaks that result in huge quantities of RAM being gradually used by these programs.

So, I'm not saying don't use TweetDeck and Seesmic Desktop. I'm just saying try everything else out first. TweetDeck and Seesmic Desktop are free, so that's a huge plus, and they're not going anywhere, since a lot of people use them (not just on the Mac—I think they're enormously popular on Windows).

There's one exception: if you're a marketing professional or a social media specialist and you live and breathe by what people are saying about your clients and products on Twitter and Facebook, then yeah, you probably should buckle down and figure out the ins and outs of one of these programs. You'll need all the extra filters and searching and sorting and everything else. But most people just don't, and that's why I'd recommend the others in this section.

Twitterrific

The Iconfactory's Twitterrific has been around on the Mac for a while, which could be causing some issues for it. Once the iPhone came out, it seems the developers jumped on that platform with both feet—which I'm sure has been financially lucrative, and bully for them!—but that also means that the Mac app hasn't seen any major love in quite some time. The company assured me in April, however, that "A new version for the Mac is in the works, but won't be out for several months." I have no idea what that will entail, but if your needs are simple, the current Twitterrific might be right for you. In a couple of months, it may have more to offer the Twitter power user.

You can get Twitterrific at http://iconfactory.com/software/twitterrific/. The free version works just like the pay version ($15), with the exception that once an hour you see an ad. That's it. Other than that, they're the same.

Twitterrific lives on your Menu Bar with a small birdie icon. Click on it, and Twitterrific opens. You can see the window in Figure 6–3.

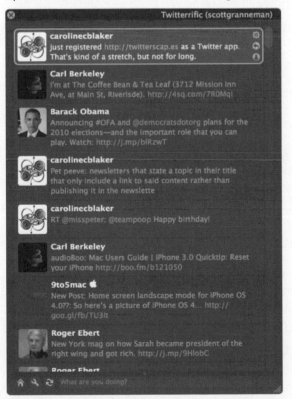

Figure 6–3. *Twitterrific follows the popular dark gray look of many modern apps.*

Twitterrific isn't that hard to use, and it has a lot of stuff you'd expect in a Twitter program:

- Public Reply and Direct Message to tweets

- Favorite tweets

- Mark all as read

- Open user's Twitter page

It also has some very cool, helpful features:

- Lots of useful keyboard shortcuts

- Navigate up and down tweets using ↑ and ↓

- Jump to the newest tweet with ⌥-↑ and the oldest with ⌥-↓

- AppleScript support

- Show and hide the app via a customizable hotkey

- Power User Preferences: advanced configuration done via the command line

- Some quirky, funny features and notes in the Read Me

However, it's missing a lot of features that are now standard with Twitter apps:

- No way to retweet easily

- No way to search tweets

- No built-in URL shortener

- No complete history, just partial

- No way to see who's following me without taking me to the Web

- No integration with Facebook (yes, I know this is a Twitter app, but most other Twitter apps have added this, and it's a natural fit)

- No simple support for multiple accounts (you can press ⌘-L to log in with a different account, but each time you do, all of your tweets are re-downloaded, a very clumsy, inelegant process)

It also has a few annoyances:

- You can't change the color scheme.

- It doesn't act like a normal Mac program: you can't ⌘-Tab to it, and there are no menus at all, which is weird.

- If you go into Preferences and uncheck Include Replies From People Who Follow You and Include Your Direct Messages, they simply don't appear in your Twitter timeline, and there's no way to see them… unless you go back into Preferences and re-check those options.

- By default, the window floats over everything, which is very annoying. Sure, you can change this in the Preferences, but it's an irritating default.

- Twitterrific pops up every time it checks Twitter (every three minutes by default, set in the **Preferences ➤ Tweets**) and discovers new tweets (also a default, at **Preferences ➤ Tweets**); since the default is to float above all other windows (see previous bullet), this means that by default, Twitterrific is quite annoying, unless you have a huge monitor, and even then it is very distracting!

So should you get Twitterrific? If you're willing to dig in the Prefs and change a few things, and if your needs are simple, sure. The fact that you can get a free version that just shows an ad every hour makes it more attractive. But unfortunately, as it currently stands, this isn't an app I would use. In the future, after a new version comes out, I'll give it another look, but for now, I'd pass.

Tweetie

Tweetie started life as a $3 iPhone app and was then re-coded as a Mac app. On the Mac, you could use it for free if you were willing to view ads, or you could pay $20 to register it and remove the ads. Then something huge happened: Twitter bought Tweetie and announced that it was going to rename the iPhone version to Twitter For iPhone and make it free. The company didn't state its plans for the desktop Tweetie, but I'm expecting that by the time you're reading this, it will be named Twitter For Mac and will be $0. So right now you need to go to www.atebits.com/tweetie-mac/ to get the program, but that will undoubtedly change. The current URL might redirect you to Twitter's site, or you might just need to go to Twitter and look around there. So be prepared to be flexible.

Here's Tweetie in summary: it's very pretty (as you can see in Figure 6–4) and very fun, but it lacks some Twitter power-user features. For casual users, or for those who don't follow that many people, it's great, and the fact that it's free (or will be soon) is a bonus. But if you're a power user and want more features and control, jump ahead to the next section, where I look at Socialite.

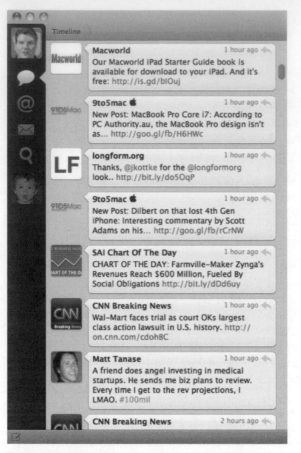

Figure 6–4. *Now that is one really nice lookin' Mac app!*

So yes, Tweetie does have some really cool things going for it:

- A pretty nifty, clean, modern UI that's actually fun to use.

- The ability to really dig down and find out details about a Twitterer (click on the person's icon and then the **i** to see what I mean).

- Direct Messages displayed by user, and then, when you select a user, in a conversation view similar to that in iChat, as shown in Figure 6–5.

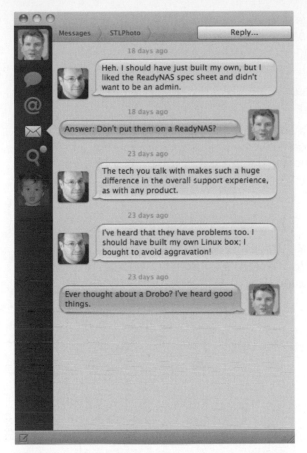

Figure 6–5. *Tweetie displays DM threads as a conversation.*

- Saved searches that let you track what people are saying about a topic of interest.

- References: Ever received an @ or DM and couldn't tell which tweet it was referring back to? Double-click on a tweet, and any related tweets show up, again with a conversation view like that in iChat.

- Easily add links to images and even videos when composing tweets.

- Support for multiple accounts, which is vital if you need it (I do).

That said, in addition to its hits, Tweetie has some misses as well (hopefully these will be fixed once Twitter devotes some of its resources to the program):

- No support for Twitter lists, which let you sort those you're following into manageable groups.

- I really don't like having to open a new window to compose a tweet. Why can't I just do it in the main window? Annoying.

- Instead of hiding read items, Tweetie fades them out, but the effect is so subtle that I had a hard time at first seeing it. Besides, I don't want them faded out; I want them *hidden*. Gone. Disappeared. Fading is not the same thing.

- No support for anything other than Twitter, which is going to stay that way, now that Twitter has bought it!

So that's Tweetie. Expect some changes soon, now that the mothership owns it. Overall, it's not a bad Twitter app at all, and it's certainly the slickest one for the Mac. It's free, and will stay that way, so download it and see if you dig it. If you don't, or if you need greater power or more features, then I suggest you check out Socialite, discussed next.

Socialite

Formerly known as EventBox, Socialite is available from Realmac Software at www.realmacsoftware.com/socialite/. You can use if for free, but you can only add two services, or you can pay $20 to unlock it completely.

Socialite supports the following services:

- Twitter
- Facebook
- Flickr
- Digg
- Google Reader
- RSS

You can add multiple accounts from Twitter, which is handy. I added a number of services quickly, giving me a window that looks like Figure 6–6.

Figure 6–6. *Socialite with two Twitter accounts and four other services.*

It's very handy to have all those services in one interface, but it can be very overwhelming, and that's the biggest negative I can think of with Socialite. After adding the various services, I found myself faced with over 1128 posts of some sort to view, which is scary. Granted, many of those I'd already seen before—Socialite had no idea what I'd already viewed using other apps—but it's still a lot to consider.

Fortunately, Socialite has a useful setting that can make it a bit easier to manage all those updates: go to **Preferences ➤ General ➤ Behavior** and check the box next to Automatically Mark Events As Read As I Scroll Past Them. That same tab's Selecting An Event Marks It As Read is checked by default, as it should be. And if you want to nuke the site from orbit, there's always a Mark All As Read button in the upper right of the main screen of the program.

So that's it for the negatives (well, it would be nice if Socialite also included support for LinkedIn and Reddit and a few other services), but what about the positives? Here are some of them, organized by service.

Common to All Services

Socialite includes an impressive list of features that are common across all supported services:

- Automatically shorten URLs using one of ten services, including bit.ly and j.mp (see **Preferences ➤ General ➤ URLs**).

- Automatically expand URLs you see when they arrive (again, **Preferences ➤ General ➤ URLs**).

- When you click on a link, have it open in your web browser in the background, so you can continue using Socialite (**Preferences ➤ General ➤ URLs**, then check Open Links In The Background).

- Set the time to refresh services (**Preferences ➤ Refresh**), or manually refresh by clicking the Refresh Selected Service button at the bottom of Socialite's window.

- For each service, set the very granular notification triggers and methods, including what is sent to Growl (**Preferences ➤ Notifications**).

- Five tabs of keyboard shortcuts that you can change and set (**Preferences ➤ Shortcuts**), including Navigation, Events, Focus, Misc, and Hotkeys.

- A Heads-Up Display (HUD) that is a slicker, more focused view of updates, as you can see in Figure 6–7. You can call up the HUD using a key command (see the previous bullet), or by going to **Window ➤ Heads-Up Display**, and then select what is shown from the title bar, which is actually a gigantic drop-down menu of all your services and their components. For more on the HUD, see **Preferences ➤ HUD**.

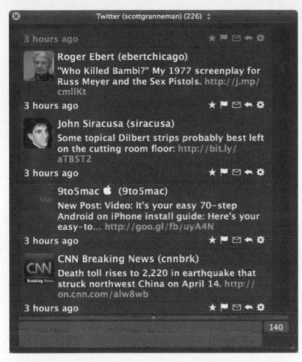

Figure 6–7. *Socialite has an attractive HUD that you can call up and dismiss easily.*

- Quick Send, a window that appears when you press a hotkey and that allows you to quickly compose a message to send to one of your selected services.

- Integration with Instapaper (www.instapaper.com), a product/service that allows you save articles and posts for reading later, on your Mac or iPhone (**Preferences ➤ Instapaper**).

- Photo uploads to one of five services, simply by dragging an image into the Socialite window (or via **Events ➤ Upload Photo**).

- Hide read items by clicking the Only Show Unread Events button in the Socialite Status Bar.

Twitter

These features are Twitter-specific:

- View your Twitter timeline, Mentions, Direct Messages, Favorites, and Retweets.

- Search: Type in a term and Socialite saves the search for you so you can keep up with the latest tweets on your area of interest.

- Profile Peek: Enter a Twitter user name and Socialite shows you her tweets, again saved for you in the left nav bar.
- For each tweet, do any of the following:
  - Favorite it
  - Send a private Direct Message or a Public Reply
  - Flag it for viewing within Socialite (to see flagged posts, check Show Flagged Folder on **Preferences ➤ General ➤ General**)
  - Retweet it
  - Quote it
  - Open it in a Web browser
  - Copy the link to it
  - Email the link to it
  - View the user's tweets
  - Follow and unfollow the user
  - Block the user
  - Add the user to your Mac's Address Book

Facebook

The 500-pound Gorilla of social networking gets these features in Socialite:

- View Status Updates, friends' photos (full size if you want!), your photos, Links, and Pages
- Upload photos
- For each post, do any of the following:
  - Like it
  - Tweet it
  - Open it in a Web browser
  - Copy the link to it
  - Email the link to it
  - Comment on it using the Input Area at the bottom of Socialite's window (if you don't see it, click the Toggle Input Area button in the Status Bar or go to **Events ➤ Toggle Input Area**)
  - View other's comments

Flickr

Yahoo's venerable photo-sharing service has these features in Socialite:

- View your photos, contacts' photos, or general Flickr photos that are "interesting"
- Upload one or more photos, with Title, Description, Tags, and more
- For each photo, do any of the following:
    - Favorite it
    - View it full size
    - Comment on it
    - Tweet it
    - Open it in a Web browser
    - Copy the link to it
    - Email the link to it

Google Reader

RSS junkies who depend upon Google Reader for their fixes can use these features in Socialite:

- View your feeds sorted into folders, just like on Google Reader
- View posts that Starred, Shared, and from friends
- Set the preview length for posts (**Preferences ➤ Google Reader**)
- For each post, do any of the following:
    - Star it
    - Share it
    - Tweet it
    - Open it in a Web browser
    - Copy the link to it
    - Email the link to it

There are other features inside Socialite—notice I didn't even discuss Digg or RSS—but I'll leave those to you to discover. If you want to keep up with some very major social networking and sharing services, then you really can't wrong with Socialite. And unlike TweetDeck and the other Adobe AIR apps, this one is native to Mac OS, so it fits in much better. It's good software that serves a very useful purpose.

Further Resources

There are certainly other Twitter apps out there that are worthy of your attention if the ones I've discussed don't float your boat:

Nambu: Totally free and available from www.nambu.com, this Mac-native program certain has plenty of features (although it is a Twitter-only app), but its UI is very crowded and not exactly pretty or clean. Further, it's still in beta, and I found it to be a little bitty bit unstable. That said, lots of people really like it.

Echofon: $20 from www.echofon.com/twitter/mac/, with syncing to the same company's iPhone app. Very minimalistic, if that's what you like (I do like its iPhone app, though).

For a ridiculously long list of over 50 Twitter programs for Mac, check out Appstorm's "The Ultimate List of Twitter Software for Mac," at http://mac.appstorm.net/roundups/communication-roundup/the-ultimate-list-of-twitter-software-for-mac-50-apps/.

Transferring Files

As both a web developer and a lover of new software, I find myself downloading (and uploading) files across the Internet on a daily basis. I'm willing to bet that most of you reading this book are in that group as well, since we all know that power users love to transfer files to and from their Macs. In this section, I'll look at three tools that do a great job moving files across networks: Cyberduck, Transmit, and Speed Download. They each have their strengths and weaknesses, as you'll see, but they're all worthy of your time, attention, and bytes.

Cyberduck

Cyberduck is open source and free (but a donation is requested), and you can get it from http://cyberduck.ch. It's a powerful file-transfer tool that supports all the essential protocols you need:

- FTP (which you shouldn't be using anyway)
- SFTP
- SCP
- WebDAV (MobileMe iDisk)
- WebDAV over SSL
- Amazon S3
- Amazon CloudFront
- Rackspace Cloud Files
- FTP-SSL (FTP over TLS)

TIP: If you connect to an Amazon S3 bucket using SSL, which is the default, and you've created a CNAME in DNS that points to the bucket, you will quickly be driven insane by an annoying, repeated process. You will first be warned that "A failure occurred during certificate trust verification" and will be given a choice of three buttons: Show Certificate, Disconnect, and Continue. Do not click Continue, or you will see that dialog box every time you connect or try to do anything with your S3 connection. Instead, click Show Certificate and then, at the top of the window, check the box next to Always Trust *.s3.amazonaws.com When Connecting To... Mac OS X will require you to type your password to make this change, so do so and click OK. You will have to do this for every bucket pointed at by a CNAME at Amazon S3, but once you authorize a bucket, you won't have to again.

I've been using Cyberduck for quite some time, and while the price is definitely right, it also has a lot of features that I really like. Here are my favorites:

Bookmark Manager: Store a list of your favorite connections so you can easily re-establish them.

Support for SSH keys: On our servers, we disable FTP completely, and when It comes to SSH, we remove the ability to log in via a password and instead rely on SSH keys for added security (for more on using SSH keys, read Apple's documentation at `http://developer.apple.com/mac/library/documentation/MacOSXServer/Conceptual/XS erver_ProgrammingGuide/Articles/SSH.html`). When you create a new connection, besides asking you all the standard questions (server, port, username, path, and so on), Cyberduck also asks if you'd like to Use Public Key Authentication, as you can see in Figure 6–8.

Mac OS X Keychain support: In Figure 6–8, you can see the checkbox next to Add To Keychain. If you're using a password to log in, you can add that password to your Mac OS X Keychain. It's smart of Cyberduck to rely on a security technology that's already proven and in place on every Mac instead of trying to create its own password storage system.

Edit remote files locally: If you're a web developer, this can be very handy. Instead of downloading a file, editing it, uploading it, and then deleting the local copy, just right-click on the file in Cyberduck (or press ⌘-K) and the file will open in your local editor. Make your changes, save it, and the remote version is automatically updated. You can set a default text editor at **Preferences ➤ Editor**; for non-text files, Cyberduck uses the default apps you have set on your Mac, so a JPG might open in Preview and an MP3 might open in iTunes.

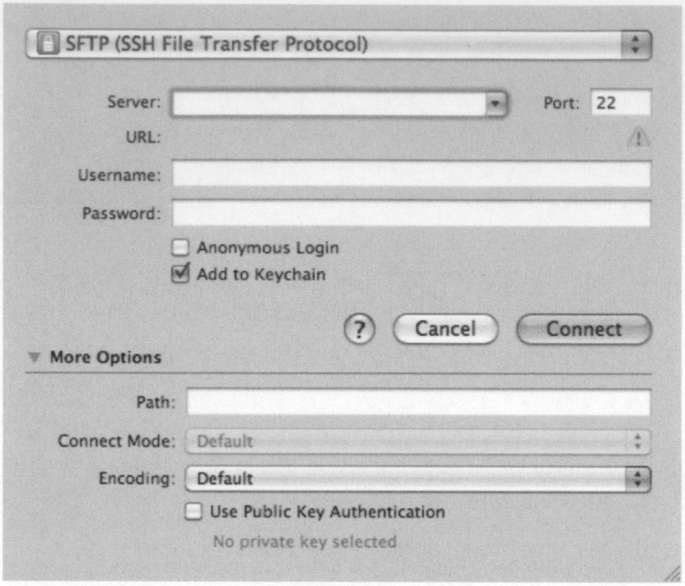

Figure 6–8. *Cyberduck asks all the right questions for a new connection, including keys.*

Create and expand archives: If you right-click on a ZIP, TAR, or GZ file on a remote machine, you can choose Expand Archive and Cyberduck will send the command to unarchive it, which is incredibly handy. You can also generate an archive by right-clicking on a selected group of files and choosing Create Archive.

Copy URL: I use this all the time, since I teach courses at Washington University in St. Louis and want students to have access to PDFs I upload to Amazon S3. I right-click on a file (or press ⌘-⇧-C), and Cyberduck copies the remote URL to my clipboard so I can paste it into my syllabus. This is a huge time-saver for me, and one that few other file-transfer programs support.

Single-pane interface: I actually prefer the single-pane interface that Cyberduck has, which you can see in Figure 6–9.

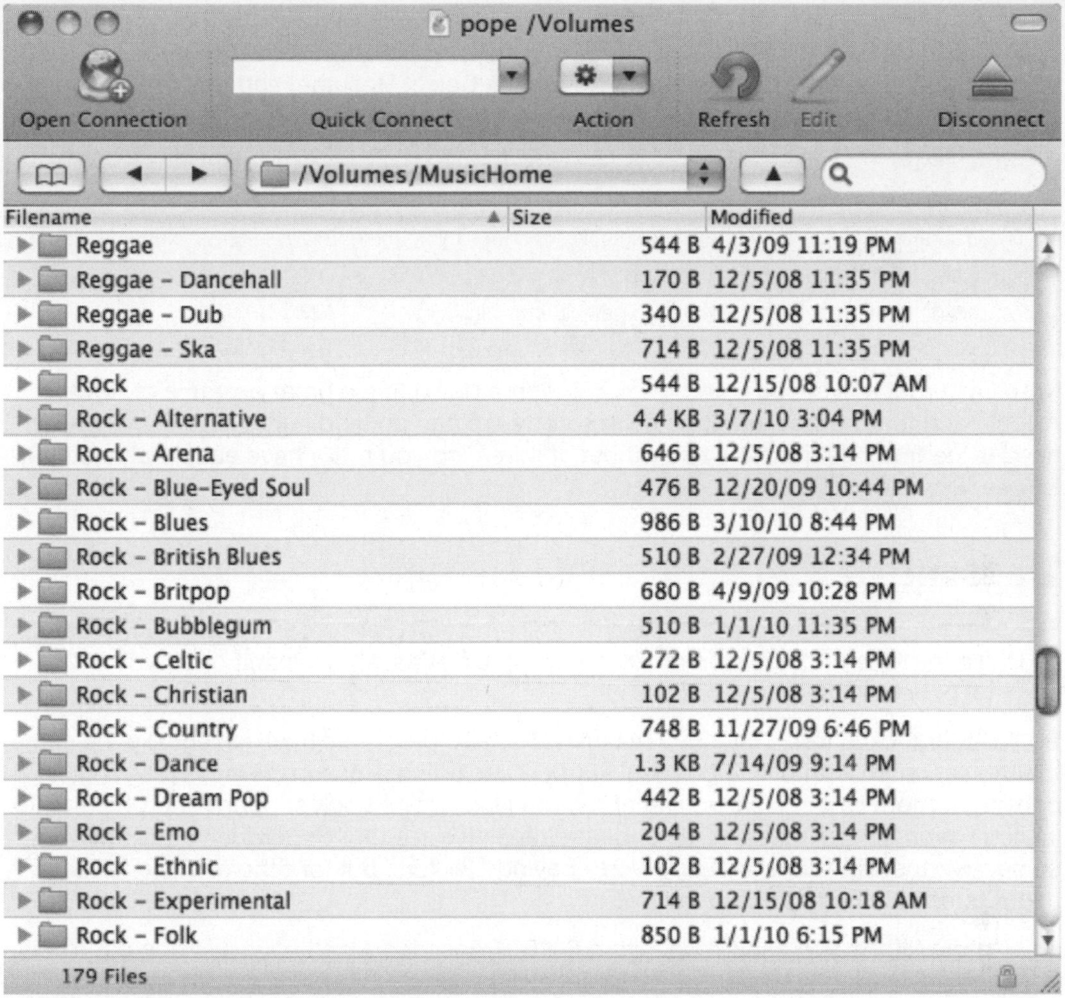
pope /Volumes
Open Connection
Quick Connect
Action
Refresh
Edit
Disconnect
/Volumes/MusicHome
Filename
Size
Modified
Reggae 544 B 4/3/09 11:19 PM
Reggae - Dancehall 170 B 12/5/08 11:35 PM
Reggae - Dub 340 B 12/5/08 11:35 PM
Reggae - Ska 714 B 12/5/08 11:35 PM
Rock 544 B 12/15/08 10:07 AM
Rock - Alternative 4.4 KB 3/7/10 3:04 PM
Rock - Arena 646 B 12/5/08 3:14 PM
Rock - Blue-Eyed Soul 476 B 12/20/09 10:44 PM
Rock - Blues 986 B 3/10/10 8:44 PM
Rock - British Blues 510 B 2/27/09 12:34 PM
Rock - Britpop 680 B 4/9/09 10:28 PM
Rock - Bubblegum 510 B 1/1/10 11:35 PM
Rock - Celtic 272 B 12/5/08 3:14 PM
Rock - Christian 102 B 12/5/08 3:14 PM
Rock - Country 748 B 11/27/09 6:46 PM
Rock - Dance 1.3 KB 7/14/09 9:14 PM
Rock - Dream Pop 442 B 12/5/08 3:14 PM
Rock - Emo 204 B 12/5/08 3:14 PM
Rock - Ethnic 102 B 12/5/08 3:14 PM
Rock - Experimental 714 B 12/15/08 10:18 AM
Rock - Folk 850 B 1/1/10 6:15 PM
179 Files

Figure 6–9. *Cyberduck always shows the remote files in its window.*

A lot of file-transfer programs use a dual-pane UI (for instance, Transmit, which I'm discussing next, does). I don't see the need, since I always have the Finder open and can just drag files back and forth between the Finder and Cyberduck. If you're dead set against a single-pane UI, then you're not going to like Cyberduck.

> **TIP:** Even though Cyberduck has a single-window UI, you can still have more than one window open at a time, each pointing at a different server and with its own transfers going on. Just go to File ➤ New Browser or press ⌘-N.

Resume downloads: If you're in the middle of a download and your connection fails, or if you have to stop for some reason, you can resume the download in Cyberduck (even if you closed and re-opened the app). Just click the Resume button at the top of the

Transfers window, or re-drag the files, and Cyberduck will show you a sheet asking what you want to do with the file. At the top of the sheet, you have a drop-down menu with three choices: Resume, Overwrite, and Rename. Select Resume, and you're good to go.

> **TIP:** Speaking of the Transfers window, there's one change I urge you to make: select the Transfers window and then go to **View ➤ Customize Toolbar**. Drag the icon for Clean Up onto the Transfers window toolbar next to Remove, and then click Done. Remove allows you to delete transfers from the window, but you can only do one at a time, while Clean Up removes all successful transfers from the window with just one click.

I use Cyberduck every day, and it's never let me down. It's a great example of how reliable and feature-packed open source software can be, and I urge Mac users who need to perform file transfers to try it out. It's free, so you really have absolutely nothing to lose. Download it today!

Transmit

The best commercial file transfer client is Transmit (www.panic.com/TRANSMIT/). Created by Panic Inc. and first released in 1998 (back in OS 9 days!), Transmit gives you a 15-day trial period. After that, it costs $30.

So if Cyberduck is free, why buy Transmit? The two programs have essentially the same feature set, such as multiple protocol support (including Amazon S3 and WebDAV), copying remote URLs, local editing of remote files, Quick Look support, and bookmarks (called *Favorites* by Transmit). What does Transmit have that Cyberduck does not? For some, the answer will be "nothing worth paying $30 for," but for others, these features might tempt them into paying money:

Dual-pane UI: As you can see in Figure 6–10, Transmit doesn't have just one pane in its interface; instead, it has two.

The left pane shows the files on your local machine, while the right contains the remote files and folders (why Transmit labels these as Your Stuff and Their Stuff is beyond me, since it's almost always *all* My Stuff). Drag and drop between the panes, or drag and drop between the Finder and the right pane, to transfer files.

Tabs: Along with the dual-pane UI, Transmit includes tabs for each connection you open. You can even drag and drop files between tabs, which is very useful.

Speed: Transmit is definitely faster than Cyberduck. Not by an enormous amount, but it is noticeable.

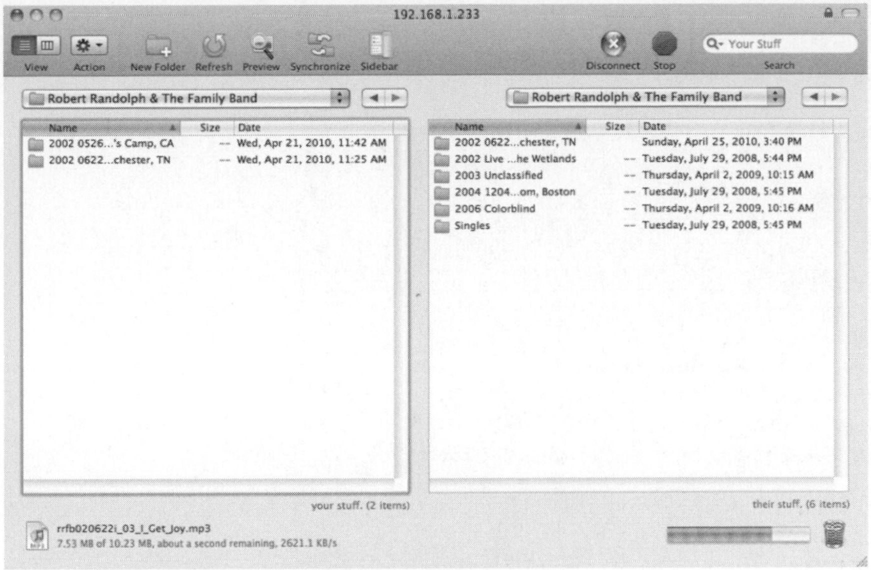

Figure 6–10. *Local stuff on the left, remote stuff on the right.*

Automator support: This is really nice. When you install Transmit, it adds three new actions under the Internet section of Automator: Download Files, Synchronize Files, and Upload Files. Any protocol supported by Transmit is available, as are all other options when creating a new connection in Transmit. If you need file transfer as part of your Automator workflow, this could be huge for you.

Droplets: If you're constantly uploading files to the same location, create what Transmit calls a drag-and-droplet by creating a bookmark and then clicking on Save As Droplet at the bottom of the bookmarks sheet. When you do, Transmit asks you to give it a name, select a location, and say whether or not you want to store the password, and then creates an app for you. Drag files onto that app, and Transmit uploads them to that location, quick and easy.

Syncing bookmarks through MobileMe: Back up your bookmarks by going to ➤ System Preferences ➤ MobileMe ➤ Sync and checking the box next to Transmit Favorites. Then forget about it, since your favorites will stay backed up without you needing to worry about it.

Synchronization: You can synchronize folders with Cyberduck, but you get more options with Transmit, which you can see in Figure 6–11.

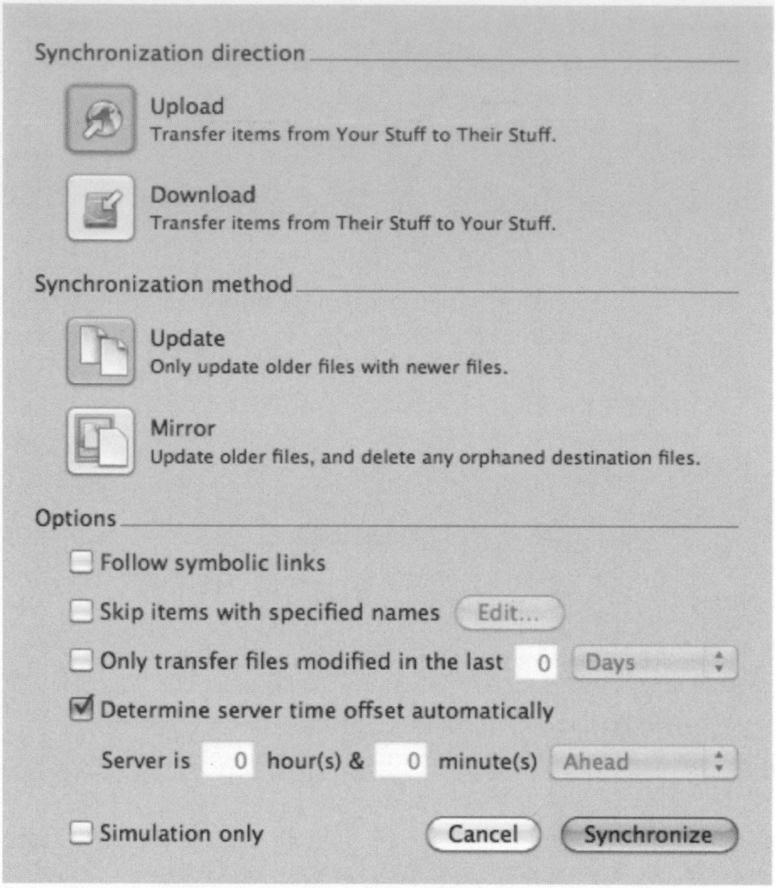

Figure 6–11. *Transmit lets you get granular with synchronization.*

Choose the direction for transfer, whether or not to delete files, which files to transfer... Transmit does it all, and even includes a simulation mode. It's really pretty sweet.

> **NOTE:** As this book was heading to production, Transmit 3 entered the world, and I gotta say, it rocks the house. Automated syncing for backups (which is way better than the syncing in Figure 6–11, for instance), a beautiful and incredibly functional new UI, and even faster speeds are just the tip of the iceberg. Go check it out for yourself at www.panic.com/transmit/. You will not be disappointed!

So, should you buy Transmit or not? If the previous features appeal to you, then abso-frickin'-lutely. My advice would be, though, to try out Cyberduck first, and if it lacks something you need, or if you just don't like it, then jump over to Transmit. Better to save your cash until you need to spend it.

Speed Download

I would be remiss if I didn't mention Speed Download in a section on file-transfer programs. Speed Download can't connect to SFTP servers at all, although it can connect to FTP and WebDAV servers. Instead, it's a download manager, a program that integrates with your Web browser to manage large or multiple downloads so you don't have to worry about what happens if Firefox or Safari crashes or a connection is lost.

The program comes in two flavors: Speed Download, a full-featured app that supports FTP and WebDAV and is available for $25 from www.yazsoft.com/products/speed-download/, and Speed Download Lite, an app that is solely a download manager and is available for $20 from the same location. Both come with a free trial. For our purposes, since I'm focusing on the browser integration, both are the same, so I'd just buy Speed Download Lite.

When you install Speed Download, you are asked if you want to run in Automatic or Manual mode. Here's the difference, as explained by Speed Download's Help:

> *With 'Automatic', SD automatically intercepts all files you are trying to download. ...if you would like to control what SD downloads, simply pick 'Manual'. Under 'Manual' mode, files are sent to SD via the contextual menu, or by simply dragging and dropping a file URL onto the Speed Download window...*

I like using Speed Download for my browser downloads, so I went with Automatic (you can always switch by going to **Speed Download** ➤ **Preferences** ➤ **General** and changing the drop-down next to Setup).

While you're working with Speed Download, I also encourage you to open its Preferences and go to the My Downloads tab. For Save Downloaded Files To, you should choose Always Prompt For Location, so you can select where you want things to go. Trust me, unless you download the same sort of thing time after time, you really don't want everything going into ~/Downloads, as it does by default.

There are many ways to use Speed Download as a download manager, but I'm going to focus on only one method that utilizes Firefox. In Firefox, go to https://addons.mozilla.org/en-US/firefox/addon/220 and install the FlashGot extension. Restart Firefox, and go to **Tools** ➤ **FlashGot** ➤ **More Options** ➤ **General**. For Download Manager, select Speed Download (or Speed Download Lite). Click OK to close the Options window.

Now if you're in Firefox and you see a list of files you want to download, click in front of the first link and drag down until all the links are selected. Now select **Tools** ➤ **FlashGot** ➤ **FlashGot Selection**, and after a moment or so Speed Download will launch if it's not already open and ask you where you want to save the first file. Choose a folder on your Mac click Save, and Speed Download will proceed to download all the selected files into that folder, quickly and efficiently, as you can see in Figure 6–12.

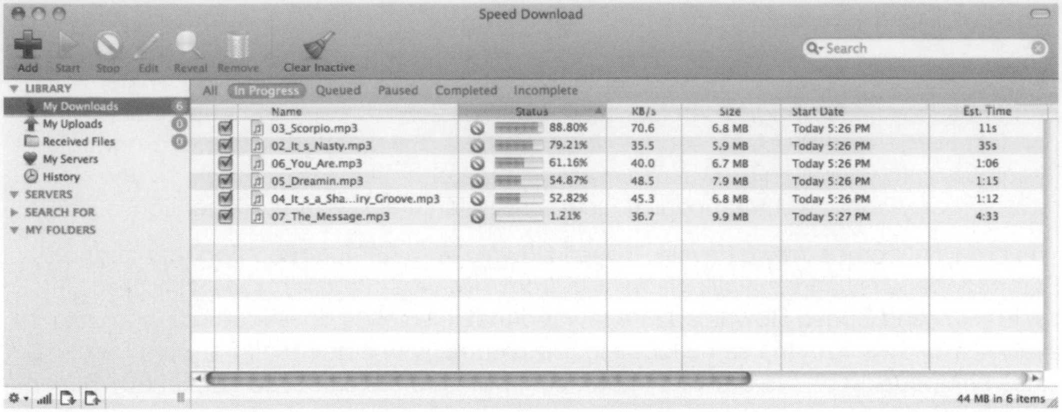

Figure 6–12. *Speed Download making short work of six files at a time.*

The best part: you can go ahead and close Firefox while Speed Download does its work, since the job is now out of Firefox's hands. I laugh at browser instability! Ha!

There's more to Speed Download than this brief example, as in fact there's more to FlashGot as well. Once you integrate FlashGot with Speed Download in Firefox, you suddenly find yourself with an extremely powerful, flexible tool that can handle just about any situation you throw at it. If you do a lot of downloading, you really ought to check out Speed Download (and FlashGot) now.

Further Resources

There are lots of file-transfer apps for Mac OS X—heck, there are lots of 'em for every operating system!—but the ones I covered here are the cream of the crop. That's not to say there aren't others that are good and that you might want to try if the programs I've covered here aren't to your liking.

ExpanDrive: Available from www.expandrive.com with a 30-day trial and costing $40, ExpanDrive actually integrates your connections directly into the Finder. When you connect to a remote server via SFTP or Amazon S3, it appears in your Finder as a mounted hard drive. You interact with the files and folders on it just as you would if they were locally mounted. It will even remount the connection if you put your Mac to sleep or lose your Internet access. However, it relies on another technology—MacFUSE—that has been pretty much abandoned by its developer (although it is open source, so it could be salvaged), it's a bit expensive, it doesn't work if you boot your Mac in 64-bit mode, and you can't quite do everything as easily as you'd like (creating a bucket at Amazon S3, for instance, is a bit of a pain). But it's worth investigating if it sounds cool to you.

Interarchy: It's been around forever, and it's super-feature-packed and powerful, but it costs a whopping $60. That seems an awful lot to me to pay for a file-transfer program. But hey, it has a free trial, so give it a go. Get it at http://nolobe.com/interarchy/.

Fetch: Another program that's been around forever (over 20 years!) and does a good job. $29 from `http://fetchsoftworks.com`, and it comes with a cute icon to boot. However, those in the previous section do a better job, or they're free.

Fugu: SFTP and SCP only—no FTP, which isn't a big deal. Free at `http://rsug.itd.umich.edu/software/fugu/`, but hasn't been updated in years and is still rockin' the pinstripe look that Mac OS X abandoned several versions ago. Add slow transfers on top of it, and this is one to avoid.

Yummy FTP: $28 with a 30-day trail at `www.yummysoftware.com`. It's not bad at all, but if you're going to pay, I really think Transmit gives you more bang for your buck.

FileZilla: A free, open source, cross-platform app that works with FTP and SFTP. Unfortunately, it's uglier than a Mississippi catfish. Don't believe me? Go look at the screenshots on `http://filezilla-project.org/client_screenshots.php`—just make sure you haven't eaten first. Snap!

Forklift: Yep, the Finder replacement software I covered in Chapter 3 also does FTP, SFTP, and Amazon S3, but it just doesn't have all the features of Cyberduck or Transmit. It'll do the basic job, but that's about it. But if you're a big ForkLift user and you just need something quick, it'll definitely come through for you.

And if you're reading this and want to learn even more about your file-transfer software options, then go read Wikipedia's "Comparison of FTP client software" at `http://en.wikipedia.org/wiki/Comparison_of_FTP_client_software`.

Torrenting Files

Despite what the goons at the MPAA and RIAA would like you to believe, there are lots of legit reasons to use BitTorrent. For instance, virtually all Linux distributions use BitTorrent to make their versions of the OS available (yes, even though I love my Mac, I also use Linux for various purposes). Lots of filmmakers and musicians distribute their work via BitTorrent as a way to save money and get their work known to a wide audience. And so on—the fact remains that BitTorrent is an awesome way to share large files using peer-2-peer technologies.

> **TIP:** If you don't know how BitTorrent works, you owe it to yourself to read Wikipedia's article on the subject, available at `http://en.wikipedia.org/wiki/BitTorrent_(protocol)`.

There are lots of BitTorrent clients out in the Macverse, and obviously I can't cover them all here. A few, though, deserve mention as ones to avoid, for various reasons.

Xtorrent: The developer of Xtorrent, David Watanabe, is very controversial within the BitTorrent and Mac communities. A lot of people like his software, but a lot of people really have strong, visceral feelings for him and his software. I'm not going to get into those issues here (if you want to find out more, just Google for `David Watanabe complaints`), but I will say that many private trackers have banned users who try to download using Xtorrent, so you should watch it. In my case, I've looked at Xtorrent and never found it be something I needed; that, coupled with the fact that I could be banned from several of my favorite BitTorrent trackers, is reason enough that I won't be using Xtorrent.

Vuze (formerly Azureus): Formerly Azureus and now known as Vuze, this is a feature-packed—and I do mean packed to the gills—BitTorrent client with a plug-in architecture that makes it easy to add even more features. So why not use it? Two reasons: it's written in Java, so it too often feels bloated and sluggish while eating up a ton of system resources, and, like Xtorrent, it's often banned by many private trackers. So no Vuze for me.

Transmission

The best stand-alone BitTorrent client is Transmission. Why? It's free and open source (both MIT and GPL licenses!), but that's just icing on the cake. It's also super simple to use, which is great. And it's cross-platform, so it runs on Mac OS X, Linux, and that other operating system.

You can download it from `www.transmissionbt.com`. When you open Transmission, it will politely ask you to support open source software by making a small donation to help out the developers. If you want to do so, click Donate; if you don't, click Nope. I encourage you to make a small donation if you use the software and like it, however. Even $5 would help—Transmission is good stuff, and it deserves some money to keep it going.

Once you find a file you want to download, grab the torrent and double-click on it or drag it into Transmission. Indicate which files you want and where you want them to go, and soon enough Transmission will start its job, as you can see in Figure 6–13.

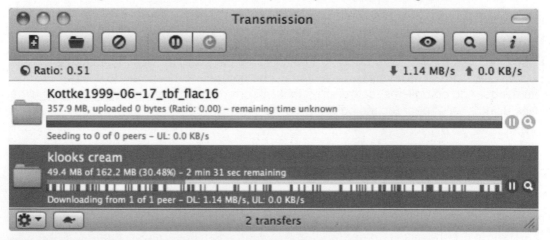

Figure 6–13. *Transmission downloading a Cream show from 40 years ago.*

Transmission supports all the features you want in a good BitTorrent client:

Small footprint: The program loads fast, and doesn't take up a lot of disk space (although the downloads can!) or RAM.

Magnet links: Magnet links are basically hashes of the files that are shared, which help BitTorrent clients directly download files while also making sure that those files are accurate and untampered with. To enable support for this feature, go to Preferences ➤ General and click Set Default Application next to Accept Magnet Links.

Default location for downloads: You can specify where each download goes every time, or you make a global setting and never get asked. To do the latter, head to Preferences ➤ Transfers ➤ Adding ➤ Default Location, where you can select ~/Downloads, Same As Torrent File, or Other. Pick a location and you're good to go.

Watched folders: Automation is a very good thing, and with that in mind, go to Preferences ➤ Transfers ➤ Adding ➤ Auto Add and check the box next to Watch For Torrent Files In, and then select a folder. When you add a .torrent file to that folder, if Transmission is running, it will see it and add it to the download queue. If you want to fully automate the process, be sure to also uncheck Preferences ➤ Transfers ➤ Display Adding Transfer Options Window.

> **TIP:** If you specify a Dropbox folder as your watched folder, then it becomes very easy to add torrents to download, even if you're not home. Just drop the .torrent file into the watched folder from your work computer, and when you get home, Transmission will have already added the file. One caveat: if you use Dropbox as your watched folder, make sure you set the Default Location on the Adding screen to something other than Same As Torrent File, or your Dropbox account will quickly fill up!

Seeding ratios: It's just basic politeness to seed a file you've downloaded at least 100%, but even more is better. To set your default ratio, go to Preferences ➤ Transfers ➤ Management ➤ Automatic. Check the box next to Stop Seeding At Ratio and set the number to something like 2.0 or 3.0—or even higher.

Groups: I like to download from various sources, and in order to keep those sources straight, I use colored groups, found at Preferences ➤ Groups. Transmission starts you out with seven different groups, but you can add more (and delete them if you wish). For each group, you can customize the color and a location for the files to go to. You can even automatically assign a download to a group based on the criteria you define, such as name, file, and tracker.

Throttling: For the sake of other programs trying to pass data back and forth on the Net, you sometimes don't want to go all out with your BitTorrent program, as it will happily use up all the bandwidth you have. To control that, go to Preferences ➤ Bandwidth ➤ Global Bandwidth Limits and check the boxes next to Download Rate and Upload Rate. Fill in values, based in KB/s, that make sense for your Net connection.

You can further refine throttling by incorporating Speed Limit Mode, on the same screen. Now you can base bandwidth limits on the time of day, with throttling in place from 6 to 11 pm (when you're home using your network for all kinds of things), for instance, while letting BitTorrent use up a much higher amount of data the rest of the time, when you're sleeping or at work. Go to **Preferences ➤ Bandwidth ➤ Speed Limit Mode** and set values next to Download Rate and Upload Rate, and then check the box next to Schedule Speed Limit and set the time.

Distributed Hash Tables (DHT): Often referred to as "trackerless torrents," DHT enables your BitTorrent client to discover others who are downloading the same file, but without having to communicate with a central BitTorrent tracker (the kind that keep getting sued out of existence). It also means that your downloads continue even if the tracker disappears. You should make sure it's enabled by looking **Preferences ➤ Peers** and seeing that Use Distributed Hash Table (DHT) For Public Torrents is checked.

Peer Exchange (PEX): This is another way to find peers, but it works by querying peers you are connected to instead of the tracker, which actually works a lot better than the old tracker-centric model. Enable this by checking Use Peer Exchange (PEX) For Public Torrents at **Preferences ➤ Peers**.

Encryption: Some ISPs try to throttle or even deny BitTorrent on their networks, and encryption can help prevent that by hiding the fact that you're using BitTorrent at all. To use encryption, go to **Preferences ➤ Peers** and check Prefer Encrypted Peers. If you're really hardcore, go ahead and check Ignore Unencrypted Peers, but keep in mind that you may not be able to access content if you do that, since a lot of BitTorrent users still don't use encryption.

> **WARNING:** Encryption is not an invisibility cloak, and certainly does *not* mean that you're anonymous or protected from malware-laden downloads!

IP blacklist: There are some companies employed by the RIAA and MPAA who try to screw up BitTorrent for everyone else, by introducing garbage files, bad connections, or by reporting (often erroneously) BitTorrent users to their ISPs for reprimand or worse. As the IP addresses used by the RIAA and MPAA's lackeys are discovered, they're added to a global blacklist, which Transmission then uses to know which addresses to avoid. I highly recommend that you enable this feature by hurrying to **Preferences ➤ Peers**, and then checking the boxes next to Prevent Known Bad Peers From Connecting and Automatically Update Weekly. If this is the first time you've enabled the feature, make sure you click the Update button to download your first list. At the time I'm writing this, there are over 224,000 addresses on the no-no list, which should make clear to you just how badly you need to turn this on.

Automatic port mapping: If you're behind a router—and I presume you are!—then you need to enable some ports on your router in order for Transmission and other BitTorrent clients to work correctly. You can fiddle around with your router directly (I've done it and it's not that hard) or you can go to **Preferences ➤ Network** and check the box next to Automatically Map Port. This should automagically talk to your router to set things up for you, but if it doesn't, you'll just have to manually do it. Fortunately, if you open Transmission's Help window and search for "port forwarding a router," you'll find some very good instructions.

Prevent sleep: Boy, this is annoying: you start a download via BitTorrent and go to sleep, only to wake up in the morning to find out that your computer went to sleep too, stopping your download in its tracks. The solution is to head to **Preferences ➤ Network** and check the box next to Prevent Computer From Sleeping With Active Transfers. Now go get your shut-eye in peace!

Remote control via the Web: If you want to connect to Transmission at home even though you're at work, you can via the Web, if you first go to **Preferences ➤ Remote** and do a few things. Check the box next to Enable Remote Access, and for goodness sakes, check the box next to Require Authentication too, as you don't want just anyone connecting to your Mac. Set a good Username and Password (1Password—discussed in Chapter 7—would be very helpful here!), and if you really want to lock things down, check the box next to Only Allow The Following IP Addresses To Connect and add your work IP address (or any other you know and will connect from). Finally, note the Listening Port, because you'll need to connect to your router and forward all traffic from that port on the Net to your Mac; you can usually find this on a router in a section called Port Forwarding, but that's all I can tell you, since there are a gazillion different routers out there).

Create torrents: You can create a torrent file using Transmission, but the process is actually a bit more complicated than that. The best thing you can do is search for "create torrent with transmission" at Google and then be prepared to experiment.

Information about the download: Select a torrent while it's downloading and then click i in the upper right of Transmission's window (or press ⌘-I) to open the Torrent Inspector window, which has six tabs:

- **General Info:** How many pieces the torrent is in, how big each piece is, the hash value of the torrent, the security of the torrent (public or private), the date of creation, comments, and the location of the files.

- **Activity:** A pretty cool screen, as you can see in Figure 6–14, this shows the current state of the transfer, the progress toward completion, the amount downloaded and uploaded, the ratio between downloads and uploads (aim for at least 1.00!), error messages, and my favorite part, a grid showing each piece of the torrent and the status of each piece. Blue means you have it, white means you don't, and orange means you're getting it.

Figure 6–14. *That grid showing the state of the torrent's pieces is almost hypnotic.*

- **Trackers:** The trackers for the torrent, including the number of seeders and leechers. If you forget the source of your torrent, this is the place to look.

- **Peers:** Who you're connected to in the BitTorrent swarm, both for downloading and uploading. In addition to their BitTorrent clients and their upload and download rates, note that you can see their IP addresses as well. Anonymity and BitTorrent don't really go together!

- **Files:** A list of all the files in the torrent. If you don't want a particular file, just uncheck it, a nice feature that all good BitTorrent clients have.

- **Options:** Set the priority of the transfer (Normal—the default—or High or Low), limit the bandwidth for the download or upload, or stay within the global settings in Preferences, seed for a particular ratio or stay with the global setting, and set how many peers can connect to you at the same time. Normally, you never need to use this screen, but it can be handy if you need to adjust something.

Transmission has one missing feature: the ability to subscribe to RSS feeds that automatically provide torrents to download. The developers have made their attitude very clear: "That really goes outside the scope of this app. There are third party applications that can work with Transmission for this, but integration is not something we currently want to do" (http://trac.transmissionbt.com/ticket/1339). In my opinion, this isn't too big of a deal—in cases where I want to auto-download torrents, I use TED or Miro. 99% of the time, RSS feeds containing torrents are for TV shows, and that's what TED and Miro specialize in. And, no surprise, that's what I'm discussing next.

> **WARNING:** On some private BitTorrent trackers, older versions of Transmission are banned due to some technical issues that were causing problems, but that's been fixed for a while. Make sure you're using the latest version of Transmission!

Transmission is just a great piece of software—it's free and open source, which is always great, but it's also well designed, with a simple base but plenty of power and customizability in the back. I use it all the time, and I'm very happy with it. Check it out today!

TED

TED (which originally stood for Torrent Episode Downloader) is a simple app that does one thing: it checks RSS feeds of TV shows to see if there's anything new. If there is, TED downloads the torrent into the folder of your choice and notifies your BitTorrent client (or, if you're using watched folders, your BitTorrent client sees that the torrent has been downloaded into a folder you told it to watch). The BitTorrent client then does the work of actually downloading the TV shows.

TED is free and open source, and you can download it from www.ted.nu. Before you start adding shows, you first need to configure it, so open Preferences. There's not a lot you need to fiddle with, but a few things are necessary.

General

Save It To: You should change this to a folder of your choice, ideally one that is watched by Transmission or your favorite BitTorrent client.

Open It In Your Default BitTorrent Client: If you're using Transmission or another client that supports watched folders, you can uncheck this; if you're not using a client that supports watched folders (and why the heck aren't you?), then you should check this.

Look And Feel

TED is written in Java and is meant to be cross-platform, and you can tell here. The "System Tray," guys? Really? Ugh.

Advanced

Do Not Download Files With These Extensions: By default, this is checked and TED doesn't download ZIP or RAR files. If this annoys you, uncheck it, or remove ZIP or RAR. Since you're using UnRarX (which I'll cover in Chapter 11), don't be afraid of RAR files!

Now that you have TED configured, it's time to add a show. Click the Add Show button, and TED displays a nice big window that lists over 200 TV shows, as shown in Figure 6–15.

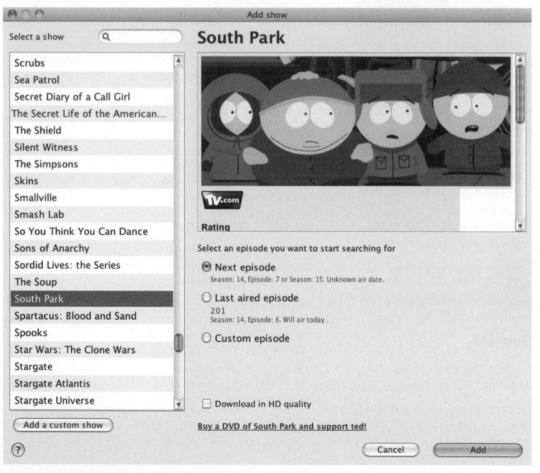

Figure 6–15. *I'm goin' down to South Park…*

Pick a show, as I've chosen South Park, and note your choice as to episode: the next one, the last one, or a custom setting. If you select Custom, a list of all episodes TED knows about will appear, along with a bar graph showing the availability of those episodes. Select the one you want—yes, you can select only one a time, although you can of course go back and select another one later—and check the box next to Download In HD Quality if you want that (keep in mind it will make your downloads a *lot* bigger). Click Add, and you'll see that your new TV episode is displayed in TED.

If you want to change how the download proceeds, select the episode and click on Edit Show. Here's a quick summary of the four screens:

- **General:** Change the name, the season, and the episode.

- **Feeds:** List the RSS feeds TED uses to grab the torrent for your show (by default, TED checks TorrentReactor, Mininova, TVRSS, The Pirate Bay, Mr. Twig, and ISOHunt). You can also delete any of those or add new ones, and reorder the feeds. TED thoughtfully provides a list of BitTorrent websites that it supports at www.ted.nu/wiki/index.php/Supported_torrent_sites.

- **Filters:** Set the minimum and maximum sizes for BitTorrent files, the minimum number of seeders for a torrent, and use keywords to filter the titles of torrents. You can also check a box to Download In HD Quality.

- **Schedule:** Use this screen if you want to check the schedule TED will use for this torrent, or manually refresh TED's check for updates.

As nice as TED is, it does have one big issue that may be a deal-killer for some users: it's written in Java, so it's a bit slow to load, and it's also not the most Mac-like app out there. The whiff of Windows is all over it, both in wording ("System Tray"?) and in UI. That said, it does work, but if the Java-y, Windows-y nature of TED is bothersome, you have other options, which I'll discuss in Further Reading ahead.

TIP: Another big annoyance, at least for someone who's as much of a neatnik as I am: TED creates a folder *without asking* at ~/ted. Note to developers: never create folders directly in my ~/ directory—or in my Documents directory—without checking with me first!

Miro

Miro is a cross-platform (in the good way, not the clumsy way as typified by TED), open source, free tool that describes itself as:

> ...a new, open mass medium of online television. We're developing the Miro internet TV platform so that watching internet video shows will be as easy as watching TV and broadcasting shows will be open to everyone. Unlike traditional TV, everyone will have a voice.

Originally known as Democracy Player, Miro is backed by the Participatory Culture Foundation, a 501(c)(3) non-profit that aims to "enable and support independent, non-corporate creativity and political engagement." Pretty lofty goals! Fortunately, Miro is excellent software that gets better all the time, one that Mac users should check out.

> **NOTE:** In the interest of full disclosure, I have donated money to the Participatory Culture Foundation in the past, and will definitely do so again.

What's interesting about Miro is that it's both a sophisticated BitTorrent client and a very powerful media player, all wrapped up in one package. I use it constantly, as its RSS subscription feature works perfectly, helping to keep me up-to-date with TV shows, videos, YouTube subscriptions, and even some audio podcasts.

Download Miro from www.getmiro.com, install it, and open it. You're asked if you want to run Miro on startup (not a bad idea if you're installing it on a Mac mini-based media center; otherwise, it's up to you) and if you want Miro to find all your media files and add them to its library (it won't move them, just index them, but I still say no, since I have a lot of videos I don't necessarily need in Miro). Miro finally appears, with the UI you can see in Figure 6–16.

There are three major parts to Miro:

- **The Sidebar:** Navigate to content and select it.

- **The Main View:** Display search contents or media as it's playing.

- **The Playback Bar:** Control playing media and show details about it.

Let's run down the Sidebar, as doing so gives a nice overview of many of Miro's features.

Miro Guide: The Miro Guide is a directory of HD videos that you can download (you can also view it on the Web, at http://miroguide.com), with content coming from indie sources to PBS to Rocketboom to NBC. There's a lot of stuff here—over 6,000 sources! And if you don't feel like browsing for cool stuff, you can filter (New, Most Popular, HD Favorites, and Genres), and if you don't feel like filtering, you can always search.

Figure 6–16. *Miro comes with a few subscriptions built-in, and it's ready for more.*

Video Search: Search many video websites in one fell swoop, including YouTube, Yahoo Video, Google Video, Blip, and many more. If you want to continually search for a term and have Miro update you with any videos, click the Save As A Feed button, and Miro creates a new entry for you under Video Feeds, further down in the Sidebar (you can also do this by going to **Sidebar ➤ New Search Feed**).

Library: Browse or search through your Miro media library by Video, Audio, or Other. You can also see the videos and audio files that are currently downloading.

Websites: View websites inside of Miro itself and then click on links to download the video inside the program. If you want to add a website, use **Sidebar ➤ Add Website.**

> **TIP:** One of the best websites for free, legal TV content is Hulu. Add `www.hulu.com` as a website, and you can watch an enormous number of TV shows and movies right in Miro, and it's all on the up and up. And if you're feeling ambitious, you can also add websites for ABC, CBS, NBC, and more.

Video Feeds: RSS feeds containing torrents to which you've subscribed (although Miro includes three subscriptions by default). When new torrents show up in the RSS feed, they are automatically downloaded for you so they're ready to play. If you want TV shows, my recommendation is to find a good TV RSS website such as showRSS, choose your favorite shows, generate an RSS feed, and then click on **Sidebar ➤ Add Feed** to start automatically downloading new and old episodes that you can watch in Miro. You can see this process in Figure 6–17.

Figure 6–17. *Some shows are old, some are new, and some are still downloading.*

Audio Feeds: Everything I just said about Video Feeds is true for this part of the Sidebar as well, except that it's for audio instead of video. Miro includes a subscription to This American Life (which is totally awesome) by default.

Playlists: Miro makes it easy to create playlists for your content—just drag videos and audio into the playlist area and bang! You have a playlist!

Playback on Miro is a crisp and clear joy, with an example in Figure 6–18.

Miro supports almost any kind of video format you can throw at it, including QuickTime, H.264, MPEG, AVI, Xvid, Divx, WMV, and even Flash. HD videos in particular look beautiful, especially if you play them full screen. If you're watching a video and you have to stop for whatever reason, Miro remembers your stopping point and starts back up at the point the next time you start the video.

Figure 6–18. *Bonus points to those who can tell me who that is!*

Miro's prefs contain some things you should know about, so here are the relevant screens:

Feeds: The default settings are here, but you can change each feed individually by selecting a feed in the Sidebar, and then clicking the Settings button at the top of the Main View. My advice: leave the defaults where they are, especially Check For New Content. Do not reduce that from Every Hour to something shorter, as most videos don't come out all that often, and BitTorrent sites really don't appreciate getting their RSS feeds hammered over and over again.

Downloads: You may want to adjust Limit Upstream Bandwidth To and Limit Downstream Bandwidth To, depending on your Internet connection and what you do with it. I really like how Ignore Unencrypted Connections is checked by default, and I'd encourage you to leave that alone. For Stop Torrent Uploads When This Ratio Is Reached, Miro uses 2 by default, which is fine, but if you're feeling generous, you might want to change this to something higher, like 3 or 4.

Folders: This is important for two reasons: it's where you tell Miro the location for downloads, and it's where you specify watched folders, if you want to use them. Think carefully about each before you make your settings.

Disk Space: It's very cool of Miro to think of this, as it's very easy to forget how much you've downloaded, only to find out that you've filled your hard drive with video. Leave the check next to Keep At Least This Much Free Space On My Drive, but I'd bump up the size from 0.2GB to more like 5 or 10GB. Only 200MB of free space on my hard drive would kind of freak me out, so I like to keep a lot more empty space just in case. Notice also that you can set the number of days after which Miro deletes video and audio here as well.

If you want to know anything more about Miro, check out the program's excellent documentation and help on its website, including screencasts and videos (duh!). One of the absolute neatest things is that it features guides to creating and publishing your own videos, so you can make your stuff available on Miro to people all over the world. Too cool!

So when should you use Transmission and when should you use Miro? I use both, because I like to keep things separated, but really, there's no need to—it's just habit. I use Miro for TV shows and RSS subscriptions, and I use Transmission for one-off's—torrents that I want to download one time and then delete. Also, Transmission has more features than Miro does when it comes to straight BitTorrenting, such as the ability to selectively choose files to download, so I would rely on Transmission when I need tighter control over what I'm downloading. But either way, they're both great, they're both free, and they're both open source, so there's no reason why you shouldn't have both.

Further Resources

If you don't like or want to use TED, Automatic (http://codingcurious.com/automatic/) does much the same thing. On the negative side, it costs 15 Euros (which isn't that much, really), but on the positive side, it's a true Mac client, unlike TED.

If you really don't want to use Transmission, µTorrent (that's the Greek letter *mu*) is free and open source, and you can find it at www.utorrent.com. It's also the official Mac client from BitTorrent the company (the company was started by Bram Cohen, the amazing programmer behind BitTorrent the protocol), but it's still in beta. That said, as nice as it is, I still prefer Transmission, but you may want to give µTorrent a try.

Summary

I've covered some major categories of apps in this chapter—e-mail, social networking and sharing, file transfer, and BitTorrent—that millions upon millions of people use every day around the world. Many of the programs I've shown you are excellent, literally the finest in their class. The funny thing is, however, in five years, who knows what new ideas about things to do and communicate and create on the Internet will have flowered, and who knows what awesome new programs will have found their places on the desktops of Mac users? That's the cool thing about the Internet, and about the Mac: it's always changing, always improving, always bringing new things to us every day.

## Chapter 7

Securing Your Mac & Networks

Security is one of those things that many Mac users don't like to think about, which is unfortunate, for several reasons. Although Mac OS X enjoys an excellent secure base thanks to its UNIX base, it's certainly not invulnerable. It behooves Mac users to take all the steps they can to protect their computers and their valuable data. Those family pictures in iPhoto? Your business' records? Your thesis? The songs you've been working on? How would you feel if they disappeared forever? If you don't protect them, they could. The final reason to learn more about security is my favorite: it's fun!

Before delving further into tips, advice, and software to enhance your Mac's security, let me make a recommendation that supersedes everything else: think strongly about paying Undercover to protect your Mac in case of loss or theft. Undercover, available from Orbicule at `www.orbicule.com/undercover/`, is a virtually undetectable software utility that you install on your Mac. Ideally, you'll never need to use it, but if your Mac is lost or stolen, you notify Orbicule, and Undercover springs into action, doing the following for you:

- Using Wi-Fi positioning, Undercover finds your Mac within a range of 30-60 feet.

- Displays screenshots that shows what your Mac is doing. If the bad guy e-mails someone, you'll see it, for instance.

- Takes pictures every eight minutes using your Mac's iSight camera, giving you a lovely mugshot of your thief.

- Simulate hardware failure, encouraging the perp to sell your Mac or take it into an Apple Store or Apple dealer.

- Once the Mac is in an Apple Store or at an Apple dealer, it will start displaying a message on-screen (and speaking, via your Mac's built-in text-to-speech) that it has been stolen and will provide Orbicule's contact info and the promise of a finder's fee.

This is a sensible series of escalating events that should give you a fighting chance at getting your Mac back. So how much does it cost? $49 for a single Mac, or $59 for a family license that covers five Macs (there are also student and site licenses as well). The famlly license is a great deal—only $12 per Mac! And there's no annual fee or anything annoying like that, which is a nice relief.

My good friend Bill Edney had his Mac stolen at a Borders bookstore a year ago. Fortunately, security cameras caught the idiot in the act, so he was busted later. But by that time, Bill's MacBook Pro was sold and long gone, and he had to buy a new laptop. One of the first things he did with that new laptop? He bought and installed Undercover. Bill's prepared now; learn from his example and get prepared too.

Managing Passwords

For the foreseeable future, we're stuck with passwords that we type into little boxes. Sure, there are other options out there—biometrics, two-factor authentication, time-synchronized one-time passwords, public key cryptography, and so on (articles about all of these are on Wikipedia)—but none of them are going to be in wide use for quite some time. As I said, we use passwords now, and we're stuck with them going forward.

One big problem with passwords, of course, is that most people choose incredibly poor passwords, and then they re-use them on every website and with every login system with which they come into contact. Want to know how bad most passwords are? Check these out:

- "Most Common Hotmail Password Revealed!"
  www.wired.com/threatlevel/2009/10/10000-passwords/

- "Depressing Analysis Of RockYou Hacked Passwords"
  http://techcrunch.com/2010/01/21/depressing-analysis-of-rockyou-hacked-passwords/

- "MySpace password exploit: Crunching the numbers (and letters)"
  www.infoworld.com/d/security-central/myspace-password-exploit-crunching-numbers-and-letters-983

- "Real-World Passwords"
  hwww.schneier.com/blog/archives/2006/12/realworld_passw.html

Horrible. There are certain rules for creating good passwords—I wrote an article about them called "Pass the Chocolate" for SecurityFocus (www.securityfocus.com/columnists/245)—but the best thing to do is generate long, complicated passwords and then use a password safe like 1Password to store them for you.

I know that some of you are saying, "Why do I need to buy 1Password when Mac OS X comes with Keychain Access in /Applications/Utilities?" Good question. Keychain Access definitely stores passwords in a secure fashion. It's also free with your OS, which is always nice. But it's clunky, especially if you want to view your saved passwords: open Keychain Access, click on the site whose password you want to view, check the box next to Show Password, enter your Mac OS X password, and click Allow.

Repeat for each subsequent password (unless you choose Always Allow, which isn't a good idea!).

The other problem with Keychain Access is that it's designed to store passwords and certificates, and that's it. Sure, there's a Secure Notes section, but using it is also clunky.

There are better ways to manage passwords and even notes—and lots of other stuff too—and you'll learn about several of them in this section. In the meantime, though, try testing some of your current passwords to see how good they are. The clearest website I found to do that is "How Secure Is My Password?" at `http://howsecureismypassword.net`. The results are given in terms of how long it would take to crack the passwords. Here are a few examples—but keep in mind that these apply to just one PC trying to crack your password. Most of the time, a bad guy uses several machines working in tandem, so these numbers are really best case scenarios:

- aaaa: "Your password is one of the 500 most common passwords. It would be cracked almost instantly."

- scottg: "It would take 30 seconds for a desktop PC to crack your password."

- 123456789: "It would take about a minute for a desktop PC to crack your password."

- a1b2c3d4: "It would take about 3 days for a desktop PC to crack your password."

- b70GqM621fh: "It would take about 164 thousand years for a desktop PC to crack your password."

> **NOTE:** You can read more about password strength in Wikipedia's article on the subject, at `http://en.wikipedia.org/wiki/Password_strength`. If you don't like the website I suggested for testing your password, you can instead use the Excel spreadsheet referenced in "Test the strength of your password policy" (`http://infoworld.com/d/security-central/test-strength-your-password-policy-437`).

1Password

The king of password safes on Mac OS X is 1Password, one of my absolute favorite programs on my Mac, one that I use too many times to count every day, and one that I couldn't work without. You can get it for yourself at `http://agilewebsolutions.com/products/1Password`, but let me say up front that it costs $40 (that said, it's often for sale at a discount in various bundles—that's how I got it—and if you look around, you can often find coupons that knock a few bucks off, too). However you have to, get it.

When you open 1Password, you find out that it can securely store several different kinds of data:

- **Logins:** Website logins, passwords, and notes, which you can see in Figure 7–1.

Figure 7–1. *See the list of logins, with one selected? Good!*

When you hit a web page that matches the domain name (test.com in Figure 7–1) stored in 1Password, you can use 1Password to fill in the username and password with just a click, which is wonderfully convenient.

- **Accounts:** Click the + at the bottom of the window to see the kinds of accounts you can add, which consist of:
  - AirPort Extreme
  - Amazon S3
  - Database
  - Email Account
  - FTP Account

- Generic Account

- Instant Messenger

- Internet Provider

- MobileMe

- Server

- iTunes

Each type of account provides you with different fields that are appropriate for the account.

- **Identities:** Creating different identities enables you to fill in forms on the Net with the information you want to provide, as you can see in Figure 7–2.

Figure 7–2. *Yes, that is the real me: Testy McTesterson.*

When you hit a web page that asks you a bunch of questions—name, birth date, job, address, phone number, and so on—you can click on 1Password and poof! all that data is filled in for you. I'm super-lazy, so I think this is just wonderiffic.

■ **Secure Notes:** Like Apple's Keychain Access, 1Password has an area where you can store notes, as you can tell from Figure 7–3.

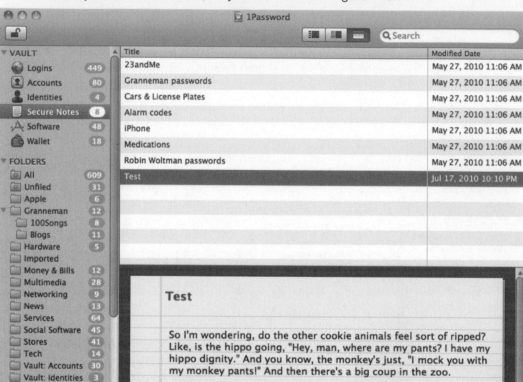

Figure 7–3. *Bonus points for knowing the source of that quotation!*

I use mine to keep license plate numbers for cars, lists of medications I'm taking, alarm codes, and things like that. Since I also sync 1Password with my iPhone (more on that in a moment), I have that information with me so I can refer to it at all times.

■ **Software:** I used to use a wiki to keep track of my software licenses, but now I use 1Password, which provides a great, encrypted storage space for that info, as you can see in Figure 7–4.

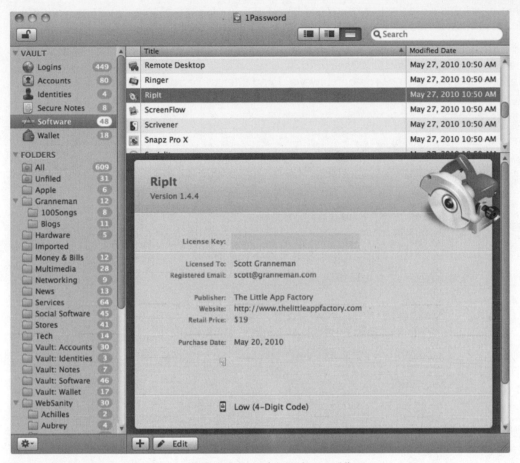

Figure 7–4. *Now I can easily keep track of all those serial numbers and licenses.*

You can even attach the external license files that some vendors use to validate software, which is another great feature of 1Password.

- **Wallet:** Click the + at the bottom of the window to see the list of items you can add to your virtual 1Password wallet:

    - Bank Account

    - Credit Card

    - Driver's License

    - Hunting License

    - Membership

    - Passport

    - Reward Program

    - Social Security Number

Again, all of this is securely stored, so I sleep well knowing that this very sensitive data is safe. And when I need it on a web page, it's just a click away.

And how is that? How is the data I'm storing in 1Password able to interface with my web browsers? When you install 1Password, you're asked if you want to install browser extensions; if you say no, you can always do so later by going to **Preferences ➤ Browsers**, which is shown in Figure 7–5.

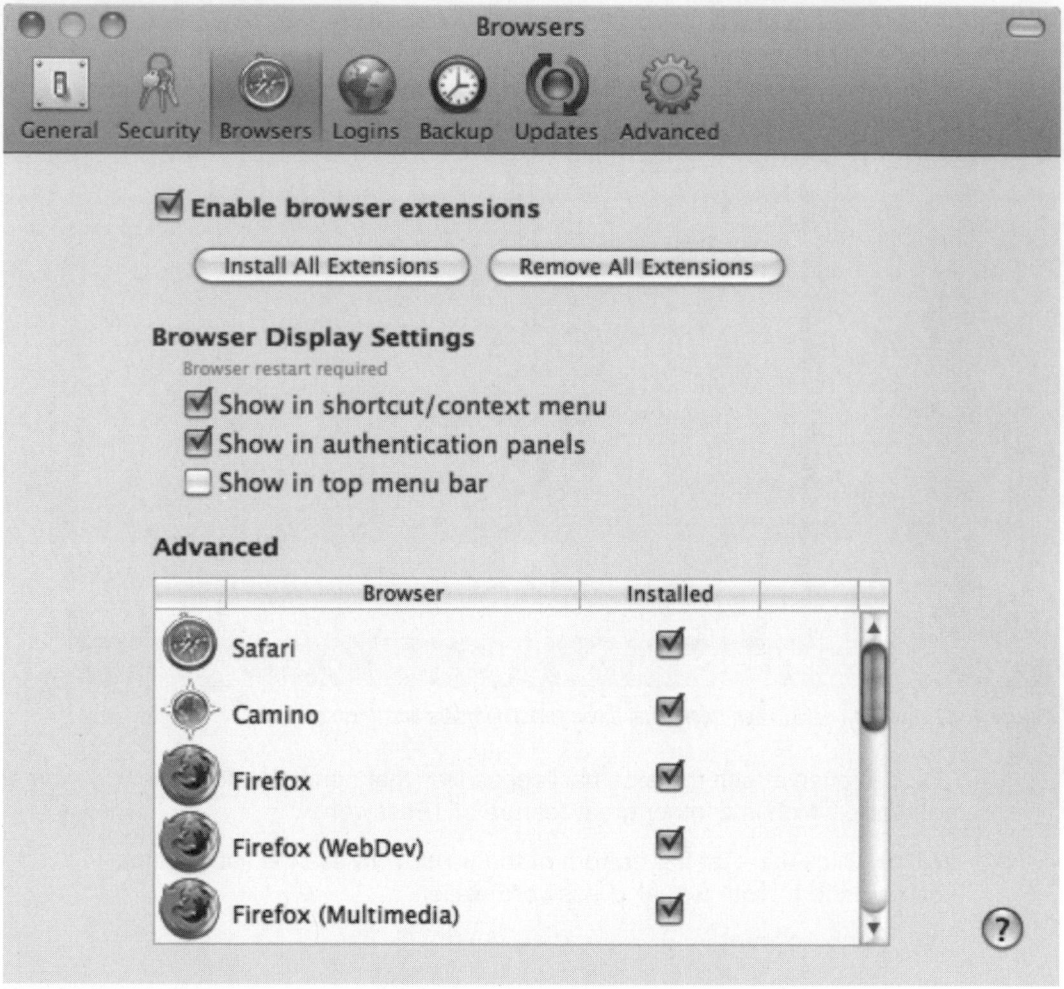

Figure 7–5. *1Password integrates nicely with almost all of your web browsers.*

The browser extensions give two-way access between 1Password and your web browsers:

- A new button appears in your browser that gives you access to your 1Password data. Click it and you can select the data you want to fill in or access.

■ As you enter names and passwords into websites, 1Password will ask you if you want it to store that data. If you say yes, it's now available the next time you visit.

There's one exception to this smooth integration: Google Chrome. To install the browser extension for Chrome, open the browser and do the following:

1. Visit `http://support.agilewebsolutions.com/forumdisplay.php?92-Chrome-extension`, which is the 1Password forum for the Chrome extension, and look for the sticky post titled "Setup instructions."

2. In that post, find the link to the extension, click on it, and install it.

3. Go to **Window** ➤ **Extensions**.

4. Click the Developer Mode link at the top of the page, which should show you something like you see in Figure 7–6.

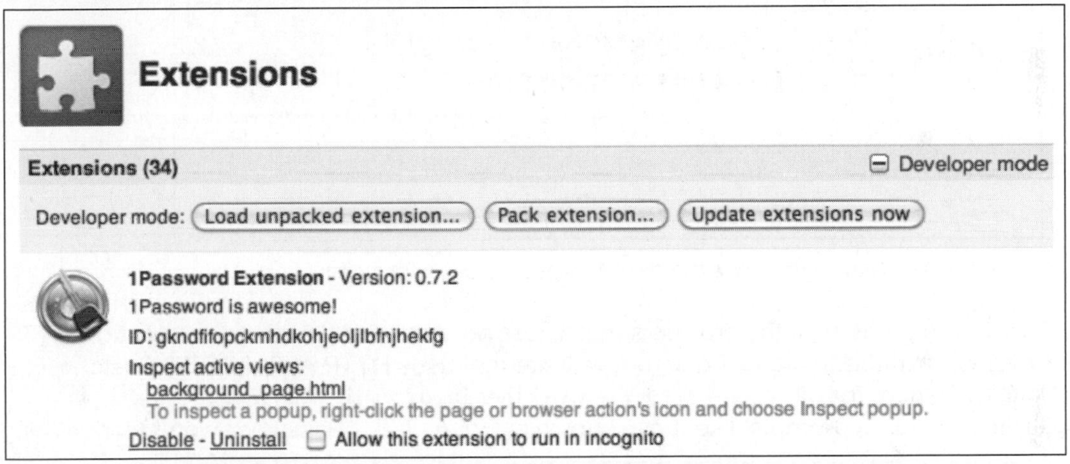

Figure 7–6. *If you use Google Chrome, it doesn't hurt to go into Developer Mode every once in a while anyway.*

5. Click the Update Extensions Now button, which should update the 1Password Extension to the latest version, which at this time is 0.7.2.

6. You can click the Developer Mode link again if you want to go back to the normal view for your extensions, but it's not necessary.

Now the extension is installed in Chrome and you can use it—pretty much. Let me explain.

In every web browser, including Chrome, when you find yourself faced with a login or any other form that asks for data stored in 1Password, you can click the 1Password button on the toolbar, or you can press ⌘-\. This inserts the login or form info as long as it's obvious to 1Password what to fill in, or the program will ask you to choose the correct log in from all those that match, as you can see in Figure 7–7.

Figure 7–7. *Yes, I have four logins somewhere at ikiped.org. Don't ask me how.*

This works great in all the browsers that 1Password supports, with one exception in Chrome. If you're trying to log in to a website that uses HTTP AUTH (HTTP Basic Authentication; for more, see `http://en.wikipedia.org/wiki/Basic_access_authentication`) prompts, like those shown in Figure 7–8, 1Password won't work at all.

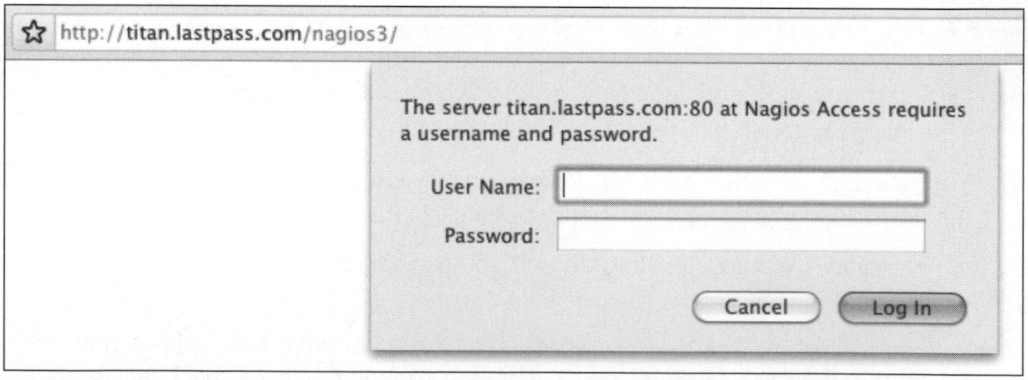

Figure 7–8. *A lot of websites use this kind of authentication. C'mon, Google—open up your browser to developers and support these!*

Why not? Because Google hasn't yet seen fit to expose the HTTP AUTH window to extensions (and unfortunately, if you read the bug report at `http://code.google.com/ p/chromium/issues/detail?id=32056`, it appears that Google doesn't consider fixing this a priority). So you have to manually copy your username and password from 1Password and paste them into HTTP AUTH windows in Chrome, which is a major drag.

If you can't think of a good password when you're registering at a site, or, better yet, if you want to use a password that will be extremely hard to break, you should use 1Password to generate a password for you. 1Password will then store this long and complicated password for you, making it easy to call up and use later when you need to get into the website.

To create a strong password in a web browser that's not Chrome, click the 1Password extension button and select Strong Password Generator, which will show you a window like Figure 7–9. If you're using Chrome, open 1Password, go to Vault ➤ Logins, and click the +, which creates a new entry in edit mode. Fill in everything but the Password, and then click Generate next to the Password field, which opens a sheet that looks like Figure 7–9.

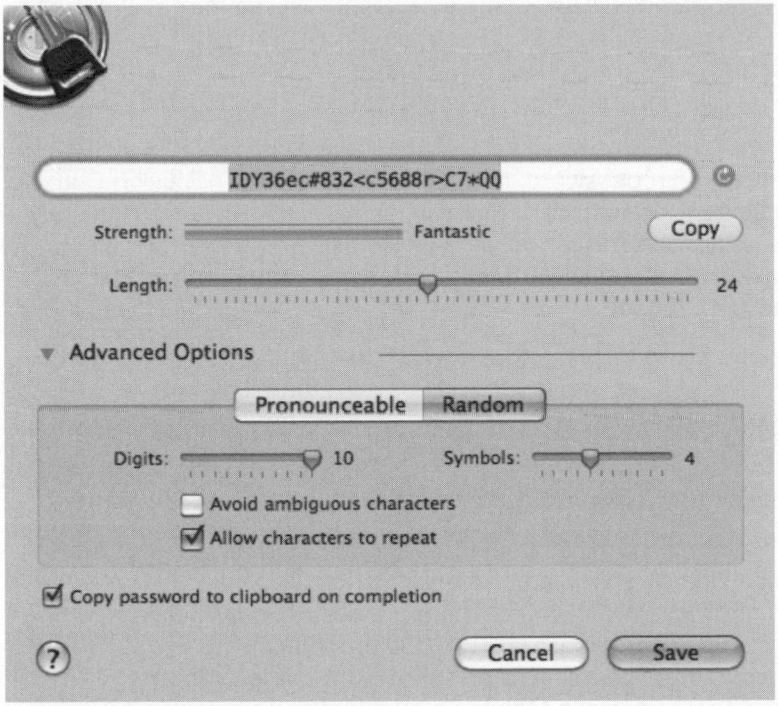

Figure 7–9. *It's ridiculously easy to generate an awesome password with 1Password.*

Make sure Advanced Options are visible, and I further recommend that you select Random over Pronounceable. The point isn't to remember this password; the point is to generate one that is so long and complicated that it would be virtually impossible for someone to crack it, but that is also so long and complicated that you have to use 1Password to keep track of it yourself.

For Length, I'd use at least 24 characters. 32 is better, although 1Password will jack it all the way up to 50 if you'd like. Really, though, anything at 24 and up will be just fine.

As for Digits, I always choose 10 to maximize the numbers that appear. Symbols is an interesting one—to be honest, I often leave it at 0, because different programs and websites sometimes choke on various symbols. For instance, some programs choke on # or ! characters in MySQL passwords, while the ' character in WordPress Secret Keys (http://api.wordpress.org/secret-key/1.1/) causes all sorts of trouble. The problem is that different programs and sites choke on different symbols, so I just disable all of them.

Before I get chastising e-mails from people warning me that I'm giving out horrible advice or that I'm following horrific security practices, let me point out two things:

- This is what I do. You are free to use as many symbols as you like in your generated password, maxing out with 10.

- If you're using 32 characters, or even 24, the fact that you have no symbols and instead just have capital letters, lowercase letters, and numbers means that you're still very, very safe. Don't believe me? Read http://en.wikipedia.org/wiki/Random_password_generator, www.garykessler.net/library/password.html, and www.redkestrel.co.uk/Articles/RandomPasswordStrength.html and then do the math for yourself!

When you're finished generating a password, click either Fill (if you're not using Chrome and used the 1Password extension button) or Save (if you're using 1Password directly either because you were using Chrome or you just felt like bypassing the extension's button). Now you have a super-long password that's super-difficult to crack, and 1Password will keep track of it for you.

Now, I know what some of you are thinking right now: "Scott, that's great, but I don't always have my Mac with me. If I use the same old password that I have memorized and have been using for years, I can still log in, even if I'm not using my Mac. But now I must have 1Password and my Mac available 24/7, and that's not possible!"

Good point. However, there are two ways around this, and you can use either or both:

- If you use an iPhone (or iPod Touch, or iPad), you can buy the 1Password app and sync your data between your Mac and your iPhone. I do this regularly, and it works. There are two apps available: 1Password (http://itunes.com/app/1Password) and 1Password Pro (http://itunes.com/app/1PasswordPro). Get Pro—it provides you with a bookmarklet that you can use in Mobile Safari and makes entering your password from 1Password about as streamlined as you can hope for on an iPhone.

- Use 1PasswordAnywhere, which I'll discuss next.

1PasswordAnywhere allows you to securely access your data anywhere on the Web (you can also use a USB flash drive; for more, see http://help.agile.ws/1Password3/1passwordanywhere.html). I recommend that you store your 1Password data in Dropbox, which does two things for you: it backs up any changes you make to your data, and it gives you a secure website that you can access to view your data.

Let's start with putting your 1Password data into Dropbox. The easy way to move it is to open 1Password and go to **Preferences ➤ General** and click Move. Pick a folder in Dropbox (I created one called Data and selected that) and click Move To Selected Folder. The file 1Password.agilekeychain (which is really a bundle, so it's actually a folder that behaves like a file) will now be located in Dropbox.

> **NOTE:** Some of you may be thinking that you could use your MobileMe iDisk instead of Dropbox, but Agile explicitly recommends against permanently moving your 1Password data there. Keeping a copy there is fine, but don't move your data there for good. For more on this issue, see http://help.agile.ws/1Password3/1passwordanywhere.html.

Every time you add a new item to track, or alter an existing item, Dropbox will instantly back up your changes. That's cool. But here's something that's even cooler.

In a web browser, go to https://www.dropbox.com (note the https) and log in. You're connecting over a secure connection (again, it's https), so what you're about to view is safe from snooping eyes. Locate the 1Password.agilekeychain file and click on it (remember, it's only Mac OS X that treats that bundle like a file; to everything else in the world, it's just a folder). You're now inside the folder, and you'll see a list of folders and a file like in Figure 7–10.

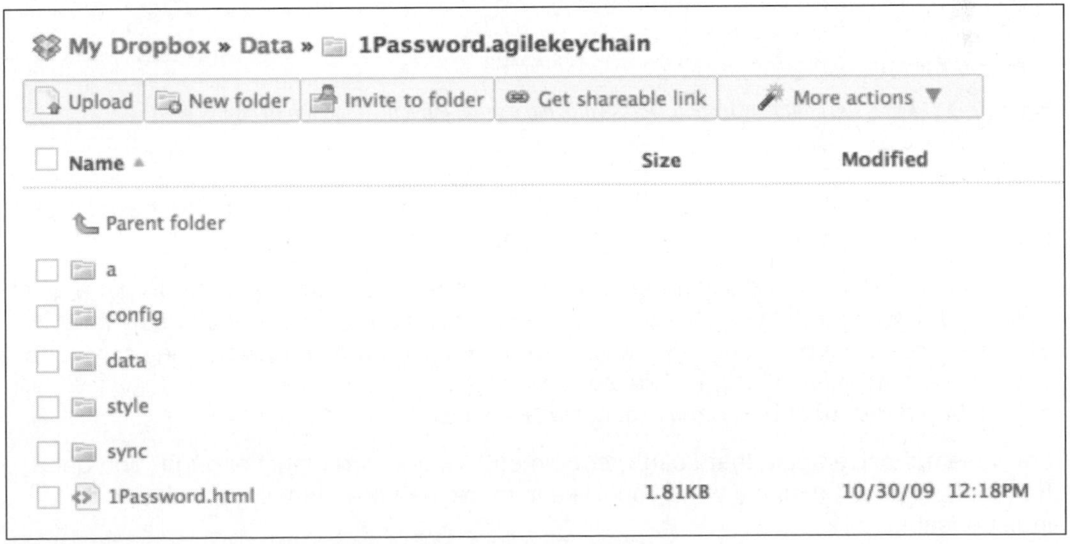

Name ▲	Size	Modified
↰ Parent folder		
▢ a		
▢ config		
▢ data		
▢ style		
▢ sync		
▢ 1Password.html	1.81KB	10/30/09 12:18PM

My Dropbox » Data » 1Password.agilekeychain
Upload   New folder   Invite to folder   Get shareable link   More actions ▼

Figure 7–10. *The contents of the 1Password bundle, as shown at Dropbox.*

Click on 1Password.html, and you'll be prompted for the same master password you use to open 1Password on your Mac. Enter that password (which had better be a good one that you have memorized, by the way, or you're hosed!), and you'll see a web-based version of 1Password's standard UI, which you can see in Figure 7–11.

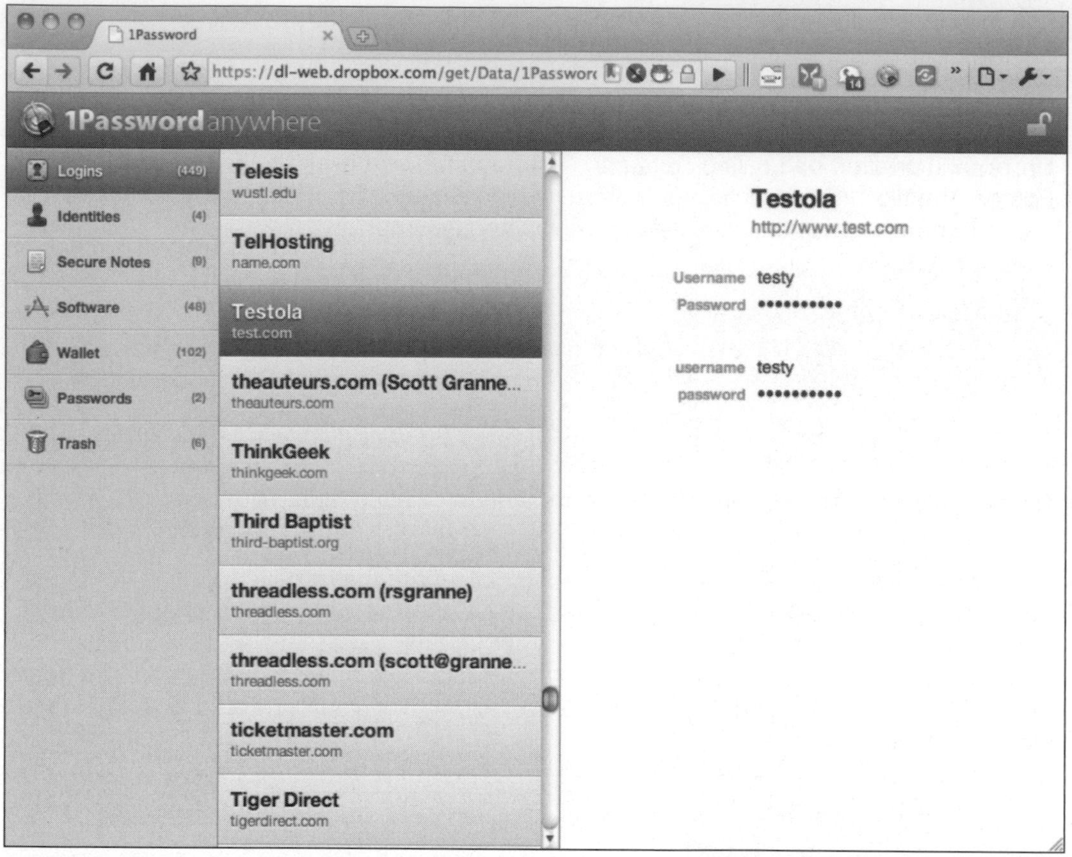

Figure 7–11. *Agile, the company behind 1Password, did a great job emulating the UI on the Web.*

You can see in Figure 7–11 that the passwords are obfuscated. If you hover your mouse over the stars, a small Reveal button appears. Click on the button, and the password is revealed. At that point, you can copy it and paste it where you need it.

There's a lot more I could say about 1Password, but my editors are about to get a giant hook and drag me offstage so I can't continue to talk about this particular software. If you want to learn more about 1Password's cool new features and what they can do for you, check out "What's New In 1Password3" at http://agilewebsolutions.com/products/1Password/whats_new.

Let me emphasize again that I can't recommend 1Password highly enough. You get a free trial, so give it a spin. I think you'll like it; more than that, I think you'll find it indispensable.

Further Resources

1Password is fantastic software, but it does cost four sawbucks. If you just can't swing the $40 (or less—remember that you can find 1Password online for a cheaper price if you look), then you have other options.

KeePassX

KeePassX is free, open source, and available from http://keepassx.sourceforge.net. You can store its data in Dropbox like you do with 1Password, though you can't really access it on the Web like you can with 1PasswordAnywhere. The other nice thing is that it supports plug-ins so it's possible to extend the app in useful ways (for more on those plug-ins, see "Eight Best KeePass Plug-Ins to Master Your Passwords" at http://lifehacker.com/5046988/eight-best-keepass-plug+ins-to-master-your-passwords).

Unfortunately, KeePassX is a cross-platform app that's been ported to Mac OS X, and it shows. It's ugly, un-Mac-like in just about every way, and not the easiest to use. Also, it doesn't integrate with the various web browsers that run on Mac OS X the way that 1Password does, which means you constantly have to switch back and forth between your web browser and KeePassX if you want to copy your data. There is a Firefox extension that integrates the program with Firefox, but it's for Windows only (boo!). Still, if you want to learn more, head over to http://keefox.org and check it out.

LastPass

LastPass, available at https://lastpass.com, is a browser-based service (Safari, Firefox, and Chrome) that is a lot like 1Password. In fact, it will happily import your data from 1Password if you give it permission. There are two editions: Free and Premium, which costs $1 per month. The Premium version enables you to store data on your mobile phone and USB flash drives, no ads, and quicker support. All in all, LastPass isn't a bad service—and you can't argue with the price.

That said, I find it to be very ugly, with a confusing UI. It's got a ton of links and options and sections, and it contrasts very unfavorably with 1Password in the interface department. In addition, remember that it runs in your web browser and that's the only way to run it. This is nice, in that it's always available while you're using the Web, but it also means that you always need to run your web browser. Granted, most power users have a web browser open all of the time anyway, but it's still something to consider.

If you don't want to spend the money for 1Password, then LastPass is a good second option. But if you care about usability, as well as the extra features that 1Password provides, then I'd definitely go with 1Password.

Clipperz

This is another web-based service (www.clipperz.com) that's fairly new, so I haven't exhaustively investigated it. It's free and open source, with a few UI complexities, but it seems based on fundamentally secure principles, and it also seems to be improving fast. Unfortunately, at this time it supports only Firefox and Opera, so Safari and Chrome users are left in the lurch.

Encrypting Your Data

Whenever I give talks to students and groups about security, I always tell them that the only way to really protect their valuable data is to use encryption of some sort. If you're using public Wi-Fi without WPA (which is the norm), encrypt your web, e-mail, and IM traffic. If you have sensitive files on your Mac that you want to protect from view, you need to encrypt them. Even if you have a desktop that never leaves your house, or you keep your MacBook glued to your side while you travel, that's no guarantee. Theft is always a possibility, and you need to prepare for that possibility. In this section, I'll cover encrypting your files on your Mac so that you're prepared.

Encrypting Your Hard Drive

If you travel a lot with your laptop and you want to safeguard its contents, you should consider encrypting a significant portion of your hard drive. Apple includes a technology called FileVault that makes this really easy to do, and there's also a free tool called TrueCrypt that's also available and very good. Turn on FileVault by going to > System Preferences > Security > FileVault and clicking the appropriate buttons. If you want to check out TrueCrypt, go to www.truecrypt.org and download the program.

> **NOTE:** A lot of people think that TrueCrypt is open source, but it isn't, according to both the Free Software Foundation and the Open Source Initiative.

I'm not going to go into exhaustive detail about the two programs, because Apple's help for FileVault is quite good, and because the TrueCrypt website has some excellent documentation. I will say this, though: both programs are worth your time if you're interested in encrypting key parts of your hard drive, but you should be aware of some big caveats associated with these two software packages:

- This may seem obvious, but it's worth repeating: if you lose the master password that decrypts your drive, you're completely, totally, 100% hosed. You absolutely need a super-strong password, but make sure you don't forget it or lose it.

- Before you turn on FileVault, make sure you have enough free space on your hard drive that's as big as your existing Home, and then a bit more, just to be careful. If you're ever going to turn off FileVault, again, you'll need free space on your drive equal to the size of the encrypted Home folder, and then again a pinch for safety.

- FileVault encrypts your entire Home folder. Don't want the whole dang thing encrypted, or only need a folder here and there locked down? Then don't use FileVault (instead, I'd recommend Knox, which I discuss soon). Worried about the contents of folders outside Home, such as /tmp, /Library, and /etc? Then don't use FileVault or TrueCrypt. In fact, you're kinda outta luck, since Mac OS X doesn't allow the encryption of boot volumes at this time.

- TrueCrypt doesn't work if you boot into the 64-bit kernel, although FileVault does.

- FileVault complicates Time Machine, so much so that you really need to choose between the two. You can use Time Machine to back up a File Vault-encrypted volume only if you're logged out, which isn't the most common scenario for most Mac users. Further, you can't use the way cool traveling through space interface to restore files; instead, you have to either restore the entire home directory (!) or manually dig around with the Finder to find the files you want and copy them yourself. Ugh.

- FileVault and TrueCrypt aren't invulnerable (see http://en.wikipedia.org/wiki/FileVault and http://en.wikipedia.org/wiki/Truecrypt for details), but they're not easily broken either. Basically, if you're worried about the punk who steals your laptop getting into your stuff, then TrueCrypt and FileVault will keep your stuff safe. If you're worried about the NSA or the Chinese government getting into your top-secret plans, then, as Public Enemy once said, I can't do nothin' for ya, man. You have a lot bigger things on your plate, and FileVault and TrueCrypt may not be enough to protect you.

So, should you use FileVault or TrueCrypt? If the preceding list of caveats doesn't scare you away, and you really feel like you need it, then try them out. To be honest, though, I don't utilize either one. I love the idea of an encrypted folder that transparently safeguards everything put into it, but the issues associated with FileVault and TrueCrypt dissuade me away from those two solutions. Instead, I use Knox, discussed next.

Knox

Knox does two things: it creates encrypted disk images into which you can place files and folders, and it manages the encrypted disk images you create. In terms of the first feature, you can do the same thing with Disk Utility, located in

/Applications/Utilities. Open the program, click New Image, enter the info, click Create, and bang! you have an encrypted disk image. However, as with many things, the built-in tools Apple provides can be improved upon. In this case, Knox makes creating those encrypted disk images much easier and clearer, and it's also an excellent tool when it comes to managing them.

You'll pay a little bit for that ease of use, however, but it's not unreasonable considering what it gives you. The cost is $35 and you get the software from http://agilewebsolutions.com/knox, the same people who make the fantastic 1Password, discussed earlier in this chapter. If you think that's too much to pay, I understand, and you should skip this section. If you're interested in learning more, read on.

To create a new encrypted volume, go to the Knox icon on your Menu Bar and select New Vault, which will show you a window like that in Figure 7–12 (OK, I kind of lied—after the window opens, you need to click on Show Advanced Options in order to see Figure 7–12).

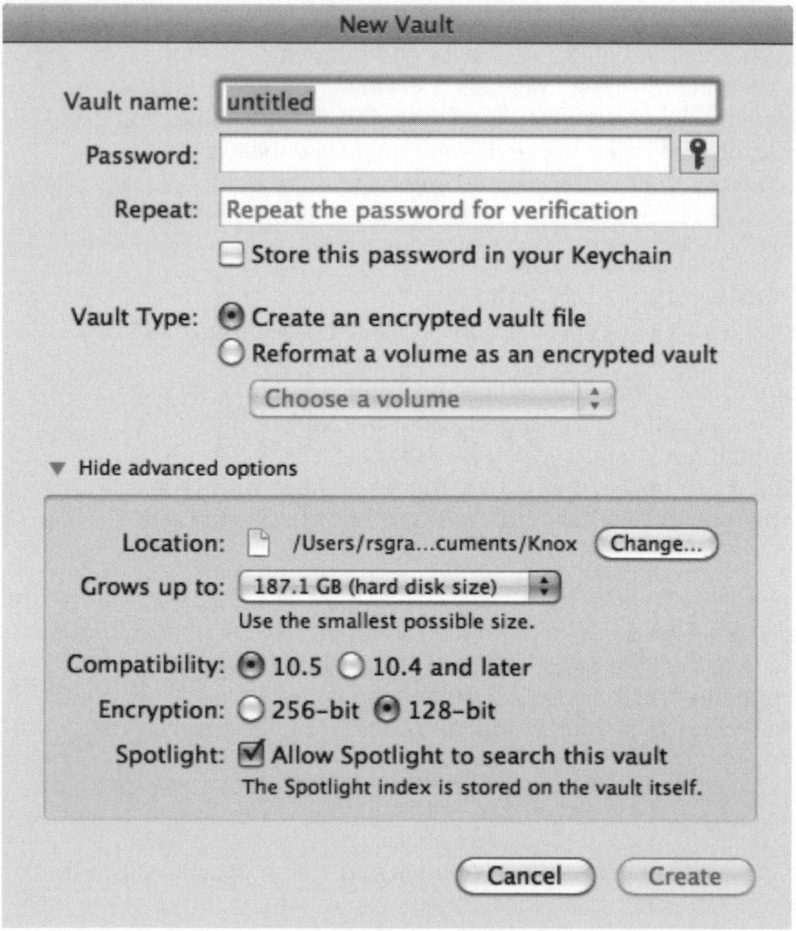

Figure 7–12. *Creating a New Vault is actually pretty simple.*

Let's say I want to keep my financial information in an encrypted volume using Knox, so I open the New Vault window. Here are my options and the choices I make:

- **Vault Name:** Finances, of course. I want something obvious that will mean something to me.

- **Password:** I want something long and complicated, since my password is going to be the weak link in the security of this data. If I'm feeling a little wacky, I could also generate something long and random with 1Password and then open that program when I want to open my Knox vault. Of course, then I need to make sure I have a really good password for unlocking 1Password, but I do. If you want to generate something good and you don't use 1Password, you could click on the key to the right of the Password field and use the Password Assistant.

- **Store This Password In Your Keychain:** I would *not* check this box, or anyone able to use my Mac has complete access to my Vault.

- **Vault Type:** If I had an entire external drive, partition, or USB flash drive that I wanted to use as a vault, I'd choose Reformat A Volume As An Encrypted Vault, but I don't, so I won't. Instead, I'm going to pick Create An Encrypted Vault File.

> **NOTE:** Strictly speaking, you're actually creating a *Sparse Bundle Disk Image*, as you can see if you look at your vaults in ~/Documents/Knox, where you'll see files with names like Finances.sparsebundle. Like the programs in /Applications, a Sparse Bundle Disk Image stores data in a folder that looks like a file to the Finder (that's the bundle part of its name). These bundles can also grow as needed, up to a maximum size that you specify when you create it. What makes them unique is that the data in a Sparse Bundle Disk Image is stored in 8 MB files called *bands*. As you add or change data, only a few bands typically change, which means that backing up a Sparse Bundle Disk Image is going to be quicker since only the relatively small number of bands have to be copied over.

- **Location:** The default location—~/Documents/Knox—is fine. If you really don't like it, click Change and pick a new place.

- **Grows Up To:** This is a very important decision that you need to make with care. Basically, how big is the vault going to be? Knox cautions you to "Use the smallest possible size," but also keep in mind that once you make a choice, you're wedded to it and cannot later adjust the size. Knox gives you several suggested sizes, including 187 GB (what it calls Hard Disk Size), 10 GB, 4.3 GB (DVD Size, according to Knox), 1024 MB (AKA 1 GB), 575 MB (termed CD Size by Knox), and 100 MB. If none of those strike your fancy, select Custom and enter your own size. In my case, I chose 100 MB, since that would more than meet my needs.

- **Compatibility:** If you have to worry about Tiger at all, select 10.4 And Later; otherwise, select 10.5.

- **Encryption:** 128-bit will definitely do the job and keep file skulkers out, but 256-bit is stronger. It's a teeny bit slower to use than 128-bit, but my rule is, the harder to crack, the better, so I'm going to go with 256-bit.

- **Spotlight:** If you think it would be helpful to search your encrypted vault with Spotlight, check the box next to Allow Spotlight To Search This Vault. This is actually a lot safer than you might presume, as the index Spotlight generates and uses is stored inside the vault, so it's safe from prying eyes, and only active when the vault is mounted and in use. That's fine with me, so I check the box.

When I'm finished with all of those settings, I click Create, and a moment later, my encrypted vault is created and mounted in the Finder under Devices. I can go ahead and drag files into Finances (the name of my vault, remember), or create new files in there. Everything is encrypted behind the scenes, so I don't have to worry about it at all.

When I'm finished, I unmount Finances just like I unmount anything else under Devices. When I want to open the vault and access the file in it again, I click on the Knox icon on the Menu Bar and select Finances, since the names of all vaults are listed under that icon.

If I ever decide to delete Finances, I click on the Knox icon on the Menu Bar and choose **Preferences > Vaults**. I select Finances and click Move Selected To Trash, clicking OK when I'm asked if I really want to do this. If you do this, read the fine print on that screen carefully and remember that you are simply moving the vault to the Trash and dissociating it from Knox. The vault, however, still exists, and if you double-click on it in the Finder, you can still open it. It is up to you to delete that vault!

If you want to easily encrypt a lot of files that you know you're going to work with on at least a semi-regular basis, or that may grow over time, you really should check out Knox. It takes a feature built into Mac OS X—FileVault—and makes it a heck of a lot easier to work with, which is great. Once again, Agile Web Solutions comes through with a great product that's powerful, easy to use, and eminently secure!

Encrypting Your Data

If you want to encrypt your own stuff, Knox or other tools like it will do the job. But what if you want to e-mail a sensitive file to someone else? As I'm sure you know, e-mail is completely insecure. The solution is obvious: encrypt the file before you send it, and then have your recipient decrypt it. Sounds easy, but it's actually a lot more complicated than you might think.

The gold standard for encrypting files that will be sent to others to decrypt is *public-key cryptography*. I'm not going to go into all the details about how it works here, so if you want to learn more about it, I'd recommend starting with http://en.wikipedia.org/wiki/Public-key_cryptography and checking out the links on that page.

For years, the software to use on your computer was PGP (Pretty Good Privacy), based on what is now an open standard, OpenPGP. Eventually, the Free Software Foundation started developing an OpenPGP-compliant suite of programs called GNU Privacy Guard, abbreviated as GnuPG or GPG.

So that's where we were. Where are we now?

When it comes to encrypting files to send to others, I'll be very honest: the situation on Macs is a mess. If this were a Linux or Windows book, it would be easy: I'd tell you to you use GnuPG, the open source and free equivalent to the criminally overpriced PGP. The problem is that GnuPG development is much more active and further along on Windows and Linux than it is on Mac OS X. In fact, the situation on Mac OS X is an embarrassment.

> **NOTE:** You can avoid most, if not all, of the problems in this section by skipping GnuPG and paying for PGP. However, PGP, now owned by Symantec, has one of the worst, most confusing websites I've ever seen. Please, be my guest—go there and try to figure out which PGP package you need. And even after you do, you'll be shocked to find out that it's going to cost you a minimum of $99 for the software, which is highway robbery as far as I'm concerned. Oh, and that gives you a "Perpetual License," but if you read the fine print, that means you have a permanent license to *use* the software, but updates require a support contract, which will run you another chunk o' change. I love it when I find a combination of greed and incompetence in a company—it makes it that much easier to run away and avoid getting burned.

Part of the problem is that there is no strong development team behind MacGPG, and another big part is that, thanks to decisions made by the GNU Project, there is no one piece of software you need to download. Instead, you're supposed to hunt down and install these:

- Mac GNU Privacy Guard v2.x (http://sourceforge.net/projects/macgpg2/files/): The heart of the software that provides the base GPG functionality.

- GPG Keychain Access (http://macgpg.sourceforge.net): A GUI for managing your private and public keys, shown in Figure 7–13.

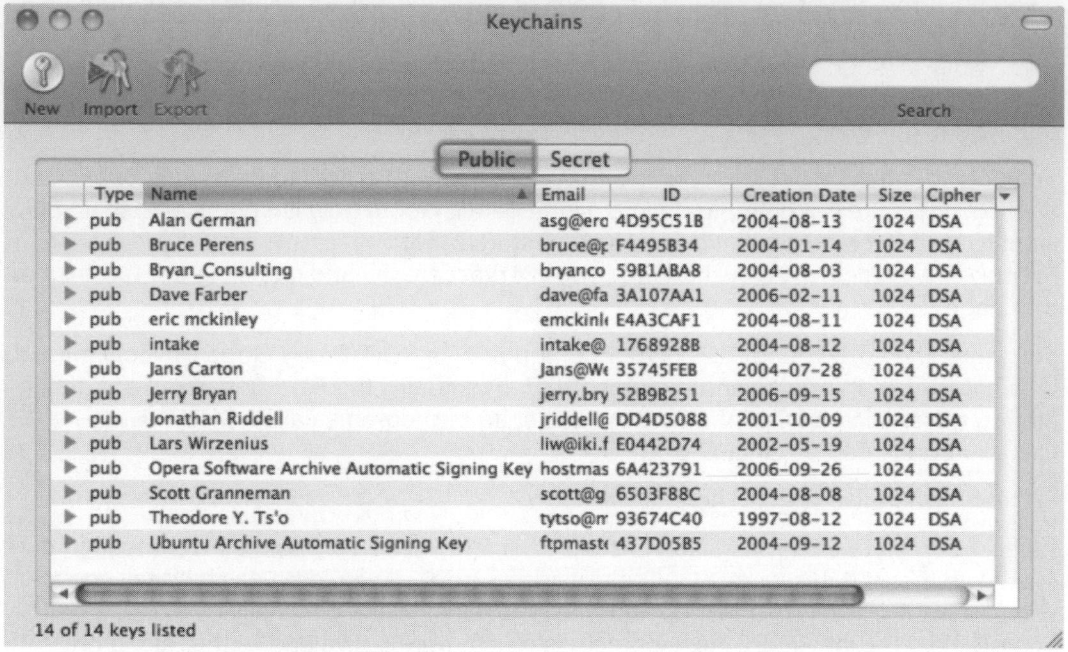

Type	Name	Email	ID	Creation Date	Size	Cipher
▶ pub	Alan German	asg@erc	4D95C51B	2004-08-13	1024	DSA
▶ pub	Bruce Perens	bruce@r	F4495B34	2004-01-14	1024	DSA
▶ pub	Bryan_Consulting	bryanco	59B1ABA8	2004-08-03	1024	DSA
▶ pub	Dave Farber	dave@fa	3A107AA1	2006-02-11	1024	DSA
▶ pub	eric mckinley	emckinl	E4A3CAF1	2004-08-11	1024	DSA
▶ pub	intake	intake@	1768928B	2004-08-12	1024	DSA
▶ pub	Jans Carton	Jans@Wε	35745FEB	2004-07-28	1024	DSA
▶ pub	Jerry Bryan	jerry.bry	52B9B251	2006-09-15	1024	DSA
▶ pub	Jonathan Riddell	jriddell@	DD4D5088	2001-10-09	1024	DSA
▶ pub	Lars Wirzenius	liw@iki.f	E0442D74	2002-05-19	1024	DSA
▶ pub	Opera Software Archive Automatic Signing Key	hostmas	6A423791	2006-09-26	1024	DSA
▶ pub	Scott Granneman	scott@g	6503F88C	2004-08-08	1024	DSA
▶ pub	Theodore Y. Ts'o	tytso@π	93674C40	1997-08-12	1024	DSA
▶ pub	Ubuntu Archive Automatic Signing Key	ftpmastε	437D05B5	2004-09-12	1024	DSA

14 of 14 keys listed

Figure 7–13. *It ain't pretty, but it works. Sorta.*

- GPGPreferences (http://macgpg.sourceforge.net): A Preferences pane for GPG's settings.

Those are the three you absolutely need if you want the basic GPG functionality. However, you can also download these:

- GPGFileTool (http://macgpg.sourceforge.net): A GUI for encrypting, decrypting, and signing files that I couldn't get to work on Snow Leopard. Useless. Since it's useless, you have to use the command line, which most Mac users won't do, not to mention that the documentation is a mess.

- GPGDropThing (http://macgpg.sourceforge.net): A GUI that takes the text you put into it and encrypts it so you can then copy it and paste it into your Mail program. How convenient! If you receive encrypted text, copy it, paste it into this program, and decrypt it. Again, how convenient! Yes, that's sarcasm. Both times. Oh, and it also doesn't work on Snow Leopard, so it's useless.

So yes, you can download those last two programs, but it's not like they'll, y'know, *work* or anything.

Even worse is the situation around GPGMail (http://sourceforge.net/projects/gpgmail/), a plug-in for Apple's Mail that makes it easy to encrypt and decrypt the contents of messages. The plug-in quit working when Apple Mail was upgraded along with Snow Leopard, and then, months later, someone got it to work. But every time Apple updates Mac OS X, even with just minor point releases like 10.6.3 to 10.6.4, GPGMail quits working again until developers tweak it.

Why all this complication? Because, as GPGMail's website says at http://www.sente.ch/software/GPGMail/English.lproj/GPGMail.html, "GPGMail is a complete hack, relying on Mail's private internal API." Apple doesn't support OpenPGP directly, and there really aren't any public APIs exposed that would make it work easily, so the developers are stuck with a "complete hack" that breaks constantly.

If you use other mail programs, you have some options. Maybe.

- **Thunderbird:** Easy—use the Enigmail extension (https://addons.mozilla.org/en-US/thunderbird/addon/71/, with more info at http://enigmail.mozdev.org), which works well.

- **Entourage:** Try EntourageGPG (http://entouragegpg.sourceforge.net). Of course, the future of this add-on is a dead end, since Microsoft is dropping Entourage in Office 2010 in favor of Outlook for the Mac.

- **Webmail through Firefox:** FireGPG (http://getfiregpg.org) worked pretty well, even with Gmail, but it's no longer under active development.

Overall, as I said, GPG on Macs is a real disappointment. So how do you e-mail or transfer a file to someone if you're worried about others snooping? You have some options, none of them super-duper easy:

- Download and compile the GNU Privacy Assistant (http://wald.intevation.org/projects/gpa/), a GUI for GPG, on your Mac. In order to do so, you'll need a bunch of dependencies. Oh, and you'll also need Apple's development environment. Or, you can use Fink (http://pdb.finkproject.org/pdb/package.php/gpa), MacPorts (www.macports.org/ports.php?by=library&substr=gnupg), or Homebrew (http://github.com/mxcl/homebrew/blob/master/Library/Formula/gnupg.rb) to install the UNIX version. However, the UI won't be Apple's, so it'll stick out like a sore thumb. But it should work. Of course, you'll also have to first figure out Fink, MacPorts, or Homebrew!

- Shell out the bucks for PGP.

- Learn to use the command line with GPG. To start, open Terminal and type in info gpg. Of course, the recipient of your encrypted file will have to use the command line as well to decrypt the file (if she's using a Mac; if she's using Windows or Linux, she'll be able to use a nice GUI, which is ironic, to say the least).

- Use a different program that doesn't depend on OpenPGP or public key cryptography to encrypt the file and then send it to the recipient. The problem comes in when you have to somehow tell the recipient how to decrypt the file without transmitting that information in an insecure fashion. In other words, you can't e-mail the password. You could read the password over the phone, but we all know how much fun that is. You can Skype it using Skype's IM feature, since that would be encrypted, except that you're relying on Skype's encryption keys to hide the conversation. Still, that will probably work, although you're now depending upon the user having Skype.

If that last option appeals to you, there are some decent programs out there that will encrypt files for you, including (but sure not limited to!) these:

- Drop Secure Pro ($57 from `www.dropsecurepro.com`): As an added bonus, this one also runs on Windows and Linux.

- R10Cipher (Around $46 from `www.r10cipher.com`): Also cross-platform.

My final piece of advice on encryption software: be very careful about what you buy. There's a lot of garbage out there selling snake oil under the guise of fancy terms and crazy claims. Do your research before you buy. It's one thing to lose your money, but it's another to lose your money and have your privacy violated because something you bought doesn't work as promised. Caveat emptor!

Further Resources

Security guru Bruce Schneier's blog (`www.schneier.com`) and monthly e-mail newsletter (`www.schneier.com/crypto-gram.html`) often cover companies that are "in the doghouse," as he puts it, because their software is junk. It's a great place to do research, but more than that, you ought to subscribe to either his blog's RSS feed or his e-mail newsletter, as they are excellent sources of information about all aspects of computer, network, and national security. Highly recommended.

SSH

SSH is one of the greatest tools on the Internet today. With it, I can securely log in to other computers and use them, without having to worry about packet sniffers grabbing my passwords and other sensitive information. In fact, you could write—and read—whole books on SSH, it's so versatile and useful (*Pro OpenSSH*, by Michael Stahnke (Apress, 2005)) is an excellent place to start). In this section, I want to walk you through two tricks that I use almost daily with SSH: changing the default port that SSH uses, and setting up Terminal so you can SSH into multiple sites simultaneously. I think you'll enjoy them, especially since they're both not documented very clearly by Apple.

Changing the Default SSH Port

Most people probably don't have SSH enabled on their desktop or laptop Macs, as it's usually more of a server thing. However, since you're a power user, you may in fact have gone to ➤ System Preferences ➤ Sharing and then checked the box next to Remote Login, which turned on the SSH server on your Mac. I certainly did that on my Mac mini at home, so that I can SSH in to the mini and run programs and get listings.

By default, an SSH server uses port 22. The problem is that every bad guy in the world knows that, and so they're all trying to get into your server via port 22. One easy method to put a nice big roadblock in the bad guys' way is to change the port that the SSH server uses.

> **NOTE:** Notice I said "roadblock" and not "impassible barrier." Criminals can still run port scans and figure out that you have an SSH port on your Mac, but trust me, changing the port number will vastly decrease the amount of hammering that SSH receives every day from jerkwads all over the Net.

Keep in mind that this means that the command you use to SSH into a server will change. Before, if you wanted to connect to a server that was using port 22, you'd use this:

```
ssh user@server.com
```

After you change the port SSH uses—to 2112 instead of 22, say—you'd have to use this:

```
ssh -p 2112 user@server.com
```

If you're cool with that—and really, it's not a huge deal—then let's proceed.

Edit ssh.plist

Using sudo, open /System/Library/LaunchDaemons/ssh.plist with your favorite text editor, such as BBEdit or vim, and look for these lines:

```
<key>SockServiceName</key>
<string>ssh</string>
```

Change them to this:

```
<key>SockServiceName</key>
<string>ssh2</string>
```

> **NOTE:** If you're a Linux user, you're probably saying to yourself, "Why the heck are you having me do this?" The answer is that Mac OS X uses launchd (discussed in more depth in Chapter 12) to start SSH, so we need to do things the Mac OS X way. I agree, by the way—it's much easier to change the port on a Linux box!

Save the file, close it, and make sure permissions are set correctly on the file you just edited:

```
$ sudo chmod 644 /System/Library/LaunchDaemons/ssh.plist
$ sudo chown root:wheel /System/Library/LaunchDaemons/ssh.plist
```

Now verify it:

```
$ ls -l /System/Library/LaunchDaemons/ssh.plist
-rw-r--r--    1 root  wheel  828B Aug 12 13:16 ssh.plist
```

Excellent.

Edit /etc/services

Now you need to figure out which port numbers you want to use instead of 22. The file that contains ports and their numbers is /etc/services. Page through it looking for ports that aren't being used by anything major. After all, you obviously don't want to change SSH to use ports 25 (SMTP), 80 (HTTP), 123 (NTP), and so on. Your best bet will probably be up in the higher end of the Registered Ports, which number from 1024-49151 (for more information, see http://en.wikipedia.org/wiki/List_of_well-known_ports_(computing)).

If you find a port that's not used, great. You can also pick ports that are already registered and then switch them over to SSH, *as long as you know for sure you don't use any software that depends on that port*. Be very careful about that, or you could cause a real problem. For instance, let's say you want to use port 2112. Open /etc/services in your text editor and find out if 2112 is used, and if so, what's using it:

```
idonix-metanet  2112/udp    # Idonix MetaNet
idonix-metanet  2112/tcp    # Idonix MetaNet
```

Hmmm. What the heck is "Idonix MetaNet"? After a bit of searching around the Web, it became apparent that not only were my servers not using Idonix MetaNet, we would also never use Idonix MetaNet (not because it's bad—I have no idea if it's awesome or sucky—but because we don't need it). So 2112 will work just fine! Time to change the port on the Mac.

Using sudo, open /etc/services with your fave text editor, and look for these lines:

```
idonix-metanet  2112/udp    # Idonix MetaNet
idonix-metanet  2112/tcp    # Idonix MetaNet
```

Change it to this:

```
# Changed by RSG 20100702 to go with port changes for SSH
# idonix-metanet  2112/udp    # Idonix MetaNet
# idonix-metanet  2112/tcp    # Idonix MetaNet
ssh2            2112/tcp
```

Notice three things about this:

- I left a comment with my initials, the date, and the reason I made the change, for future reference.

- I commented out the two lines referencing idonix-metanet instead of deleting them, which is just in case some miracle happens and Idonix MetaNet is suddenly exactly the thing we need.

- I added a line for ssh2, not ssh, because earlier, in /System/Library/LaunchDaemons/ssh.plist, we changed the line to reference ssh2. Also, I didn't create a link for UDP because SSH uses TCP only.

Now make sure your permissions are correct for /etc/services:

```
$ sudo chmod 644 /etc/services
$ sudo chown root:wheel /etc/services
```

Now verify it:

```
$ ls -l /etc/services
-rw-r--r--  1 root  wheel   662K Jun 23  2009 /etc/services
```

Excellent.

Restart and Test

OK, time to restart and test. You can reboot the Mac if you want, and then try to SSH into it, or you can use this instead and avoid a reboot:

```
$ sudo launchctl unload /System/Library/LaunchDaemons/ssh.plist
$ sudo launchctl load /System/Library/LaunchDaemons/ssh.plist
```

> **WARNING:** If you're making all these changes on a remote server to which you don't have direct access, you'd better make sure that someone is there onsite to help you out if this doesn't work and you find yourself unable to SSH in. Of course, if you're using ARD (Apple Remote Desktop) or Timbuktu or something like that, you're safe, since you can still connect and troubleshoot things yourself if SSH doesn't work. That's in fact what we did at WebSanity—kept ARD open while we futzed with the SSH settings and verified that they worked.

Now try to log in to the Mac from another machine:

```
$ ssh -p 2112 user@server.com
Last login: Thu Jul  1 19:36:43 2010 from 99.188.225.242
```

It works!

If it does not work, don't panic. Make sure you edited both /System/Library/LaunchDaemons/ssh.plist and /etc/services correctly, and try restarting the Mac just in case. It should work perfectly—I've been using this trick for years on my Mac servers, and it works beautifully.

SSH Into Multiple Sites Simultaneously

My web dev company, WebSanity, has five Mac OS X and Linux servers that I have to SSH into constantly. If I need to SSH into all of them—which I actually have to do more often than you'd imagine—I open Terminal, press ⌘-T (or go to **Shell ➤ New Tab ➤ [Name Of Shell]**) to create a new tab for each server, and then SSH in. This works, but it's tedious and way too manual. How about a faster, more efficient way to open tabs to all those servers at the same time? Here's how.

Set Up Terminal Settings

Let's begin by creating some themes for our servers.

1. Go to **Terminal ➤ Preferences ➤ Settings**.

2. Choose one of the pre-defined Terminal themes that you like. In my case, I'll select Novel.

3. **Action Menu** (the sprocket on the bottom of the list of themes) ➤ **Duplicate Settings**.

4. Configure the new, duplicate theme.

   a. Click on Novel 1 to rename it to something else. I entered wsBunyan. Why ws? Because it's short for WebSanity, and by giving all the new themes I create the same prefix, they'll all be grouped together.

   b. On the Shell tab, check Run Command. In the text box next to it, enter: `ssh -p 2112 user@bunyan.websanity.com` (note that I'm using a different port number, like I talked about in the previous section).

5. Choose another Terminal theme, such as Grass, duplicate it, and configure it.

6. Repeat as necessary for the other servers. Table 7–1 shows the five new servers I created (including the first one):

Table 7–1. *Five WebSanity Servers, Five New Themes in Terminal.*

Original Theme	New Theme	Command
Novel	wsBunyan	`ssh -p 2112 user@bunyan.websanity.com`
Grass	wsCowley	`ssh -p 2112 user@cowley.websanity.com`
Homebrew	wsDonne	`ssh -p 2112 user@donne.websanity.com`
Red Sands	wsHerrick	`ssh -p 2112 user@herrick.websanity.com`
Ocean	wsPepys	`ssh -p 2112 user@pepys.websanity.com`

You have now created the servers you need. Time to set things up so you can open connections in groups of tabs.

Create a Window Group

We've defined various servers in Terminal Preferences, and now we need to create sets of tabs.

1. Close any open tabs in Terminal.

2. Terminal ➤ Shell ➤ New Tab ➤ wsBunyan

3. Terminal ➤ Shell ➤ New Tab ➤ wsCowley

4. Terminal ➤ Shell ➤ New Tab ➤ wsDonne

5. Terminal ➤ Shell ➤ New Tab ➤ wsHerrick

6. Terminal ➤ Shell ➤ New Tab ➤ wsPepys

7. Window ➤ Save Windows As Group

8. In the Save Window Group window, enter a name. In my case, I chose something smart like `All WebSanity Servers`.

Of course, I can repeat this as many times as necessary. I can create a Window Group that comprises wsBunyan and wsPepys, or one that combines wsCowley, wsDonne, and wsHerrick, and then save it. That way, I can open the servers I need, in the groups of tabs I need, whenever I wish.

Now, if I want to open the first Window Group I created, I go to **Window ➤ Open Window Group ➤ All WebSanity Servers**, and five tabs open up, all of them using SSH to connect to different server. Now that's efficient!

> **TIP:** If you've ever used SSH before, you may be thinking that you don't want to have to enter a password for five different servers. That would be annoying, true. It would be much better if you used passwordless SSH keys so you don't need to enter a password at all. For more about how to do that, check out Chapter 15, "Working on the Network," of my *Linux Phrasebook*, or read about it at "Password-less logins with OpenSSH" (www.debian-administration.org/articles/152). Note, however, that Mac OS X for some reason doesn't include the referenced command `ssh-copy-id`, so you'll need to add your public key to your SSH server manually, or use this command:
>
> `cat ~/.ssh/id_rsa.pub | ssh account@remoteserver.com "cat->>`
> `.ssh/authorized_keys"`

Summary

Security is a topic that's as important as it is fascinating. As you read this chapter, I hope you were entertained and informed, but I also hope that you were motivated to act and try out the programs I discussed. Depending upon your needs, 1Password may be the perfect choice, but LastPass or another password safe might work better for you. Encryption can be a vital thing to have, and Knox (or Apple's built-in disk encryption) keeps your stuff safe from prying eyes. If you use SSH at all, the techniques I've shown you in this chapter can help you immensely.

## Chapter 8

Backing Up Your Mac

If you don't back up your Mac, you're going to regret it one day when you lose your data. It's that simple. As my buddy Jans likes to remind people, "There are two kinds of computer users in this world: those who have lost data and those who will." If you're in the first group, you know the pain you feel when you realize something precious you were keeping—a meaningful picture, an important paper, or a music collection—is now gone forever. If you're in the second group, you need to do everything in your power to prevent yourself from falling into the first group.

If you follow the advice in this section and the next, and do some preparation, you can make sure that you will never lose your valuable data.

Backing Up Your Files Offline

There are two places your backed-up data can go: to physical media, like hard drives that are controlled by you or a company you pay, or to the Net (or the "cloud") where it resides on a server somewhere. Both are valuable, and, in my opinion, you should use both. In this section, let's look at ways to back up your data offline, to physical media that you oversee; the next section will look at online backup.

Time Machine

Before we start delving deep into backing up, I should address the very attractive elephant in the room: Apple's Time Machine. Let me say first that Time Machine is great software, and whenever I set up a new Mac for someone, I always urge them to get an external hard drive and use Time Machine. It has some strong advantages that are too good to ignore:

- It's free with Mac OS X.

- It's super-easy to set up and pretty much out of sight, out of mind to use.

- It's got a cool, fun UI that makes restoring your data actually kinda fun!

- You can use it to restore all your data when installing Mac OS X, which is oh so handy.

For Mom and Pop and cousin Harold, Time Machine is a fantastic solution. However, that doesn't mean it's the right answer for everyone. As nice as Time Machine is, it's certainly not perfect.

- **No compression:** A lot of backup solutions compress the data to save space. Time Machine doesn't. This one doesn't concern me too much, since the price of hard drives falls ever lower ever faster.

- **No encryption:** If someone steals your Time Machine backup drive, they can read everything on it—including previous versions of files—unless you take the trouble to encrypt it (for some advice on that, see later in this chapter). Many backup programs encrypt the data they store, which is a much better way to go about things.

- **No deltas:** With most backup solutions, if a file is updated, only the changed parts of the file are backed up, which vastly speeds up the backup process. This is emphatically not how Time Machine works at all. If one bit in a file changes, Time Machine backs up the entire file. This becomes a royal pain (and waste of space!) when you have large files that change often, like videos, Entourage databases, and virtual machine images.

- **Limits on what is backed up:** Time Machine saves your last 24 hourly backups, your last month's worth of daily backups, and weekly backups for anything older than a month… as long as your external hard drive has space for all that. When your disk gets stuffed and there's no room left, Time Machine will start deleting older backups to make space. This isn't a problem with a clone—either you have enough space or you don't—and with many online backups, which let you keep all past versions of your files (granted, that often costs a bit more, but it's worth it if you want to keep everything).

- **Not flexible:** Don't like Time Machine's schedule that backs your stuff up every hour? Too bad. Apple doesn't give you a way to alter that, unless you poke around yourself in Time Machine's plist file (you can also use the free TimeMachineScheduler, available at www.klieme.com/TimeMachineScheduler.html). Want to use more than one disk for your backups? In order to switch between them so one is onsite and one is offsite? Nope. Can't do it with Time Machine. Want to exclude all files of a certain type, say disk images or virtual machine images? You can manually select files to be excluded, but otherwise Time Machine doesn't help you. In those and other ways, Time Machine is inflexible, while other backup solutions offer far more options (this can be seen as a negative of those solutions, of course—often simpler is better!).

- **No bootable clones:** Some of the backup solutions I'm going to cover create a bootable clone of your hard drive. If you have to replace your Mac's internal hard drive, or you get a new Mac, it's no problem: boot off the clone drive, open the backup software but point it in the opposite direction (so it's copying from the external drive to the Mac's internal drive), and go. An hour or so later, disconnect the external drive, reboot your Mac, and all of your files and programs and settings are back. This process isn't possible at all with Time Machine. You can restore your Mac, but you first have to boot from your Snow Leopard installation DVD. I like the much simpler reverse clone method.

- **Onsite only:** If your house burns down or your business is flooded, then it's a good chance that your Time Machine backup is going to be gone baby gone. And a thief that steals your laptop is likely to snag the external hard drive sitting next to it as well. I'm all for onsite backups— I do one every day!—but you need to do an offsite backup as well. Time Machine isn't going to help you there.

> **NOTE:** An excellent overview of Time Machine and how it works, including both positives and negatives, is at `http://arstechnica.com/apple/reviews/2007/10/mac-os-x-10-5.ars/14`.

Again, I'm not saying Time Machine is bad or that you shouldn't use it. In fact, I'd recommend it, if it meets your needs. And remember, you can use Time Machine alongside almost all the software and services I'm going to talk about in this section and the next one. I'm paranoid, so here's what my paranoid self will tell you: never rely on one backup solution. As I just said, you should have both an onsite and an offsite backup. In addition, I would recommend a daily clone as well. Your data is worth it.

Carbon Copy Cloner

Every day when I come to work, I plug my MacBook Pro into the following:

- Spare power cable, so I don't have to lug one back and forth between home and the office

- Acer 22" widescreen monitor

- USB hub, which connects my Mac to my Logitech mouse, Microsoft ergonomic keyboard, and two hard drives plugged in to a dual-enclosure: DataOffice, a back up of my home Data drive, and MusicOffice, a backup of my home Music drive

- Logitech speakers

- FireWire-connected external drive that clones my Mac's hard drive via Carbon Copy Cloner

That last item is the one I want to focus on here. Carbon Copy Cloner is fantastic software for cloning your hard drive—it's free (donation requested), it's based on robust open source software (primarily rsync, of which you can read more about at http://en.wikipedia.org/wiki/Rsync), it's configurable to meet your needs, and it just works. I've been relying on it for years, and it's never let me down.

Download Carbon Copy Cloner from www.bombich.com and install it. After opening it, you'll see the window shown in Figure 8–1.

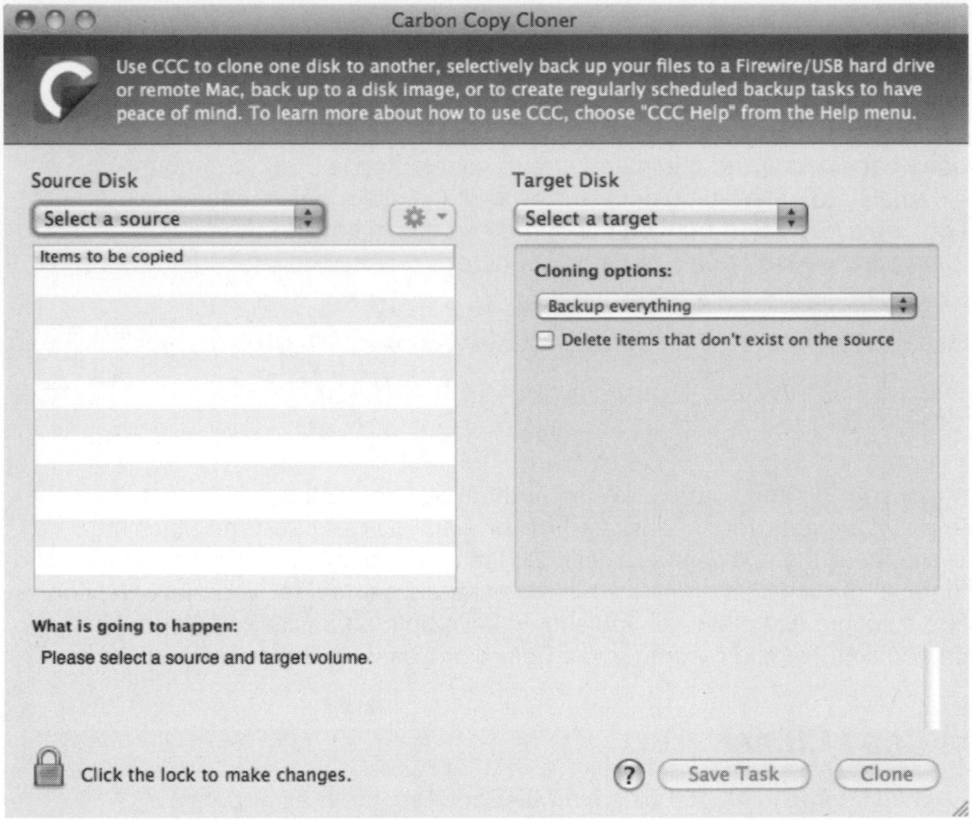

Figure 8–1. *After you open it, Carbon Copy Cloner is ready to go!*

Carbon Copy Cloner is ready to use immediately: choose a Source Disk (your Mac's internal hard drive), choose a Target Disk (your external drive), select Backup Everything under Cloning Options, check the box next to Delete Items That Don't Exist On The Source, and click Clone. A while later—with "while" greatly depends on the size and speed of your hard drive, among other factors—the job will finish. Your external hard drive will now be an exact duplicate of your Mac's hard drive.

That's cool, but Carbon Copy Cloner also makes it easy to schedule that backup to occur on a regular basis, which is the key to any good backup. After you create a backup task—and verify that it works at least once—click Save Task. The Backup Task Scheduler window opens, which you can see in Figure 8–2.

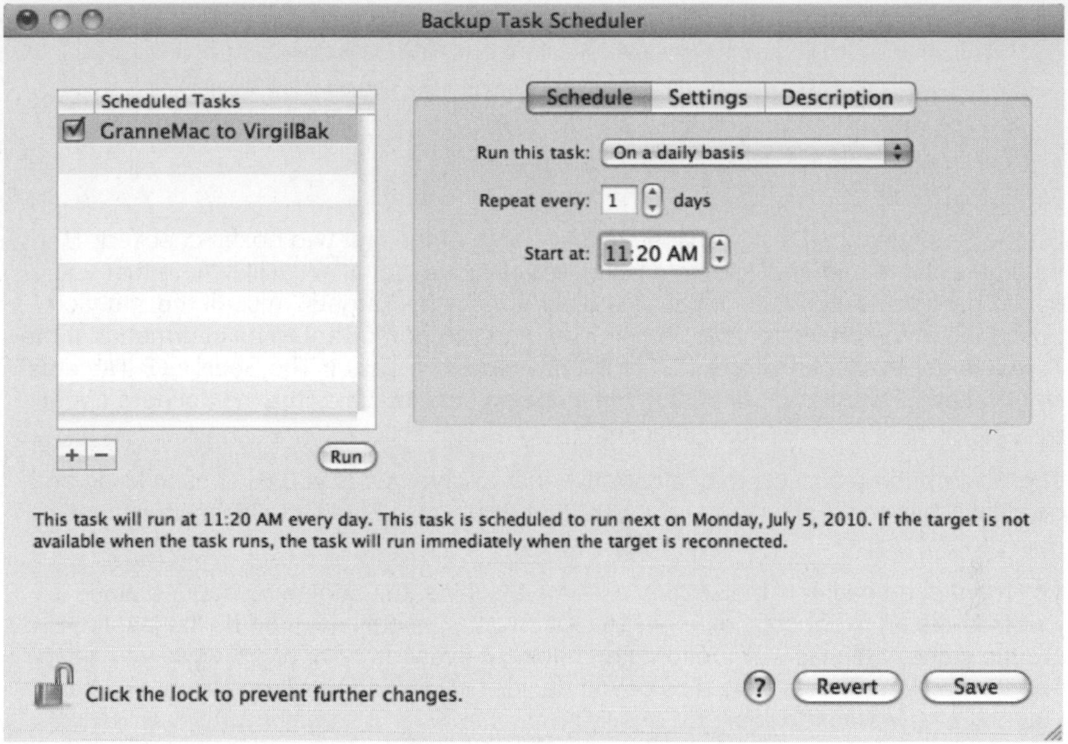

Figure 8–2. *Carbon Copy Cloner makes it very easy to create recurring backup tasks.*

Feel free to change the name of your backup job, and then head to the three tabs on the right. The first one—Schedule—is the most important, and here are your settings:

- **Run This Task:** Select from Hourly, Daily, Weekly, Monthly, and When Target Is Reconnected.

- **Repeat Every:** Select a number to correspond to what you chose for Run This Task.

- **Start At:** Pick a time.

- **Run On (Weekly only):** Allows you to pick a day, or days, of the week.

- **On The (Monthly only):** Use these drop-downs to pick a regular day of the month.

Note that no matter what you pick, Carbon Copy Cloner helpfully tells you at the bottom of the window that "If the target is not available when the task runs, the task will run immediately when the target is reconnected." This happens to me sometimes, because I'll miss a day at work, but when I come in the next day, Carbon Copy Cloner will start up as soon as I plug my backup drive in to my Mac.

NOTE: There is one little annoyance, however, but on the annoyance scale, it's not too bad: on those days when my Mac isn't plugged in to my backup drive, Carbon Copy Cloner will pop up a window complaining that it's time to run a backup job but there's no Target Disk. Just dismiss it (or change an option on the Settings tab, discussed next).

On the Settings tab, it's a good idea to leave both of the first two boxes checked: The Volume's Name and The Volume's Universally Unique Identifier (UUID) (note that you can't check the second one if you rotate hard drives for Targets). Also, if the situation I described in the previous Note bothers you, and you don't want to be informed that the Target is gone, check the box next to Silently Skip This Task If The Source Or Target Is Not Present. Personally, I like being reminded so I can make a little mental note about how many days I've missed my backup.

The Description tab is just that: a narrative that tells you what you've chosen to do and how it will happen. Fancy that—software that explains in English to its users what it's going to do! Crazy!

As I mentioned earlier in the section on Time Machine, the cool thing about a clone is just that: it's an exact copy of your Mac. Of course, it's only as good as the last time you did the clone, which is why I recommend doing it every day—or night, while you sleep. Then, when your Mac's drive dies or you decide to upgrade to a bigger one, or when you buy a new Mac, do this:

1. Plug in the external drive.

2. Reboot while holding down the ⌥ key.

3. Select the external clone as the boot drive.

4. Open Carbon Copy Cloner.

5. Select the external drive you've booted from as the Source and the Mac's internal drive as the Target.

6. Clone!

7. When it's finished, reboot, selecting the Mac's internal drive.

Total time: a couple of hours or so, depending upon the size of your drives. Total stress and involvement: nil. Now isn't that a much better system than manually reinstalling and reconfiguring everything?

There's more to Carbon Copy Cloner that I don't have space to discuss here. For instance, you can back up to another Mac over a network, or back up to a disk image. Those—and many more!—are all possibilities in Carbon Copy Cloner that you can explore in the program. But the basics are there, and they're easy to use, and you'd be crazy not to back up your Mac with Carbon Copy Cloner on a regular basis.

Synchronize! X

Carbon Copy Cloner is a great program for cloning drives—or even portions of drives—but it lacks two big features:

- Carbon Copy Cloner doesn't tell you what's going to copied or deleted. Instead, you let 'er rip and trust that it's all gonna work (and it always does—you just better know what it is you're copying or deleting).

- Carbon Copy Cloner works in one direction, from the Source to the Target. If you want to copy files from both Source to Target and Target to Source at the same time, you're out of luck.

But what if you want to know exactly what's going to be copied or deleted? Or what if you want to copy in both directions at the same time? Then, much as it pains me to say it, you should try Synchronize! X (which I shall write out as Synchronize X, because I hate extraneous exclamation points—yeah, I'm talking to you too, Yahoo). Why does it pain me? Because I haven't found anything that does as good a job as Synchronize X, but man, does that software yank my chain in a lot of ways:

- It's been years, and Synchronize X still doesn't support 512x512 icons for its app, which is pretty pathetic.

- It has nagging little UI bugs. For instance, when Synchronize X opens the Files To Copy window, if you didn't have focus on Synchronize X—if, in other words, you had another program open while you were waiting for Synchronize X to finish figuring out which files it's going to transfer—then clicking on the Files To Copy window will not bring the program back into focus. Therefore, clicking on the Start button in the Files To Copy window won't do a thing. You have to click on the main Synchronize X window first, *then* click on the Start button in the Files To Copy window, which is frustrating, to say the least.

- The Preferences are not very Mac-like, as you can see in Figure 8–3.

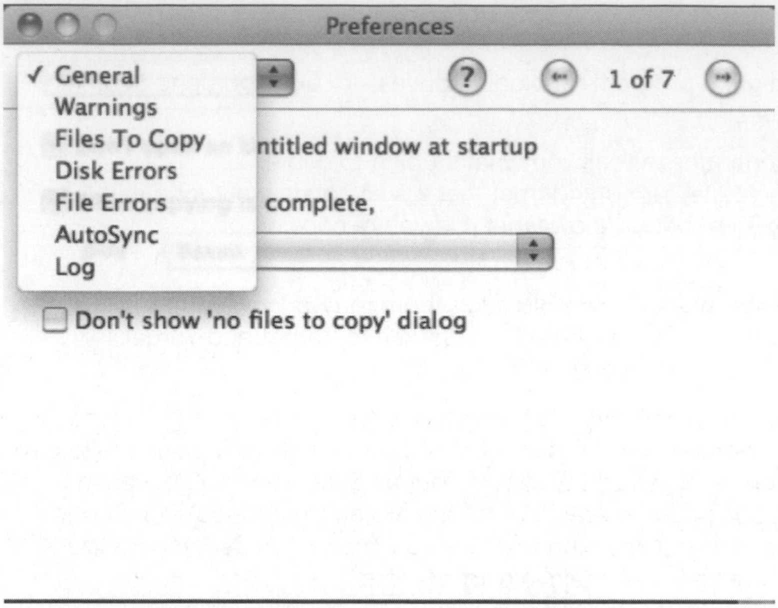

Figure 8–3. *I don't like clumsy, ugly Preferences like this.*

That is as old school as the program's icon. It's ugly, clumsy, and unlike almost every program on my Mac, which is not a good thing. Oh, there's also an **Options** menu that has a bunch of settings that aren't in the Preferences! Nice job, guys.

- It costs more than it should, in my opinion. How much? $30 for the basic version—and a whopping $100 for the advanced one! I use the basic one, by the way, and it does what I need it to do.

- It phones home every time you use it (your Mac's name and the program's serial number) in order to prevent you from using it on more than one Mac, which is annoying, especially given how much it costs.

If you're still interested, head over to `http://qdea.com` and grab a copy. Let me walk you through how I use it to back up files.

When you first open Synchronize X, a window opens like that in Figure 8–4.

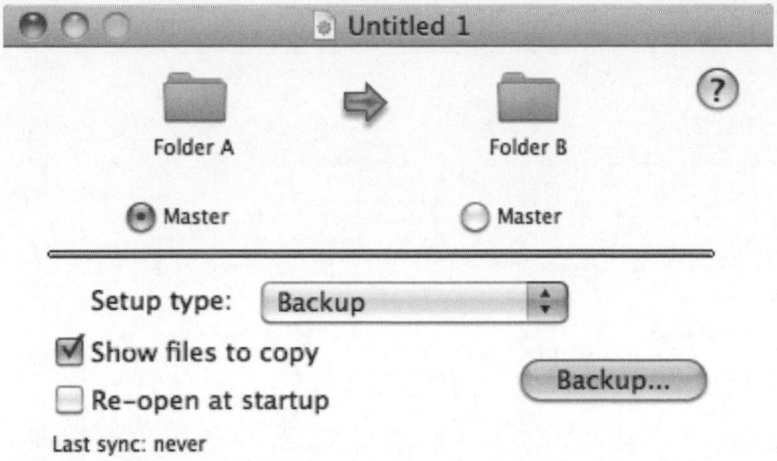

Figure 8-4. *Time to create a new job for Synchronize X.*

Before you do anything else, you need to first go to Setup Type and choose if you want to do a Backup or Synchronization (why this isn't the first thing in the window is beyond me). Backup copies the state of a Master folder (which can also be an entire volume) to a Slave folder, while Synchronization copies and deletes files back and forth between two folders so that they match. In my case, I select Backup.

I also always check the box next to Show Files To Copy, so I can review what's going to happen before it actually happens. I have several jobs that I run (more about how I save and access them in a moment), so I don't bother to check Re-Open At Startup. If, however, you always run the same job, sure, go ahead and check it.

Now for the real meat and potatoes: which folders am I going to back up? In my case, I'm going to back up my MusicHome external drive to MusicHomeBak, another external drive. I click on Folder A and select /Volumes/MusicHome and then click on Folder B and select /Volumes/MusicHomeBak. The Backup button in the window is now enabled, so I click it. A small window opens as Synchronize X shows me its progress scanning the two folders. A moment later, I see a list of all the files that Synchronize X will copy or delete, as you can see in Figure 8-5.

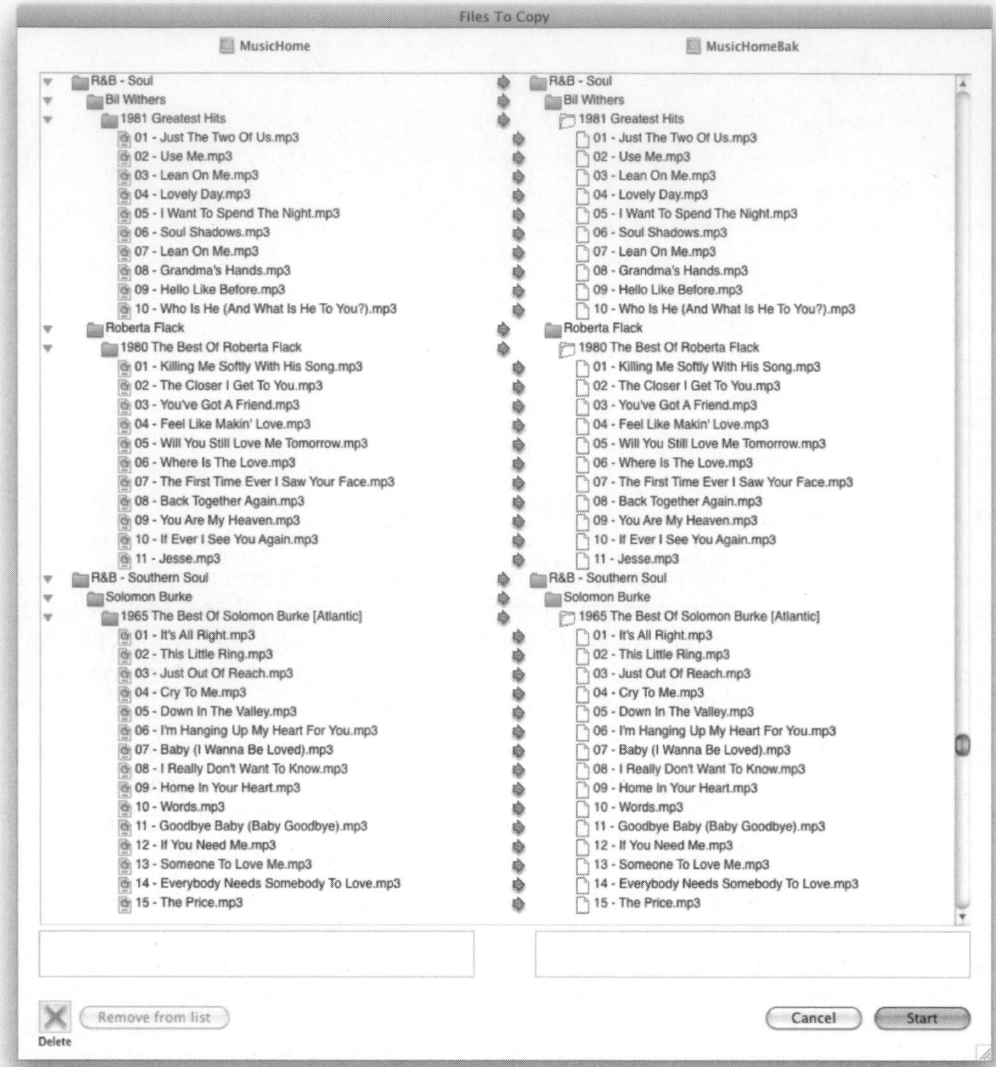

Figure 8–5. *I've been acquiring some new soul records, all good stuff.*

Figure 8–5 shows the source on the left and the target on the right. The arrows running down the middle show that I have a lot of files that will be copied from MusicHome to MusicHomeBak. If files were going to be deleted from the source—because they didn't exist on the target—the icons would indicate that as well.

If I saw files that I no longer wanted on either the source or the target, and therefore wanted to move to the Trash, I simply click the Delete button (which looks different from all the other buttons, which is indicative of the ugliness of this app). If I don't want to actually throw files into the Trash, but I don't want them to be part of the Sync, I instead click the Remove From List button.

When I'm ready to run the sync, I click the Start button, and away it goes.

You can save syncs that you run constantly by going to File ➤ Save. After that, you can recall your saved syncs by going to File ➤ Open Recent. If you want to adjust the number of saved syncs that Synchronize X remembers, or if you want to delete a sync that you no longer need, go to File ➤ Open Recent ➤ Edit.

As I said, Synchronize X isn't the greatest thing in the world, but it does the job. There are other programs that sync data like Synchronize X—in particular, ChronoSync (www.econtechnologies.com/pages/cs/chrono_overview.html) looks like a very viable competitor, but it's $40 and I find the UI a bit on the confusing side—but I've paid for Synchronize X, so I use it in spite of my grumbling. I just wish the company that makes the program would fix how ugly, weird, and clunky it is.

Further Resources

For all things backup-related, check out Wikipedia's article on the subject at http://en.wikipedia.org/wiki/Backup, as it's a good overview, with a ton of links in it.

If you want to spend some money on a commercial competitor to Carbon Copy Cloner, try SuperDuper! (again with the unnecessary exclamation point!), which is excellent but also costs $28. You can get it at www.shirt-pocket.com.

Another is ChronoSync, which I just mentioned. It's $40, but in addition to syncing selected folders like Synchronize X, it also creates bootable clones like Carbon Copy Cloner, and it will work over a network. It's got a lot of great features, but I do find the UI to be more confusing than Synchronize X. That said, if I had it to do all over again, I'd probably double down with ChronoSync and really learn that UI.

Those looking to spend zero dollars should head over to http://clonezilla.org and download Clonezilla. It doesn't feature the prettiest UI in the world; in fact, it runs on the command line, although it does feature an ncurses interface (http://en.wikipedia.org/wiki/Ncurses). Clonezilla works with just about every major file system in use today (try ext2, ext3, ReiserFS, XFS, JFS, FAT, NTFS, and HFS+!) and allows you to back up your data to both local and network targets (SSH, Samba, and NFS).

Backing Up Your Files Online

I know people who religiously back up their data to local hard drives, but just as religiously refuse to use online services. They simply don't trust those services enough, for a variety of reasons, but mostly security. They're certainly entitled to those opinions, but I think they're being a bit over-zealous, for several reasons:

- Most online services encrypt everything in transport and on their services. Further, many services allow you to specify your own encryption keys, which means that no one working at the service can read your files.

- These companies would be ruined if it became public knowledge that the integrity of their users' data was compromised. It's in their best interests to place stringent safeguards on the data with which they're entrusted.

- Most of the people who yell the loudest about how careful they are with their local data yell too loudly, methinks. The companies behind online backup services have spent millions of dollars on their offerings, hiring some of the best people in the business to secure their infrastructure. Maybe you really are their equal in your house or business, but more than likely you are not.

I certainly do not advocate that you stop doing local backups. You abso-frickin'-lutely should be using the offline tools I discussed in the last section to safeguard your data. However, you should also use an online service in this section as well. The number one reason is simple: redundancy (and redundancy!).

It's a great thing that you're backing up your files locally. But remember that those files can be stolen, or destroyed in a fire, flood, or other natural disaster. Or you just may screw up and delete things that you shouldn't have deleted. I'm paranoid as heck when it comes to my data, so I gladly use online services to make redundant copies of my data. And, I'd wager, you should too.

> **NOTE:** There is one thing you should know about backing up online: the first backup can take weeks, depending upon the amount of data you're safeguarding. You can wait it out, or, if you're willing to spend some money (usually at least $100), many services allow you to send a hard drive to them from which they will copy data, then ship the hard drive back.

Dropbox

I've been an enthusiastic user of Dropbox for years, from its existence in beta until now. It's a rousing success story as it has achieved millions of users and is one of the most-acclaimed online backup and syncing tools on the Net. If you don't know anything about Dropbox, you really should head over to www.dropbox.com and grab it. While you're waiting for Dropbox to download (it won't take long), here are ten things you should know:

1. When you install Dropbox on your Mac, it creates a new folder, at ~/Dropbox. Anything you put in that folder is immediately synced to your online Dropbox account (which uses Amazon's awesome S3—the Simple Storage Service—as its backend, by the way).

2. Your files are secure in transit—SSL is used—and in storage, with 256-bit AES encryption safeguarding your stuff. Granted, you're using Dropbox's encryption keys and can't use your own, but with stringent security policies and over four million users, I'm not too worried about Dropbox—or Amazon, for that matter—pawing around in my files.

3. If you change any files that are already in your Dropbox, those changes are written to your online Dropbox account. Notice I said "those changes" and not "the whole file." Just the bytes that have changed are transferred, so it's very fast (assuming you're not changing massive parts of an enormous file, of course, in which case it'll be a little slower!).

4. Dropbox keeps all the versions of your files that have changed, so you can view or roll back to any prior version, at any time. Keep in mind that Dropbox stores past versions for 30 days at most; if you want to keep all versions indefinitely, you gotta pay.

5. To see your files and past versions, or to download files, or to do some other neat things, log in to your Dropbox account at `www.dropbox.com`.

6. If you delete files in your Dropbox, they're marked as deleted on your online Dropbox account… but you can still recover them by logging in, navigating to the folder that contains the deleted items, and clicking on **More Actions ➤ Show Deleted Files**. At that point, click on the triangle to the right of the deleted file you want back and select Undelete File. A moment later, the file will reappear on your Mac. Once again, the free account saves deleted files for 30 days at most; if you want unlimited undelete, you need to pay for an account.

7. If you install Dropbox on your other computers—and remember that it works on Mac OS X, Windows, and Linux—and log in with your account, your files appear in the Dropbox folder on those computers. Add something on your Mac, and it appears in Dropbox on your Linux and Windows machines. Delete something on your Linux box, and it's removed from all the others as well.

8. You can easily share folders with other Dropbox users. Create a new folder in ~/Dropbox—for my brother, I created one called `Scott & Gus Share`—and then right-click on it. Go to **Dropbox ➤ Sharing Options**, which opens the page in your web browser shown in Figure 8–6.

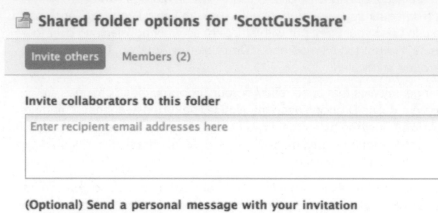

Figure 8–6. *Share your folder with others. Instant collaboration!*

Enter the e-mail addresses of those with whom you want to share the folder (they need to be Dropbox users, of course), type out a message if you want, click Invite, and tell them to check their e-mail. When they click on the e-mail, they're taken to their Dropbox account online and asked if they want to Accept or Decline the invitation. If they accept, a new folder appears in ~/Dropbox. When you add or change a file in that folder, it will appear in the folders of anyone else with whom it's shared, and vice-versa: if they add or change a file in that folder, it changes in your Dropbox as well!

9. Basic Dropbox is free, with 2 GB of storage and backup. But, keep in mind that shared folders, *even those others share with you*, count toward those 2 GB. More space, and the ability to keep prior versions and deleted files, will cost you. $100/year (or $10/month, so pay by the year!) gets you 50 GB, while $200/year (or $20/month) gets you 100 GB. You can upgrade or downgrade at any time.

10. Dropbox isn't perfect. I've already mentioned that you can't use your own encryption keys. There are other hassles, though.

- Any file that you want to backup or sync with Dropbox has to be in ~/Dropbox (kinda—I'll mention a way around that one in a sec). You can't choose random folders to sync that are in ~/Documents or ~/Pictures, for instance. You can find reasons why this is so in the discussion thread at http://forums.dropbox.com/topic.php?id=20006&replies=14#post-126194. Frankly, they make a lot of sense to me—it *is* kind of nice to know that no matter what computer you're using, your stuff is all in the Dropbox folder. And further, what happens if you try to sync C:\Documents and Settings\Scott\Documents from a Windows PC? Where the heck does that go on my Mac? At the same time, though, the next major release of Dropbox (0.9) will allow syncing of selected folders outside of ~/Dropbox, but that's going to be a while. No matter, it's going to be interesting how the developers at Dropbox solve this one!

- You can have only one Dropbox account active and running when you're logged in to your Mac. In other words, you *can* create two or more Dropbox accounts, but you can't log in to more than one while you're using your Mac. It isn't a big deal to me, but oh! the wailing and gnashing of teeth I've seen about this!

- 50 GB is a lot of storage for most people. There's nothing for people who need just 10 GB. Or 25. The jump from free and 2 GB to $100/year and 50 GB is one that causes most folks to gulp (you can submit a request to Dropbox for a smaller plan at https://www.dropbox.com/ticket, but it may or may not be successful, and don't expect a linear price drop, as there are fixed costs that Dropbox has to cover).

- Dropbox used to really stink when it came to syncing a lot of files, like over 100,000. After being impressed by the free account, I decided to pay for the 50 GB account and back up my documents and images. A week or so later, it was finally all in Dropbox, and my Mac was moving at the approximate speed of an opium-addicted tree sloth wading through honey. I contacted support at Dropbox and was told, basically, not to store that many files with Dropbox, as it would slow things down. I was not pleased to be told that after the fact, and after I'd dropped $100. However, it appears that the latest beta builds have mitigated this problem quite a bit (to get the beta, go to http://forums.dropbox.com and look for the latest discussion titled "Experimental Forum Build"). I've been testing them, and the latest versions do in fact seem to allow for thousands of files without negative effects.

It seems like a cottage industry has been growing over the last few years as people try to figure out the coolest, most interesting, most clever things they can do with Dropbox. Let me point you in the direction of some great articles that will provide you with many great ideas to try out for yourself.

- "Sync Files and Folders Outside Your My Dropbox Folder"
  `http://lifehacker.com/5154698/sync-files-and-folders-outside-your-my-dropbox-folder`
  The biggie—how to sync files that aren't in ~/Dropbox. It's actually quite easy, and it's particularly easy to create the symbolic links you need with ForkLift (discussed in Chapter 3) with Find ➤ Make Symlink. For more info, also see
  `http://wiki.dropbox.com/TipsAndTricks/SyncOtherFolders`.

- "PHP Dropbox Uploader"
  `http://wiki.dropbox.com/DropboxAddons/PHPDropboxUploader`
  Create a form on your PHP-driven website that allows others to upload files into your Dropbox. Obviously, you don't want to make this public, but it would be perfect for people who work with clients, teachers, and small teams.

- "The Dropbox Plugin"
  `http://wiki.dropbox.com/DropboxAddons/TheDropboxPlugin`
  Integrate Dropbox with WordPress.

- "Joomla Component for Dropbox"
  `http://wiki.dropbox.com/DropboxAddons/JoomlaPlugin`
  Integrate Dropbox with Joomla.

- "Drupal Dropbox Integration"
  `http://wiki.dropbox.com/DropboxAddons/DrupalPlugin`
  Integrate Dropbox with Drupal.

- "Dropbox Anywhere"
  `http://www.dropbox.com/anywhere`
  Access Dropbox on your iPod Touch, iPhone, iPad, Android device, and Blackberry.

- "Sync Safari Bookmarks Across OSX Machines"
  `http://wiki.dropbox.com/TipsAndTricks/SyncSafariBookmarks`
  I prefer Xmarks myself (see Chapter 4), but if you're strictly a Safari man or woman, this could be just what you need.

- "HowTo Keep all your Passwords in Sync"
  `http://wiki.dropbox.com/TipsAndTricks/SyncAllYourPasswords`
  Use Dropbox to sync passwords stored by KeePassX and 1Password (see earlier in this chapter).

- "15 Advanced Dropbox Hacks"
  `http://storecrowd.com/blog/dropbox-hacks/`
  A darn good list of interesting ideas for Dropbox, many of them quite clever.

I could keep going, but believe me, just spend a few minutes with Google and your imagination and you'll come up with some fantastic ideas.

> **NOTE:** If you think Dropbox sounds cool and you want to sign up, I'd really appreciate it if you use this URL: `https://www.dropbox.com/referrals/NTYzMDM5`. Since I referred you, I'll get a little bit of extra space, which would be nice (and then you can refer your friends and get extra space, too). If you don't want to use that link, no biggie: just go to `www.dropbox.com` and sign up like normal.

CrashPlan

Dropbox is a fantastic tool, and you can sure use it for backup, but its real strength is syncing and collaboration. If you have files you want to share with other people or other computers, Dropbox is easily the best solution. But if you have gigabytes of files that you just want to back up to a server online, then I'd highly recommend that you look at CrashPlan.

Why do I like CrashPlan?

- Reliable and hasn't let me down.

- Secure, both in storage (128–bit Blowfish—and you can use your own keys if you'd like!) and in transit (128–bit SSL).

- Uses very few system resources.

- Easy to configure. You can see the main screen that shows what's being backed up in Figure 8–7.

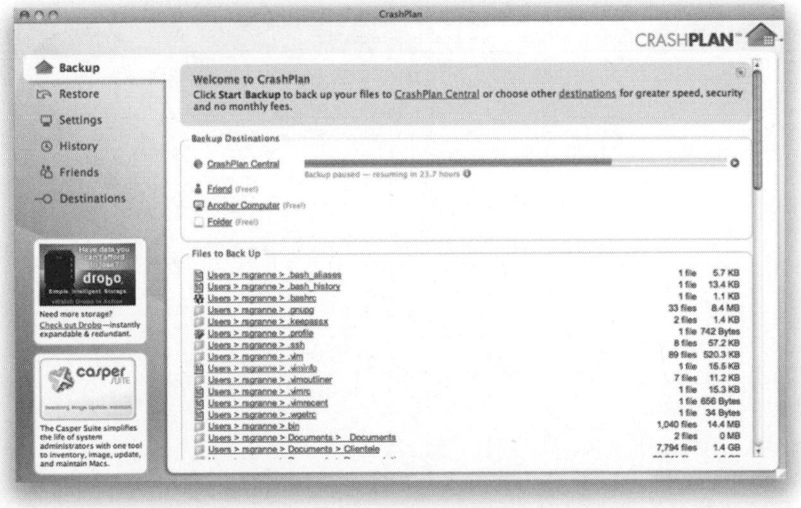

Figure 8–7. *CrashPlan shows you exactly what's you're backing up.*

- Cross-platform, so it works on Mac OS X, Windows, Linux, and Open Solaris.

- Reasonably priced (though not as cheap as Amazon S3, discussed in the next section).

When you go to www.crashplan.com to learn more or sign up, you're presented with two different, although similar, services: CrashPlan and CrashPlan Pro. The latter is really intended for businesses with at least ten computers to back up, while the former, intended for homes and individuals, is what I'll focus on here.

I said that CrashPlan's pricing is reasonable, but it's not the clearest in the world. Here's a list of its pricing segments, which I'll explain in more detail:

- CrashPlan software: Free

- CrashPlan Central: $54/year for unlimited data

- CrashPlan+: $60/year, in addition to what you pay for CrashPlan Central

So what do each of these tiers mean?

The CrashPlan software is free and surprisingly powerful. Let's start with that. The interesting thing about CrashPlan is that you can use it to back up to any of four different locations, as you can see in Figure 8–8.

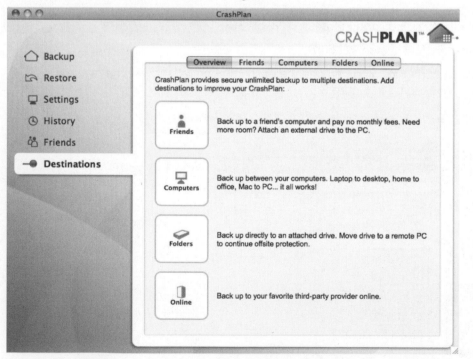

Figure 8–8. *I don't know of any other software that does this.*

You can select any combination of these four destinations, with the first three costing you nothing in terms of money:

- **Friends:** If you and a friend both install CrashPlan, you can back up to each other's computers. Yes, it's encrypted so you can't see your buddy's stuff, and vice-versa.

- **Computers:** If you have multiple computers, you can back them up to each other.

- **Folders:** The classic method of backing up to an external drive.

- **Online:** Now you start using CrashPlan's online services, and now you start paying some money.

The online service is CrashPlan Central, and it costs $54 per year for one Mac, or $100 per year for all the computers in a household (you can also pay for multiple years, which saves you some cash). There are no limitations on how much you can back up, however. For instance, I'm currently backing up 53.6 GB and it's the same price as if I was backing up 5 GB or 150 GB.

For an extra $60 per year I can get CrashPlan+ added on to CrashPlan Central. What do I get for the extra $60?

- **No ads** (the ads are tiny anyway, so this isn't a big deal for me).

- **Continual backup in real-time:** By default, CrashPlan Central backs up at a specific time every day; if you want backup that happens constantly throughout the day, get CrashPlan+.

- **Higher encryption:** 448–bit Blowfish.

- **Restore files from the Web:** If you just have CrashPlan Central, you can only restore files from within the CrashPlan software. If you have CrashPlan+, you can also restore files from the Web without having to use the CrashPlan software.

- **Phone support:** CrashPlan Central customers contact the company using e-mail or the Forums, but CrashPlan+ customers also get a phone number to call.

Personally, I've never needed those extra features, so I haven't upgraded to CrashPlan+. Even so, I can see why some people might find them attractive. For me, the combination of continual backup of super-important files with Dropbox and a nightly off-site backup with CrashPlan Central does the job.

There are plenty of other online backup services, some of which I'll cover at the end of this section, but I've been very happy with CrashPlan. Still, what's nice about almost all of these competitors is that you can try them out for a limited time, which I strongly advise you to do. Test services out before committing to them, and I'm sure you'll find something that backs up your important data in a secure, reliable way.

Amazon S3

If you ask non-techies what pops into their heads when they hear the name "Amazon," most will say books, or movies, or CDs. But if you ask technical folks, more and more they'll say "cloud computing," or "virtual server hosting," or "S3." A few years ago, Amazon decided to leverage the millions of dollars it's spent on building up some of the world's finest network operations centers and hiring people who are experts at building and running those centers. How would it leverage that money, infrastructure, and experience? By offering network services to individuals and businesses all over the globe.

Amazon Web Services (AWS), as it is now called, is one of the best and most advanced sets of services available anywhere online. They're innovative, powerful, reliable, and very reasonably priced. There's just one downside: AWS is not for the non-geeky. Amazon basically created the infrastructure but largely left the software that accesses and uses that infrastructure up to others to create. In other words, Amazon created the Tinker Toys, but how those Tinker Toys are put together and actually used is up to the developer community.

> **NOTE:** To find out more—a lot more!—about AWS, start with the Wikipedia article "Amazon Web Services" (http://en.wikipedia.org/wiki/Amazon_Web_Services) and digest that and all of its associated links. After that, when you're ready to wade into the pool and start swimming, head over to http://aws.amazon.com and start reading, and then, when you're ready, sign up at the same URL. It's so cheap that it'll cost you virtually nothing, and you may find that AWS fits your needs perfectly. In fact, it fits my company WebSanity's needs so well that we're migrating the company's infrastructure to Amazon as fast as we can.

Fortunately, they've responded in eager numbers, and AWS now boasts widespread support. In this section, I want to focus on a single service provided by AWS, one that happens to be the oldest in the AWS arsenal: S3, the Simple Storage Service. Dating all the way back to 2006, S3 is storage on the Net, using Amazon's infrastructure. It's so popular that in less than 5 years it's grown to store over 102 billion files, or *objects*, which is phenomenal.

Here are a few facts about what S3 can do and how you can use it:

- Objects you store can range from 1 B to 5 GB in size.

- You can store an unlimited number of objects.

- Objects are stored in buckets, which are like folders but not really.

- Bucket names have to be unique *across all of Amazon S3*, not just in your account. My advice: preface all of them with your last name or your company's name, so they're unique and grouped.

- Objects and buckets can be either private or public, and you can grant rights to specific users.

- HTTP and HTTPS are standard protocols, but you can easily turn any object into a BitTorrent download by adding ?torrent to the end of a URL.

- In terms of reliability, Amazon promises 99.999999999% durability and 99.99% availability over any given year.

- Versioning is available, so you can retrieve any prior version of any object.

- No minimum fees, so you pay only for what you actually use—and the prices are crazy low.

And what is that pricing? Although Amazon provides numbers for over 5000 TB (holy mackerel!), I'm going to give you some prices for only the bottom tiers to give you an idea (you can see the full listings for yourself at http://aws.amazon.com/s3/).

- Storage
    - 0-50 TB/month: $0.15/GB
    - 50-400 TB/month: $0.14/GB
- Data Transfer In
    - $0 until November 1, 2010
    - $0.1/GB after November 1, 2010
- Data Transfer Out
    - 0-1 GB/month: $0/GB
    - 1 GB-10 TB/month: $0.15/GB
- Requests
    - PUT, COPY, POST, or LIST: $0.01/1,000
    - GET & all others: $0.01/10,000
    - DELETE: $0

How does this play out in reality? Well, you can always determine what your rough costs would be by visiting the Amazon Web Services Simple Monthly Calculator, at http://calculator.s3.amazonaws.com/calc5.html. Or, Figure 8–9 shows an actual bill I received from Amazon covering June 1-30, 2010:

		Totals
⊟ **Amazon Simple Storage Service** View/Edit Service		
US Standard Region		
$0.150 per GB - first 50 TB / month of storage used	15.416 GB-Mo	2.31
$0.01 per 1,000 PUT, COPY, POST, or LIST requests	282 Requests	0.01
$0.01 per 10,000 GET and all other requests	93,979 Requests	0.09
	Download Usage Report »	**2.41**
⊟ **AWS Data Transfer (excluding Amazon CloudFront)** View/Edit Service		
$0.000 per GB - data transfer in (Until June 30, 2010)	0.262 GB	0.00
$0.000 per GB - first 1 GB / month data transfer out	1.000 GB	0.00
$0.150 per GB - up to 10 TB / month data transfer out	3.688 GB	0.55
		0.55
Taxes		0.00
Total Charges due on July 1, 2010		**$2.96**

Figure 8–9 *Cheap!*

That's right—over 15 GB of storage and thousands of requests, and it cost me $2.96 for the month. That's an amazingly great price!

So I hope you're convinced that Amazon S3 is a viable, if not preferable, way to back up and store files. There's just one little problem you have to solve before you can use it, though, which I mentioned at the start of this section: it's up to you to learn how to get your files into S3 and sync them there. Remember, Amazon just provides the services, not the software that interacts with those services. So what can you use?

There are actually a lot of methods available to you now (a few years ago, it was far more difficult). I'm going to focus on two, and then give you a list of others you can check out.

WARNING: This isn't an "Ohmygosh something horrible will happen!" warning as much as it is a "You could find yourself annoyed by this" warning. Remember earlier when I said that S3 buckets are like folders but aren't really? Well, that's true. But further than that, S3 doesn't really have a defined concept for folders inside buckets.

The result is that every different program that accesses S3 has to define how it's going to create a "folder" and put files inside that "folder." I've mixed and matched S3 software over the last several years, and things seem to somehow work together without major issue (for instance, Cyberduck likes to create a file for each folder; it hides those files but they're shown by other programs, which is annoying). That's not saying that different programs might not completely wig out with my data on S3 and mess things up royally, though, so it's probably best to pick a program and stick with it.

Transmit

Panic's Transmit, which I discussed in Chapter 6, connects to Amazon S3 *and* has a powerful Sync feature built right in. It's easy to use, fast, and it works perfectly. The only downside: it's manual. So if you want to back up ten directories into ten buckets, you have to do each one by hand. Blech.

However, you're in luck, because the folks at Panic created Automator actions (for more on Automator, see Chapter 12) that you can use to automate the process! Open Automator and go to the Internet category under Library, and you'll see four actions courtesy of Transmit:

- Download
- Mount
- Synchronize
- Upload

The third is the one we want. Drag Synchronize into the workflow and set things up. After I did, I saw the interface shown in Figure 8–10.

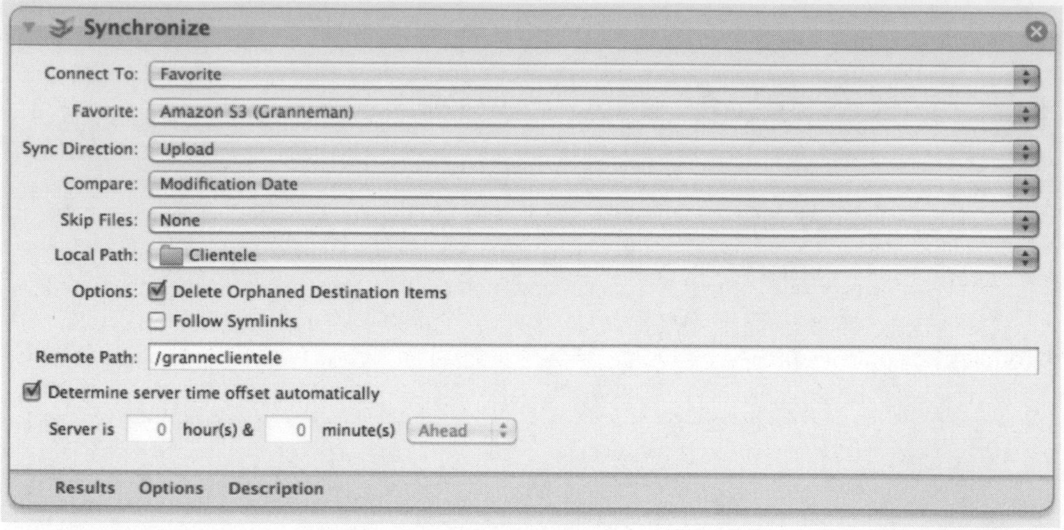

Figure 8–10. *Panic did a good job thinking of all the right options.*

Let me walk you through my choices:

- **Connect To:** Your choices are Specified Server and Favorite. If you choose the former, you'll have to enter a lot of information in fields that appear when you select it. I recommend using a Favorite, so you'll already have the info entered.

- **Favorite:** Select the Favorite you want to use. In my case, it's Amazon S3.

- **Sync Direction:** Do you want to Upload or Download? I want to copy the contents of my Mac's hard drive up to S3, so it's Upload.

- **Compare:** You can compare files using Modification Date or Size. Date makes more sense, especially given the potential file size differences of my Mac's file system and that at S3.

- **Skip Files:** I chose None, but I could also use rules to exclude certain files if I wanted.

- **Local Path:** Which folder on my Mac do I want to synchronize with S3? In this case, I chose my Clientele folder (you could always select your entire Documents folder, but I didn't want to have one giant bucket at S3, so I created buckets for each of the main subfolders in ~/Documents).

- **Options:** I want files I deleted on my Mac to be removed from S3, so I definitely check the box next to Delete Orphaned Destination Items. I don't need soft links followed, so I did not check Follow Symlinks.

- **Remote Path:** Which bucket do I want to sync with at S3? The path name for S3 follows the pattern of /[name of bucket], so I enter /granneclientele.

- **Determine Server Time Offset Automatically:** Transmit does a fine job of figuring out the server time automatically, so this one's checked.

To test the settings, click the Run button and make sure that your files appear at S3 in the correct bucket. If they do, repeat the process and add the Synchronize action again, configuring it for a different local folder and S3 bucket. Do this as many times as you have folders and buckets that you want to sync, testing all the while.

When you're done, it's time to save your workflow. In actuality, you should have made a choice from the list of templates when you started the workflow: is this going to be an Application or an iCal Alarm (you could choose one of the others, of course, but those are the two that make the most sense)?

If you select Application, then you'll need to either run it manually (boo!) or somehow set things up so it runs on a recurring basis, say every night at 3AM. You can easily do that with Lingon, discussed in Chapter 12. If you instead want to create an iCal Alarm to automate the process, I gave you an example of how to do that in Chapter 2. Pick the method that suits you.

And there you go—thanks to the excellent developers at Panic, who had the thoughtfulness to create Automator actions for Transmit, as well as those at Apple who gave us Automator in the first place, you can couple the two to automatically back up your key files to Amazon S3 as often as you'd like.

s3sync

This one is for the command-line junkies out there (I'm in the group myself), especially if you're familiar with the awesome rsync, which this program emulates. Download the free and open source s3sync from www.s3sync.net and then put the s3sync directory somewhere you can get to easily. In my case, I put it in ~/bin.

The README.txt file that comes inside the download has good instructions about how to use s3sync, but here's a quick run-through.

To start with, you need Ruby, since that's what s3sync uses, but that's not an issue, since Ruby comes with Mac OS X.

Next, you should create a file named s3config.yml and place it in ~/.s3conf (it must have that name, and it must go in that location). Edit s3config.yml so it contains the following:

```
# Your AWS Access Key, similar to the one listed below (it's not mine!).
aws_access_key_id: OG6OEWSOAZO9JTFCB2P2
# Your AWS Secret Key, similar to the one listed below (still not mine!).
aws_secret_access_key: b9w5ytreBH8jfGTyplZaaOX2lnZx/uOHWgrymU+
# The path to your Certificate Authority keys that s3sync will use, like the one listed.
# Be sure to create this directory before you use s3sync.
ssl_cert_dir: /Users/[username]/bin/s3sync/s3certs
```

```
# The number of HTTP errors before s3sync exits.
s3sync_retries: 5
# The character set s3sync uses. The default is ISO-8859-1, but you should use UTF.
s3sync_native_charset: UTF-8
```

Now you can use s3sync on the command line or in shell scripts (or in Automator workflows by including bash shell scripts, for that matter). On the command line, do something like this:

```
~/bin/s3sync/s3sync.rb --ssl --delete --verbose --progress --recursive
/Users/rsgranne/Documents/Clientele/ granneclientele:
```

Here's what those options do:

- `--ssl` (or `-s`)
  Encrypt your connection to S3 via SSL, a very good idea.

- `--delete`
  Delete files on the target (S3) if they're missing on the source (my Mac).

- `--verbose` (or `-v`)
  Show me more info about what's happening.

- `--progress`
  Show the progress of the sync.

- `--recursive` (or `-r`)
  Proceed recursively down through the source folder.

- `/Users/rsgranne/Documents/Clientele/`
  The source. The / at the end means to copy the contents of the directory; if you leave off the /, the directory *and* its contents will be copied (yes, just like rsync).

- `granneclientele:`
  The target at S3. Buckets need a : after them, but you can put paths after the : if you need to. The README contains more info if you're interested.

If you want the world to be able to access your files, then use `--public-read` or `-p` in your list of options.

And here are extra ones you should use for testing:

- `--dryrun` (or `-n`): This shows you what would happen if you actually ran the command. When you're satisfied with the test results, remove the `--dryrun` or `-n` and let 'er rip!

- `--debug` (or `-d`): Want a *lot* more info about what's going on? Turn this one on!

Once you know that complete command and all of its options work, try it with other paths and buckets. Once you know those work, put them in a bash shell script, set up a recurring job with Lingon, and you're set. Nice!

Further Resources

It seems like there are new online backup services coming out of the woodwork nowadays. Here are a few that are worth checking out:

- Mozy and Mozy Pro (http://mozy.com)

- Carbonite (www.carbonite.com)

- SugarSync (www.sugarsync.com)

- Box.net (www.box.net)

- Wuala (www.wuala.com)

- Backblaze (www.backblaze.com)

Besides Transmit, which I covered in this chapter, here are some other GUI programs you can use with S3:

- **Cyberduck:** Discussed in Chapter 6, this free and open source program will not only access S3, but will also sync local folders with buckets.

- **Jungle Disk:** A lot of people like this service, which starts at $2/month and is available from https://www.jungledisk.com, but the fact that it creates a large disk cache (see http://support.jungledisk.com/entries/19300-jungle-disk-cache) turned me off.

- **JetS3t:** A free program available from http://jets3t.s3.amazonaws.com/index.html (be sure to include the index.html). The cross-platform JetS3t relies on Java, which always seems to run slowly. And it's ugly as a mud fence, as my Mom would say. But it does provide a GUI for accessing S3.

- **S3Fox:** A free Firefox extension that puts a nice GUI for working with S3 right inside a great web browser. Read about it at www.s3fox.net and download it from https://addons.mozilla.org/en-US/firefox/addon/3247/.

- **S3Hub:** This free program doesn't support syncing, but if you want to manually manage your files, it will do the job. Get it at http://s3hub.com.

- **Arq:** It looks promising, with a nice GUI and a total focus on using S3 to back up your data. Try it out for yourself at www.haystacksoftware.com/arq/. Keeping it will cost you $29 (that price should be a bit lower, IMHO), plus Amazon fees, of course.

There are other command-line programs you can use with S3 as well, beyond s3sync:

- **s3cmd:** Another free and open source tool, available at `http://s3tools.org/s3cmd`. For syncing, you should read "s3cmd sync HowTo" (`http://s3tools.org/s3cmd-sync`).

- **Jets3t:** The program, which I mentioned in the previous list, contains a command-line program called Synchronize that does the job. I used to use this quite a bit, but I found s3sync to be easier to configure and use.

These are just a few. A Google search will turn up lots of others. Try out the ones that seem interesting, but be sure to use test data!

Summary

The last chapter contained information that is important to know and that I strongly suggested you use. Backup, though, is a different story. That's not a suggested activity; that's a mandatory obligation. I can't stress that enough. You must back up your Mac and your data, and I urge you to think of those as two separate things. Use an external hard drive and the software of your choice to copy your Mac so that you can easily restore the whole furshlugginer thing if you have to, use another external drive to back up key data, and use an online service to back up your vital data to a cloud service in the event of a disaster.

The writer William S. Burroughs once said, "A paranoid is someone who knows a little of what's going on," and that's great advice for computer users as well. Be paranoid, because you know what's going on with computers, and you understand that entropy rules the universe. One day your Mac's hard drive *will* die. Be prepared!

## Chapter 9

Manipulating and Sharing Pictures

Let me be very clear up front—I'm not a graphics guy. I don't know how to use Photoshop, and more importantly, it's just not a program for which I have a use. I don't even really use the main commercial Photoshop replacements on the Mac, Pixelmator and Acorn (GIMP is free, open source, and available for Macs at http://gimp.lisanet.de, but it's also far more than I need). Oh sure, I have Acorn, and I occasionally open it, but it's usually to perform some very basic task.

So if you're a graphics professional, you're probably not going to get a huge amount out of this chapter. I'm not discouraging you from reading it; I'm just trying to let you know that you're not going to get *mad skillz* about Photoshop and Pixelmator in this chapter. Instead, I'm going to focus on the quick and dirty stuff that I—and many others!—need to do on our Macs: take screenshots, create screencasts, share pictures, and convert and manipulate images. Fortunately, there are some useful, often free, options that make those tasks easy to do, as you'll see.

Taking Screenshots

In contrast to Windows, which has always had an incredibly clumsy method for taking screenshots, Mac OS X features a powerful, yet simple, built-in set of commands (to stop a screenshot in progress, simply press ⎋):

- ⌘-⇧-3: Takes a screenshot of everything on your screen; if you have a dual-monitor setup, a separate image is created for each monitor.

- ⌘-⇧-4: Lets you draw a box onscreen that becomes the screenshot.

- ⌘-⇧-4, Space: After you press Space, your cursor turns into a camera. As you mouse over a window (or the Desktop), it grays out to indicate that it will become the source of the screenshot. That's how 98% of the screenshots in this book were taken.

When you press any of these key combos, your Mac plays a wonderful sound like a shutter closing and creates an image in the TIFF format on your Desktop with the date and time in it, something along the lines of Screen shot 2010-04-30 at 3.33.13 PM.

When you press those key commands, you're actually invoking Apple's built-in Grab.app, located in /Applications/Utilities. You can open that program yourself, which then allows you to both select which pointer you want to appear in your screenshot and delay the screenshot by ten seconds. Those are nice, but a lot's missing from Grab.app, including:

- You can't take screenshots of DVDs you're playing for silly copyright reasons.

- You can take an automatic screenshot of a window, but if you have a menu open in that window, you can get either the window or the menu, not both. You can of course take a screenshot manually and capture both, but I want to do it automatically.

- You can't do anything to the image without opening it in another program. No cropping, editing, and adding shapes, for instance.

So, if Apple's built-in tool isn't enough for you, there are always third parties that make software to take screenshots. Of course, most of the big graphics programs for Mac OS X include screenshot capabilities, but I'm instead going to focus on smaller apps that focus on one or two things. Some of the more popular screenshot programs in that category are:

LittleSnapper: This is more than just an app that takes screenshots; it's basically an iPhoto or iTunes for screenshots. You take the screenshots, and then you can organize them into folders, collections, and more, as you can see in Figure 9–1. And don't forget ratings, tags, and all the other fun stuff you can use in iPhoto. It also goes beyond Grab.app in that you can takes shots of a complete web page (even the stuff that's not visible on screen), annotate and mark it up in a wide variety of ways, and finally publish it online to many different places. If you're interested, LittleSnapper is available at www.realmacsoftware.com/littlesnapper/ for $35 (with a free trial period that allows you to use it as long as you like, but limits you to storing only 30 screenshots in your library). If you like the library feature, go for it, but if all you want is a better screenshot program, there are cheaper options available.

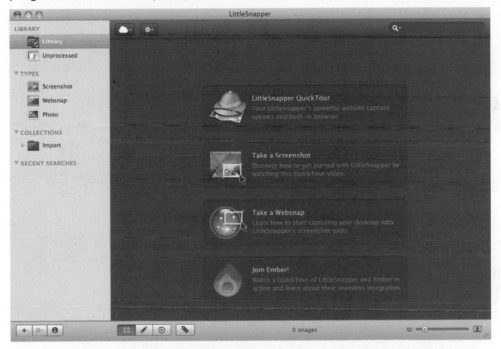

Figure 9–1. *LittleSnapper is as much about organizing screenshots as it is about taking them.*

Skitch: This is a program that people either love or hate. On the one hand, it's a powerful screenshot app that allows you to edit your images in many ways, and then publish your changes online (not surprisingly, Skitch would love it if you used Skitch.com for your free hosting, but you don't have to). On the other hand, it's got a very unconventional UI that can be confusing and difficult (see for yourself in Figure 9–2; personally, I hate it). Download it for yourself at http://skitch.com; it's free, so you have nothing to lose but your time.

Figure 9–2. *Skitch has one weird, non-standard UI that some folks really like.*

Snapz Pro X: This is a program that's been around a while, and the interface shows it, as you can tell from Figure 9–3. It's not slick or spiffy, but it does take screenshots (and record screencasts, too). Interestingly, when you run Snapz Pro X, it's a hidden app that finally appears when you press ⌘-⇧-3, so it takes the place of Apple's normal key commands. Grab the program at www.ambrosiasw.com/utilities/snapzprox/ and play with it over its 15-day free trial, and then be prepared to quit using it or pay the price: a whopping $69. That's an awful lot of money for a program that does what Snapz Pro X does, and I'll just leave it at that.

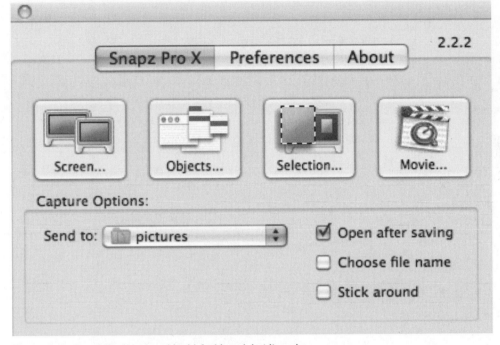

Figure 9–3. *Snapz Pro X looks a bit old-fashioned, but it works.*

Jing: Quick, easy, and free—that's what Jing is. Screenshots are PNG only, but you can add captions, highlights, and arrows to them, and it's easy to post the results online to servers you like (just like Skitch, Jing has a preferred service: screencast.com). You can also record screencasts as well, but they time out at five minutes max. If you really want, you can pay $15 a year, which gets you Jing Pro, giving you extra features for screencasts, but nothing for screenshots. Download Jing from www.jingproject.com, and check out the UI in Figure 9–4.

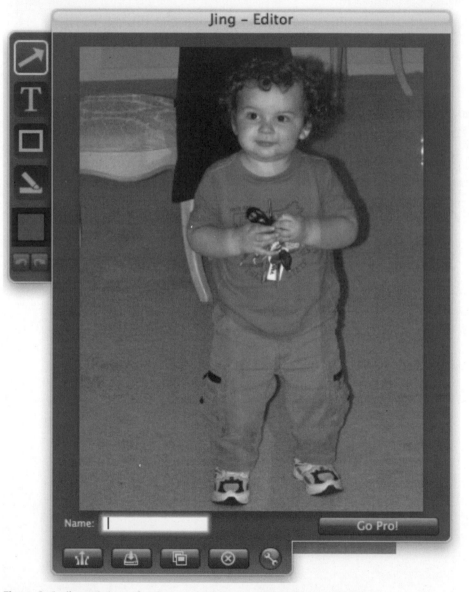

Figure 9–4. *Jing only has a few features, and they're all right there on the side.*

If those aren't enough for you, here are some others that you might want to investigate:

- **Voila:** $30 (free trial first) at www.globaldelight.com/voila/voila_overview.html

- **Snapplr:** $20 with a free trial at http://snapplr.com

- **SnapNDrag:** Free at www.yellowmug.com/snapndrag/

Here are a few specialized screenshot tools that are aimed at those with very specific needs. Are they for everyone? Nope. But they may be for you.

- **Layers:** Instead of a single image in TIFF, PNG, or JPG format, Layers saves the image as a layered Photoshop document (PSD), with each window and Mac OS X element (Menu Bar, icons, Dock, and so on) becoming a separate layer. $25 at http://layersapp.com.

- **Paparazzi:** Takes screenshots of entire web pages, even what you can't currently see in the browser. Free at http://derailer.org/paparazzi/.

- **DropImageURL:** Another program like Paparazzi whose job is taking screenshots of web pages. Donation requested at www.limit-point.com/Utilities/DropImageURL.html.

A Note on Screencasts

Some may wonder why I don't devote several long pages to tools for recording screencasts on the Mac. Granted, this is a chapter on images, but as with Jing, you'll often see tools that bundle together the ability to take both screenshots and screencasts. The bigger reason, though, is that the choices are so clear-cut.

If you're prepared to spend money and you want the best screencast tool for Mac OS X, it's an easy decision: ScreenFlow from www.telestream.net/screen-flow/ for $99. That's a decent chunk o' change, but it's worth it. I've used it extensively to make videos for my classes, and it's a great piece of software. There are other commercial packages—such as Camtasia ($149 at www.techsmith.com/camtasiamac/) and iShowU ($30 or $60 at http://store.shinywhitebox.com)—but they're not as easy to use or as sophisticated as ScreenFlow. If you're going to buy screencasting software, just save your coins and purchase ScreenFlow.

If you don't have any coins to spend, there are some free options, but the only three I'd bother with are:

- **Jing:** Remember, as I discussed previously, it does screencasts up to five minutes long.

- **QuickTime X:** The QuickTime X Player will record screencasts (**File ➤ New Screen Recording**), but it records the full screen and you can't change that. If you want to edit the resulting movie, you can trim it with QuickTime X, and that's it, which means you'll probably want to import it into iMovie for more sophisticated cuts and effects.

- **Screencast-O-Matic:** This is a free or ultra-cheap ($5!) web-based solution (www.screencast-o-matic.com) that uses Java. You can record 15-minute screencasts if you use the free account, but if you pay the $5, you can create hour-long movies, which is a pretty good bargain. Just don't expect a lot of editing options and you'll be happy.

For more on screencasting, see the Wikipedia article on the subject (http://en.wikipedia.org/wiki/Screencast). And if you want to view the best Mac-centric screencasts on the entire InterWebs, you can't do any better than Don McAllister's weekly, in-depth examinations of Mac software at ScreenCastsOnline (www.screencastsonline.com). Subscriptions are $57 for three months, but that gives you complete access to all previous shows (over 250 currently, and in HD to boot!) and the quality is really first-rate. Highly recommended!

iPhoto

iPhoto is one of Apple's flagship apps on the Mac, and the company has been pushing it for years as a reason to choose the Mac over Windows. It's certainly a great program, and yeah, it's no match for Windows Photo Manager or whatever Microsoft is calling its program this week. But even though iPhoto is quality stuff, it still doesn't mean it's perfect. In this section, I'm going to talk about some ways to make an already-good program even better.

Speeding up iPhoto

In Chapter 6, I discussed how to speed up Mail by cleaning its database out so that old, deleted stuff is removed. It turns out that you can do the same thing with iPhoto, using the same command. However, where Mail only has one library that needs vacuuming, iPhoto has four, as you can see (I took some of the detail out of the listings so you could focus on the important stuff):

```
$ cd ~/Pictures/iPhoto\ Library
$ ls -lh
-rw-r--r--  rsgranne  staff   2.3M face.db
-rw-r--r--  rsgranne  staff   4.5M face_blob.db
-rw-r--r--  rsgranne  staff    23M iPhotoAux.db
-rw-r--r--  rsgranne  staff   5.7M iPhotoMain.db
$ sqlite3 face.db vacuum
$ sqlite3 face_blob.db vacuum
$ sqlite3 iPhotoAux.db vacuum
```

```
$ sqlite3 iPhotoMain.db vacuum
$ ls -lh
-rw-r--r--  rsgranne  staff   2.2M face.db
-rw-r--r--  rsgranne  staff   4.5M face_blob.db
-rw-r--r--  rsgranne  staff    19M iPhotoAux.db
-rw-r--r--  rsgranne  staff   5.4M iPhotoMain.db
```

How often should you do this? It depends, of course, on how much you use iPhoto and how often you delete items from your library. If you're busy with the camera and make a habit of deleting photos that just don't work, then you should try to vacuum the iPhoto database files once a month or so. Of course, this would be easy-peasy to turn into a script that you could set to run at intervals with Lingon (see Chapter 12) or Automator (see Chapter 3).

```
#!/bin/bash
sqlite3 /Users/YOURUSERNAME/Pictures/iPhoto\ Library/face.db vacuum
sqlite3 /Users/YOURUSERNAME/Pictures/iPhoto\ Library/face_blob.db vacuum
sqlite3 /Users/YOURUSERNAME/Pictures/iPhoto\ Library/iPhotoAux.db vacuum
sqlite3 /Users/YOURUSERNAME/Pictures/iPhoto\ Library/iPhotoMain.db vacuum
```

Enter this, save it to a file named something like vacuumiphoto.sh, make it executable (chmod 755 vacuumiphoto.sh), and you're good to go.

Integrating iPhoto with Flickr

Starting with iLife '09, iPhoto includes built-in support for Flickr, one of the best photo-sharing sites on the Net. Unfortunately, iPhoto's built-in support stinks, as Fraser Speirs explained in "On the Flickr support in iPhoto '09," which you still can—and definitely should—read at http://speirs.org/blog/2009/1/30/on-the-flickr-support-in-iphoto-09.html. After reading it, I think you'll refuse to use iPhoto's Flickr button (if you'd like to remove it, unselect **View ➤ Show In Toolbar ➤ Flickr**). Instead of using it, my advice is to look at two alternatives, both of which are far better than iPhoto's native Flickr tool.

NOTE: Yes, Speirs is the programmer behind FlickrExport, software that competes with the new Flickr feature in iPhoto, and also software that I'm going to cover in this section. But that doesn't mean that he's not correct. Read his critique, and then try it out yourself if you still don't believe him. After that, you'll want to use one of the solutions I discuss in this section, I guarantee.

Photonic

Photonic does double duty: it allows you to view—but not download—Flickr photos (your own, your contacts', your favorites, and your groups') and also makes it easy to upload your own pix to Flickr. It costs $25 and you download it from www.photonicapp.com.

Uploading is an easy affair: under your username on the left pane, choose Upload Photos. Drag the photos you want to upload from iPhoto into the big blank middle area, and then make any selections you want on the right pane. You can select multiple images at once to apply data about the photos in bulk, leaving you with a window that looks something like Figure 9–5.

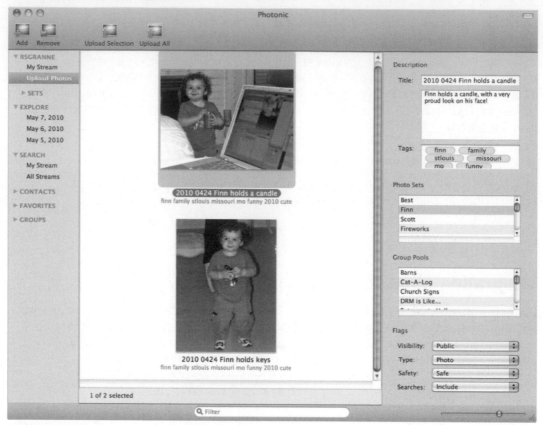

Figure 9–5. *Uploading pictures of a cute little toddler!*

When you have everything set up the way you want it, click the Upload All button, and Photonic will go to work (if for some reason you only want a subset to go to Flickr, click Upload Selection). A few moments later, depending upon the size of your images and the speed of your Internet connection, your images will be on Flickr, and Photonic will open Flickr in your default web browser so you can check out your work.

I use Photonic, but I haven't for a while. Why not? Because it's another program outside of iPhoto, and FlickrExport, which I'm covering next, does the data management and upload inside of iPhoto. That said, if you like to look at Flickr images and upload to Flickr, then Photonic is for you.

And on top of that, every once in a while, FlickrExport won't export. Something just does not compute, and the images won't leave iPhoto for the World Wide Web. It doesn't happen very often—hardly at all—but when it does, I turn to Photonic, and it always works. So I think of FlickrExport as my slightly clumsier fail-safe program for uploading to Flickr. But as I said, it's what I use the vast majority of the time, and you're about to see why.

FlickrExport

Invoking FlickrExport is easy: select the photos you want to upload from within iPhoto, and then go to File ➤ Export ➤ FlickrExport. If you've never used the program before, press Log In to link FlickrExport to Flickr; to do so, just follow the instructions. You'll have to do that once. Normally, in a few moments, after FlickrExport communicates with Flickr and verifies that everything is copacetic, you'll see something like Figure 9–6.

Figure 9–6. *Six cute photos of Finny & Uncle Gussie, ready to upload to Flickr.*

FlickrExport automatically fills in whatever you enter in iPhoto as each picture's Title, Description, Tags, and Latitude and Longitude. Of course, you can change all those in FlickrExport, if you feel like it. Nicely, if you click the sprocket next to Longitude, you can select from saved presets, save the current location as a preset, or open up Google Earth and grab the coordinates from that program, which can be a tremendously useful feature if your camera doesn't have built-in GPS support.

There are also several Flickr-specific elements as well:

- **Privacy:** Choose from Public or Private, and limit to Friends and Family.

- **Safety:** Indicate to Flickr if your images are Safe, Moderate, or Restricted (in other words, is there nudity or something quote-unquote adult?).

- **Content:** Photo, Screenshot, or Other. Flickr also supports short videos of 90 seconds or less, so for those you'll have to use Other.

- **Hide From Public Areas:** Limit your photos' exposure to areas of Flickr that anyone can see, such as Search and Interestingness.

- **Groups:** All of your Groups are listed; to add your images to your groups, simply check the appropriate boxes.

- **Scale Longest Side To:** If you want to resize your images, do so here.

- **Quality:** If you want to adjust the quality of your pix, you can select Low, Medium, High, or Maximum (the default).

- **Add Photo To:** You can choose from the following:

  - **Photostream:** Your list of photos, but not into any of your sets.

  - **Photostream And Existing Photoset:** Next to this is a drop-down list of all your sets, allowing you to select one to which you can add your images.

  - **Photostream And New Photoset:** Select this, and you can enter a title and description for the set, as well as choose the default picture that represents it.

- **Open Flickr When Export Complete:** If this is checked, Flickr opens in your default web browser so you can give your upload the once over before approving it.

When you've made all your choices, click Export and stand back as FlickrExport does its job. If you chose to open the Flickr website at the end of the process, eventually you'll see that, which means that FlickrExport is finished.

So why use FlickrExport? Because you're already in iPhoto, and it's the easiest path to Flickr! If it sounds good to you, go to http://connectedflow.com/flickrexport/iphoto/

and download the program. You get a limited 30-day trial, and then it costs only $17. If you use iPhoto and Flickr, give it a try.

Integrating iPhoto with Facebook

The other big news about iPhoto '09 was that in addition to including support for Flickr, it also added support for uploading images to Facebook, which is now the world's largest photo site. Unfortunately, just as iPhoto's built-in support for Flickr wasn't that useful, the same is true for its Facebook support as well.

> **NOTE:** Just how many pix does Facebook host? Try 14,000,000—that's fourteen million— photos uploaded per day. You can find that factoid and more on the Wikipedia article on Facebook, at http://en.wikipedia.org/wiki/Facebook.

And what are some of the issues? Try these:

- iPhoto file names show up as captions for uploaded photos on Facebook, so you have to manually change them on Facebook.

- If you use Faces in iPhoto to identify people and then upload the pictures to Facebook, the people are tagged on Facebook. Kinda. The names don't link on Facebook to your friends' accounts, so one big purpose of Facebook tagging is thrown out the window, and you end up having to manually tag your friends. Apple provides a sort-of workaround at www.apple.com/ilife/tutorials/#iphoto-facebook, but it's tedious and sometimes difficult to implement.

- This is a huge one: when it's time to upload your pix, you can't put them into existing photo albums on Facebook. Bad Apple, bad!

For all those reasons, it's best just to remove the Facebook button from iPhoto so you don't even see it. To do so, unselect **View ➤ Show In Toolbar ➤ Facebook**.

Fortunately, there is a free solution that does the right things: Facebook Exporter for iPhoto, available from http://developers.facebook.com/iphoto/. Install it, and when you're ready to send some pictures up to Facebook, select the images and then go to **File ➤ Export ➤ Facebook**.

If you've never used the Facebook Exporter before, click Login to link it to Facebook; just follow the instructions to walk through the process and you won't have to do it again. If you've already finished that process, then you'll see the window shown in Figure 9–7.

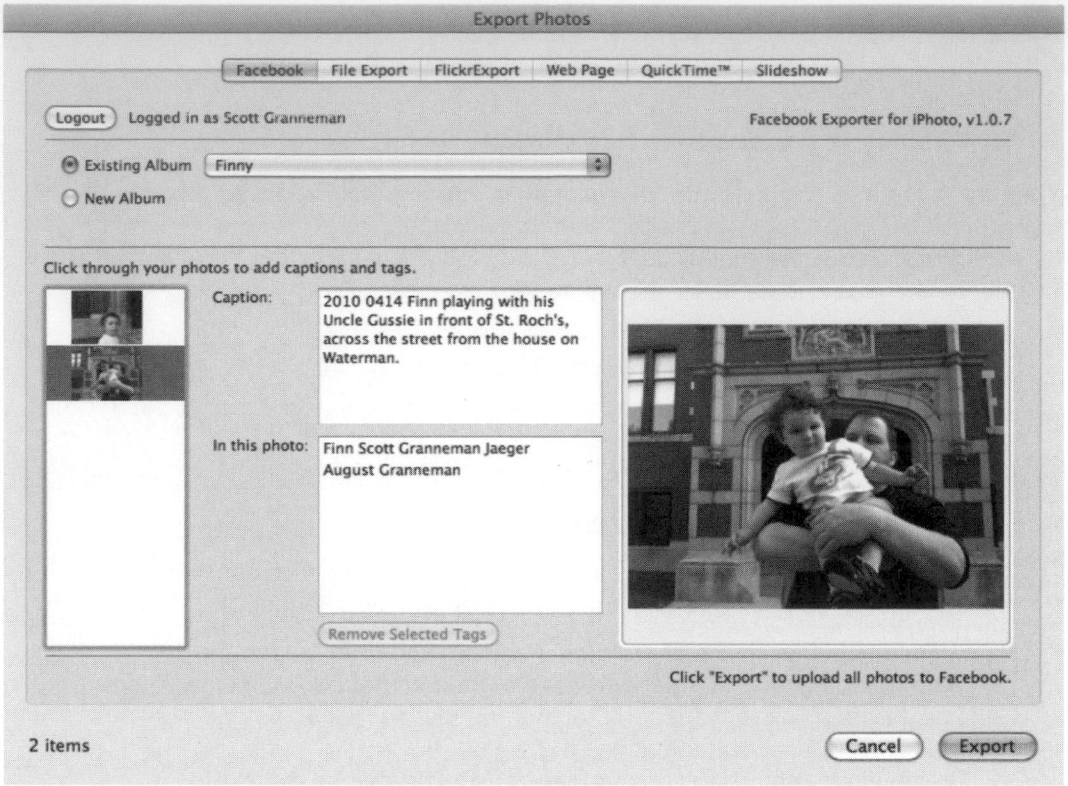

Figure 9–7. *Facebook Exporter for iPhone is simple and fun to use.*

As you can tell, there are only a few settings, and they're easy to use:

- **Album:** You can select either Existing Album—in which case you select which of your albums to use—or you can create a New Album. If you select New Album, you have to enter a Name, and you can also enter, if you'd like, a Description and Location.

- **Caption:** For each photo, you can enter a caption.

- **In This Photo:** Click on each person's face, and a box appears around it. At that point, you can select from a list of your Facebook friends or enter a name if that person isn't on Facebook ... yet.

When you're done, click Export and a few moments later your Facebook friends can see your pix on the fastest-growing social networking site in the world. It's that easy! Why Apple can't do that is a mystery for the ages, but thank goodness the free Facebook Exporter for iPhoto exists.

Further Resources

If you want to learn more about iPhoto, Apple has a lot of great resources available on the Web.

- Guided Tour: www.apple.com/ilife/iphoto/guided-tour/

- Apple support for iPhoto: www.apple.com/support/iphoto/

- Apple discussions for iPhoto:
  http://discussions.apple.com/category.jspa?categoryID=143

- iPhoto Feedback: www.apple.com/feedback/iphoto.html

- iPhoto Tutorials: www.apple.com/ilife/tutorials/#iphoto

Manipulating & Converting Images Quickly

If you need to convert or manipulate (resize, crop, rotate, and so on) one image, you can just open Preview and it will usually handle whatever you need to do. If you need to convert or manipulate several images at once, however, doing it with Preview will quickly grow tedious. If you have Photoshop or one of the other well-known commercial image apps for Mac OS X, you can probably automate your task using that software by creating a droplet or some other automated package. But if you don't have those apps, or if you want to perform your changes quickly and easily, what do you do?

That's the question this section is going to try to answer. There are actually a large number of Mac programs out there that perform batch manipulations of images, but most of them are pretty bad. They might work—or they might not!—but the real problem is that their UIs are substandard and often very confusing. Yuck.

It actually turns out that you don't really need to buy or even download a program to batch manipulate images, although I'm still going to point you to one. And what is the built-in app that will change images in bulk? Why, it's our old friend Automator!

Automator

Open Automator, tell it you want to create a new Workflow, and then go to **Library ➤ Photos**, as that's where you'll be spending (almost) all your time. The first step to our workflow is selecting the images you want to change. You can do this in several ways, using different actions depending upon the source of the images, which can be either in your file system or in iPhoto:

- **Files & Folders ➤ Ask for Finder Items:** Prompts the user to choose photos or folders containing photos. Probably the one I'd use most often.

- **Files & Folders ➤ Filter Finder Items:** Given input (such as Get Specified Finder Items, which passes a folder along to Get Folder Contents), this action allows you to set up multiple conditions (Name, Kind, Date, Size, File Extension, and so on) and then look for files that match those conditions.

> **TIP:** When you're building your workflow in Automator, if you want to see the list of files that Automator has discovered as a means of debugging, plug the View Results action onto the end.

- **Files & Folders ➤ Find Finder Items:** Recursively search a specified folder looking for files that match your conditions.

- **Files & Folders ➤ Get Selected Finder Items:** After selecting pix, you would either right-click on one of them and select **Services ➤ Your New Service** or go to **Finder ➤ Services ➤ Your New Service**. The selected items would then be used in your workflow.

- **Files & Folders ➤ Get Specified Finder Items:** Select files and folders ahead of time and they become part of the workflow. Good if you're constantly working with a particular folder all the time, and really handy if you plug in Filter Finder Items (discussed previously) after it if you want to work only on specific kinds of files.

- **Photos ➤ Ask For Photos:** Opens an iPhoto media browser window, shown in Figure 9–8, which enables you to choose images to use.

- **Photos ➤ Filter iPhoto Items:** Find photos or albums that match specified criteria, including Title, File Name, Date, Rating, Height or Width, Size, and even technical things like Aperture, ISO speed, and Focal length. Just like Filter Finder Items, this action is only really useful with input provided by other actions such as Get Specified iPhoto Items.

- **Photos ➤ Find iPhoto Items:** Search for photos or albums based on criteria you set.

- **Photos ➤ Get Selected iPhoto Items:** After selecting images in iPhoto, you would go to **Finder ➤ Services ➤ Your New Service**. The selected items would then be used in your workflow.

- **Photos ➤ Get Specified iPhoto Items:** Select albums and photos ahead of time and then process them as part of the workflow. If you're converting images in a particular album a lot, this makes sense, but generally I don't see it as that useful.

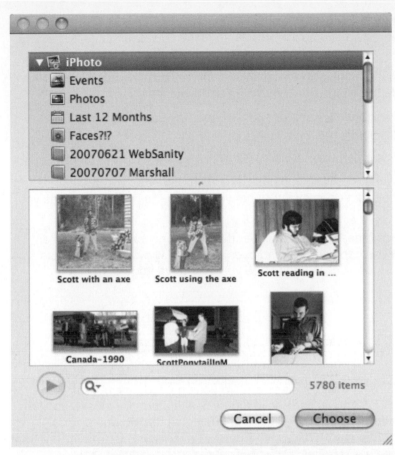

Figure 9–8. *You can choose or search for images you want to use from within iPhoto.*

After choosing which images you want to manipulate, it's time to add actions that define how they are to be manipulated. All of the following are found in the Photos library.

> **NOTE:** Most of these will, when you insert them into the workflow, prompt you to let Automator insert the Copy Finder Items action "so that the copies are changed and your originals are preserved." Needless to say, unless you're abso-frickin'-lutely sure about what you're doing, it is a very good idea to click the Add button and put that backup action into your workflow.

- **Change Type Of Images:** Convert the images to BMP, GIF, JPEG, JPEG 2000, PDF, PICT, PNG, or TIFF. Keep in mind that you cannot specify the quality level for JPEGs, or any other specifics for any of the other formats. But for quick conversions, it does the job.

- **Crop Images:** Crop based on a percentage or pixels, and select which side, if any, you'd like to use for scaling. A nice little preview is provided, which is very helpful.

- **Flip Images:** Flip your images horizontally, vertically, or both ways. Again, Automator provides a useful preview to make your change clear.

- **Pad Images:** Adjust the height or width of the canvas size of your photos, and scale the image first. Another preview guides you.

- **Rotate Images:** Rotate left, right, or 180 degrees. The same little boy preview from Flip Images reappears here.

- **Scale Images:** Scale by pixels or percentage.

Of course, you can daisy-chain as many of these actions together as you'd like, creating a powerful, customized app that does exactly what you want to as many images as you can select.

Automator requires a few moments to set up, but after you save your workflow as an app, you have a tool that you can use over and over again. It's wonderful that Apple makes Automator a part of Mac OS X, and I hope you take advantage of it.

Shrink O'Matic

If for whatever reason you don't want to use Automator to manipulate images, you can always download one of a gazillion programs off the Net to do so. Some cost money, and many are free. The one I turn to for super-quick-and-dirty changes is actually an Adobe AIR app called Shrink O'Matic. It's free and you can get it at `http://toki-woki.net/p/Shrink-O-Matic/`. As you can see in Figure 9–9, it's not the most Mac-like app (it uses the cross-platform Adobe AIR, after all), but it gets the job done.

Figure 9–9. *Shrink O'Matic isn't pretty or Mac-like, but it works.*

Shrink O'Matic only does a few things, but those things are really easy to do:

- **Output Size:** Select either pixels or a ratio (percentage). If you use pixels, only resize height or width to auto-resize the other side to the right length.

- **Output Name:** Keep the original name (which means you're overwriting the file!) or auto-rename to a new one (which appends the width and height).

- **Specify An Output Folder:** If you don't pick a new folder, the new image will appear in the same location as the original one.

- **Output Format:** You can keep the same format, or you can select JPEG, GIF, or PNG. You can select a quality level for JPGs using a slider.

And that's it! As I said, it's simple, but that's why I like it. If I need to quickly change some images, I usually fire up Shrink O'Matic, and I'm finished a few moments later. If I need more power or choices, then Automator is my next software option. And if I need more than Automator, it's time to look for something else, but in my admittedly limited experience, the combination of Shrink O'Matic and Automator has always satisfied my needs.

Summary

Most Mac users aren't graphics experts (although a lot of them are!), but that doesn't mean they don't need to occasionally work with images. In this chapter, I focused on the day-to-day tasks that many people want to do with pictures: take screenshots or screencasts, send pix from iPhoto to various online services, and convert and manipulate images. And for each of those tasks, I wanted to call out free, simple, or highly useful tools that will do those jobs as efficiently as possible. Photoshop is great, but it's not necessary for everything, and I hope that's obvious after reading this chapter.

## Chapter 10

Having More Fun With Audio & Video

For years, Windows users tried to put down Macs by saying that the only things Macs were good for was multimedia (a word coined by Apple, by the way). What's funny about that is that Windows users were implicitly confirming that yes, Macs were better than PCs at viewing and creating audio and video (and images, of course). Nowadays, it's *still* true: Macs are *still* far better than PCs for multimedia. It's just that now Macs are far better than PCs at virtually everything (except gaming, but even that's changing—thank you, Valve and Steam!).

NOTE: Steam is the biggest gaming platform in the world, but for years it's been available for Windows only. Earlier this year, Valve, the company behind Steam, announced that it would be supporting Mac OS X as well, and since then has released the Steam gaming platform and many hugely popular games for Macs. For gamers, this is fantastic news! Find out more at www.steampowered.com.

When it comes to multimedia, Mac users have a cornucopia of amazing options from which to choose. In fact, this chapter could have been its own book, if I had the time, inclination, and editors' approval. The hard part was narrowing it down to just a few areas, but I tried to hit the high points.

If you're going to own a multimedia library of video and audio, there are some things that you just have to concern yourself with, and that's what I'm covering here:

- Codecs and containers, the building blocks of all multimedia
- Great multimedia players, besides QuickTime and iTunes
- How to convert video and audio files to new formats
- How to rip DVDs
- How to edit ID3 tags on audio files

And finally, I give you some warnings about some software and companies you should definitely avoid.

This is a long chapter, but there's a ton of great information in here. Dig in and have fun!

Codecs and Containers

Before I dive into all the fun stuff in this chapter, I first need to explain the difference between codecs and converters. Understanding what each one is will help prevent a lot of confusion later.

A *codec* is software (or hardware, but in this case let's just stick to software) that encodes and decodes, and compresses and decompresses, data. On a music CD, the music isn't compressed at all, so if you copy tracks straight off of a CD, you end up with WAVs, which are enormous (roughly 10 MB per minute) precisely because they aren't compressed. When you convert the tracks on a CD to MP3 or AAC, you use a codec to compress the data so that the files are smaller but still sound good. Common audio codecs include MP3, AAC, Ogg Vorbis, WMA (Windows Media Audio), and FLAC (Free Lossless Audio Codec).

Video is kind of a different beast, in that you'll almost never find yourself working with uncompressed video unless you do video post-production work. However, there are still common video codecs that you've undoubtedly run across, such as WMV (Windows Media Video), DivX (and its open source rival, XviD), MPEG-2 (used on DVDs), Ogg Theora, and H.264 (AKA MPEG-4 Part 10 AVC).

> **TIP:** If you want to see a huge list of audio and video codecs so you can learn more about them, check out http://en.wikipedia.org/wiki/List_of_codecs.

Now, H.264 is great for video, but it doesn't handle audio at all, and MP3 is widely popular for audio, but it sure doesn't do a thing with video. That's where *container* formats come in: they basically provide a wrapper that holds everything you need to watch a movie: video (created with a video codec) and audio (generated by an audio codec), as well as subtitles and chapters. In addition, the container also makes sure that everything plays in sync. Some common container formats include:

- **AVI (Audio Video Interleave):** an ancient container created by Microsoft and still widely used.

- **MP4:** used widely by Apple (and many others—it's actually owned by the MPEG consortium), a modern, versatile container.

- **ASF (Advanced Systems Format):** another Microsoft-owned container used mainly for streaming.

- **Ogg:** A royalty-free, patent-free (supposedly) container popular with the open source crowd.

- **Matroska:** An open standard, open source container format with some sophisticated features.

- **FLV (Flash Video):** Adobe's container for video on the Web—if you've ever been to YouTube, you've used FLV.

- **WebM:** Recently released by Google at the time I'm writing this, and claimed by the company to be royalty- and patent-free (we'll see!), this container format is based on Matroska and is intended for web video.

> **NOTE:** To find out more about audio and video containers, check out Wikipedia's articles on the subject: `http://en.wikipedia.org/wiki/Container_format_(digital)` ("Container format (digital)") and `http://en.wikipedia.org/wiki/Comparison_of_container_formats` ("Comparison of container formats"). Gizmodo has an excellent article about video codecs and containers: "Giz Explains: Every Video Format You Need to Know" (`http://gizmodo.com/5093670/giz-explains-every-video-format-you-need-to-know`).

Even if your Mac can handle the container, that doesn't necessarily mean that it can deal with the codecs inside that container, which is where complications can ensue. It's easy to find out the container—just look at the file's extension. But how do you find out what codecs are inside the container? Actually, you have several options:

- Open Terminal and use the file command, like this (I've formatted the output so you can see it better):

```
$ file 30\ Rock\ S04E21.avi
30 Rock S04E21.avi: RIFF (little-endian) data,
  AVI, 624 x 352, 23.98 fps,
  video: XviD,
  audio: MPEG-1 Layer 3 (stereo, 48000 Hz)
$ file gus-as-elf.mov
gus-as-elf.mov: ISO Media, Apple QuickTime movie
```

As you can see, sometimes you get a ton of info, and sometimes you don't. But it's still a great command (try it with different types of files).

- Open the movie in VLC, discussed later in this chapter, and then go to **Window ➤ Media Information**.

- Open the movie in MPEG Streamclip (covered later in this section), and then go to **File ➤ Show Stream Info**.

- Download and install MediaInfo Mac (`http://mediainfo.massanti.com`) and then, after you open it, drag the video onto the app to see a wealth of detail, as in Figure 10–1.

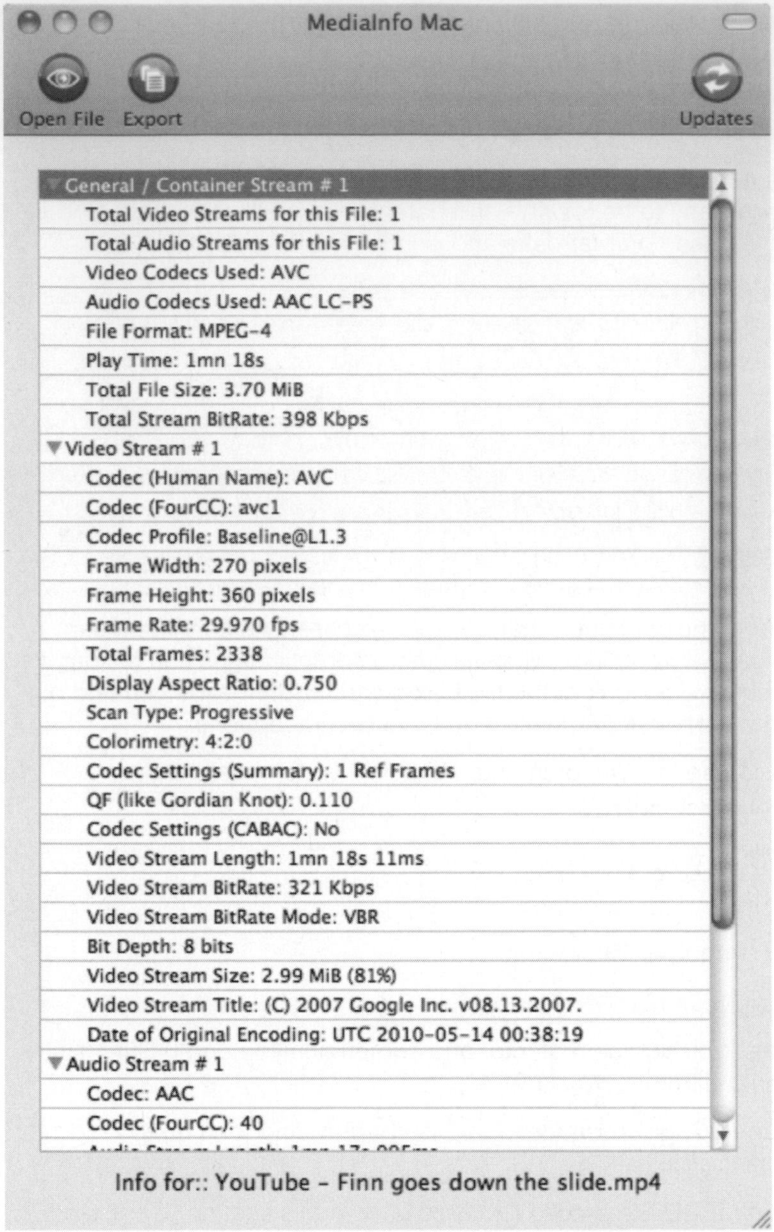

```
                              MediaInfo Mac

    Open File   Export                                    Updates

   ▼ General / Container Stream # 1
        Total Video Streams for this File: 1
        Total Audio Streams for this File: 1
        Video Codecs Used: AVC
        Audio Codecs Used: AAC LC-PS
        File Format: MPEG-4
        Play Time: 1mn 18s
        Total File Size: 3.70 MiB
        Total Stream BitRate: 398 Kbps
   ▼ Video Stream # 1
        Codec (Human Name): AVC
        Codec (FourCC): avc1
        Codec Profile: Baseline@L1.3
        Frame Width: 270 pixels
        Frame Height: 360 pixels
        Frame Rate: 29.970 fps
        Total Frames: 2338
        Display Aspect Ratio: 0.750
        Scan Type: Progressive
        Colorimetry: 4:2:0
        Codec Settings (Summary): 1 Ref Frames
        QF (like Gordian Knot): 0.110
        Codec Settings (CABAC): No
        Video Stream Length: 1mn 18s 11ms
        Video Stream BitRate: 321 Kbps
        Video Stream BitRate Mode: VBR
        Bit Depth: 8 bits
        Video Stream Size: 2.99 MiB (81%)
        Video Stream Title: (C) 2007 Google Inc. v08.13.2007.
        Date of Original Encoding: UTC 2010-05-14 00:38:19
   ▼ Audio Stream # 1
        Codec: AAC
        Codec (FourCC): 40

   Info for:: YouTube - Finn goes down the slide.mp4
```

Figure 10–1. *MediaInfo Mac shows you everything you need to know about your video's container and codecs.*

With the info you get about your container and codecs, you can help figure out why things might not be working with your video player of choice. And, even more fun, you can convert between containers and codecs more effectively, as you'll find out.

Codecs You Need

It might seem as though Apple has taken over the world of multimedia even more so than it used to. iPods are the number-one portable music player by far, iTunes is one of the most widely installed software packages in the world, and billions of songs have been sold through the iTunes Store.

If you stay completely within Apple's media ecosystem—you buy songs and movies only from iTunes, and you only use QuickTime Player to view movies and iTunes to listen to music, then you don't need this next bit of advice.

However, I frankly don't know anyone apart from Steve Jobs who actually lives like that. Most other Mac users get music and movies from many different sources, or they want to watch videos and listen to songs that are not blessed by Apple. The question I'm trying to address is, how do you play a video encoded as an AVI file? Or Matroska? Or DivX? Or listen to a song encoded as a WMA? Or MP2?

The solution is easy—simply install the following, which provide QuickTime components that add support for a wide variety of formats. If you install these packages, you'll basically take care of pretty much any video or audio file that you'll commonly find.

- **Perian.** Free from `http://perian.org`, this is a must-have, as it provides support for over 20 audio, video, subtitle, and container formats. One of the first pieces of software I install on a new Mac.

- **Flip4Mac.** Free from `www.microsoft.com/windows/windowsmedia/player/wmcomponents.mspx` (yes, Microsoft pushes this to Mac users as a preferred solution for viewing files formatted with its software!), this allows you to view and hear virtually all Microsoft formats in QuickTime. Make sure you don't pay for this software—it's free, unless you want to save in a Microsoft format (and why would you want to do that?), and only then must you pay for it.

- **Xiph QuickTime Components (XiphQT).** Free from `http://xiph.org/quicktime/`, you need this only if you want to view or hear files that were encoded with the Xiph.Org Foundation's open source codecs and containers, including Ogg Theora (video), Ogg Vorbis (audio), and (mostly) FLAC (audio). For full FLAC support in QuickTime and iTunes, read `http://barelyfocused.net/blog/2006/10/12/native-flac-in-itunesquicktime/`.

- **DivX.** Free from `www.divx.com/en/software/mac`. You don't need to buy DivX Pro unless you want to create DivX files; to simply view them, the free software is enough. You need this only if Perian's support for DivX isn't enough for you.

Much of the software I'm going to discuss in this chapter needs at least Perian installed, and if you want to work with Microsoft or Xiph formats that you may run in to on the Net, you'll need those software packages as well.

Exploring Alternatives to QuickTime and iTunes

Apple is justifiably proud of its two main multimedia players built in to Mac OS X: QuickTime and iTunes (which uses QuickTime). They're both great, and millions of people use them every day to listen to music and watch movies and videos. But that doesn't mean they're perfect, and here are some reasons why they're not:

- Some videos just don't play correctly in QuickTime. That doesn't mean they're unplayable on your Mac, however.

- Apple has implemented ridiculously over-broad restrictions, such as disabling screenshots of DVD content.

- In order to play a really wide variety of audio and video encoded in non-Apple-supported codecs, you need to install the software I listed in the introduction to this chapter. Some people don't like installing extra codecs and want to keep QuickTime and iTunes lean and mean, without extra software loading—but they still want to watch video and audio that don't work natively in Apple's software.

- The interface of QuickTime Player in Snow Leopard is very different from previous versions, and a lot of very valid criticisms have been made about it (see www.paulsahner.net/home/2009/8/29/quicktime-x-sucks.html, http://imnotbruce.blogspot.com/2009/08/snow-leopard-tips.html, and http://arstechnica.com/apple/reviews/2009/08/mac-os-x-10-6.ars/16)

- To play audio in iTunes, you have to add it to the iTunes library, which can be a drag if you just want to, y'know, *listen* to some MP3s that you have.

- You don't want or need to put your videos into a library to view them. You've already organized your videos into a directory structure that makes sense to you and you don't want to organize them via iTunes.

- Even on a Mac, iTunes can be slooooooooow (on Windows, it's even more painful, but that's just yet another reason not to use Windows). That said, iTunes is also one of the only apps I've ever seen that can handle my absolutely gi-normous music collection (80,000 or so songs and growing).

If you can relate to any of those reasons, or if you have your own, you're in luck, because there are other choices for your Mac. There aren't a lot of choices—Apple's dominance has affected that—but fortunately the ones that are available are good, and free, and open source, all of which are very positive developments.

VLC

The king of QuickTime Player replacements is VLC. First unveiled in 2001, this free and open source software acts as a player, encoder, and streamer for video and audio. It really is pretty awesome, incredible stuff, and if you haven't already downloaded it from www.videolan.org, get yourself to that site and get it downloaded.

32 or 64?

When you get there, you might notice that the versions available are all 32-bits, and of course Snow Leopard supports 64-bit apps, so where are the 64-bit versions of VLC? Unfortunately, there's been a bit of turmoil lately when it comes to Mac development of VLC. Apparently there is a shortage of developers for the Mac version of VLC, which means that while 32-bit releases are still coming out regularly, as the website explains on the download page, "VLC will not be available for 64-bit Intel-based Macs until further notice."

Strictly speaking, however, this isn't quite true, since there are still nightly (read: unstable and potentially crashy) builds of VLC for Mac that are both 32- and 64-bit, as you can see for yourself at http://nightlies.videolan.org/build/macosx-intel/?C=M;O=D (the ?C=M;O=D at the end will make the listing chronological). Go there and click on Mac OS X Intel and then look for links with "vlc-git-intel64" in them. But I've also read that 1.1.0 will be the last 64-bit version for Mac. At this point, let's all hope that Mac developers turn out to help keep VLC for the Mac alive and thriving. One way to help if you're not a coder would be to contribute time, materials, help, documentation, and, yes, money to the project at www.videolan.org/contribute.html.

> **NOTE:** I've been running the nightly build of the 64-bit version of VLC for quite a while, and it's been just fine. Your mileage, as they say, may vary. However, if you're nervous about using a nightly build, version 1.0.2 of VLC was the last official build with 64-bit support, and it works. Get it at http://download.videolan.org/pub/videolan/vlc/1.0.2/macosx/vlc-1.0.2-intel64.dmg.

Before leaving this issue entirely, let me complicate it further (that's a joke ... kinda). There is a new GUI being developed for Mac users of VLC: Lunettes. This is an effort to create a better, more Mac-friendly UI that is 64-bits from the get-go. The code is still pretty rough, but it's usable. If you want to keep up with Lunettes as it develops, you can follow along on these web pages:

- http://wiki.videolan.org/Lunettes: The official web page explaining why Lunettes is being developed.

- http://github.com/pdherbemont/Glasses: Code to compile, and, for those who just want an actual build they can install, ZIPs are available by following the Downloads link.

■ http://wiki.github.com/pdherbemont/Glasses/: Information about the project, including goals, how to compile the code, and more.

Keep in mind, though, that this is a project focused on VLC's GUI for Macs, not the underlying core of the software that does the heavy lifting. That part still needs developers, so keep your fingers crossed.

Basic Features

When you open VLC and start playing videos with it, you'll see that it's pretty straightforward, as you can tell from Figure 10–2.

Figure 10–2. *Yours truly interviewed on a local TV news segment. Note the two windows VLC uses.*

VLC has a dizzying array of features, as you can see when you peruse www.videolan.org/vlc/features.html. Wow! Here are a few key things you should know about VLC, and then we'll dig down for a few more advanced items:

Codecs codecs codecs! VLC comes with all the codecs it needs already built-in, and it will play just about anything you can throw at it.

Damaged is OK. Even more amazing, VLC can play back videos that are damaged or missing part of the files! This can be especially nice if you want to preview a movie you're downloading via BitTorrent, and it's only partly done. Check it out with VLC to make sure it's the file you want, even if the download is still in progress. Try doing *that* with QuickTIme!

Streaming. VLC will play back streaming media as well as files on your Mac. Go to **File ➤ Open Network** and enter the URL you want to stream, click Open, and enjoy your streaming media.

Discs. VLC will play CDs, VCDs, DVDs, and VIDEO_TS folders you've copied from DVDs (for more on that, see Ripping DVDs later in this chapter). Use **File ➤ Open Disc**.

Playlist services. VLC has a playlist area that appears when you click the Playlist button on the bottom right of the VLC Media Player window. What's really interesting is that you can add sources for audio and video media to that playlist area by using **File ➤ Services Discovery**. In that menu, you'll find My Videos and My Music (pointing to ~/Movies and ~/Music, respectively), Free Music Charts, Freebox TV, Icecast Directory (a huge list of free streaming music stations), and more. Some of this is obviously yours, and some of this comes from other people, but it makes it easy to mix and match stuff you know with new things as well.

Save streams and files. You can save the stream or file you're viewing or hearing. When you open a source, look at the bottom of the window and check the box next to Streaming/Saving and then click the Settings button, which will show you a window like that in Figure 10–3.

Don't take care of File first; instead, select an Encapsulation Method (I suggest MP4, which means your file name better end in MP4) and *then* choose File and select a place and file name for saving. If you set the Encapsulation Method first, VLC will automatically enter the extension (MP4, AVI, and so on) for you when you specify the File.

For Transcoding Options, check Video and Audio and try the following for each:

- **Video:** Choose H264, enter 1024 for Bitrate, and leave Scale at 1.

- **Audio:** Choose MP4A, enter 128 for Bitrate, and set Channels to 2.

Click OK and VLC should save your streamed file. If something doesn't work, mess around with the Settings you chose—for instance, try Ogg for the Encapsulation Method, Theo for Video, and Vorb for Audio.

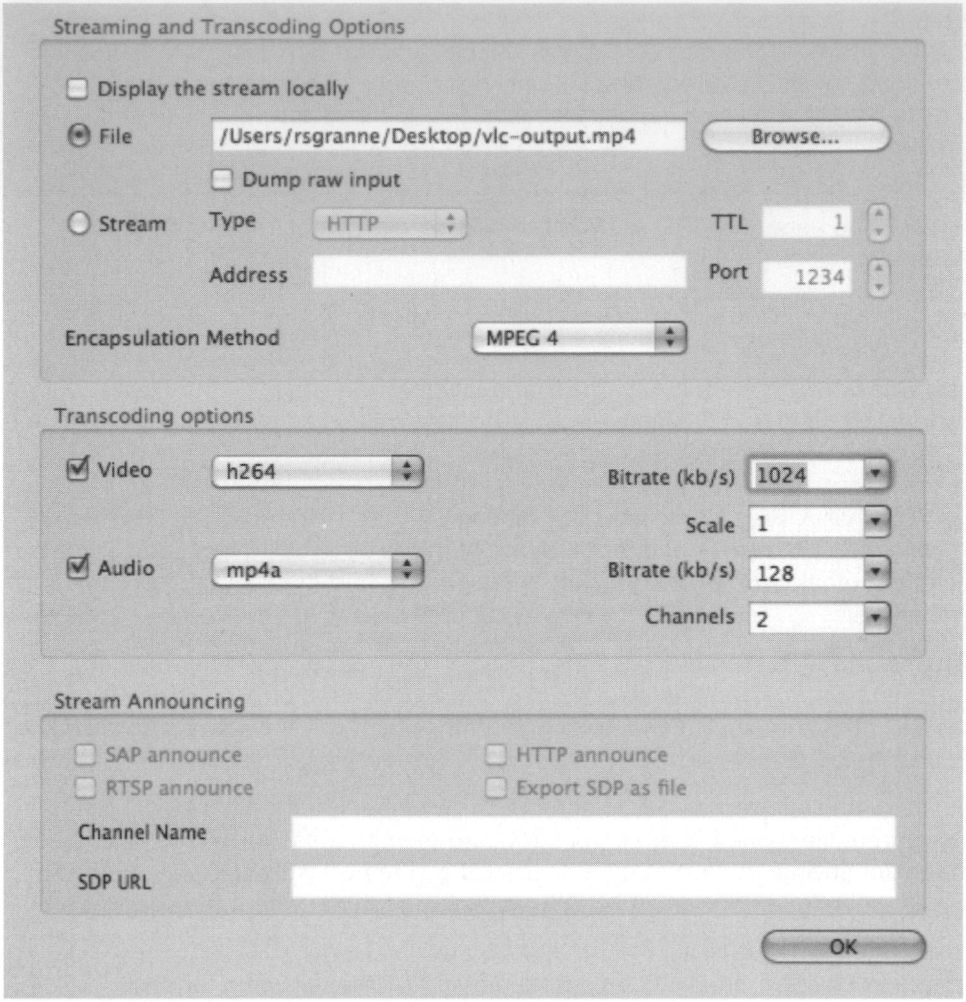

Figure 10–3. *Settings for saving files and streams in VLC.*

Screenshots. VLC will take screenshots of the videos you're watching—even if you're watching a DVD. Go into **Preferences ➤ Video**, and in the Video Snapshots section, set the Folder in which you want the screenshots to go (I usually just use the Desktop). Set a Prefix or use the default, check the box next to Sequential Numbering if you plan to take a lot, and set the format—either PNG or JPG. Click Save to close Preferences, and when you want to save an image of your movie, use **Video ➤ Snapshot**.

Video effects. You can have fun with your videos while you watch them. During playback, use **Window ➤ Extended Controls**. You can then check boxes next to Wave, Gradient, Blue, and Ripple, for instance, to produce some really weird effects on-the-fly, while the video is playing. For example, Wave is in Figure 10–4. See if you can identify the TV show.

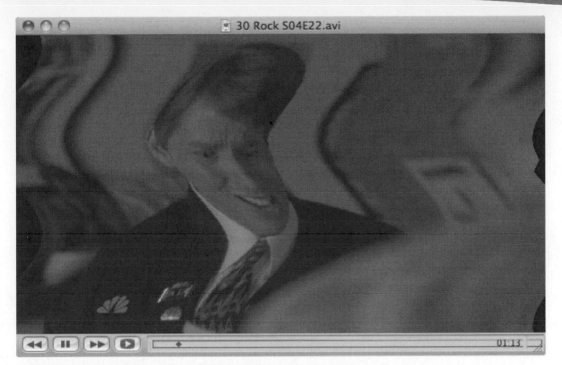

Figure 10–4. *Is this something you'll do all the time? I should hope not!*

Key commands. VLC provides key commands for almost every aspect of the program. Unfortunately, some of them are hardly standard to Mac users. ⌘-N to Open Network, for instance? ⌘-P for Play? Not good. That annoyance aside, you can also set and change key commands in VLC's Preferences, on the Hotkeys tab.

Prefs for Prefs. Speaking of Preferences, VLC provides two ways to view them: Basic and All. Look at the bottom left of the Preferences window, and you'll see that you can toggle between a simpler view and a far more complex one.

Skins? One feature not available on Mac OS X but available on other platforms: skins. You can change how VLC looks if you use Windows or Linux, but not if you use a Mac. That should change with the final release of Lunettes, however.

Advanced Features

As you can see, there are a lot of cool things that VLC can do. If you poke around the VLC wiki at http://wiki.videolan.org, however, you'll find that the app can do some pretty advanced tasks.

NOTE: VLC can do a lot of advanced things, but that doesn't mean it should be your first choice for those tasks. For instance, VLC will record screencasts, but I'd still use a tool designed for that task, such as ScreenFlow or even QuickTime Player X, and it will rip DVDs, but I'd use the tools I'll discuss later in this chapter. So why cover this stuff? Because it gives you an idea about just how powerful and versatile VLC is, and it's also good to have in a pinch, so if you need to rip a DVD or record a screencast and your only tool is VLC, you can still get the job done.

Record Screencasts. You can record simple screencasts with VLC by using **File ➤ Open Capture Device**. From the pick list, select Screen, and for Frames Per Second, enter something reasonable, like 5 (if you need a sharper video, enter 10, but you're also going to have a larger file). Now the fun part—what to enter in for the Subscreen options. In typical nerd fashion, these are jargon-y terms that basically set how much of your screen that VLC will record. If you leave all four at 0, your entire screen will be recorded, which may be fine. But if you need a smaller area, here's how you set it:

- **Subscreen Left:** The top left corner of the box in which VLC will record, measured from the left side of your screen

- **Subscreen Width:** The width of the box in which VLC will record, starting from the Subscreen Left value

- **Subscreen Top:** The top left corner of the box in which VLC will record, measured from the top of your screen

- **Subscreen Height:** The height of the box in which VLC will record, starting from the Subscreen Left value

If you want to record an 800x600 pixel area of your screen, starting about 200 pixels from the left and about 20 pixels from the top (so you exclude the Menu Bar), you'd enter these numbers:

- **Subscreen Left:** 200

- **Subscreen Width:** 800

- **Subscreen Top:** 21

- **Subscreen Height:** 600

If you want to record an area that's a set size (again, 800x600, say), but move that area around your screen as you do things, check the box next to Follow The Mouse, and VLC will do just that as it records.

Once you've set up VLC to record the properly sized area of your Mac's screen, click Open and the recording immediately starts. To stop it, click the Pause button on VLC. It would be nice if setting the recording area was a bit easier, but remember that VLC started life as a command-line program, and still exists very much as one. The only way to specify an area for recording via the command line is with the Subscreen values, so that's what you have to use until some developer creates a nice GUI that lets you draw an area on your screen and then maps it to them. I just wish VLC used clearer terminology!

Rip DVDs. Use File ➤ Open Disc to open your DVD, paying close attention to the number next to Title. Your job is to find what Title number corresponds to the part of the DVD you want to rip. You could increment it by 1 and click Open until you find it, which will possibly take forever, or you could just be lazy and first open the DVD in Apple's DVD Player, find the part you want to play in the DVD's menu and start playing it, and then open Go ➤ Title and see which number has a check next to it. Much easier! Enter that number back in Title, check the box next to Streaming/Saving, and click Settings.

Earlier in this section, I discussed this same screen in regard to saving files and streams you view. It's the same principle: set your Encapsulation Method, select File and Browse to where you want the ripped file to go, then decide Video and Audio Transcoding Options. Click OK to close these options, and then Open to close the Open Source window and begin the rip. Sometime later, your video will be ready.

> **TIP:** It's very cool that you can do this with VLC, but it's a lot easier to use the tools I discuss later in Ripping DVDs. Still, it could be very handy to know that VLC will do the job, and in fact, some of the tools I'll cover in Ripping DVDs actually use VLC on the backend!

Convert video. It's pretty easy to convert videos using VLC (if you think about it, that's really what you're doing when you rip a DVD). Go to File ➤ Advanced Open File and select the file you wish to convert. Check the box next to Streaming/Saving, click Settings, and enter your choices (it's the same screen we've previously covered). When you've made your choices, click OK and then click Open, and VLC will convert your video.

Or it will crash, apparently for no reason. I tried converting a video I took with my iPhone (MP4 container, using H.264 AVC video and AAC audio codecs) to OGG, AVI, and several other containers/codecs, and VLC immediately crashed every time. Other videos worked just fine, however. Weird.

There are other advanced things that VLC will do, but this should give you a taste. For more, go read the VLC wiki, at http://wiki.videolan.org.

MPlayer OSX Extended

In the open source world, there are two big video players: VLC and MPlayer. Both work on the Mac, although the back-story of MPlayer is a bit more complicated.

The MPlayer project began in 2000, and it's since expanded to encompass a large project that supports MPlayer on several operating systems, including several you've never heard of. In actuality, MPlayer is a command-line program; no matter the OS, the GUI is built on top of that CLI app. In the case of Mac OS X, you have several to choose from, but in reality, there's only one you should pursue: MPlayer OSX Extended. It's the "official" one supported by the MPlayer project, and it really is the most full-featured of your options, with continual development.

The main website for the free MPlayer OSX Extended is at http://mplayerosx.sttz.ch, but if you go to the official website for the MPlayer project, at http://www.mplayerhq.hu, you can read more about it. Just make sure that you're downloading MPlayer OSX Extended, shown playing a video in Figure 10–5, and not any other version of MPlayer.

Figure 10–5. *Yours truly interviewed on a local TV news segment.*

MPlayer supports a huge number of containers and codecs, including (but not limited to!) the following:

- **Containers:** AVI, ASF, FLV, Matroska, MOV, MP4, Ogg, RealMedia

- **Video codecs:** H.264/MPEG-4 AVC, MPEG-1, MPEG-2, MPEG-4 Part 2, RealVideo, Sorenson, Ogg Theora, WMV

- **Audio codecs:** AAC, ALAC, FLAC, MP3, RealAudio, Shorten, Ogg Vorbis, WMA

Not to mention that MPlayer also handles subtitles, images, and streaming over the Internet as well!

NOTE: For the full, complicated, crazily long list of codecs and their status in MPlayer, see www.mplayerhq.hu/DOCS/codecs-status.html. Warning: unless you are a codec-head, you will probably not understand much of this page.

MPlayer is nice, but it's not a program I recommend over VLC; instead, I break it out only for those files that neither QuickTime Player nor VLC will play. Why not use it above VLC? First, I think VLC works more often with more videos. Second, more software on the Mac uses VLC to do some sort of work—such as Handbrake, discussed later in this chapter, ad Miro, found in Chapter 6, for instance—so it seems to have wider support in Mac-land. Third, I've found that MPlayer is quite a bit flakier than VLC. Opening short videos sometimes takes *minutes*, and there's no apparent reason for that.

And fourth, although the main interface of MPlayer is pretty usable, its preferences are pretty geeky. Really, really geeky in that way that only certain open source apps can be (and I speak as an open source lover!). For instance, in **General ➤ Default Lanuages** [sic], it tells you to "Enter your preferred languages in the order you want them selected as either two or three letter ISO codes or using their names." Wow. Would most users have the foggiest what that meant? Nope.

So MPlayer is not a day-to-day tool I use, but it's nice to have it in your arsenal when you just have to watch the funny video of a monkey doing something funny.

Cog

iTunes is nice, but sometimes you just want to play some music without having to put it in a library. In fact, that's my situation at work—I have a hard drive there with a copy of all my music on it (all 750 GB of it), neatly organized in folders, and plugged in to my MacBook Pro. I don't want to use iTunes to listen to all that music, as I already have iTunes set up with its own small library, and I just don't need all the complexity and overhead that iTunes brings. But I want to listen to music. My solution? Cog, shown in Figure 10–6.

Cog is a free, open source music player available from http://cogx.org. It is incredibly easy to use, and it supports these formats out of the box: MP3, Ogg Vorbis, FLAC, Musepack, Monkeys Audio, Shorten, WavPack, AAC, Apple Lossless, WAV, and AIFF.

If you ever used Winamp on Windows, or are even familiar with that style of player, you'll have no problem using Cog (if you haven't used Winamp, check out http://en.wikipedia.org/wiki/Winamp to see what I'm talking about). Using Cog couldn't be easier: simply drag the songs you want to hear into Cog, or use the standard **File ➤ Open** dialog box to select the songs. Click Play, and you're listening to your tunes.

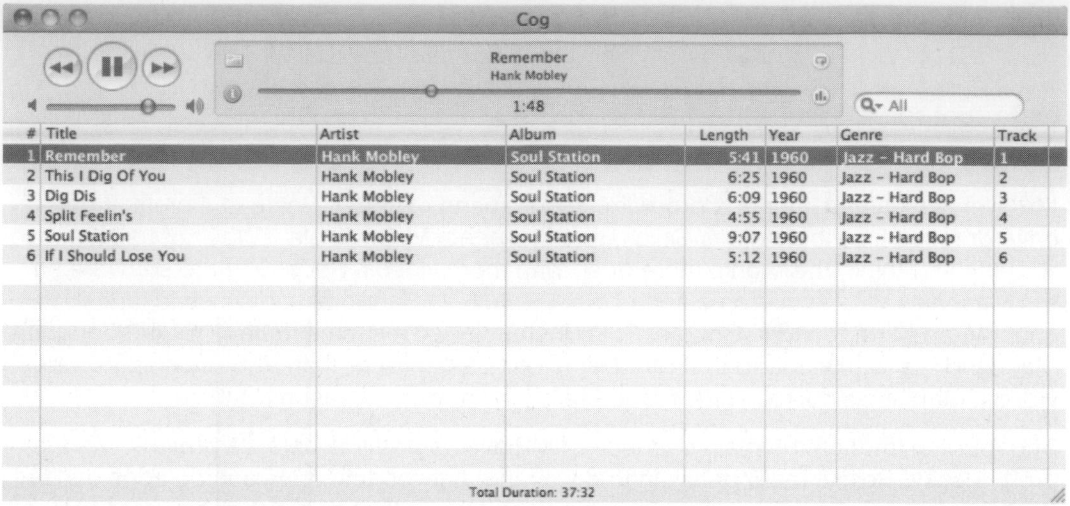

Figure 10–6. *Cog, a simple music player that just … plays … music. Crazy!*

You can do all the typical things you'd expect with a music player:

- Jump to the Previous and Next tracks.
- Filter the list of songs.
- Shuffle and repeat your playlist.

Cog has some interesting features in its Preferences, including:

- **Preferences ➤ Remote ➤ Enable Remote Control:** Want to use your Apple Remote with Cog? Check this box.

- **Preferences ➤ Last.fm ➤ Enable Last.fm Support:** If you want Last.fm (a social networking service focused on music) to know about the songs you listen to, check this box. Needless to say, you need to have the Last.fm app installed.

Cog isn't the most sophisticated program in the world. It's a simple app that does a great job playing music—and that's just fine. If you don't need everything that iTunes brings to the table, then give Cog a whirl.

Further Resources

There are of course other alternatives to QuickTime and iTunes, but I only have room for a few and I wanted to focus on the well-known and interesting ones. That said, here are a few others you might want to look into:

Amazon MP3 Store. Not really a competitor to iTunes the software, this is more a competitor to the iTunes Music Store. As nice as the iTunes Store is, you can buy millions of albums and songs through the Amazon MP3 Store, available at www.amazon.com/MP3. Amazon uses the MP3 format (duh!) without any DRM, and encoded at a great-sounding 256 kilobits-per-second variable bitrate. To download the music you buy, you'll need the free Amazon MP3 Music Downloader, available at www.amazon.com/gp/dmusic/help/amd.html. Check the website out—Amazon provides a great selection at very good prices. To be honest, I use it far more than I've ever used the iTunes Store.

Songbird. When I tried Songbird a few years ago, it stunk. Now it's quite good in many ways. Basically a GUI that combines Firefox, VLC, and the SQLite database, this open source software, shown in Figure 10–7, is a great music player and manager. You can get it at www.getsongbird.com.

Figure 10–7. *Songbird sure looks like a darker version of a very popular music player from Apple.*

If you let it, Songbird will happily sync its library with iTunes' (in both directions!), which is very convenient, and it also supports a nice variety of extensions, with these installed as defaults:

- **Last.fm:** Publishes songs you play to Last.fm, a social networking site for music

- **mashTape:** Find out more about the music and musicians you're listening to

- **Concerts:** Keep track of tours and tickets

- **7digital Music Store:** Buy music encoded as 320 kbps MP3s—no DRM

- **LyricMaster:** Lyrics

- **Gracenote:** Look up info about your CDs

- **QuickTime Playback:** Listen to FairPlay-protected files you bought from the iTunes Store

Other nice features include tabs (so you can play music in one tab while you look up info in another and buy music from Amazon's MP3 Store in another), integrated lyrics and art, support for open source formats such as Ogg and FLAC, and powerful playlist creation tools.

However, there are negatives, and some are substantial.

- No CD ripping in the current version (it's in the Mac beta), and even when it will be there, you will only be able to rip to Ogg, FLAC, and WMA. No MP3, as that costs too much to license. Note that none of those formats play on the iPod, which makes it pretty much useless for most folks.

- Not the most Mac-like looking app. Still, it's not ugly, at least to my eyes.

- It can be a bit complex, since it has a lot of Firefox under it. There are a lot of features that are completely based on the fact that Songbird is in many ways a web browser for media as much as a music player.

- Songbird will work with some iPods, but not all of them by any means, and not with the iPhone or iPod Touch (see http://wiki.songbirdnest.com/Docs/Device_Support/IPod_Device_Su pport for more info).

Still, it's free, so give it a spin—you might find that the substantial positives outweigh the negatives. Speaking for myself, support for lyrics and other metadata, as well as built-in access to the Amazon MP3 Store makes Songbird definitely worth playing with.

Vox. A simple music player in the vein of Cog (as you can see in Figure 10–8) that plays a wide variety of formats and also comes with effects, extensive audiophile preferences, and even exporting to AAC, ALAC, and WAV. My only complaint—it doesn't show a playlist and there appears to be no playlist editor. You just choose songs and it plays them. Available for free at www.voxapp.uni.cc.

Figure 10–8. *Vox is a music player. That's it. No library, no videos. Just music.*

With all these options—all of them free, by the way—you have no excuse. If you're annoyed in any way by QuickTime Player or iTunes, try something else! Heck, try all of them and use the ones that work with you. I do, and many others do as well.

Converting & Manipulating Movies

It's nice that so many different media players on Mac OS X support so many different formats, but sometimes you need a video or song to be in a particular format because that's what a device supports. Or maybe you just want a sense of consistency. Several years ago, I went through my huge video collection and converted everything to MP4 and its associated codecs so it would all work with QuickTime. It took a lot of time, but I'm glad I did it.

In this section, I'm going to introduce you to several tools that convert videos (music is coming up) between different containers and codecs. While we're at it, I'm also going to talk about some software that can manipulate movies as well, allowing you to do things such as rotate, edit, and flip what you want to watch.

TIP: Don't forget that VLC, which I just discussed in the previous section, can convert videos for you, too. And so can Handbrake, which I'm going to cover in the next section, on ripping DVDs. Lots of the software programs in this chapter do lots of different things, but some are easier to use or better than others.

FFmpeg & its Many Descendents

When it comes to conversion programs, virtually all of the ones I'm covering in this chapter are based in some way on FFmpeg. FFmpeg is a cross-platform, open source project encompassing many powerful tools, libraries, and programs that enable you to convert and manipulate audio and video files. The website of the project is http://ffmpeg.org, and it contains all that you need to know about the software...

...which is going to frustrate most Mac users, because it turns out that FFmpeg is a command-line app! If you want to be really hardcore about this, then by all means, go right ahead and install it and use it. It's obviously exactly what you need for scripts, and it does work great in its natural element. It's just not exactly easy or quick to get going.

The best instructions are Stephen Jungels' "Installing and using FFmpeg on Mac OS X," at http://stephenjungels.com/jungels.net/articles/ffmpeg-howto.html. They're linked to from FFmpeg's documentation page, at http://ffmpeg.org/documentation.html, and they are about as clear as you can get. Just keep in mind that often he tells you to download a specific file, and a newer one may very well have appeared since his directions were written in 2009, so you'll need to find those yourself.

Once you have FFmpeg installed and working, head to FFmpeg Documentation for information about how to use the program. You can also use Google to find examples and tips from users. Eventually, though, you're going to find yourself using commands like this one:

```
$ ffmpeg -i original.mpg -vcodec mpeg4 -s 640x480 -b 300k -r 10 -acodec mp3 -ar 22050 -
ab 64k -f avi new.avi
```

What that does and how it works I'll leave as an exercise to my readers. However, it's not really that complicated. If you're comfortable with the command line, you shouldn't have too much trouble with FFmpeg.

That said, there are also GUIs that make FFmpeg a whole heck of a lot easier to use. Much as I love the command line—as I've mentioned, I wrote a book about it—I still like using GUIs when they make my life easier.

One of the most popular GUIs is ffmpegX, an oldie but goodie that unfortunately hasn't been updated since 2008. The developer explains that he's busy, but that doesn't change the fact that it's been several years since the program was updated, and in that time new tools have appeared. Still, ffmpegX is free to try at http://ffmpegx.com, so give it a spin (you're supposed to pay $15 to register it, but I'm not sure the program ever times out). You can see it in Figure 10–9.

Figure 10–9. *ffmpegX was revolutionary for its time, but has its time passed?*

To really use it, though, you're going to have to install some codecs the program needs, and the instructions for doing so have proven hellishly complex for many people. You can read the official steps at http://ffmpegx.com/download.html, but users at VersionTracker have explained things well at www.versiontracker.com/dyn/moreinfo/macosx/15473&mode=feedback, so check that one out too.

OK, so what about some that are in active development?

VisualHub & Its Children

Another program that was really just a nice shell for FFmpeg—but oh what a shell it was!—VisualHub was a great, and popular, Mac app for converting videos to different formats. It was $24, and I was happy to pay it, because VisualHub just worked. It could translate between wide numbers of formats, or you could instead choose a device (iPod,

Apple TV, and so on) to target. And on top of that, it had a comprehensible UI that was actually kind of fun, as you can see in Figure 10–10.

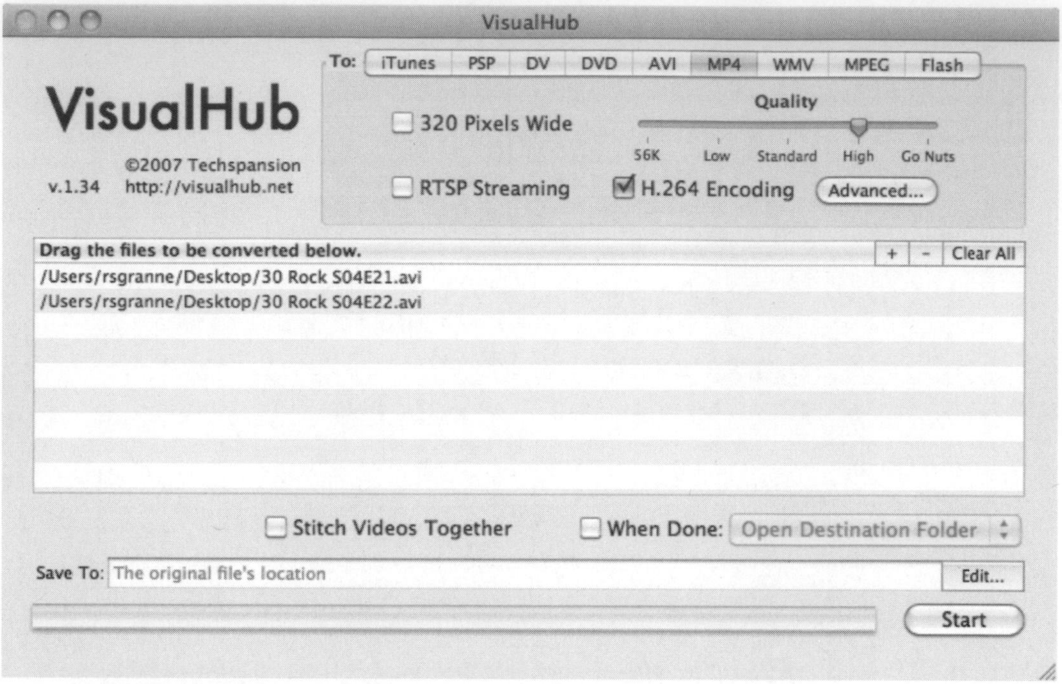

Figure 10–10. *VisualHub was easy to use, with a nice UI.*

I used it constantly.

And then Techspansion, the company behind VisualHub, killed it "for personal reasons," according to the website (www.techspansion.com). As a consolation prize, the code was open sourced. So why am I telling you about VisualHub? Well, if you look around online, you can still find copies of the program. But more importantly, the successors to VisualHub live on, so if you can't get the original, you'll have to use one of the apps based on it.

At this time, these are all the successors to VisualHub that are available today that I know of:

- **FilmRedux:** Source code that was going to be VisualHub 2.0 before it was killed. If you're a coder or you want to try compiling your own stuff, get it at http://transcoderredux.svn.sourceforge.net/viewvc/transcoderredux/FilmRedux/.

- **VideoMonkey:** A free app you can download from http://videomonkey.org, but at this time—and after years of development—it still only targets Apple devices, not formats, as you can see in Figure 10–11.

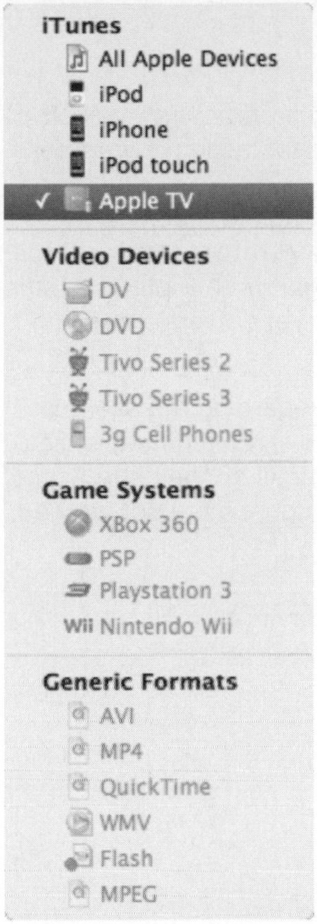

iTunes
- 🎵 All Apple Devices
- ▪ iPod
- 📱 iPhone
- 📱 iPod touch
- ✓ 📺 Apple TV

Video Devices
- 📹 DV
- 💿 DVD
- 📺 Tivo Series 2
- 📺 Tivo Series 3
- 📱 3g Cell Phones

Game Systems
- 🎮 XBox 360
- ▭ PSP
- ▱ Playstation 3
- Wii Nintendo Wii

Generic Formats
- AVI
- MP4
- QuickTime
- WMV
- Flash
- MPEG

Figure 10–11. *VideoMonkey still has a long way to go, but what is there works.*

- ■ **ReduxEncoder:** Another free program, available from `http://blog.easelnet.net/category/reduxencoder/` (scroll to the very bottom to see the downloads), and also limited, but also supporting more than VideoMonkey: DVD, AVI, MP4, and WMV. ReduxEncoder is much further along than VideoMonkey in every way, so it's the one to use. Add videos, make your choices, and go. It's really easy, and it works very well.

It's too bad that VisualHub shuffled off this mortal coil, but the fact that it's open source now and that there are successors to it is a heartening sign. Let's just hope that ReduxEncoder keeps improving going forward, so we're not stranded again.

Evom

In the next big section, on ripping DVDs, I'll talk about a fantastic program called RipIt. The company that makes it, The Little App Factory, also makes a fantastic program for converting videos called Evom, which you can get at http://thelittleappfactory.com/evom/. Like the others I've mentioned, Evom is basically a GUI wrapper for FFmpeg (it puts the library it uses at ~/Library/Application Support/Evom/ffmpeg), but it's the best I've seen. As you'll see again with RipIt, The Little App Factory specializes in software that is incredibly easy to use yet powerful, and Evom fits that description well.

Right now Evom is free, and I've seen contradictory information regarding the eventual direction The Little App Factory is going with Evom. Some say it will remain free, while others claim that it will eventually cost some money. Given the prices of The Little App Factory's other software, I can't imagine it will be very much, though, so I'm not worried.

Evom starts with a super-simple UI, as you can see in Figure 10–12.

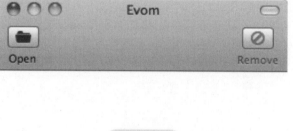

Drop movies, folders, or movie links.

Figure 10–12. *Now what do I need to do? Oh yeah! There it is!*

After you drop videos onto Evom, a window opens that asks you, Where Do You Want To Send The Video? Your choices are:

- **iTunes:** Convert to a format that works in iTunes and adds it to an Evom playlist. If you want, save just the audio as an MP3.

- **iPod:** Same as iTunes, but for the iPod.

- **Apple TV:** Same as iTunes, but without the audio-only option.

- **YouTube:** Convert to a format that works on YouTube and then upload it to the service. You first have to enter in your YouTube account info, of course, and you have to fill in the usual YouTube metadata: Title, Description, Category, and whether or not you want it to be Private.

- **Folder:** Shown in Figure 10–13, this is a straight video conversion that let's you pick the Title, Location, Format (AVI, FLV, HTML5, OGG, OGV, MOV, MP3, MP4, MPG, or WMV), and Quality (Low, Medium, or High).

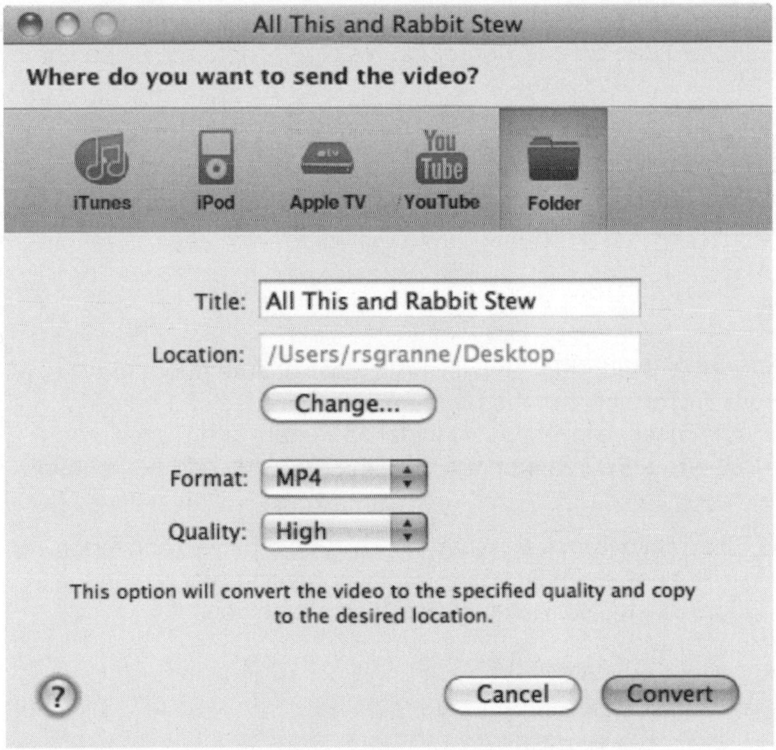

Figure 10–13. *Simple controls make converting videos a simple task.*

Make your choice, click Convert, and a little bit later you're done. As easy as pie!

> **NOTE:** Interestingly, if you select HTML5 as a Format, you actually end up with two new videos, one ending with MP4 and one with OGV. This reflects the fragmentation of the HTML5 video standard, which doesn't specify which format is to be used (see `http://en.wikipedia.org/wiki/HTML5_video` for background). As a result, some browser makers (Firefox, Google, Opera) support Ogg Theora as a format, while others (Apple, Microsoft, Google again) support MP4. Recently, however, Google announced a new format—WebM—that it, Firefox, and Opera will support, so it will be interesting to see what Evom will do about that. Will choosing HTML5 result in *three* videos? We'll see.

As nice as Evom is, it's still in beta, so some things don't yet work well. For instance, Evom supposedly lets you download and convert YouTube videos by simply clicking a bookmarklet. However, I couldn't find the bookmarklet anywhere on The Little App Factory's website (c'mon, guys), and when I finally found it at `www.marklets.com/Bookmarklets/Evom+Convert+.aspx`, it never worked for me. Evom would say that it couldn't find a video on that web page. No biggie, actually, since I grab my YouTube videos using other methods, but still.

Even though Evom isn't fully baked, it looks fantastic. I'm excited to use it, because it's simple and it just works. Granted, it doesn't give you detailed control over the conversion, but most people don't need that. For the vast majority of folks who want to convert videos, it's going to be a perfect fit.

MPEG Streamclip

The most popular format for downloaded TV shows is AVI (I'm not sure about movies, as I never download movies via BitTorrent), but the problem is that iTunes can't "see" AVI files. Try to drag AVI files into iTunes, even if you've installed Perian, and iTunes won't see the files and won't add them. MPEG Streamclip fixes the problem, and boy oh boy does it work!

Download the free MPEG Streamclip from `www.squared5.com`. It's a player, converter, and editor, and to be honest, it's not the most aesthetically appealing program in the world, as you can see in Figure 10–14. But don't let that discourage you.

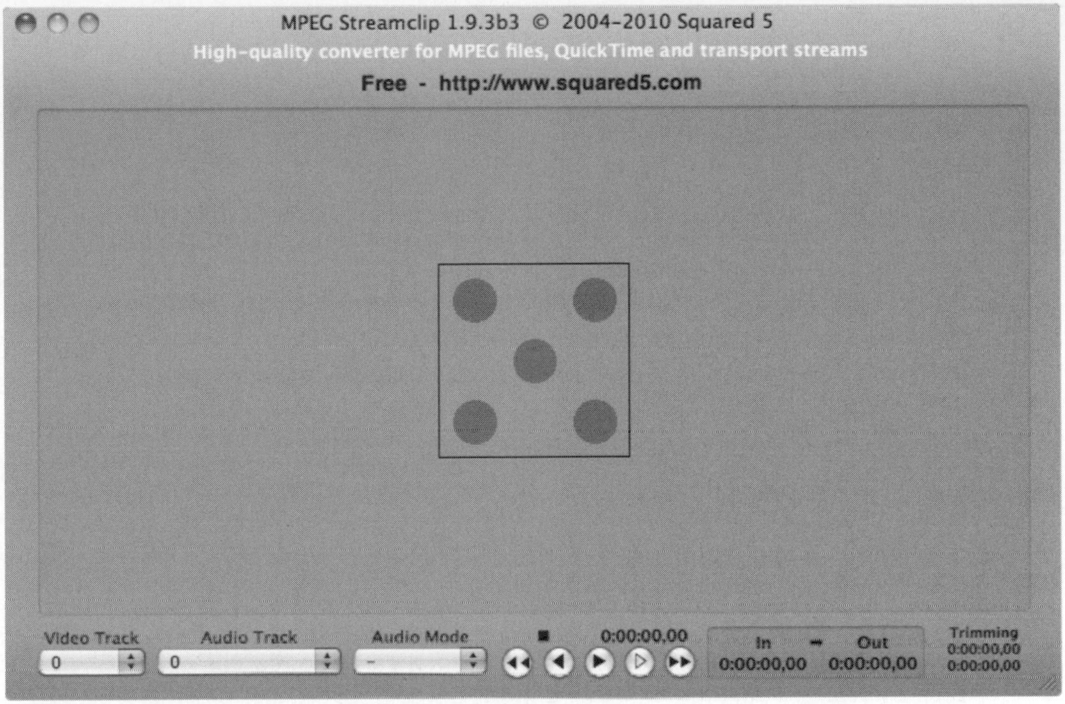

Figure 10–14. *When you first open MPEG Streamclip it isn't what you'd call an eye-catcher.*

The list of input formats it supports is impressive: MPEG, VOB, PS, M2P, MOD, VRO, DAT, MOV, DV, AVI, MP4, TS, M2T, MMV, REC, VID, AUD, AVR, VDR, PVR, TP0, TOD, M2V, M1V, MPV, AIFF, M1A, MP2, MPA, and AC3 (I have no idea what several of those are!). You can export to a smaller number of formats, with QuickTime MOV, DV, AVI, and MP4 preferred, but if you want you can select others as well, including Windows Media. In addition, you can also pick a device to target, such as iPod, iPhone, and Apple TV.

NOTE: To work with some of those formats, you need third-party software. If you go to MPEG Streamclip's web page for Macs, at `http://www.squared5.com/svideo/mpeg-streamclip-mac.html`, it lists that software in the Requirements section.

The list of things you can do with MPEG Streamclip is long; here are a few of them, in no particular order:

- Download YouTube videos: Go to File ➤ Open URL and type in the web page at YouTube. Choose Download (or Open if you just want to view it in MPEG Streamclip), choose a format (HD, MP4, or FLV), and click the Download button.

- Set In and Out points (Edit ➤ Select In and Edit ➤ Select Out) and then trim the video (Edit ➤ Trim).

- Jump to various points in the video, including Keyframe, Time, In, and Out (all through the Edit menu).

- Rotate the video, either clockwise or counter-clockwise (again, through the Edit menu).

- Remove the audio track (**Edit ➤ Delete Audio Track**) or save just the video (**File ➤ Save Track ➤ Save Video Track**) or just the audio (**File ➤ Save Track ➤ Save Audio Track**).

- Find out what codecs are being used for the audio and video (**File ➤ Show Stream Info**).

- Join two or more videos, or selections from videos, with Cut, Copy, and Paste.

That's all cool, but here's the thing that really makes MPEG Streamclip a contender: support for mass conversions. Yep, that's right. Let's say you have a folder full of videos in the AVI format that you want to convert to MP4. Go to **List ➤ Batch List** and click Add Files when the Batch List window appears. Select the files you want to add and click the To Batch button. When you do, a wizard will walk you through several screens on which you can make your choices:

- **Please Choose A Task:** You can select from a variety of subtasks, all based on four main master tasks: Export, Save, Convert, and Demux. In this case, we want to select Save As (I'll explain why in a moment) and then click OK.

- **Select The Destination Folder:** Where do you want your newly converted videos to go? I like to put 'em right back in the same folder as the originals and then delete the old ones. Click Select.

- **Please Choose The File Format:** I said I wanted to do a Save As, and now I tell MPEG Streamclip what I want to save them as. I'd like to use MP4, but I usually end up selecting MOV because MP4 doesn't work with the TV shows I download (AVIs encoded with XviD for video and MP3 for audio—why it doesn't work with those, I dunno). You have a few other choices, if MP4 and MOV don't do it for you. Click OK.

At this point, the Batch List window shows my chosen files and what I'm going to do to them, as you can see in Figure 10–15.

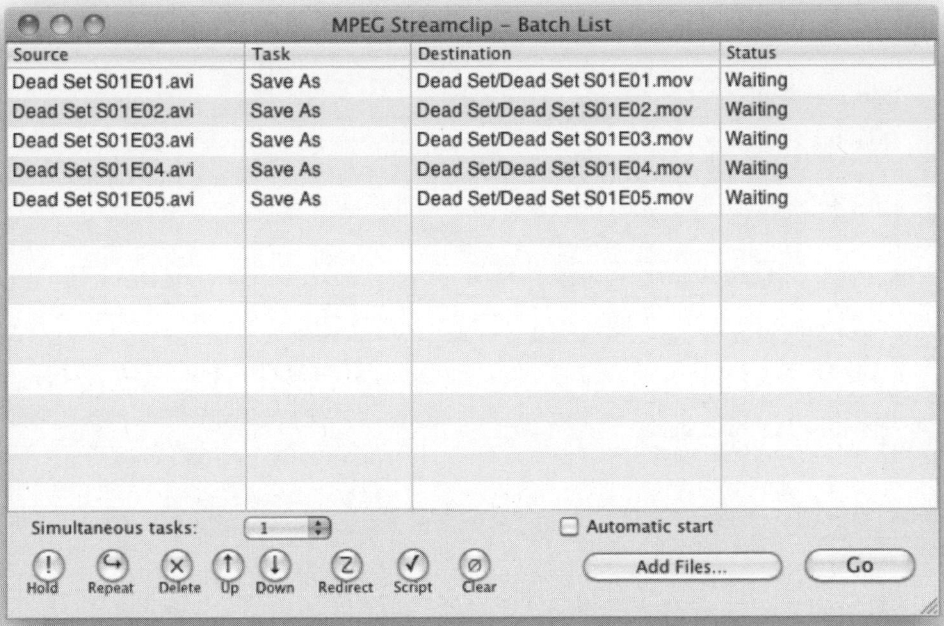

Figure 10–15. *MPEG Streamclip's Batch List function is ready to run.*

If you want to add other files for the mass conversion, repeat as necessary with other folders of videos. When you're finally ready, simply click Go. A while later, depending upon how many movies you're changing, MPEG will be done. Check out your new videos to make sure they work, and then get rid of the old versions.

Now, why did I use Save As instead of Convert? One simple reason: speed. Save As simply changes the container but doesn't do anything to the codecs, so it's pretty fast—about 2 minutes for a 30-minute TV show. As long as I could play the original file using QuickTime, I'll be able to play the newly saved file as well. It's a matter of QuickTime's ability to handle the codecs inside the container, which I take care of with Perian and the other codec packs I talked about at the beginning of this chapter.

If you want to actually convert the container and codecs, you can easily do so. Instead of selecting Save As, choose Export to MPEG-4. You'll have to make a lot of decisions about the codecs, as you can see in Figure 10–16:

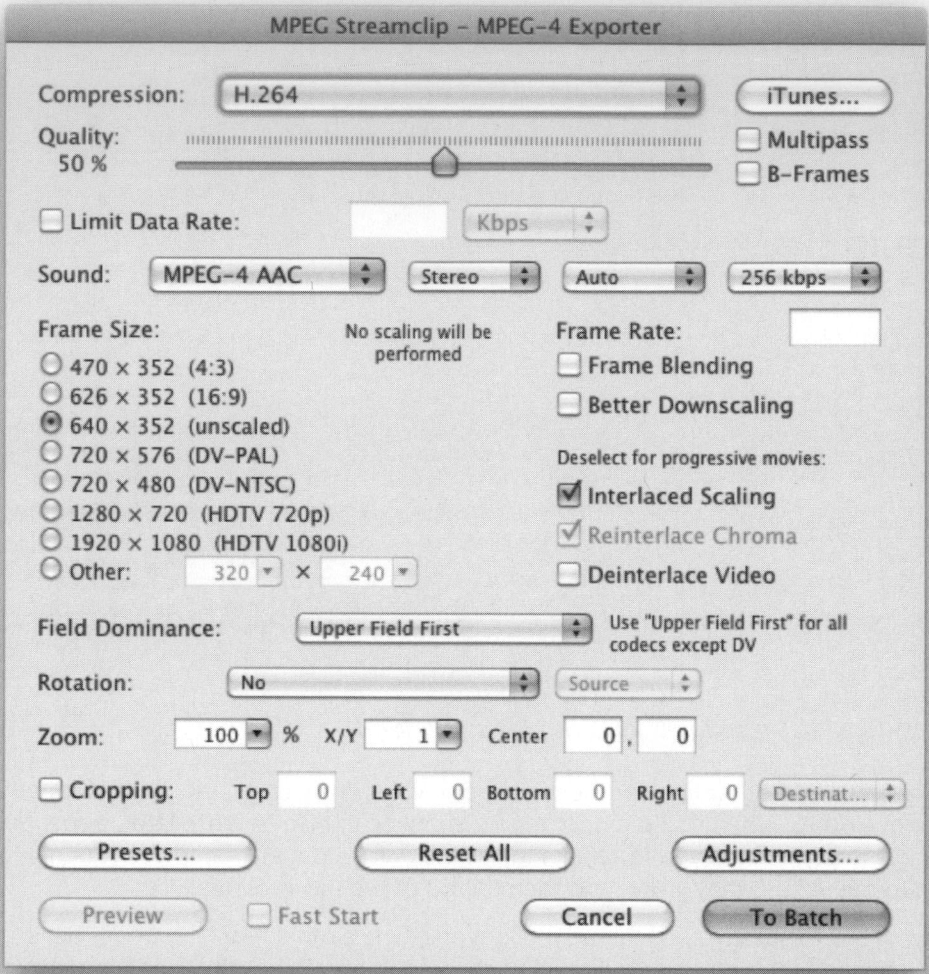

Figure 10–16. *It looks a bit complicated, and it can be.*

Fortunately, the defaults should be fine most times, with these changes:

- You'll probably want to dial the sound down on the last drop-down from 256 kbps to something more like 128 kbps, which is the usual rate. 256 is just not necessary for most TV.

- For video Compression Quality, pick something between 60% and 80%. Anything lower will look bad, and anything higher just increases your file size without bringing much benefit in quality.

For anything else on the screen shown in Figure 10–16, I encourage you to click on the buttons and to read MPEG Streamclip's documentation, located at **Help ➤ MPEG Streamclip Guide**. It's actually quite informative!

When you first open it, MPEG Streamclip doesn't look like much, but trust me, once you start messing around with it, I think you'll be pretty impressed. It's really a nice piece of work, and it comes highly recommended.

Ripping DVDs

Yes, the MPAA and its stooges in the copyright-maximalist lobby have succeeded in basically making it illegal to copy a DVD. But I cry foul to that—if I want to rip a DVD I own so that my toddler can't destroy it, or so that I have a backup, and the law says that it's illegal to do so, then the law is wrong. My fair use rights (see http://en.wikipedia.org/wiki/Fair_use) and my right to control the things I've purchased trumps bad law.

So I'm *not* telling you to go nuts copying DVDs and distributing them over the Internet. That's not cool, and it's also dangerous—you can get sued or disconnected by your ISP, and neither would be fun. But if you want to rip DVDs you already own for backup purposes, or simply because it's more convenient to watch them as part of a digital library, I say, go for it.

You have two ways you can rip a DVD:

1. Rip the DVD as a complete copy of the entire DVD. This preserves all the extras, which is the good part. Unfortunately, the rip will be the same size as the original DVD—roughly 4 or 8 GB, which is a lot of space, even with today's enormous hard drives—and it will also preserve all the annoyances, like the stuff you can't skip past and the region codes that limit which DVD players will play which DVDs (http://en.wikipedia.org/wiki/DVD_region_code).

2. Rip selected parts of the DVD as converted video files. In other words, the movie ends up as a 1.5 GB MP4 file, and a featurette about the filming of the movie becomes a 400 MB MP4 file. You don't have a complete copy of the DVD, but you end up with the stuff you care about, in a format that video players and media centers understand. And you certainly take up less space on your hard drive. Oh, and there's nothing you have to wait for (FBI warning, trailers) and no region codes. The quality isn't as high as that of the DVD, but you can change the settings on your ripper to get pretty close, and frankly, I never notice much of a difference.

Here's the small detail, though—even if you want to only do the second method, you may very well still want to do step one first, and then convert from the ripped DVD. Why?

■ Speed. It's often faster to rip selections from a big file on your hard drive than it is to rip those same selections from an actual DVD.

■ Efficiency. You can copy all of your DVDs bim bam boom, and then rip them later, making things more efficient.

■ Reliability. Copying the DVD first and then ripping selections from it can be more stable and successful than attempting a straight rip of selections.

But if you usually do your ripping overnight while you sleep, it really doesn't matter if it takes extra time, so you can skip the first method and proceed directly to the second, especially if you're seeing good success with your rips.

In this section, I'm going to look at two software packages: RipIt (http://thelittleappfactory.com/ripit/) and Handbrake (http://handbrake.fr). RipIt copies the entire DVD to your hard drive, while Handbrake converts selected chapters from the DVD to MP4 files, so they serve different purposes. Of course, as I've explained, you can first use RipIt and then point Handbrake at the copied DVD that RipIt has created, a method I use quite often. No matter which method you use, both RipIt and Handbrake are excellent at what they do.

> **NOTE:** You may have noticed that I haven't said a word about ripping Blu-Ray discs. That's because right now there is no good or easy way to rip Blu-Ray discs on Macs, a major reason I haven't gotten into Blu-Ray (well, there's also having to buy a Blu-Ray player and discs and the fact that DVDs are "good enough"). If you absolutely want to rip Blu-Ray discs, your best bet is to get a Windows machine and buy a copy of AnyDVD for about $80 at www.slysoft.com/en/anydvdhd.html. Yup, it's expensive, but it works, and they keep on top of the latest Blu-Ray shenanigans.

RipIt

Mac users that have been around a while may wonder why I'm not going to examine MacTheRipper, a program that copies DVDs like RipIt. The basic version of MacTheRipper is free, while RipIt costs $19 (a pittance for what it does, in my book). Here's why I recommend RipIt over MacTheRipper:

■ RipIt is about the simplest program you've ever seen on a Mac. Insert DVD, watch as RipIt does its job, and then it's finished. That's it. MacTheRipper is far more complex.

■ MacTheRipper isn't the most stable program in the world. RipIt has been nothing but stable.

- MacTheRipper is free, but that's for an old version of the software (2.6.6). The current version is 4.x; to get that, you need to send a "gift" to the project, and then the developer e-mails you a copy of the program. Yes, you read that right. That "gift" also gets you access to the developer's forums; no "gift," no access.

- MacTheRipper isn't nearly as good about recognizing and successfully ripping DVDs as RipIt is. RipIt has, according to their website, successfully ripped over 250,000 unique DVDs, with a success rate of 99.9999%. If you run into a DVD that doesn't work with MacTheRipper, you get to head to the forums (which, remember, you have to pay to access!); if a DVD doesn't work with RipIt, report it to the developers, and they'll figure out how to make it work (in fact, on their website, they promise "If a DVD doesn't work, we'll buy it ourselves and fix it as soon as possible." Wow!).

- Development on MacTheRipper is sporadic at best and the developer often disappears, and on top of that, the forums (which you had to pay to access, remember) are not friendly at all. RipIt is constantly improved and support is much more helpful and friendly. Oh, and you don't need to pay to access RipIt's forums.

For all these reasons, I recommend you avoid MacTheRipper and proceed to RipIt.

Open RipIt and there's just about the simplest interface ever, as you can see in Figure 10–17.

Figure 10–17. *Well, it doesn't get much easier or more obvious than that!*

Put a DVD in, and you now have a whopping three buttons to choose from, as Figure 10–18 shows.

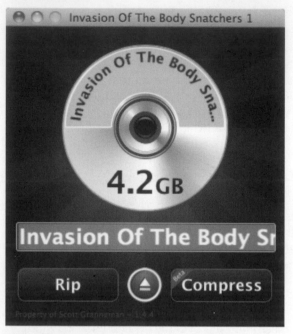

Figure 10–18. *Rip, Eject, or Compress. Still simple!*

Before you actually start ripping, I recommend you make a few small changes in RipIt's Preferences.

On the General tab, I went ahead and checked every single box. By default, When A Disc Is Inserted, Start Ripping isn't checked, and neither is When A Rip Completes, Eject The Disc. Both of those made sense to me, so I checked them. Also, by default RipIt inserts its rips into the ~/Movies folder, but I wanted them to go onto the Desktop, since I immediately convert them via Handbrake and then delete them, so I changed it.

You'll also notice a Compress tab in Preferences, and you may have noticed a Compress button in Figure 10–18. The idea behind Compress is that RipIt will eventually do the same thing that Handbrake does: create an MP4 file from the video. At this time, however your options with Compress are very limited and it's still very much in beta, so I don't recommend using it and instead sticking with Handbrake (in fact, RipIt is really just using Handbrake's command-line interface to do the job!). That said, things may change in the future, so keep an eye out on RipIt's website.

Close the Preferences, and now Figure 10–18 makes a bit more sense. Click Rip, and a little bit later (around 45 minutes or so, depending upon the speed of your Mac), you'll have a file named Name Of Your Movie.dvdmedia sitting where you told RipIt to put it. You can open that file with your Mac's DVD Player (or any other DVD player software, for that matter) or point Handbrake at it and rip selected portions of it to MP4 files. If you want to get to the VIDEO_TS folder that contains the meat of the DVD, just right-click on the dvdmedia file and choose Show Package Contents (that's right—a dvdmedia file is really a folder that appears as a file to the Finder).

That's really about it for RipIt. If you find that you use RipIt a lot, I highly recommend you make opening it the default action when you insert a DVD. To do so, go to > **System Preferences > CDs & DVDs**. Next to When You Insert a Video DVD, select Open Other Application and then choose RipIt. As I mentioned, RipIt is only $19, and this seems like a bargain to me, since I rip a lot of movies. Even if I didn't, knowing that I can copy a DVD quickly, easily, and hassle-free makes it worth it.

HandBrake

As cool as RipIt is, you'll still be left with a complete copy of the DVD (sure, the Compress feature could eventually fix that, but it's not there right now, so I'm not going to act like it is). Immediately after copying a DVD with RipIt, I open Handbrake (available for free at `http://handbrake.fr`) to convert selected chapters of the DVD to more usable, portable MP4 files, so that's what I'm going to focus on in this section.

> **TIP:** Handbrake can also convert video files between selected formats, but, as much as I love Handbrake, I've never found that it's particularly great at that task. Oh, it'll do it, but I've experienced crashes and failures, so I use the tools I mentioned earlier in Converting and Manipulating Movies, instead. My brother, however, reports that Handbrake encodes videos perfectly for his iPod Touch, so maybe it's me. So give it a try with Handbrake—if it works well for you, great!

Where RipIt is super-duper simple, Handbrake is far more complex, with a gazillion options and choices you can make to tweak your video files exactly the way you want them, as you can see in Figure 10–19.

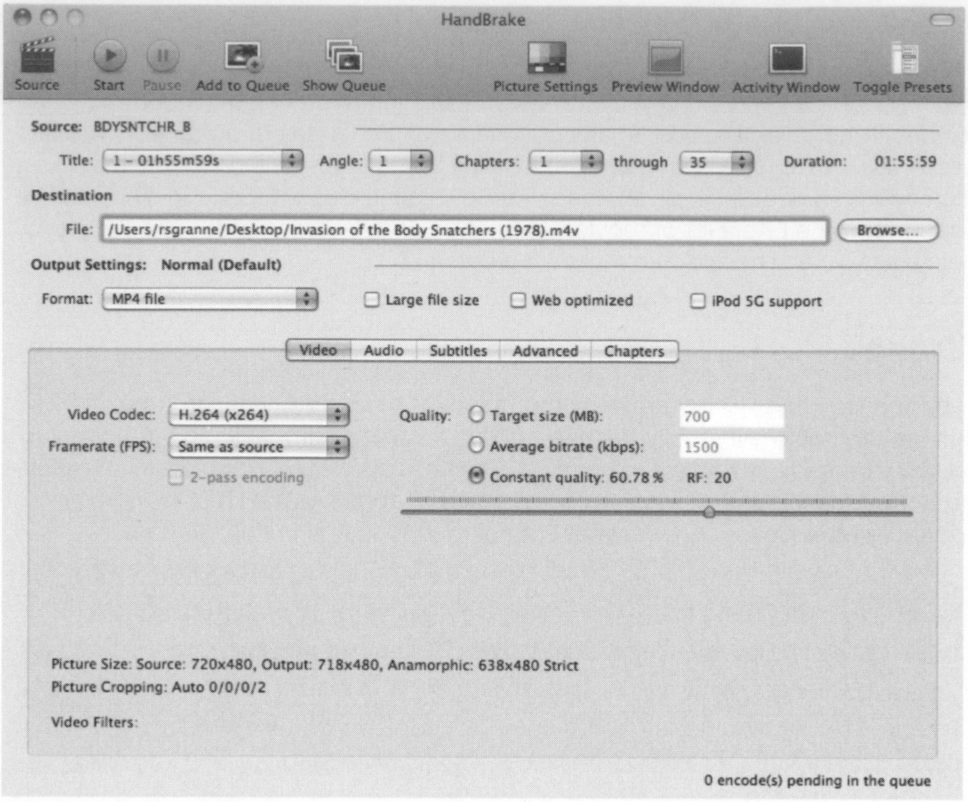

Figure 10–19. *Handbrake looks complex, but there are shortcuts that make it a lot easier.*

Fortunately for those of us not trained in the minutiae of video formats and encoding, Handbrake comes with a set of preset options that are more than satisfactory for most folks; if you don't see them, click the Toggle Presets button to see the drawer slide out on the right:

- Apple

  - **Universal:** Full resolution settings for all current Apple devices, both computers and portable devices

  - **iPod:** Low resolution and small file size

  - **iPhone & iPod Touch:** Same as above, but for these devices

  - **AppleTV:** Includes Dolby Digital 5.1 AC3 sound for better audio on TVs and stereos

- Regular

  - **Normal:** Just fine for most people, with H.264 video and AAC audio

- **High Profile:** Described by Handbrake's devs as H.264 video and AAC audio, but "with automated filtering and all the H.264 bells and whistles"

- Legacy: don't use any of these

    - Classic

    - AppleTV Legacy

    - iPhone Legacy

    - iPod Legacy

If you don't like any of those presets, you can create your own (click the + at the bottom of the Presets drawer and go to town), and if you like a preset but want to tweak it, you can do that as well (select a preset, tweak it, and then click + at the bottom of the Presets drawer to give it a name and save it). In either case, you can save the new preset and even make it the default using Make Default on the action menu at the bottom of the drawer.

> **TIP:** Handbrake features excellent tooltips that appear as you hover over the various options in the app. They're long and detailed, and usually contain enough information that, even if you still don't know what it means, you can look things up on Google to learn more.

Really, what you ought to do is try both the Normal and High Profile with the same DVD and see which one you prefer. In my case, I usually go with Normal, and I'm quite happy with the results. More than likely, you would be too.

There's a lot more to Handbrake, including:

- Queuing of conversions, which can be really helpful if you're trying to get several chapters on a disc.

- Subtitles, both burned in and available upon request (for more on this, look up "soft subtitles" on the Handbrake website).

- Live Preview lets you test your preset before you actually rip the movie; to use this feature, make your choices and then click on the Preview Window button to see how things will look.

- If scanning an entire DVD is hanging on a certain chapter (*Looney Tunes Golden Collection Volume 4*, I'm looking at you), you can instead open a particular chapter and bypass the troublesome scan. To do so, go to **File ➤ Open Source (Title Specific)** and make your choice there.

TIP: How do you know which chapter to open? Easy—open the DVD (or ripped DVD) in Apple's DVD Player, navigate to the part you want to rip, and click Play. Head to **Go ➤ Title** and see which chapter has the checkmark next to it—that's the one you want! Close DVD Player, go back to Handbrake, and open just that chapter.

Before I leave Handbrake, there's one very important gotcha you need to know—to use Handbrake, you have to have VLC on your Mac first, and you have to have opened VLC at least once before using Handbrake. Now, that doesn't sound too bad—VLC is a worthy program to have on your Mac, anyway—but it's a bit more complicated than that.

On its download page at `http://handbrake.fr/downloads.php`, Handbrake comes in two flavors: 32- and 64-bit. The 64-bit version is faster, but in order to use it, you need the 64-bit version of VLC (and, no surprise, to use the 32-bit version of Handbrake you need the 32-bit version of VLC). No problem, right? Not so fast.

Remember earlier in this chapter when I said that VLC is having difficulties finding Mac developers, so consequently things are a bit messy and disjointed now for the Mac VLC? One big result of that is that you're going to have to hunt for a 64-bit version of VLC—to find it, refer back to that earlier section.

With all of that 32- and 64-bit *mishegoss* going on, here are your choices:

- If you're the careful type, stick with 32-bit VLC and 32-bit Handbrake. You're good to go, but it's slower, and the future of Mac OS X is 64-bits, but for now you'll be fine.

- If you're the adventurous type, download the 64-bit nightly build and use that along with the 64-bit version of Handbrake. If the nightly of VLC is a bug farm, try another one until you get one that works. Most of the 64-bit versions I've played with have been fine, but to be honest, a few haven't. So be prepared to be flexible—maybe keep the old installer until you know the new one works!

- If you're the middle of the road type, you could do what I do: download the 32- and the 64-bit versions of VLC (crazy, I know!), but rename the 32-bit version VLC32.app before you put it in /Applications. Leave the 64-bit version as VLC.app and put it in /Applications too. Download the 64-bit version of Handbrake; when it starts, it will see VLC.app in /Applications and use that, but for regular video watching, fire up VLC32.app and use that instead. As the 64-bit nightly build matures, however, I'm growing more likely to just use that for everything and completely bag on the 32-bit version.

- Say "screw it" to the whole VLC thing and just use RipIt to copy the DVDs first, and then point Handbrake at the resulting .dvdmedia file. I don't recommend that, though. Really, just get VLC—it's a great program to have anyway, and more and more apps are depending upon it.

Regardless of the choice you make, Handbrake is a fantastic app that I use constantly, and if you want to rip DVDs into MP4s, you'll want to use it too. If you want to learn more about it, you can find out a wealth of info at http://trac.handbrake.fr, and the forums are at http://forum.handbrake.fr.

Further Resources

If RipIt and Handbrake aren't your cup of tea, then I'd urge you to check out Fairmount and its companion app, DVDRemaster. Fairmount is free at www.metakine.com/products/fairmount/; basically, it mounts a DVD free of copy protection so you can then drag the contents of the disc to your hard drive. DVDRemaster costs $40 or $50 (depending upon which version you pick) at http://www.metakine.com/products/dvdremaster/, and it does a lot of what Handbrake does. I find DVDRemaster to be a lot more confusing to use than Handbrake—not to mention that it costs a lot more than free—but it does work and it's a powerful program.

Editing, Converting, & Fixing Music & Audio

Several years ago, I went through my huge music collection and converted anything that wasn't MP3 to that format. Why? Consistency and device support. Everything in the world supports MP3 playback, and I grew tired of having to remember which software would play which formats I had. Now I don't have to think about it, which is much nicer.

When it came to ripping CDs, I just used iTunes, which does a great job. However, I was careful to go into the program's settings to tell it to use MP3 when ripping. To do that, go to Preferences ➤ General ➤ Import Settings and change the following:

- Import Using: MP3 Encoder
- Setting: Custom

In the resulting MP3 Encoder window, I recommend these settings:

- Stereo Bit Rate: 256 kbps
- Use Variable Bit Rate Encoding (VBR): Check this box
- Quality: High
- Sample Rate: Auto
- Channels: Auto
- Stereo Rate: Joint Stereo

- Smart Encoding Adjustments: Check this box
- Filter Frequences Below 10 Hz: Check this box

Click OK to close the MP3 Encoder window, OK to close the Import Settings window, and OK to close Preferences, and iTunes will now rip CD tracks into MP3 files at a very nice bitrate.

To get my music collection ready, I had to do more than convert everything to MP3. I also had to fix the metadata that MP3 files store—called ID3—which is then used by iTunes to display key information about each track, including (but not limited to):

- Artist name
- Track name
- Album name
- Track number
- Total number of tracks
- Year
- Genre
- Composer
- Comments

The tools I used to do all that will be covered in this chapter; amazingly, here's how many it took: two. That's right. Two. With just two pieces of software—Max and Media Rage—you can fix up your entire music library and whip it into prime shape for iTunes, or any other music player you choose. Let's learn how.

> **NOTE:** If you actually need to edit your music files for some reason—split long files into shorter ones, or trim off the ends or beginnings of songs, or do any other sort of surgery—then you need Audacity, a free, open source audio editing tool available at `http://audacity.sourceforge.net`. I'm not going to go much into Audacity here, since I wrote an entire book about it, along with the inventor of the software, Dominic Mazzoni: *Podcasting with Audacity: Creating a Podcast with Free Audio Software* (Prentice Hall, 2007; available solely as an ebook). Yes, there's a lot in it about podcasting, but the info about Audacity is good no matter what you're doing with it.

Max

Max is an audio conversion program (it's also a CD ripper, but I never use it for that—as I just said, I prefer iTunes for that). Available at `http://sbooth.org/Max/`, it's free and open source. It's not super-slick, but it works well.

After you install the program, you need to make a few settings before you can really use it. Open Preferences, and make changes on these tabs:

- **General ➤ Automatically Check For New Versions:** I recommend checking this. Why not?

- **Formats:** This is where you specify the various output formats you want to be available to Max. I only use one—256 VBR—but if you want more, you'll just need to repeat this process until you have all you want. Make sure you check any that you want to use, but keep in mind that *all* the ones that are checked will be used for conversions! To create a new format rule, click + and then do this:

  - **Encoder Quality:** Custom

  - **Encoder Target:** Bitrate

  - **Encoding Engine Quality:** High

  - **Stereo Mode:** Default

  - **Bitrate:** 256

  - **Restrict Encoder To Constant Bitrate:** Do not check this box, so that you have a variable instead of constant bitrate (for more on why this is good, see http://en.wikipedia.org/wiki/Variable_bitrate).

- **Output ➤ Output Files:** Try Same As Source File, but if you don't like that idea, select a folder on your hard drive instead.

- **iTunes ➤ Use iTunes Compatability Mode:** Check this box.

Once you've set up the Preferences, you're ready to convert. Let's say you have a folder of FLAC files and you want to convert them to MP3. Drag the folder of files into Max, and you should next see a list of files, as in Figure 10–20.

If you want to set the information in a song's ID3 tags, select it and click the Metadata button. Enter what you want and move on to the next song. If you want to set similar ID3 tags on several files (such as an album title), select the files, click Metadata, and make your changes.

When you're ready for Max to get to work, click Convert. Max is a fast program, so within a minute you should start seeing results.

And that's that. Max is a simple program to use, and it does a fantastic job. I think you'll be happy with it, especially when you're faced with folder after folder of songs you want to convert to a new format.

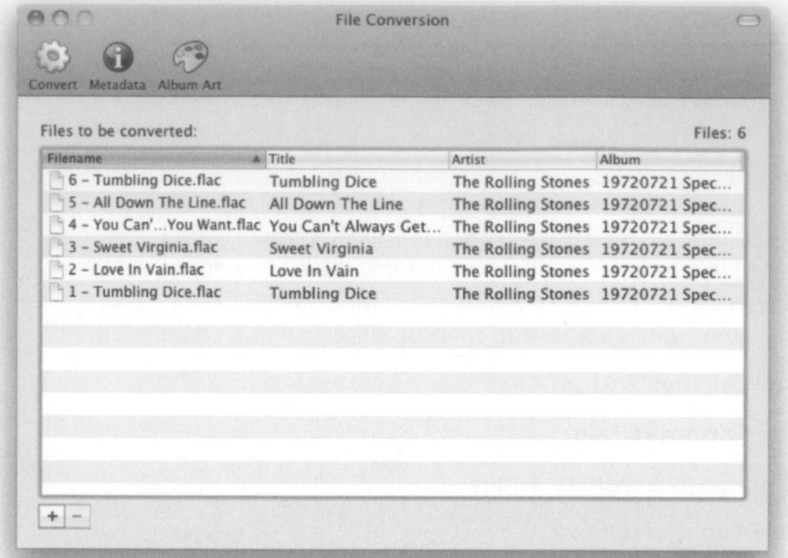

Figure 10–20. *A great concert available as FLAC files, ready to convert to MP3s.*

Media Rage

The best software I've ever used on any platform—Mac OS X, Windows, and Linux—for editing ID3 tags is easily Media Rage. It has every sort of tool you'd need to whip your ID3 tags into shape, quickly and efficiently. I've used it over 1,000 times, and it continues to be the only tool I'll use for fixing MP3 files so their metadata is 100% correct.

Download Media Rage at `www.chaoticsoftware.com/ProductPages/MediaRage.html`. You get a free trial, but after that you have to buy it for $30, which is more than reasonable based on my experience.

Media Rage works with audio files in these formats: AAC, Ogg Vorbis, FLAC, BWF, and MP3, of course. It also supports tagging metadata (artist, track name, album, and so on) in many different formats, which necessitates talking about ID3 for a moment.

> **NOTE:** In actuality, the only format that directly supports ID3 is MP3. Ogg Vorbis and FLAC don't actually support ID3; instead, they use Vorbis comments, which are not the same thing. AAC doesn't really support tagging, which is why AAC files are often wrapped in an MP4 container to become M4A (or MP4 Audio only) files, since MP4 does have a documented tagging standard. Here's a post comparing the different tag formats, which some of you might find interesting: `www.hydrogenaudio.org/forums/index.php?showtopic=29120&st=0&p=251686&#entry251686`. That said, Media Rage supports tagging for all of its supported formats, so just use it without worrying.

ID3 has been around since 1996, and it has gone through several versions, all of which work with Media Rage. However, that doesn't mean you want to support all of them.

- **ID3v1:** Avoid. Ancient and very limited.

- **ID3v2.2:** Avoid, as it's considered obsolete... yet it is the default format used by iTunes.

- **ID3v2.3:** The most widely used version of ID3. You can convert songs that are already in iTunes to 2.3 by right-clicking on them, selecting Convert ID3 Tags, checking the box next to ID3 Tag Version, and then selecting 2.3.

- **ID3v2.4:** The latest version of the ID3 standard (even it dates from 2000!). Supports UTF-8, so it handles non-Western characters perfectly. Unsupported by Windows Media Player (which is pathetic). You can convert songs that are already in iTunes to 2.4 by following the same procedure I just outlined.

So which should you use? If you rip CDs with iTunes, you're going to end up with ID3v2.2, which is considered obsolete, but if you convert them to ID3v2.4, your songs won't play in Windows Media Player, and who knows what else. My advice is to use ID3v2.3, which is easy to do with Media Rage.

> **NOTE:** For more than you ever wanted to know about ID3, see www.id3.org.

It's easy to take care of that while we're in Media Rage's Preferences. Go to the Miscellaneous screen, and for Use ___ Tags When None Specified, choose ID3v2.3.0. By the way, as for the rest of this screen, I don't have anything else checked, especially not Write Sync-Safe ID3v2.4, which has caused lots of folks problems in iTunes.

The only other thing I'd set on this tab is Custom Genres. Media Rage allows you to enter in a list of genres, separated by commas, which are then available to use throughout the program in drop-downs and text fields. You can enter your own list, but I've also provided one for you on my website, at www.granneman.com/personal/music/musicgenres.htm. It has 176 genres in the list, but feel free to change or delete whatever you want. Click OK to close Preferences. It's time to tag some songs!

When you start up Media Rage, you'll see the Dashboard, shown in Figure 10–21.

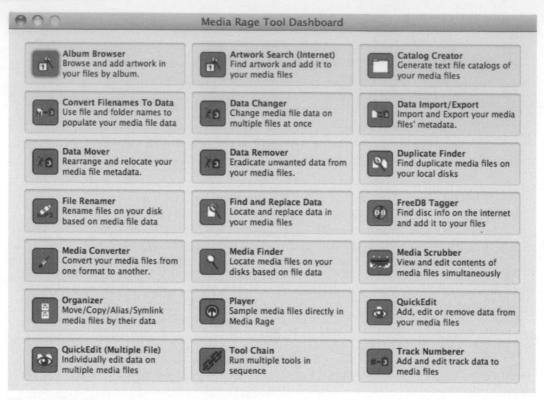

Figure 10–21. *These are the various tools that Media Rage provides you.*

As you can see, Media Rage consists of 21 different tools. I'm not going to go through all 21—Media Rage's Help does that for you, and many of them are obvious once you open them. Instead, I wanted to walk through an actual series of steps I'd use after downloading a torrent of a live concert by Bruce Springsteen and the E Street Band recorded on September 17, 1978.

After downloading the torrent, I have the following folders and files (I've hidden the text files that contain info about the recording, which Media Rage would ignore anyway):

```
$ cd Bruce\ Springsteen\ -\ 1978-09-17
$ ls -1
bs1/
bs2/
bs3/
$ ls -1 *
bs1:
Track01.mp3
Track02.mp3
Track03.mp3
Track04.mp3
Track05.mp3
Track06.mp3
Track07.mp3
Track08.mp3
```

```
Track09.mp3
Track10.mp3
bs2:
Track01.mp3
Track02.mp3
Track03.mp3
Track04.mp3
Track05.mp3
Track06.mp3
Track07.mp3
Track08.mp3
Track09.mp3
bs3:
Track01.mp3
Track02.mp3
Track03.mp3
Track04.mp3
Track05.mp3
Track06.mp3
```

Three folders inside the main Bruce Springsteen - 1978-09-17 folder, each with songs in it. OK, now I know the lay of the land, here are the steps I'd go through, based on the tools in Media Rage.

Track Numberer

The songs come in three different folders, and they're numbered starting at 1 in each folder. I don't like that; instead, I like to put all the songs into one folder and number them from 1 to whatever the last song is. To do that, it's time to break out the Track Numberer, shown in Figure 10–22.

To start with, I'll make sure the songs in bs1 are numbered correctly. I probably don't need to do this, but it can't hurt. I drag the folder bs1—not the files, but the actual folder—into the area under Folder Of Files To Change. Then, under Setup, I indicate how I want the numbering to be done; in this case, I want the second option: Sort Files In Folders By Name, And Then Renumber. In addition, I always like to check Show Changed Files In A Results Window, so I can verify what happens, and Update MP3 Tags To Version, so my ID3 tags are correct. I click Start.

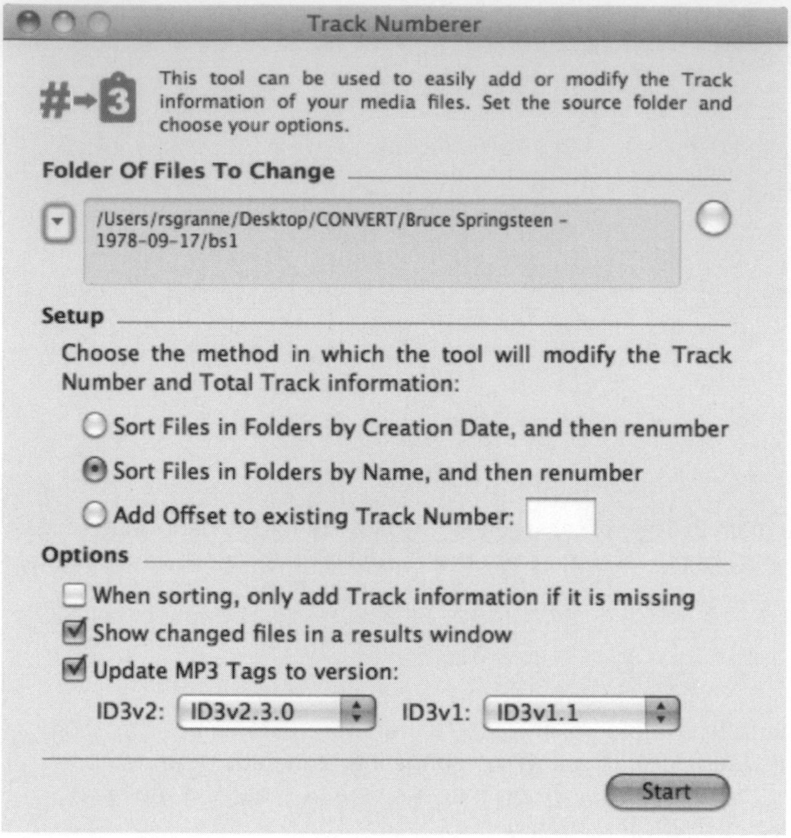

Figure 10–22. *You can use the Track Numberer in several different ways.*

A window opens like the one you can see in Figure 10–23.

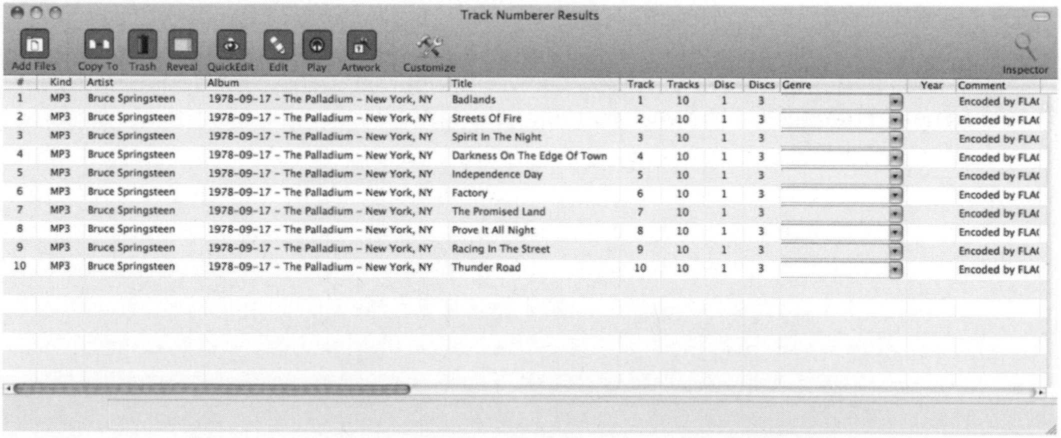

Figure 10–23. *1-10 of … 10? But what about the other songs? No worries—that can be fixed.*

The Track Numberer Results window shows me that yes, the files have been numbered (they very well could have been numbered correctly before I began, but by this point, they've been renumbered, so it doesn't matter), but there's a problem: the Tracks column says 10, as if there are only 10 tracks total on this album. In fact, if you count all the songs listed previously, there are 25 tracks total. Don't worry about it now, though, as I'll fix it shortly.

I close the Track Numberer window, but not before remembering that there were 10 tracks in the first folder. Now I drag bs2 onto Track Numberer, but this time, under Setup, I select Add Offset To Existing Track Number, and in the box after that I enter 10. When I click Start and the Track Numberer Results window appears, the Tracks column is now empty, while the songs have been given Track numbers 11 though 19, as the excerpt of the window in Figure 10–24 shows.

Title	Track	Tracks
Meeting Across The River	11	
Jungeland	12	
Kitty's Back	13	
Fire	14	
Candy's Room	15	
Because The Night	16	
Point Blank	17	
Not Fade Away	18	
She's The One	19	

Figure 10–24. *11–19 with nothing under Tracks. Now we're getting somewhere.*

I do the same thing with the third folder, bs3, that I did with the second, but this time I add an offset of 19, since that was the last number produced in the second folder. This time, the Results window shows me tracks numbered 20 through 25.

Now that my songs are all numbered correctly, I would normally move them all out of their individual folders—bs1, bs2, and bs3—and into the main enclosing folder, Bruce Springsteen - 1978-09-17. Even if the files themselves were out of order, it wouldn't matter, because the track numbers in the ID3 tags are correct, and I'm eventually going to rename the files. However, I can't do that with these files, because each folder contains a Track01.mp3, Track02.mp3, and so on, and I obviously can't have three files named Track01.mp3 in the same folder!

Media Scrubber

Now I'm done with Track Numberer and it's time to work on the rest of the metadata. I drag the Bruce Springsteen - 1978-09-17 folder onto Media Scrubber and it opens, displaying what's shown in Figure 10–25.

#	Kind	Artist	Album	Title	Track	Tracks	Disc	Discs	Genre	Year	Comment
1	MP3	Bruce Springsteen	1978-09-17 – The Palladium – New York, NY	Badlands	1	10	1	3			Encoded by
2	MP3	Bruce Springsteen	1978-09-17 – The Palladium – New York, NY	Streets Of Fire	2	10	1	3			Encoded by
3	MP3	Bruce Springsteen	1978-09-17 – The Palladium – New York, NY	Spirit In The Night	3	10	1	3			Encoded by
4	MP3	Bruce Springsteen	1978-09-17 – The Palladium – New York, NY	Darkness On The Edge Of Town	4	10	1	3			Encoded by
5	MP3	Bruce Springsteen	1978-09-17 – The Palladium – New York, NY	Independence Day	5	10	1	3			Encoded by
6	MP3	Bruce Springsteen	1978-09-17 – The Palladium – New York, NY	Factory	6	10	1	3			Encoded by
7	MP3	Bruce Springsteen	1978-09-17 – The Palladium – New York, NY	The Promised Land	7	10	1	3			Encoded by
8	MP3	Bruce Springsteen	1978-09-17 – The Palladium – New York, NY	Prove It All Night	8	10	1	3			Encoded by
9	MP3	Bruce Springsteen	1978-09-17 – The Palladium – New York, NY	Racing In The Street	9	10	1	3			Encoded by
10	MP3	Bruce Springsteen	1978-09-17 – The Palladium – New York, NY	Thunder Road	10	10	1	3			Encoded by
11	MP3	Bruce Springsteen	1978-09-17 – The Palladium – New York, NY	Meeting Across The River	11		2	3			Encoded by
12	MP3	Bruce Springsteen	1978-09-17 – The Palladium – New York, NY	Jungeland	12		2	3			Encoded by
13	MP3	Bruce Springsteen	1978-09-17 – The Palladium – New York, NY	Kitty's Back	13		2	3			Encoded by
14	MP3	Bruce Springsteen	1978-09-17 – The Palladium – New York, NY	Fire	14		2	3			Encoded by
15	MP3	Bruce Springsteen	1978-09-17 – The Palladium – New York, NY	Candy's Room	15		2	3			Encoded by
16	MP3	Bruce Springsteen	1978-09-17 – The Palladium – New York, NY	Because The Night	16		2	3			Encoded by

Figure 10–25. *The Media Scrubber, where you'll spend most of your time.*

The Media Scrubber allows you to fix up most of your songs' metadata, so you'll find yourself using it a lot. As you can see in Figure 10–25, we need to fix the following:

- **Artist:** It should be Bruce Springsteen & the E Street Band.

- **Album:** If it's a live bootleg, I like the title to be named with the date and then the location of the concert. In this case, I want it to be 19780917 The Palladium, NYC.

- **Tracks:** This should be 25, the real total number of tracks.

- **Disc and Discs:** I always combine multiple discs and folders into one, so it would be 1 Disc out of 1 Discs. For a long time, I would empty out Disc and Discs and just leave them blank, since it wasn't necessary, but then I realized that many times iTunes wouldn't group songs together correctly. When I began entering 1 for Disc and 1 for Discs, that issue went away. So that's what I need to enter here: 1 and 1.

- **Genre:** Click the drop-down menu, and my long list of custom genres appears first, and then a list of built-in genres. I put Bruce into Rock - Heartland (if you don't agree, see what AllMusic says at www.allmusic.com/cg/amg.dll?p=amg&opt1=1&sql=bruce+springsteen —and besides, it works for me).

- **Year:** 1978, of course.

- **Comment:** I make this blank generally. Sometimes I enter some info about a song—the names of contributors, for instance—but most of the time it's blank, so I need to empty out the stuff that's in there now.

That's my plan. How do I do it?

I go to **Edit ➤ Select All** so all the songs are chosen, and then I click Edit, bringing up a drawer that allows me to change up to four attributes at a time. I make four settings so the drawer looks like Figure 10–26, and click OK.

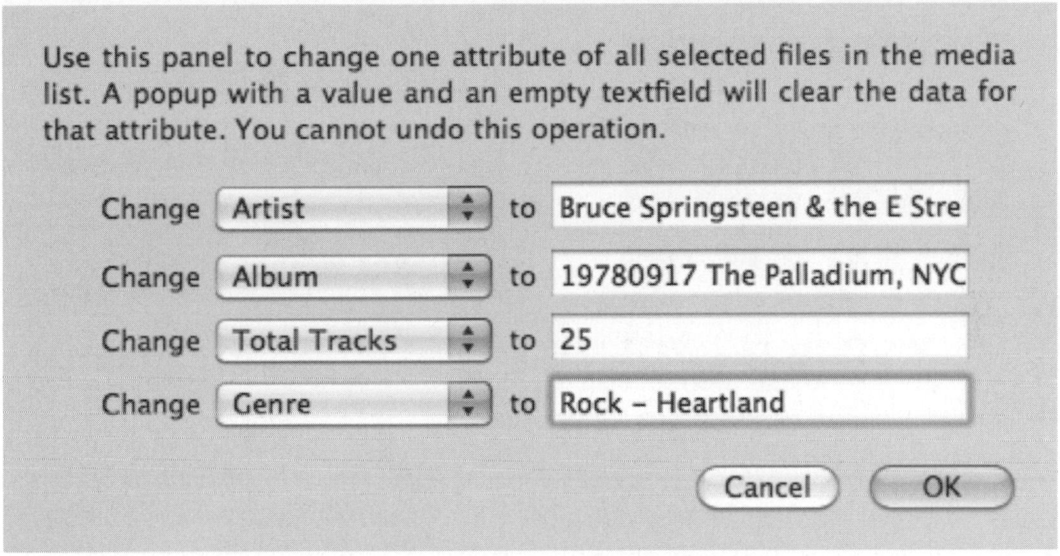

Use this panel to change one attribute of all selected files in the media list. A popup with a value and an empty textfield will clear the data for that attribute. You cannot undo this operation.

Change Artist to Bruce Springsteen & the E Stre

Change Album to 19780917 The Palladium, NYC

Change Total Tracks to 25

Change Genre to Rock – Heartland

Cancel   OK

Figure 10–26. *I can change up to four attributes at a time, which makes things much more efficient.*

A few seconds later, the Media Scrubber displays the changes I made. I then click Edit and repeat as necessary until I've made all of my changes.

Time to move on to album covers!

Artwork Search

If this was a commercially released album and not a bootleg, while I was in the Media Scrubber, I would clicked the Artwork button, and Media Rage would search Amazon.com and a few other sites for cover art. To show you what I'm talking about, let's assume I was instead using Media Rage with Bruce Springsteen's *Nebraska*, in which case you'd see the drawer in Figure 10–27.

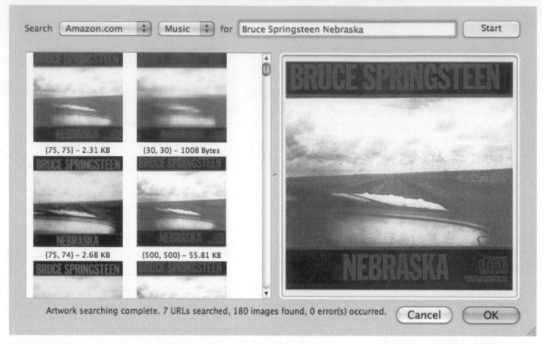

Figure 10–27. *I can pick a cover from a wide number of sizes.*

The Artwork drawer displays covers in a number of sizes, but you really shouldn't choose anything less than 300x300, with 500x500 optimal, and then click OK to apply it.

> **TIP:** I've noticed that apostrophes and other punctuation can screw the Artwork search up, resulting in no results at all. If that happens, click Stop, edit the textbox at the top of the Artwork drawer to remove punctuation, and then click Start to search again.

However, this is not a commercially released album. It's a boot, so Amazon and other websites Media Rage searches aren't going to have squat. If I'm really lucky, the torrent includes custom album art that you can use, but too often it doesn't (and also, too often the included album art is tiny, something like 200x200, which makes it useless). So instead, I search the Net for images of the artist or band in concert, and then I use that.

In the case of Bruce Springsteen, the Brucebase site at www.brucebase.org.uk has an index of virtually every concert he's ever played, along with pictures for a lot of them. Perfect! So I'll use that. I copy an image to my hard drive and then open the Artwork Search (Internet) tool from the Media Rage Dashboard. The main part of the window is for searching Amazon and other Internet sites, but if you look at the bottom of the window, you'll see a button labeled Add Artwork To Files. Click that, and a panel opens, as you can see in Figure 10–28.

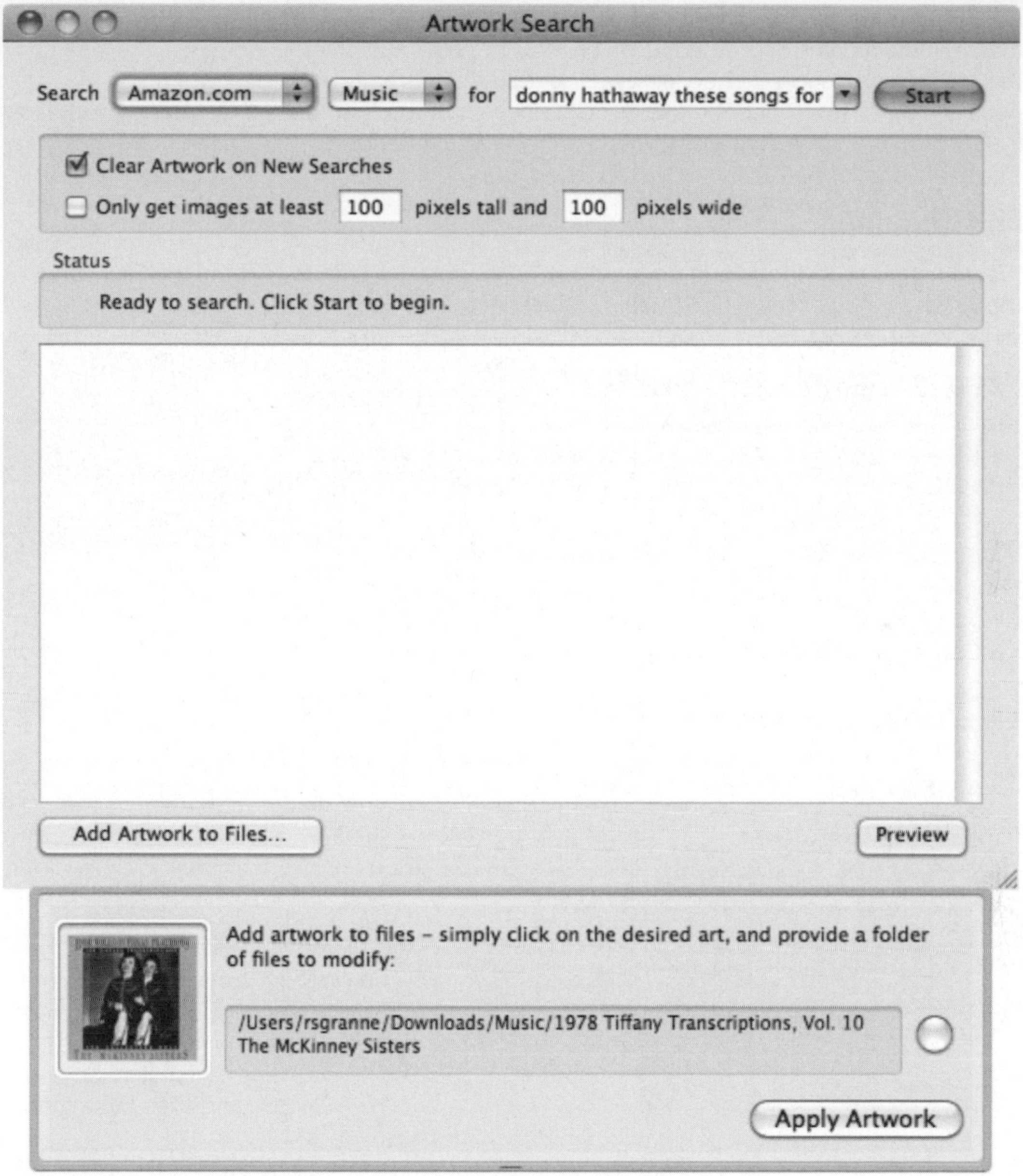

Figure 10–28. *All that you should care about is the panel at the bottom.*

By default, Artwork Search shows you the last folder I was working with, which is why you see the cover of a Bob Wills & the Texas Playboys album. Now, though, I drag the Bruce Springsteen - 1978-09-17 folder to the box that shows the path, and I drag the album cover I downloaded on top of the image you see in Figure 10–28.

Click Apply Artwork, and Media Rage actually adds the image to the music files themselves, as part of their data, which is what you want. Sure, it increases the size of the MP3s by a hundred or so kilobytes, but that's not really a big deal when you consider the cheap cost of massive hard drives and the fact that you're dealing with files that are several megabytes, so what's a few extra kilobytes?

File Renamer

We've fixed our ID3 tags and added artwork, so now it's time to rename the files. Drag the Bruce Springsteen - 1978-09-17 folder onto the File Renamer tool and the window you can see in Figure 10–29 opens.

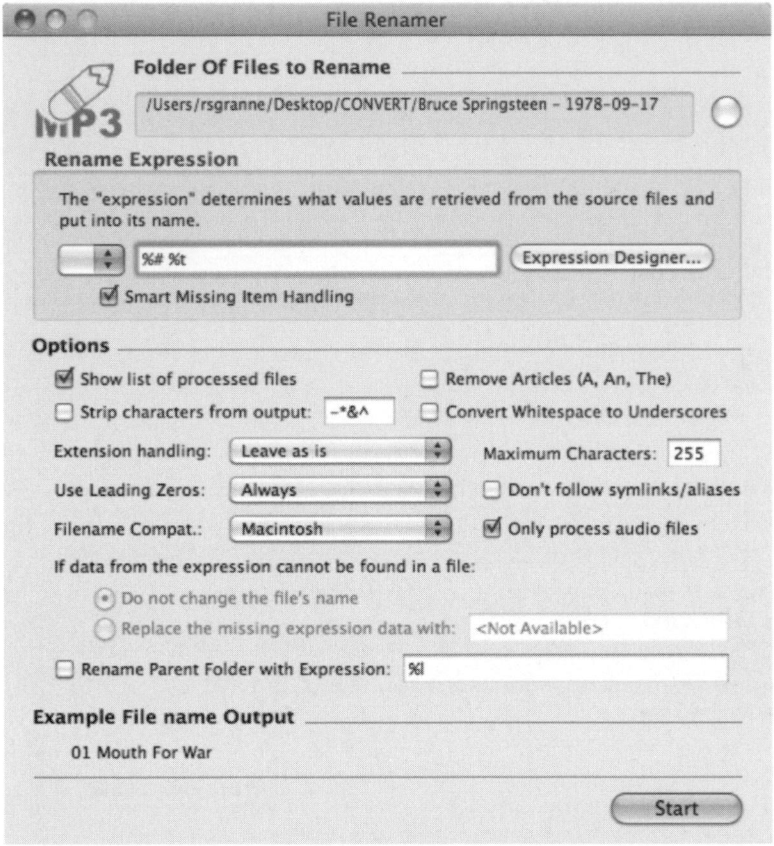

Figure 10–29. *You have a tremendous amount of flexibility naming your files.*

In the Rename Expression text field, you can see that it has %# %t in it; the result of that is at the bottom of the window, under Example File Name Output; given my Bruce Springsteen files, the result would be something like 01 Badlands. If you want something else, click the Expression Designer button and you can see the other codes; for instance, Album is %l and Year is %y. For punctuation marks like parentheses and hyphens, just type them in.

Click Start and Media Rage will rename your files according to your Rename Expression. Now that my files all have unique names, I drag the MP3s out of bs1, bs2, and bs3 into the containing Bruce Springsteen - 1978-09-17 folder and then delete those subfolders. I then rename the actual containing folder too so that it's now 19780917 The Palladium, NYC.

After having used Media Rage to fix up my MP3s, I have the following, which is quite a bit different than what I started with!

```
$ cd 19780917\ The\ Palladium\,\ NYC/
$ ls -1
01 Badlands.mp3
02 Streets Of Fire.mp3
03 Spirit In The Night.mp3
04 Darkness On The Edge Of Town.mp3
05 Independence Day.mp3
06 Factory.mp3
07 The Promised Land.mp3
08 Prove It All Night.mp3
09 Racing In The Street.mp3
10 Thunder Road.mp3
11 Meeting Across The River.mp3
12 Jungeland.mp3
13 Kitty's Back.mp3
14 Fire.mp3
15 Candy's Room.mp3
16 Because The Night.mp3
17 Point Blank.mp3
18 Not Fade Away.mp3
19 She's The One.mp3
20 Incident On 57th Street.mp3
21 Rosalita.mp3
22 Born To Run.mp3
23 Tenth Avenue Freeze-Out.mp3
24 Detroit Medley.mp3
25 Quarter To Three.mp3
```

It might look like the entire process took a long time, but it really doesn't. I can usually whip through a folder now in just a few minutes or so—and it makes a huge difference when it comes to finding, organizing, and enjoying your music in iTunes. I've covered some of the major tasks you'll do with Media Rage, but with 21 total tools, you can tell that there's plenty more left for you to discover.

Further Resources

A popular tool for tagging MP4 and other video files is MetaX; it's free and available at www.kerstetter.net/index.php/projects/software/metax. If you're interested in the nerdy details of exactly how MP4 files handle tagging, check out http://atomicparsley.sourceforge.net/mpeg-4files.html.

Danger, Will Robinson! Danger!

In this chapter, I've been delving into programs that you should be using, but before I leave this subject, I need to warn you about several you should **avoid at all costs**. They have names like these:

- Wondershare Video Converter Pro for Mac

- Aimersoft Video Converter for Mac

- Aiseesoft Video Converter for Mac

- Xilisoft Video Converter for Mac

- AppleMacSoft Video Converter

Notice a pattern (go look at the websites to see even more of a visual pattern)? Know why? They're all the same software, sold by the same company, using different front companies and names! And they're all ripoffs of FFmpeg, a fact the group has publicized on its Hall of Shame, at `http://ffmpeg.org/shame.html`.

So we have one company operating under at least 50 names, most of which you can read at "Hunting Blog-Spamming Scumbags," found at `http://oncallnerd.com/blog-spam-hunt/`. Even worse, the sleazeballs behind this crapware have created an enormous number of fake websites that supposedly review multimedia software, like this one here: "Mac DVD Rippers Comparison - 4 Products Reviewed," at `http://www.dvd-tutorials.com/mac-dvd-ripper-review-for-aimersoft-wondershare-iskysoft.html`. However, notice that all four of the products being reviewed are from the same company! Nice review!

If you do a search at Google for "mac video conversion software" or "mac dvd rip software," I guarantee that the vast majority of the results will be Potemkin websites set up by the Wondershare/Aimersoft/Aiseesoft crew. Of course, they all review only their own stuff, and they only link to each other, but it works. Too bad Google doesn't clean that garbage out.

Who's behind this junk? Here's who registered aimersoft.com:

```
Aimersoft tobee@sina.com +86.75526038199
        Aimersoft
        High Tech Industry Park
        SHENZHEN,Guangdong,CN 518000
```

Someone in China is creating website after website to push their software in about as sleazy a manner as possible. Of course, this explains why they're pushing the boundaries of ethics and licensing—they figure they'll never get caught. And they probably won't. So it's up to you to protect yourself.

Before buying any software online that promises to rip DVDs, convert videos, or do anything else multimedia-related, you really should do the following:

- Check the page at "Hunting Blog-Spamming Scumbags" to see if the company is listed.

- Search for reviews and comments at VersionTracker
  (www.versiontracker.com/macosx/) and MacUpdate
  (http://macupdate.com).

- See if Macworld (www.macworld.com) or The Unofficial Apple Weblog
  (www.tuaw.com) has ever reviewed the software.

- Look up the company on Wikipedia and verify that it's legit.

- Search for info at Google.

- Do a whois lookup for the domain name (use whois domain.com in
  Terminal or www.dnsstuff.com) to see who owns it.

Don't freak out if one of those sources comes up with nothing, but I would definitely investigate before handing my money over to a company that could be nothing but a front operation for dirtbag scammers.

For instance, in researching this chapter, I found several references to Kigo Video Converter for Mac, at www.kigo-video-converter.com, shown in Figure 10–30.

Figure 10–30. *Kigo's website looks pretty suspicious to me.*

That website looks a lot like many of the others in the Aimersoft orbit of sites, but mere looks aren't enough for certainty, so I did more research. Here's what I found out about the company and its software:

- It's not listed on "Hunting Blog-Spamming Scumbags" (gotta love that name!).

- There's only one review at VersionTracker, and it's negative.

- Nothing at MacUpdate.

- Nothing at Macworld.

- Nothing at TUAW.

- Nothing at Wikipedia (all of these "nothings" are not a good sign—I mean, *nothing* on *any* of those sites? Not good at all.)

- Google lists thousands of sites, many on domains that sound fishy… aha! About the 15th or so listing, I see that Kigo is listed on `http://mac.brothersoft.com`, one of the sites listed on "Hunting Blog-Spamming Scumbags." Busted!

- Just to be sure, whois `kigo-video-converter.com` gives me this as the owner:

```
Registrant:
   Domains by Proxy, Inc.
   DomainsByProxy.com
   15111 N. Hayden Rd., Ste 160, PMB 353
   Scottsdale, Arizona 85260
   United States
```

Yes, I know that lots of people choose to hide their contact info when they register a domain (I don't, as I think that it breaks a fundamental aspect of the Net, the ability to know who owns and operates a domain), but this is the final straw. After guilt by association with brothersoft.com, the fact that the domain's owners are hiding their identities makes me certain that Kigo is another piece of junk to add to the garbage pile.

Basically, you have to be careful out there!

Summary

Whew! This has been quite a read, but by now you should know how to take care of almost all issues involved with maintaining a multimedia library. You know the codecs you need to install to view the widest range of videos and listen to the most different kinds of audio files. You've learned about the amazingly versatile VLC and the simple but effective Cog. If you need to convert a video or a song, you should be able to do that easily. Ripping DVDs should be easy as pie. If you need to edit ID3 tags on your MP3s, you know where to turn.

After all that, I just have one word for the power users reading this chapter, a word that some of you know already. If you don't, then I urge you to investigate it further, as you can consider it the culmination of everything I've covered in this chapter. I'll leave it up to you to learn more about this great software that brings together all your multimedia into one cool package: Boxee, free at `www.boxee.tv`. Enjoy!

## Chapter 11

Key Utility Tools for Text & Archives

Productivity has become something of a cottage industry in the last few years, with blogs (such as Lifehacker, at `http://lifehacker.com`), books (*Getting Things Done: The Art of Stress-Free Productivity*, by David Allen (Penguin, 2002), is a sacred text), and even videos (just search YouTube for productivity tips). Many people would argue that Mac OS X itself makes people more productive than other operating systems, due to its elegance, logic, and consistency, but even the most knowledgeable Mac user can always add new software that helps him work more efficiently. In this chapter, I'm going to look at two types of utility tools that can help people get things done on their Macs: macro expanders that automatically insert text, and archiving and compression tools.

Automatically Inserting Text System-Wide

One of the most important—and easily most-used—apps on my Mac is a text expander. I do a lot of writing, and I get tired of having to enter "Mac OS X" in by hand all the time, so instead, I just type `mx` and in a flash it automatically expands to `Mac OS X`. If I want to type in my e-mail address, I type `sem` and immediately it changes into scott@granneman.com. I constantly misspell "version," so I have things set up such that when I once again fat finger `verstion`, it gets immediately corrected to `version`. I have hundreds of these shortcuts defined, and I use them constantly.

NOTE: To be precise, these are *macro* apps. A computer macro allows you to type a short sequence of characters, which then generates another sequence that you can use, just like the examples in the previous paragraph; for more, see http://en.wikipedia.org/wiki/ Macro_(computer_science). The programs in this chapter don't tend to use the word "macro" in their documentation, though; instead, they use such words as *clipping* and *snippet*. I'll use all of those throughout the chapter, so just know that they mean the same thing.

When Snow Leopard came out, it included a text expansion and correction feature, one that most users probably don't know about. To get to it, go to > **System Preferences** > **Language & Text** > **Text**. By default, only six substitutions are enabled, all for inserting special symbols such as ©, ®, and ™. Unfortunately, while it's nice that Apple included this feature, it's actually not that great, especially when compared with the apps in this chapter:

- It works in Cocoa apps only, and even then, not in every one.

- Adding substitutions is a pain, as there's no way to import or export those you create or enable.

- There's no way to sync your substitutions between Macs.

- You can only do text substitutions; you can't do anything else, such as incorporate shell scripts or AppleScripts, which several of the other apps can do.

For those reasons, I'd skip Apple's built-in solution and look at some of the ones I cover here.

Before I go on, I want to sell the need for macro programs to those of you who still aren't convinced. Here are some of the things you can do with this class of software:

- Insert e-mail signatures, and it's even more fun when you use shell scripts (I'll show you how)!

- Fill in forms on web pages.

- Automatically fix typos.

- Instead of having to remember special key combinations to insert accented characters, use your text expander, so you type n~ to create ñ.

- Insert boilerplate text that you're constantly typing out ("Thank you for your interest, but none of my body parts need enhancement").

- Insert the date and time into letters.

- If you're a coder, insert snippets. A good text expander makes HTML a lot easier to write, for instance.

In addition to those I've already provided, take a look at Table 11-1 to see a few other examples that I use. Before you start looking at the table, let me point out that you're going to see %| in Table 11-1, which indicates where I want the cursor to be when the expansion finishes. By putting it between <h2> and </h2>, for instance, I can immediately start typing the text I want between those two HTML tags.

Table 11-1. *Common Abbreviations and Expansions I Use with My Text Expander Programs*

Abbreviation	Expansion
embarass	embarrass
,h2	<h2>%|</h2>
,ie	Internet Explorer
loremipsum	Lorem ipsum dolor sit amet, consectetur adipisicing elit, sed do eiusmod tempor incididunt ut labore et dolore magna aliqua.
ooo	OpenOffice.org
,p	<p>%|</p>
,sig	% do shell script "cat /Users/rsgranne/bin/email/rsg_sig_gmail.txt | pbcopy" %-
tcpip	TCP/IP
teh	the
,ul	<ul> <li>%|</li> <li></li> <li></li> </ul>
,ws	WebSanity
wyg	WYSIWYG
.....	&hellip;

WARNING: Here's one major caveat, though: do not use these kinds of apps to expand and type out passwords! Most of the time, the programs I'm discussing store their data in plain text, which means that your passwords would be easily viewable by anyone who looks at the data files.

As you can see, the possibilities are really endless. I do have some advice on creating snippets, however, no matter what program you choose:

- Use sets or folders, if the program makes them available. In other words, put all your HTML macros in one set, and your spelling corrections in another, and all your expansions into another. This will help keep things organized and will help find clippings if you need to change them.

- Pick different delimiters for different kinds of macros, so that those in one set or of one type start with one type of delimiter and others start with a different one. Examples will make this clear. I don't use this method, but Timothy in Ohio has a smart system that the makers of TextExpander presented on their blog, at http://smileonmymac.net/blog/2006/08/21/textexpander-organize-abbreviations-by-context/:

  - HTML shortcuts start with <, so <3 becomes <h3>%|</h3>.

  - IRC administrative commands start with i, so ikick fills in the syntax for kicking someone off.

  - IM shortcuts start with !, so !ty becomes Thank you!

  - E-mail shortcuts start with /, so /sig enters his signature and /add fills in his mailing address.

  - Of course, typos don't have any delimiter, so teh becomes the.

There are others, but you get the idea. In my case, I often start with a comma, so I might type ,wu to expand to Washington University in St. Louis, where I teach. Just pick a schema that's logical to you and use it!

All of these expander programs have certain features in common:

- Choose whatever clippings you want.

- Speed. You want the expansions to happen as quickly as possible, so you don't have to wait for them to occur and slow your thoughts. All of the programs here are plenty fast, but you may experience occasional slowdowns if your CPU is busy or you're low on RAM.

- You can insert rich text (bold, italic, custom fonts and colors) in addition to plain text.

- You can insert pictures, such as a signature.

- If you like, the case you type for the macro can change the case of the expansion. In other words, you state that comp will expand to computer; if you type comp, it does expand to computer, but if you type Comp it expands to Computer, and if you type COMP, it expands to COMPUTER.

- You can specify where you want to position the cursor when the expansion is finished, often with %|, as in <h2>%|</h2>.

- Sort snippets, either by what is typed or what is eventually displayed.

- Insert the date and time easily.

- Specify which Mac apps work with the macro program, either by including or excluding them.

- Use multiple snippet files (not the same as multiple snippet sets, however).

> **WARNING:** Here are two other similarities that are not obvious at all: first, in order for the apps in this section to work, you must go to ▸ ➤ System Preferences ➤ Universal Access ➤ Seeing, and check Enable Access For Assistive Devices. This monitors all keystrokes you type, thus making clipping expanders possible.
>
> Second, if you want to use Microsoft Word with your program, you need to dig around in Word's preferences and uncheck the box next to Use Smart Cut And Paste, or Word won't append the space you use to trigger an expansion. Of course, if you don't care, or you never use a space as a trigger, don't worry about it.

Before moving on to take a look at the actual macro apps, I need to stress that everyone has different needs when it comes to programs of this type. The best way to figure out if one of these programs is for you is to try it. Fortunately, all of them have free trials, so you can try 'em out to find the one you like. In this section, these are the questions I'll be asking for each program:

- Does the app live in the Dock, the Menu Bar, or is it a Preference Pane?

- What are the key commands to add new clippings? To temporarily pause the app (for those times when I really do need to type msft and not expand it to Microsoft)?

- Can I control what causes the expansion? In other words, does it happen automatically when I type the whole word, or do I have to type a delimiter, such as Space, Tab, or Return? Can different snippets have different controls?

- Can I search or filter snippets?

- Can I use shell scripts and AppleScripts in my expansions?

- How do I organize my macros? In groups, sets, or something else?

- Does the program provide any predefined sets or clippings?

- Can I import and export snippets?

- Can I sync my snippets, so they're easy to use on my other machines?

- Can I insert special keys, such as Tab and Return?

- Can I set the cursor's position once the expansion completes? How?

- Can I insert the clipboard as part of a clipping?

- Does the program provide any statistics about how many characters I've saved myself from typing? It's not necessary, but it's fun to know—it helps me feel more productive!

I think that's a good list for anyone to keep in mind when evaluating these types of apps, but I realize that these are my concerns, and they may not be yours. However, I wanted to be up-front and let you know what I'll be looking for in the rest of this section. With that in mind, let's look at the big three text expansion programs for the Mac: TypeIt4Me, Typinator, and TextExpander.

TypeIt4Me

TypeIt4Me is the really old guy in your office that's been around forever but knows where everything is and how everything is done, so he's amazingly useful, even if he doesn't dress snappily or know the latest tunes. That's TypeIt4Me—it's been around since 1989 (!) and while it isn't the slickest or nicest-looking app in this roundup, it still works beautifully.

You can get it at `www.ettoresoftware.com/products/typeit4me/`, and you have a 30-day free trial before you have to pay up. A single-user license is $27, but students can get it for $14, and upgrades are only $9.

When you first open TypeIt4Me, you'll be prompted to create a file for your macros. Here are a few ideas:

- In a Dropbox folder, so it's automatically backed up and saved. When it comes to synchronization, I'd be careful—since everything is stored in one file, I would not try to edit a TypeIt4Me file on two computers at the same time. Running it on two computers at the same time is probably fine, but if users on the two Macs try to edit the clippings at the same time, it could cause corruption.

- In TypeIt4Me's Library file at `~/Library/Application Support/TypeIt4Me/`.

- Wherever you'd like—before Dropbox, I used to put it in `~/bin`.

So how does TypeIt4Me do with regard to my questions? Let's find out.

Does TypeIt4Me live in the Dock, the Menu Bar, or is it a Preference Pane?

It's a pref pane (32-bit), as you can see in Figure 11–1.

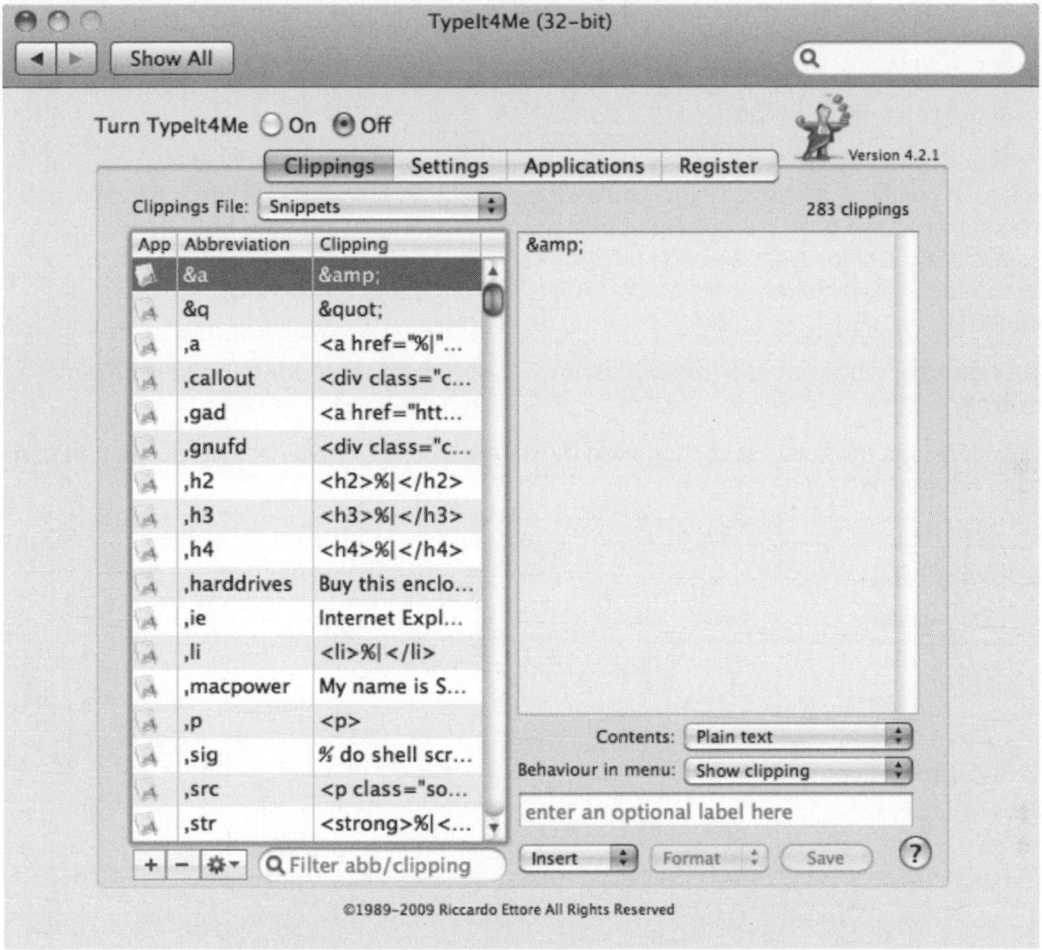

Figure 11–1. *TypeIt4Me is a pref pane, but it's still very powerful and complete.*

You install it, go to the Clippings tab, and select the radio button next to Turn TypeIt4Me On. Done! Now it just runs automatically along with your Mac so you don't have to think about it at all.

By default, TypeIt4Me displays an icon on the Menu Bar, but if you want to control what shows up when you click on the icon, or if you want to turn it off altogether, go to Settings ➤ Menu and check the appropriate radio button.

What are the key commands for TypeIt4Me?

While TypeIt4Me supports key commands, by default there are none set. To create them, open up the TypeIt4Me pref pane and then go to Settings ➤ HotKeys. You can set key commands for any of the following:

- Add A Clipping
- Edit Clippings
- Pause/Resume
- Add Word To Ignore
- Autocorrect On/Off

The last two are there because TypeIt4Me has a unique feature, which you can see at **Settings ▶ AutoCorrect**: the ability to correct typos with an autocorrect dictionary of your choice and/or the built-in AppleSpell dictionary that comes with your Mac. I tried using this feature, but it drove me absolutely bonkers, as it constantly "corrected" words that were in fact not mistakes at all, so I disabled it and instead rely on snippets that I've defined.

Can I control what causes the expansion? Can different snippets have different controls?

TypeIt4Me has the best list of triggering delimiters of any of these programs, as you can see in Figure 11–2.

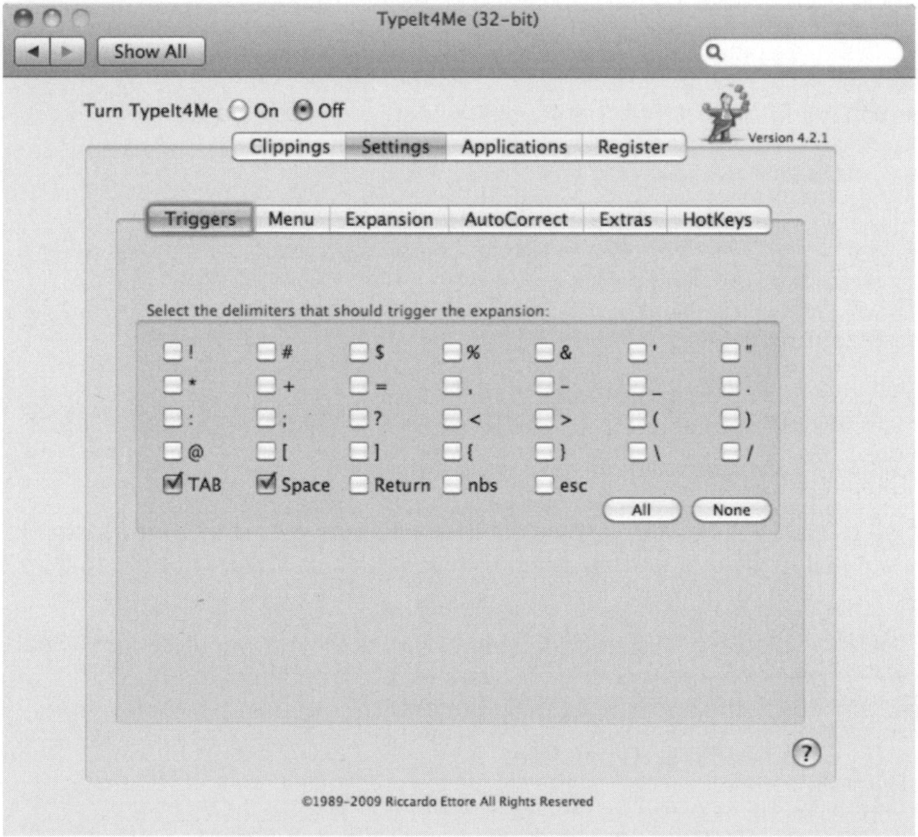

Figure 11–2. *You can choose just about any combination of symbols as delimiters.*

In my case, Tab and Space are good enough, but you can add a wide array of different symbols and keys to the mix. But that's not all! Go to **Settings** ➤ **Expansion**, and you can check or uncheck the box next to Don't Append Trigger, so that your delimiters are kept or discarded.

Keep in mind that these are all or none settings, however, that affect every snippet in the same way. What if you check the box next to Don't Append Trigger, because that applies to the majority of your expansions, but then in a few cases you want to go ahead and append the space (or whatever you use)? Select the specific abbreviation on the Clippings screen and then, on the bottom of the screen, click on **Insert** ➤ **Special** ➤ **Append Trigger**, which inserts %+ at the end of your clipping.

Likewise, if the reverse situation is true, and you by default append the delimiter but want it to be discarded for specific snippets, select **Insert** ➤ **Special** ➤ **Don't Append Trigger**, which inserts %- at the end of your clipping.

Can I search or filter snippets?

There is a filter box on the bottom of the Clippings screen that works with both abbreviations and clippings.

Can I use shell scripts and AppleScripts in my expansions?

Yes on AppleScripts, no on shell scripts… but remember that you can use AppleScripts to run shell scripts (by putting do shell script, followed by the contents of the shell script in quotation marks, into your AppleScript), so there's an easy way around the problem.

To insert an AppleScript, click the + at the bottom left of the Clippings screen to create a new snippet, type in an abbreviation, and then, after clicking in the Clipping box to place your cursor there, go to **Insert** ➤ **Special** ➤ **% (Execute As AppleScript)**, or you can also just type % in front of your script, if you can remember that.

How do I organize my macros?

This is one area that TypeIt4Me falls down compared to the other offerings in this section. You can have multiple files containing clippings (one for spelling mistakes, one for abbreviations, one for HTML, and so on), but you can have only *one active at a time*. Ugh. On the Clippings screen is a drop-down next to Clippings File, which is where you select the file you want to use. This basically means that you have to put all your clippings in one big file, which can grow unwieldy.

> **TIP:** The Clippings File drop-down is also where you go to create new files and delete old ones. You can also use it to print your clippings, which could be handy if you want a cheat sheet on your wall, for instance.

Fortunately, TypeIt4Me enables you to sort your active snippets in a variety of ways, including by abbreviation, clipping, date created, date last used, use frequency, and more. That's nice, but support for more than one file at a time would be much better.

Does the program provide any predefined sets or clippings?

Nope, which is too bad. That said, as you're about to see in the next question, you can import sets from other apps or from the Web. People have created sets for TextExpander that you can find if you search Google for "textexpander snippet file," which you can then import into TypeIt4Me.

Can I import and export snippets?

Kind of. There's no command for exporting, but when you first started the program, you were prompted to save your clippings somewhere. Find that file (do a Spotlight search for files with an extension of .typeit4me) and you can import it into TextExpander and Typinator easily.

Can I sync my snippets, so they're easy to use on my other machines?

TypeIt4Me doesn't have built-in support for syncing, but you can place your TypeIt4Me files in Dropbox for backup and syncing. Just don't edit the files on two machines at the same time!

Can I insert special keys, such as Tab and Return?

Sure. On the Clippings screen, create or select your clipping and click on Insert ➤ Special, and you'll see that you can insert any of these:

- Backspace
- Tab
- Return

Why do this? Forms are a great use, especially for Tabs. If there's a form you fill out constantly, define a clipping for it, separating the fields with Tabs and then finishing everything off with a Return.

Can I set the cursor's position once the expansion completes? How?

Absolutely. On the Clippings screen, create or select your abbreviation and click on Insert ➤ Special ➤ Position Cursor Here, which places %| in your clipping. This works most of the time, but I have a few macros in which the cursor ends up a couple of characters away from where it's supposed to go, which is weird and annoying. None of the other programs that support cursor positioning have that bug, which is good.

Can I insert the clipboard as part of a clipping?

Easily. On the Clippings screen, create or select your clipping and click on Insert ➤ Special ➤ ⌘ (Paste Clipboard Here), or type Command in your macro.

Does the program provide any statistics about how many characters I've saved myself from typing?

Go to the Register screen, and TypeIt4Me tells you how long you've been using it, how many abbreviations have been expanded, how many keystrokes you've saved, and, based on your typing speed (which I guess TypeIt4Me calculates—mine is apparently 72 WPM, which isn't too awful), how much typing time you've saved. All of that is really good to know, and TypeIt4Me does the best job with that information of all the programs in this section.

Typinator

You can download Typinator from www.macility.com/products/typinator/, and it has an interesting evaluation method. Instead of giving 30 days or so to try out the program, you're allowed to use it as much as you want, as long as you do all your typing in TextEdit. If you try to use Typinator in any other program, it will work, but you'll be constantly reminded to register it, so in that sense, it's nagware.

If you want to buy it, it's 20 Euros, with discounts for multiple purchases available. Here again, Typinator does things a bit differently from other programs: upgrades are free for two years after you purchase the program, but after two years, you need to buy it again. This means there's no upgrade price. It also means that your license does *not* expire after two years, just your ability to get free updates.

Time to see how Typinator matches up to questions.

Does the app live in the Dock, the Menu Bar, or is it a Preference Pane?

In the previous version of Typinator, the program ran as a Preference Pane, but it now runs as an app that appears as an icon in the Menu Bar. Click that icon to open the Typinator app, shown in Figure 11–3.

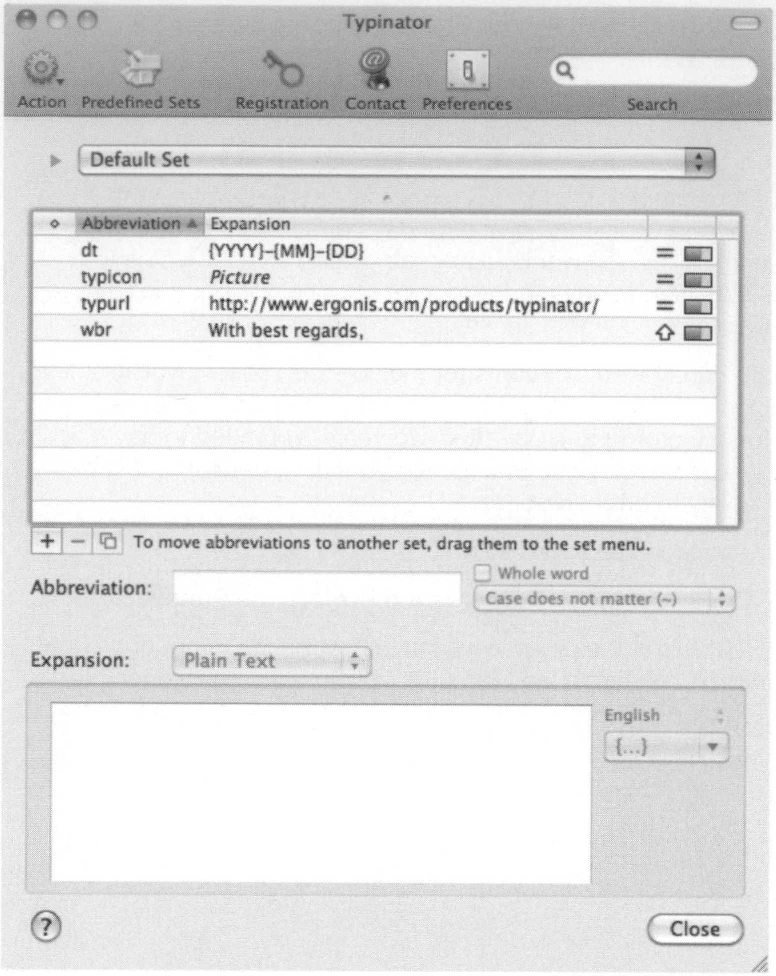

Figure 11–3. *Typinator's main screen, which immediately focuses on your macros.*

If you click the Menu Bar icon and hold, you can access key features quickly. To remove the icon entirely, go to **Actions ➤ Preferences ➤ Activation** and uncheck Show Typinator In Menu Bar. Keep in mind that if you hide that Menu Bar icon, you'll need to double-click on Typinator in /Applications or use a key command in order to add, edit, or delete macros.

What are the key commands?

There aren't that many. To see them, go to **Action ➤ Preferences ➤ Activation**, where you can see the shortcuts for Show Window (^-T) and Pause Expansions (^-⇧-T). Too bad there's so few.

Can I control what causes the expansion? Can different snippets have different controls?

You sure can. When you create a new macro, Typinator makes a few defaults, as you can see in Figure 11–4.

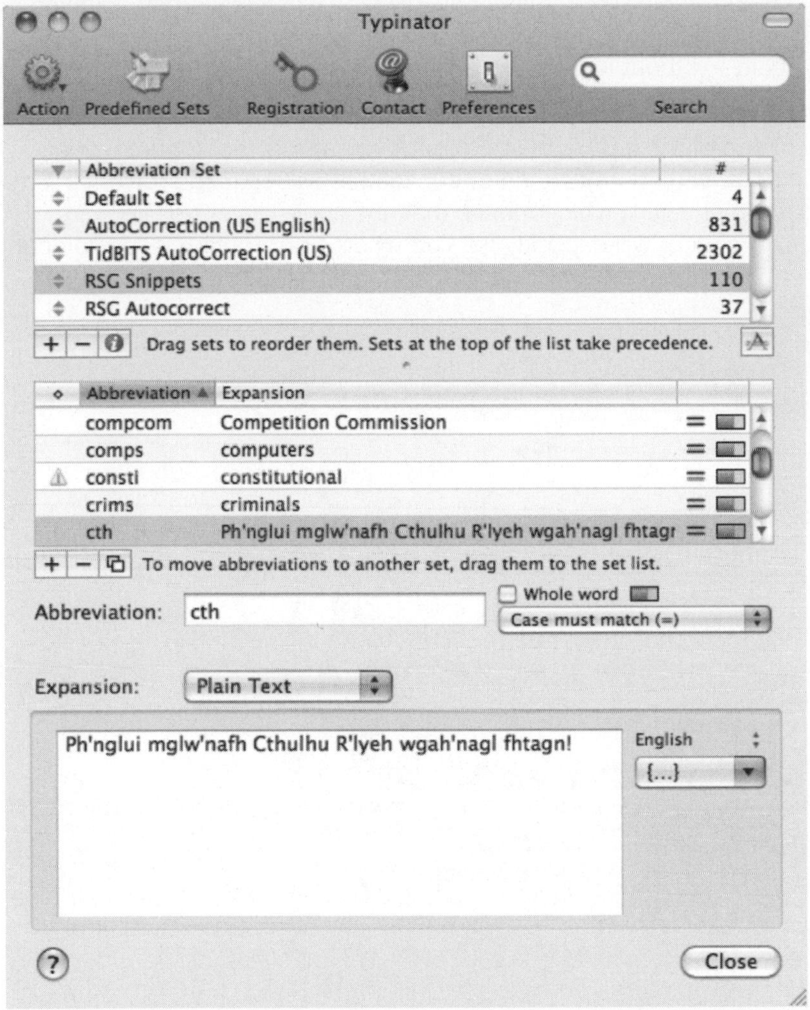

Figure 11–4. *Creating a new clipping automatically requires matching case but not the whole word.*

By default, a whole word is not required. In my example, my abbreviation is cth, which expands to Ph'nglui mglw'nafh Cthulhu R'lyeh wgah'nagl fhtagn! (if you don't know what that means, Google it). Since Typinator didn't check the box next to Whole Word, any time I type cth, even if it's in the middle of a word, or even if I want to continue typing letters after it, it immediately expands to Ph'nglui mglw'nafh Cthulhu R'lyeh wgah'nagl fhtagn!. Notice also that Case Must Match is chosen by default; if I click on that drop-down, my other choices are Case Does Not Matter and Case Affects Expansion.

So if I type Cth and then continue with ulhu, no problem, since the abbreviation is cth and Case Must Match. But if I'm typing ecthyma (don't look it up; it's gross), I'll get ecth out, but as soon as I type the h it will immediately turn into ePh'nglui mglw'nafh Cthulhu R'lyeh wgah'nagl fhtagn!—see the e at the beginning?

On the other hand, if I check Whole Word, then I have to type cth followed by anything except a letter or a digit in order to expand it. So I can now type ecthyma—which I hope never to have to type again—without having to worry about a sudden expansion in the middle.

Related to these issues, one of the best features about Typinator is that if one of your clippings conflicts with another, either because of duplication or because of overlap (one abbreviation is ub and another is ubt, which means that ubt could never be fired because ub would first), Typinator will explicitly tell you where the problem is, as you can see in Figure 11–5.

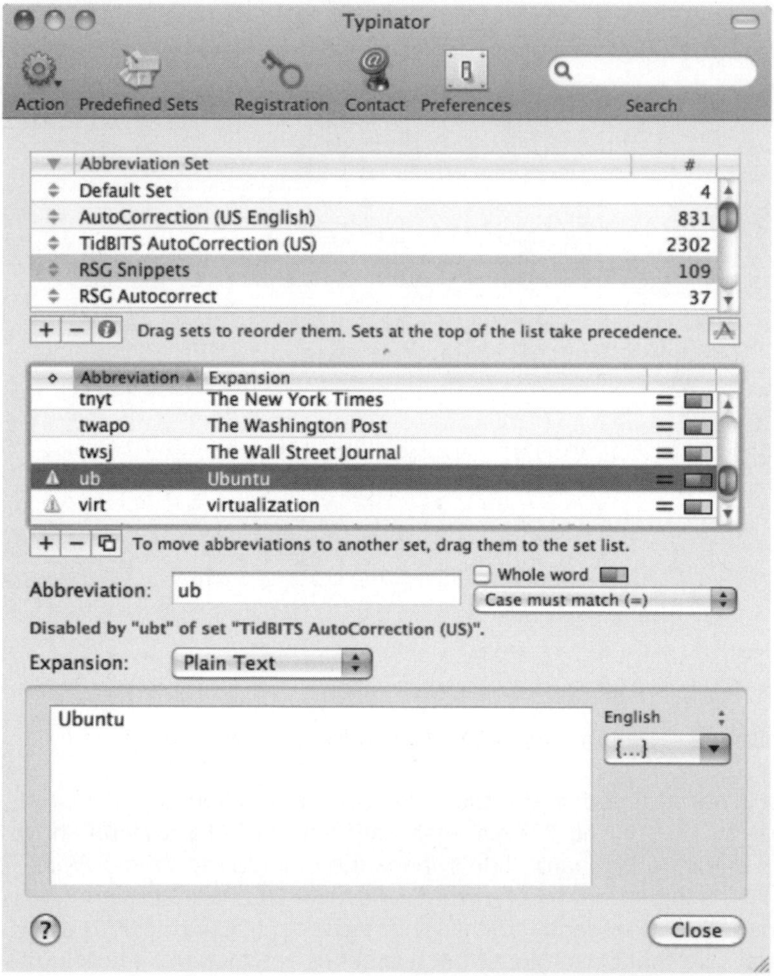

Figure 11–5. *Typinator makes it very clear where the conflicts are, making it easy to fix them.*

As you can see in Figure 11–5, ub conflicts, so I see the little yellow warning sign to the left of the macro. This is as far as TypeIt4Me and TextExpander go, which isn't that useful, because it means I have to search and try to figure out where the conflict lies. Typinator makes things much easier by telling me exactly what the conflicting abbreviation *is*, and in which set I can find it. This is incredibly user friendly, and the other text expansion apps should immediately copy this idea.

Can I search or filter snippets?

Yes you can—there's a search box in the upper right that let's you look across all of your abbreviations and expansions.

Can I use shell scripts and AppleScripts in my expansions?

No, you can't, which is a major weakness for Typinator. The ability to run AppleScripts and shell scripts and then place the output into your documents is incredibly useful, and it's too bad that Typinator doesn't support this.

How do I organize my macros?

At the top of Figure 11–3, you can see a drop-down menu that says Default Set. If you click that drop-down, Typinator shows you all of your sets, or if you click the little triangle to the left of the drop-down, Typinator gets rid of the drop-down and instead shows you the interface in Figure 11–6.

Now you can see five sets at a time, and in addition to the name of the set, you can also see the number of expansions in the set on the right. On the far left is a double-sided arrow that enables you to drag and drop the sets to reorder them as you please. At the bottom is a + to create new sets, a – to delete sets, and an i that displays information about the set. Finally, on the right is the Mac OS Applications icon, which allows you to specify specific applications that may have only a few sets—or none—available to them.

> **TIP:** The reverse side of that coin is that there are a few programs that don't play well with Typinator. To see that list, as well as tips about getting around those issues, check out www.macility.com/products/typinator/faq.html.

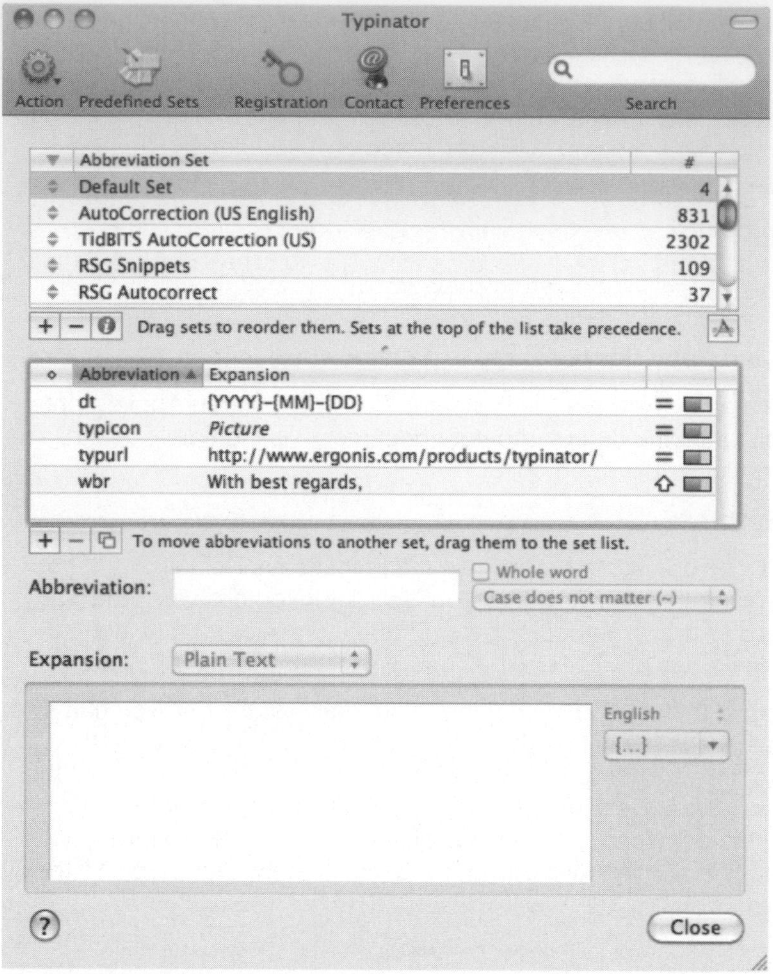

Figure 11–6. *I prefer this to the drop-down; you may not, but then you'd be wrong. :)*

Does the program provide any predefined sets or clippings?

Typinator comes with several predefined macros that you can easily install. Go to **Action** ➤ **Add Predefined Sets**, or just click on the Predefined Sets button, and you can check boxes next to ten sets, including Auto-Correction in four languages, TidBITS Auto-Correction in two dialects, FileMaker, HTML, and more. In addition, if you search Google for "typinator snippet file," you can find more.

Can I import and export snippets?

This really makes me pretty annoyed, and it's a major reason I can't recommend Typinator. It will happily import from TextExpander, TypeIt4Me, and text files formatted using tabs between abbreviations and expansions. Great. You can also export files from Typinator by going to **Action** ➤ **Export**, which creates files with the .tyset extension.

However, other programs can't import .tyset files. Why? Because .tyset files are actually bundles (directories that act and look like files to the Finder), and the contents of those bundles are binary files, not text. This means that neither TypeIt4Me nor TextExpander can import Typinator's macros, which is ridiculous. So Typinator will import, but it won't export in any way that is useful to other programs.

Think about this—if you don't like TypeIt4Me, you can take your macros and move them into TextExpander and Typinator. Same thing with TextExpander. But if you don't like Typinator, you're stuck. Either that, or if you decide to move to another program, you get to retype all of your snippets, which could be painful—if not impossible—if you have a lot. Does that sound appealing to you? If you don't care, then by all means, get Typinator. But if that sounds like a raw deal to you—and it sure does to me—then it's a very good reason not to go with Typinator.

Can I sync my snippets, so they're easy to use on my other machines?

Yes, and it's super easy to do. Go to **Action ➤ Preferences ➤ Expansion**, and click the Change button next to Sets Folder. Select a location in Dropbox, and you can now rest secure that your snippets are backed up and synced.

In fact, this is the positive side of the ".tyset is actually a bundle" issue I brought up in the last question. Because Typinator uses bundles to store expansions, each individual expansion is actually stored in a separate file (this is different from TypeIt4Me and TextExpander, which store each set's expansions in a single file, one for each set). You can feel much safer editing macros on multiple Macs because the likelihood that you're editing the same snippet at the same time on the other Mac is very small.

Translation? It's OK to use Dropbox to back up and sync your macros if you use TypeIt4Me, Typinator, or TextExpander, but if you have multiple Macs, I'd be wary of editing your TypeIt4Me and TextExpander macros unless you know for certain no one else is editing them at the same time on another Mac. I wouldn't worry about that issue if you use Typinator.

Is that nice benefit enough to outweigh the fact that the binary format used by Typinator with each of those individual macros is proprietary and can't be read by either TypeIt4Me or TextExpander? Not for me. But if it is for you, then full steam ahead.

Can I insert special keys, such as Tab and Return?

No, you cannot, something that both TypeIt4Me and TextExpander allow. I find this kind of weird.

Can I set the cursor's position once the expansion completes?

Yep. Create or select your snippet, click where you want the cursor to end up, and then click on {...} (the drop-down menu to the right of the Expansion field) ➤ **Cursor Position**, which inserts {^} into the clipping.

Can I insert the clipboard as part of a clipping?

You can. Create or select your snippet, click where you want the content of the clipboard to go, and then click on {...} ➤ **Clipboard**, which inserts {clip} into the macro.

Does the program provide any statistics about how many characters I've saved myself from typing?

Yes it does, but it's well hidden. Click on the Menu Bar icon and select About Typinator. On that screen, you can find out how many corrections and how many expansions you've run, how many keystrokes you've saved, and how much time you've saved, based on your number of keystrokes per minute.

TextExpander

TextExpander started life as Textpander, which was purchased by Smile On My Mac in 2006, fixed up, and released as TextExpander, a commercial software product. Since then, it's gotten very popular in many circles (text expanders such as TypeIt4Me, Typinator, and TextExpander seem to inspire fierce loyalties in their users!).

You can download it from `www.smileonmymac.com/TextExpander/`, with a 30-day free trial. After that, it will cost you $35, but you get a 90-day money-back guarantee, which is something of a rarity in the software world. I think this is a great move on Smile On My Mac's part, and I thank them for it.

One thing I need to mention: Smile On My Mac prides itself on its tech support, promising that they will answer any tech support e-mail within 24 hours. I found a bug and e-mailed the company, and received an acknowledgment back within a few hours confirming it and promising that they would fix it in a future release. In addition, I also needed help with an issue, and again, the company came through quickly. I was impressed. There have been times when the developer of TypeIt4Me has been very busy and hasn't been timely with replies, although that seems to have improved. I have no idea how Typinator's support is, so please don't take my positive experience with Smile On My Mac as a condemnation of Typinator. But I did want to let my readers know that TextExpander's support was excellent.

Does the app live in the Dock, the Menu Bar, or is it a Preference Pane?

What's cool about TextExpander is that you can decide where it lives. Choose Preferences ➤ Appearance, and you'll see check boxes next to Show TextExpander In Menu Bar and Hide TextExpander Icon In Dock. I checked both, since I don't want another icon taking up space on my Dock and also showing up when I cycle between apps with Command-Tab. If you check Hide TextExpander Icon In Dock, the program warns you that the Menu Bar menus will be hidden, which means that the only way to access those features is through the detailed menu you see by clicking on the Menu Bar icon.

Regardless of which location you choose—Dock or Menu Bar—when you open TextExpander, you'll see a window like that in Figure 11–7.

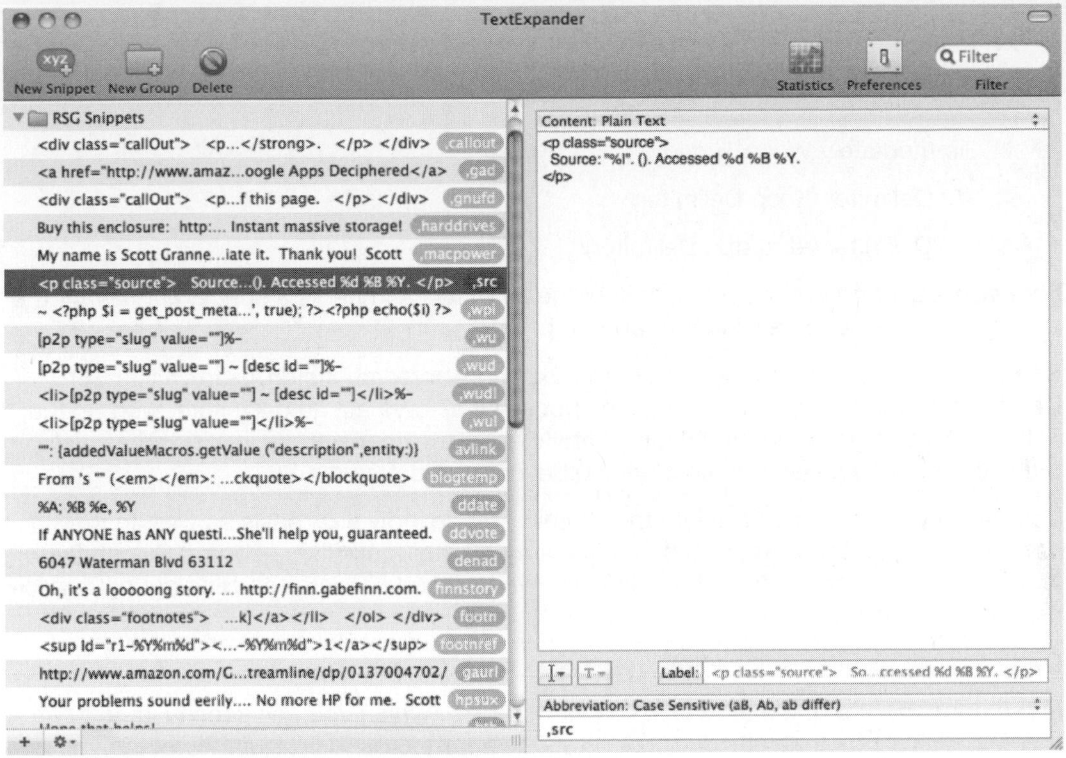

Figure 11–7. *TextExpander, with a macro selected*

On the left are my snippets, while on the right is a clipping's Content (the stuff that appears after expansion), buttons to determine what goes in the Content, the Label that appears on the left side, and the Abbreviation (the stuff you type to cause the expansion).

What are the key commands?

Open **Preferences ➤ Hotkeys**, and you can set keys for the following, all of which are very handy:

- Enable/Disable TextExpander
- Create New Snippet
- Create Snippet From Selection
- Create Snippet From Clipboard
- Edit Last Expanded Snippet
- Suggest Matching Abbreviation

These are in addition to the many other key commands that TextExpander supports for using the program, many of which I'll cover in this section. If you like key commands, TextExpander is the program for you.

Can I control what causes the expansion?

Sure. Go to Preferences ➤ Expansion, and you'll see Expand Abbreviations, followed by a drop-down with the following choices:

- Immediately When Typed
- At Delimiter (Keep Delimiter)
- At Delimiter (Abandon Delimiter)

I prefer the second option, since 99% of the time my delimiter is a space, and I want the space to follow the expansion that appears.

Speaking of Delimiters, to the right of the Expand Abbreviations drop-down is a Set Delimiters button. Click it, and you can choose what keys act as delimiters, with Space, Tab, and Return selected by default. Pretty much any other symbol is allowed as well, but I find that I've never needed anything beyond the defaults.

You can choose to keep or delete the delimiter on an individual basis as well. In the bottom left under the Content box, there's a menu that looks like a cursor. Select [Cursor] ➤ Cursor, and you can choose Keep Delimiter, which inserts %+ into the clipping, or Abandon Delimiter, which inserts %-.

Can I search or filter snippets?

In the upper right of the main TextExpander window, which you can see in Figure 11–7, there is a Filter box that let's you look through your macros to find just the string you're looking for.

Can I use shell scripts and AppleScripts in my expansions?

Yes, you can, but it's a bit hidden, which is unfortunate. When you create a new snippet by choosing + ➤ New Snippet, notice at the top of the Content box shown in Figure 11–7 that it says Content: Plain Text. Notice also that Content: Plain Text is actually on a very thin drop-down menu. Click on that drop-down menu, and *voila!*: it turns out that you actually have four Content types:

- Plain Text
- Formatted Text, Pictures
- AppleScript
- Shell Script

Choose AppleScript, and you can type AppleScripts into the Content box; choose Shell Script and you can enter UNIX shell scripts. It's that simple, and it's right in front of your face, but it's easy to miss.

How do I organize my macros? In groups, sets, or something else?

Your snippets are organized into groups of folders. You can drag to reorder the folders. You can sort the macros themselves by clicking on the Action menu (the sprocket icon), which enables you to sort by Content (or press ⌘-1), Abbreviation (⌘-2), Date Created

(⌘-3), Date Modified (⌘-4), Most Recently Used (⌘-5), or Label (⌘-6). You can also Duplicate a folder or clipping by choosing (**Action menu**) ➤ **Duplicate** (or press ⌘-D).

If a macro is a duplicate or conflicts with another, the abbreviation will turn orange as a warning. Unfortunately, you need to figure out where the conflict lies on your own; unlike Typinator, TextExpander doesn't tell you exactly where you can find the problem. You can use the Filter box in the upper right to search for the abbreviation, but more info would definitely be nice.

Does the program provide any predefined sets or clippings?

Absolutely. Open TextExpander and click on the + in the bottom left, then choose Add Predefined Group, which shows you seven different sets you can add, including Accented Words, AutoCorrect (two different ones), CSS and HTML, Symbols, and Internet Productivity. In addition, you can instead select Add Group From URL if you know of a set online (to find some, check out `http://smileonmymac.net/blog/?s=%22add+group+from+url%22` or search Google for textexpander "add group from url".

However, there's one little gotcha that you need to know about the Predefined Groups: you can't edit or delete the snippets in them. The only way to get around that restriction is to select the set, click on the sprocket in the bottom left of the window, and choose Duplicate (or press ⌘-D). You'll see a copy of the set appear. Rename it (I duplicated TidBITSAutoCorrect and changed the new name from `TidBITSAutoCorrect copy` to `TidBITSAutoCorrect - editable`), and you can now edit and delete entries.

Can I import and export snippets?

Absolutely. To export, select the set and then go to [**Action Menu**] ➤ **Save A Copy Of Group** (or press ⌘-S). That's easy enough. To import, go to + ➤ **Add Group From File** and you can select any file created by TypeIt4Me or SpellCatcher shorthand files that were exported into XML (but not Typinator, thanks to its proprietary format, as I discussed earlier in the section on Typinator). You can also import from TXT, RTF, and RTFD files, if they are formatted with either commas or tabs between the abbreviations and clippings.

Can I sync my snippets, so they're easy to use on my other machines?

You can, and TextExpander is the only app that has built-in support for both Dropbox and MobileMe. Click the Preferences button and select the Sync screen, and from there you can select which method, if any, you'd like to use. If you really want to get slick, you can check the box next to Share Snippets On Local Network With Other Devices (iPhone, iPod, iPad). Of course, you'll need to get TextExpander for those devices as well, but once you do, you can use your snippets on them.

Can I insert special keys, such as Tab and Return?

Yes. Create or select a clipping, and then click [**Cursor**] ➤ **Key**, and you can insert Enter (which puts %key:enter% in your Content), Escape (%key:esc%), Return (%key:return%), or Tab (%key:tab%).

Can I set the cursor's position once the expansion completes? How?

You can. Create or select your macro, click [Cursor] ➤ Cursor, and you can choose Position Cursor Here, which is the same as inserting %| yourself (the same characters that TypeIt4Me uses, by the way). You can also use ←, →, ↑, and ↓, if you want to move the cursor one position at a time.

Can I insert the clipboard as part of a clipping?

Yes sirree. Create or select a macro, place your cursor in the Content box, choose [Cursor] ➤ Clipboard, and it inserts %clipboard into your snippet. Simple.

> **TIP:** With this capability plus the previous one, you can do some interesting things, particularly if you code HTML. For instance, you can create an abbreviation called ,img with this content: `<img class="center" src="%clipboard" alt="%|">`. Copy the URL of an image to your Mac's clipboard using ⌘-C and then type ,img. Instantly you'll see something like `<img class="center" src="http://www.granneman.com/images/banth.jpg" alt="%|">`, with your cursor positioned ready to enter something in the `alt` value. If you think about it for a while, you'll come up with lots of things like this that will save you hours of time.

In addition, TextExpander makes it very easy to insert other snippets into a snippet, by going to [Cursor] ➤ Snippet ➤ [Snippet Group] ➤ [Snippet]. Why would you want to do that? Here's an example that I use every day.

A long time ago, I had a friend create a Perl script for me that parses an XML-like file that contains quotations I collect there, and then pulls out one quote at random and writes it to a file on my Mac, at `~/bin/email/rsg_sig.txt`, along with my standard e-mail signature info: name, e-mail address, website address, and so on. I use Lingon (more about that in Chapter 12, "Digging Deep as an Admin") to run that Perl script every couple of minutes, so my signature file at `rsg_sig.txt` is constantly changing with a new quotation.

> **NOTE:** Yes, this is just like the fortune command, but this was something I wanted to do on my own in order to learn about several different technologies. I've been using it for so long now that it's part of my computer, and I'd be as lost without it as I would be without a web browser.

I created an abbreviation in TextExpander named ,siga, with a Content type of AppleScript, that contains the following:

```
do shell script "cat /Users/rsgranne/bin/email/rsg_sig.txt | pbcopy"
```

This ridiculously simple AppleScript actually runs a UNIX shell script that prints the contents of `rsg_sig.txt` and then immediately pipes it to `pbcopy`, an old NeXTSTEP command that takes whatever input you give it and puts it into the clipboard (`pbcopy` is actually short for "pasteboard copy," as "pasteboard" was the NeXTSTEP name for what is now the Mac clipboard).

NOTE: My more observant readers are probably wondering, "Hey Scott—you earlier said that TextExpander supports Content types of both AppleScript and Shell Script. All that your AppleScript is doing is calling a shell script, so why not just use the Shell Script type and leave out the `do shell script` part?" The answer is silly but true: in this case, it's faster to call a shell script inside an AppleScript than it is to run a shell script directly! I know, I know.

I next created an abbreviation named `,sig`, with a Content type of Plain Text. For the actual Content, I first went to [Cursor] ➤ Snippet ➤ RSG Email ➤ ,siga, which inserted code calling the `,siga` snippet. I then went to [Cursor] ➤ Clipboard, which inserted code that tells TextExpander to paste in the contents of the clipboard. The final result looks like this:

```
%snippet:,sig%%clipboard
```

So when I am done writing an e-mail—no matter if I'm writing it in Gmail, Apple Mail, or Thunderbird—at the end, I type `,sig`, and my signature is inserted. TextExpander first calls the `,siga` snippet, which copies the contents of my dynamically generated, constantly updated signature file to the Mac clipboard, and then pastes the contents of the clipboard into my message, giving me something like this:

```
--
R. Scott Granneman
scott@granneman.com ~ www.granneman.com ~ granneman.tel
Full list of publications @ http://www.granneman.com/publications
  My new book: Mac OS X for Power Users @ http://www.granneman.com/books

"Now, in general, Stick to the boat, is your true motto in whaling; but cases will
sometimes happen when Leap from the boat, is still better."
   ---Ishmael in Herman Melville's Moby-Dick, chap. 93, 'The Castaway'
```

NOTE: If you want the Perl script, feel free to e-mail me at scott@granneman.com and I'll shoot you a copy. It's not anything special, but it does the job for me.

Does the program provide any statistics about how many characters I've saved myself from typing?

Yes, and it's really easy to find them—just click on the big Statistics button on the TextExpander toolbar! A new window opens that tells you how many snippets TextExpander has expanded, how many characters you've saved, and how many hours of typing you've saved, based on your typing speed, which you have to set yourself.

Other Programs

There are other programs I haven't covered in this section, but you might find one of those to be a better fit for your needs, so if you're not happy with TypeIt4Me, Typinator, or TextExpander, you may want to try one of them out:

- FastFox Typing Expander (www.nch.com.au/fastfox/)

- Spell Catcher X (www.rainmakerinc.com/products/spellcatcherx/)

- Keyboard Maestro (www.keyboardmaestro.com)

I want to say something quick about Keyboard Maestro, which at first looked great. It's an automation app that is incredibly powerful, but it also does text expansion. When it comes to the automation, it's definitely worth testing. But I quickly found two problems with it when it comes to text macros.

First, there's no way to position the cursor after an expansion like there is with the others. Well, to be more accurate, there is one way: you can insert commands to move the cursor up, down, left, and right, one position at a time. So instead of simply inserting a few characters that mean "put the cursor here," you have to insert command after command after command to move the cursor left left left left up up, into exactly where you want it. Ugh. Too tedious for me!

Second, and far worse, it has no facility for importing clippings from any of the three programs I've examined in this chapter (it also has no export mechanism either, but that's a different issue). That means you'll have to retype everything manually into Keyboard Maestro, and if you have a lot of snippets, that could be awful.

Which One Should You Get?

I wanted to focus on TypeIt4Me, Typinator, and TextExpander because they are the three most popular programs of their type used on the Mac, so even though I mentioned others in the previous section, I'm going to focus only on those three. So here are my thoughts.

Typinator is fast and has some great features, but it also has some curious omissions:

- You can't run AppleScripts and shell scripts as parts of the macros.

- You can't easily import or export your macros from other, popular programs such as TypeIt4Me and TextExpander.

- You can't insert the clipboard into a clipping.

To me, then, Typinator is useless. You might not find my complaints compelling though, which is fine.

So for me, it comes down to TypeIt4Me and TextExpander. Both do the job well and both are full-featured (including all the things that Typinator lacks). TextExpander costs a few bucks more, but it's not that much. If you get either one, you won't go wrong. But for me, even though I've been a long-time TypeIt4Me user, I'm going to move to TextExpander.

TextExpander is a more modern-looking app, and the developers seem to be on top of things better—and faster—than the developer of TypeIt4Me. Also, I've found weird little bugs in TypeIt4Me, such as the misplacement of the cursor after an expansion, that I haven't seen in TextExpander (that's not to say that TextExpander is perfect; after all, I found a bug in it as well). I also like how I can group my macros into folders with TextExpander, which I can't do in TypeIt4Me. The predefined clippings that TextExpander provides are nice, especially since I can copy them to a new folder, making them editable.

Still, you can't go wrong with TypeIt4Me. It's just that I prefer TextExpander because it suits my needs better. I stand by the advice I gave at the beginning of this section: make a list of the features that are important to you and then download trial copies of each of these programs to see which one most closely meets your criteria.

Archiving & Compressing Files & Folders

When you saw the title of this section, you might have thought, "Why do we need this? After all, Mac OS X comes with a perfectly fine program that will unarchive ZIP and other archiving and compression formats: Archive Utility. Heck, Archive Utility will even archive and compress files using ZIP." You'd be absolutely correct.

> **NOTE:** Strictly speaking, archiving and compressing are very different. Archiving simply takes files and globs them all together without reducing their size; in other words, if you have 10 files that are each 1 MB and archive them, you'll have one 10 MB file. Compressing takes files and globs them all together, but it also compresses their data (if it can; sometimes files are already compressed, such as GIFs); in other words, if you have 10 files that are each 1 MB and archive and compress them, you'll have one file that may be 500 KB, or 4 MB, or something else—it depends on what's in the files and what compression program you're using.

Archive Utility is built in to Mac OS X, and is located (on Leopard and Snow Leopard) at /System/Library/CoreServices/Archive Utility.app, although I've never invoked it directly (doing so lets you set a few preferences that you might want to check out). Instead, almost everyone runs Archive Utility by double-clicking on a ZIP file and watching as it does its job, or by selecting files, right-clicking on them, and choosing Compress X Items, where X is the number of files (or folders) you've chosen.

As easy and efficient as Archive Utility is to use, it still has a few shortcomings. It supports ZIP files, which are definitely the most common format in use, but it doesn't work with password-protected ZIP archives, either reading or creating. It supports several other formats, but only those that are available as command-line utilities built in to Mac OS X:

- .bz, .bz2
  Compressed using bzip2; uncompressed with bunzip2

- .cbz
  Comic Book Zip; really just ZIP files

- .cpgz
  Compressed by cpio and then gzipped

- .cpio
  Extracts from `ar`, `cpio`, ISO 9660 CD-ROM images, `jar`, `pax`, `tar`, `zip`

- .gz, .gzip
  Compressed using `gzip`; uncompressed with `gunzip`

- .jar
  Java Archive, based on `zip`

- .tar
  Tape Archive, archiving only

- .tbz, .tbz2
  A tar archive that's compressed with `bzip2`

- .tgz
  A tar archive that's compressed with `gzip`

- .Z
  An old UNIX utility that uses the `compress` program

- Uuencode
  An ancient UNIX utility for turning binary data into text for mail attachments

That seems like a lot, but it doesn't cover everything. In order to be prepared for pretty much any kind of file thrown my way, there are two other archiving and compression tools I always install on my Mac, which I'm going to cover here: The Unarchiver and UnRarX.

The Unarchiver

The Unarchiver is free and open source, and you can get it at http://code.google.com/p/theunarchiver/ (you can read more about it at http://wakaba.c3.cx/s/apps/unarchiver.html, even though that site's pretty much a mess). This is the kind of program that you set up and basically forget about until you use it, and even then it does its job and then disappears again.

The Unarchiver supports an astonishing number of archiving and compression formats, some more than others. For instance, The Unarchiver supports all of the formats that Archive Utility does, and then these tooi(and even more if you wanted!):

- .adf
  Amiga Disk File

- .adz
  Amiga Disk File compressed with `gzip`

- .cab
  Cabinet, the native compressed archive format on Windows

- .dd
  DiskDoubler, an obsolete format for Mac OS

- .dms
  Amiga DMS Disk Archive

- .lzh, .lha
  Almost totally found in Japan

- .lzma
  Files compressed with the Lempel-Ziv-Markov chain Algorithm

- .lzx
  Amiga LZX Archive, subsequently used by several Microsoft formats, including Cabinets, Compressed HTML Help, Microsoft Reader, and Windows Imaging Format

- .msi
  Microsoft Windows Installer Package

- .pit
  PackIt for Mac; long obsolete

- .pp
  Amiga PowerPacker

- .rar, .r00, .r01
  Roshal ARchive, a popular format on Windows; The Unarchiver supports encryption and multiple volumes

- .rpm
  Linux RPM; originally developed by Red Hat, now widely used

- .sar
  Bitmap image created with Saracen Paint, found on the Commodore 64

- .xar
  eXtensible ARchive format, used in Mac OS X and RPM

- .xz
  Mostly used with Slackware Linux

- .zip
  The Unarchiver supports encryption

- .zoo
  Mostly used by VAX and Amiga

The Unarchiver also has partial support for these formats (and keep in mind that partial support is probably enough for most people):

- .7z
  An open source format; The Unarchiver supports the format, but not with encryption

- .ace
  Mostly used on Windows, The Unarchiver supports older versions, but not 2.0 and up

- .alz
  ALZip for Windows, very popular in Korea; The Unarchiver doesn't support encryption

- .arj
  Stands for Archived by Robert Jung, an old Windows format that never had a GUI; The Unarchiver doesn't support multi-part files

- .cpt
  Compact Pro for Mac, but now obsolete; The Unarchiver doesn't work with encryption

- Split files
  Can join files named .001, .002 that do not use any extra wrapper format

- .sit
  StuffIt, an old format for Mac that's still around (why?); The Unarchiver won't decrypt files

- .sitx
  StuffIt X, a newer version of StuffIt for Mac OS with more up-to-date features; The Unarchiver doesn't support "some more obscure features" and JPEG compression

When you open The Unarchiver, its preferences window opens showing three screens, which I'll now walk you through.

Archive Formats

Shown in Figure 11–8, this is the key screen for The Unarchiver, as it lists all the various file formats the program works with.

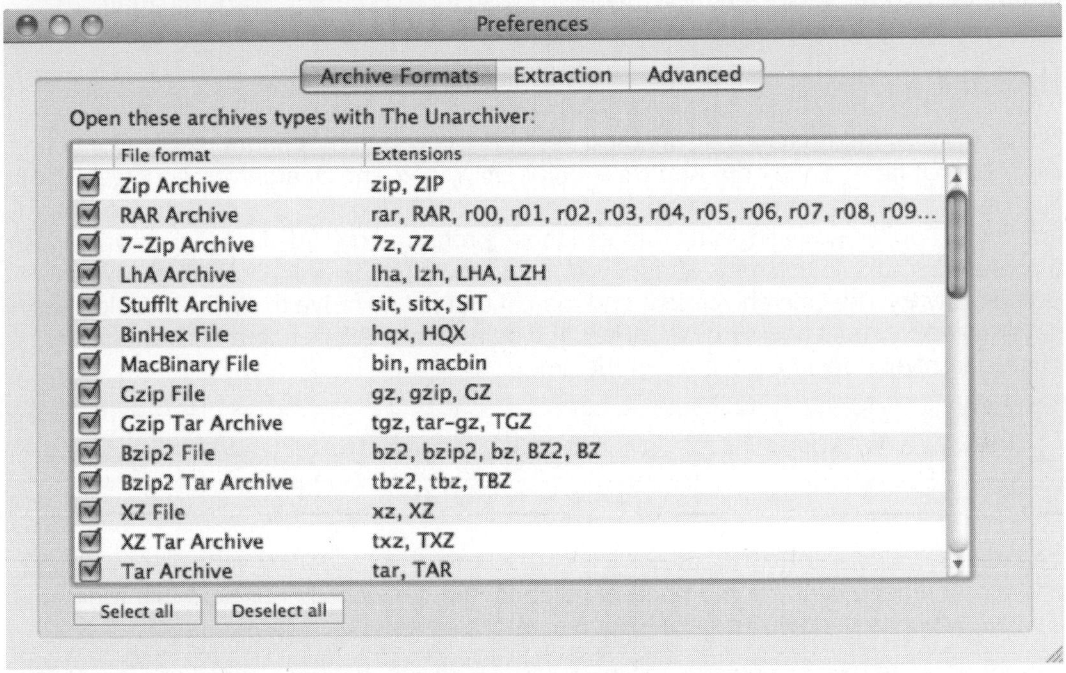

Figure 11–8. *You can tell how many formats The Unarchiver supports by the size of the scroll bar's scroller.*

Simply check the box next to a format, and The Unarchiver becomes the default for opening it. I recommend just clicking Select All and being done with it.

Extraction

This screen allows you to control what happens when you extract files using The Unarchiver. Frankly, the defaults are good enough for me, but I know some people that like to extract an archive into a different folder than the one the archive is in, or that like to move the archive to the Trash automatically after extracting it. If those options interest you, check this screen out.

Advanced

This screen is interesting, as it allows The Unarchiver to detect filename encoding automatically. You can set the threshold level for automatic file-name encoding, below which the program will ask you for an encoding to use; the default level is 80%, which again is good enough for most people (I've never been asked by The Unarchiver, and I use it all the time).

The Unarchiver is small, free, and it works perfectly. It should be one of the first programs you install on a new Mac, so it's there when you need it. Otherwise, you'll never need to worry, or even think, about it. I wish more programs were like that!

UnRarX

UnRarX is a program that, well, uncompresses RAR files. You're undoubtedly wondering why I have it here, since both Apple's Archive Utility and The Unarchiver work with RAR files, even if they're in multiple volumes (foo.rar, foo.r01, foo.r02, and so on). The simple reason is that I've sometimes tried to use those programs on RAR files I've downloaded that were in multiple volumes, and they just didn't work. However, UnRarX always does. So I usually try The Unarchiver first, and then, if that fails, I move to UnRarX, which has never failed for me. I could make UnRarX the default for RAR files, but I haven't, since The Unarchiver does the job most of the time.

> **NOTE:** Older multivolume RAR files used .rar, .r01, .r02, and so on, but newer versions use a naming convention like foo.part001.rar, foo.part002.rar, foo.part003.rar, and so on.

You can download UnRarX from www.unrarx.com. It's free, and it says it's open source and that the code is going to be published soon, but the website has said that for quite a while, which isn't cool. If it's open source, publish it and be done with it.

I'm not going to give any awards to UnRarX for UI design. It's bare bones and crude, as you can see in Figure 11–9.

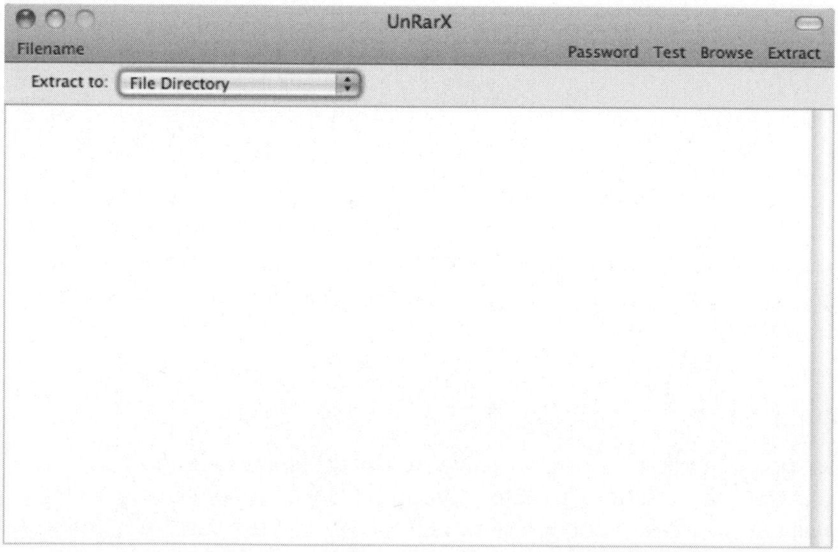

Figure 11–9. *Yep, that's it for UnRarX.*

It's just a window with a few text buttons, but the easiest way to use it is just to select your RAR files and drag them into the window. UnRarX will go to work, and a few moments later, the extracted files will be in the same directory as the original RAR files. UnRarX will show a window with messages that looks a lot like a log file (actually, it *is* a log file) to give you feedback. That part's easy, but there are a few gotchas you need to know.

- If the person who created the RAR archive didn't enclose the files in a folder first, UnRarX will happily spew those files into the same directory as the RAR files, which could create a confusing mess. The safest thing to do is to create a folder for the RAR files, put them into it, and then use UnRarX. That way any unsightly spewage is kept under control.

- You have to reset preferences every time. If you go into **UnRarX ➤ Preferences** and uncheck Overwrite Existing Files, you'll have to do it again the next time you use UnRarX. No fun, I know.

> **TIP:** Speaking of which, definitely check out UnRarX's preferences. You only have five choices, but some of them may be of interest to you, such as Recurse Subdirectories and Assume Yes To All Queries.

- If a RAR archive is password-protected, you have to click on the Password text button and enter the password *before* you drag the files into UnRarX. If you don't, UnRarX will try to expand the RAR archive and look like it's succeeding, with your only clue of failure being a short error message at the end of the log report.

- If extraction fails with a CRC error, look for a PAR2 file that came with your RAR archive and drag that into the UnRarX window.

Like I said, UnRarX isn't much to look at, but it does the job when I need it to. It's free and a good thing to have around.

Further Resources

For more on any compression format, see Wikipedia. Start with "List of archive formats" (http://en.wikipedia.org/wiki/List_of_archive_formats) and go from there. In particular, some of the historical and technical info on ZIP and RAR is pretty interesting.

You might wonder why I didn't mention StuffIt, the venerable Mac archiving and compression program. The reason is that it's simply not needed any longer. ZIP is a standard format on Windows, Mac OS X, and Linux, while SIT (StuffIt's format) most assuredly is not. And there are free tools—such as Archive Utility, The Unarchiver, and UnRarX—that do everything that StuffIt does and more, so why buy it or use it? Unfortunately for StuffIt, its day in the sun is past.

Summary

This chapter has focused on two types of software tools that I consider indispensible to a well-functioning Mac: macro expanders that turn abbreviations into text, and unarchivers. Most everyone has used unarchivers, even if was just the built-in Archive Utility that Apple provides, but I hope I've convinced you to install The Unarchiver and UnRarX on your machine. Not as many folks have used text expanders, so if you haven't, take advantage of free trial periods to give the three I discussed in this chapter a whirl and see if you don't find yourself typing less. If you already use a macro tool, I hope I've given you some ideas about new ways to make it still better. Now get busy and make your Mac even more productive than it already is!

## Chapter 12

Digging Deep as an Admin

For years, Microsoft and, yes, Apple have sold computers by telling people that they're easy to use. While that is certainly truer when it comes to Macs than it is for Windows PCs, it's still not completely factual. Computers are complex beasts, and even such "easy" operating systems as Mac OS X have to be administered in some way. This chapter will cover some of the administrative tasks that Mac users have to deal with: monitoring what their Macs are doing, automating tasks, improving your network connections by changing DNS, and making your hardware work a little bit better.

> **NOTE:** The complexity of modern desktop operating systems is one reason, of course, that the iPhone and iPad are doing so well and have a very bright futures ahead of them. Those devices—which run iOS, a vastly simplified branch of Mac OS X—are truly easier to use and leave behind most of the headaches associated with such OSs as Windows and, yes, Mac OS X.

Monitoring & Notifying

Part of administering your Mac is keeping track of what it's doing. This sounds obvious, but it's easy to overlook. A modern computer is doing so many things, at so many different levels, that it's not surprising some things just slip by. In this section, I'll talk about a few of my favorite monitoring and notification tools.

Before I begin, I'm assuming that you already have the mighty Growl (http://growl.info) on your Mac, so I'm not going to address it here. For those of you who don't know, Growl is a notification system that any Mac app can use to send alerts and information to users, which looks something like what you see in Figure 12–1.

Figure 12–1. *I like the Smoke theme with Growl, but there are around 20 from which you can choose.*

A lot of programs install Growl as part of their installation process (like Dropbox, Adobe Creative Suite 5, and Adium), so you probably already have it on your Mac. But if you don't, it's definitely worth getting it on there. I've been using it for years, and I find it indispensable to my Mac usage.

iStat Menus

The premier tool for monitoring what's going on with your Mac *right now*—"premier" both in terms of the information provided and the beauty of the program—is without a doubt Bjango's iStat Menus, available at `http://bjango.com/apps/istatmenus/`. The software was free prior to the last major release, but it was proving to be a financial drain on the company, so Bjango had to start charging. The new price? A measly $16 (after a two-week free trial). It's worth it. Oh man, is it worth it.

> **NOTE:** Yes, there is a free alternative—MenuMeters, from `http://ragingmenace.com/software/menumeters/`—but it's not nearly as full-featured or pretty. But it's free. I love free and open source software, but I'll never understand why people complain bitterly when developers explain that they have to charge some small amount of money for their software, especially when that software does something incredibly useful. After all, the $16 that iStat Menus charges is equivalent to three lattes from Starbucks!

When you install iStat Menus, you'll be asked if you want to install sensors for monitoring your CPU's temperature. You need to do that only if you in fact want to use that monitoring tool. If you have no interest in tracking your CPU's temperature, then don't install the sensors. If you change your mind, you can always go to **iStat Menus ➤ Install Sensors Module** at a later date.

You first interact with iStat Menus as an app, which you can see in Figure 12–2.

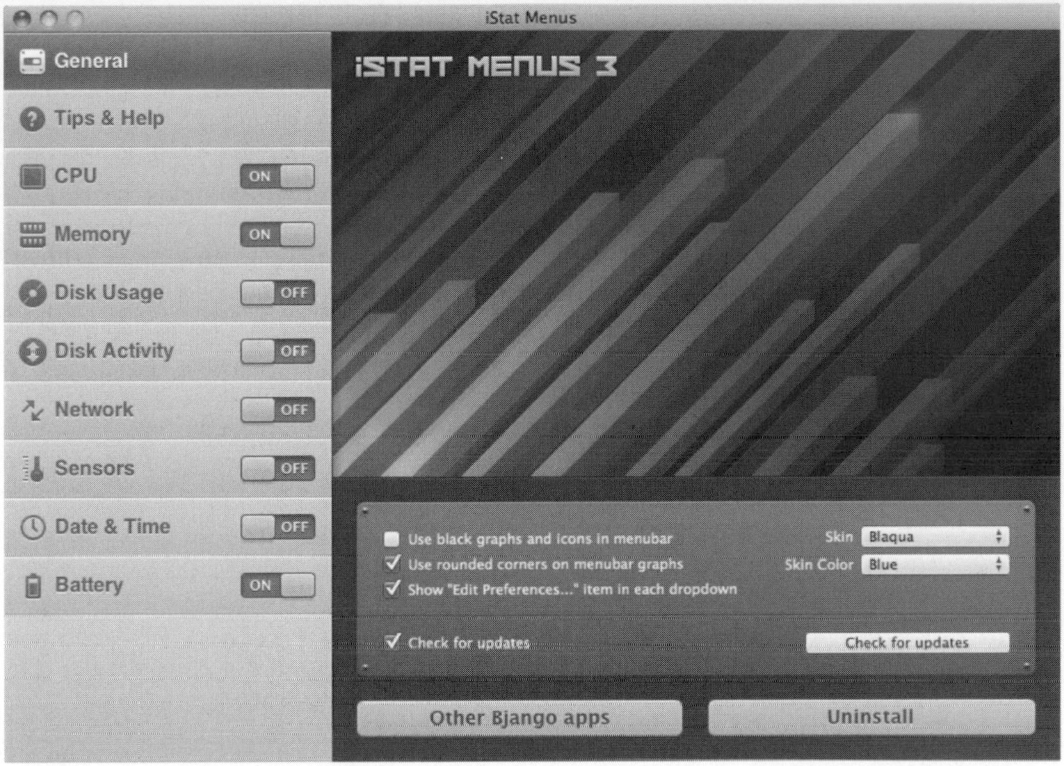

Figure 12–2. *It shore is purty, ain't it?*

Use the app to decide what you want to monitor and then choose your settings. As you do, the actual monitoring tools appear as status icons in your Menu Bar that are updated every few seconds. If you want to move the icons around and re-order them, hold down ⌘ as you click on an icon and then drag it to where you want it (this actually works with any icon on the Menu Bar, not just those for iStat Menus). To remove an icon, disable it in the iStat Menus app or just drag it off the Menu Bar. When you quit the iStat Menus program, the icons happily continue to run in the Menu Bar—you only need the app to add, remove, or change the monitoring icons.

That said, before we dive into the various monitoring graphs and icons that iStat Menus offers, let me say two things:

- Don't worry about CPU and memory usage. On my MacBook Pro, iStat Menus consists of two processes: iStatLocal, which uses 0% of the CPU and 4.6 MB of RAM, and iStatLocalDaemon, which uses 1.5% of my CPU and 2.2 MB of RAM. This is negligible, especially considering all the information I'm getting from the program.

- It's probably not a good idea to enable all of the various icons and graphs on your Menu Bar, unless you have a super-giant monitor and the scanning skills of Star Trek's Data. On my MacBook Pro, for instance, I have only three running all the time—Battery, Memory, and CPU—while my Mac mini media center has four: Network, Memory, Disks, and CPU.

The first screen in the iStat Menus app is General, and it allows you to set the look of the graphs and icons. Choose one that appeals to you. I also like checking the box next to Show Edit Preferences Item In Each Dropdown so I can quickly open the iStat Menus app.

Moving down the left side of the program, lets walk through the monitoring tools that iStat Menus offers.

CPU: As you can see in Figure 12–3, this menu displays your CPU's activity as it happens, so you can tell if your Mac is working its tail off.

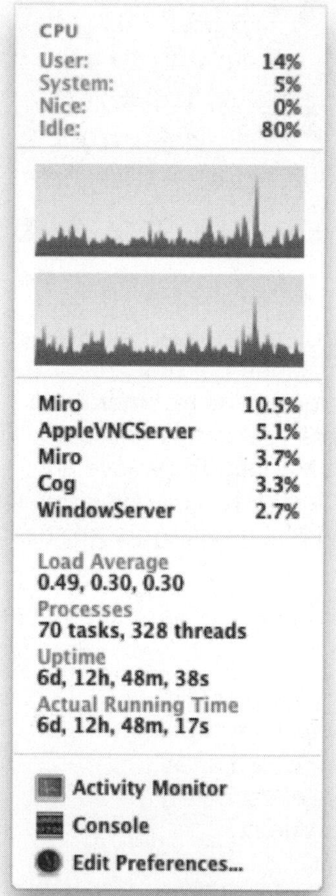

Figure 12–3. *Miro's working, but overall things are fine.*

The settings have a check box next to Show Top 5 Processes, which I advise you to check. You can see the top five in Figure 12–3. When your CPU is spiked, it's nice to figure out what's doing the spiking so you can kill it if necessary (speaking of which, it would be nice if I could kill any of those top five processes from within iStat Menus, so I didn't have to open Activity Monitor or Terminal).

There's also a check box in the app for Show Multiple CPU Cores As One Item, which is handy to save space on your Menu Bar.

Memory: Want to know how your RAM is being divvied up? This menu shows you how much is currently in use and how it's allocated. The app lets you determine how you want to see the info on your Menu Bar (this is common to many of the modules): as a pie chart, graph, bar, numeric percentage, or any combination of those. If you check the box in the app next to Show Top 5 Processes, one click on the menus will show you who the current RAM hogs are so you can kill them (again, I wish I could do that from within iStat Menus, but that functionality doesn't exist).

Disk Usage: Worried you're filling up your hard drive? How about any external drives? If so, use this module. My Mac mini serves as my media center, so this menu, shown in Figure 12–4, is important to me.

You can choose which disks are monitored in the iStat Menus app, so I've been careful to include my external disks on the list. I don't enable this one on my MacBook Pro since I normally have only one hard drive—the internal one—to worry about, and I keep an eye on it anyway. But you may very well want to enable it anyway, which is just fine and dandy.

Disk Activity: If you're fascinated by disk I/O, then be my guest. I'm not so worried about it, so I've never enabled this one. But as they say, different strokes for different folks.

Network: On my MacBook Pro, I don't really need to enable this particular menu, mostly because Little Snitch, which I'm covering later, already provides a nice graph on my Menu Bar that displays how much traffic is sent and received by my Mac. An added bonus with Little Snitch is that when I click on the Menu Bar graph, I can see the top 15 apps that are using the Net, in addition to how much activity they're responsible for, which is way more than iStat Menus show.

However in iStat Menus' favor, its graph shows me my current public IP address, which is great info to have at just a click away. If you're using Little Snitch along with iStat Menus, play around with both Menu Bar menus to see which you like; if you're just using iStat Menus, you might very well find the Network graph to be useful, especially if you need access to your public IP address more than every once in a while.

Figure 12–4. *Better keep an eye on my mini's internal hard drive!*

Sensors: Your Mac is constantly tracking all sorts of different things about your hardware, and that's where this module comes in, as it allows you to follow your Mac's temperature (even of the hard drive!), fans, and battery voltage and amps. You can also control your fan speeds, and can set different rules for the fan when you're running on battery power or are charging. I know some people have reported issues with their laptops running overly hot, and this module can help track that—and, if you use the fan judiciously, can help alleviate some of the issues.

Date & Time: Yes, your Mac comes with a date and time widget for the Menu Bar that you can configure in your System Preferences. But the one that iStat Menus provides is quite a bit nicer, as you can see in Figure 12–5, so much so that you may want to turn off what Mac OS X provides and just use iStat Menus instead.

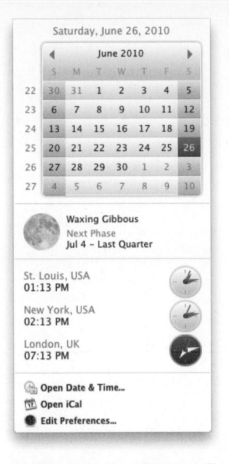

Figure 12-5. *Now that is one fine Date and Time menu!*

In addition to allowing you to exactly customize how you want the date and time to be displayed on your Menu Bar, you can see from Figure 12-5 that you get a lot of useful data when you click on the widget. A calendar is great, but the moon's phase is neat and the world clocks (over 20,000 cities) can be very handy. But the really cool stuff shows up when you hover your mouse over the moon—you get full information about the moon's phases for the next two months—and the world clocks: each one shows you the times for sunrise, sunset, moonrise, and moonset. That's a lot of information packed smartly into one menu!

> **TIP:** As nice as the Date & Time menu is that iStat Menus provides, I still don't use it. Instead, I use a nice little utility called MenuCalendarClock for iCal, available at `www.objectpark.net/mcc.html`, and free with basic features or $20 for advanced features (which I use, so I bought it). Why do I use it? Because it integrates with iCal to show me what's happening every day, as you can see in Figure 12-6.

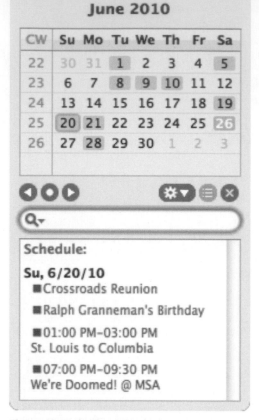

Figure 12–6. *Sunday, June 20, is a busy day!*

> Sure, I could have iCal open all the time, or Google Calendar in my web browser, but with MenuCalendarClock for iCal, I don't have to. If I need to quickly check a date, I just click on the date and time in my Menu Bar and run my mouse over the dates in the calendar. It's quick, it's easy, and it's highly configurable. I've been using it for years and like it a lot.

Battery: If you use a laptop, you really must switch from Apple's battery monitor to the one provided by iStat Menus. The proof is in the pudding—just look at Figure 12–7.

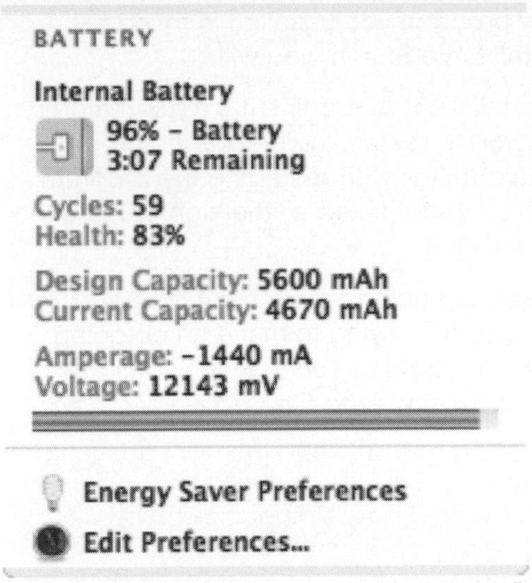

BATTERY

Internal Battery

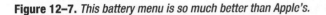

**96% – Battery
3:07 Remaining**

Cycles: **59**
Health: **83%**

Design Capacity: **5600 mAh**
Current Capacity: **4670 mAh**

Amperage: **–1440 mA**
Voltage: **12143 mV**

Energy Saver Preferences

Edit Preferences...

Figure 12-7. *This battery menu is so much better than Apple's.*

First of all, you can customize the actual Menu Bar item so that it shows an icon, a percentage, the time left, or any combination of the three. In addition, you can set a percentage left at which the icon turns red, and percentages at which you start getting warned that you're almost out of juice.

That's cool, but then look at the data you get in the menu shown in Figure 12-7. If you're using battery power (as I am for the screenshot), you see your percentage and time remaining. More importantly, no matter the power source you're using, you always see the battery's health and the number of charge cycles it's been through. As someone who's had to have his battery replaced at the Apple Store a few times, take my word for it—that's good to know (you can get the same information by going to ➤ About This Mac ➤ More Info ➤ Hardware ➤ Power and looking for the Cycle Count, but using iStat Menus is obviously a heckuva lot quicker!).

Those are the modules that come with iStat Menus, and I think you can now see that it's a complete, powerful, informative package. I have no idea how many times a day I glance at the iStat Menus icons on my Menu Bar, but I know it's a bunch. Is my Mac slow? Take a gander at iStat Menus. Do I hear the hard drive thrashing? Up to iStat Menus. How's my battery life? A quick look at iStat Menus. Once you have it installed, I think you'll find it indispensable too.

Little Snitch

Mac OS X comes with a nice firewall, but it's limited in one key way: it blocks incoming traffic only. It does nothing about outgoing traffic, which can be a concern. After all, worms and Trojans can grab data or try to infect other computers, but that's not much of a Mac problem. No, the bigger issue is from software that you install, which then tries to phone home surreptitiously, whether for good or for more nefarious reasons.

Normally, you have absolutely no idea that a new program you installed is trying to connect over the Net for some reason. If you install Little Snitch, you will.

Download Little Snitch from www.obdev.at and install it. At that point, it's a full-featured demo that runs for three hours before prompting you to restart the program. This will continue forever until you uninstall it, buy it, or learn to live with restarting the program every three hours. My advice? Buy it. It's $30, which might seem a little high, but it's the best of breed in its class and, I think, completely worth it.

Basically, Little Snitch sits in the background, taking up next to no system resources, and watches your network interfaces. If it sees a program trying to make an outgoing Internet connection that wasn't instantiated by you, it stops the connection in its tracks and prompts you to approve it by displaying a window similar to Figure 12–8.

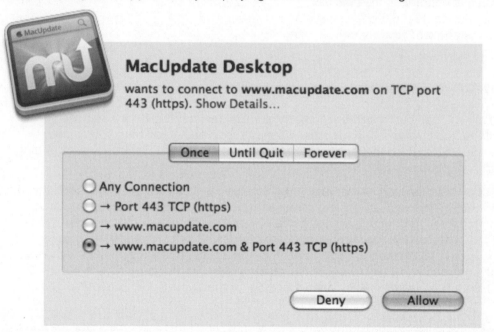

Figure 12–8. *Right after I installed MacUpdate Desktop, Little Snitch popped up this window.*

Figure 12–8 appeared right after I first opened MacUpdate Desktop, because the program was trying to connect back to the MacUpdate website. I have three decisions to make, which will ultimately lead me to one choice:

- Do I want to Allow or Deny the connection?
- What kind of connection am I allowing or denying?
  - Any Connection
  - → Port 443 TCP (https)
  - → www.macupdate.com
  - → www.macupdate.com & Port 443 TCP (https)

- How long should my allowance or denial last?
  - Once (which means I'll be asked again the next time the program attempts to make a connection)
  - Until Quit (but when the program restarts, I'll get asked again)
  - Forever (I'll never get asked again—but I can go into the Little Snitch Rules and do something else if I change my mind later)

Most of the time, I choose Forever, Any Connection, Allow. There are some cases, though, where I'll limit the kind of connection that can be made, but ensure the limit is Forever, and there are a very few cases in which I will Deny the connection forever.

Earlier in this chapter, in my discussion of iStat Menus, I mentioned that I really like the Network Monitor that Little Snitch adds to my Mac's Menu Bar. The graph in the menu bar lets me know of any incoming or outgoing traffic, which is nice, but when you hover your mouse over the graph, a useful transparent window appears, as shown in Figure 12–9.

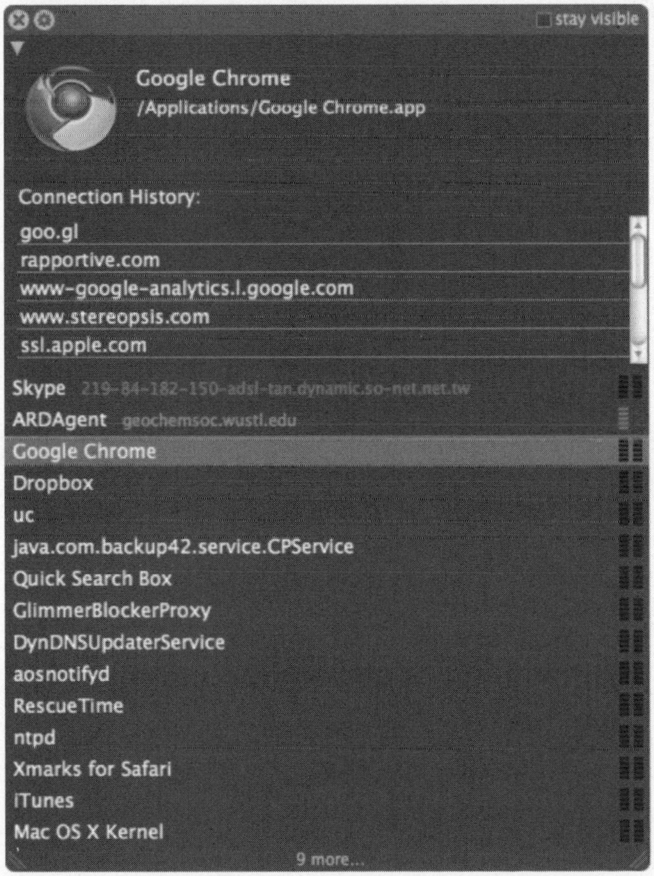

Figure 12–9. *What programs are using the network and where are they going?*

At the top of the window in Figure 12–9 you'll see a small triangle. Normally, the triangle is closed, so that you see just a list of about 15 or so programs that have been using the network, which is shown at the bottom of the window. If a program is currently accessing the network, the green (for downloads) and red (for uploads) bars show, and the current connection is listed in green. In Figure 12–9, therefore, I can tell that Skype is connecting to a peer in Taiwan (by the .tw extension) and ARD is connecting to one of our clients.

If you select an app on the list and then expand that triangle, as I've done in Figure 12–9 with Google Chrome, you get the full path to the app and a list of the last ten connections that the app has made, which can be very interesting, perhaps even surprising.

> **TIP:** If you don't see the Network Monitor on your Menu Bar after installing Little Snitch, go to **Applications ➤ Little Snitch Configuration** and open the program's Preferences. Go to the Monitor tab, select On next to Network Monitor, and then check the boxes next to Show In Menu Bar and Show Automatically When Mouse Enters Menu Bar Icon. I'll leave the other check boxes to you, but I didn't check them.

The other tool that Little Snitch comes with is the Little Snitch Rules, which you can get to by either clicking on the Network Monitor graph on the Menu Bar and choosing Little Snitch Rules, or by choosing **Applications ➤ Little Snitch Configuration**. Either way, you'll see a window something like the one in Figure 12–10.

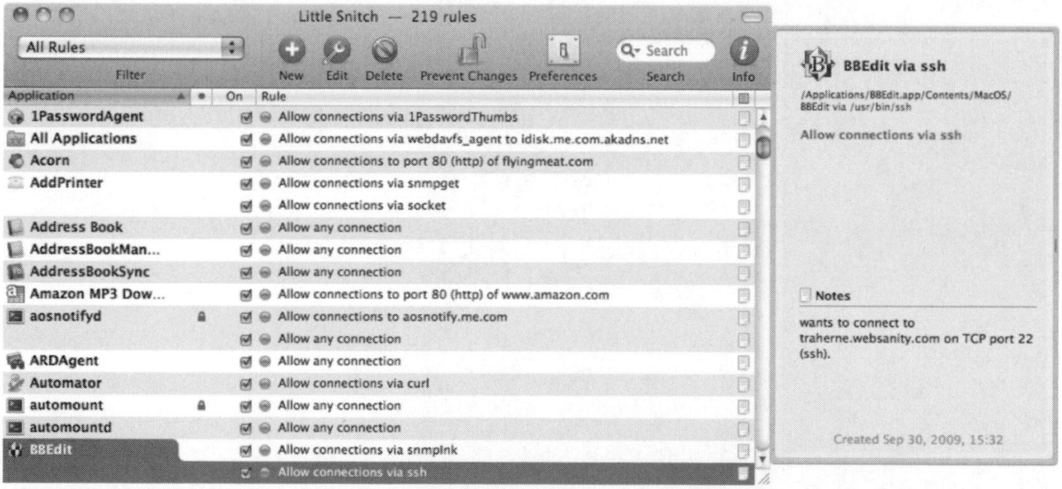

Figure 12–10. *Review, delete, or change the rules you've set up for Little Snitch.*

The smaller sheet you see on the right is there because I clicked the Info button on the toolbar (I could also go to **View ➤ Show Info** or press ⌘-I). It shows more details about the rule, such as:

- The full path to the application

- The rule you chose

- The initial connection that sparked the creation of the rule in the first place

- The date the rule was created

In the main window is the list of rules. Select one, and you can view, edit, or delete it. You can also create new rules, but really, I'd just let them appear organically as you use your Mac. And if you see a rule in which the app's name is red, that means that the rule is no longer necessary, since the program has been deleted, so you can nuke the rule.

Little Snitch is an essential app that I put on my Mac almost immediately when I'm configuring a new machine. It adds an extra layer of protection and notification that makes me feel safer and more informed, and that's always a good thing.

Automating

It's funny—I work with an older guy who will sometimes ask me what I've been doing for the last hour. "Writing a script to automate the ABC task," I'll reply.

"But it only takes you five minutes to do that task!" he'll shout back, astonished. "You just spent over ten times the time it would have taken you to just do it by hand!"

"That's true," I'll say, "but you're forgetting I have to do it every week. I spent an hour now, but in the future it will be automatically done, so I'll never have to worry about it again."

And that, my dear readers, is what computers—and this section—are really all about.

Automator

If you've been following along, you'll notice that I've mentioned Automator already several times throughout this book:

- Chapter 2: "Repair Permissions Weekly With Automator"

- Chapter 3: "Forklift"

- Chapter 4: "Speeding Up Safari"

- Chapter 6: "Making Mail Faster"

- Chapter 9: "Speeding Up iPhoto" and "Manipulating & Converting Images Quickly"

I've shown you how to use Automator for specific tasks (or given you pointers for doing so), but I haven't really walked through it in a more general sense. That's what I'm going to do here.

Ever since Mac OS X 10.4 Tiger, Apple has included Automator with every Mac. Automator provides a drag-and-drop interface that makes it easy to automate tasks and even create programs that will do some very powerful things (as you may have noticed earlier in this book). By default, it comes with over 250 *Actions*—individual steps that you link together to create a workflow—but other programs and third-party developers can create and add more. Once you build a workflow, you can then save it for editing later or to reuse in other workflows, or you can save it as an Application, Service, Folder Action, iCal Alarm, Image Capture Plugin, or Print Plugin.

When you first open Automator, you're asked to pick a template that corresponds to what you eventually want to do with your workflow, as you can see in Figure 12–11.

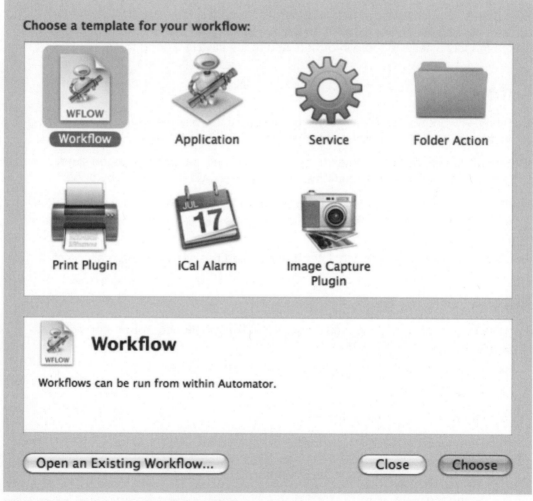

Figure 12–11. *What you want to automate today?*

Click on each template, and you'll see Apple's description of its purpose below. What I'd like to do is walk through several of those templates to give you some ideas about how you can use Automator, one of my absolute favorite tools in Mac OS X. Before doing that, though, let me discuss the Automator interface and how to use it.

On the far left is the Library, a list of Actions sorted by category. Actions are the building blocks of workflows, each one an individual step that you link together to form a complete workflow. When you find an Action that you want to use in your workflow, simply drag it into the main part of the window. As you drag Actions into your workflow, they'll lock together, indicating that the output of the previous one becomes the input of the next one.

> **NOTE:** Automator also supports variables, which, if you know anything about programming, sounds pretty cool. Unfortunately, not every Action supports the insertion of variables, even when it appears that it will. There's also no visual indication if a field in an Action will support a variable or not, which means you won't know until you try to insert a variable and fail. Which pretty much stinks. You can try the solution at Mac OS X Hints' "Use Automator variables anywhere in a workflow" (www.macosxhints.com/article.php?story=20080213200213250), but I couldn't get it to work. The bottom line: Apple has some work to do when it comes to supporting Variables in Automator.

With the UI under your belt, I'm now going to walk through some examples for the templates that appear when you create a new workflow.

Application

This is one of the most common uses for Automator—make a program that you can use in the same way you can use any other program on your Mac. Drag files onto it, open it and then work with other files, use it to interact with other programs and services on your Mac. The possibilities really are endless. Here are two little apps I've whipped up that I use constantly to make my life a little bit easier.

Update Times Reader

I'm a subscriber to *The New York Times*, and one of my benefits is that I can use the Times Reader (https://timesreader.nytimes.com). Basically, Times Reader is an Adobe AIR app (I know, I know—but before version 2, it was a Microsoft Silverlight app, so at least it's not *that* any longer) that allows me to read a huge number of *Times* articles going back seven days. The nice thing is that it works offline as well as online, so if I'm in a car or away from Wi-Fi, I can still catch up on the news.

I don't use the Times Reader every day, though, and I never know when I'll want to open it up and read the news. This presents a problem, because in order to grab the news, Times Reader needs to be online at least once a day. I could try to remember to manually open the program once every day, just in case I might want to later use it to read the news, but that's silly and will never happen. And here comes Automator to solve the problem!

1. Open Automator and select Application as a template.

2. Add **Actions ➤ Utilities ➤ Launch Application** to your workflow.

3. Choose Times Reader.app from the drop-down menu.

4. Add **Actions ➤ Utilities ➤ Pause** to the workflow.

5. Change the drop-down to Minutes and enter 5 in the textbox. That should be enough time for a daily update.

6. Add **Actions ➤ Utilities ➤ Quit Application** to your workflow.

7. Choose Times Reader.app from the drop-down menu. Do not check the box next to Ask To Save Changes.

8. Go to **File ➤ Save** (or press ⌘-S).

9. Save it in /Applications. Enter a name for the Application, like Update Times Reader, and click Save.

I've now created the app, but how do I run it automatically every day at 4AM, so that Times Reader is ready if I want to read the news when I wake up hours later? To do that, I use Lingon, discussed later in this section, and it works perfectly.

I know that the workflow I gave you was ridiculously simple, but that's the cool thing about Automator—it was also ridiculously simple to create that workflow, and it took next to no time at all. But it solves a very real need for me, and that's the nifty thing about Automator that I'm trying to get across.

> **NOTE:** Yes, I could have also done this whole thing with an iCal Alarm template too, and skipped Lingon. That just goes to show that there's very often more than one good way to do something on a Mac.

Login Apps

If you were to sit at my Mac a few months ago and go to ➤ System Preferences ➤ Accounts ➤ Scott Granneman ➤ Login Items, you would've seen a very long list of software. Some would say too long of a list, and if you were nice to me, I might very well agree. Even so, I need all of them, and they're staying!

The problem was that booting my Mac took a looooooong time before everything was finally loaded. Part of the problem was all those Login Items, which just loaded one after the other, without waiting to see if the previous ones had finished yet, and which really gummed up the works. If only there was some way to set the order of those Login Items, with a pause after each one launches to give it time to get started before the next one begins. If only...

Look! Up there in the sky! It's a script! It's an automation tool! It's … Automator! Yes, Automator to the rescue once again.

> **NOTE:** For all the gory details about the Mac OS X boot process, see the article at `http://developer.apple.com/mac/library/documentation/MacOSX/Conceptual/B PSystemStartup/Articles/BootProcess.html`.

I started by looking at the Login Items window to see what my Mac was trying to load. The first thing I did was delete anything I didn't want starting by selecting it and clicking the –. Then I started tracking everything that was loading and tried to figure out exactly which app was loading, which can be kind of tricky.

Why? Well, some of the items in Login Items were apps that I knew were sitting in /Applications, such as these:

- TextExpander (see Chapter 11): `/Applications/TextExpander.app`

- Skype: `/Applications/Skype.app`

- MenuCalendarClock for iCal (see earlier in this chapter): `/Applications/MenuCalendarClock iCal.app`

But some of them were not to be found in /Applications at all. SteerMouse Manager? There was a SteerMouse.app in /Applications/Utilities, but no SteerMouse Manager.app. GrowlHelperApp? Nope. Nothing like that anywhere in /Applications. Choosy? Again, nada. So where are these programs?

In Login Items, right-click on each app listed and choose Reveal In Finder. The mystery is revealed!

- SteerMouse Manager: `/Applications/Utilities/SteerMouse.app/Contents/Resources/Steer Mouse Manager.app`

- GrowlHelperApp: `/Library/PreferencePanes/Growl.prefPane/Contents/Resources/Grow lHelperApp.app`

- Choosy: `~/Library/PreferencePanes/Choosy.prefPane/Contents/Resources/Ch oosy.app`

Wow—those are all over the place. So now that I know where my Login Items are, how do I use that with Automator? Simple: I create a workflow that launches apps that I want to open when I log in, but after each app, I introduce a delay to give it time to finish opening before the next one starts. Then I save that workflow as an app and add *that* to Login Items.

In my case, I didn't want to add everything listed in Login Items to an Automator workflow. I could, but in my experience, adding just half of the items sped up boot times by quite a bit. If I'm feeling ambitious, one day I'll go ahead and add everything.

WARNING: Before beginning this process, you should back up the file that Mac OS X created to keep track of the programs listed in Login Items. That way, if your Automator app doesn't quite work the way you want it, you can revert back to the way things were and try again with Automator.

The file you want to safeguard is `~/Library/Preferences/com.apple.loginitems.plist`. If you want to view it (look but don't touch!), you can do so in a good text editor such as TextWrangler or BBEdit, or if you've installed Apple's Developer Tools, try Property List Editor.

And here's a note inside my warning: instead of right-clicking on each item listed in Login Items and choosing Reveal In Finder, you could always open up `com.apple.loginitems.plist` to see the paths to each app there.

There's one other caveat before I walk you through the Automator action (which ain't that hard, actually). You'll notice that I have the same delay time after each app opens. That's done out of sheer laziness. If I wanted to do it the correct way, I'd close the apps that I'm going to add to the Automator workflow and then reopen each one, timing how long it takes to fully open. The result would be that Skype would have a longer delay after its launch than would MenuCalendarClock iCal, for instance. But again, I'm pleading laziness. Since you're not nearly as lazy as I am, I'm sure you'll do better.

I'm going to show you what you're going to create first. Figure 12–12 is what my particular workflow looks like; yours, of course, will be different.

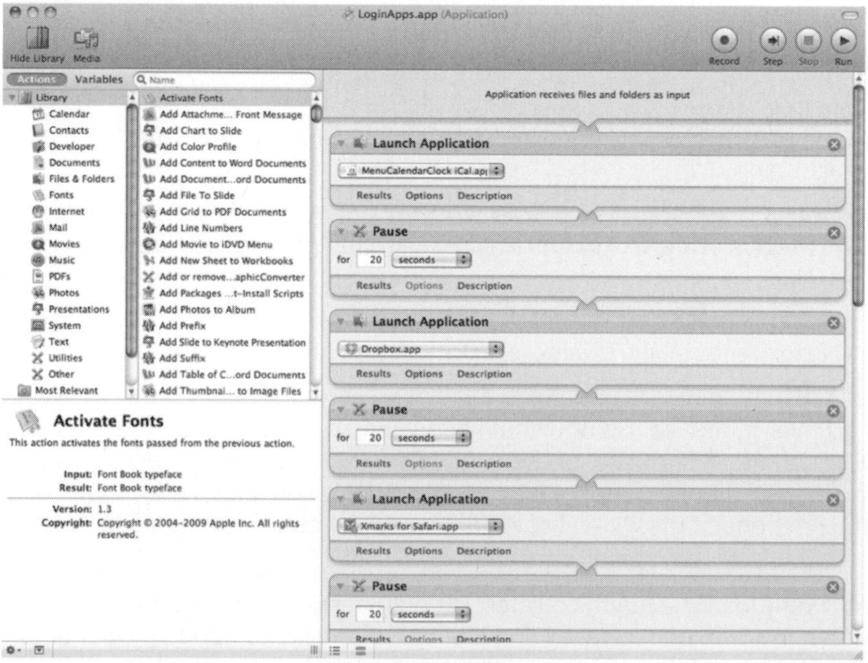

Figure 12–12. *Who's in control of the apps that start on login? I am!*

And here's the (again, mind-bogglingly simple) Automator workflow:

1. Open Automator and select Application as a template.

2. Add **Actions ➤ Utilities ➤ Launch Application** to your workflow.

3. Choose the first program you want to open from the drop-down menu. I chose MenuCalendarClock iCal.app.

4. Add **Actions ➤ Utilities ➤ Pause** to your workflow.

5. In the textbox, enter 20. Choose Seconds from the drop-down menu.

6. Repeat steps 2-5 until you're finished. Here's a shortcut: select the last Launch Application action you inserted into your workflow and go to **Edit ➤ Duplicate** (or press ⌘-D). Automator will copy the action and place it at the very end of the workflow, exactly where you were going to create a new one. Then choose a new program from the drop-down menu. You can do the same thing with the Pause action as well.

7. Go to **File ➤ Save** (or press ⌘-S).

8. Save it in /Applications. Enter a name for the Application, such as LoginApps.app, and click Save.

Your Application is now ready to use. Delete any of the apps you added to the workflow from Login Items and then click the + at the bottom of the Login Items window. Select /Applications/LoginApps.app and click Add. Reboot to test. You should notice a faster boot time, and your apps should open in the order you specified. All thanks to Mr. Automator.

Service

Services are easy to create and even easier to use in Snow Leopard than in any previous version of Mac OS X (in fact, I'd contend that Services were pretty much unusable in any previous version of Mac OS X and are finally where they should have been all along in Snow Leopard). Here are a few simple ones that I've created to solve my needs over the years.

Convert Images to PNG

This is a common need for me—I'll take a screenshot and need to e-mail or Skype it to someone. I used Onyx (see Chapter 2) to change my settings so that the default format for screenshots is uncompressed TIFFs, which can be many megabytes in size (Why TIFF? Because I write books and that's what publishers want!). Instead of sending those, I'd like to convert the TIFFs to smaller PNGs so I can send them. Here's how I created a super-simple Automator Service to do just that.

1. Open Automator and select Service as a template.

2. At the very top of the workflow, you'll see two select lists. For Service Receives Selected, choose Image Files. For In, choose Finder.app.

3. Add **Actions ➤ Photos ➤ Change Type Of Images** to your workflow (I recommend clicking Add when you're asked if you want to include the Copy Finder Items action, just to be safe, but you don't have to do it).

4. For Copy Finder Items (if you added it), I set the To drop-down to Desktop, which is fine, since that's where screenshots go by default.

5. For Change Type Of Images, set the To Type select list to PNG

6. Go to **File ➤ Save** (or press ⌘-S).

7. Enter a name for the Service, such as `Convert To PNG`, and click Save.

Your Service is now saved (at `~/Library/Services`) and ready to use. Create a screenshot by pressing ⌘-⇧-3 and you should hear the camera noise and see a file named something like `Screen Shot 2010-06-25 At 10.56.31 AM.TIF` appear on your Desktop (unless you've changed something on your Mac, in which case you're on your own!). Right-click on the file and choose **Services ➤ Convert To PNG**. A moment later, you'll have another file on your Desktop: `Screen Shot 2010-06-25 At 10.56.31 AM.PNG`. Now wasn't that easy?

Attach Files to Messages in Mail

So I now have a much smaller PNG to send. If I'm using Skype, I just drag the file into the chat window and it gets transferred. But what if I'm using e-mail? I could open a new message in Mail and then drag the PNG into the message, but I'm lazier than that. Here's how to create a Service that automatically creates a new message and adds your PNG to it as an attachment.

1. Open Automator and select Service as a template.

2. At the very top of the workflow, you'll see two select lists. For Service Receives Selected, choose Files Or Folders (yes, I know you can't attach folders, but plain ol' Files isn't an option, and even though my example is with a PNG, this Service will allow you to attach any kind of file, so I'm not going to pick Image Files). For In, choose Finder.app.

3. Add **Actions ➤ Mail ➤ New Mail Message** to your workflow. If you want to pre-fill in some of the fields (To, CC, Subject, and so on), be my guest, but I don't.

4. Add **Actions ➤ Mail ➤ Add Attachments To Front Message** to your workflow.

5. Go to **File ➤ Save** (or press ⌘-S).

6. Enter a name for the Service, such as `Grab Files & Attach To New Mail`, and click Save.

Your Service is now saved (again, at ~/Library/Services) and ready to use. Right-click on the PNG we created using the other service and go to **Services ➤ Grab Files & Attach To New Mail**. A moment later, Mail will open if it wasn't already and a new message will appear, with your PNG image attached. Fill in the fields, click Send, and you're done with work for the day. Go have a beer on me.

Are You Thinking What I'm Thinking?

I know some of you are saying out loud, "Dude! Why not combine the two different Services into one big Service and call it something like Convert To PNG & Attach To New Mail?!"

That's a great idea! However, I actually end up using Skype to send files more than e-mail, so I keep the two Services separate. But you sure could combine them—heck, just create a third Service.

And anyway, the point of this is to give you ideas. If you're thinking about better ways to combine Services, you're ready to start using Automator, so jump on in!

Folder Action

You probably know what an FTP dropbox is: a public folder into which anyone can deposit files meant for you. But what if you could have folders on your Mac that each did something useful when files were deposited into them? That's the whole idea behind Folder Actions, which are basically scripts attached to folders. Automator makes it easy to create Folder Actions, although actually attaching the finished products to folders isn't the most obvious activity in the world, as you'll see.

So let's assume you have some videos that you want to convert to watch on your shiny new iPhone. I'm going to create a Folder Action that automatically converts any video placed into the watched folder into a movie suitable for the iPhone, and then adds the resulting iPhone-ready video to iTunes so you can sync it.

1. Open Automator and select Folder Action as a template.

2. At the very top of your workflow, you need to select the folder that will have your Folder Action attached to it. In my case, I used ~/Downloads/Convert For iPhone, which I had previously created.

3. Add **Actions ➤ Files & Folders ➤ Get Specified Finder Items** to your workflow (do not add the Copy Finder Items action when prompted).

4. Add **Actions ➤ Movies ➤ Export Movies** to the workflow.

5. For Format, select iPhone. For Save To, choose Other and then navigate to ~/Music/Automatically Add To iTunes (betcha didn't know that folder was there, didja?!). Click Choose so that folder is now the target for your converted movies. Check the box next to Delete Original Movies When Done so that the original files are deleted out of Convert For iPhone once they're converted (if you want to save the originals, don't check that box—but remember to remove them once you're finished converting them).

6. Go to File ➤ Save (or press ⌘-S).

7. Enter a name for the Folder Action, such as Convert Movies To View On iPhone, and click Save.

Your Folder Action is now saved (at ~/Library/Workflow/Applications/Folder Actions) and ready to use. Here's how to apply it to ~/Downloads/Convert For iPhone.

1. Right-click on ~/Downloads/Convert For iPhone and choose Services ➤ Folder Actions Setup.

2. A sheet titled Choose A Script To Attach should appear. Select Convert Movies To View On iPhone and click Attach.

3. Close the Folder Actions Setup window.

Now test your new Automator workflow by putting a couple of short videos into ~/Downloads/Convert For iPhone. While Mac OS X is converting the videos, you'll see a sprocket icon in your Menu Bar. Once it's finished, you should see new movies in iTunes, under Library ➤ Movies. To add them to your iPhone, drag them to a playlist you sync with your iPhone and then sync that playlist the next time you plug your iPhone in to your Mac.

There are a lot of interesting things you can do with Folder Actions if you put your mind to it: FTPing files, converting images, moving new torrent files in a Dropbox folder to a folder watched by Transmission (see Chapter 6), and merging several PDFs into one all come to mind. If you can think of a regular action involving a particular folder that you'd like to make easier and more efficient, think of turning to Automator to help you do it.

Print Plugin

At first, this might not seem that useful. I mean, doesn't Mac OS X already do everything you could already want when it comes to printing? It even has built-in support for printing any document to PDF!

It turns out that when you create a workflow using the Print Plugin template, it actually works with those PDFs. So yes, it's the Print Plugin template, but it could almost instead be called the Print to PDF Plugin.

Here's an example of a task you can do with this template: rename and move PDFs as you print them.

I print a lot of web pages into PDFs for later reading, and I like the resulting PDFs stored in a folder I've created: ~/Downloads/To Read. Here's how to automatically put those files where I want them, named the way I like them.

1. Open Automator and select Print Plugin as a template.

2. Add **Actions ➤ Files & Folders ➤ Rename Finder Items** to your workflow (do not add the Copy Finder Items action when prompted).

3. For Rename Finder Items, select the following in the first column:

    a. Add Date Or Time

    b. Date/Time: Created

    c. Where: Before Name

    d. Separator: Space

    And in the second column:

    a. Format: Year Month Day

    b. Separator: None

    c. Check the box next to Use Leading Zeros

    The Example should now say: 20100628 Item Name.xxx.

4. Add **Actions ➤ Files & Folders ➤ Move Finder Items** to the workflow.

5. For To, select where you'd like your PDFs to end up. In my case, I chose ~/Downloads/To Read.

6. Go to **File ➤ Save** (or press ⌘-S).

7. Enter a name for the Print Plugin, such as To Read For Later, and click Save.

Your Print Plugin is now saved (at ~/Library/PDF Services) and ready to use. Open a web page and go to **File ➤ Print ➤ PDF ➤ To Read For Later**. The Print dialog will close and if you go look at ~/Downloads/To Read, you'll see a new PDF. Success!

> **NOTE:** If you're using Safari, the title of the web page is automatically inserted so that, for instance, if I was printing a story from *The New York Times*, the eventual file name would be 20100628 36 Hours in St. Louis—NYTimes.com.pdf. If you're using Chrome, however, the dang browser spits out 20100628 Untitled.pdf, which is really flippin' annoying.
>
> That's where the Choosy bookmarklet comes in (remember Choosy, which I talked about back in Chapter 5?), which you can grab at the bottom of this page: www.choosyosx.com/browsers. If you're in Chrome and want to print a page using the Print Plugin you create, click on the Choosy bookmarklet and re-open the page in Safari, and then print from there. I really like Chrome, but its print support kinda stinks.

Here's another idea: if you have Dropbox installed (discussed in Chapter 7) and you have an iPad, you could create a Print Plugin called Send To Dropbox that does just that: automatically saves a new PDF to a predefined folder in Dropbox, so you can then read those files on your iPad at your leisure.

iCal Alarm

I already covered this one earlier in this book. Go back to Chapter 2's "Repair Permissions Weekly With Automator" for a nice walkthrough of how you can use iCal Alarms to keep your Mac running smoothly, or to Chapter 6's "Making Mail Faster" for a hint about how to regularly compact Mail's database files. If you think about it, you can do pretty much any task you need to do on a timed basis with an iCal Alarm (or you could create an Application instead and then run it on recurring basis using Lingon, discussed earlier in this chapter).

Image Capture Plugin

If you're very particular about what happens to your photos when you plug in your digital camera or iPhone to your Mac, then you may find a good use for an Image Capture Plugin. Here's one example—let's say that you're really into black and white images, and you want the opportunity to review the new images on your digital camera, select the ones you wish to convert to black and white, convert them, and then import them into iPhoto, deleting them from your camera after doing so. That's actually really easy with Automator.

1. Open Automator and select Image Capture Plugin as a template.

2. Add **Actions > Photos > Apply Quartz Composition Filter To Image Files** to your workflow (do not add the Copy Finder Items action when prompted).

3. Select Black And White from the drop-down menu.

4. Add **Actions > Photos > Import Files Into iPhoto** to the workflow.

5. For the first drop-down menu, choose Existing Album. For the second, select Events. Check the box next to Delete The Source Images After Importing Them (if you want to keep the images so you can import them without the black and white effect, don't check that box).

6. Go to **File > Save** (or press ⌘-S).

7. Enter a name for the Image Capture Plugin, such as `Save As B&W For iPhoto`, and click Save.

Your Image Capture Plugin is now saved (at `~/Library/Workflows/Applications/Image Capture`) and ready to use, if you set a few things up. Namely, open `/Applications/Image Capture.app` and then plug in your digital camera or iPhone. Select the camera under Devices on the left side of the Image Capture window and you should see Device Settings at the bottom left, under your Devices. If you don't, click the Show Device Settings button at the very bottom left of the Image Capture window.

If you want to use Image Capture as the first interface that opens when you plug in your camera, select Image Capture for the drop-down under Connecting This iPhone Opens. If you don't, you'll have to open Image Capture every time you plug in your device.

> **NOTE:** I'm going to talk about Image Capture and these settings a bit more in the last section of this chapter, in which I discuss hardware.

By now, you should see all the images that are on your camera listed in the main part of the Image Capture window. If you see the list view and have a hard time making out the actual images, switch to the icon view by clicking the Show Items As Icons button at the bottom of the window.

Select the photos to which you want to apply the Image Capture Plugin, and then, in the Import To select menu, choose Save As B&W For iPhoto.workflow. Click Import, and a few moments later iPhoto will open and your new black and white images will be imported as a new Event (or Events, depending upon how far apart in time you took the pix). I've noticed that this process can take a bit of time, so be patient, especially if you have a lot of shots to process.

Of course, you don't have to import pictures into iPhoto. You could also save them to a folder in the Finder where you can manipulate them or view them. Or you can string together a whole series of Actions to process the images in several different ways. Or you can rename the images before importing them into iPhoto. And so on. If you want more control over what happens to your digital photos, Automator can come through for you.

> **TIP:** If you have the full-featured A Better Finder Rename (mentioned in Chapter 3 in my discussion of ForkLift), read "How to use Image Capture to import images to a specific folder and run A Better Finder Rename" (`www.publicspace.net/blog/a-better-finder-rename/2009/10/09/how-to-use-image-capture-to-import-images-to-a-specific-folder-and-run-a-better-finder-rename/`) for instructions about how to integrate it into a workflow for extremely sophisticated renaming of images when you import them.

Scheduling Programs, Scripts, and Jobs

Cron is a job-scheduling daemon that's been around in UNIX systems for decades. To this day, every UNIX box I've ever used has had cron on it, and I've scheduled many a recurring job by editing `/etc/crontab`. It's easy to set up, powerful, and works about as reliably as a nuclear clock.

You can still use cron on Mac OS X, and `/etc/crontab` is still there, but Apple actively discourages users from dabbling with cron. Starting with Mac OS X 10.4 Tiger, Apple introduced *launchd*, a program that is like cron on steroids. Make that steroids, five Red Bull energy drinks, and a few cups of coffee. So while cron is still on your Mac running Snow Leopard, Apple has made it very clear (at `http://developer.apple.com/mac/library/documentation/Darwin/Reference/ManPages/man8/launchd.8.html`) that you really shouldn't use it—or any of the other legacy methods for launching programs, scripts, and anything else:

> *In Darwin, the canonical way to launch a daemon is through launchd as opposed to more traditional mechanisms or mechanisms provided in earlier versions of Mac OS X. These alternate methods should be considered deprecated and not suitable for new projects.*

So that means I'm not going to say much more about cron and instead focus on launchd.

> **TIP:** If you want to learn about cron—and really, it's not all that complicated, it does still work on Mac OS X, and, frankly, I find it easier to set up and use than launchd, but that could be because I've been using it so long—then start with the Wikipedia article at `http://en.wikipedia.org/wiki/Cron`. If you need more, follow the links at the end of the article, or just search Google for `cron tutorial` and you'll find a gazillion hits.

However, in order to keep this book from becoming even longer, I'm also not going to go into the deep technical details of launchd, plists, and all the other stuff that makes launchd the powerhouse that it is.

Instead, I'm going to focus on a nice, free, open source tool for creating plists for launchd jobs: Lingon. Before detailing how to use Lingon, however, let's first understand why we need it in the first place.

Basically, the problem is that plist files are a lot more complicated to create than cron job entries. To demonstrate this, here's how I'd set up a job in `/etc/crontab` to run every day at 5 AM:

```
0 5 * * * rsgranne open /Users/rsgranne/bin/Automator/Update\ Times\ Reader.app
```

And this plist file—`com.granneman.UpdateTimesReader.plist`—performs the same function:

```
<?xml version="1.0" encoding="UTF-8"?>
<!DOCTYPE plist PUBLIC "-//Apple//DTD PLIST 1.0//EN"
"http://www.apple.com/DTDs/PropertyList-1.0.dtd">
<plist version="1.0">
<dict>
        <key>Label</key>
        <string>com.granneman.UpdateTimesReader</string>
        <key>ProgramArguments</key>
```

```
    <array>
            <string>/Users/rsgranne/bin/Automator/Update\ Times\ Reader.app</string>
    </array>
    <key>StartCalendarInterval</key>
    <dict>
            <key>Hour</key>
            <integer>5</integer>
            <key>Minute</key>
            <integer>0</integer>
    </dict>
</dict>
</plist>
```

As you can see, plist files are really XML files that are formatted a certain way, to Apple's exact specifications. The file indicates what you want to run, when, and how, along with any other particulars. Then you save the file in a folder. The particular folder you choose determines whom the plist runs as (you, root, someone else) and when the job runs. Table 12–1 shows you those folders, what they mean, and what Lingon calls them in its GUI:

Table 12–1. *Mac OS X Attaches Different Significance to Different Startup Items Depending upon Their Locations*

Folder	User	When It Loads	Notes	Lingon Name
~/Library/LaunchAgents	You	You login	Affect your files or run jobs specific to you	My Agents
/Library/LaunchAgents	Any user	Any user logs in	Run the same program for all users	Users Agents
/Library/LaunchDaemons	Root	Boot	Run no matter the user or run as root	Users Daemons
/System/Library/LaunchAgents	Root	Boot	Do not modify	System Agents
/System/Library/LaunchDaemons	Root	Boot	Preinstalled by Mac OS X; do not modify	System Daemons

Now that you understand why you need Lingon, let's talk about how to get it and use it. Download the program from http://sourceforge.net/projects/lingon/files/, but do not click the big green Download Now! button, as that is a very old version. Instead, download the latest version, 2.1.1, and install that.

Open Lingon and you'll see a window like the one in Figure 12–13 (I have a lot of entries under My Agents because I've been using Lingon for a while).

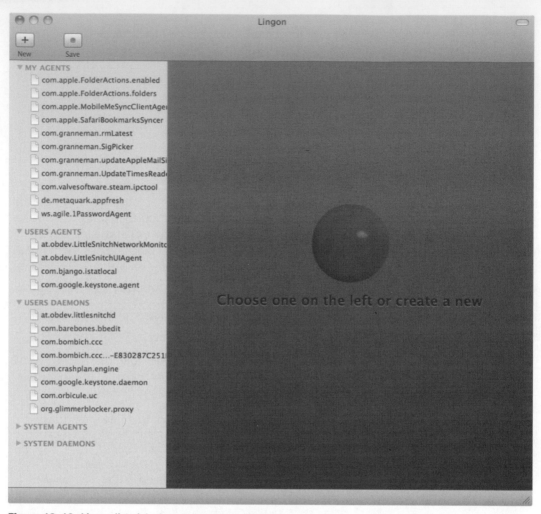

Figure 12–13. *Lingon lists jobs by category down the left.*

The five categories shown in Table 12–1 are listed down the side in Figure 12–13. Keep in mind that the bottom two—System Agents and System Daemons—should be considered look but don't touch. If you mess with those and you don't know exactly what you're doing, you can mess up your Mac, so *be careful*. In fact, approach any job that you didn't create with caution, but especially if they're in those two groups.

To create a new plist file, click on the New button (or go to **File ➤ New** or press ⌘-N). You're immediately asked which kind of launchd configuration file you want to create: My Agents, Users Agents, or Users Daemons. Let's assume that you want to create a job that runs when you log in, so choose My Agents and click Create. When you do, the right side of Lingon will reload to show what you see in Figure 12–14.

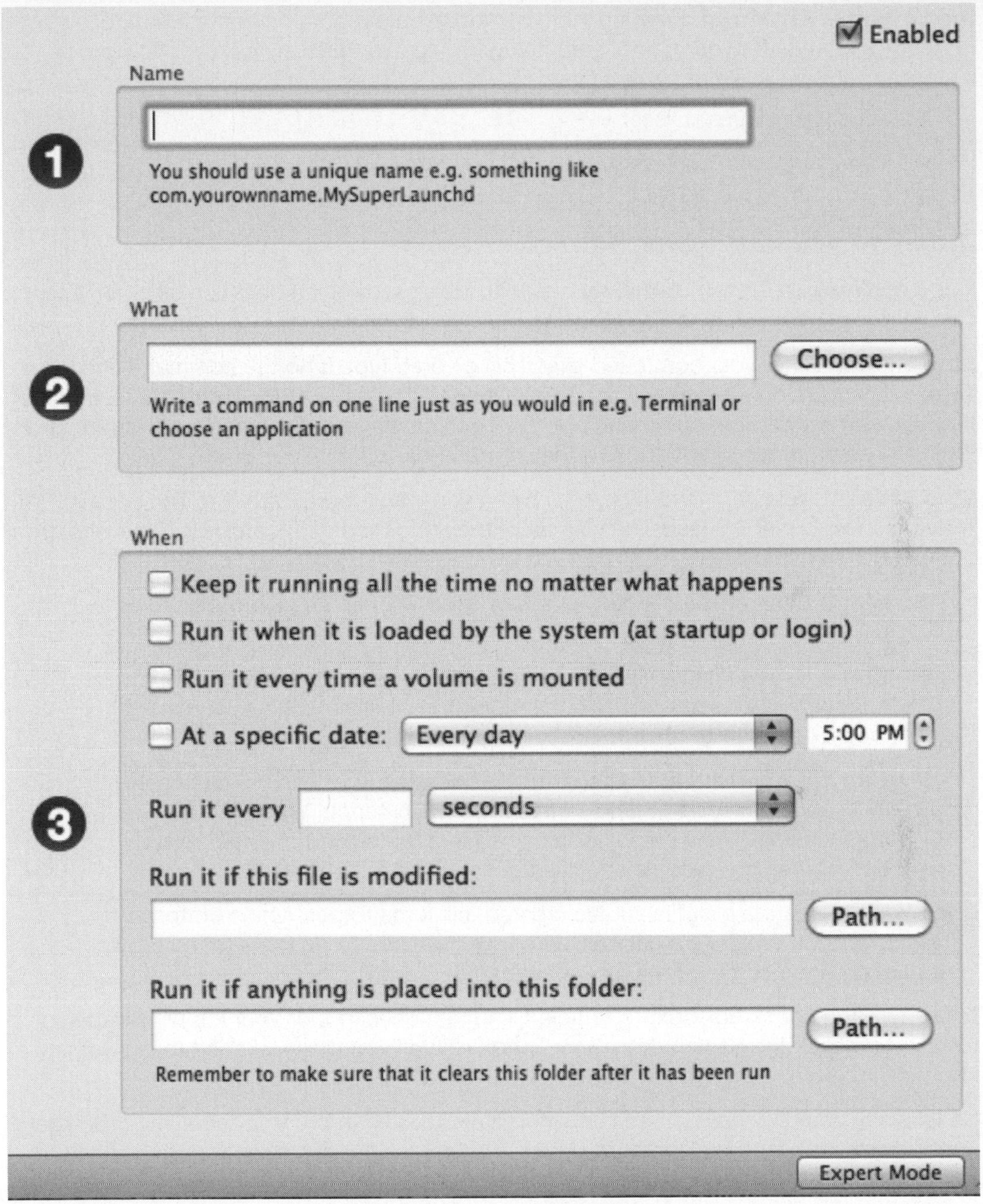

☑ Enabled

Name

1

You should use a unique name e.g. something like
com.yourownname.MySuperLaunchd

What

2

Choose...

Write a command on one line just as you would in e.g. Terminal or
choose an application

When

3

☐ Keep it running all the time no matter what happens

☐ Run it when it is loaded by the system (at startup or login)

☐ Run it every time a volume is mounted

☐ At a specific date: Every day   ▼   5:00 PM ⬍

Run it every [   ]   seconds   ▼

Run it if this file is modified:

Path...

Run it if anything is placed into this folder:

Path...

Remember to make sure that it clears this folder after it has been run

Expert Mode

Figure 12–14. *Lingon makes it pretty easy to create a plist file for launchd.*

You can see why Lingon is so popular from Figure 12–14—it makes it very easy to
create a launchd job by just going step by step.

Step 1 Name: Enter a unique name for your job. Apple recommends that you follow a reverse-DNS style for your name, something like `com.granneman.jobname`. So, for instance, here are a few of my job titles:

- `com.granneman.rmLatest`

- `com.granneman.SigPicker`

- `com.granneman.updateAppleMailSig`

- `com.granneman.UpdateTimesReader`

If you don't own a domain name, no big deal. Make something up, such as `com.yourname.jobname`, and you'll be fine.

Step 2 What: Enter your command exactly like you'd type it on the command line in Terminal. If you don't feel like typing, click Choose and navigate to your app. Remember that sometimes, though, commands on the Terminal have options and parameters after them, so don't forget to add those if they're necessary.

Step 3 When: Now you need to specify when you want your job to run. The options are fairly obvious, but notice especially some of the things that you can't easily do with cron but can do with launchd:

- **Run It Every Time A Volume Is Mounted:** Plug in an external hard drive and immediately have a script run.

- **Run It If This File Is Modified:** If you have a semaphore file that is modified when something you're monitoring happens, have launchd look for that file to change and then act accordingly.

- **Run It If Anything Is Placed Into This Folder:** This can be very useful if you're monitoring an app's instability, for instance. When the app crashes and a new crash file is placed in a folder, launchd will notice and will react as you've specified.

If you want to see the plist file you've created, click the Expert Mode button at the bottom of Lingon and take a gander. When you're ready to go back to the easier interface, click the same button, now changed to Basic Mode.

Make sure the check box next to Enabled is in fact checked, or your job will not be set to run. Now click the Save button, and Lingon will tell you that you need to log out and log back in for your changes to work. In fact, you don't need to do that.

So let's say your job was named `com.granneman.foobar`. In order to make my new Agent active, I'd type this on the command line:

```
$ launchctl load -w ~/Library/LaunchAgents/com.granneman.foobar
```

Of course, I used that particular path—`~/Library/LaunchAgents`—because the job I created was in My Agents. Refer to Table 12–1 to know what the path should be when you want to use launchctl.

If you want to disable jobs without deleting them, open Lingon, select the Agent, and then uncheck the box next to Enabled. Then type this on the command line:

```
$ launchctl unload -w ~/Library/LaunchAgents/com.granneman.foobar
```

Lingon makes something that's complicated—creating plist files for launchd—into something that's much quicker and easier. That's the great part. But there's one problem with Lingon: it's no longer in active development. The last release was in December 2008, and the developer has announced that he's no longer working on the project.

That said, Lingon is open source and pretty popular in the Macverse, so I'm hoping (and pretty certain) that someone else will take it over. At any rate, Lingon works with Snow Leopard just fine, and barring some major changes in the successor to Snow Leopard, it should work fine then too. But when that successor comes out, do some research first before relying on it.

Further Resources

If you want to learn more about launchd and plists—and it is interesting, so I encourage you to do some reading on the subject—I'd start with these:

- "Getting Started with launchd"
  http://developer.apple.com/macosx/launchd.html
  Apple's semi-canonical article on the subject. The place to start.

- "launchd"
  http://en.wikipedia.org/wiki/Launchd
  Wikipedia has a nice introduction to the subject, with lots of good pointers to other resources.

- "All About launchd Items (and How To Make One Yourself)"
  www.macgeekery.com/tips/all_about_launchd_items_and_how_to_make
  _one_yourself
  A nice walkthrough that teaches you how to do everything by hand.

There's a wealth of infomation, even entire websites, about Automator out there on the Interwebs. Here's where I'd go first:

- "Automator Programming Guide"
  http://developer.apple.com/mac/library/documentation/AppleAppli
  cations/Conceptual/AutomatorConcepts/Automator.html
  If you want to develop Automator Actions, or learn more about the technical parts of Automator, start here.

- "Automator Actions"
  www.apple.com/downloads/macosx/automator/
  At this time, 137 third-party Actions you can download, install, and use in Automator. There's some excellent stuff here!

- Mac OS X Automation
  www.macosxautomation.com
  An entire website devoted to automating tasks on Mac OS X. Be sure
  to check out the download page, at
  http://macosxautomation.com/services/download/, as there are vital
  Services and Actions there.

- Automator • Leopard
  http://automator.us
  Even though this website hasn't been updated for Snow Leopard,
  that's OK, since almost all of it still works fine.

Switching Your DNS

I'll just say it up front: if we didn't have DNS, the Domain Name Service, using the
Internet would be much more difficult and tedious, and far less widespread. When you
type www.apple.com into your web browser, you're using DNS. Behind the scenes, lots of
DNS servers and services are translating that domain name into an IP address such as
96.7.29.15. The same thing happens when you send an e-mail to scott@granneman.com,
download a file from www.panic.com, or SSH to www.myserver.com—DNS translates those
domain names into IP addresses so that you get where you want to go, without having
to type in an IP addresses.

NOTE: We're in the middle of a slow transition (though it will speed up soon) to the next
generation of IP, IPv6. With the current generation of IP—v4—we have a total of 4,294,967,296
addresses, and we're running out quickly. With IPv6, addresses will now consist of eight groups
of four hexadecimal (0-9 and A-F) digits, and will look something like this:

2001:0db8:85a3:0000:0000:8a2e:0370:7334

How many IP addresses will we have available once we've moved to IPv6? Are you sitting down?
Try 340 trillion trillion trillion. Written out, that's:

340,282,366,920,938,463,463,374,607,431,768,211,456

Spoken aloud, it's 340 undecillion, 282 decillion, 366 nonillion, 920 octillion, 938 septillion, 463
sextillion, 463 quintillion, 374 quadrillion, 607 trillion, 431 billion, 768 million, 211 thousand, and
456!

For more on this mind-boggling number, check out
www.wolframalpha.com/input/?i=2^128.

Most of the time, people use the DNS they've been assigned. Either the office they work
in has DNS already configured, or they use their ISP's DNS settings, or their DNS is
auto-assigned via DHCP. However, it doesn't have to be that way. You can change your

DNS settings and use a third-party service instead, which is what I'm going to cover in this section.

Why & How to Switch DNS

So if DNS is so critical, why switch it? There are actually several reasons you might want to do so:

- **Reliability:** Back when I was using AT&T DSL at home, DNS seemed to go out regularly. The Internet connection was still up, and I could get to locations via an IP address, but DNS was broken. In cases like that, switching to a more reliable DNS provider would mean that I would never have to deal with AT&T's incompetence (of course, I also own an iPhone, so I get to deal with AT&T's incompetence every day).

- **Response speed:** Some DNS servers are slower than others, and that slows down use of the Internet. Faster DNS servers mean faster web browsing. Who doesn't want faster?

- **Propagation speed:** When my company, WebSanity, builds websites, we often have to set up DNS for a test site. We then have to wait for the DNS to propagate through the major DNS servers of the world, which can take some time. We've found that waiting for our ISP's DNS servers can take a while, but if we use a third-party DNS provider, we can view the client's testing website much sooner.

> **NOTE:** Yes, we could just as easily edit our `/etc/hosts` file (more info at `http://en.wikipedia.org/wiki/Hosts_file`), but too often we forget to edit it back, and that causes boo-boos later. So we find it's better to wait for DNS propagation instead.

- **Additional features:** Some third-party DNS providers go beyond mere DNS and provide additional services that make using the Net safer or more efficient.

Why wouldn't you want to switch your DNS? Well, there are really only a couple of reasons:

- Your IT guys at work don't want you to use anyone's DNS but your company's and will blow a gasket if you do.

- Some networks don't play well with your Mac when you don't use their DNS. When I bring my laptop to Washington University in St. Louis to teach, I switch my Network location to one that uses straight DHCP, which means that I'm using Wash U's DNS. If I use one of my other locations, which all have third-party DNS hard-coded in, I can't get anywhere on the Net. Switch to the location that's just DHCP, and I'm flying.

For that last reason, you should create multiple locations in the Network System Preference. Although you can create as many as you like, I currently have four:

- Automatic (which is straight DHCP)
- OpenDNS
- Google DNS
- DynDNS

Set up a different DNS in each one by going to > System Preferences > Network and then, in the Location select list, selecting Edit Locations and adding the appropriate information. For DNS, click on Advanced, go to the DNS tab, and click on the + to add the DNS records I'll give you in the next section. Click OK to save your additions, and you can quickly switch between your various locations as you need from > Location.

OpenDNS vs. Google Public DNS vs. DynDNS

There are several different DNS providers out there, but I want to focus on three that I've used and that do a great job: OpenDNS, Google Public DNS, and DynDNS.

OpenDNS

Started in 2006 by David Ulevitch, a recent Washington University in St. Louis grad (go Wash U!), OpenDNS is growing like Topsy and currently serves over 20 billion DNS requests every day. Switching to OpenDNS couldn't be easier—just change your DNS to use these addresses (complete, step-by-step instructions for Mac OS X are at `https://store.opendns.com/setup/operatingsystem/apple-osx-leopard`):

- 208.67.222.222
- 208.67.220.220

In fact, OpenDNS provides clear instructions (including screencasts) for setting up more than your Mac to use its services. Head to `https://store.opendns.com/setup/` and you'll find details for:

- **Operating systems:** Mac OS X, of course, but also Windows, Linux, and Wii
- **Routers:** 18 different models, as well as generic instructions
- **DNS Servers:** Windows, Mac OS X, and Linux, including the ubiquitous BIND (the Berkeley Internet Name Daemon, the most commonly used DNS server on the Net)

If you want to use the many services provided by OpenDNS, however, you need to set up an account. The company has three levels—Basic, Deluxe, and Enterprise—that are reasonably priced at, respectively, free, $10 per household or $5 per user per year, and $2,000 per year. In this section, I'll focus on what you get with the free account, but if you want to learn more, head to www.opendns.com/start/ and check out the useful chart there that breaks down the differences between the accounts.

Here are some of the more interesting services you get with a free account:

Web content filtering: Block access to various websites in over 50 categories, including gambling, drugs, dating, sports, pornography, movies, and radio (a good list is at www.opendns.com/community/domaintagging/categories). You can select categories yourself, or choose Low, Medium, and High levels. Or you can do as I do and select None.

Block proxies and anonymizers used to bypass blocking: Those who want to get past site blocks often can by using proxies and anonymizer websites. OpenDNS prevents that so that blocked sites stay blocked.

> **NOTE:** Personally, I'm not a big fan of blocking access to sites, but I know many people—and businesses—are, and OpenDNS makes that free and easy to do. I'm not endorsing it, but it is a major service provided by OpenDNS.

Whitelist and blacklist domains: You can limit access to only a few websites (a whitelist) or deny access to specific websites (a blacklist). Either way, the free account limits you to 25 domains.

Phishing protection: If you hate phishing (http://en.wikipedia.org/wiki/Phishing) like I do, you'll be thrilled to learn that OpenDNS does an excellent job of blocking phishing websites. In fact, OpenDNS runs PhishTank (http://en.wikipedia.org/wiki/Phishtank), a huge collection of data about scam websites that is constantly updated and so far, according to the company, has identified over a half-million phishing frauds. In fact, it's so good that it's used by many other companies and software, including Yahoo, Mozilla, 1Password, and even Google Chrome!

Botnet protection: OpenDNS blocks access to sites known to serve up malware that infects computers and brings them under the control of criminals (granted, this is 99.999% a Windows problem, but still, it's good to have the protection available). If machines are already compromised, OpenDNS will alert users that it detects certain bot activity on their networks.

Detailed reports and statistics: You can see charts showing statistics for total DNS requests, total unique domains, top domains, blocked domains, and more. The free account archives the data for two weeks.

Typo correction: I constantly type .cmo instead of .com into my browsers' address bars, and OpenDNS automatically fixes my request for me. It will also make sure you don't accidentally end up on a website in Cameroon by accidentally typing .cm instead of .com as well.

Shortcuts: Basically, on your OpenDNS shortcuts page, you enter something like fb and point it to www.facebook.com. Then you just type fb into your browser's address bar,

OpenDNS sees it, and it then redirects you to Facebook's website. That is, unless you're using Google Chrome, in which case you need to enter `http://fb` into your browser's address bar (since Google Chrome allows you to enter URLs and searches into what it calls the Omnibox). Set up shortcuts and you'll be able to jump to your favorite websites with next-to-no typing at all.

With all that, OpenDNS must be perfect, right? Well, as great as it is—and I really like OpenDNS a lot—there are some caveats you should know about.

Failed requests: If you try to go to a domain that doesn't exist, or hasn't propagated yet, DNS specifications say that you should receive an error (see `http://en.wikipedia.org/wiki/DNS_hijacking` and `www.faqs.org/rfcs/rfc2308.html`). If you're using OpenDNS, however, you'll end up at a search page with ads and search results from Yahoo, which you can see in Figure 12–15.

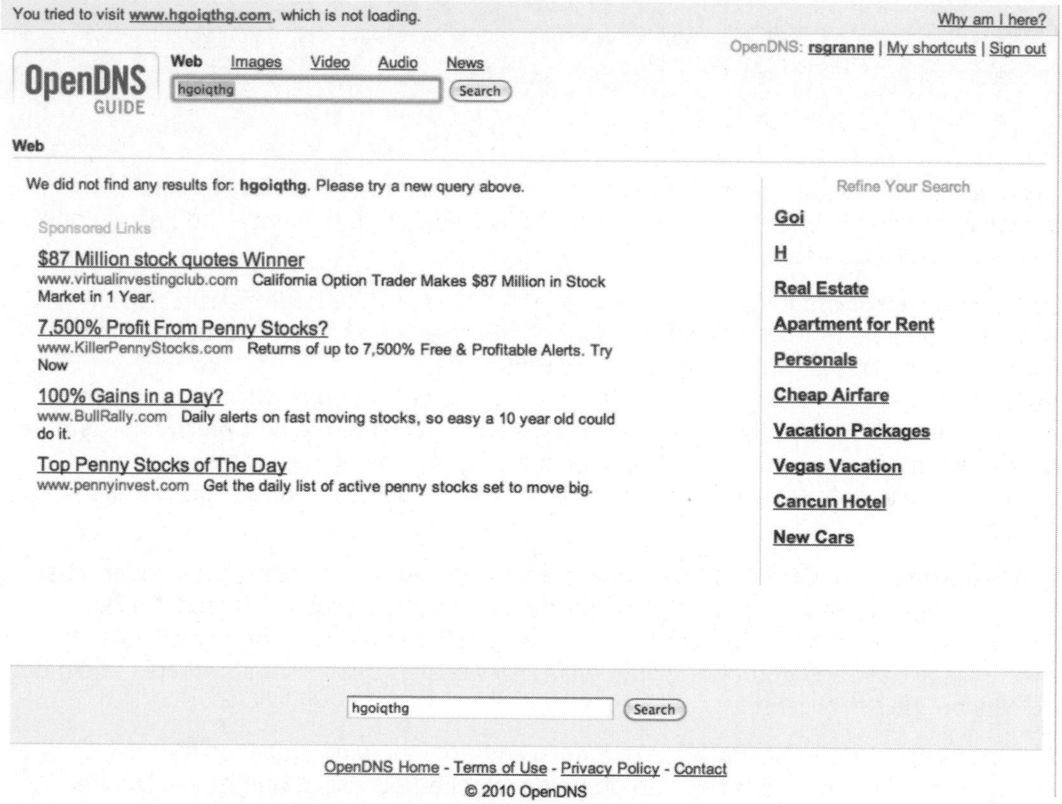

Figure 12–15. *Not the prettiest sight, is it?*

This can be particularly annoying if you're doing network tests to see if a domain has propagated yet, and instead of an error, you get results from OpenDNS. When I need to verify failure, I need to see failure, not false positives.

I understand why OpenDNS creates this page—David Ulevitch and his team are offering a free service to millions of people, after all, and they have to pay their bills. Fortunately, you can turn this "feature" off in your account's settings, but if you do, you'll lose the ability to filter content. In my case, I don't want to filter content, but if you do, you need to weigh the negatives of doing that along with the benefits.

Not-so-obvious redirections: Sometimes, OpenDNS resolves DNS requests without the user realizing it; however, in most of those cases, the user was about to be sneakily redirected by a piece of software on her computer, so it's kind of a wash. Still, you should know that OpenDNS can and does do these redirections. In my opinion, what OpenDNS is doing is less bad than what the sneakware is doing, and OpenDNS is actually trying to right a perceived wrong, so I give the company a pass. For all the gory technical details, read Ulevitch's blog post at `http://blog.opendns.com/2007/05/22/google-turns-the-page/` and Amit Agarwal at `http://www.labnol.org/software/browsers/prevent-opendns-google-redirects-firefox-address-bar-ie/2662/`.

Overall, OpenDNS is a great service that I use constantly, at home and while I travel. If I have issues with it—I can't use it at a particular location, for instance, or I'm testing DNS propagation and need to see error messages—I either switch to DHCP or use Google's service, discussed next.

Google Public DNS

Late in 2009, Google announced that it too was getting into the free DNS game with a service called Google Public DNS. Why did Google do this? To make the Web faster, according to the company. Remember, for Google, the better the Web, the more people will use the Web, and the more people using the Web, the more advertising that Google can sell.

Switching to Google Public DNS is super-duper simple, because Google's DNS addresses are easy to remember:

- 8.8.8.8
- 8.8.4.4

That's it! If you want more info, feel free to check out Google's pages about their service at `http://code.google.com/speed/public-dns/`, but there's not much more to it.

But how does Google's service compare to that offered by OpenDNS?

- Google doesn't offer any of the other services provided by OpenDNS. Oh, there are a few security features—which you can read about at `http://code.google.com/speed/public-dns/docs/security.html`—but the main focus is on providing DNS. If you want all those other services, you want OpenDNS. If you just want a rock-solid DNS service, then Google will do the trick.

- Unlike OpenDNS, Google doesn't filter or redirect anything. Failed queries result in an error message, which is in accordance with the DNS protocol's standards, and Google doesn't even show you a page of Google ads and search results. This is laudable, and for people who constantly deal with DNS and domains, this may be enough to convince them to go with Google Public DNS.

If you want to use Google Public DNS, you don't need a Google account. In fact, you can't tie your DNS queries to your Google account, because there's no way to associate an account with Google Public DNS! Any information Google collects about IP addresses is deleted after 24 hours, which is great for privacy.

It doesn't hurt to set up a Network Location for Google Public DNS on your Mac, so why not do it? Try it, test it, and see what you think.

DynDNS

I'm biased to like DynDNS (www.dyndns.com) quite a bit. I've been using it personally for close to a decade, and my company has been using it in one way or another for almost that long. In all that time, I've been thrilled with its service and support. The company originally provided DNS server hosting—I would use DynDNS to manage where www.granneman.com, ftp.granneman.com, and mail.granneman.com all pointed—but it's branched out to offer domain registrations, SSL certificates, URL redirection, and recursive DNS, which is what we're looking at here.

> **NOTE:** DNS server hosting meant that the rest of the world would know how to get to my domains. Recursive DNS—which, again, is what I've been discussing in this section—allows me to find the rest of the world's domains.

To use DynDNS's DNS service, you need an account with DynDNS. I'm going to go ahead and tell you what number you need to add into the DNS tab in your Network System Preferences:

- 216.146.35.35

- 216.146.36.36

However, you have to associate your computer's IP address with a DNS record at DynDNS or it won't work. If you have a static IP address that never changes, no problem—you could even just set things up on your home or business router, assuming your ISP lets you use a static IP address, and you'd be done. But if you have a dynamic IP address, either because your ISP changes it regularly or because you travel around to different networks (like I do), then you need to install some free software from DynDNS that will keep things up-to-date for you. I'll walk you through the process, though, so it won't be too complicated.

Ready? Start by going to the web page at www.dyndns.com/services/dynguide/ for DynDNS Internet Guide, which is what DynDNS calls its service. Table 12–2 shows you the three levels of the service that you can use.

Table 12–2. *DynDNS Offers Three Levels, All Reasonably Priced*

Internet Guide Service	Cost	Dynamic Networks	Defense Plans	Whitelists & Blacklists	Static Addresses & Network Ranges
Free	Free	1	1	0	No
Pro	$20/year	3	3	100 of each	Yes
Premium	$40/year	10	10	240 of each	Yes

Let me explain what some of those columns mean.

- **Defense Plan:** This is a customized set of restrictions that you set up for your Dynamic Network, discussed next. There are three components to your Defense Plan:

    - Defense Strategy: A quick configuration corresponding to None (nothing blocked), Low (viruses, phishing, and fraud), Medium (NSFW websites), and High (not suitable for children). This is good if you want something quick.

    - Blocked Categories: Block certain kinds of websites by category, such as Adult, Gambling, Hacking, Game, and Conficker Worm (that last one seems useful for Windows users!).

    - Advanced Settings: Whitelists and blacklists, and whether or not you want non-existent domains to display a DNS error (like Google Public DNS does) or search results and other "help" (like OpenDNS does).

- **Dynamic Network:** You associate your Defense Plan with a network, but that network can consist of several different things: a dynamic or custom DNS hostname, a static IP address, or a CIDR block if you're managing a large network (for more on CIDR, see http://en.wikipedia.org/wiki/CIDR). In this section, I'll assume you want to associate a Defense Plan with a dynamic DNS hostname, a process I'll go through soon.

- **Whitelists & Blacklists:** You can specify addresses that are never banned and ones that are always banned. Free accounts can't do this, but paying accounts can, within limits.

■ **Static Addresses & Network Ranges:** You can use the service with more than just dynamic DNS hosts; in fact, you can also use it with DNS addresses that don't change or even network ranges like 10.0.0.1/24. Again, this is something free accounts can't do.

To begin actually signing up for the service you want, you have to have an account with DynDNS. Go to `https://www.dyndns.com/account/entrance/` and create one. After that, you need to create a domain name to which you will link your Mac. If you already have domains at DynDNS, you can use any that have A records, but if you don't, it's not a problem—just create a free dynamic DNS name that's tied to your Mac's IP address. It's easy, and did I mention that it's free? To start, go to `https://www.dyndns.com/services/dns/dyndns/` and click Create Hostname.

> **NOTE:** If you don't know an A record from a CNAME and you want to learn more about DNS, check out `http://en.wikipedia.org/wiki/Domain_Name_System` and then move on to `http://en.wikipedia.org/wiki/List_of_DNS_record_types`.

On the next page, select a domain name from the long select list and then type in a subdomain in the text box next to Hostname. In my case, I selected dyndns.org and entered *granneman* (clever, I know). I left Wildcard Status disabled and set Service Type to Host With IP Address.

Under the IP Address text box is a URL with your current IP address in it. If you click it, the web page will automatically fill in that text box with your IP address. I did so, ignored everything on the page, scrolled down to the bottom, and clicked Add To Cart. On the following page I clicked Next, and on the following page I clicked Activate Services. Now that part's done.

> **NOTE:** Again, if you have your own domain name—like I have granneman.com—and you manage the DNS for that domain with DynDNS (which I heartily recommend), then you can just create a subdomain like `mac.granneman.com`, create an A record for it, point it to your current IP public address (not your private address, like 192.168.x.x, or 10.0.x.x, but a public IP address), and use that with the DynDNS Updater.

The next step: download and install the DynDNS Updater for Mac OS X from `www.dyndns.com/support/clients/`. Start the program and enter your DynDNS account information. A few seconds later, the program will download information from DynDNS and display your domain names with A records, including the free dynamic one you just set up. Select that domain, and you'll see something like Figure 12–16.

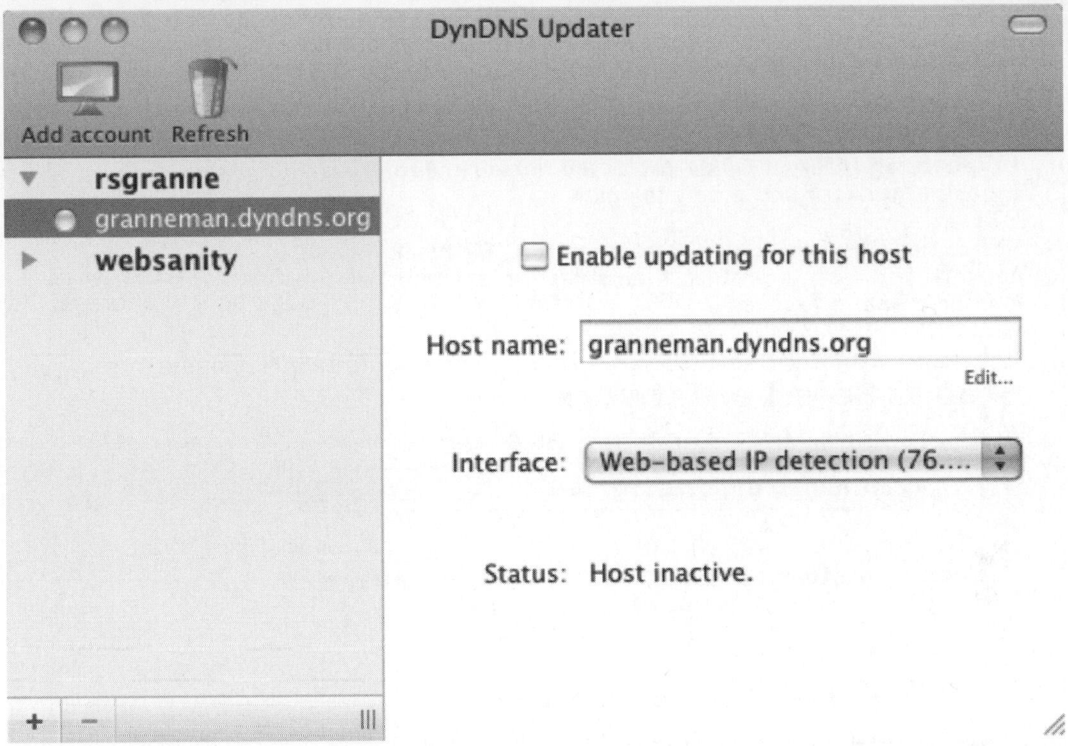

Figure 12–16. *Setting up the DynDNS Updater is easy-peasy.*

Check the box next to Enable Updating For This Host—that's the magic that will keep everything working. Of course, to work effectively, DynDNS needs to know your current IP address, which will be reported to the website by the Updater whenever that address changes. But how does it get your IP address? That's where Interface comes in. The safest thing to pick is Web-Based IP Detection, but if that proves problematic, choose Web-Based IP Detection (Bypassing Proxy).

At that point, you're done with the DynDNS Updater, although if you want it to start automatically when you boot your Mac, you should add it to > System Preferences > Accounts > Login Items.

Now go to where you'll manage your DynDNS Internet Guide, at https://www.dyndns.com/account/services/dynguide/. Click the Add New button, and you'll see a popup window similar to Figure 12–17.

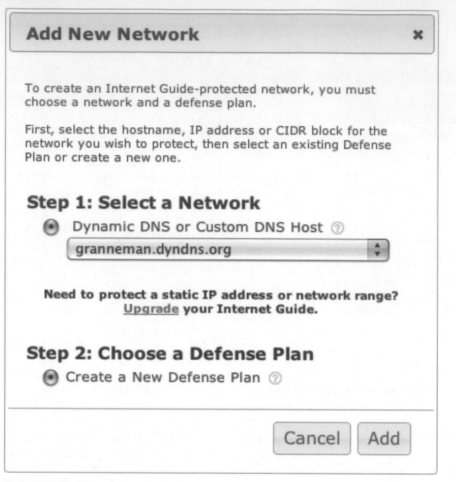

Figure 12–17. *We're so close to the finish!*

Under Step 1, choose a network. If you've been following along, you'll have only one choice. In my case, it was granneman.dyndns.org.

Under Step 2, choose a Defense Plan. However, I don't have one yet, so I have to go with Create A New Defense Plan.

Click Add, and I'm there! I can finally create my Defense Plan and decide what I want to block, if anything! Give your Defense Plan a name, make your settings, save them, and you're good to go. DynDNS is now defending your Mac—or your network, if you set it up on your router—along with providing you with fast, reliable DNS. It's a few steps to set up, but once you do it should work beautifully, without much involvement from you again.

DynDNS is a bit more complicated to set up than OpenDNS or Google Public DNS—OK, it's a lot more complicated—but if you're already using DynDNS, or you're a DNS junkie, or you want really great service at a very reasonable price, then you might find it to be perfect for your needs.

Testing Your DNS

As I said earlier in this section, it's easy to change your DNS. As long as you won't get in trouble for doing it, I say go for it, switch between the ones you have, and see what you like. However, if you're a numbers person, if you like to test and measure first before you make a move, then you might find this section particularly interesting.

Before you actually change your DNS, you can test the various options to see which one would deliver the best speed for you. Thomas Stromberg, an engineer at Google, created a fantastic tool called Namebench that will perform over two hundred different tests of various DNS servers—including several I haven't even covered!—to give you some numbers that you can use to make a decision. You can download the free (and open source!) Namebench from http://code.google.com/p/namebench/.

When you open Namebench, you'll see a window like Figure 12–18.

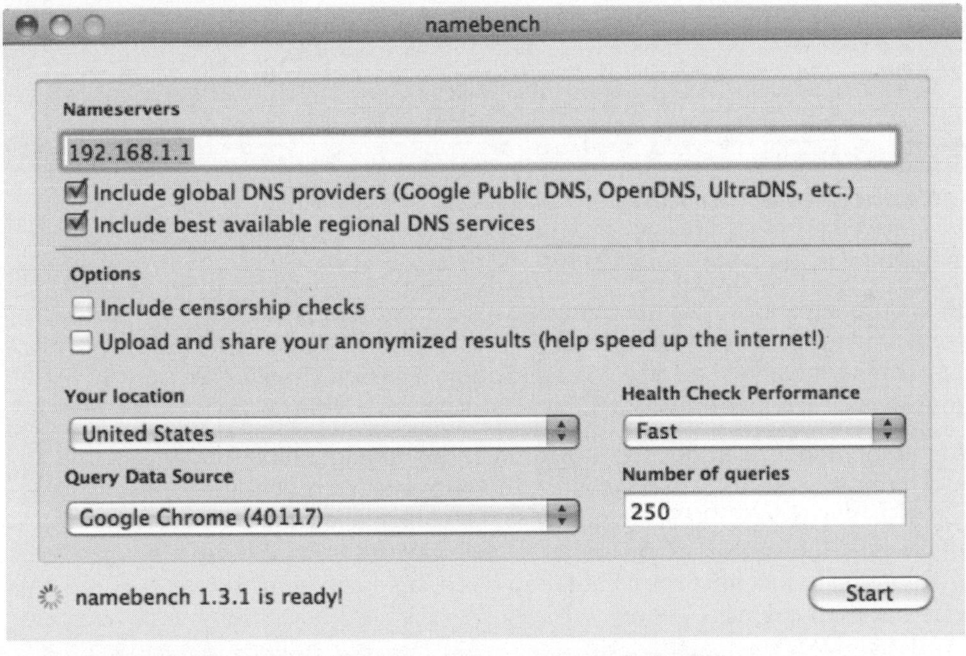

Figure 12–18. *Namebench is pretty much ready to use when you first open it.*

You can go ahead and click Start if you'd like, but it would be nice if you checked the box next to Upload And Share Your Anonymized Results, so that others can benefit from your results. If you check Include Censorship Links, Namebench will test to see if your ISP is blocking your access to certain sites, with the full list at http://code.google.com/p/namebench/source/browse/trunk/config/hostname_reference.cfg.

Namebench will run its suite of tests, which can take a while, and at the end it will prompt you to open a local web page with your results. You can see the top part of my results (I cut off several graphs, a link to a CSV file of the results, and details about Namebench's config file) in Figure 12–19.

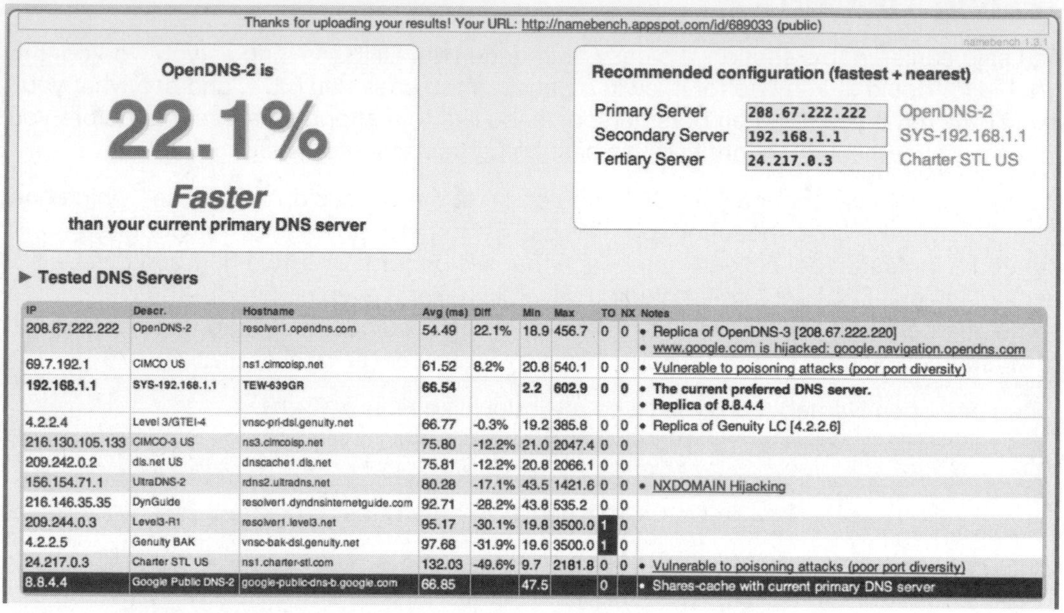

IP	Descr.	Hostname	Avg (ms)	Diff	Min	Max	TO	NX	Notes
208.67.222.222	OpenDNS-2	resolver1.opendns.com	54.49	22.1%	18.9	456.7	0	0	• Replica of OpenDNS-3 [208.67.222.220] • www.google.com is hijacked: google.navigation.opendns.com
69.7.192.1	CIMCO US	ns1.cimcoisp.net	61.52	8.2%	20.8	540.1	0	0	• Vulnerable to poisoning attacks (poor port diversity)
192.168.1.1	**SYS-192.168.1.1**	**TEW-639GR**	**66.54**		**2.2**	**602.9**	**0**	**0**	• **The current preferred DNS server.** • **Replica of 8.8.4.4**
4.2.2.4	Level 3/GTEI-4	vnsc-pri-dsl.genuity.net	66.77	-0.3%	19.2	385.8	0	0	• Replica of Genuity LC [4.2.2.6]
216.130.105.133	CIMCO-3 US	ns3.cimcoisp.net	75.80	-12.2%	21.0	2047.4	0	0	
209.242.0.2	dls.net US	dnscache1.dls.net	75.81	-12.2%	20.8	2066.1	0	0	
156.154.71.1	UltraDNS-2	rdns2.ultradns.net	80.28	-17.1%	43.5	1421.6	0	0	• NXDOMAIN Hijacking
216.146.35.35	DynGuide	resolver1.dyndnsinternetguide.com	92.71	-28.2%	43.8	535.2	0	0	
209.244.0.3	Level3-R1	resolver1.level3.net	95.17	-30.1%	19.8	3500.0	1	0	
4.2.2.5	Genuity BAK	vnsc-bak-dsl.genuity.net	97.68	-31.9%	19.6	3500.0	1	0	
24.217.0.3	Charter STL US	ns1.charter-stl.com	132.03	-49.6%	9.7	2181.8	0	0	• Vulnerable to poisoning attacks (poor port diversity)
8.8.4.4	Google Public DNS-2	google-public-dns-b.google.com	66.85		47.5		0		• Shares-cache with current primary DNS server

Figure 12–19. *Namebench gives you results and recommendations for what to do next.*

There are three main parts to Figure 12–19:

- In the top left, in nice big numbers and letters, the overall recommendation. In my case, OpenDNS's second DNS server is 22% faster than the one I had been using (Google's, which I had set on my router).
- In the top right is Namebench's recommended configuration for my top three DNS servers. In my case, it recommends, in order, OpenDNS's second DNS server, my router (which it knows is a replica of Google Public DNS), and Charter's DNS. Charter is my ISP, so it's not surprising that it finished in the top three, but keep in mind that it *was* still third overall!
- Under those two sections is a table showing the 11 Tested DNS Servers, with a wealth of information about each, including IP address, hostname, times in milliseconds, and notes (interestingly, those notes also point out that several of the DNS providers hijack incorrect results to show ads).

If you want more details, there's even more if you scroll down the web page, including the full test results in CSV format, which the super-nerdy might find fun to play with.

I had Google Public DNS set in my router when I ran the test the first time, so I thought it might be interesting to change to DynDNS and see what happened when I ran the test a second time. The results? OpenDNS is 46% faster than DynDNS on my router! Namebench recommends that I set my three recommended DNS servers to, in order:

- OpenDNS
- My router (DynDNS)
- Charter, my ISP

Verrry interesting!

Now that you know a lot more about your DNS options, try them out. Create some Locations in the Network System Preferences, run some tests with Namebench, and see what works best for you and your network. You may be in for a big surprise!

Hardware

Before leaving this chapter, I wanted to quickly cover a few tools that will help you work with your hardware a little more efficiently. Some of these fix annoyances, some provide functionality, and some do both.

Acquiring Better Mouse Drivers

Plug in pretty much any Bluetooth or USB mouse, and Mac OS X will work with it out of the box. That doesn't mean, though, that the Mouse System Preference is all that and a bag of chips, however. There are several alternatives that I have found to be much better in terms of giving me more control over my mouse.

I use a USB mouse (a Logitech MX500, to be precise), and I don't particularly like the Logitech Control Center software that comes with the mouse. It didn't allow me to middle-click (click on the Wheel, in other words) on hyperlinks in web browsers to open them in new background tabs, which I consider essential. Further, Logitech made a practice for quite a while of basing their mouse drivers on Unsanity's Application Enhancer, which they secretly installed without it being clear to users. When it came time to upgrade to Leopard, a lot of people had major problems booting (for more on this, see `http://daringfireball.net/2007/10/blue_in_the_face`). Logitech later stopped this practice, but for me, the damage was done.

Those are just my problems with the Logitech Control Center, but others report lots of other issues, as you can see for yourself at VersionTracker (`www.versiontracker.com/dyn/moreinfo/mac/14421`) and MacUpdate (`www.macupdate.com/reviews.php?id=8154`).

You have other options, and two that I've used over the years are USB Overdrive and SteerMouse.

USB Overdrive is good software that you can download from `www.usboverdrive.com/USBOverdrive/`. It works with any USB or Bluetooth mouse and any USB trackball, joystick, gamepad, and media keyboard. If you boot your Mac using either the 32- or 64-bit kernel, you're covered, as it supports both. USB Overdrive costs $20, but it's one of the least annoying shareware apps I've ever used, with a reminder when you log in and a short countdown when you launch the program.

Because it allows you to try it for free, I definitely recommend that you download USB Overdrive and give it a whirl. I don't use it now, because I like SteerMouse a teeny bit better for my needs, but I happily used USB Overdrive for years.

SteerMouse works with USB or Bluetooth mice and is available from http://plentycom.jp/en/steermouse/ (Apple Magic Mouse users should head to http://plentycom.jp/en/magicdriver/). You get a generous 30-day free trial period, but after that it will cost you $20.

SteerMouse is a System Preference, but when you click it you launch the SteerMouse app, which has four tabs: Buttons, Wheel, Tilt Wheel, and Cursor. You can see the first tab, Buttons, in Figure 12–20.

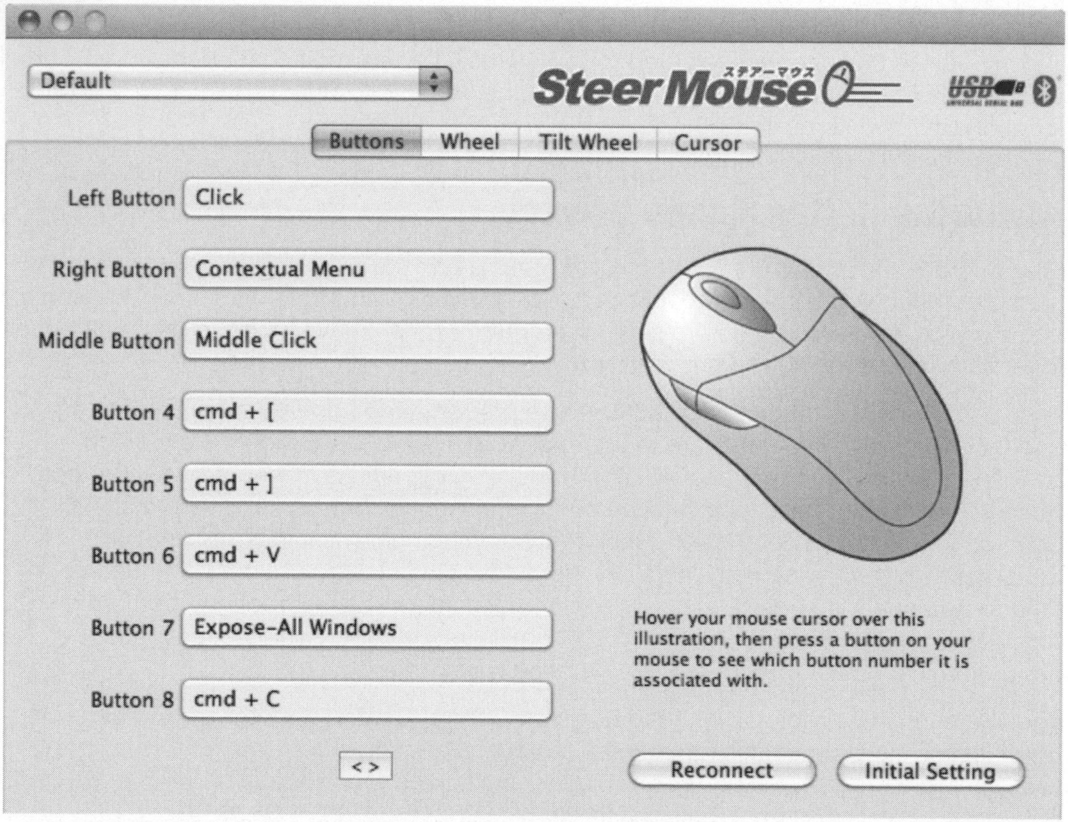

Figure 12–20. *Make your mouse buttons do what you want them to do.*

My mouse has eight buttons, and I can program them all to do what I want them to do, so that no buttons are wasted. This is wonderfully useful, but notice the drop-down menu on the top left in Figure 12–20, the one that says Default? By default, my settings on the Buttons tab work in every program on my Mac. But what if I need different settings in other programs? No problem. Click on that drop-down, choose Add/Remove Applications, and make your new settings.

For instance, even though I had Middle Click set for the Middle Button, Safari wouldn't open a link in a new background tab when I middle-clicked on it. Every other browser worked fine, but not Safari. So I created a new group of Settings for Safari, which you can see in Figure 12–21.

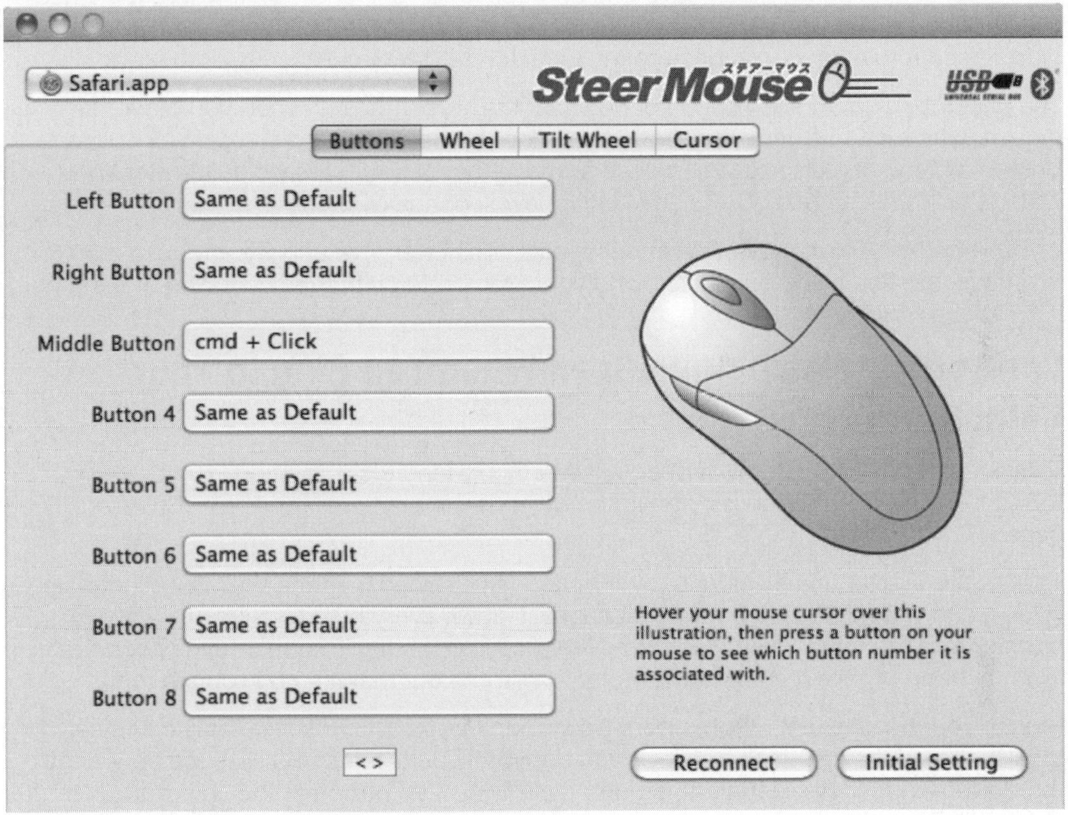

Figure 12–21. *Now middle-clicking does what I want in Safari!*

Everything else is the same except the Middle Button. By default, it gives a Middle Click, but in Safari, it instead does a ⌘-Click, which works to open a link in a new background tab. Woohoo!

If you game, you'll love this feature, as you can load different weapons or do different things with your mouse in each different game. If you're a big Microsoft Office user, map your buttons for that program. Mail? Sure, why not? The point is, customize your buttons for your apps to be more productive (or to solve problems, like I did with Safari).

NOTE: It's not just the buttons you customize for each app; it's all the tabs in SteerMouse. But I was focusing on Buttons because that's the most-used tab. At least it is for me.

The next tab, Wheel, allows you to control what happens when you roll the wheel up or down, and if you want the scrolling to accelerate or decelerate.

Tilt Wheel is only handy if you have one of those fancy-shmancy mice where the wheel tilts left and right in addition to scrolling up and down. I've tried them before, and I just didn't need it very much, so back to my Logitech MX500 I went.

The final tab, Cursor, allows you set how fast the cursor moves when you move the mouse, which can be very nice, both if you find the default speed too slow or too fast. Best of all, you can also set the mouse to move the cursor to the default button in dialogs, which is a great way to save just a few seconds every day.

If you want to fix or improve your mouse, give USB Overdrive and SteerMouse a try for a few days and see if you don't like using your Mac better with them installed. It can't hurt!

Controlling Which Apps Open When You Plug In Your Camera/iPhone

This is one that annoys a lot of people, even though there's a solution. The problem, though, is that the solution isn't obvious, which is a bit unusual for Apple. Still, here goes.

The problem: every time I plug in my iPhone, iTunes opens. That's fine. But iPhoto also opens, and that drives me bonkers because it slows everything to a crawl. I want to open iPhoto manually when I want to either copy pix off my iPhone or sync pix onto my iPhone, but not have it automatically start up. Turns out that it's no problem to fix.

Plug in your iPhone. Let iPhoto open. Now open **/Applications** ➤ **Image Capture** and select the iPhone on the left sidebar. When you do, you should see some settings appear at the bottom of the left sidebar; if you don't, click the little button at the very bottom of the sidebar, which should make those settings appear, and you'll see something like Figure 12–22.

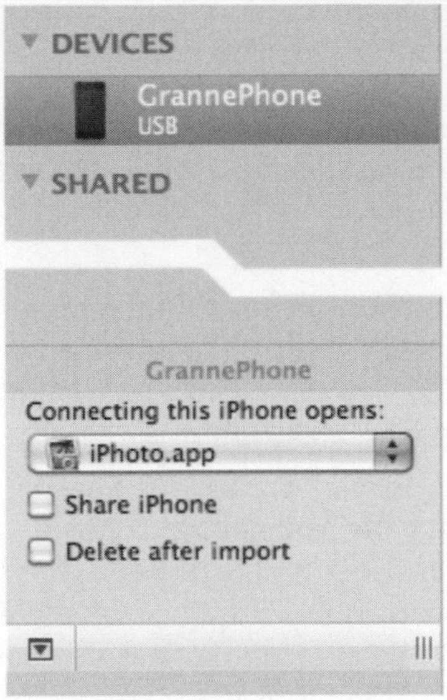

Figure 12–22. *By default, the iPhone opens iPhoto. Let's change that!*

As you can see, by default iPhoto opens when you connect the iPhone to your Mac. Click on the select menu, however, and you can choose any of the following:

- No Application
- iPhoto.app
- Image Capture.app
- Preview.app
- AutoImporter.app
- Other

The solution is obvious: choose No Application. If you want to work with the images on your iPhone using iPhoto, you must now manually open iPhoto after you've plugged in your iPhone. This trick works with your other digital cameras as well—simply plug them in and then open Image Capture. Change the settings for each device as you'd like.

Problem solved!

Keeping Your Monitor from Dimming

I know this has happened to everyone—you're watching a video on YouTube, rapt with attention as a monkey bathes a cat, when the screen suddenly dims because you haven't touched the mouse or keyboard for a few minutes. So you reach out and wiggle the mouse, and now things brighten again. Back to the video. A few minutes later, the whole scene is repeated. How will you ever see just how that monkey bathes the cat?!

Here's how to get around that: install Caffeine, available for free from www.lightheadsw.com/caffeine/. When you run the app, you'll see a little empty coffee cup icon on your Menu Bar. Click the icon and the icon turns into a full coffee cup, steaming with yummy coffee goodness. Now your Mac won't automatically go to sleep, dim your screen, or start any screen savers. When you're done, click the icon again and you go back to the empty coffee cup and normal Mac behavior. Is that not ridiculously easy or what?

Right-click on the Caffeine icon on your Menu Bar to get to the program's Preferences: Do you want it start automatically when you login? Do you want Caffeine to activate when it starts and immediately prevent your Mac from going to sleep, or do you want to initiate that manually? How long do you want Caffeine to work by default?

In addition to Preferences, you can also choose how long you want Caffeine to keep your Mac awake. Go to the Activate For menu and select a time. You have everything from 5 minutes to 5 hours to Indefinitely available to you.

And that's it for Caffeine!

Further Resources

If you're looking for better drivers for your Mac's trackpad, you have a few options, all of which add extra features and more control.

- SideTrack: $15 at http://ragingmenace.com/software/sidetrack/

- Jitouch: $6 at www.jitouch.com

- BetterTouchTool: Free at http://blog.boastr.net

In general, though, it appears to me that the mouse-centric options are slicker, more professional, and better maintained.

Summary

Many of the items in this chapter made me very happy when I discovered them, and I was happy to write about them because I wanted to share them with my readers. iStat Menus is a great product, and Little Snitch is an indispensible complement to the Mac OS X firewall. There's nothing like Automator on any other operating system, and I consider it a jewel in Mac OS X's crown. I love networking, and I've always been fascinated by DNS, so I'll seize on any opportunity to talk about that subject. And even the hardware improvements I discuss are fun and help to make my day-to-day use of Mac OS X a bit more enjoyable. I hope you enjoyed reading about all of these tools, and I encourage you to try the stuff in this chapter out on your own Macs. I think you'll find administering your Mac a little easier, and maybe even a bit more fun.

Index

■H

■ X

You Need the Companion eBook

Your purchase of this book entitles you to buy the companion PDF-version eBook for only $10. Take the weightless companion with you anywhere.

We believe this Apress title will prove so indispensable that you'll want to carry it with you everywhere, which is why we are offering the companion eBook (in PDF format) for $10 to customers who purchase this book now. Convenient and fully searchable, the PDF version of any content-rich, page-heavy Apress book makes a valuable addition to your programming library. You can easily find and copy code—or perform examples by quickly toggling between instructions and the application. Even simultaneously tackling a donut, diet soda, and complex code becomes simplified with hands-free eBooks!

Once you purchase your book, getting the $10 companion eBook is simple:

❶ Visit **www.apress.com/promo/tendollars/**.

❷ Complete a basic registration form to receive a randomly generated question about this title.

❸ Answer the question correctly in 60 seconds, and you will receive a promotional code to redeem for the $10.00 eBook.

THE EXPERT'S VOICE™

233 Spring Street, New York, NY 10013

Offer valid through 3/11.